NX-OS and Cisco Nexus Switching

Next-Generation Data Center Architectures

Second Edition

Ron Fuller, David Jansen,
Matthew McPherson

W9-BUA-648

Cisco Press

800 East 96th Street

Indianapolis, IN 46240

NX-OS and Cisco Nexus Switching
Next-Generation Data Center Architectures, Second Edition

Copyright © 2013 Cisco Systems, Inc.

Published by:
Cisco Press
800 East 96th Street
Indianapolis, IN 46240 USA

First Printing March 2013

Library of Congress Cataloging-in-Publication data is on file.

ISBN-13: 978-1-58714-304-5
ISBN-10: 1-58714-304-6

Warning and Disclaimer

This book is designed to provide information about the Nexus Operating system and Nexus family of products. Every effort has been made to make this book as complete and as accurate as possible, but no warranty or fitness is implied.

The information is provided on an "as is" basis. The authors, Cisco Press, and Cisco Systems, Inc., shall have neither liability nor responsibility to any person or entity with respect to any loss or damages arising from the information contained in this book or from the use of the discs or programs that may accompany it.

The opinions expressed in this book belong to the author and are not necessarily those of Cisco Systems, Inc.

Trademark Acknowledgments

All terms mentioned in this book that are known to be trademarks or service marks have been appropriately capitalized. Cisco Press or Cisco Systems, Inc. cannot attest to the accuracy of this information. Use of a term in this book should not be regarded as affecting the validity of any trademark or service mark.

Corporate and Government Sales

The publisher offers excellent discounts on this book when ordered in quantity for bulk purchases or special sales, which may include electronic versions and/or custom covers and content particular to your business, training goals, marketing focus, and branding interests. For more information, please contact:
U.S. Corporate and Government Sales 1-800-382-3419 corpsales@pearsontechgroup.com

For sales outside of the U.S. please contact: International Sales international@pearsoned.com

Feedback Information

At Cisco Press, our goal is to create in-depth technical books of the highest quality and value. Each book is crafted with care and precision, undergoing rigorous development that involves the unique expertise of members from the professional technical community.

Readers' feedback is a natural continuation of this process. If you have any comments regarding how we could improve the quality of this book, or otherwise alter it to better suit your needs, you can contact us through e-mail at feedback@ciscopress.com. Please make sure to include the book title and ISBN in your message.

We greatly appreciate your assistance.

Publisher: Paul Boger	**Business Operation Manager, Cisco Press:** Anand Sundaram
Associate Publisher: Dave Dusthimer	**Executive Editor:** Brett Bartow
Development Editor: Eleanor C. Bru	**Copy Editor:** Apostrophe Editing Services
Managing Editor: Sandra Schroeder	**Technical Editors:** Jeff Fry, Chad Hintz
Project Editor: Seth Kerney	**Proofreader:** Megan Wade
Editorial Assistant: Vanessa Evans	**Indexer:** Ken Johnson
Cover Designer: Gary Adair	**Composition:** Jake McFarland
Book Designer: Louisa Adair	

CISCO

Americas Headquarters
Cisco Systems, Inc.
San Jose, CA

Asia Pacific Headquarters
Cisco Systems (USA) Pte. Ltd.
Singapore

Europe Headquarters
Cisco Systems International BV
Amsterdam, The Netherlands

Cisco has more than 200 offices worldwide. Addresses, phone numbers, and fax numbers are listed on the Cisco Website at www.cisco.com/go/offices.

CCDE, CCENT, Cisco Eos, Cisco HealthPresence, the Cisco logo, Cisco Lumin, Cisco Nexus, Cisco StadiumVision, Cisco TelePresence, Cisco WebEx, DCE, and Welcome to the Human Network are trademarks; Changing the Way We Work, Live, Play, and Learn and Cisco Store are service marks; and Access Registrar, Aironet, AsyncOS, Bringing the Meeting To You, Catalyst, CCDA, CCDP, CCIE, CCIP, CCNA, CCNP, CCSP, CCVP, Cisco, the Cisco Certified Internetwork Expert logo, Cisco IOS, Cisco Press, Cisco Systems, Cisco Systems Capital, the Cisco Systems logo, Cisco Unity, Collaboration Without Limitation, EtherFast, EtherSwitch, Event Center, Fast Step, Follow Me Browsing, FormShare, GigaDrive, HomeLink, Internet Quotient, IOS, iPhone, iQuick Study, IronPort, the IronPort logo, LightStream, Linksys, MediaTone, MeetingPlace, MeetingPlace Chime Sound, MGX, Networkers, Networking Academy, Network Registrar, PCNow, PIX, PowerPanels, ProConnect, ScriptShare, SenderBase, SMARTnet, Spectrum Expert, StackWise, The Fastest Way to Increase Your Internet Quotient, TransPath, WebEx, and the WebEx logo are registered trademarks of Cisco Systems, Inc. and/or its affiliates in the United States and certain other countries.

All other trademarks mentioned in this document or website are the property of their respective owners. The use of the word partner does not imply a partnership relationship between Cisco and any other company. (0812R)

About the Authors

Ron Fuller, CCIE No. 5851 (Routing and Switching/Storage Networking), is a technical marketing engineer (TME) on the Nexus 7000 team for Cisco. He has 21 years of experience in the industry and has held certifications from Novell, HP, Microsoft, ISC2, SNIA, and Cisco. His focus is working with customers worldwide to address their challenges with comprehensive end-to-end data center architectures and how they can best use Cisco technology to their advantage. He has had the opportunity to speak at Cisco Live on VDCs, NX-OS Multicast, and general design. He lives in Ohio with his wife and four wonderful children and enjoys travel and auto racing. He can be found on Twitter @ccie5851.

David Jansen, CCIE No. 5952, is a technical solutions architect for Data Center for Enterprise Central Area. David has more than 20 years' experience in the information technology industry. He has held multiple certifications from Microsoft, Novell, Checkpoint, and Cisco. His focus is to work with Enterprise customers to address end-to-end data center Enterprise architectures. David has been with Cisco for 15 years, has been working as a technical solutions architect for 6 years, and has provided unique experiences helping customers build architectures for Enterprise data centers. David has also been instrumental in developing and delivering the following Cisco Live presentations:

> Data Center Interconnect solutions to address L2 requirements between multiple data centers to meet application clusters and virtualization requirements (for the past five years)
>
> Next-generation data center architectures and operations tectorial and breakout sessions (for the past three years)
>
> Deploying NX-OS Nexus devices in the network infrastructure best practices

David holds a B.S.E. degree in computer science from the University of Michigan (Go Blue!) and an M.A. degree in adult education from Central Michigan University.

Matthew McPherson is a senior systems engineer and solutions architect for Cisco in the Central Select Operation, specializing in data center architectures. Matt has been with Cisco for more than 2 1/2 years and has more than 12 years of experience in the industry working for service providers and large enterprise customers in the financial and manufacturing verticals. He has held certifications from Juniper, Netscreen, and Cisco, and possesses a deep technical background in the areas of routing, switching, and security. His primary focus is working with strategic customers in greater Michigan to address their overall infrastructure challenges. He lives in Michigan with his wife and enjoys biking and collecting cars.

About the Technical Reviewers

Jeff Fry, CCIE No. 22061 (Routing and Switching), is a senior network engineer and data center architect for a large data center hosting company in the United States. Prior to working at the hosting company, Jeff designed and oversaw a globally diversified data center and call center network in a large call center environment. Jeff has designed and implemented several Cisco data center networks using the Catalyst 6500 and Nexus 7000, 5000, and 2000 devices. Jeff has more than 20 years of experience in the industry and has certifications from Microsoft, CompTIA, Novell, and Cisco. Jeff lives in Pennsylvania with his wife and their three sons, and they enjoy vacationing at Disney World. Jeff can be found on twitter at @fryguy_pa.

Chad Hintz, CCIE No. 15729, is a technical solutions architect for Cisco focusing on designing enterprise solutions for customers around Cisco data center technologies. He also holds three CCIEs in routing and switching, security, and storage. He has more than 10 years of experience in the industry and has held certifications from Novell, VMware, and Cisco. His focus is working with enterprise/commercial customers to address their challenges with comprehensive end-to-end data center architectures. Chad is a regular speaker at Cisco and industry conferences for data center technologies. Chad lives near Buffalo, New York, with his wife and two wonderful children.

Dedications

Ron Fuller: This book is dedicated to my loving wife Julie and my awesome children: Max, Sydney, Veronica, Emerson, and Wu. Thank you for showing me the world through your perspective and helping me appreciate the true joy of children. I can't thank you enough for believing in me when I told you I was going to write another book. Your support and encouragement has and always will be the key to any success I enjoy. Thank you for your love and support. I can't forget to acknowledge my parents, Gene and Joan. Your guidance and upbringing are what showed me what commitment and "getting it done right the first time" were all about. I've tried to make good use of my spare time and use my God-given gifts correctly.

David Jansen: This book is dedicated, again, to my loving wife Jenise and my three children: Kaitlyn, Joshua, and Jacob. You are the inspiration that gave me the dedication and determination to complete this project. Kaitlyn, Joshua, Jacob, you are three amazing kids; you are learning the skills to be the best at what you do and accomplish anything; keep up the great work. Thank you for all your love and support; I could not have completed (yet another) this without your help, support, and understanding. I also promise you that I am not going to take on another commitment like this for a long time; I promise. Second, I would also like to further dedicate this book to my parents, Michael and Dolores; you have given me proper tools, guidance, attitude, drive, and education to allow me to do what I do. I'm so grateful to God, who gives endurance, encouragement, and motivation to complete such a large project like this.

Matthew McPherson: This book is dedicated to my wonderful wife Carey who is the love of my life! Without your strength, support, and encouragement, I would never have been able to complete this project. I would also like to further dedicate this book to my parents, Steve and Kathy. Without your guidance and wisdom growing up, I would never have had the opportunity to write this book. Thank you both for always making me strive for greatness.

Acknowledgments

Ron Fuller: First, I'd like to thank my co-authors Dave Jansen and Matt McPherson. Dave, thank you for being such a good friend, a trusted co-worker, and a leader in our organization. You set the bar the rest of us try to reach. It has been great sharing a brain with you, and I look forward to more challenges and fun. Keep the goat rodeos coming! Matt, thank you for stepping in to help complete this project. You are awesome to work with, and your technical acumen is top-notch. People like you and Dave are the reason I love my job. We need to find some more concerts to go to, but hopefully I won't have to walk so far in the cold.

I'd like to thank Brett Bartow for his (almost) infinite patience with this project. It is a huge undertaking, and his persistence, understanding, and encouragement were greatly appreciated. You gave us the extra time we needed to make sure this was a fantastic and comprehensive second edition.

Chris Cleveland, it has been a pleasure working with you. Your guidance on the formatting and consistency makes the book something we all can be proud of. Thank you for making three propeller heads from Cisco look good.

To our technical editors, Jeff Fry and Chad Hintz: Thank you for the detail-oriented work and assistance making the book accurate and concise.

I'd like to thank my team, in particular Nikhil Kelshikar and Jeff Raymond, for giving me the time needed to complete this project. The rest of the TMEs, thank you for explaining some of these topics, some more than once, so I could make sure this book is accurate.

A special thanks to Lucien Avramov for the Python script example used in Chapter 7. I also appreciate the help getting around Moscow—my Russian isn't very good.

To my family, thank you for the time away from you while I worked on a book on a topic on things you don't get to see. Your understanding and support through the weekends and late nights are truly appreciated.

Finally, I want to thank God for the gifts he has given me and the opportunity to do what I love to do with people I enjoy to support my family. I couldn't ask for more.

David Jansen: This is my third book, and it has been a tremendous honor to work with the great people at Cisco Press. There are so many people to thank; I'm not sure where to begin. I'll start with Brett Bartow: Thank you for allowing me to publish another book; this is something I enjoy doing. As we are a year late on this, I appreciate your patience and tolerance on this project. I really appreciate you keeping me on track to complete the project in a timely manner, as we have missed several completion dates.

First, I would like to thank my friends and co-authors Ron Fuller and Matthew McPherson. Both of you guys are great friends and co-workers that ROCK. I can't think of two better people to work with to complete such a project. Cisco is one of the most amazing places I've ever worked, and it's people like you, who are wicked smart and a lot of fun to work with, that make it such a great place. I look forward to working on other projects in the future. I look forward to continuing to work with you and grow the friendship into the future. We need to find another heavy concert to top the Megadeth one we went to together the winter of 2011; Brett, this is why we were a year late on the project ☺.

I want to thank Kevin Corbin for your contributions to the second editions. Thank you for being a great friend and peer co-worker.

Chris Cleveland, again it was a pleasure to work with you. Your expertise, professionalism, and follow-up as a development editor is unsurpassed; thank you for your hard work and quick turnaround; this helped to meet the deadlines set forth.

To our technical editors—Jeff Fry and Chad Hintz—thank you for the time, sharp eyes, and excellent comments/feedback; both of you created a ton more work for me just when I thought I was done. It was a pleasure having you as part of the team. I would like to thank Yuri Lukin for allowing me access to his lab to complete the Nexus 1000V chapter and all the services. Yuri you are a true professional; thank you for your time and expertise.

Thanks to my manager at Cisco, Robert Fisher—I appreciate your guidance and your trust in my ability to juggle the many work tasks along with extra projects like working on a book. Thank you for all your support Bob!

I would like to thank the heavy metal music world out there—it allowed me to stay focused when burning the midnight oil; I would not have been able to complete this without loud rock 'n roll music. Thank you.

I want to thank my family for their support and understanding while I was working on this project late at night and being patient with me when my lack of rest may have made me a little less than pleasant to be around. I know it is also hard to sleep when Dad is downstairs writing and not realizing the db levels of the music while the rest of the family sleeps.

Most important, I would like to thank God for giving me the ability to complete such a task with dedication and determination and for providing me the skills, knowledge, and health needed to be successful in such a demanding profession.

Matthew McPherson: I'd like to thank both David and Ron for asking me to be a part of such an amazing opportunity. Dave, thank you again for being such an awesome friend and great mentor. You are a technical rock star who is always there to help in any situation, and for that reason I have the utmost respect for you. I cannot thank you enough your continued guidance and wisdom. Ron, you have become a great friend, and it's been a privilege to work more closely with you. I look forward to our continued friendship and am eagerly awaiting the next laser-sword match! It is so amazing to be at Cisco and have an opportunity to work with such amazing people!

Brett Bartow and Chris Cleveland, thank you both for your patience and support through my first publication. It has certainly been a privilege working with you both, and I look forward to starting on the third edition!

Chad Hintz and Jeff Fry, it has been great working with you both. Thank you for your time, attention to detail, and technical knowledge that have helped shape this book.

Gary Witt, thank you for stepping up to mentor me when I joined Cisco. You are such a great leader, and I certainly appreciate your insight and encouragement. I look forward to continuing our conversations and learning as much as I can.

I'd also like to thank my manager, Rajeev Grover. Your guidance and support for this project are truly appreciated!

Contents at a Glance

Contents

Icons Used in This Book

Nexus
7000

Nexus
5000

Nexus 2000
Fabric Extender

Nexus 1000

Nexus 1KV VSM

Route/Switch
Processor

ASR 1000
Series

Router

Network
Management
Appliance

Web
Server

Laptop

Server

PC

Network Cloud

Ethernet
Connection

Serial Line
Connection

Command Syntax Conventions

The conventions used to present command syntax in this book are the same conventions used in the IOS Command Reference. The Command Reference describes these conventions as follows:

- **Boldface** indicates commands and keywords that are entered literally as shown. In actual configuration examples and output (not general command syntax), boldface indicates commands that are manually input by the user (such as a **show** command).

- *Italic* indicates arguments for which you supply actual values.

- Vertical bars (|) separate alternative, mutually exclusive elements.

- Square brackets ([ ]) indicate an optional element.

- Braces ({ }) indicate a required choice.

- Braces within brackets ([{ }]) indicate a required choice within an optional element.

Foreword

With more than 30,000 customers across every vertical, segment, and corner of the Earth, nobody can dispute that NX-OS is delivering on the requirements for the next-generation data center. In five quick years, seven product families have been released that are powered by NX-OS and provide end-to-end solutions in data centers large and small. These environments are as varied as ultra low latency trading environments, massively scalable data centers, cloud providers, and commercial and enterprise customer networks. NX-OS has the flexibility, reliability, security, and scalability to meet these demands and more.

The success of these products is driven by a team within Cisco that is committed to providing world-class solutions and solving challenges for customers with innovative technologies. Capabilities such as In-Service Software Upgrade (ISSU), modularity of the operating system, and stateful process restart lay a foundation for emerging technologies to build upon while preserving the investment in training and operations of the network. Game-changing capabilities such as Overlay Transport Virtualization (OTV), Locator Separator/ID Protocol (LISP), FabricPath, Fabric Extender architecture, vPath, Unified Ports, and dense 10G, 40G, and 100G interfaces provide customers a breadth of flexibility unparalleled in the industry—all running a common operating system, NX-OS.

To that end, a book like this can become a convenient reference for best practices deployment of these new technologies. It is written by two enterprise data center technology solutions architects and a technical marketing engineer on the Nexus 7000 team who all work with our customers on a daily basis and help them develop next-generation data center architectures. Their breadth of experience makes them perfect candidates to drive a project such as this.

We hope that as you read this book and learn more about the Nexus series of switches, and NX-OS specifically, you'll see the years of effort that made this product the Cisco flagship data center operating system now and in the years to come. Enjoy!

David Yen, SVP & GM
Data Center Business Unit
Cisco, San Jose

Introduction

The modern data center is rapidly changing and evolving to support the current and future demands of technology. At the center of this change is the network—the single entity that connects everything and touches all components of the data center. With that in mind, Cisco has launched a new series of switches, Nexus, based on a revolutionary new operating system, NX-OS, to meet these changes and provide a platform with the scalability, reliability, and comprehensive feature set required in the next-generation data center.

The purpose of this book is to provide a guide for the network administrator who might not be familiar with Nexus and NX-OS. It is intended to be used as a "go-to" resource for concise information on the most commonly used aspects of NX-OS across the Nexus 7000, 5000, 5500, and 1000V platforms.

Goals and Methods

The goal of this book is to provide best practice configurations to common internet-working scenarios involving Nexus products. Having been network administrators, the authors are conscious of the pressures and challenges with finding accurate and relevant information, especially on new technology. They intend this book to be a resource network administrators reach for first.

Although there might be more than one way to accomplish a networking requirement, this book focuses on the best way that minimizes operational complexity and maximizes supportability. The authors realize and respect that there might be corner-case scenarios that call for configurations not described in this book but sincerely hope they address the vast majority of common configurations.

Who Should Read This Book?

This book is targeted for the network administrator, consultant, or student looking for assistance with NX-OS configuration. It covers the three major Cisco Nexus products and highlights key features of them in a way that makes it easy to digest and implement.

How This Book Is Organized

This book has been organized following the OSI system model with the initial chapters starting with Layer 2 and then moving to Layer 3. Network-based services such as IP multicast, security, and high availability are then added. Next, the embedded serviceability features of NX-OS are explored, before moving to emerging data center architecture, Unified Fabric. With the drive toward virtualization, the need for increased visibility and control arises, and the Nexus 1000V meets these goals, which are covered next. Quality of service (QoS) is detailed before moving to the next topic, Overlay Transport Virtualization (OTV), where L2 segments can be safely extended between data centers.

The last chapter features a case study of an Enterprise customer who migrated from a Cisco Catalyst-based architecture to a Nexus-based one. The detailed step-by-step process is illustrated to provide a cookbook that can be used in many places.

Chapters 1 through 14 cover the following topics:

- **Chapter 1, "Introduction to Cisco NX-OS":** Provides the reader with the foundation for building NX-OS configurations, including command-line interface (CLI) differences, virtualization capabilities, and basic file system management.

- **Chapter 2, "Layer 2 Support and Configurations":** Focuses on the comprehensive suite of Layer 2 technologies supported by NX-OS, including vPC, Spanning Tree Protocol, and Cisco FabricPath.

- **Chapter 3, "Layer 3 Support and Configurations":** Delves into the three most-common network Layer 3 protocols, including EIGRP, OSPF, and BGP. In addition, HSRP, GLBP, and VRRP are discussed.

- **Chapter 4, "IP Multicast Configuration":** Provides the information needed to configure IP Multicast protocols such as PIM, Auto-RP, and MSDP.

- **Chapter 5, "Security":** Focuses on the rich set of security protocols available in NX-OS, including CTS, SGTs, ACLs, CoPP, DAI, and more.

- **Chapter 6, "High Availability":** Delves into the high-availability features built into NX-OS, including ISSU, stateful process restart, stateful switchover, and non-stop forwarding.

- **Chapter 7, "Embedded Serviceability Features":** Provides the ability to leverage the embedded serviceability components in NX-OS, including SPAN, ERSPAN, configuration checkpoints and rollback, packet analysis, Smart Call Home, NTP, Python, and PoAP.

- **Chapter 8, "Unified Fabric":** Explores the industry-leading capability for Nexus switches to unify storage and Ethernet fabrics with a focus on FCoE, NPV, and NPIV.

- **Chapter 9, "Nexus 1000V":** Enables you to implement Nexus 1000V in a virtualized environment to maximum effect leveraging the VSM, VEM, and port profiles.

- **Chapter 10, "Quality of Service (QoS)":** Illustrates the QoS capabilities of the Nexus platforms and covers the MQ CLI, queuing, and marking.

- **Chapter 11, "Overlay Transport Virtualization (OTV)":** Delves into the details of this technology used to extend L2 networks across a L3 infrastructure.

- **Chapter 12, "Layer 3 Virtualization and Multiprotocol Label Switching (MPLS)":** Covers how the integration of MPLS application components, including Layer 3 VPNs, traffic engineering, QoS, and mVPN-enable the development of highly efficient, scalable, and secure networks that guarantee service-level agreements.

- **Chapter 13, "LISP"**: Provides an introduction and overview of Locator ID Separation Protocol (LISP) in NX-OS and how this new routing architecture and paradigm shift decouples the server identity and the server location to allow for mobility, scalability, and security.

- **Chapter 14, "Nexus Migration Case Study"**: Detailed step-by-step description of a customer's implementation of Nexus technology in their data center and the migration from a Catalyst-based architecture.

Chapter 1

Introduction to Cisco NX-OS

This chapter provides an introduction and overview of NX-OS and a comparison between traditional IOS and NX-OS configurations and terminology. The following sections will be covered in this chapter:

- NX-OS overview
- NX-OS user modes
- Management interfaces
- Managing system files

NX-OS Overview

Cisco built the next-generation data center class operating system designed for maximum scalability and application availability. The NX-OS data center class operating system was built with modularity, resiliency, and serviceability at its foundation. NX-OS is based on the industry-proven Cisco Storage Area Network Operating System (SAN-OS) Software and helps ensure continuous availability to set the standard for mission-critical data center environments. The self-healing and highly modular design of Cisco NX-OS enables for operational excellence, increasing the service levels and enabling exceptional operational flexibility. Several advantages of Cisco NX-OS include the following:

- Unified data center operating system
- Robust and rich feature set with a variety of Cisco innovations
- Flexibility and scalability
- Modularity
- Virtualization
- Resiliency

- IPv4 and IPv6 IP routing and multicast features

- Comprehensive security, availability, serviceability, and management features

Key features and benefits of NX-OS include

- **Virtual device contexts (VDCs):** Cisco Nexus 7000 Series switches can be segmented into virtual devices based on customer requirements. VDCs offer several benefits such as fault isolation, administration plane, separation of data traffic, and enhanced security.

- **Virtual Port Channels (vPCs):** Enables a server or switch to use an EtherChannel across two upstream switches without an STP-blocked port to enable use of all available uplink bandwidth.

- **Continuous system operation:** Maintenance, upgrades, and software certification can be performed without service interruptions because of the modular nature of NX-OS and features such as In-Service Software Upgrade (ISSU) and the capability for processes to restart dynamically.

- **Security:** Cisco NX-OS provides outstanding data confidentiality and integrity, supporting standard IEEE 802.1AE link-layer cryptography with 128-bit Advanced Encryption Standard (AES) cryptography. In addition to CTS, there are many additional security features such as access control lists (ACLs) and port-security, for example.

- **Overlay Transport Virtualization (OTV):** Enables the Layer 2 extension between distributed data centers over any transport Layer 3 network.

- **NX-OS Persistent Storage Service (PSS):** The PSS is a lightweight database that maintains runtime information state. PSS provides reliable persistent storage to the software components to *checkpoint* their internal state and data structures enabling nondisruptive restart. If a fault occurs in a process (such as OSPF), the NX-OS high-availability (HA) manager determines best recovery action:

  - Restart a process.

  - Switch over to a redundant supervisor module.

Note   The process restart does not have any impact in the data plane operations; the total control plane recovery is approximately 10 milliseconds.

- **FabricPath:** Enables each device to build an overall view of the topology; this is similar to other link state routing protocols. Each device in the FabricPath topology is identified by a switch-id. The Layer 2 forwarding tables are built based on reachability to each switch-id, not by the MAC address. Eliminates spanning-tree to maximize network bandwidth and flexibility in topological configurations, as well as simplify operational support and configuration. This enables a tremendous amount of flexibility on the topology because you can now build FabricPath topologies for Layer 2-based networks the same as for Layer 3-based networks.

NX-OS Supported Platforms

An NX-OS data center-class operating system, designed for maximum scalability and application availability, has a wide variety of platform support, including the following:

- **Nexus 7000:** Provides an end-to-end data center architecture on a single platform, including data center core, data center aggregation, and data center access layer. The data center access layer could be end-of-row or top-of-rack or a combination of end-of-row and top-of-rack with a Fabric Extender (FEX). Depending on the requirements, the Nexus 7000 has many different form factors; the form factors include the following (note that all the chassis share common supervisor modules, I/O modules, NX-OS software, and power supplies):

  - **Nexus 7018:** An 18-slot chassis that supports 16 I/O modules. Slots 9 and slot 10 are reserved for supervisor modules on the Nexus 7018 chassis. The I/O module slots for the Nexus 7018 chassis are reserved 1 through 8 and 11 through 18. The supervisor module slots (9 and 10) can have only a supervisor module installed in them; I/O modules will not work in the supervisor slots. All I/O module slots have full fabric connections of up to 230 Gbps with Fabric-1 installed or 550 Gbps with Fabric-2 installed. The fabric bandwidth depends on the number of fabric modules installed and the I/O modules installed in any given I/O module slot; the Nexus 7018 chassis is side-to-side airflow.

  - **Nexus 7010:** A 10-slot chassis that supports 8 I/O modules. Slot 5 and slot 6 are reserved for supervisor modules on the Nexus 7010 chassis. Slot 1 through slot 4 and slot 7 through slot 10 are reserved for I/O modules on the Nexus 7010 chassis. The supervisor module slots (5 and 6) can have only a supervisor module installed in them; I/O modules do not work in the supervisor slots. The Nexus 7010 is front-to-back-airflow, to meet hot isle or cold isle data center design. All I/O module slots have full fabric connections of up to 230 Gbps with Fabric-1 installed or 550 Gbps with Fabric-2 installed. The fabric bandwidth depends on the number of fabric modules installed and the I/O modules installed in any given I/O module slot

  - **Nexus 7009:** A 9-slot chassis that supports 7 I/O modules. The Nexus 7009 chassis I/O modules have a horizontal orientation of the line modules and side-to-side airflow. Slot 1 and slot 2 are reserved for supervisor modules in the Nexus 7009 chassis. Slots 3 through 9 are reserved for I/O modules on the Nexus 7009 chassis. The supervisor module slots (1 and 2) can have only a supervisor module installed in them; I/O modules will not work in the supervisor slots. The Nexus 7009 chassis is side-to-side airflow. All I/O module slots have full fabric connections of up to 550 Gbps with Fabric-2 installed. The fabric bandwidth depends on the number of fabric modules installed and the I/O modules installed in any given I/O module slot.

  - **Nexus 7004:** A four-slot chassis that supports two I/O modules. The Nexus 7004 chassis I/O modules have a horizontal orientation of the line modules and side-to-rear airflow. Slot 1 and slot 2 are reserved for supervisor modules in the Nexus

7004 chassis. Slot 3 and slot 4 are reserved for I/O modules on the Nexus 7004 chassis. The supervisor module slots (1 and 2) can have only a supervisor module installed in them; I/O modules do not work in the supervisor slots. The 7004 does not have fabric modules. The I/O modules installed in a 7004 chassis use one of the fabric connections for communications between the modules.

Note   The Nexus 7004 chassis is supported only with the Supervisor 2 and Supervisor 2e. In addition, the Nexus 7004 supports M1-XL, F2, M2, and F2e I/O modules.

- **Nexus 5000:** Ideal for the data center server access layer providing architectural support for virtualization and Unified Fabric Environments while maintaining consistent operational models.

  - **Nexus 5010:** Twenty fixed wire-speed 10-Gigabit Ethernet interfaces that support IEEE data center bridging (DCB) and FCoE. In addition to the fixed interfaces, the Nexus 5010 has one expansion module. The expansion module supports Native Fibre Channel, Ethernet, and FCoE interfaces. The first eight interfaces of the Nexus 5010 support 1 GbE and 10 GbE.

  - **Nexus 5020:** Forty fixed wire-speed 10-Gigabit Ethernet interfaces that support IEEE DCB and FCoE. In addition to the fixed interfaces, the Nexus 5010 has one expansion module. The expansion module supports Native Fibre Channel, Ethernet, and FCoE interfaces. The first 16 interfaces of the Nexus 5010 support 1 GbE and 10 GbE.

  - **Nexus 5548P:** Thirty-two fixed 1/10 Gbps fixed SFP+ on the base chassis along with one expansion slot. In addition to the fixed interfaces, the Nexus 5548P has one expansion module. The expansion module supports Native Fibre Channel, Ethernet, and FCoE interfaces, for a total of 48 interfaces. In addition to these expansion modules, the 5548P supports a Layer 3 daughtercard that can be ordered with the system or as a spare.

Note   The default airflow for the Nexus 5000/5500 platforms is front-to-back, with the back of the chassis being the network port side of the chassis. The Nexus 5548UP and 5596UP support reversed airflow with power supplies and fan trays with "B" SKU /PID. A sample SKU or PID for the Nexus 5548UP reversed airflow for the power supply and fan tray is N55-PAC-750W-B= and N5548P-FAN-B=.

- **Nexus 5548UP:** Thirty-two fixed Unified ports 1/10 Gbps fixed SFP+ on the base chassis along with one expansion slot. In addition to the fixed interfaces, the Nexus 5548UP has one expansion module. The expansion module supports native Fibre Channel, Ethernet, and FCoE interface for a total of 48 interfaces. Unified ports on the Nexus 5500 platforms enable an interface to have one of the following characteristics depending on the licensing and pluggable transceiver installed: traditional Ethernet, Fibre Channel (FC), or FCoE. Depending on the configuration, the interface can have the following physical characteristics: 1-Gigabit Ethernet, 10-Gigabit Ethernet, 10-Gigabit Ethernet with FCoE, and 1/2/4/8-G native Fibre Channel. In addition to these expansion modules, the 5548UP supports a Layer 3 daughtercard that can be ordered with the system or as a spare.

■ **Nexus 5596UP:** Forty-eight fixed Unified ports 1/10-Gbps fixed SFP+ on the base chassis along with three expansion slots. The expansion module supports native Fibre Channel, Ethernet, and FCoE interfaces, for a total of 96 interfaces. Another expansion module option is the Layer 3 modules for the 5596UP. Unified ports on the Nexus 5500 platforms enable an interface to have one of the following characteristics depending on the licensing and pluggable transceiver installed: traditional Ethernet or FCoE. Depending on the configuration, the interface can have the following physical characteristics: 1-Gigabit Ethernet, 10-Gigabit Ethernet, 10-Gigabit Ethernet with FCoE, and 1/2/4/8 G native Fibre Channel.

Note The Nexus 5010 and Nexus 5020 do not support the following features:

1. Layer 3 module
2. Reversible airflow
3. FabricPath/TRILL
4. Adapter-FEX
5. VM-FEX

■ **Nexus 3000:** Delivers high-performance and high-density switching at ultra-low latencies. The Cisco Nexus 3000 Series switches are positioned for use in environments with ultra-low latency requirements such as financial High-Frequency Trading (HFT), chemical genomics, and automotive crash-test simulation applications. These applications require support for advanced unicast and multicast routing protocol features and ultra-low latency; low latency is measured <1 μsecs (microseconds) where below 1 μsecs is measuring ns (nanoseconds):

■ **Nexus 3064:** Forty-eight fixed 1/10-Gigabit Ethernet and four fixed Quad SFP+ (QSFP+) ports. (Each QSFP+ port is 4 × 10 GbE-capable.)

■ **Nexus 3048:** Forty-eight 1GE and 4 10GE.

■ **Nexus 3016:** Sixteen QSFP+ (40GE) ports.

- **Nexus 3548:** Forty-eight fixed Enhanced Small Form-Factor Pluggable (SFP+) ports (1 Gbps or 10 Gbps).

- **Nexus 2000 Fabric Extenders:** A building block in the architecture for the virtualized data center access layer. The FEX architecture provides flexible data center deployment models to meet growing server demands. FEX can be deployed with end-of-row, middle-of-row, top-of-rack, or in any combination leveraging the Fabric interfaces between the FEX and the parent switch. The parent switch can be a Nexus 5000, Nexus 5500, or Nexus 7000. When a FEX is deployed, all the configuration and management is performed on the parent switch. Think of FEX as a remote line card and module to create a virtual chassis; there is not any spanning tree or FabricPath control plane passed between the FEX fabric interface and the parent switches. FEX has several different hardware SKUs based on server requirements:

  - **Nexus 2148:** FEX, 1000BaseT Host Interfaces (server interfaces), and four 10-Gigabit Ethernet fabric uplinks.

  - **Nexus 2248:** FEX, 48 100/1000BaseT Host Interfaces (server interfaces), and four 10-Gigabit Ethernet fabric uplinks.

  - **Nexus 2248TP-E:** Forty-eight ports 100M/1000BaseT Enhanced Host interfaces (server interfaces) and four 10-Gigabit Ethernet Fabric uplinks. The enhanced FEX is buffer optimized for specific data center workloads such as big data, Hadoop, video applications, and distributed storage.

  - **Nexus 2224:** FEX, 24 100/1000BaseT Host interfaces (server interfaces) and two 10 Gigabit Ethernet fabric uplinks.

  - **Nexus 2232TP:** FEX, 32 1/10 Gigabit Ethernet SFP+ server interfaces and eight 10-Gigabit Ethernet SFP+ Fabric uplinks. The 2232TP supports IEEE DCB to transport FCoE.

  - **Nexus 2232TM:** FEX, 32 1000BaseT/10000BaseT Gigabit Ethernet server interfaces, and eight SFP+ 10-Gigabit Ethernet Fabric uplinks. Today, the industry does not support FCoE over 10GBaseT cabling due to the bit-error rate requirements.

  - **Nexus 2232TM-E:** Thirty-two 1/10GBASE-T host interfaces and uplink module (eight 10-Gigabit Ethernet fabric interfaces [SFP+]). The 2232TM-E enables 10GBASE-T PHY, enabling lower power and improved bit error rate (BER).

- **Nexus 1000v:** An NX-OS Software switch that integrated into VMware hypervisor virtualized platforms. The Nexus 1000v architecture has two components: the Virtual Ethernet Module (VEM) and the Virtual Supervisor Module (VSM). The VEM is a software switch embedded in the hypervisor; the VSM is the control plane and management plane to create policies and quality of service (QoS) for virtual machines for each VEM across multiple physical hypervisor hosts.

- **Cisco MDS 9000:** Multilayer SAN switches running Cisco NX-OS. The MDS 9000 offers director-class platforms and Fabric switches. The MDS 9000 offers native fibre channel, storage services, and FCoE.

- **Cisco Unified Computing System (UCS):** Offers a unified, model-based management, end-to-end provisioning, and migration support that come together in this next-generation data center platform to accelerate and simplify application deployment with greater reliability and security. Cisco UCS integrates the server, network, and I/O resources into a single converged architectural system.

- **Nexus 4000:** A purpose-built blade switch for IBM's BladeCenter H and HT chassis. Nexus 4000 is a line-rate, low-latency, nonblocking 10 Gigabit Ethernet and DCB switch module. The Nexus 4000 has 14 fixed 10-Gigabit Ethernet server-facing downlinks (1/10G) and 6 fixed 10-Gigabit Ethernet SFP+ uplinks (1/10G). The Nexus 4000 is a FIP-Snooping Bridge, meaning that it cannot provide Fibre Channel Forwarder (FCF) functionality. The Nexus 4000 cannot participate in FCoE without a Nexus 5000/5500/7000 FCF.

- **B22HP HP-FEX:** Sixteen × 10GBASE-KR internal host interfaces and 8 × 10-Gigabit Ethernet fabric interfaces (Enhanced Small Form-Factor Pluggable).

NX-OS Licensing

Licensing enables specified features to be on a device after you install the appropriate license.

Nexus 7000

The following list outlines the Nexus 7000 licensing options: feature-based licenses, which make features available to the entire physical device, and module-based licenses, which make features available to one module on the physical device.

- **Base services:** The default license that ships with NX-OS covers Layer 2 protocols including such features such as Spanning Tree, virtual LANs (VLANs), Private VLANS, Unidirectional Link Detection (UDLD), and Cisco Trustsec (CTS).

Note CTS has been moved to base services as of NX-OS 6.1.1.

- **Enterprise Services Package:** Provides Layer 3 protocols such as OSPF, Border Gateway Protocol (BGP), Intermediate System-to-Intermediate System (ISIS), Enhanced Interior Gateway Routing Protocol (EIGRP), Policy-Based Routing (PBR), Protocol Independent Multicast (PIM), and Generic Routing Encapsulation (GRE).

- **Advanced Services Package:** Provides VDC

- **Virtual Device Context:** Provides licensing for four VDCs for Supervisor 2 and Supervisor 2e

- **Transport Services License:** Enables OTV support and in NX-OS 5.2(1) enables LISP

- **DCNM for LAN Enterprise License for one Nexus 7000 Chassis:** Enables data center network manager (DCNM) management support on a per chassis basis.

- **Nexus 7010 Scalable Feature License:** Enables XL capabilities and is enabled on a per-chassis basis

- **Enhanced Layer 2 License:** Enables FabricPath

- **Nexus 7000 MPLS License:** Enables MPLS features, including MPLS forwarding, QoS, L3VPN, 6PE/VPE, and OAM

- **FCoE License:** Enables FCoE features on a per F-Series module basis

- **Storage License:** Enables Inter-VSAN Routing (IVR), fabric binding, and access control for FCoE environments.

- **DCNM for SAN Advanced Edition for Nexus 7000:** Enables DCNM SAN management support on a per-chassis basis

Nexus 5500

The Nexus 5500 offers the following licensing options:

- **Nexus 5500 Storage License, 8 Ports:** The Storage Protocol Services License is required to enable an FC or FCoE operation.

- **Nexus 5000 DCNM SAN:** Fabric Manager is licensed per switch and enforced by Fabric Manager.

- **Layer 3 License for Nexus 5500 Platform:** The Nexus 5500 Layer 3 module has two license types: basic license and enterprise license. The base license includes the following Layer 3 feature support: Connected, Static, RIPv2, OSPF (256 Dynamically Learned Routes), EIGRP-Stub, HSRP, VRRP, IGMPv2/3, PIMv2, RACLs, and uRPF. The Nexus 5500 Layer 3 enterprise license includes the following support: EIGRP, OSPF routes (Unrestricted), BGP, and VRF-Lite.

Nexus 3000

The Nexus 3000 offers the following licensing options:

- **Base Layer-3 Services:** Includes Static Routes, Ripv2, EIGRP Stub, OSPF with limited routes, and PIM

- **Enterprise Layer-3 Services:** Includes OSPF unlimited routes, BGP, VRF-lite, and requires the base license

Nexus 2000

For the Nexus 2000, all the licensing is on the parent switch, Nexus 5010, 5020, 5548, 5596, or Nexus 7000.

Nexus 1000v

The Nexus 1000v offers the following licensing options:

- One 1000V license is needed for each installed server CPU/Socket on every VEM in the distributed architecture. There is no limit to the number of cores per CPU or socket.

- Cisco Virtual Security Gateway (VSG) requires one license for each installed server CPU or socket on every VEM.

- Release of Nexus 1000V v2.1 enables a free Essential licensing mode.

  - **Essential Edition:** Available at no cost, the Nexus 1000V Essential Edition provides all the rich Layer 2 networking features to connect virtual applications to the network and integrate into VMware environments, including VXLAN capability, Cisco vPath service insertion, integration with vCloud Director, and a plug-in for management and monitoring in VMware's vCenter Server.

  - **Advanced Edition:** Priced per CPU, the same price as the current Nexus 1000v 1.5 release, the Advanced Edition includes

    - The Cisco VSG for Nexus 1000V, a virtual firewall with visibility to virtual machine attributes for building sophisticated compliance policies, and logical trust zones between applications

    - Support for advanced security capabilities, such as DHCP snooping, IP Source Guard, Dynamic ARP inspection, and Cisco TrustSec Security Group Access (SGA)

Installing the NX-OS License File

Example 1-1 shows the simplicity of installing the NX-OS license file.

Example 1-1 *Displaying and Installing the NX-OS License File*

```
! Once a license file is obtained from Cisco.com and copied to flash, it can be in-
stalled for the chassis.
! Displaying the host-id for License File Creation on Cisco.com:
congo# show license host-id
License hostid: VDH=TBM14404807
```

```
! Installing a License File:
congo# install license bootflash:license_file.lic
Installing license ..done
congo#
```

Note   NX-OS offers feature testing for a 120-day grace period. Here is how to enable a 120-day grace period:

```
congo(config)# license grace-period
```

The feature is disabled after the 120-day grace period begins. The license grace period is enabled only for the default admin VDC, VDC1.

Using the grace period enables customers to test, configure, and fully operate a feature without the need for a license to be purchased. This is particularly helpful for testing a feature prior to purchasing a license.

Cisco NX-OS and Cisco IOS Comparison

If you are familiar with the traditional Cisco IOS command-line interface (CLI), the CLI for NX-OS is similar to Cisco IOS. There are key differences that should be understood prior to working with NX-OS, however:

- When you first log in to NX-OS, you go directly into EXEC mode. Because this is different from IOS, you have the option to configure an operational model similar to 6500 IOS for privilege mode (15).

- NX-OS has a setup utility that enables a user to specify the system defaults, perform basic configuration, and apply a predefined Control Plane Policing (CoPP) security policy.

- NX-OS uses a feature-based license model. This enables flexibility in licensing for uses in different areas of the network in which not all features are required.

- NX-OS has the capability to enable and disable features such as OSPF, BGP, and so on via the **feature** configuration command. Configuration and verification commands are not available until you enable the specific feature.

- Interfaces are labeled in the configuration as Ethernet. There aren't any speed designations in the interface name. Interface speed is dynamically learned and reflected in the appropriate **show** commands and interface metrics.

- NX-OS supports VDCs, which enable a physical device to be partitioned into logical devices. When you log in for the first time, you are in the default VDC.

- By default, Cisco NX-OS has two preconfigured instances of Virtual Routing Forwarding (VRF): management and default-default. All Layer 3 interfaces and routing protocols exist in the default VRF. The mgmt0 interface exists in the management VRF and cannot be moved to another VRF. On the Nexus 7000, mgmt0 is accessible from any VDC. If VDCs are configured, each VDC has a unique IP address for the mgmt0 interface.

- Secure Shell version 2 (SSHv2) is enabled by default. (Telnet is disabled by default.)

- The default login administrator user is predefined as admin; a password must be specified when the system is first powered up. With NX-OS, you must enter a username and password; you cannot disable the username and password login. In contrast, in IOS you can simply type a password; you can optionally set the login to require the use of a username.

- NX-OS uses a kickstart image and a system image. Both images are identified in the configuration file as the kickstart and system boot variables. The first image that boots is the kickstart image, which provides the Linux kernel, basic drivers, and initial file system. The NX-OS system image boots after the kickstart image; the system image provides L2, L3, infrastructure and feature support such as OTV, multicast, FEX, and so on.

- NX-OS removed the **write memory** command; use the **copy running-config startup-config**. The alias command syntax can be used to create an alias for a shortcut.

- The default Spanning Tree mode in NX-OS is Rapid-PVST+.

Caution In NX-OS, you must enable features such as OSPF, BGP, and CTS. If you remove a feature via the **no** feature command, all relevant commands related to that feature are removed from the running configuration.

For example, when configuring vty timeouts and session limits, consider Example 1-2, which illustrates the difference between IOS and NX-OS syntax.

Example 1-2 *vty Configurations and Session Limits, Comparing the Differences Between Traditional IOS and NX-OS*

```
! IOS:
congo#
congo(config)# line vty 0 9
congo(config)# exec-timeout 15 0
congo(config)# login
congo# copy running-config startup-config
----------------------------------------------------------------
! NX-OS:
congo(config)# line vty
```

```
congo(config)# session-limit 10
congo(config)# exec-timeout 15

congo# copy running-config startup-config
```

NX-OS User Modes

Cisco NX-OS CLI is divided into command modes, which define the actions available to the user. Command modes are "nested" and must be accessed in sequence. As you navigate from one command mode to another, an increasingly more specific set of commands becomes available. All commands in a higher command mode are accessible from lower command modes. For example, the **show** commands are available from any configuration command mode. Figure 1-1 shows how command access builds from the EXEC mode to the global configuration mode.

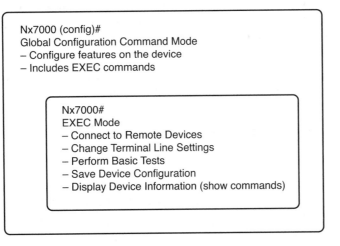

Figure 1-1   *NX-OS Command Access from EXEC Mode to Global Configuration Mode*

EXEC Command Mode

When you first log in, Cisco NX-OS Software places you in EXEC mode. As demonstrated in Example 1-3, the commands available in EXEC mode include the **show** commands that display device status and configuration information, the **clear** commands, and other commands that perform actions that you do not save in the device configuration.

Example 1-3   *Cisco NX-OS EXEC Mode*

```
Congo# show interface ethernet 1/15
Ethernet1/15 is down (SFP not inserted)
  Hardware: 10000 Ethernet, address: 001b.54c2.bbc1 (bia 001b.54c1.e4da)
```

```
    MTU 1500 bytes, BW 10000000 Kbit, DLY 10 usec,
       reliability 255/255, txload 1/255, rxload 1/255
    Encapsulation ARPA
    auto-duplex, auto-speed
    Beacon is turned off
    Auto-Negotiation is turned off
    Input flow-control is off, output flow-control is off
    Switchport monitor is off
    Last link flapped never
    Last clearing of "show interface" counters never
    30 seconds input rate 0 bits/sec, 0 packets/sec
    30 seconds output rate 0 bits/sec, 0 packets/sec
    Load-Interval #2: 5 minute (300 seconds)
      input rate 0 bps, 0 pps; output rate 0 bps, 0 pps
    L3 in Switched:
      ucast: 0 pkts, 0 bytes - mcast: 0 pkts, 0 bytes
    L3 out Switched:
      ucast: 0 pkts, 0 bytes - mcast: 0 pkts, 0 bytes
! Output omitted for brevity

Congo#
```

Global Configuration Command Mode

Global configuration mode provides access to the broadest range of commands. The term *global* indicates characteristics or features that affect the device as a whole. You can enter commands in global configuration mode to configure your device globally or enter more specific configuration modes to configure specific elements such as interfaces or protocols as demonstrated here:

```
Nx7000# conf t
Nx7000(config)# interface ethernet 1/15
```

Interface Configuration Command Mode

One example of a specific configuration mode that you enter from the global configuration mode is the interface configuration mode. To configure interfaces on your device, you must specify the interface and enter interface configuration mode.

You must enable many features on a per-interface basis. Interface configuration commands modify the operation of the interfaces on the device, such as Ethernet interfaces or management interfaces (mgmt 0).

NX-OS supports different Ethernet interface types such as Gigabit Ethernet and 10-Gigabit Ethernet interfaces. All interfaces are referred to the Ethernet; NX-OS does not designate Gigabit or 10-Gigabit Ethernet interfaces. In Example 1-4, interface 1/15 is a 10-Gigabit Ethernet interface. With NX-OS 5.1(1) and 5.2(1) and later, the default interface is added to NX-OS; this enables the administrator to quickly reset the interface configuration back to the default settings.

Example 1-4 demonstrates moving between the different command modes in NX-OS.

Example 1-4 *Interface Ethernet1/5 Is a 10-Gigabit Ethernet Interface—Show How the Interface Is Designated at the Ethernet and Not the Interface Ten1/15*

```
congo# conf t
congo(config)# interface ethernet 1/15
congo(config-if)# exit
Congo# show interface ethernet 1/15
Ethernet1/15 is down (SFP not inserted)
  Hardware: 10000 Ethernet, address: 001b.54c2.bbc1 (bia 001b.54c1.e4da)
  MTU 1500 bytes, BW 10000000 Kbit, DLY 10 usec,
      reliability 255/255, txload 1/255, rxload 1/255
  Encapsulation ARPA
  auto-duplex, auto-speed
  Beacon is turned off
  Auto-Negotiation is turned off
  Input flow-control is off, output flow-control is off
  Switchport monitor is off
  Last link flapped never
  Last clearing of "show interface" counters never
  30 seconds input rate 0 bits/sec, 0 packets/sec
  30 seconds output rate 0 bits/sec, 0 packets/sec
  Load-Interval #2: 5 minute (300 seconds)
    input rate 0 bps, 0 pps; output rate 0 bps, 0 pps
  L3 in Switched:
    ucast: 0 pkts, 0 bytes - mcast: 0 pkts, 0 bytes
  L3 out Switched:
    ucast: 0 pkts, 0 bytes - mcast: 0 pkts, 0 bytes

Congo#
```

Management Interfaces

NX-OS has many different types of management interfaces, all of which the following section covers:

- **Controller Processor (CP)/Supervisor:** Has both the management plane and control plane and is critical to the operation of the network.

- **Connectivity Management Processor (CMP):** Provides a second network interface to the device for use even when the CP is not reachable. The CMP interface is used for out-of-band management and monitoring; the CMP interface is independent from the primary operating system. The CMP interface is only available on the Nexus 7000 Supervisor Module 1.

- **MGMT0:** Provides true out-of-band management through a dedicated interface and VRF to ensure 100 percent isolation from either control plane or data plane. MGMT0 enables you to manage the devices by the IPv4 or IPv6 address on the MGMT0 interface; the mgmt0 interface is a 10/100/1000 Ethernet interface. When implementing vPC, a best practice is to use the MGMT0 interface for the vPC keepalive link.

- **Telnet:** Provides an unsecure management connection to the NX-OS device.

- **SSH:** Provides a secure management connection to the NX-OS device.

- **Extended Markup Language (XML) management interfaces:** Use the XML-based Network Configuration Protocol (NETCONF) that enables management, monitoring, and communication over the interface with an XML management tool or program.

- **Simple Network Management Protocol (SNMP):** Used by management systems to monitor and configure devices via a set of standards for communication over the TCP/IP protocol.

Controller Processor (Supervisor Module)

The Cisco Nexus 7000 series supervisor module is designed to deliver scalable control plane and management functions for the Cisco Nexus 7000 Series chassis. The Nexus 7000 supervisor module is based on an Intel dual-core processor that enables a scalable control plane. The supervisor modules controls the Layer 2 and Layer 3 services, redundancy capabilities, configuration management, status monitoring, power, and environmental management. The supervisor module also provides centralized arbitration to the system Fabric for all line cards. The fully distributed forwarding architecture enables the supervisor to support transparent upgrades to higher forwarding capacity-capable I/O and Fabric modules. Two supervisors are required for a fully redundant system, with one supervisor module running as the active device and the other in hot standby mode, providing exceptional high-availability features in data center class products. Additional features and benefits of the Nexus 7000 supervisor modules to meet demanding data center requirements follow:

- Active and standby supervisor.

- ISSU with dual supervisor modules installed in the Nexus 7000. As of NX-OS 4.2(1)N1 for the Nexus 5000/5500 supports ISSU, the following caveats need to be adhered to for ISSU support:

- ISSU on the Nexus 5500 is not support with a Layer 3 module installed.

- ISSU on the Nexus 5000/5500 is not supported if the Nexus 5000/5500 is the STP Root Bridge. The reason is that the root bridge needs to generate BPDUs every hello interval (2 sec). During the ISSU, the process restart time is too long to ensure that the process comes back prior to three times the hello dead interval. Because the Nexus 5000/5500 is positioned for the data center access layer, this typically is not an issue because the STP root would sit at the L2/L3 boundary of the data center aggregation layer.

- Virtual output queuing (VoQ), which is a QoS-aware lossless Fabric, avoids the problems associated with head-of-line blocking.

- USB interfaces that enable access to USB flash memory devices for software image loading and recovery.

- Central arbitration that provides symmetrical control of the flow of traffic through the switch Fabric helps ensure transparent switchover with no losses.

- Segmented and redundant out-of-band provisioning and management paths.

- Virtualization of the management plane via VDC is available on the Nexus 7000.

- Integrated diagnostics and protocol decoding with an embedded control plane packet analyzer; this is based on the Wireshark open source. (No additional licenses are required.) The *EthAnalyzer* provides a real-time, on-the-device protocol analyzer to monitor traffic from inband and mgmt0 interfaces to the Control Processor (supervisor module). The *EthAnalyzer* also provides extensive capture and display options and capturing to a standard .pcap file.

- Fully decoupled control plane and data plane with no hardware forwarding on the module.

- Distributed forwarding architecture, enabling independent upgrades of the supervisor and Fabric.

- With Central arbitration and VoQ, enabling Unified Fabric.

- Transparent upgrade capacity and capability; designed to support 40-Gigabit and 100-Gigabit Ethernet.

- System locator and beacon light-emitting diodes (LEDs) for simplified operations.

- Dedicated out-of-band management processor for lights-out management, the CMP.

Connectivity Management Processor (CMP)

The supervisor incorporates an innovative dedicated CMP to support remote management and troubleshooting of the complete system. The CMP provides a complete out-of-band management and monitoring capability independent from the primary operating system. The CMP enables lights-out management of the supervisor module, all modules, and the Cisco Nexus 7000 Series system without the need for separate terminal servers with the associated additional complexity and cost. The CMP delivers the remote control through its own dedicated processor, memory, and boot flash memory and a separate Ethernet management port. The CMP can reset all system components and can also reset the host supervisor module to which it is attached, enabling a complete system restart.

Note   The CMP interface is only on the Supervisor-1; CMP is not an option on the Supervisor-2 and the Supervisor-2e.

The CMP offer many benefits, including the following:

- Dedicated processor and memory, and boot flash.

- The CMP interface can reset all the system components, which include the supervisor module, and system restart.

- An independent remote system management and monitoring capability enables lights-out management of the system.

- Remote monitoring of supervisor status and initiation of resets that removes the need for separate terminal server devices for out-of-band management.

- System reset while retaining out-of-band Ethernet connectivity, which reduces the need for onsite support during system maintenance.

- Capability to remotely view boot-time messages during the entire boot process.

- Capability to initiate a complete system power shutdown and restart, which eliminates the need for local operator intervention to reset power for devices.

- Login authentication, which provides secure access to the out-of-band management environment.

- Access to supervisor logs that enables rapid detection and prevention of potential system problems.

- Capability to take full console control of the supervisor.

Example 1-5 shows how to connect to the CMP interface and the available **show** commands available from the CMP interface. Also, note the escape sequence of "~," to get back to the main NX-OS interface. You can also connect from the CMP back to the CP module.

Example 1-5 *Connecting to the CMP Interface, Displaying Available show Commands*

```
N7010-1# attach cmp
Connected
Escape character is '~,' [tilde comma]

N7010-1-cmp5 login: admin
Password:
Last login: Tue Aug 11 23:58:12 2009 on ttyS1

N7010-1-cmp5# attach cp
This command will disconnect the front-panel console on this supervisor, and will
clear all console attach sessions on the CP - proceed(y/n)? y
N7010-1#

N7010-1# attach cmp
Connected
Escape character is '~,' [tilda comma]

N7010-1-cmp5 login: admin
Password:
Last login: Wed Aug 12 00:06:12 2009 on ttyS1
N7010-1-cmp5# show ?
  attach         Serial attach/monitor processes
  clock          Display current date
  cores          Show all core dumps for CMP
  cp             Show CP status information
  hardware       Show cmp hardware information
  interface      Display interface information
  line           Show cmp line information
  logging        Show logging configuration and contents of logfile
  logs           Show all log files for CMP
  processes      Show cmp processes information
  running-config Current operating configuration
  sprom          Show SPROM contents
  ssh            SSH information
  system         Show system information
  users          Show the current users logged in the system
  version        Show cmp boot information
```

Telnet

NX-OS provides support for the Telnet server and client. The Telnet protocol enables TCP/IP terminal connections to a host. Telnet enables a user at one site to establish a

TCP connection to a login server at another site and then passes the keystrokes from one device to the other. Telnet can accept either an IP address or a domain name as the remote device address. Telnet sessions are not encrypted, and SSH is recommended instead.

Note Remember that the Telnet server is disabled by default in NX-OS.

Example 1-6 demonstrates how to enable a Telnet server in NX-OS.

Example 1-6 *Enabling a Telnet Server in NX-OS*

```
N7010-1# conf t
Enter configuration commands, one per line. End with CNTL/Z.
N7010-1(config)# feature telnet
N7010-1(config)# show telnet server
telnet service enabled
N7010-1(config)# copy running-config startup-config
[########################################] 100%
```

SSH

NX-OS supports an SSH server and SSH client. Use an SSH server to enable an SSH client to make a secure, encrypted connection to a Cisco NX-OS device; SSH uses strong encryption for authentication. The SSH server in Cisco NX-OS Software can interoperate with publicly and commercially available SSH clients. The user authentication mechanisms supported for SSH are Remote Authentication Dial-In User Service (RADIUS), Terminal Access Controller Access Control System Plus (TACACS+), and the use of locally stored usernames and passwords.

The SSH client application enables the SSH protocol to provide device authentication and encryption. The SSH client enables a Cisco NX-OS device to make a secure, encrypted connection to another Cisco NX-OS device or to any other device that runs the SSH server.

SSH requires server keys for secure communications to the Cisco NX-OS device. You can use SSH server keys for the following SSH options:

■ SSH version 2 using Rivest, Shamir, and Adelman (RSA) public-key cryptography

■ SSH version 2 using the Digital System Algorithm (DSA)

Be sure to have an SSH server key-pair with the appropriate version before allowing the SSH service. You can generate the SSH server key-pair according to the SSH client version used. The SSH service accepts two types of key-pairs for use by SSH version 2:

- The *dsa* option generates the DSA key-pair for the SSH version 2 protocol.

- The *rsa* option generates the RSA key-pair for the SSH version 2 protocol.

By default, Cisco NX-OS Software generates an RSA key using 1024 bits.

SSH supports the following public key formats:

- OpenSSH

- IETF Secure Shell (SECSH)

Example 1-7 demonstrates how to enable an SSH server and configure the SSH server keys.

Example 1-7   *Enabling an SSH Server and Configuring SSH Server Keys*

```
N7010-1# conf t
Enter configuration commands, one per line. End with CNTL/Z.
N7010-1(config)# no feature ssh
XML interface to system may become unavailable since ssh is disabled
N7010-1(config)# ssh key rsa 2048
generating rsa key(2048 bits).....
..
generated rsa key
N7010-1(config)# feature ssh
N7010-1(config)# exit
N7010-1# show ssh key
**************************************
rsa Keys generated:Thu Aug 13 23:33:41 2009
ssh-rsa AAAAB3NzaC1yc2EAAAABIwAAAQEA6+TdX+ABH/mq1gQbfhhsjBmm65ksgfQb3Mb3qbwUbNlc
Aa6fjJCGdHuf3kJox/hjgPDChJOdkUXHjESlV59OhZP/NHlBrBq0TGRr+hfdAssD3wG5oPkywgM4+bR/
ssCzoj6jVG41tGmfPip4pr3dqsMzR21DXSKK/tdj7bipWKy1wSkYQzZwatIVPIXRqTJY7L9a+JqVIJEA
0QlJM1l0wZ5YbxccB2GKNKCM2x2BZl4okVgl80CCJg7vmn+8RqIOQ5jNAPNeb9kFw9nsPj/r5xFC1RcS
KeQbdYAjItU6cX1TslRnKjlWewCgIa26dEaGdawMVuftgu0uM97VCOxZPQ==


bitcount:2048
fingerprint:
1f:b7:a3:3b:f5:ca:a6:36:19:93:98:c7:37:ba:27:db
**************************************
could not retrieve dsa key information
**************************************
N7010-1# show ssh server
ssh version 2 is enabled
N7010-1(config)# username nxos-admin password C1sc0123!

N7010-1(config)# username nxos-admin sshkey ssh-rsa
AAAAB3NzaC1yc2EAAAABIwAAAQEA6+TdX+ABH/mq1gQbfhhsjBmm65ksgfQb3Mb3qbwUbNlcAa6fjJCG-
```

```
dHuf3kJox/hjgP
DChJOd-
kUXHjESlV59OhZP/NHlBrBq0TGRr+hfdAssD3wG5oPkywgM4+bR/ssCzoj6jVG41tGmfPip3dqsMz-
R21DXSKK/tdj7b
ip-
WKy1wSkYQzZwatIVPIXRqTJY7L9a+JqVIJEA0QlJM1l0wZ5YbxccB2GKNKCM2x2BZl4okVgl80CCJg7vmn+8
RqIOQ5jNAP
Neb9kFw9nsPj/r5xFC1RcSKeQbdYAjItU6cX1TslRnKjlWewCgIa26dEaGdawMVuftgu0uM97VCOxZPQ==
N7010-1(config)# show user-account
user:admin
        this user account has no expiry date
        roles:network-admin
user:nxos-admin
        this user account has no expiry date
        roles:network-operator
        ssh public key: ssh-rsa AAAAB3NzaC1yc2EAAAABIwAAAQEA6+TdX+ABH/mq1gQbfhh-
sjBmm65ksgfQb3Mb3qbwUbNlcAa6fjJCGdHuf3kJox/hjgP
DChJOd-
kUXHjESlV59OhZP/NHlBrBq0TGRr+hfdAssD3wG5oPkywgM4+bR/ssCzoj6jVG41tGmfPip3dqsMz-
R21DXSKK/tdj7b
ip-
WKy1wSkYQzZwatIVPIXRqTJY7L9a+JqVIJEA0QlJM1l0wZ5YbxccB2GKNKCM2x2BZl4okVgl80CCJg7vmn+8
RqIOQ5jNAP
Neb9kFw9nsPj/r5xFC1RcSKeQbdYAjItU6cX1TslRnKjlWewCgIa26dEaGdawMVuftgu0uM97VCOxZPQ==
N7010-1(config)#
N7010-1# copy running-config startup-config
[#####################################] 100%
N7010-1#
```

NX-OS has a robust XML management interface, which can be used to configure the entire switch. The interface uses the XML-based NETCONF that enables you to manage devices and communicate over the interface with an XML management tool or a program. NETCONF is based on RFC 4741, and the NX-OS implementation requires you to use an SSH session for communication with the device.

NETCONF is implemented with an XML Schema (XSD) that enables you to enclose device configuration elements within a remote procedure call (RPC) message. From within an RPC message, you select one of the NETCONF operations that matches the type of command that you want the device to execute. You can configure the entire set of CLI commands on the device with NETCONF.

The XML management interface does not require any additional licensing. XML management is included with no additional charge.

XML/NETCONF can be enabled via a web2.0/ajax browser application that uses XML/NETCONF to pull all statistics off all interfaces on the Nexus 7000 running NX-OS in a dynamically updating table.

Figures 1-2, 1-3, and 1-4 demonstrate sample output from the XML/NETCONF interface.

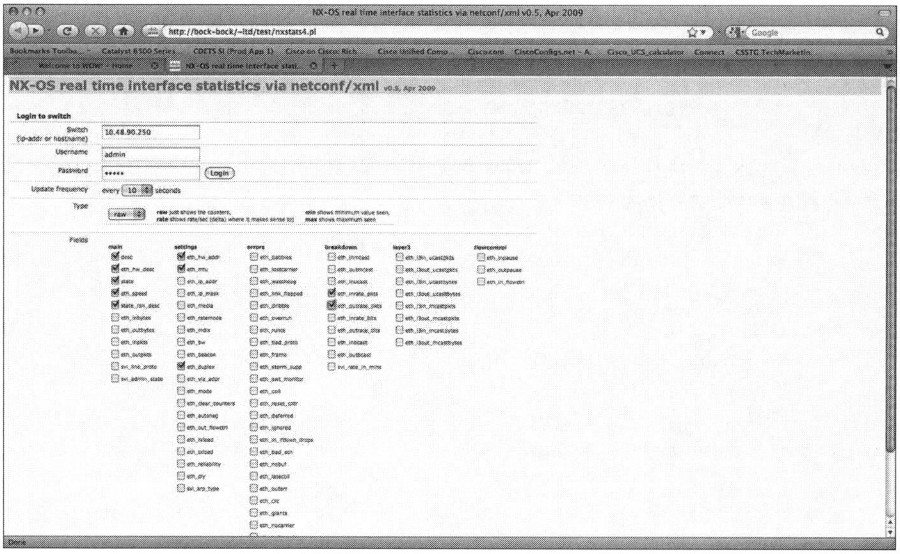

Figure 1-2 *Obtaining NX-OS Real-Time Interface Statistics via NETCONF/XML; the IP Address Entered Is the NX-OS mgmt0 Interface*

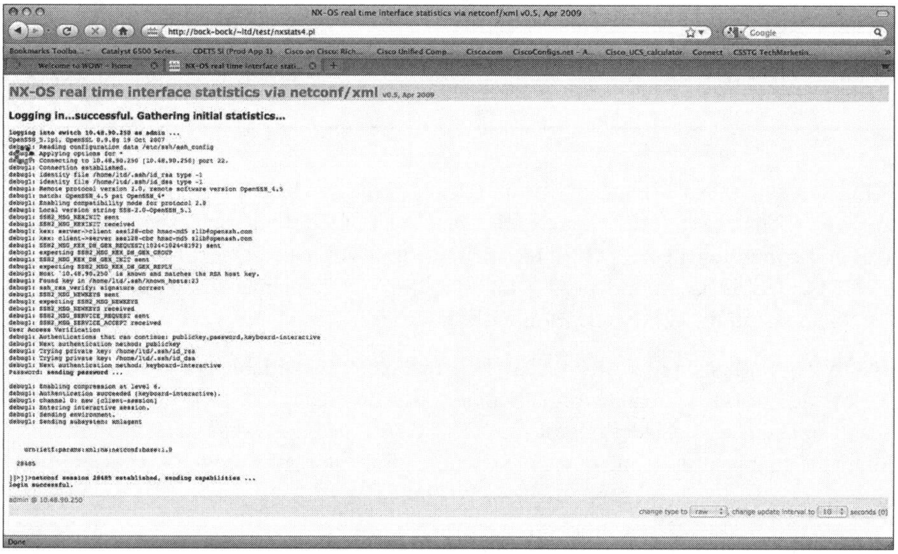

Figure 1-3 *Login Results to the NX-OS Devices via NETCONF/XML*

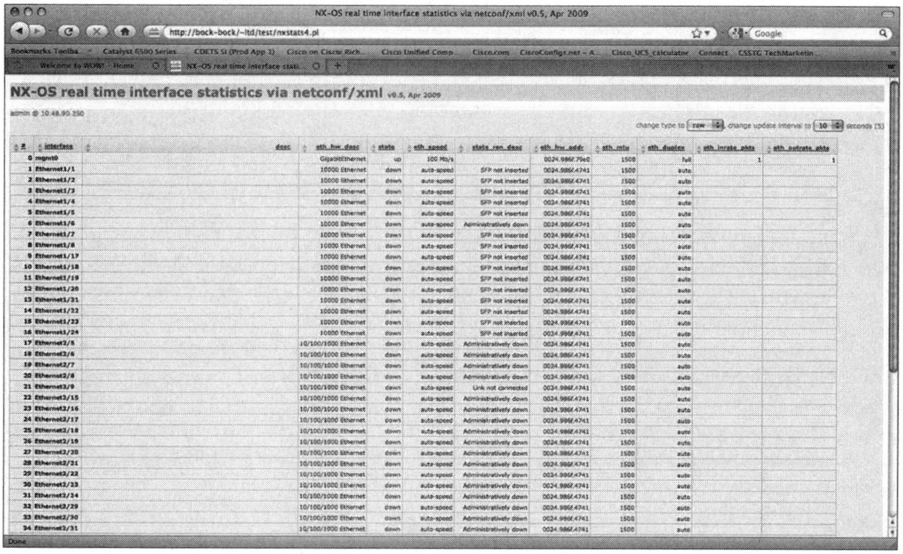

Figure 1-4   *Results of the Selected Attributes, Such as Speed, Duplex, Errors, Counters, MAC Address; the Page Refreshes Every 10 Seconds*

SNMP

The Simple Network Management Protocol is an application layer protocol that provides a message format for communication between SNMP managers and agents. SNMP provides a standardized framework and a common language used for the monitoring and management of devices in a network.

SNMP has different versions such as SNMPv1, v2, and v3. Each SNMP version has different security models or levels. Most Enterprise customers want to implement SNMPv3 because it offers encryption to pass management information (or traffic) across the network. The security level determines if an SNMP message needs to be protected and authenticated. Various security levels exist within a security model:

- **noAuthNoPriv:** Security level that does not provide authentication or encryption

- **authNoPriv:** Security level that provides authentication but does not provide encryption

- **authPriv:** Security level that provides both authentication and encryption

Cisco NX-OS supports the following SNMP standards:

- **SNMPv1:** Simple community-string based access.

- **SNMPv2c:** RFC 2575-based group access that can be tied into RBAC model.

■ **SNMPv3:** Enables for two independent security mechanisms, authentication (Hashed Message Authentication leveraging either Secure Hash Algorithm [SHA-1] or Message Digest 5 [MD5] algorithms) and encryption (Data Encryption Standard [DES] as the default and AES), to ensure secure communication between NMS station and NX-OS. Both mechanisms are implemented, as shown in Example 1-8.

Because NX-OS is truly modular and highly available, the NX-OS implementation of SNMP supports stateless restarts for SNMP. NX-OS has also implemented virtualization support for SNMP; NX-OS supports one instance of SNMP per VDC. SNMP is also VRF-aware, which enables you to configure SNMP to use a particular VRF to reach the network management host.

Example 1-8 demonstrates how to enable SNMPv3 on NX-OS.

Example 1-8 *Enabling SNMPv3 on NX-OS*

```
N7010-1# conf t
Enter configuration commands, one per line. End with CNTL/Z.
N7010-1(config)# snmp-server user NMS auth sha Cisc0123! priv Cisc0123! engineID
00:00:00:63:00:01:00:10:20:15:10:03
N7010-1(config)# snmp-server host 10.100.22.254 informs version 3 auth NMS
N7010-1(config)# snmp-server community public ro
N7010-1(config)# snmp-server community nxos rw
N7010-1(config)# show snmp
sys contact:
sys location:
0 SNMP packets input
        0 Bad SNMP versions
        0 Unknown community name
        0 Illegal operation for community name supplied
        0 Encoding errors
        0 Number of requested variables
        0 Number of altered variables
        0 Get-request PDUs
        0 Get-next PDUs
        0 Set-request PDUs
        0 No such name PDU
        0 Bad value PDU
        0 Read Only PDU
        0 General errors
        0 Get Responses
45 SNMP packets output
        45 Trap PDU
        0 Too big errors
        0 No such name errors
```

```
            0 Bad values errors
            0 General errors
            0 Get Requests
            0 Get Next Requests
            0 Set Requests
            0 Get Responses
            0 Silent drops
Community             Group / Access        context      acl_filter
---------             --------------        -------      ----------
nxos                  network-admin
public                network-operator


_____

                SNMP USERS

_____

User                        Auth   Priv(enforce)  Groups
____                        ____   _____   _____
admin                       md5    des(no)        network-admin

nxos-admin                  sha    des(no)        network-operator

_____

  NOTIFICATION TARGET USERS (configured  for sending V3 Inform)

_____

User                        Auth   Priv
____                        ____   ____
NMS                         sha    des
(EngineID 0:0:0:63:0:1:0:10:20:15:10:3)
SNMP Tcp Authentication Flag : Enabled.
--------------------------------------------------------------------------------
Port Monitor : enabled
--------------------------------------------------------------------------------
Policy Name  : default
Admin status : Not Active
Oper status  : Not Active
Port type    : All Ports
--------------------------------------------------------------------------------
Counter         Threshold  Interval Rising Threshold event Falling Threshold  event
In Use
-------         ---------  -------- ---------------- ----- ------------------ --
Link Loss       Delta      60       5                     4  1         4      Yes
Sync Loss       Delta      60       5                     4  1         4      Yes
Protocol Error  Delta      60       1                     4  0         4      Yes
Signal Loss     Delta      60       5                     4  1         4      Yes
Invalid Words   Delta      60       1                     4  0         4      Yes
Invalid CRC's   Delta      60       5                     4  1         4      Yes
RX Performance  Delta      60       2147483648            4  524288000 4      Yes
```

```
TX Performance    Delta      60      2147483648    4    524288000  4    Yes
----------------------------------------------------------------------------
SNMP protocol : Enabled
----------------------------------------------------------------
Context                          [Protocol instance, VRF, Topology]

N7010-1# show snmp user
_____
                    SNMP USERS
_____


User                      Auth  Priv(enforce) Groups
____                      ____  _____ _____
admin                     md5   des(no)       network-admin

nxos-admin                sha   des(no)       network-operator

_____
 NOTIFICATION TARGET USERS (configured  for sending V3 Inform)
_____


User                      Auth  Priv
____                      ____  ____
NMS                       sha   des
(EngineID 0:0:0:63:0:1:0:10:20:15:10:3)
N7010-1(config)# exit
N7010-1# copy running-config  startup-config
 [#######################################] 100%
N7010-1#
```

DCNM

Cisco Data Center Network Manager is a management solution that supports NX-OS devices. DCNM maximizes the overall data center infrastructure uptime and reliability, which improves service levels. Focused on the operational management requirements of the data center, DCNM provides a robust framework and rich feature set that fulfills the switching, application, automation, provisioning, and services needs of today's data centers and tomorrow's data center requirements.

DCNM is a client-server application supporting a Java-based client-server application. The DCNM client communicates with the DCNM server only, never directly with managed Cisco NX-OS devices. The DCNM server uses the XML management interface of Cisco NX-OS devices to manage and monitor them. The XML management interface is a programmatic method based on the NETCONF protocol that complements the CLI functionality.

DCNM has a robust configuration and feature support on the NX-OS platform. The following features can be configured, provisioned, and monitored through DCNM enterprise management:

- Physical ports.

- Port channels and vPCs.

- Loopback and management interfaces.

- VLAN network interfaces (sometimes referred to as switched virtual interfaces [SVI]).

- VLAN and private VLAN (PVLAN).

- Spanning Tree Protocol, including Rapid Spanning Tree (RST) and Multi-Instance Spanning Tree Protocol (MST).

- Virtual Device Contexts.

- Gateway Load Balancing Protocol (GLBP) and object tracking.

- Hot Standby Router Protocol (HSRP).

- Access control lists.

- IEEE 802.1X.

- Authentication, authorization, and accounting (AAA).

- Role-based access control.

- Dynamic Host Configuration Protocol (DHCP) snooping.

- Dynamic Address Resolution Protocol (ARP) inspection.

- IP Source Guard.

- Traffic storm control.

- Port security.

- Hardware resource utilization with Ternary Content Addressable Memory (TCAM) statistics.

- Switched Port Analyzer (SPAN).

- Network Path Analysis (PONG); the PONG feature enables you to trace the path latency between two nodes at a given time interval and to monitor the latency information in the form of statistics, based on the polling frequency.

- MDS 9000 support.

- Nexus 1000v Support.

- Nexus 4000 Support.

- Nexus 3000 Support.

- Catalyst 6500 support.

- Nexus 7000.

- Nexus 5000.

- Nexus 5500.

- UCS Support.

- FCoE Provisioning and Management—the wizard-based provisioning enables for simple configuration of Fibre Channel and FCoE interfaces. The performance monitoring of the FCoE path can show how much Fibre Channel versus Ethernet traffic moves through the path. The topology view can display the FCoE path through SAN or LAN switches out to the VMware virtual infrastructure.

- Port Profile Support enables the administrator to create, delete, and modify the Layer 2 parameters of port profiles on Cisco Nexus 7000 Series devices. You can also view the interface types that inherit a given profile.

- FabricPath monitoring enables the administrator to view the switch ID for devices enabled for FabricPath and view the conflicts between switches.

- FEX Layer 3 Routed Port for HIF Ports enables the administrator to configure and manage Layer 3 interfaces for FEX interfaces.

- Shared interfaces enable the administrator to create a new storage VDC, share ports across the Ethernet and storage VDC, and configure allowed VLANs from the Ethernet VDC to the storage VDC.

DCNM also includes end-end enterprise visibility including topology views, event browsers, configuration change management, device operating system management, hardware asset inventory, logging, and statistical data collection management.

Managing System Files

Directories can be created on bootflash: and external flash memory (slot0:, usb1:, and usb2:); you can also navigate through these directories and use them for files. Files can be created and accessed on bootflash:, volatile:, slot0:, usb1:, and usb2: file systems. Files can be accessed only on the system: file systems. A debug file system can be used for debug log files specified in the **debug** *logfile* command. System image files, from remote servers using FTP, Secure Copy (SCP), Secure Shell FTP (SFTP), and TFTP, can also be downloaded.

File Systems

Table 1-1 outlines the parameters for the syntax for specifying a local file system, which is

```
filesystem:[//module/]
```

Example 1-9 demonstrates some file system commands and how to copy a file.

Table 1-1 *Syntax for Specifying a Local File System*

File System Name	Module	Description
Bootflash	sup-active sup-local sup-1 sup-2	Internal CompactFlash memory located on the active supervisor module used for storing image files, configuration files, and other miscellaneous files. The initial default directory is bootflash.
Bootflash	sup-standby sup-remote sup-1 sup-2	Internal CompactFlash memory located on the standby supervisor module used for storing image files, configuration files, and other miscellaneous files.
slot0	sup-standby sup-remote sup-1 sup-2	External CompactFlash memory installed in a supervisor module used for storing system images, configuration files, and other miscellaneous files.
volatile	Not applicable	Volatile random-access memory (VRAM) located on a supervisor module used for temporary or pending changes.
Nvram	Not applicable	Nonvolatile random-access memory (NVRAM) located on a supervisor module used for storing the startup-configuration file.
Log	Not applicable	Memory on the active supervisor that stores logging file statistics.
system	Not applicable	Memory on a supervisor module used for storing the running-configuration file.
debug	Not applicable	Memory on a supervisor module used for debug logs.
usb1	Not applicable	External USB flash memory installed in a supervisor module used for storing image files, configuration files, and other miscellaneous files.

File System Name	Module	Description
usb2	Not applicable	External USB flash memory installed in a supervisor module used for storing image files, configuration files, and other miscellaneous files.

Example 1-9   *File System Commands/Copying a File*

```
N7010-1# dir bootflash:
      43032    Jul 26 17:20:27 2011  .sksd_crypt_service_1
      49445    Jul 26 16:48:31 2011  .sksd_crypt_service_2
      39969    Jul 26 16:48:32 2011  .sksd_crypt_service_3
      30317    Jul 26 16:48:32 2011  .sksd_crypt_service_4
        315    Oct 04 11:19:14 2010  Advanced.lic
       7615    Jul 29 13:10:08 2011  DubPoc-7K1-PreConfig.txt
        308    Oct 04 11:19:30 2010  Enhancedl2.lic
        317    Oct 04 11:19:00 2010  Enterprise.lic
        257    Aug 29 14:43:49 2011  N7K-AIDA-FCoE
        257    Aug 29 14:45:24 2011  N7K-AIDA-FCoE.lic
        257    Aug 29 14:44:01 2011  N7K-AIDA-FCoE2
        257    Aug 29 14:45:34 2011  N7K-AIDA-FCoE2.lic
        300    Aug 23 00:36:46 2011  N7K1-FCOE1.lic
        300    Aug 23 00:37:04 2011  N7K1-FCOE2.lic
        298    Aug 23 00:37:17 2011  N7K1-MPLS.lic
        301    Aug 23 00:37:33 2011  N7K1-SAN.lic
        311    Oct 04 11:17:57 2010  Otv.lic
      33766    Jul 26 16:48:32 2011  dana1.txt
        309    Mar 21 15:43:51 2011  dc1-fp.lic
       4096    Aug 05 17:04:31 2011  lost+found/
  146701191    Jul 28 18:49:31 2011  n7000-s1-dk9.5.1.3.bin
  146247835    Jul 01 15:26:11 2011  n7000-s1-dk9.5.1.4.bin
  161980383    Aug 04 13:48:52 2011  n7000-s1-dk9.5.2.1.bin
   13564350    Oct 26 12:04:14 2010  n7000-s1-epld.5.1.1.img
   13574595    Aug 04 13:56:45 2011  n7000-s1-epld.5.2.1.img
   30674944    Jul 28 18:50:31 2011  n7000-s1-kickstart.5.1.3.bin
   30691328    Jul 26 16:49:37 2011  n7000-s1-kickstart.5.1.4.bin
   29471232    Aug 04 13:52:46 2011  n7000-s1-kickstart.5.2.1.bin
       4096    Jul 29 13:39:58 2011  vdc_2/
       4096    Jul 29 13:40:39 2011  vdc_3/
       4096    Aug 12 13:01:23 2011  vdc_4/

Usage for bootflash://sup-local
 705400832 bytes used
```

```
 1104498688 bytes free
 1809899520 bytes total
CMHLAB-DC1-SW2-OTV1#
Usage for bootflash://sup-local
  982306816 bytes used
  827592704 bytes free
 1809899520 bytes total
N7010-1# dir bootflash://sup-remote
      12349    Dec 05 02:15:33 2008  7k-1-vdc-all.run
       4096    Apr 04 06:45:28 2009  eem/
      18180    Apr 02 23:47:26 2009  eem_script.cfg
   99851395    Aug 03 05:20:20 2009  congo-s1-dk9.4.2.0.601.bin
  100122301    Aug 12 04:46:18 2009  congo-s1-dk9.4.2.1.bin
      19021    Apr 03 21:04:50 2009  eem_script_counters.cfg
      19781    Apr 05 23:30:51 2009  eem_script_iptrack.cfg
      29104    Jun 19 22:44:51 2009  ethpm_act_logs.log
          0    Jun 19 22:44:51 2009  ethpm_syslogs.log
        175    Jun 20 04:14:37 2009  libotm.log
      49152    Jun 19 22:38:45 2009  lost+found/
   87755113    Apr 07 23:54:07 2009  congo-s1-dk9.4.0.4.bin
   92000595    Apr 16 21:55:19 2009  congo-s1-dk9.4.1.4.bin
   92645614    Apr 08 06:08:35 2009  congo-s1-dk9.4.1.5.bin
   92004757    Jun 02 04:29:19 2009  congo-s1-dk9.4.1.5E2.bin
   10993389    Mar 22 04:55:13 2009  congo-s1-epld.4.1.3.33.img
   23785984    Apr 07 23:47:43 2009  congo-s1-kickstart.4.0.4.bin
   24718848    Apr 16 21:52:40 2009  congo-s1-kickstart.4.1.4.bin
   25173504    Apr 08 06:00:57 2009  congo-s1-kickstart.4.1.5.bin
   23936512    Jun 02 04:26:35 2009  congo-s1-kickstart.4.1.5E2.bin
   25333248    Aug 03 05:19:26 2009  congo-s1-kickstart.4.2.0.601.bin
   25234944    Aug 12 04:45:24 2009  congo-s1-kickstart.4.2.1.bin
        310    Sep 19 03:58:55 2008  n7k-rhs-1.lic
      12699    Jan 23 14:02:52 2009  run_vpc_jan22
      11562    Mar 13 07:52:42 2009  startup-robert-cfg
      16008    Mar 12 02:02:40 2009  startup-vss-cfg
      17315    Mar 19 06:24:32 2009  startup-vss-cfg_roberto_mar18
         99    Apr 04 06:51:15 2009  test1
       9991    Jun 19 23:12:48 2009  vdc.cfg
       4096    Jan 22 13:37:57 2009  vdc_2/
       4096    Jan 22 00:40:57 2009  vdc_3/

       4096    Sep 11 12:54:10 2008  vdc_4/
     111096    Dec 20 04:40:17 2008  vpc.cap
          0    Feb 03 08:02:14 2009  vpc_hw_check_disable
      18166    Apr 03 03:24:22 2009  vpc_vss_apr02
      18223    Apr 02 22:40:57 2009  vss_vpc_apr2
```

```
Usage for bootflash://sup-remote
  863535104 bytes used
  946364416 bytes free
 1809899520 bytes total
N7010-1# copy bootflash://sup
bootflash://sup-1/          bootflash://sup-active/     bootflash://sup-remote/
bootflash://sup-2/          bootflash://sup-local/      bootflash://sup-standby/

N7010-1# copy bootflash://sup-local/congo-s1-epld.4.0.4.img bootflash://sup-
remote/congo-s1-epld.4.0.4.img
N7010-1# dir bootflash://sup-remote
       12349      Dec 05 02:15:33 2008  7k-1-vdc-all.run
        4096      Apr 04 06:45:28 2009  eem/
       18180      Apr 02 23:47:26 2009  eem_script.cfg
       19021      Apr 03 21:04:50 2009  eem_script_counters.cfg
       19781      Apr 05 23:30:51 2009  eem_script_iptrack.cfg
       29104      Jun 19 22:44:51 2009  ethpm_act_logs.log
           0      Jun 19 22:44:51 2009  ethpm_syslogs.log
         175      Jun 20 04:14:37 2009  libotm.log
       49152      Jun 19 22:38:45 2009  lost+found/
    87755113      Apr 07 23:54:07 2009  congo-s1-dk9.4.0.4.bin
    92000595      Apr 16 21:55:19 2009  congo-s1-dk9.4.1.4.bin
    92645614      Apr 08 06:08:35 2009  congo-s1-dk9.4.1.5.bin
    92004757      Jun 02 04:29:19 2009  congo-s1-dk9.4.1.5E2.bin
    99851395      Aug 03 05:20:20 2009  congo-s1-dk9.4.2.0.601.bin
   100122301      Aug 12 04:46:18 2009  congo-s1-dk9.4.2.1.bin
     9730124      Aug 12 22:02:57 2009  congo-s1-epld.4.0.4.img
    10993389      Mar 22 04:55:13 2009  congo-s1-epld.4.1.3.33.img
    23785984      Apr 07 23:47:43 2009  congo-s1-kickstart.4.0.4.bin
    24718848      Apr 16 21:52:40 2009  congo-s1-kickstart.4.1.4.bin
    25173504      Apr 08 06:00:57 2009  congo-s1-kickstart.4.1.5.bin
    23936512      Jun 02 04:26:35 2009  congo-s1-kickstart.4.1.5E2.bin
    25333248      Aug 03 05:19:26 2009  congo-s1-kickstart.4.2.0.601.bin
    25234944      Aug 12 04:45:24 2009  congo-s1-kickstart.4.2.1.bin
         310      Sep 19 03:58:55 2008  n7k-rhs-1.lic
       12699      Jan 23 14:02:52 2009  run_vpc_jan22
       11562      Mar 13 07:52:42 2009  startup-robert-cfg
       16008      Mar 12 02:02:40 2009  startup-vss-cfg
       17315      Mar 19 06:24:32 2009  startup-vss-cfg_roberto_mar18
          99      Apr 04 06:51:15 2009  test1

        9991      Jun 19 23:12:48 2009  vdc.cfg
        4096      Jan 22 13:37:57 2009  vdc_2/
        4096      Jan 22 00:40:57 2009  vdc_3/
```

```
    4096      Sep 11 12:54:10 2008  vdc_4/
  111096      Dec 20 04:40:17 2008  vpc.cap
       0      Feb 03 08:02:14 2009  vpc_hw_check_disable
   18166      Apr 03 03:24:22 2009  vpc_vss_apr02
   18223      Apr 02 22:40:57 2009  vss_vpc_apr2

Usage for bootflash://sup-remote
  873283584 bytes used
  936615936 bytes free
 1809899520 bytes total
N7010-1#
```

Configuration Files: Configuration Rollback

The configuration rollback feature enables you to take a snapshot, or *checkpoint*, of the Cisco NX-OS configuration and then reapply that configuration to your device at any point without reloading the device. Rollback enables any authorized administrator to apply this checkpoint configuration without requiring expert knowledge of the features configured in the checkpoint.

You can create a checkpoint copy of the current running configuration at any time. Cisco NX-OS saves this checkpoint as an ASCII file that you can use to roll back the running configuration to the checkpoint configuration at a future time. You can create multiple checkpoints to save different versions of your running configuration.

When you roll back the running configuration, you can trigger the following rollback types:

- **Atomic:** Implement the rollback only if no errors occur. This is the default rollback type.

- **Best-effort:** Implement a rollback and skip any errors.

- **Stop-at-first-failure:** Implement a rollback that stops if an error occurs.

- **Verbose mode:** Shows the execution log and enables the administrator to see what the switch does during a configuration rollback.

When you are ready to roll back to a checkpoint configuration, you can view the changes that will be applied to your current running configuration before committing to the rollback operation. If an error occurs during the rollback operation, you can choose to cancel the operation or ignore the error and proceed with the rollback. If you cancel the operation, Cisco NX-OS provides a list of changes already applied before the error occurred. You need to clean up these changes manually.

Configuration rollback limitations are as follows:

■ You are allowed to create up to 10 checkpoint copies per VDC.

■ You are not allowed to apply a checkpoint file of one VDC into another VDC.

■ You are not allowed to apply a checkpoint configuration in a nondefault VDC if there is a change in the global configuration portion of the running configuration compared to the checkpoint configuration.

■ The checkpoint filenames must be 75 characters or less.

■ You are not allowed to start a checkpoint filename with the word *auto*.

■ You cannot name a checkpoint file with *summary* or any abbreviation of the word *summary*.

■ Only one user can perform a checkpoint or rollback or copy the running configuration to the startup configuration at the same time in a VDC.

■ After execution of the **write erase** and **reload** commands, checkpoints are deleted. You can use the **clear checkpoint database** command to clear out all checkpoint files.

■ Rollback fails for NetFlow if during rollback you try to modify a record that is programmed in the hardware.

■ Although rollback is not supported for checkpoints across software versions, users can perform rollback at their own discretion and can use the best-effort mode to recover from errors.

■ When checkpoints are created on bootflash, differences with the running-system configuration cannot be performed before performing the rollback and the system reports No Changes.

Example 1-10 demonstrates how to create a configuration rollback.

Note   You need to make sure you are in the correct VDC. If you need to change VDCs, use the **switchto vdc** syntax.

Example 1-10   *Creating a Configuration Rollback*

```
N7010-1# checkpoint changes
...........Done
N7010-1# show diff rollback-patch checkpoint changes running-config
Collecting Running-Config
Generating Rollback Patch
Rollback Patch is Empty
N7010-1# conf t
Enter configuration commands, one per line. End with CNTL/Z.
```

```
N7010-1(config)# no snmp-server user nxos-admin
N7010-1(config)# exit
N7010-1# show diff rollback-patch checkpoint changes running-config
Collecting Running-Config
Generating Rollback Patch
!!
no username nxos-admin sshkey ssh-rsa AAAAB3NzaC1yc2EAAAABIwAAAQEA6+TdX+ABH/mq1gQbf-
hhsjBmm65ksgfQb3Mb3qbwUbNlcAa6fjJCGdHuf3kJ
ox/hjgPDChJOd-
kUXHjESlV59OhZP/NHlBrBq0TGRr+hfdAssD3wG5oPkywgM4+bR/ssCzoj6jVG41tGmfPip4pr3dqsMz-
R21DXSK
K/tdj7bipWKy1wSkYQzZwatIVPIXRqTJY7L9a+JqVIJEA0QlJM1l0wZ5YbxccB2GKNKCM2x2BZl4okVgl80C
CJg
7vmn+8RqIOQ5jNAPNeb9kFw9nsPj/r5xFC1RcSKeQbdYAjItU6cX1TslRnKjlWewCgIa26dEaGdawMVuft-
gu0uM
97VCOxZPQ==
no username nxos-admin
N7010-1# rollback running-config checkpoint changes
Note: Applying config in parallel may fail Rollback verification
Collecting Running-Config
Generating Rollback Patch
Executing Rollback Patch
Generating Running-config for verification
Generating Patch for verification
N7010-1# show snmp user nxos-admin

_____

                  SNMP USER

_____


User                         Auth  Priv(enforce) Groups

____                         ____  _____ _____

nxos-admin                   sha   des(no)       network-operator


You can also enable specific SNMP traps:
N7010-1(config)# snmp-server enable traps eigrp
N7010-1(config)# snmp-server enable traps callhome
N7010-1(config)# snmp-server enable traps link
N7010-1(config)# exit
N7010-1#
```

Operating System Files

Cisco NX-OS Software consists of three images:

- **The kickstart image:** Contains the Linux kernel, basic drivers, and initial file system.

- **The system image:** Contains the system software, infrastructure, and Layers 4 through 7.

■ **The Erasable Programmable Logic Device (EPLD) image:** EPLDs are found on the Nexus 7000 currently shipping I/O modules. EPLD images are not released frequently; even if an EPLD image is released, the network administrator is not forced to upgrade to the new image. EPLD image upgrades for I/O modules disrupt traffic going through the I/O module. The I/O module powers down briefly during the upgrade. The EPLD image upgrades are performed one module at a time. Starting with NX-OS 5.2.1 and higher, ELPD images can be installed in parallel upgrade on all I/O modules.

On the Nexus 7000 with dual-supervisor modules installed, NX-OS supports ISSU. NX-OS ISSU upgrades are performed without disrupting data traffic. If the upgrade requires EPLD to be installed onto the line cards that causes a disruption of data traffic, the NX-OS software warns you before proceeding so that you can stop the upgrade and reschedule it to a time that minimizes the impact on your network.

NX-OS ISSU updates the following images:

■ Kickstart image

■ System image

■ Supervisor module BIOS

■ Data module image

■ Data module BIOS

■ SUP-1 CMP image

■ SUP-1 CMP BIOS

The ISSU process performs a certain sequence of events, as outlined here:

1. Upgrade the BIOS on the active and standby supervisor modules and the line cards (data cards or nonsupervisor modules).

2. Bring up the standby supervisor module with the new kickstart and system images.

3. Stateful Switchover (SSO) from the active supervisor module to the upgraded standby supervisor module.

4. Bring up the old active supervisor module with the new kickstart image and the new system image.

5. Upgrade the CMP on both supervisor modules.

6. Perform a nondisruptive image upgrade for the line card (data cards or nonsupervisor modules), one at a time. With NX-OS 5.2.1 and higher, I/O modules on the Nexus 7000 can be upgraded in parallel.

7. ISSU upgrade is complete.

Virtual Device Contexts

The Nexus 7000 NX-OS software supports Virtual Device Contexts (VDC), which enable the partitioning of a single physical Nexus 7000 device into multiple logical devices. This logical separation provides the following benefits:

- Administrative and management separation

- Change and failure domain isolation from other VDCs

- Address, VLAN, VRF, and vPC isolation

Each VDC appears as a unique device and enables separate Roles-Based Access Control Management (RBAC) per VDC. This enables VDCs to be administered by different administrators while still maintaining a rich, granular RBAC capability. With this functionality, each administrator can define VRF names and VLAN IDs independent of those used in other VDCs safely with the knowledge that VDCs maintain their own unique software processes, configuration, and data plane forwarding tables.

Each VDC also maintains an individual high-availability (HA) policy that defines the action that the system takes when a failure occurs within a VDC. Depending on the hardware configuration of the system, there are various actions that can be performed. In a single supervisor system, the VDC can be shut down or restarted or the supervisor can be reloaded. In a redundant supervisor configuration, the VDC can be shut down or restarted or a supervisor switchover can be initiated.

Example 1-11 shows how to monitor VDC resources.

Example 1-11   *How to Monitor VDC Resources*

```
egypt(config)# show resource

    Resource                Min     Max     Used    Unused   Avail
    --------                ---     ---     ----    ------   -----
    vlan                    16      4094    28      0        4066
    monitor-session         0       2       0       0        2
    monitor-session-erspan-dst 0    23      0       0               23

    vrf                     2       1000    3       0        997
    port-channel            0       768     1       0        741
    u4route-mem             96      96      1       95       95
    u6route-mem             24      24      1       23       23
    m4route-mem             58      58      1       57       57
    m6route-mem             8       8       1       7        7
egypt#
```

The output shows how much shared memory in a specific VDC is used for a specific type of routes; the **u4route-mem** row indicates memory usage for unicast IPv4 routes. The first five items up to the port-channel are in numbers; the remaining –mem information is in MBs.

> **Note**   Refer to Chapter 6, "High Availability," for additional details.

Components are shared between VDCs, which include the following:

- A single instance of the kernel which supports all the processes and VDCs
- Supervisor modules
- Fabric modules
- Power supplies
- Fan trays
- System fan trays
- CMP
- CoPP
- Hardware SPAN resources

Figure 1-5 shows the logical segmentation with VDCs on the Nexus 7000. A common use case is horizontal consolidation to reduce the quantity of physical switches at the data center aggregation layer. There are two physical Nexus 7000 chassis; the logical VDC layout is also shown.

The default VDC is a fully functional VDC with all capabilities. The default VDC has special tasks that are unique to the default VDC. Tasks unique to the default VDC are

- VDC creation/deletion/suspend
- Resource allocation: interfaces and memory
- NX-OS Upgrade across all VDCs
- EPLD Upgrade (for new hardware features)
- Ethanalyzer captures: control plane/data plane (with ACL) traffic
- Feature-set installation for Nexus 2000, FabricPath and FCoE
- CoPP
- Port Channel load balancing
- Hardware IDS checks control

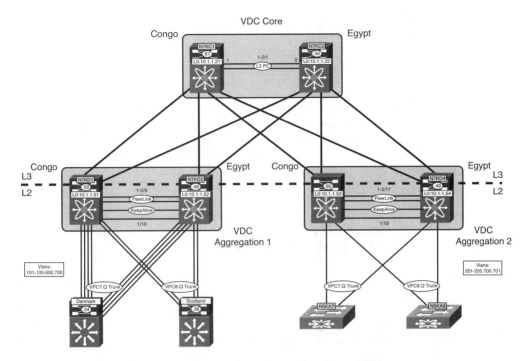

Figure 1-5 *Logical Segmentation with VDCs on the Nexus 7000*

If the operational and administrative requirements or tasks are met, the default VDC can be used for production traffic with no issues; some customers may choose to reserve it for administrative functions.

The non-default VDC is also a fully functional VDC with all capabilities and scale. The VDC feature offers a superset of functionality; the following features are a subset of VDC functionality:

■ Changes in nondefault VDC affect only that particular VDC.

■ Independent processes started for each protocol in each VDC.

■ Discrete configuration file per VDC.

■ Discrete checkpoints per VDC.

■ Discrete RBAC, TACACS, SNMP, and so on.

■ Discrete VLAN, VRF, Spanning-tree control-plane or topology, routing protocols, private-VLANs, and so on.

In NX-OS release 5.1, a module-type parameter that defines the behavior for each VDC was introduced. There are five different I/O module types that can be specified:

■ **m1:** Specifies that VDC can contain only M1 modules

■ **m1-xl:** Specifies that VDC can contain only M1-XL modules

- **f1:** Specifies that VDC can contain only F1 modules

- **f2:** Specifies that VDC can contain only F2 modules

- **m2xl:** Enables m2 type modules in this VDC

The default VDC is **limit-resource module-type f1 m1 m1-xl m2-xl (default):** It enables a mix of M1, M1-XL, and F1 modules in the VDC. Example 1-12 shows how to create a VDC and limit the resources module type to F1 modules only.

Example 1-12   *Creating VDC Module Type*

```
For an F1-only VDC
egypt# conf t
Egypt (config)# vdc egypt-dc1-fcoe
Egypt(config-vdc)# limit-resource module-type f1
Egypt(config-vdc)# end
egypt#
For an M1/M1-XL-only VDC:
egypt# conf t
Egypt (config)# vdc egypt-dc1-core
Egypt(config-vdc)# limit-resource module-type m1 m1-xl
Egypt(config-vdc)# end
egypt#
For an M1-XLwith F1 Modules for L3 proxy-mode
egypt# conf t
Egypt (config)# vdc egypt-dc1-agg
Egypt(config-vdc)# limit-resource module-type m1-xl f1
Egypt(config-vdc)# end
egypt#
```

Note   When configuring these VDC types, the following results will occur based on the following conditions. Conflicting modules are placed in a"suspended" state. With online insertion and removal (OIR), power is supplied, the module is in ok status but the interfaces are not available for configuration. Only VDC allocation is allowed for such interfaces, meaning, to move F1 interfaces from an M1-only VDC to an F1 or mixed-mode VDC.

The introduction of NX-OS 5.2.1 for the Nexus 7000, enables the creation of an FCoE Storage VDC with F1series I/O modules. For FCoE support on F2 and F2-e, a Supervisor-2 or Supervisor-2e must be deployed with NX-OS 6.1.1 and higher. The storage VDC enables traditional Fibre Channel SANs topologies: Fabric A and Fabric B separation. Today, there is support only for one Storage VDC; the default VDC cannot be the storage VDC. The storage VDC enables separation of job functions for LAN and SAN administrators to preserve current operational models. The storage VDC creates a "virtual" MDS within the Nexus 7000 with the following feature sets:

- Participates as a full FCF in the network.

- Zoning, FC alias, fcdomains, IVR, Fabric Binding, and so on.

- FCoE target support.

- FCoE ISLs to other switches: Nexus 7000, 5000, and MDS.

- Only one storage VDC per chassis.

- Does not require Advanced License (VDC).

- Does count toward total VDC count; currently support for four per Nexus 7000 with Supervisor 1, 4+1 for Supervisor 2, and 8+1 for Supervisor 2e.

- Shared interfaces, exception to the rule allowing an interface to exist in only one VDC. The shared interface concepts are for F1, F2, and F2e modules with a CNA installed in a server. The traffic is based on the L2 Ethertype; Ethernet VDC "owns" the interface, and the storage VDC sees the interface as well.

The shared interface is the only exception to have an interface shared between two VDCs. The shared interface is supported when an F1 interface has a Converged Network Adapter (CNA) attached running FCoE. Depending on the Layer 2 Ethertype, the traffic is separated. There are two components to FCoE. The two Ethertypes are directed only to the storage VDC running FCoE; all other Ethertypes are directed to the Ethernet VDC (non-storage VDC):

1. Control plane, FCoE Initialization Protocol (FIP) Ethertype 0x8914

2. Data plane, FCoE 0x8906

Figure 1-6 shows the shared interface concept with a CNA installed in a server connected to the Nexus 7000 F-Series modules.

Following are the requirements for a shared interface on the Nexus 7000:

- Minimum of NX-OS 5.2(1).

- The interfaces must be on F1, F2, or F2e I/O modules.

- Shared between Default VDC and Storage VDC.

- Shared between nondefault VDC and Storage VDC.

- Ethernet VDC is where the interface is allocated.

- Must be configured as an 802.1q trunk in the Ethernet VDC.

- Both ports on the ASIC must be configured for sharing. Storage VDC is allocated shared interfaces.

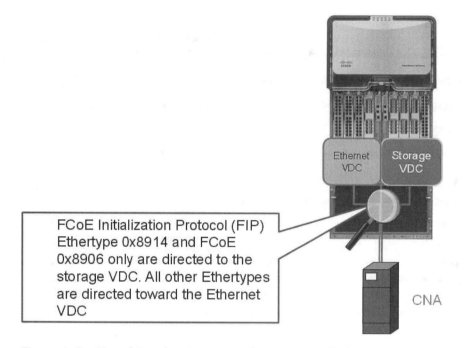

FCoE Initialization Protocol (FIP) Ethertype 0x8914 and FCoE 0x8906 only are directed to the storage VDC. All other Ethertypes are directed toward the Ethernet VDC

Figure 1-6   *Shared Interface Concept with a CNA Installed in a Server Connected to the Nexus 7000 F-Series Modules*

Example 1-13 shows how to configure shared interfaces on the Nexus 7000.

Example 1-13   *Configuring Shared Interfaces on the Nexus 7000*

```
N7K1-VDC1# config
N7K1-VDC1(config)# vdc fcoe
N7K1-VDC1(config-vdc)# allocate fcoe-vlan-range 2000-2100 from vdc N7K1-VDC1
N7K1-VDC1(config-vdc)# allocate shared interface e3/25-26
Ports that share the port group of the interfaces you have specified will be affected
as well. Continue (y/n)? [yes] yes
N7K1-VDC1(config-vdc)# end
N7K1-VDC1# switchto vdc fcoe
FCoE# show int brief
Eth3/25        1      eth  trunk  down    Administratively down      auto(D) --
Eth3/26        1      eth  trunk  down    Administratively down      auto(D) --
FCoE#
```

Because each VDC is its own switch, to communicate between VDCs, the following criteria must be met:

■ Must use front panel port to communicate between VDCs; today there are not soft cross-connect or backplane inter-VDC communications.

- Storage shared ports.

- Front panel ports align security models; ensure QoS, ACL, NetFlow, and so on resources.

- No restrictions on L2/L3 or line card models.

- When using vPC or vPC+ between VDCs, ensure domain IDs are unique.

VDC Configuration

This section shows the required steps to creating a VDC; after the VDC is created, you will assign resources to the VDC. VDCs are always created from the default admin VDC context, VDC context 1.

Note The maximum number of VDCs that can be configured per Nexus 7000 chassis is four with Supervisor-1: the default VDC (VDC 1) and three additional VDCs. Additional VDCs can be configured with the Supervisor-2 and Supervisor-2e. The Supervisor 2 supports four VDC + the admin VDC. The Supervisor-2e supports eight VDCs + the admin VDC. The admin VDC cannot have any data-plane interfaces allocated; only mgmt0 is allowed in the admin VDC.

Example 1-14 shows how to configure the VDC core on Egypt.

Example 1-14 *Creating a VDC Core on Egypt*

```
egypt(config)# vdc core
Note:  Creating VDC, one moment please ...
egypt# show vdc
vdc_id  vdc_name                          state           mac
------  --------                          -----           ----------

1       egypt                             active          00:1b:54:c2:38:c1
2       core                              active          00:1b:54:c2:38:c2


egypt# show vdc core detail
vdc id: 2
vdc name: core
vdc state: active
vdc mac address: 00:1b:54:c2:38:c2
vdc ha policy: RESTART
vdc dual-sup ha policy: SWITCHOVER
vdc boot Order: 2
vdc create time: Mon Feb 22 13:11:59 2010
vdc reload count: 1
vdc restart count: 0
egypt#
```

After the VDC is created, you must assign physical interfaces to the VDC. Depending on the Ethernet modules installed in the switch, interface allocation is supported as follows.

For the 32-port 10-Gigabit Ethernet module (N7K-M132XP-12 and N7K-M132XP-12L) interfaces can be allocated on a per-port-group basis; there are eight port-groups. For example, port-group 1 interfaces are e1, e3, e5, e7; port-group 2 interfaces e2, e4, e6, and e8.

Figure 1-7 shows the Nexus 7000 M1-32-port 10-Gb Ethernet Module.

Figure 1-7   *Nexus 7000 M1-32-Port 10-Gb Ethernet Module*

Figure 1-8 shows the 48-port 10/100/1000 I/O module (N7K-M148GT-11 and N7K-M148GT-11S) can be allocated on a per-port basis.

Figure 1-8   *Nexus 7000 M1-48 10/100/1000 Ethernet Module*

Figure 1-9 shows the 48-port 1000BaseX I/O module (N7K-M148GS-11 and N7K-M148GS-11S) can be allocated on a per-port basis.

Figure 1-9   *Nexus 7000 M1 48-Port 1000BaseX Ethernet Module*

Figure 1-10 shows the N7K-F132XP-15, 32-port 1G/10G L2 Only Ethernet module; SFP/SFP+ interfaces will be allocated per 2 ports per VDC. (1–2, 3–4, 5–6...).

Figure 1-10   *Nexus 7000 F1 32-Port L2 Ethernet Module*

Figure 1-11 shows the N7K-M108X2-12L, eight-port 10GbE with an XL option does not have port allocation requirements.

Figure 1-11   *Nexus 7000 M1-08 10-Gb Ethernet Module with Two EARL-8 Forwarding Engines*

Figure 1-12 shows the N7K-F248XP-25 - F2-series I/O module 48-port L2/L3 1/10GE SFP+ Module (req. SFP).

Figure 1-12   *N7K-F248XP-25 - F2-series I/O Module 48-Port L2/L3 1/10GE SFP+ Module (req. SFP)*

Figure 1-13 shows the N7K-F248XT-25e - F2-series I/O module 48-Port L2/L3 1/10-GBase-T RJ45 Module.

Figure 1-13   *Nexus 7000 F2e 48-Port L2/L3 1/10GBase-T Ethernet Module RJ45*

The F2/F2e module is 12 groups of four. The ports will be in sequence (1–4, 5–8, and so on). The F2 module will operate only in a VDC or chassis with other F2 modules. So you could have a chassis composed of only F2 modules in the default VDC and not need the advanced license, or you could have F2 modules in their own VDC in a chassis with other M1/M2 or F1 modules in their own VDC. The F2/F2e module will provide for 550 Gbps of Fabric bandwidth with the Fabric-2 modules, and provide line-rate L2/L3 performance.

Figure 1-14 shows the N7K-M206FQ-23L – M2-Series I/O modules 6-port 40-G Module L2/L3 QSFP.

Figure 1-14   *Nexus 7000 M2-Series I/O modules 6-Port 40Gbe Ethernet Module*

Figure 1-15 shows the N7K-M224XP-23L – M2-Series I/O modules 24-port 10-G Module L2/L3 SFP+.

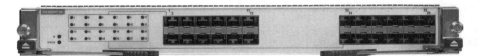

Figure 1-15   *N7K-M224XP-23L – M2-Series I/O modules 24-port 10G Module L2/L3 SFP+*

Figure 1-16 shows the N7K-M202CF-22L – M2 Series 2-port 100-G Module CFP Optics.

Figure 1-16   *N7K-M202CF-22L – M2 Series 2-Port 100-G Module CFP Optics*

The M2 modules can operate in a VDC or a chassis with M1/F1.

VDC Interface Allocation

Depending on the hardware modules installed in the Nexus 7000 chassis, the interface allocation can vary. The following sections provide the details for each hardware module and port-allocation VDC allocation.

Interface Allocation: N7K-M132XP-12 and L

Interfaces are assigned on a per-VDC basis and cannot be shared across VDCs. After an interface has been assigned to a VDC, all subsequent configuration is done from within that VDC. The N7K-M132XP-12 and L require allocation in port groups of four to align ASIC resources:

- Ports are assigned on a per-VDC basis and cannot be shared across VDCs.

- After a port has been assigned to a VDC, all subsequent configuration is done from within that VDC.

- N7K-M132XP-12 and L require allocation in port groups of four to align ASIC resources.

Figure 1-17 shows the interface allocation for the N7K-M132XP-12 and L modules.

Interface Allocation

Interface Allocation N7K-M132XP-12 and L

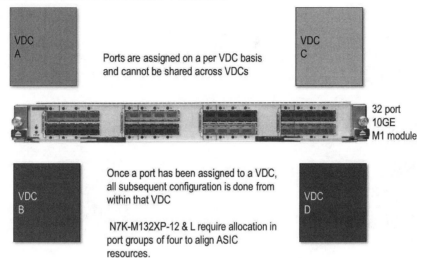

Figure 1-17   *N7K-M132XP-12 and L Module Interface Allocation*

Interface Allocation: N7K-F132XP-15

Interfaces are assigned on a per-VDC basis and cannot be shared across VDCs unless using FCoE. When an interface has been assigned to a VDC, all subsequent configuration is done from within that VDC. The N7K-F132XP-15 requires allocation in port groups of two to align ASIC resources:

■ Ports are assigned on a per-VDC basis and cannot be shared across VDCs unless using FCoE.

■ After a port has been assigned to a VDC, all subsequent configuration is done from within that VDC.

■ N7K-F132XP-15 requires allocation in port groups of two to align ASIC resources.

Figure 1-18 shows the interface allocation for the N7K-F132XP-15 modules.

Interface Allocation

Interface Allocation N7K-F132XP-15

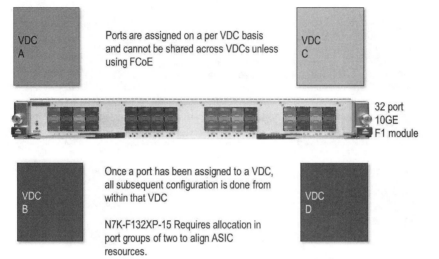

Figure 1-18   *N7K-F132XP-15 Module Interface Allocation*

Interface Allocation: N7K-M108X2-12L

Interfaces are assigned on a per-VDC basis and cannot be shared across VDCs. When a port has been assigned to a VDC, all subsequent configuration is done from within that VDC. Each port on a N7K-M108X2-12L has its own ASIC:

- Ports are assigned on a per-VDC basis and cannot be shared across VDCs.
- After a port has been assigned to a VDC, all subsequent configuration is done from within that VDC.
- Each port on a N7K-M108X2-12L has its own ASIC.

Figure 1-19 shows the interface allocation for the N7K-M108X2-12L modules.

Interface Allocation: 10/100/1000 Modules

Interfaces are assigned on a per VDC basis and cannot be shared across VDCs. After a port has been assigned to a VDC, all subsequent configuration is done from within that VDC. The M1 48 port line cards have four port groups of 12 ports:

- Ports are assigned on a per-VDC basis and cannot be shared across VDCs.
- After a port has been assigned to a VDC, all subsequent configuration is done from within that VDC.
- The M1 48-port line cards have four port groups of 12 ports.
- The recommendation is to have all members of a port group in the same VDC.

Interface Allocation

Interface Allocation N7K-M108X2-12L

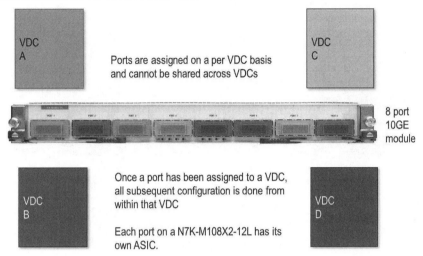

Figure 1-19   *N7K-M108X2-12L Module Interface Allocation*

Figure 1-20 shows the interface allocation for the N7K-M148GS-11 and L and N7K-M148GT-11 and L modules.

Interface Allocation

Interface Allocation N7K-M148GS-11 and L and N7K-M148GT-11 and L

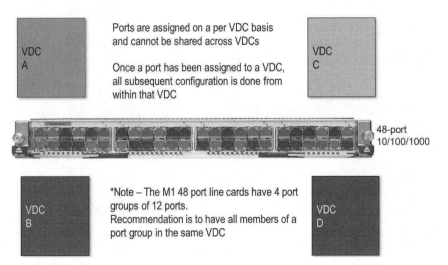

Figure 1-20   *N7K-M148GS-11 and L Module, N7K-M148GT-11 and L Module Interface Allocation*

Figure 1-21 shows the interface allocation for the N7K-F248XP-25 I/O modules.

Interface Allocation
Interface Allocation N7K-F248XP-25

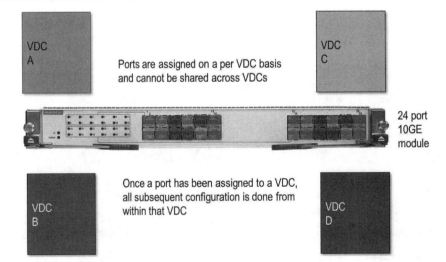

VDC
A

Ports are assigned on a per VDC basis
and cannot be shared across VDCs unless
using FCoE*

VDC
C

48 port
10GE
F2 module

Once a port has been assigned to a VDC,
all subsequent configuration is done from
within that VDC

VDC
B

N7K-F248XP-25 Requires allocation in
port groups of four to align ASIC
resources.

VDC
D

*FCoE on F2 requires
SUP2 or SUP2E and
NX-OS 6.1

Figure 1-21 *N7K-F248XP-25 I/O Modules Interface Allocation*

Figure 1-22 shows the interface allocation for the N7K-M224XP-23L I/O modules.

Interface Allocation
Interface Allocation N7K-M224XP-23L

VDC
A

Ports are assigned on a per VDC basis
and cannot be shared across VDCs

VDC
C

24 port
10GE
module

Once a port has been assigned to a VDC,
all subsequent configuration is done from
within that VDC

VDC
B

VDC
D

Figure 1-22 *N7K-M224XP-23L I/O Module Interface Allocation*

Figure 1-23 shows the interface allocation for the N7K-M206QF-23L I/O modules.

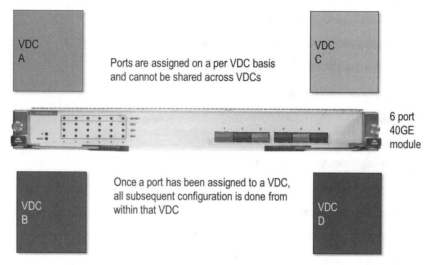

Figure 1-23   *N7K-M206QF-23L I/O Module Interface Allocation*

Figure 1-24 shows the interface allocation for the N7K-M202CF-22L I/O modules.

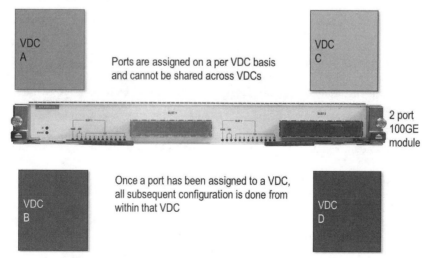

Figure 1-24   *N7K-M202CF-22L I/O Module Interface Allocation*

A common question is, "Can you explain the Nexus 7000 I/O module part number?" For example:

Part Number: N7K-M108X2-12L:

- **N7K:** Nexus 7000 i/o module

- **M1:** M1 forwarding engine

- **08:** Number of interfaces on the module

- **X2:** Optics Interface Type

- **1:** Module h/w version

- **2:** Requires two fabric without N+1 Fabric redundancy

- **L:** XL version and requires XL License

Part Number: N7K-F132XP-15:

- **N7K:** Nexus 7000 i/o module

- **F1:** Fabric module

- **32:** Number of interfaces on the module

- **XP:** Optics Interface Type SFP+

- **1:** Module h/w version

- **5:** Requires five fabric without N+1 Fabric redundancy

Interface Allocation on M2 Modules

On M2 modules, ports are assigned on a per VDC basis and cannot be shared across VDCs.

Note   You cannot virtualize a physical interface and associate the resulting logical interfaces to different VDCs. A supported configuration is to virtualize a physical interface and associate the resulting logical interfaces with different VRFs or VLANs. By default, all physical ports belong to the default VDC.

Example 1-15 demonstrates how to allocate interfaces to a VDC.

Example 1-15   *Allocating Interfaces to a VDC*

```
egypt(config)# vdc core
egypt(config-vdc)# allocate interface Ethernet1/17
egypt(config-vdc)# allocate interface Ethernet1/18
```

To verify the interfaces allocation, enter the **show vdc membership** command, as demonstrated in Example 1-16.

Example 1-16   *Verifying Interface Allocation to a VDC*

```
egypt(config-vdc)# show vdc membership

vdc_id: 1 vdc_name: egypt interfaces:
        Ethernet1/26        Ethernet1/28        Ethernet1/30
        Ethernet1/32        Ethernet2/2         Ethernet2/4
        Ethernet2/6         Ethernet2/8         Ethernet2/26
        Ethernet2/28        Ethernet2/30        Ethernet2/32
        Ethernet3/4         Ethernet3/5         Ethernet3/6
        Ethernet3/7         Ethernet3/8         Ethernet3/9
        Ethernet3/11        Ethernet3/12        Ethernet3/13
        Ethernet3/14        Ethernet3/15        Ethernet3/16
        Ethernet3/17        Ethernet3/18        Ethernet3/19
        Ethernet3/20        Ethernet3/21        Ethernet3/22
        Ethernet3/23        Ethernet3/24        Ethernet3/25
        Ethernet3/26        Ethernet3/27        Ethernet3/28
        Ethernet3/29        Ethernet3/30        Ethernet3/31
        Ethernet3/32        Ethernet3/33        Ethernet3/34
        Ethernet3/35        Ethernet3/36        Ethernet3/39
        Ethernet3/40        Ethernet3/41        Ethernet3/42
        Ethernet3/43        Ethernet3/44        Ethernet3/45
        Ethernet3/46        Ethernet3/47        Ethernet3/48


vdc_id: 2 vdc_name: core interfaces:
        Ethernet1/17        Ethernet1/18        Ethernet1/19
        Ethernet1/20        Ethernet1/21        Ethernet1/22
        Ethernet1/23        Ethernet1/24        Ethernet1/25
        Ethernet1/27        Ethernet1/29        Ethernet1/31
        Ethernet2/17        Ethernet2/18        Ethernet2/19
        Ethernet2/20        Ethernet2/21        Ethernet2/22
        Ethernet2/23        Ethernet2/24        Ethernet2/25
        Ethernet2/27        Ethernet2/29        Ethernet2/31
        Ethernet3/1         Ethernet3/2         Ethernet3/3
        Ethernet3/10
```

In addition to interfaces, other physical resources can be allocated to an individual VDC, including IPv4 route memory, IPv6 route memory, port-channels, and SPAN sessions. Configuring these values prevents a single VDC from monopolizing system resources. Example 1-17 demonstrates how to accomplish this.

Example 1-17   *Allocating System Resources*

```
egypt(config)# vdc core
egypt(config-vdc)# limit-resource port-channel minimum 32 maximum equal-to-min
egypt(config-vdc)# limit-resource u4route-mem minimum 32 maximum equal-to-min
egypt(config-vdc)# limit-resource u6route-mem minimum 32 maximum equal-to-min
egypt(config-vdc)# limit-resource vlan minimum 32 maximum equal-to-min
egypt(config-vdc)# limit-resource vrf minimum 32 maximum equal-to-min
```

Defining the VDC HA policy is also done within the VDC configuration sub-mode. Use the ha-policy command to define the HA policy for a VDC as demonstrated in Example 1-18.

Example 1-18   *Changing the HA Policy for a VDC*

```
egypt(config)# vdc core
egypt(config-vdc)# ha-policy dual-sup bringdown
```

The HA policy will depend on the use case or VDC role. For example, if you have dual-supervisor modules in the Nexus 7000 chassis or if the VDC role is development/test, the VDC HA policy may be to just shut down the VDC. If the VDC role is for the core and aggregation use case, the HA policy would be switchover.

Troubleshooting

The troubleshooting sections introduce basic concepts, methodology, and general troubleshooting guidelines for problems that might occur when configuring and using Cisco NX-OS.

show Commands

Table 1-2 lists sample EXEC commands showing the differences between IOS and NX-OS.

Table 1-2   *Sample EXEC Commands Showing the Differences Between IOS and NX-OS*

Operation	IOS	NX-OS
Displays the running configuration	show running-config	show running-config
Displays the startup configuration	show startup-config	show startup-config
Displays the status of a specified port-channel interface	show etherchannel #	show port channel #

Operation	IOS	NX-OS
Displays the current boot variables	show boot	show boot
Displays all environmental parameters	show environment	show environment
Displays the percentage of Fabric used per module	show fabric utilization	show hardware fabric-utilization [detail]
Displays the supervisors high-availability status	show redundancy	show system redundancy status
Displays CPU and memory usage data	show process cpu	show system resources
Displays specific VRF information	show ip vrf *name*	show vrf *name*

debug Commands

Cisco NX-OS supports an extensive debugging feature set for actively troubleshooting a network. Using the CLI, you can enable debugging modes for each feature and view a real-time updated activity log of the control protocol exchanges. Each log entry has a timestamp and is listed chronologically. You can limit access to the debug feature through the CLI roles mechanism to partition access on a per-role basis. Although the **debug** commands show real-time information, you can use the **show** commands to list historical and real-time information.

> **Caution**   Use the **debug** commands only under the guidance of your Cisco technical support representative because **debug** commands can impact your network/device performance.
>
> Save **debug** messages to a special log file, which is more secure and easier to process than sending the **debug** output to the console.

By using the **?** option, you can see the options available for any feature. A log entry is created for each entered command in addition to the actual **debug** output. The **debug** output shows a timestamped account of the activity that occurred between the local device and other adjacent devices.

You can use the **debug** facility to track events, internal messages, and protocol errors. However, you should be careful when using the **debug** utility in a production environment because some options might prevent access to the device by generating too many messages to the console or creating CPU-intensive events that could seriously affect network performance.

You can filter out unwanted **debug** information by using the **debug-filter** command. The **debug-filter** command enables you to limit the **debug** information produced by related **debug** commands.

Example 1-19 limits EIGRP hello packet **debug** information to Ethernet interface 1/1.

Example 1-19   *Filtering debug Information*

```
switch# debug-filter ip eigrp interface ethernet 1/1
switch# debug ip eigrp  packets hello
```

Topology

Throughout the book, you see a common topology for demonstration purposes. Figure 1-25 depicts the physical topology.

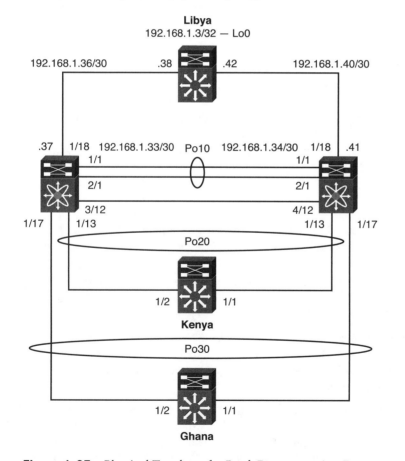

Figure 1-25   *Physical Topology for Book Demonstration Purposes*

Further Reading

NX-OS Nexus 7000 Supported MIB List: ftp://ftp-sj.cisco.com/pub/mibs/supportlists/nexus7000/Nexus7000MIBSupportList.html

- NX-OS Nexus 4000 Support MIB List: ftp://ftp.cisco.com/pub/mibs/supportlists/nexus4000/Nexus4000MIBSupportList.html

- NX-OS Nexus 5000/5500 Supported MIB List: ftp://ftp-sj.cisco.com/pub/mibs/supportlists/nexus5000/Nexus5000MIBSupportList.html

- NX-OS Nexus 1000V Supported MIB List: ftp://ftp.cisco.com/pub/mibs/supportlists/nexus1000v/Nexus1000VMIBSupportList.html

- IOS to NX-OS Conversion tool on CCO: http://tools.cisco.com/nxmt/

NX-OS is a full-featured, modular, and scalable network operating system that enables the entire Cisco Data Center switching portfolio. NX-OS has a modular building-block approach to quickly integrate new innovations and evolving industry standards.

NX-OS helps ensure continuous availability and sets the standard for mission-critical environments. Its self-healing, highly modular design makes zero-impact operations a reality and provides you with exceptional operational flexibility and scalability. Delivering the critical features for next-generation networks, NX-OS is designed with the following requirements: resiliency, virtualization, efficiency, and extensibility.

NX-OS resiliency delivers highly secure, continuous operations, with failure detection, fault isolation, self-healing features, and hitless ISSU that helps reduce maintenance outages.

NX-OS virtualization enhances virtual machine portability and converges multiple services, platforms, and networks to reduce infrastructure sprawl and total cost of ownership.

NX-OS efficiency, operational tools, and clustering technologies reduce complexity and offer consistent features and operations without compromising functionality.

NX-OS extensibility is designed to scale current and future multi-processor hardware platforms and offers easy portability across varying platforms with consistent features. It facilitates the integration of new innovations and evolving standards, delivering long-term feature extensibility.

Chapter 2

Layer 2 Support and Configurations

The Nexus line of switches provides a robust Layer 2 feature set. This chapter covers common implementations and syntax for Layer 2 features such as virtual local-area networks (VLANs), Private VLANs (PVLANs), Spanning Tree Protocol (STP), Unidirectional Link Detection (UDLD), virtual Port Channel (vPC), and Cisco FabricPath.

This chapter covers the following topics, as they relate to the Nexus family of switches:

- **Layer 2 overview:** Describes the functionality of Layer 2 features and interfaces for the Nexus family of switches

- **VLANs and Private VLANs:** Describes VLAN and Private VLAN support available within the Nexus family of switches

- **Spanning Tree Protocol:** Outlines the different STP options available within the Nexus switches and the configuration parameters

- **Virtual Port Channel:** Describes the functionality of configuring virtual Port Channels between a pair of Nexus switches and provides configuration examples and best practices

- **Unidirectional Link Detection:** Describes how to use UOLD to prevent unwanted conditions in a Layer 2 environment

- **FabricPath:** Provides an overview of Cisco FabricPath, use cases, and configuration examples

Layer 2 Overview

Although NX-OS is a single operating system for the Nexus line of switches, the hardware architecture of the switches might differ slightly. This section begins by reviewing some basic switching concepts and then discusses the forwarding behavior of both the Nexus 5000 and Nexus 7000 switches.

Layer 2 forwarding deals with the capability to build and maintain Media Access Control (MAC) address tables stored in a Content Addressable Memory (CAM) table. MAC tables are built by learning the MAC address of the stations plugged into them. The process of learning MAC addresses is done in large part dynamically; however, in certain cases, a network administrator might need to create static MAC entries prepopulated into the CAM table. When populated, the CAM tables are used to make forwarding decisions at Layer 2 by analyzing the destination MAC (DMAC) address of the frame. When this table lookup occurs and any other decisions such as dropping the frame or flooding the frame, it determines whether the switch is said to implement a store-and-forward or cut-through method.

Store-and-Forward Switching

Store-and-forward switching waits until the entire frame has been received and then compares the last portion of the frame against the frame check sequence (FCS) to ensure that no errors have been introduced during physical transmission. If the frame is determined to be corrupt, it is immediately dropped. Store-and-forward switching also inherently addresses any issues that might arise when a packet's ingress and egress ports have dissimilar underlying physical characteristics, that is, 100 Mbps versus 1 Gbps versus 10 Gbps. Latency measurements in a store-and-forward switch are typically measured on a Last In First Out (LIFO) basis. The Nexus 7000 series of switches implements store-and-forward switching.

Cut-Through Switching

Although store-and-forward switches wait for the entire frame to be received into a buffer, cut-through switches can perform the L2 lookup as soon as the DMAC is received in the first 6 bytes of the frame. Historically, cut-through switching provided a method for forwarding frames at high speeds while relying on another station to discard invalid frames. The latency of cut-through switching platforms is typically measured on a First In First Out (FIFO) basis. As application-specific integrated circuit (ASIC) process technology matured, cut-through switches gained the capability to look further into the frame without the performance penalty associated with store-and-forward switches. In addition, over time, physical mediums have become more reliable than in the past. With the maturity of both ASIC process technology and physical transmission reliability, the industry has seen a reemergence of cut-through switching technology. The Nexus 5000 series of switches uses the cut-through switching method, except when dissimilar transmission speeds exist between the ingress and egress ports.

Fabric Extension via the Nexus 2000

The Nexus 5000 and 7000 offer a unique capability by combining with the Nexus 2000 Fabric Extenders. The Nexus 2000 operates as a linecard for the Nexus parent switch, without being constrained to a physical chassis as is the case with most modular switch platforms. To continue this analogy, the Nexus parent switch operates as a supervisor module for the *virtual chassis*. Although physically separate, the Nexus parent switch and 2000 are managed as a single entity from a software image, configuration, and spanning tree perspective. This functionality enables data center engineers to gain the cabling benefits of an in-rack switching solution, with the simplicity of management of a centralized or end-of-row topology. The following Nexus 2000s are currently available:

- **Nexus 2148T:** 48 1000BASE-T host interfaces and four 10 Gbps SFP+ uplinks

- **Nexus 2224TP:** 24 100/1000BASE-T host interfaces and two 10 Gbps SFP+ uplinks

- **Nexus 2248TP and 2248TP-E:** 48 100/1000BASE-T host interface and four 10 Gbps SFP+ uplinks.

- **Nexus 2232PP:** 32 1/10Gbps SFP+ host interfaces and eight 10 Gbps SFP+ uplinks

- **Nexus 2232TM:** 32 1/10GBASE-T host interfaces and a modular uplink module with eight 10 Gbps SFP+ uplinks

The Nexus 2000 does not perform any local switching functions, and all traffic is switched in a centralized fashion by the parent switch. The front panel ports on a Nexus 2000 do not operate the same way that a normal switch port would and should be used only for host connectivity. One of the most apparent differences in operations between the Nexus 2000 and other switches is the implementation of BPDUGuard on all front-panel ports. BPDUGuard is covered in depth later in this chapter.

The initial configuration of the Nexus 2000 is simple and when configured can then be treated as additional ports configurable on the Nexus 5000 or 7000. The Nexus 2000 can be connected to the 5000 or 7000 in one of two distinct modes:

- **Static pinning:** This configuration creates a direct relationship between front-panel ports and their uplinks. The pinning is based on the number of uplinks available. For example, if one uplink is active, all front-panel ports are mapped. Static pinning is a good option in which tight control over the bandwidth and oversubscription is preferable. The drawback of static pinning is that if uplinks are added or removed, the host ports are bounced to repin the hosts across the uplinks. One to four uplinks are supported in this configuration.

- **Etherchannel:** This configuration aggregates the uplink ports into a single logical interface that all front-panel ports are mapped to. As discussed later in the chapter, in an Etherchannel configuration only one, two, or four uplinks should be used. In this configuration hosts' ports remain up if uplinks are added or removed. The uplink port-channel can also be a vPC to two different Nexus 5000s.

Configuring Nexus 2000 Using Static Pinning

This section demonstrates a basic Nexus 2000 configuration using the topology shown in Figure 2-1.

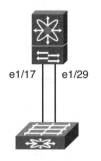
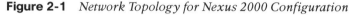

e1/17   e1/29

Figure 2-1 *Network Topology for Nexus 2000 Configuration*

Example 2-1 demonstrates how to configure Nexus 2000 to 5000 connectivity using two uplinks in static pinning mode.

Example 2-1 *Nexus 2000 Static Pinning Configuration*

```
NX5000(config)# fex 100
NX5000(config-fex)# pinning max-links 2
Change in Max-links will cause traffic disruption

NX5000(config-fex)# description FEX100
NX5000(config-fex)# exit
NX5000(config)#


NX5000# conf t
NX5000(config)# interface ethernet 1/17
NX5000(config-if)# switchport mode fex-fabric
NX5000(config-if)# fex associate 100
NX5000(config-if)# no shutdown
NX5000(config-if)# exit
NX5000(config)# interface ethernet 1/29
NX5000(config-if)# switchport mode fex-fabric
NX5000(config-if)# fex associate 100
NX5000(config-if)# no shutdown
NX5000(config-if)# exit
NX5000(config)# exit
```

Nexus 2000 Static Pinning Verification

You can monitor the Nexus 2000 using the following commands:

■ **show fex:** Displays a list of fabric extension (FEX) units, their description, state, model, and serial number.

■ **show fex fex-id detail:** Provides verbose status information about a particular Nexus 2000. The output of this command provides details as to the software versions, operational configuration, uplink status, and much more.

■ **show interface status fex fex-id:** Displays the status of front-panel host ports on a particular FEX.

■ **show interface ethernet mod/slot fex-intf:** Displays front-panel hosts' ports pinned to a particular Nexus 5000 interface.

Example 2-2 shows sample output from the previous commands.

Example 2-2 *Nexus 2000 Static Pinning Verification*

```
NX5000# show fex
  FEX          FEX             FEX                    FEX
Number        Description      State    Model         Serial
-----------------------------------------------------------------
  100          FEX100          Online   N2K-C2148T-1GE JAF1318AALS
NX5000# show fex 100 detail
FEX: 100 Description: FEX100    state: Online
  FEX version: 4.0(1a)N2(1a) [Switch version: 4.0(1a)N2(1a)]
  FEX Interim version: 4.0(1a)N2(1a)
  Switch Interim version: 4.0(1a)N2(1a)
  Extender Model: N2K-C2148T-1GE, Extender Serial: JAF1318AALS
  Part No: 73-12009-05
  Card Id: 70, Mac Addr: 00:0d:ec:cd:26:c2, Num Macs: 64
  Module Sw Gen: 19 [Switch Sw Gen: 19]
 pinning-mode: static    Max-links: 2
  Fabric port for control traffic: Eth1/17
  Fabric interface state:
    Eth1/17 - Interface Up. State: Active
    Eth1/29 - Interface Up. State: Active
  Fex Port          State  Fabric Port  Primary Fabric
        Eth100/1/1    Up     Eth1/17      Eth1/17
        Eth100/1/2    Up     Eth1/17      Eth1/17
        Eth100/1/3    Up     Eth1/17      Eth1/17
        Eth100/1/4  Down     Eth1/17      Eth1/17
        Eth100/1/5  Down     Eth1/17      Eth1/17
        Eth100/1/6  Down     Eth1/17      Eth1/17
        Eth100/1/7  Down     Eth1/17      Eth1/17
        Eth100/1/8  Down     Eth1/17      Eth1/17
        Eth100/1/9  Down     Eth1/17      Eth1/17
        Eth100/1/10   Up     Eth1/17      Eth1/17
        Eth100/1/11   Up     Eth1/17      Eth1/17
        Eth100/1/12   Up     Eth1/17      Eth1/17
        Eth100/1/13   Up     Eth1/17      Eth1/17
```

```
         Eth100/1/14   Down     Eth1/17      Eth1/17
         Eth100/1/15   Down     Eth1/17      Eth1/17
         Eth100/1/16   Down     Eth1/17      Eth1/17
         Eth100/1/17   Down     Eth1/17      Eth1/17
         Eth100/1/18   Down     Eth1/17      Eth1/17
         Eth100/1/19   Down     Eth1/17      Eth1/17
         Eth100/1/20   Down     Eth1/17      Eth1/17
         Eth100/1/21   Down     Eth1/17      Eth1/17
         Eth100/1/22   Down     Eth1/17      Eth1/17
         Eth100/1/23   Down     Eth1/17      Eth1/17
         Eth100/1/24   Down     Eth1/17      Eth1/17
         Eth100/1/25   Down     Eth1/29      Eth1/29
         Eth100/1/26   Down     Eth1/29      Eth1/29
         Eth100/1/27   Down     Eth1/29      Eth1/29
         Eth100/1/28   Down     Eth1/29      Eth1/29
         Eth100/1/29   Down     Eth1/29      Eth1/29
         Eth100/1/30   Down     Eth1/29      Eth1/29
         Eth100/1/31   Down     Eth1/29      Eth1/29
         Eth100/1/32   Down     Eth1/29      Eth1/29
         Eth100/1/33   Down     Eth1/29      Eth1/29
         Eth100/1/34   Down     Eth1/29      Eth1/29
         Eth100/1/35   Down     Eth1/29      Eth1/29
         Eth100/1/36   Down     Eth1/29      Eth1/29
         Eth100/1/37   Down     Eth1/29      Eth1/29
         Eth100/1/38   Down     Eth1/29      Eth1/29
         Eth100/1/39   Down     Eth1/29      Eth1/29
         Eth100/1/40   Down     Eth1/29      Eth1/29
         Eth100/1/41   Down     Eth1/29      Eth1/29
         Eth100/1/42   Down     Eth1/29      Eth1/29
         Eth100/1/43   Down     Eth1/29      Eth1/29
         Eth100/1/44   Up       Eth1/29      Eth1/29
         Eth100/1/45   Up       Eth1/29      Eth1/29
         Eth100/1/46   Up       Eth1/29      Eth1/29
         Eth100/1/47   Up       Eth1/29      Eth1/29
         Eth100/1/48   Up       Eth1/29      Eth1/29
Logs:
[02/08/2010 18:26:44.953152] Module register received
[02/08/2010 18:26:44.954622] Registration response sent
[02/08/2010 18:26:44.989224] Module Online Sequence
[02/08/2010 18:26:46.868753] Module Online
NX5000# sho interface status fex 100
--------------------------------------------------------------------------------
Port         Name             Status   Vlan     Duplex  Speed   Type
--------------------------------------------------------------------------------
Eth100/1/1   --               up       trunk    full    1000    --
```

Eth100/1/2	--	up	trunk	full	1000	--
Eth100/1/3	--	up	trunk	full	1000	--
Eth100/1/4	--	down	1	full	1000	--
Eth100/1/5	--	down	1	full	1000	--
Eth100/1/6	--	down	1	full	1000	--
Eth100/1/7	--	down	1	full	1000	--
Eth100/1/8	--	down	1	full	1000	--
Eth100/1/9	--	down	1	full	1000	--
Eth100/1/10	--	up	89	full	1000	--
Eth100/1/11	--	up	trunk	full	1000	--
Eth100/1/12	--	up	trunk	full	1000	--
Eth100/1/13	--	up	trunk	full	1000	--
Eth100/1/14	--	down	1	full	1000	--
Eth100/1/15	--	down	1	full	1000	--
Eth100/1/16	--	down	1	full	1000	--
Eth100/1/17	--	down	1	full	1000	--
Eth100/1/18	--	down	1	full	1000	--
Eth100/1/19	--	down	1	full	1000	--
Eth100/1/20	--	down	1	full	1000	--
Eth100/1/21	--	down	1	full	1000	--
Eth100/1/22	--	down	1	full	1000	--
Eth100/1/23	--	down	89	full	1000	--
Eth100/1/24	--	down	89	full	1000	--
Eth100/1/25	--	down	100	full	1000	--
Eth100/1/26	--	down	100	full	1000	--
Eth100/1/27	--	down	1	full	1000	--
Eth100/1/28	--	down	1	full	1000	--
Eth100/1/29	--	down	1	full	1000	--
Eth100/1/30	--	down	1	full	1000	--
Eth100/1/31	--	down	1	full	1000	--
Eth100/1/32	--	down	1	full	1000	--
Eth100/1/33	--	down	1	full	1000	--
Eth100/1/34	--	down	1	full	1000	--
Eth100/1/35	--	down	1	full	1000	--
Eth100/1/36	--	down	1	full	1000	--
Eth100/1/37	--	down	89	full	1000	--
Eth100/1/38	--	down	89	full	1000	--
Eth100/1/39	--	down	89	full	1000	--
Eth100/1/40	--	down	89	full	1000	--
Eth100/1/41	--	down	89	full	1000	--
Eth100/1/42	--	down	89	full	1000	--
Eth100/1/43	--	down	89	full	1000	--
Eth100/1/44	--	up	89	full	1000	--
Eth100/1/45	--	up	89	full	1000	--
Eth100/1/46	--	up	89	full	1000	--

```
Eth100/1/47     --              up      89      full    1000    --
Eth100/1/48     --              up      89      full    1000    --
NX5000#


NX5000# show interface ethernet 1/17 fex-intf
Fabric          FEX
Interface       Interfaces
---------------------------------------------------
 Eth1/17        Eth100/1/24   Eth100/1/23   Eth100/1/22   Eth100/1/21
                Eth100/1/20   Eth100/1/19   Eth100/1/18   Eth100/1/17
                Eth100/1/16   Eth100/1/15   Eth100/1/14   Eth100/1/10
                Eth100/1/9    Eth100/1/8    Eth100/1/7    Eth100/1/6
                Eth100/1/5    Eth100/1/4    Eth100/1/13   Eth100/1/12
                Eth100/1/11   Eth100/1/3    Eth100/1/2    Eth100/1/1


NX5000# show interface ethernet 1/29 fex-intf
Fabric          FEX
Interface       Interfaces
---------------------------------------------------
 Eth1/29        Eth100/1/48   Eth100/1/47   Eth100/1/46   Eth100/1/45
                Eth100/1/44   Eth100/1/43   Eth100/1/42   Eth100/1/41
                Eth100/1/40   Eth100/1/39   Eth100/1/38   Eth100/1/37
                Eth100/1/36   Eth100/1/35   Eth100/1/34   Eth100/1/33
                Eth100/1/32   Eth100/1/31   Eth100/1/30   Eth100/1/29
                Eth100/1/28   Eth100/1/27   Eth100/1/26   Eth100/1/25
```

Configuring Nexus 2000 Using Port-Channels

This section demonstrates the configuration of the Nexus 2000 for the topology in Figure 2-2, using port-channels instead of static pinning.

Figure 2-2   *Nexus 2000 Port-Channel Topology*

The next example configures a similar topology using port-channels instead of static pinning. The configuration in Example 2-3 is similar to that of Example 2-1; however, in this method the **pinning max-links** parameter is set to one, and the individual interfaces are configured for a Port-Channel.

Example 2-3   *Nexus 2000 Port-Channel Configuration*

```
NX5000# config t
NX5000(config)# fex 100
NX5000(config-fex)# pinning max-links 1
Change in Max-links will cause traffic disruption.
NX5000(config-fex)# exit
NX5000(config)# interface port-channel 100
NX5000(config-if)# switchport mode fex-fabric
NX5000(config-if)# fex associate 100
NX5000(config-if)# no shutdown
NX5000(config-if)# exit
NX5000(config)# int e1/17,e1/29
NX5000(config-if-range)# channel-group 100 mode on
NX5000(config-if-range)# no shutdown
NX5000(config-if-range)# exit
NX5000(config)# exit
```

Nexus 2000 Static Pinning Verification

Verification of the Nexus 2000 is similar whether port-channels or static pinning is used; however, all ports will now be pinned to the logical port-channel interface, as shown in Example 2-4.

Example 2-4   *Nexus 2000 Port-Channel Verification*

```
NX5000# show fex
  FEX           FEX           FEX                    FEX
Number        Description     State    Model         Serial
-----------------------------------------------------------------
  100           FEX100        Online   N2K-C2148T-1GE  JAF1318AALS
NX5000# sho fex 100 det
FEX: 100 Description: FEX100    state: Online
  FEX version: 4.0(1a)N2(1a) [Switch version: 4.0(1a)N2(1a)]
  FEX Interim version: 4.0(1a)N2(1a)
  Switch Interim version: 4.0(1a)N2(1a)
  Extender Model: N2K-C2148T-1GE, Extender Serial: JAF1318AALS
  Part No: 73-12009-05
  Card Id: 70, Mac Addr: 00:0d:ec:cd:26:c2, Num Macs: 64
  Module Sw Gen: 19 [Switch Sw Gen: 19]
```

```
pinning-mode: static    Max-links: 1
 Fabric port for control traffic: Eth1/29
 Fabric interface state:
   Po100 - Interface Up. State: Active
   Eth1/17 - Interface Up. State: Active
   Eth1/29 - Interface Up. State: Active
 Fex Port        State  Fabric Port  Primary Fabric
      Eth100/1/1    Up       Po100         Po100
      Eth100/1/2    Up       Po100         Po100
      Eth100/1/3    Up       Po100         Po100
      Eth100/1/4    Down     Po100         Po100
      Eth100/1/5    Down     Po100         Po100
      Eth100/1/6    Down     Po100         Po100
      Eth100/1/7    Down     Po100         Po100
      Eth100/1/8    Down     Po100         Po100
      Eth100/1/9    Down     Po100         Po100
     Eth100/1/10    Up       Po100         Po100
     Eth100/1/11    Up       Po100         Po100
     Eth100/1/12    Up       Po100         Po100
     Eth100/1/13    Up       Po100         Po100
     Eth100/1/14    Down     Po100         Po100
     Eth100/1/15    Down     Po100         Po100
     Eth100/1/16    Down     Po100         Po100
     Eth100/1/17    Down     Po100         Po100
     Eth100/1/18    Down     Po100         Po100
     Eth100/1/19    Down     Po100         Po100
     Eth100/1/20    Down     Po100         Po100
     Eth100/1/21    Down     Po100         Po100
     Eth100/1/22    Down     Po100         Po100
     Eth100/1/23    Down     Po100         Po100
     Eth100/1/24    Down     Po100         Po100
     Eth100/1/25    Down     Po100         Po100
     Eth100/1/26    Down     Po100         Po100
     Eth100/1/27    Down     Po100         Po100
     Eth100/1/28    Down     Po100         Po100
     Eth100/1/29    Down     Po100         Po100
     Eth100/1/30    Down     Po100         Po100
     Eth100/1/31    Down     Po100         Po100
     Eth100/1/32    Down     Po100         Po100
     Eth100/1/33    Down     Po100         Po100
     Eth100/1/34    Down     Po100         Po100
     Eth100/1/35    Down     Po100         Po100
     Eth100/1/36    Down     Po100         Po100
     Eth100/1/37    Down     Po100         Po100
     Eth100/1/38    Down     Po100         Po100
```

```
    Eth100/1/39   Down        Po100        Po100
    Eth100/1/40   Down        Po100        Po100
    Eth100/1/41   Down        Po100        Po100
    Eth100/1/42   Down        Po100        Po100
    Eth100/1/43   Down        Po100        Po100
--------------------------------------------------------------------
    Eth100/1/44   Up          Po100        Po100
    Eth100/1/45   Up          Po100        Po100
    Eth100/1/46   Up          Po100        Po100
    Eth100/1/47   Up          Po100        Po100
    Eth100/1/48   Up          Po100        Po100
Logs:
[02/08/2010 18:26:44.953152] Module register received
[02/08/2010 18:26:44.954622] Registration response sent
[02/08/2010 18:26:44.989224] Module Online Sequence
[02/08/2010 18:26:46.868753] Module Online
[02/08/2010 19:15:20.492760] Module disconnected
[02/08/2010 19:15:20.493584] Offlining Module
[02/08/2010 19:15:20.494099] Module Offline Sequence
[02/08/2010 19:15:20.905145] Module Offline
[02/08/2010 19:15:57.354031] Module register received
[02/08/2010 19:15:57.355002] Registration response sent
[02/08/2010 19:15:57.383437] Module Online Sequence
[02/08/2010 19:15:59.212748] Module Online
NX5000#
```

Layer 2 Forwarding on a Nexus 7000

The Nexus 7000 is an entirely distributed Layer 2 forwarding platform. This means that every module in the system contains its own forwarding table. When a packet is received on a port, the ingress module performs both an ingress L2 lookup and an initial egress L2 lookup. When the packet arrives at the egress module, a second egress lookup is performed to ensure that the table has not changed. Each module is also responsible for learning MAC addresses in the local hardware. MAC addresses learned by an individual module are flooded across the fabric to all other modules in the system, and an additional software process ensures that MAC addresses are properly synchronized across the hardware modules. Aging of MAC addresses is also done locally by each linecard but only for primary entries (entries learned locally). When a module ages a MAC address, it also notifies the supervisors so that the address can be removed from the other modules. MAC address aging is configurable on a per-VLAN basis, with a limit of 14 unique aging values per system.

To configure the MAC address aging timer, enter the following commands:

```
N7K-1# config t
N7K-1(config)# mac address-table static 0A11.1111.1111 vlan 10 interface e1/1
N7K-1(config)# exit
```

To create a static MAC entry, enter the following command:

```
N7K-1# config t
N7K-1(config)# mac address-table aging-time 1800
N7K-1(config)# exit
```

Note   The Nexus 7000 has the following default Layer-2 mac-address aging time of 1800 seconds (30 minutes) and ARP aging-timer: 1500 seconds (25 minutes). By setting the default, ARP < CAM timeout results in refreshing the CAM entry before it expires and preventing unicast flooding in the network.

L2 Forwarding Verification

During the normal operation of a switched infrastructure, certain tasks are required to validate the L2 forwarding process. These tasks include displaying the MAC address table to identify connected nodes or validate switching paths. In certain cases, it might also be necessary to clear the MAC address table, forcing the switch to repopulate with the latest information. The following examples clear the MAC table and validate that it is synchronized across all modules within the system. Example 2-5 shows how to display the MAC address table, and Example 2-6 shows how to clear the MAC table.

Example 2-5   *Displaying the MAC Address Table*

```
Congo# show mac address-table static
Legend:
        * - primary entry, G - Gateway MAC, (R) - Routed MAC
        age - seconds since last seen,+ - primary entry using vPC Peer-Link
   VLAN     MAC Address      Type      age     Secure NTFY     Ports
---------+-----------------+--------+---------+------+----+------------------
G    -      001b.54c2.bbc1   static     -        F     F    sup-eth1(R)
* 1         12ab.47dd.ff89   static     -        F     F    Eth2/1
```

Example 2-6   *Clearing MAC Address Table*

```
Congo# clear mac address-table dynamic
```

Because of the distributed forwarding nature of the Nexus 7000, each linecard maintains its own forwarding table, which is synchronized across all cards. To verify the synchronization of tables, use **the show forwarding consistency l2** command, as shown in Example 2-7. Please note that this command is module specific, so remember to specify the module number. In Example 2-7, module 1 is used.

Example 2-7 *Checking Forwarding Table Consistency*

```
Congo# show forwarding consistency l2 1
Legend:
        * - primary entry, G - Gateway MAC, (R) - Routed MAC
Missing entries in the MAC Table
    VLAN     MAC Address      Type      age      Secure NTFY    Ports
---------+-----------------+--------+---------+------+----+-----------------


Extra and Discrepant entries in the MAC Table
    VLAN     MAC Address      Type      age      Secure NTFY    Ports
---------+-----------------+--------+---------+------+----+-----------------
Congo#
```

If there were any discrepancies between the two linecards, they would appear in the preceding output. Under normal circumstances, the two linecards should always be consistent and thus produce no output.

VLANs

VLANs provide a mechanism to segment traffic on a single switch into isolated networks. VLANs can be used to segment a switch for many reasons including security, business unit, or application/function. VLANs are configured on each switch in a given topology but can span multiple physical switches using 802.1Q trunks.

The assumption is made that a Nexus supports up to 4 VDCs. The Nexus 7000 switch supports 4096 VLANs per Virtual Device Context (VDC). Some of these VLANs are used by system-level functions and are not user-configurable. You can display the internal VLANs by using the **show vlan internal usage** command, as shown in Example 2-8.

Example 2-8 *Internal VLAN Usage*

```
Congo# show vlan internal usage
VLAN        DESCRIPTION
---------   -----------------------------------------------------
3968-4031   Multicast
4032        Online diagnostics vlan1
4033        Online diagnostics vlan2
4034        Online diagnostics vlan3
```

```
4035         Online diagnostics vlan4
4036-4047    Reserved
4094         Reserved
```

Configuring VLANs

VLANs are configured in global configuration mode with the **vlan** *vlan-id configuration* command.

Example 2-9 shows how to add a VLAN to the local database.

Example 2-9   *Creating a New VLAN*

```
Congo# config t
Enter configuration commands, one per line. End with CNTL/Z.
Congo(config)# vlan 10
Congo(config-vlan)# name newvlan
```

Example 2-10 shows how you can create multiple VLANs by specifying a range using the **vlan** *vlan-range* command.

Example 2-10   *Creating Multiple VLANs*

```
Congo# config t
Enter configuration commands, one per line. End with CNTL/Z.
Congo(config)# vlan 10-15
Congo(config-vlan)# exit
```

VLAN Trunking Protocol

In large switched networks, VLAN Trunking Protocol (VTP) is sometimes used to allow the dissemination of VLAN definition across a large number of switches.

With VTP, devices can operate in one of four distinct modes:

- **Off:** By default, NX-OS devices do not run VTP. Devices that are not running VTP will not send or receive VTP advertisements and will break the flow of VTP advertisements when inserted between two VTP devices.

- **VTP server mode:** In VTP server mode, VLANs can be created, modified, and deleted. VTP servers also define domainwide parameters such as a version and whether VTP pruning will be in effect. VTP servers send VTP advertisements to other devices within the VTP domain and update the VLAN database with advertisements received from other devices in the domain.

- **VTP Client mode:** VTP clients send and receive VTP advertisements and update their local VLAN database based on these advertisements; however, you cannot create, modify, or delete VLANs locally on the device.

- **VTP transparent mode:** Devices operating in VTP transparent mode relay messages received from other devices but do not advertise changes made to the devices' local database, nor will they modify the local database based on information received from other devices.

To configure VTP transparent mode, the code base must be loaded into memory by using the **feature** command, as shown in Example 2-11.

Example 2-11 *Enabling the VTP Feature*

```
Congo# config t
Enter configuration commands, one per line. End with CNTL/Z.
Congo(config)# feature vtp
```

Example 2-12 shows how to specify VTP parameters in global configuration mode.

Example 2-12 *Specifying VTP Parameters*

```
Congo# config t
Enter configuration commands, one per line. End with CNTL/Z.
Congo(config)# vtp domain cisco
Congo(config)# vtp mode transparent
```

Assigning VLAN Membership

After the VLAN database has been created, ports can now be added to the VLAN based on the requirements of the devices connected to the switch. In addition, links between switches might be required to carry multiple VLANs.

Example 2-13 shows how to add a port to a VLAN.

Example 2-13 *Adding a Port to a VLAN*

```
Kenya# conf t
Enter configuration commands, one per line. End with CNTL/Z.
Kenya(config)# interface ethernet 2/20
Kenya(config-if)# switchport
Kenya(config-if)# switchport mode access
Kenya(config-if)# switchport access vlan 10
Kenya(config-if)#
```

Example 2-14 shows how to create a trunk interface.

Example 2-14 *Configuring a Trunk Interface*

```
Kenya# conf t
Enter configuration commands, one per line. End with CNTL/Z.
Kenya(config)# interface ethernet 2/11
Kenya(config-if)# switchport
Kenya(config-if)# switchport mode trunk
Kenya(config-if)#
```

With this configuration, the trunk port carries all VLANs that are active in the local VLAN database. It is best practice to manually prune unnecessary trunk ports, limiting the VLANs carried to only those necessary using the following syntax:

```
Kenya(config-if)# switchport trunk allowed vlan 10-20
```

As requirements change, it might be necessary to add or remove VLANs from a trunk port, using the **add** or **remove** keywords to the **switchport trunk allowed** command, as shown in Example 2-15.

Example 2-15 *Adding and Removing VLANs from a Trunk*

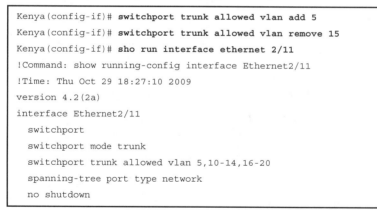

```
Kenya(config-if)# switchport trunk allowed vlan add 5
Kenya(config-if)# switchport trunk allowed vlan remove 15
Kenya(config-if)# sho run interface ethernet 2/11
!Command: show running-config interface Ethernet2/11
!Time: Thu Oct 29 18:27:10 2009
version 4.2(2a)
interface Ethernet2/11
  switchport
  switchport mode trunk
  switchport trunk allowed vlan 5,10-14,16-20
  spanning-tree port type network
  no shutdown
```

Verifying VLAN Configuration

You can view the configured VLANs and the interfaces assigned to them with the **show vlan** command, as shown in Example 2-16.

Example 2-16 *View Configured LANs and Interfaces*

```
Kenya# show vlan
VLAN Name                             Status    Ports
---- -------------------------------- --------- ------------------------------
1    default                          active    Eth2/12, Eth2/40
2    VLAN0002                         active    Eth2/12
3    VLAN0003                         active    Eth2/12
4    VLAN0004                         active    Eth2/12
5    VLAN0005                         active    Eth2/11, Eth2/12
6    VLAN0006                         active    Eth2/12
7    VLAN0007                         active    Eth2/12
8    VLAN0008                         active    Eth2/12
9    VLAN0009                         active    Eth2/12
10   VLAN0010                         active    Eth2/11, Eth2/12, Eth2/20
11   VLAN0011                         active    Eth2/11, Eth2/12
12   VLAN0012                         active    Eth2/11, Eth2/12
13   VLAN0013                         active    Eth2/11, Eth2/12
14   VLAN0014                         active    Eth2/11, Eth2/12
15   VLAN0015                         active    Eth2/12
16   VLAN0016                         active    Eth2/11, Eth2/12
17   VLAN0017                         active    Eth2/11, Eth2/12
18   VLAN0018                         active    Eth2/11, Eth2/12
19   VLAN0019                         active    Eth2/11, Eth2/12
20   VLAN0020                         active    Eth2/11, Eth2/12
VLAN Type
---- -----
1    enet
2    enet
3    enet
4    enet
5    enet
6    enet
7    enet
8    enet
9    enet
10   enet
11   enet
12   enet
13   enet
14   enet
15   enet
16   enet
17   enet
18   enet
```

```
19    enet
20    enet
Remote SPAN VLANs

--------------------------------------------------------------------------

Primary  Secondary  Type            Ports
-------  ---------  --------------- -----------------------------------------
```

Private VLANs

PVLANs offer a mechanism to divide a single VLAN into multiple isolated Layer 2 networks. PVLANs can be configured on a single Nexus switch or extended across multiple devices by trunking all the primary, isolated, and community VLANs to any other devices that need to participate in the PVLAN domain. Private VLANs are useful in several scenarios:

- **IP address management:** Typically speaking, a one-to-one relationship exists between a VLAN and an IP subnet. In situations in which many VLANs are required with a relatively small number of hosts per subnet, PVLANs can be used to configure an aggregation layer with a larger subnet and configure each isolated group of hosts into isolated VLANs, thus not requiring an IP address or subnet mask change if the host is moved from one isolated VLAN to another.

- **Security:** PVLANs offer an additional level of security at Layer 2. Isolated VLANs are allowed to communicate only at Layer 2 with other members of the same isolated VLAN. If communication between isolated VLANs is required, the communication must flow through an upstream router or firewall, making it possible to apply security policy on hosts within the same broadcast domain.

- **Broadcast suppression:** PVLANs can also be used to control the propagation of broadcast traffic only to those devices that can benefit from receiving certain broadcasts.

Within a PVLAN domain, the two major types of VLANs follow:

- **Primary:** The primary VLAN is where the broadcast domain is defined. Promiscuous ports are part of the primary VLAN and can communicate with all other ports in the primary VLAN and all isolated and community VLAN ports.

- **Secondary:** Subdomains that share IP address space with the primary VLAN but are isolated from each other in one of two ways:

  - **Isolated VLANs:** Each port within an isolated VLAN is restricted such that it can communicate only with promiscuous ports in the primary VLAN. Ports within the isolated VLANs cannot receive broadcasts from any other devices.

  - **Community VLANs:** Community VLAN ports are restricted from communicating with other community VLANs but might communicate with other ports in the same community VLAN and promiscuous ports belonging to the primary VLAN.

Multiple secondary VLANs can be associated with a single primary VLAN. These associations define a PVLAN domain.

Configuring PVLANs

In the following examples, you see the configuration of six hosts to meet the following requirements:

- **Host1(192.168.100.21):** Communicates only with Host2 and its default gateway

- **Host2(192.168.100.22):** Communicates only with Host1 and its default gateway

- **Host3(192.168.100.23):** Communicates only with Host4 and its default gateway

- **Host4(192.168.100.24):** Communicates only with Host3 and its default gateway

- **Host5(192.168.100.25):** Sends traffic only to its default gateway

- **Host6(192.168.100.26):** Sends traffic only to its default gateway

Figure 2-3 provides a visual representation of the configuration in the following examples.

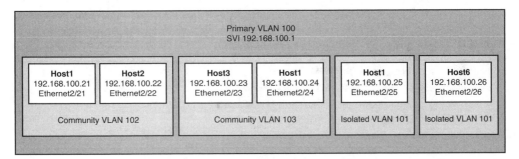

Figure 2-3   *Network Topology for PVLAN Configuration*

First, activate the code base for private VLANs by using the **feature** command, as demonstrated in Example 2-17.

Example 2-17   *Enable Private VLANs*

```
Congo# config t
Enter configuration commands, one per line. End with CNTL/Z.
Congo(config)# feature private-vlan
```

Example 2-18 demonstrates how to configure the primary VLAN, isolated, and community VLANs and define their relationship.

Example 2-18   *Defining Private VLANs*

```
Congo(config)# vlan 101
Congo(config-vlan)# name VLAN100-ISOLATED
Congo(config-vlan)# private-vlan isolated
Congo(config-vlan)# vlan 102
Congo(config-vlan)# name VLAN100-COMMUNITY1
Congo(config-vlan)# private-vlan community
Congo(config-vlan)# vlan 103
Congo(config-vlan)# name VLAN100-COMMUNITY2
Congo(config-vlan)# private-vlan community
Congo(config-vlan)#
Congo(config)# vlan 100
Congo(config-vlan)# name VLAN100-PRIMARY
Congo(config-vlan)# private-vlan primary
Congo(config-vlan)# private-vlan association add 101-103
Congo(config-vlan)# exit
```

Example 2-19 shows how to define a Layer 3 switched virtual interface (SVI) and associate secondary Layer 2 VLANs.

Example 2-19   *Creating an SVI for the Primary VLAN*

```
Congo(config)# interface vlan 100
Congo(config-if)# ip address 192.168.100.1/24
Congo(config-if)# private-vlan mapping add 101-103
Congo(config-if)# exit
Congo(config)#
```

Example 2-20 shows how to define the PVLAN configuration on the access switch and assign the host ports into the appropriate secondary VLANs.

Example 2-20   *Private VLAN Access Switch Configuration*

```
Kenya(config)# feature private-vlan
Kenya(config)# vlan 101
Kenya(config-vlan)# name VLAN100-ISOLATED
Kenya(config-vlan)# private-vlan isolated
Kenya(config-vlan)# vlan 102
Kenya(config-vlan)# name VLAN100-COMMUNITY1
Kenya(config-vlan)# private-vlan community
Kenya(config-vlan)# vlan 103
```

```
Kenya(config-vlan)# name VLAN100-COMMUNITY2
Kenya(config-vlan)# private-vlan community
Kenya(config-vlan)# vlan 100
Kenya(config-vlan)# name VLAN100-PRIMARY
Kenya(config-vlan)# private-vlan primary
Kenya(config-vlan)# private-vlan association add 101-103
Kenya(config-vlan)#
Kenya(config)# interface ethernet2/21
Kenya(config-if)# description HOST1
Kenya(config-if)# switchport
Kenya(config-if)# switchport mode private-vlan host
Kenya(config-if)# switchport private-vlan host-association 100 102
Kenya(config-if)# exit
Kenya(config)# interface ethernet2/22
Kenya(config-if)# description HOST2
Kenya(config-if)# switchport
Kenya(config-if)# switchport mode private-vlan host
Kenya(config-if)# switchport private-vlan host-association 100 102
Kenya(config-if)# exit
Kenya(config)# interface ethernet2/23
Kenya(config-if)# description HOST3
Kenya(config-if)# switchport
Kenya(config-if)# switchport mode private-vlan host
Kenya(config-if)# switchport private-vlan host-association 100 103
Kenya(config-if)# exit
Kenya(config)# interface ethernet2/24
Kenya(config-if)# description HOST4
Kenya(config-if)# switchport
Kenya(config-if)# switchport private-vlan host-association 100 103
Kenya(config-if)# exit
Kenya(config)# interface ethernet2/25
Kenya(config-if)# description HOST5
Kenya(config-if)# switchport mode private-vlan host
Kenya(config-if)# switchport
Kenya(config-if)# switchport mode private-vlan host
Kenya(config-if)# switchport private-vlan host-association 100 101
Kenya(config-if)# exit
Kenya(config)# interface ethernet2/26
Kenya(config-if)# description HOST6
Kenya(config-if)# switchport
Kenya(config-if)# switchport mode private-vlan host
Kenya(config-if)# switchport private-vlan host-association 100 101
Kenya(config-if)# exit
```

Verifying PVLAN Configuration

Example 2-21 shows how to verify the mapping of the SVI for the primary VLAN and associated secondary VLANs.

Example 2-21 *Verifying Layer 3 SVI PVLAN Mapping*

```
Congo# show interface private-vlan mapping
Interface Secondary VLAN Type
--------- -------------- ----------------

vlan100   101            isolated
vlan100   102            community
vlan100   103            community
```

Example 2-22 shows how to verify the mapping of the primary VLANs, the associated secondary VLANs, and the host ports that belong to each on the access switch Kenya.

Example 2-22 *Verifying PVLAN Mapping*

```
Kenya# show vlan private-vlan
Primary  Secondary  Type            Ports
-------  ---------  --------------  -----------------------------------------

100      101        isolated        Eth2/25, Eth2/26
100      102        community       Eth2/21, Eth2/22
100      103        community       Eth2/23, Eth2/24
```

Spanning Tree Protocol

The Spanning Tree Protocol provides a mechanism for physically redundant network topologies to remain logically loop-free. All devices in a bridging domain run spanning tree calculations to discover the topology and calculate the best path to the root bridge. Through the spanning tree process, redundant network links are placed into a blocking state preventing loops from occurring at Layer 2.

The Nexus series of switches implements two forms of standards-based Spanning Tree Protocols:

- **Rapid Per-VLAN Spanning Tree (Rapid-PVST/802.1w):** Rapid-PVST is the default spanning tree mode on Nexus 7000 switches. As the name implies, in Rapid-PVST, each VLAN elects a single root bridge, and all other devices determine the lowest cost path to the root bridge. With Rapid-PVST topology, changes are isolated to that particular VLAN. One additional characteristic worth noting is that 802.1w is backward compatible with standard Per-VLAN Spanning Tree (PVST/802.1d) for migration or interoperability purposes.

■ **Multiple Spanning Tree (MST/802.1s):** In large Layer 2 environments, MST can be used to provide a much simpler configuration with lower control-plane overhead than Rapid-PVST. When MST is leveraged, VLANs with similar topologies share a single spanning tree instance. MST instances with identical names, revision numbers, and VLAN mappings create a construct called an MST region. For further simplification of complex Layer 2 domains, each MST region is presented to the network as a single bridge. It is also worth noting that MST is backward compatible with Rapid-PVST.

For the following common data center configuration examples, refer to the topology illustrated in Figure 2-4.

In Figure 2-4, Congo and Egypt are redundant data center aggregation switches. First, the aggregation switches will be configured for Rapid-PVST+ with Congo configured as the root bridge for VLANs 1 to 10 (shown in Figure 2-5) and Egypt as root for VLANs 11 to 20 (shown in Figure 2-6) in the aggregation block. This type of *root staggering* is often preferable to maximize the amount of bandwidth available by reducing the number of blocking links within the spanning tree.

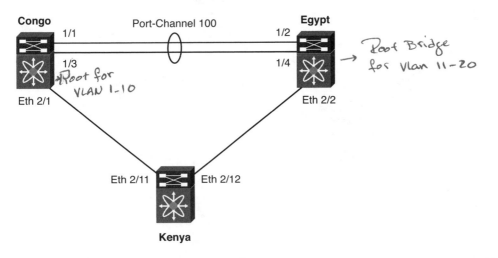

Figure 2-4 *Common Data Center Topology*

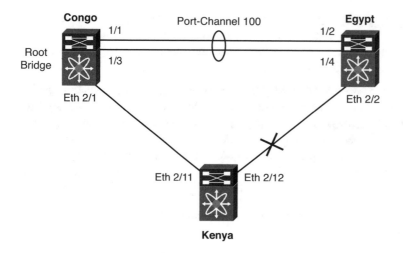

Figure 2-5   *STP Topology for VLANs 1 to 10*

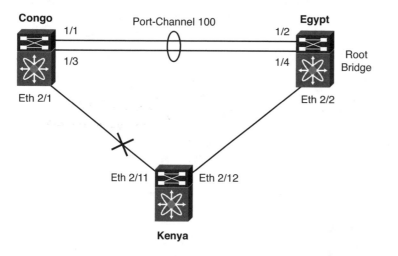

Figure 2-6   *STP Topology for VLANs 11 to 20*

Rapid-PVST+ Configuration

Typically, root bridge placement is influenced by modifying the priority. On NX-OS and most IOS devices, the default bridge priority is 32768, so you will be configuring considerably lower values on the aggregation switches.

Example 2-23 shows how to configure the spanning tree priority on a range of VLANs.

Example 2-23 *Configuring Spanning Tree Bridge Priority*

```
Congo# conf t
Enter configuration commands, one per line. End with CNTL/Z.
Congo(config)# spanning-tree mode rapid-pvst
Congo(config)# vlan 1-20
Congo(config-vlan)# exit
Congo(config)# spanning-tree vlan 1-10 priority 4096
Congo(config)# spanning-tree vlan 11-20 priority 8192
Congo(config)#
-------------------------------------------------------------------------
Egypt# conf t
Enter configuration commands, one per line. End with CNTL/Z.
Egypt(config)# spanning-tree mode rapid-pvst
Egypt(config)# vlan 1-20
Egypt(config-vlan)# exit
Egypt(config)# spanning-tree vlan 1-10 priority 8192
Egypt(config)# spanning-tree vlan 11-20 priority 4096
Egypt(config)#
```

Alternatively, you can manipulate the spanning tree priority values using the **root** keyword, as demonstrated in Example 2-24.

Example 2-24 *Using the **spanning tree root** Keyword*

```
Configuration on Congo
Congo(config)#spanning-tree vlan 1-10 root primary
Congo(config)#spanning-tree vlan 11-20 root secondary
-------------------------------------------------------------------------
Egypt(config)#spanning-tree vlan 1-10 root secondary
Egypt(config)#spanning-tree vlan 11-20 root primary
```

Verifying Spanning Tree State for a VLAN

Understanding the spanning tree topology on a specific VLAN is important to ensure that the topology behaves as expected if a link or bridge failure occurs. Inconsistent spanning tree configurations can lead to unexpected outages or slower reconvergence. Example 2-25 shows how to verify the spanning tree state for a particular VLAN.

Example 2-25 *Displaying Spanning Tree Information for a Specific VLAN*

```
Congo# show spanning-tree vlan 10
VLAN0010
  Spanning tree enabled protocol rstp
  Root ID    Priority    4106
             Address     001b.54c2.bbc1
             This bridge is the root
             Hello Time   2  sec  Max Age 12 sec  Forward Delay 9  sec
  Bridge ID  Priority    4106   (priority 4096 sys-id-ext 10)
             Address     001b.54c2.bbc1
             Hello Time   2  sec  Max Age 12 sec  Forward Delay 9  sec
Interface        Role Sts Cost      Prio.Nbr Type
---------------- ---- --- --------- -------- --------------------------------
Po100            Desg FWD 1         128.4195 Network P2p
Eth2/1           Desg FWD 4         128.257  Network P2p
```

Example 2-26 shows how to verify that Kenya has selected the best path to root; in this case, Ethernet 2/11 is blocking the redundant connection to Egypt.

Example 2-26 *Confirming Spanning Tree Bridge Priority*

```
Kenya# show spanning-tree vlan 10
VLAN0010
  Spanning tree enabled protocol rstp
  Root ID    Priority    4106
             Address     001b.54c2.bbc1
             Cost        4
             Port        267 (Ethernet2/11)
             Hello Time   2  sec  Max Age 12 sec  Forward Delay 9  sec
  Bridge ID  Priority    32778  (priority 32768 sys-id-ext 10)
             Address     001b.54c2.bbc3
             Hello Time   2  sec  Max Age 20 sec  Forward Delay 15 sec
Interface        Role Sts Cost      Prio.Nbr Type
---------------- ---- --- --------- -------- --------------------------------
Eth2/11          Root FWD 4         128.267  Network P2p
Eth2/12          Altn BLK 4         128.268  Network P2p
Kenya#
```

Spanning Tree Timers

The hello, forward-delay, and max-age timers determine the operational characteristics of the spanning tree bridge.

The hello timer defines how often the bridge sends Bridge Protocol Data Units (BPDU) to connected devices. On NX-OS, the default is 2 seconds but can be configured for 1 to 10 seconds.

The forward-delay timer specifies how long the bridge stays in the listening and learning states before transitioning into a forwarding state. By default, NX-OS waits 15 seconds before transitioning the port from listening to learning, and from learning to forwarding. The forward-delay timer is configurable from 15–30 seconds.

The max-age timer ensures backward compatibility with traditional 802.1D spanning tree environments by specifying the length of time a BPDU received on a given port is stored. The default NX-OS max-age time is 20 seconds and can be configured from 6 to 40 seconds.

Example 2-27 shows how to verify the spanning tree timers for a specific VLAN.

Example 2-27 *Default Spanning Tree Timers*

```
Congo# show spanning-tree vlan 10
VLAN0010
  Spanning tree enabled protocol rstp
  Root ID    Priority    4106
             Address     001b.54c2.bbc1
             This bridge is the root
             Hello Time  2  sec  Max Age 20 sec  Forward Delay 15 sec
  Bridge ID  Priority    4106    (priority 4096 sys-id-ext 10)
             Address     001b.54c2.bbc1
             Hello Time  2  sec  Max Age 20 sec  Forward Delay 15 sec
Interface        Role Sts Cost      Prio.Nbr Type
---------------- ---- --- --------- -------- -------------------------------
Po100            Desg FWD 1         128.4195 (vPC peer-link) Network P2p
```

In smaller L2 domains, faster reconvergence can be achieved by manipulating these timers. Example 2-28 shows how to manually adjust the hello, forward-delay, and max-age timers.

> **Caution**   Although it might be desirable to manipulate spanning tree timers for faster reconvergence, these timers and the Layer 2 topology should be well understood. Incorrect spanning tree timers can produce unwanted results.

Example 2-28 *Modifying Spanning Tree Timers*

```
Congo(config)# spanning-tree mode rapid-pvst
Congo(config)# spanning-tree vlan 10 hello-time 1
Congo(config)# spanning-tree vlan 10 forward-time 10
Congo(config)# spanning-tree vlan 10 max-age 15
Congo(config)#
Congo(config)# sho spanning-tree vlan 10
VLAN0010
  Spanning tree enabled protocol rstp
  Root ID    Priority    4106
             Address     001b.54c2.bbc1
             This bridge is the root
             Hello Time  1  sec  Max Age 15 sec  Forward Delay 10 sec
  Bridge ID  Priority    4106    (priority 4096 sys-id-ext 10)
             Address     001b.54c2.bbc1
             Hello Time  1  sec  Max Age 15 sec  Forward Delay 10 sec
Interface         Role Sts Cost      Prio.Nbr Type
---------------- ---- --- --------- -------- --------------------------------
Po100      e    Desg FWD 1         128.4195 (vPC peer-link) Network P2p
```

To mitigate some of the risk associated with the manual manipulation of spanning tree timers, NX-OS provides the **diameter** keyword, and if needed, adjusts these timers according to best practices. In this topology, a single-tier Layer 2 design is implemented with access switches connecting to both aggregation switches; therefore, the maximum number of bridges between any two stations (diameter) is 3. If no diameter is specified, the default of 7 applies. By specifying the diameter of the spanning tree domain, hello, forward-delay, and max-age timers are adjusted for optimal reconvergence in the event that a spanning tree recalculation occurs.

Example 2-29 demonstrates how the **diameter** keyword is used to manipulate spanning tree timers.

Example 2-29 *Specifying the Spanning Tree Diameter*

```
Congo(config)#spanning-tree mode rapid-pvst
Congo(config)#spanning-tree vlan 1-10 root primary diameter 3
Congo(config)#spanning-tree vlan 11-20 root secondary diameter 3
--------------------------------------------------------------------------
Egypt(config)# spanning-tree vlan 1-10 root primary diameter 3
Egypt(config)# spanning-tree vlan 11-20 root secondary diameter 3
Egypt(config)# show spanning-tree vlan 10
VLAN0010
  Spanning tree enabled protocol rstp
  Root ID    Priority    4106
             Address     001b.54c2.bbc1
```

```
              This bridge is the root
              Hello Time   2  sec  Max Age 12 sec  Forward Delay 9  sec
  Bridge ID  Priority     4106    (priority 4096 sys-id-ext 10)
             Address      001b.54c2.bbc1
             Hello Time   2  sec  Max Age 12 sec  Forward Delay 9  sec
Interface         Role Sts Cost      Prio.Nbr Type
---------------- ---- --- --------- -------- --------------------------------
Po100             Desg FWD 1          128.4195 (vPC peer-link) Network P2p
Egypt(config)# spanning-tree vlan 1-10 root primary diameter 3
Egypt(config)# spanning-tree vlan 11-20 root secondary diameter 3
Egypt(config)# show spanning-tree vlan 10
VLAN0010
  Spanning tree enabled protocol rstp
  Root ID    Priority    4106
             Address      001b.54c2.bbc1
             This bridge is the root
             Hello Time   2  sec  Max Age 12 sec  Forward Delay 9  sec
  Bridge ID  Priority     4106    (priority 4096 sys-id-ext 10)
             Address      001b.54c2.bbc1
             Hello Time   2  sec  Max Age 12 sec  Forward Delay 9  sec
Interface         Role Sts Cost      Prio.Nbr Type
---------------- ---- --- --------- -------- --------------------------------
Po100             Desg FWD 1          128.4195 (vPC peer-link) Network P2p
```

As you can see in the previous example, the hello time, max age, and forward delay have been adjusted based on the STP diameter keyword.

MST Configuration

The examples in this section demonstrate the same configuration as the previous section using MST instead of Rapid-PVST. The configuration steps are similar; however, you see the additional steps of creating an instance, defining a revision number, and associating VLANs with an instance. These steps are required to define which VLANs share the same spanning tree topology within MST.

Example 2-30 demonstrates basic MST configuration.

Example 2-30 *Basic MST Configuration*

```
Congo# conf t
Enter configuration commands, one per line. End with CNTL/Z.
Congo(config)# spanning-tree mode mst
Congo(config)# spanning-tree mst configuration
Congo(config-mst)# name AGG1
Congo(config-mst)# revision 10
```

```
Congo(config-mst)# instance 1 vlan 1-10
Congo(config-mst)# instance 2 vlan 11-20
Congo(config-mst)#
```

Prior to exiting from MST configuration mode, it is recommended to review the changes being proposed. Existing MST mode commits all changes prior to exiting.

Example 2-31 shows MST verification.

Example 2-31   *MST Verification*

```
Congo(config-mst)# show pending
Pending MST Configuration
Name       [AGG1]
Revision   10      Instances configured 3
Instance   Vlans mapped
--------   ----------------------------------------------------------------------
0          21-4094
1          1-10
2          11-20
--------   ----------------------------------------------------------------------
Congo(config-mst)# exit
Congo(config)#
```

Because MST changes are not committed until you exit MST configuration mode, the administrator has the ability to back out of the configuration without committing the changes. During the configuration of Egypt, you can misconfigure the instance mapping, abort the changes, and reconfigure appropriately.

Example 2-32 shows how to abort pending MST changes.

Example 2-32   *MST Misconfiguration*

```
Egypt(config)# spanning-tree mode mst
Egypt(config)# spanning-tree mst configuration
Egypt(config)# name AGG1
Egypt(config-mst)# revision 10
Egypt(config-mst)# instance 1 vlan 1-9
Egypt(config-mst)# instance 2 vlan 11-20
Egypt(config-mst)# show pending
Pending MST Configuration
Name       [AGG1]
Revision   10      Instances configured 3
Instance   Vlans mapped
--------   ----------------------------------------------------------------------
0          10,21-4094
```

```
1          1-9
2          11-20
-------------------------------------------------------------------------------
Egypt(config-mst)# abort
Aborting and exiting region configuration mode
Egypt(config)# spanning-tree mst configuration
Egypt(config-mst)# spanning-tree mst configuration
Egypt(config-mst)# name AGG1
Egypt(config-mst)# revision 10
Egypt(config-mst)# instance 1 vlan 1-10
Egypt(config-mst)# instance 2 vlan 11-20
Egypt(config-mst)# show pending
Pending MST Configuration
Name      [AGG1]
Revision  10     Instances configured 3
Instance  Vlans mapped
--------  ---------------------------------------------------------------------
0          21-4094
1          1-10
2          11-20
--------------------------------------------------------------------------------
Egypt(config-mst)# exit
Egypt(config)#
```

Because the instance 1 VLAN mapping was input incorrectly, the pending changes were aborted and reconfigured correctly before exiting/committing.

If PVLANs are used within the environment, it is required that all secondary VLANs share the same MST instance as their associated primary VLAN. MST provides a mechanism to automatically enforce this.

Example 2-33 shows VLAN synchronization for MST.

Example 2-33   *Private VLAN Synchronization*

```
Congo(config)# spanning-tree mst configuration
Congo(config-mst)#private-vlan synchronize
```

Example 2-34 shows how to verify the spanning tree configuration with the **show running-config spanning tree** command.

Example 2-34   *Verifying MST Configuration*

```
Egypt(config)# show run spanning-tree
spanning-tree mode mst
spanning-tree port type edge bpduguard default
```

```
spanning-tree port type edge bpdufilter default
spanning-tree mst configuration
  name AGG1
  revision 10
  instance 1 vlan 1-10
  instance 2 vlan 11-20
interface port-channel1
  spanning-tree port type network
  spanning-tree guard root
interface port-channel100
  spanning-tree port type network
interface Ethernet2/2
  spanning-tree port type network
```

Like Rapid-PVST+, the spanning tree root placement can be influenced by modifying the priority for each bridge; however, instead of configuring the priority on a per-VLAN basis, MST switches are configured with a priority per-instance.

Example 2-35 shows how to adjust the priority for an MST instance.

Example 2-35   *MST Priority Configuration*

```
Congo(config)# spanning-tree mst 1 priority 4096
Congo(config)# spanning-tree mst 2 priority 8192
----------------------------------------------------------------------
Egypt(config)# spanning-tree mst 1 priority 8192
Egypt(config)# spanning-tree mst 2 priority 4096
```

Alternatively, Example 2-36 shows how to use the **root** keyword as done previously in the Rapid-PVST section.

Example 2-36   *MST Root Configuration*

```
Configuration on Congo
Congo(config)#spanning-tree mst 1 root primary
Congo(config)#spanning-tree mst 2 root secondary
```

Example 2-37 shows how to verify the configuration of an MST instance.

Example 2-37   *MST Verification*

```
Congo# show spanning-tree mst 1
##### MST1    vlans mapped:   1-10
Bridge          address 001b.54c2.bbc1  priority      4097  (4096 sysid 1)
Root            this switch for MST1
```

```
Interface          Role Sts Cost       Prio.Nbr Type
---------------- ---- --- --------- -------- -------------------------------
Po100              Desg FWD 1000       128.4195 Network P2p
Eth2/1             Desg FWD 20000      128.257  Network P2p Bound(PVST)
Congo#
```

The example shows that Congo is the root bridge for MST instance 1, which has VLANs 1–10 mapped to it.

Additional Spanning Tree Configuration

The following sections cover the configuration required to manipulate some additional spanning tree parameters.

Port Cost

Port cost is used to calculate the shortest path to the root bridge. By default, port costs are automatically calculated by the device based on the transmission speed of the physical link. Table 2-1 illustrates the default port costs.

From time to time, it might be necessary to statically define port costs; an example of this is with port-channels in which the cost might change depending on the number of links active within the bundle.

Example 2-38 shows the root ports on Kenya prior to change to port cost.

Table 2-1   *Default Spanning Tree Costs*

Link Speed	Default Spanning Tree Cost
10 Mbps	100
100 Mbps	19
1000 Mbps	4
10,000 Mbps	2

Example 2-38   *MST Verification*

```
Kenya# show spanning-tree root

                              Root  Hello Max Fwd
Vlan              Root ID     Cost  Time  Age Dly  Root Port
---------------- ----------------- ------- ----- --- ---  ----------------
VLAN0001          4097 001b.54c2.bbc1    4    2   12   9     Ethernet2/11
VLAN0002          4098 001b.54c2.bbc1    4    2   12   9     Ethernet2/11
VLAN0003          4099 001b.54c2.bbc1    4    2   12   9     Ethernet2/11
VLAN0004          4100 001b.54c2.bbc1    4    2   12   9     Ethernet2/11
```

```
VLAN0005         4101 001b.54c2.bbc1      4    2    12    9      Ethernet2/11
VLAN0006         4102 001b.54c2.bbc1      4    2    12    9      Ethernet2/11
VLAN0007         4103 001b.54c2.bbc1      4    2    12    9      Ethernet2/11
VLAN0008         4104 001b.54c2.bbc1      4    2    12    9      Ethernet2/11
VLAN0009         4105 001b.54c2.bbc1      4    2    12    9      Ethernet2/11
VLAN0010         4106 001b.54c2.bbc1      4    2    12    9      Ethernet2/11
VLAN0011         4107 001b.54c2.bbc2      4    2    12    9      Ethernet2/12
VLAN0012         4108 001b.54c2.bbc2      4    2    12    9      Ethernet2/12
VLAN0013         4109 001b.54c2.bbc2      4    2    12    9      Ethernet2/12
VLAN0014         4110 001b.54c2.bbc2      4    2    12    9      Ethernet2/12
VLAN0015         4111 001b.54c2.bbc2      4    2    12    9      Ethernet2/12
VLAN0016         4112 001b.54c2.bbc2      4    2    12    9      Ethernet2/12
VLAN0017         4113 001b.54c2.bbc2      4    2    12    9      Ethernet2/12
VLAN0018         4114 001b.54c2.bbc2      4    2    12    9      Ethernet2/12
VLAN0019         4115 001b.54c2.bbc2      4    2    12    9      Ethernet2/12
VLAN0020         4116 001b.54c2.bbc2      4    2    12    9      Ethernet2/12
Kenya#
```

Example 2-39 shows the configuration of port cost on a link.

Example 2-39 *Configuring Port Cost*

```
Kenya# conf t
Enter configuration commands, one per line. End with CNTL/Z.
Kenya(config)# interface ethernet 2/11
Kenya(config-if)# spanning-tree cost 128
Kenya(config-if)# exit
Kenya(config)# exit
```

Example 2-40 shows the output after adjusting the port cost. Now Ethernet 2/12 is the root port for all VLANs.

Example 2-40 *Spanning Tree Root Verification*

```
Kenya# show spanning-tree root

                                  Root  Hello Max Fwd
Vlan                 Root ID      Cost  Time  Age Dly  Root Port
---------------- -------------------- ------- ----- --- ---  ----------------
VLAN0001         4097 001b.54c2.bbc1      5    2    12    9      Ethernet2/12
VLAN0002         4098 001b.54c2.bbc1      5    2    12    9      Ethernet2/12
VLAN0003         4099 001b.54c2.bbc1      5    2    12    9      Ethernet2/12
VLAN0004         4100 001b.54c2.bbc1      5    2    12    9      Ethernet2/12
VLAN0005         4101 001b.54c2.bbc1      5    2    12    9      Ethernet2/12
VLAN0006         4102 001b.54c2.bbc1      5    2    12    9      Ethernet2/12
VLAN0007         4103 001b.54c2.bbc1      5    2    12    9      Ethernet2/12
```

```
VLAN0008              4104 001b.54c2.bbc1      5    2   12   9    Ethernet2/12
VLAN0009              4105 001b.54c2.bbc1      5    2   12   9    Ethernet2/12
VLAN0010              4106 001b.54c2.bbc1      5    2   12   9    Ethernet2/12
VLAN0011              4107 001b.54c2.bbc2      4    2   12   9    Ethernet2/12
VLAN0012              4108 001b.54c2.bbc2      4    2   12   9    Ethernet2/12
VLAN0013              4109 001b.54c2.bbc2      4    2   12   9    Ethernet2/12
VLAN0014              4110 001b.54c2.bbc2      4    2   12   9    Ethernet2/12
VLAN0015              4111 001b.54c2.bbc2      4    2   12   9    Ethernet2/12
VLAN0016              4112 001b.54c2.bbc2      4    2   12   9    Ethernet2/12
VLAN0017              4113 001b.54c2.bbc2      4    2   12   9    Ethernet2/12
VLAN0018              4114 001b.54c2.bbc2      4    2   12   9    Ethernet2/12
VLAN0019              4115 001b.54c2.bbc2      4    2   12   9    Ethernet2/12
VLAN0020              4116 001b.54c2.bbc2      4    2   12   9    Ethernet2/12
Kenya#
```

Example 2-41 shows the configuration of port cost on a per-VLAN basis.

Example 2-41 *Per-VLAN Cost Configuration*

```
Kenya(config)# interface ethernet 2/11
Kenya(config-if)# spanning-tree vlan 1,3,5,7,9 cost 4
Kenya(config-if)# exit
```

Example 2-42 shows the result of the changes in the previous example. Ethernet2/11 is now the root for VLANs 1, 3, 5, 6, and 9.

Example 2-42 *Spanning Tree Root Verification*

```
Kenya# show spanning-tree root

                                 Root  Hello Max Fwd
Vlan                  Root ID    Cost  Time  Age Dly  Root Port
----------------  --------------------  -------  -----  ---  ---  ----------------
VLAN0001              4097 001b.54c2.bbc1      4    2   12   9    Ethernet2/11
VLAN0002              4098 001b.54c2.bbc1      5    2   12   9    Ethernet2/12
VLAN0003              4099 001b.54c2.bbc1      4    2   12   9    Ethernet2/11
VLAN0004              4100 001b.54c2.bbc1      5    2   12   9    Ethernet2/12
VLAN0005              4101 001b.54c2.bbc1      4    2   12   9    Ethernet2/11
VLAN0006              4102 001b.54c2.bbc1      5    2   12   9    Ethernet2/12
VLAN0007              4103 001b.54c2.bbc1      4    2   12   9    Ethernet2/11
VLAN0008              4104 001b.54c2.bbc1      5    2   12   9    Ethernet2/12
VLAN0009              4105 001b.54c2.bbc1      4    2   12   9    Ethernet2/11
VLAN0010              4106 001b.54c2.bbc1      5    2   12   9    Ethernet2/12
VLAN0011              4107 001b.54c2.bbc2      4    2   12   9    Ethernet2/12
VLAN0012              4108 001b.54c2.bbc2      4    2   12   9    Ethernet2/12
VLAN0013              4109 001b.54c2.bbc2      4    2   12   9    Ethernet2/12
```

```
VLAN0014          4110 001b.54c2.bbc2      4   2   12    9     Ethernet2/12
VLAN0015          4111 001b.54c2.bbc2      4   2   12    9     Ethernet2/12
VLAN0016          4112 001b.54c2.bbc2      4   2   12    9     Ethernet2/12
VLAN0017          4113 001b.54c2.bbc2      4   2   12    9     Ethernet2/12
VLAN0018          4114 001b.54c2.bbc2      4   2   12    9     Ethernet2/12
VLAN0019          4115 001b.54c2.bbc2      4   2   12    9     Ethernet2/12
VLAN0020          4116 001b.54c2.bbc2      4   2   12    9     Ethernet2/12
VLAN0100         32868 001b.54c2.bbc1      5   2   20   15     Ethernet2/12
Kenya#
```

Port Priority

With a well-planned root placement in the aggregation switches, manipulation of other spanning tree parameters is seldom needed; however, in certain cases it might be necessary to manipulate port-priority to influence the forwarding path. With VLAN access ports, the port-priority applies to the VLAN to which the port belongs. For interfaces carrying multiple VLANs using 802.1Q trunking, a port-priority can be specified on a per-VLAN basis. The default port priority is 128.

Example 2-43 shows the configuration of port-priority on an interface.

Example 2-43 *Spanning Tree Port Priority Configuration*

```
Kenya# conf t
Enter configuration commands, one per line. End with CNTL/Z.
Kenya(config)# interface ethernet 2/12
Kenya(config-if)# spanning-tree port-priority 64
Kenya(config-if)# exit
Kenya(config)# exit
```

Spanning Tree Toolkit

NX-OS provides many extensions to the operation of spanning tree. When used properly, these extensions can improve the resiliency, performance, and security of the spanning tree. The following sections look at some of the specific enhancements and then discuss some basic spanning tree port types. They conclude by combining the techniques covered in this section with some sample port-profiles for various configurations.

BPDUGuard

BPDUGuard shuts down an interface if a BPDU is received. This option protects the spanning tree from unauthorized switches being placed into the topology. BPDUGuard can also be useful in protecting against host misconfiguration that could introduce a loop into the environment.

To enable BPDUGuard on all edge ports, enter the following command:

```
Congo(config)# spanning-tree port type edge bpduguard default
```

Example 2-46 shows how to enable BPDUGuard on a specific interface.

Example 2-46 *Enabling BPDUGuard on a Specific Interface*

```
Congo(config)# int ethernet 2/1
Congo(config-if)# spanning-tree bpduguard enable
Congo(config-if)#
2009 Oct 28 14:45:20 Congo %STP-2-BLOCK_BPDUGUARD: Received BPDU on port Ethernet2/1
with BPDU Guard enabled. Disabling port.
2009 Oct 28 14:45:21 Congo %ETHPORT-2-IF_DOWN_ERROR_DISABLED: Interface Ethernet 2/1
is down (Error disabled. Reason:BPDUGuard)
```

Example 2-47 shows how to disable BPDUGuard on a specific interface.

Example 2-47 *Disabling BPDUGuard on a Specific Interface*

```
Congo(config)#
Congo(config)# interface ethernet 2/21
Congo(config-if)# spanning-tree bpduguard disable
Congo(config-if)# exit
```

To decrease administrative overhead in a dynamic environment, it might be desirable to leverage the protection provided by BPDUGuard but undesirable to require manual intervention to enable ports that have been shut down. Ports that have been disabled because of BPDUGuard can be automatically enabled after a period of time by specifying an errdisable recovery time.

Example 2-48 shows how to configure errdisable recovery.

Example 2-48 *errdisable Recovery*

```
Congo(config)# errdisable recovery cause bpduguard
Congo(config)# errdisable recovery interval 60
```

BPDUFilter

BPDUFilter prevents a port from sending or receiving BPDUs. BPDUFilter is usually used with BPDUGuard to prevent an inadvertent misconfiguration that could introduce loops into the environment. When BPDUGuard is not enabled, BPDUFilter still provides some safeguard against accidental misconfiguration. When configured globally, BPDUFilter applies to ports that are operationally spanning tree-type edge ports. Also, when BPDUFilter is configured globally, a port initially sends a series of at least 10 BPDUs. If the device receives the BPDUs, it returns to the initial port state and transitions through the listening and learning phases. However, when BPDUFilter is configured on a per-port basis, BPDUFilter does not send any BPDUs. Take caution when enabling BPDUFilter, especially on a per-port basis, as bridging loops may occur if BPDUFilter is enabled on non-host facing interfaces.

To enable BPDUFilter on all edge ports, enter the following command:

```
Congo(config)# spanning-tree port type edge bpdufilter default
```

Example 2-44 shows how to enable BPDUFilter on a specific interface.

Example 2-44   *BPDU Interface Configuration*

```
Congo(config)# int ethernet 2/21
Congo(config-if)# spanning-tree bpdufilter enable
Congo(config-if)#
Congo(config-if)# exit
```

Example 2-45 shows how to disable BPDUFilter on a specific interface.

Example 2-45   *Disabling BPDUFilter*

```
Congo(config)# int ethernet 2/21
Congo(config-if)# spanning-tree bpdufilter disable
Congo(config-if)#
```

RootGuard

RootGuard protects the root placement in the bridging domain. If a port configured with RootGuard receives a superior BPDU, the port is immediately placed into an inconsistent state. RootGuard is typically implemented in the data center aggregation layer to prevent misconfigured access switches from becoming the root bridge for the entire data center aggregation block. RootGuard can be implemented only on a port-by-port basis.

Example 2-49 shows how to enable RootGuard on a specific interface.

Example 2-49   *RootGuard Configuration*

```
Congo(config)# int ethernet 2/1
Congo(config-if)# spanning-tree guard root
Congo(config-if)#
```

Now, test RootGuard by changing the priority of a Kenya to a lower value.

Example 2-50 shows RootGuard in action.

Example 2-50   *RootGuard Verification*

```
Kenya(config)# spanning-tree vlan 1 priority 0
Output from Congo
Congo# 2009 Oct 28 14:50:24 Congo %STP-2-ROOTGUARD_BLOCK: Root guard blocking port
Ethernet2/1 on VLAN0001.
Congo#
! When we remove the priority command, port connectivity is restored.
Kenya(config)# no spanning-tree vlan 1 priority 0
Output from Congo
Congo# 2009 Oct 28 14:51:19 Congo %STP-2-ROOTGUARD_UNBLOCK: Root guard unblocking
port
Ethernet2/1 on VLAN0001.
Congo#
```

Example 2-51 shows how to remove RootGuard.

Example 2-51   *Disabling RootGuard*

```
Congo(config)# int ethernet 2/1
Congo(config-if)# no spanning-tree guard root
Congo(config-if)#
```

LoopGuard

LoopGuard prevents any alternative or root ports from becoming designated ports. This situation is typically caused by a unidirectional link.

To enable LoopGuard globally, enter the following command:

```
Egypt(config)# spanning-tree loopguard default
```

Example 2-52 shows how to enable LoopGuard on a specific interface.

Example 2-52   *Enabling LoopGuard on a Specific Interface*

```
Egypt# conf t
Enter configuration commands, one per line. End with CNTL/Z.
Egypt(config)# int port-channel 100
Egypt(config-if)# spanning-tree guard loop
```

To disable LoopGuard on a specific interface, the **no** form of this command should be used, as shown in Example 2-53.

Example 2-53   *Disabling LoopGuard on a Specific Interface*

```
Egypt# conf t
Enter configuration commands, one per line. End with CNTL/Z.
```

```
Egypt(config)# int port-channel 100
Egypt(config-if)# no spanning-tree guard loop
```

Dispute Mechanism

The 802.1D-2004 standard specifies a dispute mechanism that can prevent loops created for a variety of reasons. Two common cases in which the dispute mechanism helps are unidirectional links or port-channel misconfiguration. Dispute mechanism is enabled by default and cannot be disabled.

Bridge Assurance

Bridge Assurance is a new feature that can eliminate issues caused by a malfunctioning bridge. With Bridge Assurance, all ports send and receive BPDUs on all VLANs regardless of their states. This creates a bidirectional keepalive using BPDUs, and if a bridge stops receiving BPDUs, these ports are placed into an inconsistent state. This functionality can prevent loops that can be introduced as a result of a malfunctioning bridge. Bridge Assurance is enabled by default on any port configured with a spanning tree port type network but can be disabled globally with the following command:

```
Congo(config)# no spanning-tree bridge assurance
```

To enable Bridge Assurance by setting the spanning tree port type, enter the following commands:

```
Congo(config)# int port-channel 1
Congo(config-if)# spanning-tree port type network
```

An interesting side effect of Bridge Assurance is an automatic *pruning* function. In the topology from Figure 2-5, if a VLAN is defined on Congo but not on Egypt, Bridge Assurance puts that VLAN into a blocking state because it is not receiving BPDUs for that VLAN from Egypt. Example 2-54 demonstrates this functionality.

Example 2-54 *Bridge Assurance as a Pruning Mechanism*

```
Congo# conf t
Enter configuration commands, one per line. End with CNTL/Z.
Congo(config)# vlan 500
Congo(config-vlan)# exit
Congo(config)# 2009 Oct 28 14:06:53 Congo %STP-2-BRIDGE_ASSURANCE_BLOCK: Bridge
Assurance blocking port Ethernet2/1 VLAN0500.
2009 Oct 28 14:06:53 Congo %STP-2-BRIDGE_ASSURANCE_BLOCK: Bridge Assurance
  blocking port port-channel100 VLAN0500.
```

After the VLAN is defined on Egypt, Bridge Assurance can detect the presence of BPDUs for that VLAN and allow it to move into a forwarding state, as demonstrated in Example 2-55.

Example 2-55 *Detecting VLAN BPDUs and Advancing in State*

```
Egypt(config)# vlan 500
Egypt(config-vlan)# exit
Egypt(config)#
Congo#
Congo# 2009 Oct 28 14:10:42 Congo %STP-2-BRIDGE_ASSURANCE_UNBLOCK: Bridge
  Assurance unblocking port port-channel100 VLAN0500.
Congo#
```

Spanning Tree Port Types

NX-OS provides three basic switch port types that ease the administrative burden of con-figuring STP extensions:

- **Normal ports:** By default, a switchport is a normal port for the purpose of spanning tree. Normal ports remain unmodified and operate as standard bridge ports.

- **Network ports:** Network ports define connections between two bridges. By default, Bridge Assurance is enabled on these ports.

- **Edge ports:** Previously known as PortFast, a port configured as a spanning tree edge denotes that the port should transition immediately into a forwarding state, bypass-ing the listening and learning states. Only nonbridging Layer 2 devices should be configured as edge ports. This port type should be reserved for data center hosts that cannot create a Layer 2 loop; this includes single attached hosts, Layer 3 routers and firewalls, or multihomed devices that leverage some form of NIC teaming.

Example 2-56 shows how to specify the default spanning tree port type.

Example 2-56 *Defining Default Spanning Tree Port Type*

```
Congo(config)#
Congo(config)# spanning-tree port type edge default
Warning: this command enables edge port type (portfast) by default on all inter-
faces.
You should now disable edge port type (portfast) explicitly on switched ports lead-
ing to hubs, switches and bridges as they may create temporary bridging loops.
! -OR-
Congo(config)#
Congo(config)# spanning-tree port type network default
Congo(config)#
```

To define the spanning tree port type on a specific interface, enter the following commands:

```
Kenya(config)# interface ethernet 2/11
Kenya(config-if)# spanning-tree port type network
```

Virtualization Hosts

Because of the recent trend of virtualization in the data center, a hybrid of the two interface types exists as well. Although historically, 802.1Q trunks were reserved for interconnecting network devices only, virtualization hosts often require 802.1Q trunk connectivity directly to hosts. Even though these hosts tag traffic with 802.1Q headers, they are typically not true bridges and therefore can be treated as hosts and bypass the listening and learning stages of spanning tree initialization. This configuration is sometimes referred to as *TrunkFast*.

Example 2-57 shows how to enable TrunkFast on a specific interface.

Example 2-57   *Enabling TrunkFast*

```
Kenya(config)# interface ethernet 2/40
Kenya(config-if)# switchport
Kenya(config-if)# spanning-tree port type edge trunk
Warning: Edge port type (portfast) should only be enabled on ports connected to
a single host. Connecting hubs, concentrators, switches, bridges, etc... to this
  interface when edge port type (portfast) is enabled, can cause temporary bridging
loops.
 Use with CAUTION
Kenya(config-if)#
```

Caution   Virtualization techniques vary greatly; consult your vendor's documentation to determine whether this feature should be implemented.

Configuring Layer 2 Interfaces

Now that the initial spanning tree configurations are complete, you can begin adding additional interfaces into the switching environment. The following examples discuss three different types of switchports: edge, trunk, and an edge trunk port.

Trunk Ports

Example 2-58 shows a sample configuration that would be used for access to aggregation links where multiple VLANs exist.

Example 2-58 *Standard Trunk Port Configuration*

```
interface Ethernet 2/9
switchport
switchport mode trunk
switchport trunk allowed vlan 100-103
```

Standard Host

Example 2-59 shows a sample configuration that would be used for standard Linux/ Windows hosts that belong to a single VLAN.

Example 2-59 *Sample Access Port Configuration*

```
interface Ethernet1/7
  no shutdown
  switchport
  switchport mode access
  switchport access vlan 10
  spanning-tree port type edge
  spanning-tree bpduguard enable
  spanning-tree bpdufilter enable
```

Link to Virtualization Host

Virtualization has changed the way that network administrators must think about edge and trunk ports. In the past, physical hosts typically hosted a single MAC/IP pair, which mapped to a single VLAN. With virtualization, internal software provides some level of switching function, making it possible for a virtualized host to contain many different MAC/IP pairs that might map to more than one VLAN. To perform optimally, special consideration should be made for these hosts at the physical network edge. Example 2-60 shows a sample configuration used for a virtualization host that uses an internal softswitch and guests that reside on multiple VLANs.

Example 2-60 *Sample Virtualization Host Port Configuration*

```
Kenya(config-if)# interface Ethernet1/7
Kenya(config-if)# no shutdown
Kenya(config-if)# switchport mode trunk
Kenya(config-if)# switchport trunk allowed vlan 101-103
Kenya(config-if)# spanning-tree port type edge trunk
Kenya(config-if)# spanning-tree bpduguard enable
```

Port-Profiles

Beginning in NX-OS 4.2(2), port-profiles can simplify the configuration of multiple ports that share common configuration components.

Example 2-61 shows a sample configuration of a port profile and how it is applied and verified.

Example 2-61   *Port Profiles*

```
Kenya(config)# port-profile COMMUNITY1
Kenya(config-ppm)# switchport
Kenya(config-ppm)# switchport mode access
Kenya(config-ppm)# switchport private-vlan host-association 100 102
Kenya(config-ppm)# spanning-tree port type edge
Kenya(config-ppm)# spanning-tree bpdufilter enable
Kenya(config-ppm)# spanning-tree bpduguard enable
Kenya(config-ppm)# no shutdown
Kenya(config-ppm)# state enabled


Kenya# conf t
Enter configuration commands, one per line. End with CNTL/Z.
Kenya(config)# interface ethernet 2/28
Kenya(config-if)# inherit port-profile COMMUNITY1
Kenya(config-if)# exit
Kenya(config)# exit
Kenya# sho run int ethernet 2/28
!Command: show running-config interface Ethernet2/28
!Time: Fri Oct 30 08:52:29 2009
version 4.2(2a)
interface Ethernet2/28
  inherit port-profile COMMUNITY1
Kenya#
Kenya# sho port-profile
port-profile COMMUNITY1
 type: Ethernet
 description:
 status: enabled
 max-ports: 512
 inherit:
 config attributes:
  switchport
  switchport mode access
  switchport private-vlan host-association 100 102
  spanning-tree port type edge
  spanning-tree bpdufilter enable
```

```
    spanning-tree bpduguard enable
    no shutdown
evaluated config attributes:
    switchport
    switchport mode access
    switchport private-vlan host-association 100 102
    spanning-tree port type edge
    spanning-tree bpdufilter enable
    spanning-tree bpduguard enable
    no shutdown
  assigned interfaces:
    Ethernet2/21
    Ethernet2/28
Kenya#
```

Port-Channels

Where multiple links exist between two switches, it is often preferable to treat them as a single link from a spanning tree perspective. The benefit of this logical bundling is that redundant physical connectivity is not blocked by spanning tree, making more bandwidth available for data traffic. Port-channels also create a level of redundancy because the failure of a physical link can no longer cause spanning tree to reconverge. The Nexus 7000 enables up to eight links to be aggregated in a port-channel. For optimal performance, it is recommended that the number of links be a power of 2 (for example, 2, 4, or 8 links). Members of a port-channel can be on the same linecard or protect against linecard failure and can be distributed across multiple modules in the system. Port-channels use various algorithms to hash frames as they arrive and load-balance traffic across the physical interfaces, where any given flow always hashes to the same physical interface. A common misconception about port-channels is that the logical interface is a 20/40/80-Gbps link. For 10-Gbps member links, however, no single flow would exceed the transmission speed of the physical links that are members. An analogy here would be that port-channels add new lanes to the highway but do not increase the speed limit. A port-channel can be configured as either a Layer 2 or Layer 3 link depending on the requirements.

The hashing used to load balance traffic across the links is user-configurable, and the following options are available on the Nexus 7000:

- Source IP

- Destination IP

- Source MAC

- Destination MAC

- Source port

- Destination port

- Source and destination IP

- Source and destination MAC

- Source and destination port

You can configure these options globally or, because of the distributed nature of the Nexus 7000, on a linecard-by-linecard basis. If VDCs are used, these parameters are defined in the default VDC.

Example 2-62 shows how to configure and verify the load-balancing algorithm.

Example 2-62 *Port-Channel Load-Balancing Algorithm*

```
Congo(config)# port-channel load-balance ethernet source-dest-ip-vlan
Congo(config)# show port-channel load-balance
Port Channel Load-Balancing Configuration:
System: source-dest-ip-vlan
Port Channel Load-Balancing Addresses Used Per-Protocol:
Non-IP: source-dest-mac
IP: source-dest-ip-vlan
```

Assigning Physical Ports to a Port-Channel

Two options exist for assigning members to the logical interface:

- Configure member links to run the industry-standard 802.3ad Link Aggregation Control Protocol (LACP).

- Statically configure the port as a member of the port-channel. This mode is on, and no aggregation protocol information is exchanged between the devices.

There is no right or wrong method to use, and implementations vary based on personal preference. Some administrators like the environment to be deterministic and opt for the static configuration, whereas others might want to take advantage of some of the enhanced features that LACP offers. One of the benefits offered by LACP is a level of protection against misconfigured ports inadvertently becoming a member of the channel that could lead to Layer 2 loops, or black-holing data traffic. This level of protection is preferable in virtual Port Channel configurations, which are discussed later in this chapter.

The **channel-group** command associates member interfaces with the port-channel. If an existing configuration is applied to the interface that makes it incompatible with the port-channel, the channel-group might be rejected from time to time. In these instances, channel compatibility can be ensured by adding the **force** command.

To assign a physical port to a port-channel without LACP, enter the following commands:

```
Egypt(config)# interface ethernet 1/4
Egypt(config-if)# channel-group 100 mode on
```

LACP is a modular process within NX-OS and must be explicitly enabled before configuration can begin. This is accomplished with the **feature** command.

When enabled, ports can be negotiated into a channel by specifying one of two modes:

- **Active:** This mode actively tries to negotiate channel membership by sending LACP packets.

- **Passive:** This mode listens for LACP packets and responds to them but does not send LACP negotiation packets.

For a link to bundle between two devices, the ports must be configured in either an active/active or active/passive fashion. If both sides of the link are configured for passive, they will not be bundled.

Example 2-63 shows how to assign a physical port to a port-channel with LACP.

Example 2-63 *LACP Configuration*

```
Congo(config)# feature lacp
Congo(config)# show feature | inc lacp
lacp                   1            enabled

Congo(config)# interface ethernet 1/1,ethernet1/3
Congo(config-if-range)# channel-group 100 mode active
Congo(config-if-range)#
-----------------------------------------------------------------------
Egypt(config)# interface ethernet 1/2, ethernet 1/4
Egypt(config-if-range)# channel-group 100 mode active
Egypt(config-if-range)#
```

During the negotiation phase, many parameters are verified to ensure that the port is compatible with the port-channel.

Example 2-64 shows the compatibility parameters that must match for a port to bundle.

Example 2-64 *Channel Compatibility*

```
Egypt# show port-channel compatibility-parameters
* port mode
Members must have the same port mode configured, either E,F or AUTO. If
they are configured in AUTO port mode, they have to negotiate E or F mode
when they come up. If a member negotiates a different mode, it will be
suspended.
```

* speed

Members must have the same speed configured. If they are configured in AUTO speed, they have to negotiate the same speed when they come up. If a member negotiates a different speed, it will be suspended.

* MTU

Members have to have the same MTU configured. This only applies to ethernet port-channel.

* MEDIUM

Members have to have the same medium type configured. This only applies to ethernet port-channel.

* Span mode

Members must have the same span mode.

* load interval

Member must have same load interval configured.

* sub interfaces

Members must not have sub-interfaces.

* Duplex Mode

Members must have same Duplex Mode configured.

* Ethernet Layer

Members must have same Ethernet Layer (switchport/no-switchport) configured.

* Span Port

Members cannot be SPAN ports.

* Storm Control

Members must have same storm-control configured.

* Flow Control

Members must have same flowctrl configured.

* Capabilities

Members must have common capabilities.

* Capabilities speed

Members must have common speed capabilities.

* Capabilities duplex

Members must have common speed duplex capabilities.

* rate mode

Members must have the same rate mode configured.

* 1G port is not capable of acting as peer-link

Members must be 10G to become part of a vPC peer-link.

* port

Members port VLAN info.

* port

Members port does not exist.

* switching port

Members must be switching port, Layer 2.

* port access VLAN

Members must have the same port access VLAN.

* port native VLAN

```
Members must have the same port native VLAN.
* port allowed VLAN list
Members must have the same port allowed VLAN list.
* port egress queuing policy
10G port-channel members must have the same egress queuing policy as the
port-channel.
* Port Security policy
Members must have the same port-security enable status as port-channel
Egypt#
```

Example 2-65 shows how to quickly verify the channel configuration with the **show port-channel summary** command.

Example 2-65 *LACP Configuration*

```
Egypt# show port-channel summary
Flags:  D - Down         P - Up in port-channel (members)
        I - Individual   H - Hot-standby (LACP only)
        s - Suspended    r - Module-removed
        S - Switched     R - Routed
        U - Up (port-channel)
--------------------------------------------------------------------------------
Group Port-        Type     Protocol   Member Ports
      Channel
--------------------------------------------------------------------------------
100   Po100(SU)   Eth       LACP       Eth1/2(P)   Eth1/4(P)
```

Logical interfaces parameters apply to all the member links, giving the administrator an easy way to manipulate multiple ports.

Note   In IOS devices, port-channel interfaces are initially put into an administratively down state, whereas in NX-OS newly created port-channels are active as soon as they are created.

Port-Channel Flow Control

Flow control is supported on port-channel interfaces as well. For flow control to work properly, both sides of the port-channel must be configured. By default, the port-channel flow control is preferred. Flow control can be statically configured for on or off and for each direction.

Example 2-66 shows how to configure and verify port-channel flow control.

Example 2-66 *Port-Channel Flow Control*

```
Congo(config)# interface port-channel 100
Congo(config-if)# flowcontrol send on
Congo(config-if)# flowcontrol receive on
Congo# show interface port-channel 100 flowcontrol
--------------------------------------------------------------------------------

Port      Send FlowControl  Receive FlowControl  RxPause TxPause
          admin    oper     admin    oper
--------------------------------------------------------------------------------

Po100     on       on       on       on           0       0
Congo#
```

Verifying Load Distribution Across a Port-Channel

Unequal traffic distribution across physical ports can be caused for a variety of reasons, including configuration of a suboptimal load balancing algorithm, or a nonpower of 2 number of links, (for example, 3). From time to time, it is good to verify that traffic is load-balanced across all the available members. A useful command to get a quick snapshot of these statistics is **show port-channel traffic**. Example 2-67 shows example output from this command.

Example 2-67 *Verifying Load Distribution*

```
Congo# show port-channel rbh-distribution
ChanId    Member port    RBH values        Num of buckets
--------  ------------   ----------------  ----------------

  11      Eth2/17        4,5,6,7           4
  11      Eth1/17        0,1,2,3           4
--------  ------------   ----------------  ----------------

  13      Eth2/18        4,5,6,7           4
  13      Eth1/18        0,1,2,3           4
--------  ------------   ----------------  ----------------

  15      Eth2/25        4,5,6,7           4
  15      Eth1/25        0,1,2,3           4
francevdc1#
Congo(config)# show port-channel traffic
ChanId    Port Rx-Ucst Tx-Ucst Rx-Mcst Tx-Mcst Rx-Bcst Tx-Bcst
------    ---------  -------  ------  -------  -------  -------  ------

  100     Eth1/1     53.67%   46.32%  97.39%   97.27%   0.0%     0.0%
  100     Eth1/3     46.32%   53.67%   2.60%    2.72%   0.0%     0.0%
```

In the previous output, the first command shows the number of hash buckets that each member link is assigned to, and the second shows the amount of traffic each link has forwarded. When troubleshooting port-channels, one additional task is to determine which link a particular flow will be hashed to. As shown in Example 2-68, the **show port-channel loadbalance forwarding-path** command can be used to gather this information.

Example 2-68   *Determining Which Link a Particular Flow Will Use*

```
francevdc1# show port-channel load-balance forwarding-path interface port-channel 11
src-ip 172.16.30.25 dst-ip 192.168.10.236 module 2
Missing params will be substituted by 0's.
Module 2: Load-balance Algorithm: source-dest-ip-vlan
RBH: 0x2        Outgoing port id: Ethernet1/17
francevdc1# show port-channel load-balance forwarding-path interface port-channel 11
src-ip 172.16.30.25 dst-ip 192.168.10.235 module 2
Missing params will be substituted by 0's.
Module 2: Load-balance Algorithm: source-dest-ip-vlan
RBH: 0x5        Outgoing port id: Ethernet2/17
```

By specifying inputting in the required values based on the hash algorithm in use, you've identified that for traffic from 172.16.30.25 destined for 192.168.10.236 interface, Ethernet1/17 forwards traffic, and traffic destined for 172.16.30.25 selects Ethernet2/17 to forward traffic.

Virtual Port Channels

The Nexus 7000 and 5000 series switches the take port-channel functionality to the next level by enabling links connected to different devices to aggregate into a single, logical link. This technology was introduced in NX-OS version 4.1(4) and is called virtual Port Channel. In addition to link redundancy provided by port-channels, vPCs offer some additional benefits:

- Device level redundancy with faster convergence than multiple port-channels using traditional Spanning Tree

- Further elimination of spanning tree blocked ports by providing a loop-free topology

- Better bandwidth utilization

Caution   Port-channels configured as vPCs can be used only as Layer 2 links, and no dynamic routing protocol should be used across the link.

vPCs are configured by associating two Nexus devices into a vPC domain. Within the vPC domain, information is exchanged between vPC peers across two special links:

- **vPC peer-keepalive link:** Provides heartbeating between vPC peers to ensure that both devices are online, and also to avoid active/active or split-brain scenarios that could introduce loops into the vPC topology. The vPC peer-keepalive link can be either 1 Gbps or 10 Gbps.

- **vPC peer link:** Used to exchange state information between the vPC peers and also provides additional mechanisms that can detect and prevent split-brain scenarios.

Some other terminology that you must understand for vPCs follows:

- **vPC link:** A link configured as a vPC on the Nexus. The downstream device sees the vPC link as a normal port-channel.

- **vPC Role:** Each of the members of a vPC domain participates in an election to determine the primary and secondary devices in the vPC domain. Only the vPC operational primary devices generate and receive BPDUs. This election can be manipulated by way of a **role priority**, which is defined under the vPC domain configuration mode.

- **Orphan Port:** An orphaned port is a link that is not configured as a vPC link that is carrying a VLAN present on a vPC link, or the vPC peer-link. Orphan ports should generally be avoided if possible. Orphan ports can be displayed by using the **show vpc orphan-ports** command. Orphan ports can be avoided by keeping the vPC domain "pure," which is to say that all devices are dual homed to both members of the vPC domain with vPC links.

Note   On the Nexus 7000, the mgmt0 interface can be used as the vPC peer-keepalive link but should be avoided if at all possible. On the Nexus 7000, the mgmt0 is actually a logical interface representing the physical management port of the active supervisor. During processes such as supervisor switchover during hardware failure or In-Service Software Upgrades (ISSU), the physical link supporting the mgmt0 interface might change, causing a disruption of the keepalive messages. By using normal switch interfaces, additional levels of redundancy in the port-channels can be used. If the mgmt0 interface is used as the peer-keepalive link, it is critical to ensure that all physical management ports are connected to an external device, such as a management switch.

The remainder of this section demonstrates configuration based on the topology shown in Figure 2-7.

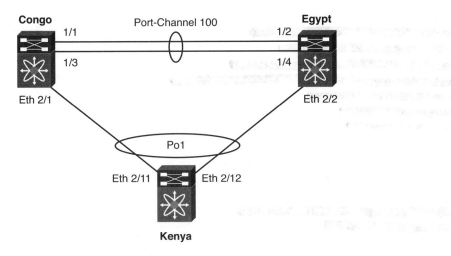

Figure 2-7 *vPC Topology*

To configure vPC, perform the following steps.

1. Enable the vPC feature on each vPC peer:

```
! Congo
Congo# conf t
Enter configuration commands, one per line. End with CNTL/Z.
Congo
Congo(config)# feature vpc
Congo(config)# exit
! Egypt
Egypt(config)# feature vpc
Egypt(config)# exit
```

2. Create VRF for the vPC keepalive link:

```
! Congo
Congo(config-if)# vrf context vpc-keepalive
Congo(config-vrf)# exit
! Egypt
Egypt(config)# vrf context vpc-keepalive
Egypt(config-vrf)# exit
! Congo
Congo(config)# int ethernet 2/47
Congo(config-if)# vrf member vpc-keepalive
Congo(config-if)# ip address 1.1.1.1 255.255.255.252
Congo(config-if)# no shutdown
Congo(config-if)# exit
Congo(config)# exit
```

```
! Egypt
Egypt(config)# interface ethernet 2/48
Egypt(config-if)# no switchport
Egypt(config-if)# vrf member vpc-keepalive
Egypt(config-if)# ip address 1.1.1.2 255.255.255.252
Egypt(config-if)# no shutdown
Egypt(config-if)# exit
Egypt(config)# exit
! Congo
Congo(config-if)# vrf context vpc-keepalive
Congo(config-vrf)# exit
! Egypt
Egypt(config)# vrf context vpc-keepalive
Egypt(config-vrf)# exit
! Congo
Congo(config)# int ethernet 2/47
Congo(config-if)# vrf member vpc-keepalive
Congo(config-if)# ip address 1.1.1.1 255.255.255.252
Congo(config-if)# no shutdown
Congo(config-if)# exit
Congo(config)# exit
! Egypt
Egypt(config)# interface ethernet 2/48
Egypt(config-if)# no switchport
Egypt(config-if)# vrf member vpc-keepalive
Egypt(config-if)# ip address 1.1.1.2 255.255.255.252
Egypt(config-if)# no shutdown
Egypt(config-if)# exit
```

3. Verify connectivity of the vPC peer keepalive link:

```
Congo# ping 1.1.1.2 vrf vpc-keepalive
PING 1.1.1.2 (1.1.1.2): 56 data bytes
64 bytes from 1.1.1.2: icmp_seq=0 ttl=254 time=0.958 ms
64 bytes from 1.1.1.2: icmp_seq=1 ttl=254 time=0.617 ms
64 bytes from 1.1.1.2: icmp_seq=2 ttl=254 time=0.595 ms
64 bytes from 1.1.1.2: icmp_seq=3 ttl=254 time=0.603 ms
64 bytes from 1.1.1.2: icmp_seq=4 ttl=254 time=0.645 ms
--- 1.1.1.2 ping statistics ---
5 packets transmitted, 5 packets received, 0.00% packet loss
round-trip min/avg/max = 0.595/0.683/0.958 ms

Congo(config)# vpc domain 1
Congo(config-vpc-domain)# peer-keepalive destination 1.1.1.2 source 1.1.1.1
vrf vpc-
```

```
keepalive
Congo(config-vpc-domain)# exit
Egypt(config)# vpc domain 1
Egypt(config-vpc-domain)# peer-keepalive destination 1.1.1.1 source 1.1.1.
  2 vrf vpc-keepalive
Egypt(config-vpc-domain)# exit
```

4. Verify that vPC peer keepalive link is working:

```
Congo# show vpc
Legend:
                    (*) - local vPC is down, forwarding via vPC peer-link
vPC domain id                    : 1
Peer status                      : peer link not configured
vPC keep-alive status            : peer is alive
Configuration consistency status: failed
Configuration consistency reason: vPC peer-link does not exists
vPC role                         : none established
Number of vPCs configured        : 0
Peer Gateway                     : Disabled
Dual-active excluded VLANs       : -
Congo#
```

5. Configure the vPC peer-link:

```
! Congo
Congo# conf t
Enter configuration commands, one per line. End with CNTL/Z.
Congo(config)# interface port-channel 100
Congo(config-if)# vpc peer-link
Please note that spanning tree port type is changed to "network" port type on
vPC peer-
link.
This will enable spanning tree Bridge Assurance on vPC peer-link provided the
STP
Bridge Assurance (which is enabled by default) is not disabled.
Congo(config-if)#
! Egypt
Egypt# conf t
Enter configuration commands, one per line. End with CNTL/Z.
Egypt(config-if)# switchport mode trunk
Egypt(config)# interface port-channel 100
Egypt(config-if)# vpc peer-link
Please note that spanning tree port type is changed to "network" port type on
vPC peer-link.
```

```
This will enable spanning tree Bridge Assurance on vPC peer-link provided the
STP Bridge Assurance.(which is enabled by default) is not disabled.
Egypt(config-if)#
```

> **Note**   On the Nexus 7000, interfaces that are members of the vPC peer-link must be 10-GbE ports, and it is recommended that they are in dedicated rate-mode if they reside on an M1 card.

6. Verify configuration consistency checks pass, and you have an active vPC configuration:

```
Egypt# show vpc
Legend:
                (*) - local vPC is down, forwarding via vPC peer-link

vPC domain id                  : 1
Peer status                    : peer adjacency formed ok
vPC keep-alive status          : peer is alive
Configuration consistency status: success
vPC role                       : secondary
Number of vPCs configured      : 0
Peer Gateway                   : Disabled
Dual-active excluded VLANs      : -
vPC Peer-link status
---------------------------------------------------------------------
id   Port   Status Active vlans
--   ----   ------ -------------------------------------------------
1    Po100  up     1-20,100
```

If the configuration consistency status returns anything other than success, additional information about the inconsistencies can be derived with the following command:

```
Congo# show vpc consistency-parameters global

    Legend:
        Type 1 : vPC will be suspended in case of mismatch


Name                    Type   Local Value           Peer Value
-------------           ----   --------------------- --------------------
---
STP Mode                1      Rapid-PVST            Rapid-PVST
STP Disabled            1      VLANs 91              VLANs 91
STP MST Region Name     1      customer              customer
STP MST Region Revision 1      1                     1
STP MST Region Instance to  1
```

```
 VLAN Mapping
STP Loopguard                 1    Disabled           Disabled
STP Bridge Assurance          1    Enabled            Enabled
STP Port Type, Edge           1    Normal, Disabled,  Normal, Disabled,
BPDUFilter, Edge BPDUGuard         Disabled           Disabled
STP MST Simulate PVST         1    Enabled            Enabled
Interface-vlan admin up       2    40-43,50,60,70-71,1 40-43,50,60,70-
71,91,1
                                   00-103             00-103
Allowed VLANs                 -    40-43,50,60,91,100-103 9,40-
43,50,60,91,100-1
                                   ,1000              03,1000
Local suspended VLANs         -    -                  -
```

7. Add port-channels to a vPC:

```
! Congo
Congo(config-if)# exit
Congo(config)# interface ethernet 2/1
Congo(config-if)# channel-group 1 mode active
Congo(config-if)# no shutdown
Congo(config-if)# exit
Congo(config)# interface port-channel 1
Congo(config-if)# switchport
Congo(config-if)# switchport mode trunk
Congo(config-if)# vpc 1
! Egypt
Egypt(config)# int ethernet 2/2
Egypt(config-if)# channel-group 1 mode active
Egypt(config-if)# no shutdown
Egypt(config-if)# exit
Egypt(config)# int port-channel 1
Egypt(config-if)# switchport
Egypt(config-if)# switchport mode trunk
Egypt(config-if)# vpc 1
! Kenya
Kenya(config)# interface ethernet 2/11-12
Kenya(config-if-range)# switchport
Kenya(config-if-range)# channel-group 1 mode active
Kenya(config-if-range)# no shutdown
Kenya(config-if-range)# exit
Kenya(config)# exit
Kenya(config)# int port-channel 1
Kenya(config-if)# switchport
Kenya(config-if)# switchport mode trunk
Kenya(config-if)#
```

8. Verify that the vPC is operational:

```
Congo# show vpc
Legend:
                    (*) - local vPC is down, forwarding via vPC peer-link
vPC domain id                 : 1
Peer status                   : peer adjacency formed ok
vPC keep-alive status         : peer is alive
Configuration consistency status: success
vPC role                      : primary
Number of vPCs configured     : 1
Peer Gateway                  : Disabled
Dual-active excluded VLANs    : -
vPC Peer-link status
---------------------------------------------------------------------
id   Port   Status Active vlans
--   ----   ------ ------------------------------------------------
1    Po100  up     1-20,100
vPC status
---------------------------------------------------------------------
id   Port   Status Consistency Reason                   Active vlans
--   ----   ------ ----------- ------------------------ -----------
1    Po1    up     success     success                  1-20,100
```

vPC Peer-Gateway

The vPC Peer-Gateway feature was introduced in NX-OS 4.2(1). This feature is designed to enable certain storage, application servers, or load balancers to implement *fast-path functionality*. This causes nodes to send return traffic to a specific MAC address of the sender rather than HSRP address. By default, this traffic might be dropped as vPC loop avoidance does not enable traffic received on a vPC peer-link to be forwarded out a vPC interface (loop avoidance). A vPC Peer-Gateway enables the vPC peer device to forward packets destined for its peer router MAC locally.

To enable the peer-gateway, enter the following command:

```
Congo(config-vpc-domain)# peer-gateway
```

vPC Peer-Switch

vPC creates an environment in which two devices are seen as a single device for purposes of Etherchannel. Peer-Switch extends this to make the vPC domain appear as a single spanning tree domain to the entire topology. To accomplish this, the switches in a vPC domain synchronize their Bridge IDs; both generate BPDUs. For this to completely work, the Priorities contained within those BPDUs must match on both switches. The configuration in Example 2-69 demonstrates how to enable the peer-switch feature and configure the priorities the same on both switches.

Example 2-69   *Configuring vPC peer-switch Functionality*

```
Congo(config)# vpc domain 1
Congo(config-vpc-domain)# peer-switch
Congo(config)# spanning-tree vlan 1-4094 priority 4096

Egypt(config)# vpc domain 1
Egypt(config-vpc-domain)# peer-switch
Egypt(config)# spanning-tree vlan 1-4094 priority 4096
```

The peer switch feature is useful in a pure vPC topology; however, if there are both vPCs and non-vPC links into the vPC domain, spanning tree "pseudo" information should also be configured. These are the values that STP uses when generating BPDUs for non-vPC links. Example 2-70 demonstrates the configuration of spanning tree pseudo-information.

Example 2-70   *Configuring STP Pseudo-Information*

```
fp-spine-1(config)# spanning-tree pseudo-information
fp-spine-1(config-pseudo)# vlan 1-4094 root priority 4096
fp-spine-1(config-pseudo)# vlan 1-4094 designated priority 8192
```

ARP Synchronization

Because of the high level of asymmetric traffic flows that can arise in a vPC environment combined with ECMP back into the aggregation layer, one of the largest delays in reconvergence when a vPC domain member comes online is the time that it takes to restore the ARP table. To overcome this delay, the ARP tables between the two devices in the vPC domain can be synchronized using ARP Table Sync.

The configuration of ARP synchronization is simple and is usually preferable by most network administrators. Example 2-71 shows the configuration of ARP synchronization.

Example 2-71   *Configuring ARP Synchronization*

```
Congo(config)# vpc domain 1
Congo(config-vpc-domain)# ip arp synchronize
```

Unidirectional Link Detection

Full-duplex communication creates a situation in which a node can receive traffic but cannot transmit or vice versa; this condition is known as a *unidirectional link* and can be problematic for protocols that require a bidirectional exchange of information. This condition is most-often attributed to fiber-optic cabling as the physical medium. Unidirectional link conditions can exist in other mediums such as twisted-pair copper cabling. Although upper-layer protocols can overcome this scenario easily, this scenario can produce unexpected results at Layer 2. For these Layer 2 protocols, Cisco provides a mechanism for detecting and disabling links where bidirectional traffic flow is not possible. Cisco developed Unidirectional Link Detection to eliminate any negative behavior associated with the failure of bidirectional communication. UDLD enables each device to send packets to the directly connected device at periodic intervals (15 seconds by default); the sending and receiving of these packets ensure that traffic flow is bidirectional. The Cisco UDLD implementation defines two modes that devices can operate:

- **Aggressive mode:** Typically used for copper-based mediums such as twisted-pair copper

- **Nonaggressive mode:** Typically used for fiber-based networks

Example 2-72 shows the configuration and verification of UDLD.

Example 2-72 *UDLD Configuration*

```
! Enabling UDLD
Congo(config)# feature udld
Congo(config)#
! Verifying UDLD global status
Congo# show udld global
UDLD global configuration mode: enabled
UDLD global message interval: 15
Congo# show udld
Interface Ethernet1/1
--------------------------------
Port enable administrative configuration setting: device-default
Port enable operational state: enabled
Current bidirectional state: bidirectional
Current operational state:  advertisement - Single neighbor detected
Message interval: 7
Timeout interval: 5
        Entry 1
        ---------------
        Expiration time: 20
        Cache Device index: 1
        Current neighbor state: unknown
        Device ID: TBM12224047
```

```
        Port ID: Ethernet1/2
        Neighbor echo 1 devices: TBM12224047
        Neighbor echo 1 port: Ethernet1/1
        Message interval: 7
        Timeout interval: 5
        CDP Device name: Egypt(TBM12224047)
! Enabling UDLD aggressive mode
Congo(config-if)# udld aggressive
Congo(config-if)# exit
Congo(config)# show udld ethernet 1/1
Interface Ethernet1/1
--------------------------------
Port enable administrative configuration setting: enabled-aggressive
Port enable operational state: enabled-aggressive
Current bidirectional state: bidirectional
Current operational state:  advertisement - Single neighbor detected
Message interval: 15
Timeout interval: 5
        Entry 1
        ---------------
        Expiration time: 44
        Cache Device index: 1
        Current neighbor state: bidirectional
        Device ID: TBM12224047
        Port ID: Ethernet1/2
        Neighbor echo 1 devices: TBM12224047
        Neighbor echo 1 port: Ethernet1/1
        Message interval: 15
        Timeout interval: 5
        CDP Device name: Egypt(TBM12224047)
Congo# show udld neighbors
Port            Device Name     Device ID   Port ID       Neighbor State
-------------------------------------------------------------------------
Ethernet1/1     TBM12224047     1           Ethernet1/2   bidirectional
Ethernet1/3     TBM12224047     1           Ethernet1/4   bidirectional
```

Cisco FabricPath

Historically, Layer 2 networks did not require high levels of scalability because network administrators designed networks based on the limitations of spanning tree, hardware MAC address tables, and L2 flooding characteristics. Doing so limited Layer 2 to small pockets and separated them from one another via L3 routing devices. Leveraging L3 boundaries around these small pockets of L2 infrastructure allowed network administrators to rely on more scalable resilient routing protocols to scale their networks. Trends today in the areas of high-performance computing (HPC), virtualization, and a demand for a more flexible infrastructure requires many organizations to revisit Layer 2 technologies. New technologies such as virtual Port Channel (vPC) are emerging to help customers build larger L2 domains; however, these technologies still fundamentally rely on spanning tree. Spanning tree creates topologies where local problems such as a link flap can have catastrophic impacts to the entire infrastructure, whereas more intelligent Layer 3 routing protocols such as OSPF and EIGRP assume these types of failures and have sophisticated algorithms to handle such events. These challenges have created the demand for a more flexible protocol, which takes the best characteristics of Layer 2 and Layer 3 and combines them to meet these demands.

Cisco FabricPath introduces a new way to build and operate Layer 2 networks. FabricPath enables network operators to build large-scale L2 networks and eliminate challenges associated with various spanning tree implementations. FabricPath takes well-understood technologies that have been leveraged at Layer 3 for routing IP packets and uses them to carry Layer 2 reachability information. In this manner, network administrators gain the flexibility of large L2 networks and still have the resiliency of large L3 networks.

Cisco FabricPath can be broken down into two distinct areas of operations: control plane and data plane. The control plane is responsible for building and disseminating information about the reachability of devices within the network, whereas the data plane is responsible for the encapsulation, de-encapsulation, and forwarding of data packets across a FabricPath network.

The FabricPath control plane uses Intermediate System-to-Intermediate System (IS-IS) to replace spanning tree. IS-IS is a multi-area (level) routing protocol that has no IP dependencies and is easily extensible using custom TLVs. These characteristics make IS-IS an attractive way to exchange routing information at Layer 2. The FabricPath control-plane functions can be broken down into two main areas. First, the FabricPath domain is composed of a number of switches, which must be uniquely identified. The FabricPath domain may also consist of a number of disparate logical topologies for isolation of various types of traffic. Dynamic Resource Allocation Protocol (DRAP) provides the mechanism for switches to be auto-assigned a unique 12-bit switch ID (SID). This protocol is built on IS-IS adjacencies, which are formed when an interface first connects to another FabricPath switch. In addition, the network administrator may choose to statically configure the SID. FabricPath IS-IS adjacencies are then used to exchange routing information used to populate the Unicast Layer 2 Routing Information Base (U2RIB), where a shortest path calculation determines the optimal path or paths to a destination. FabricPath IS-IS selects the lowest cost path, including equal cost paths, up to 16.

For multidestination traffic such as broadcast, multicast, or unknown unicast, FabricPath IS-IS creates multidestination trees. These multidestination trees are automatically created by way of a root election process in which one switch based on priority, system ID, and Switch ID becomes the root switch. The root switch then assigns a Fabric Path Topology identifier or FTAG to the tree.

The FabricPath data plane is responsible for the encapsulation, de-encapsulation, and forwarding of data packets across the FabricPath network. The FabricPath encapsulation uses a MAC-in-MAC encapsulation. This encapsulation technique takes existing L2 frames and prepends them with a 16-byte header that contains instructions on how the frame should be forwarded through the fabric. The FabricPath header is shown in Figure 2-8.

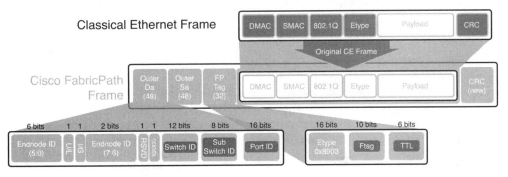

Figure 2-8 *FabricPath Header*

On the surface, the FabricPath header appears as simply another Layer 2 header containing source and destination addresses; however, these are not MAC addresses in the normal sense. The Outer Destination Address (ODA) header contains specific information on which SID the frame is destined for, along with the port information." In addition, the FP header tag contains the Fabric Path FTag, which specifies which topology the frame should be switched on.

As mentioned previously, FabricPath also takes advantage of a classic L3 technology by implementing a Time-To-Live (TTL) field. Each time the frame is switched by a FabricPath device, the TTL is decremented. If the TTL is decremented to zero, the frame is dropped. This provides packets from looping to infinity and creating storm conditions.

There are two primary types of interfaces within a FabricPath topology; a FabricPath edge port and a FabricPath core port. As the name implies, FabricPath edge ports represent the edge of the FabricPath network. FabricPath edge ports are where hosts or other switches connect via Classic Ethernet (CE). These are ports where traditional MAC learning is done, and frames are transmitted with standard Ethernet headers. FabricPath core ports are where FabricPath IS-IS adjacencies are formed, and where frames transmitted will be encapsulated in a FabricPath header. From these interface types, three roles are defined for switches carrying traffic across the fabric.

First, the ingress FabricPath switch receives a frame on one of its connected edge ports. The ingress FabricPath switch is responsible for performing a MAC table lookup to determine which SID has advertised reachability for the destination MAC address. The ingress FabricPath switch also determines to which interface the frame should be forwarded. The ingress FabricPath switch forwards the frame accordingly. Next, a core FabricPath switch receives frames on a FabricPath core port and determines the next-hop interface based on the SID in the FabricPath header. The core FabricPath switch forwards the frame accordingly. Finally, the egress FabricPath switch receives frames on a FabricPath core port and examines the FabricPath header. Upon seeing that it is the destination SID, it uses the Local Identifier (LID) field to determine which FabricPath edge port the frame needs to be forwarded on. The egress FabricPath switch removes the FabricPath header and forwards the frame to the appropriate CE port. The ingress and egress FabricPath switches are also sometimes referred to as Layer 2 gateways.

Through the use of these defined functions, MAC address learning can be optimized through conversational learning. In traditional Ethernet implementations each switch unconditionally populates its MAC address table based on the source address of the frame. This causes the switch to consume valuable resources, even if it is just a transit switch. In the case of FabricPath, traditional learning is done only on FabricPath edge ports. FabricPath core switches do not need to learn any MAC addresses. At the FabricPath edge, only local MAC addresses are unconditionally learned. The edge switch learns only the source MAC address if the destination MAC is already present in its local MAC table.

Enabling FabricPath on a Nexus 7000 has the following prerequisites:

- You must install the Enhanced Layer 2 license.
- You must be using F1, F2, or F2e linecards for all FabricPath interfaces.

The first step in FabricPath configuration is to enable the corresponding feature-set, as shown in Example 2-73.

Example 2-73   *Enabling the FabricPath feature-set*

```
fp-spine-1(config)# install feature-set fabricpath
fp-spine-1(config)# feature-set fabricpath
```

When the prerequisites are met, and the FabricPath feature set is enabled, you can begin the configuration tasks associated with FabricPath. For the remainder of this chapter, the topology shown in Figure 2-9 will be used.

As discussed previously, FabricPath IS-IS can automatically assign a unique switch ID; however, these values are usually statically assigned via the network administrator. The switch ID is a 12-bit identifier, giving the administrator 4094 unique switch IDs to choose from. The switch ID can be configured, as shown in Example 2-74.

Example 2-74   *Configuring the Switch ID*

```
 ! Configure Fabric Path Switch ID on fp-spine-1
fp-spine-1(config)# fabricpath switch-id 1
 ! Configure Fabric Path Switch ID on fp-spine-1
fp-spine-2(config)# fabricpath switch-id 2
 ! Configure Fabric Path Switch ID on fp-edge-3
fp-edge-3(config)# fabricpath switch-id 3
 ! Configure Fabric Path Switch ID on fp-edge-4
fp-edge-4(config)# fabricpath switch-id 4
```

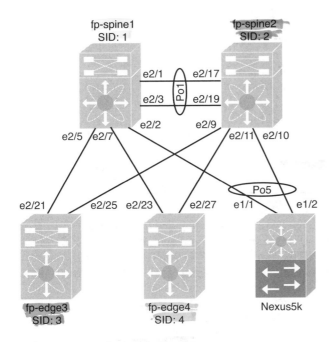

Figure 2-9   *FabricPath Topology*

After defining the switch IDs for the sample topology, you must next define which VLANs will be transported through the FabricPath network. VLANs must be defined and configured as FabricPath VLANs on each switch. The configuration in Example 2-75 is used to configure a set of VLANs as a FabricPath VLANs.

Caution   After a VLAN is placed into FabricPath mode, that VLAN can no longer be carried on any M Series linecards.

Example 2-75   *Configuring VLANs for FabricPath Mode*

```
fp-spine-1# conf t
Enter configuration commands, one per line. End with CNTL/Z.
fp-spine-1(config)# vlan 10-20
fp-spine-1(config-vlan)# mode fabricpath
fp-spine-1(config-vlan)# end

fp-spine-2# conf t
Enter configuration commands, one per line. End with CNTL/Z.
fp-spine-2(config)# vlan 10-20
fp-spine-2(config-vlan)# mode fabricpath
fp-spine-2(config-vlan)# end
```

```
fp-edge-3# conf t
Enter configuration commands, one per line. End with CNTL/Z.
fp-edge-3(config)# vlan 10-20
fp-edge-3(config-vlan)# mode fabricpath
fp-edge-3(config-vlan)# end

fp-edge-4# conf t
Enter configuration commands, one per line. End with CNTL/Z.
fp-edge-4(config)# vlan 10-20
fp-edge-4(config-vlan)# mode fabricpath
fp-edge-4(config-vlan)# end
```

Now that switch IDs have been defined and VLANs configured to operate in FabricPath mode, you can now begin to configure interfaces so that they form FabricPath IS-IS adjacencies. For an interface to form a FabricPath adjacency, it must be configured with the **switchport mode fabricpath** command. Per the sample topology in Figure 2-10, the following configuration would be applied.

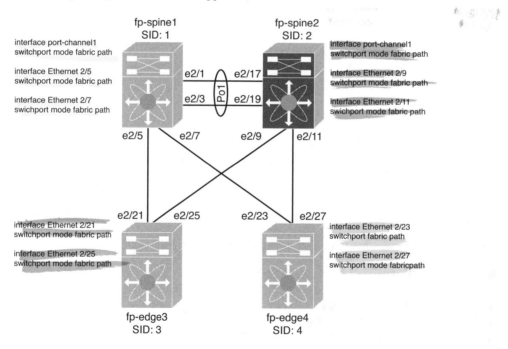

Figure 2-10 *FabricPath Interface Configuration*

To verify that the FabricPath adjacencies have been established, the **show fabricpath isis adjacency** command can be used, as shown in Example 2-76.

Example 2-76 *FabricPath Adjacency Verification*

```
fp-spine-1# show fabricpath isis adjacency
Fabricpath IS-IS domain: default Fabricpath IS-IS adjacency database:
System ID       SNPA          Level  State  Hold Time  Interface
fp-spine-2      N/A           1      UP     00:00:28   port-channel1
fp-edge-3       N/A           1      UP     00:00:23   Ethernet2/5
fp-edge-4       N/A           1      UP     00:00:25   Ethernet2/7


fp-spine-2# show fabricpath isis adjacency
Fabricpath IS-IS domain: default Fabricpath IS-IS adjacency database:
System ID       SNPA          Level  State  Hold Time  Interface
fp-spine-1      N/A           1      UP     00:00:32   port-channel1
fp-edge-3       N/A           1      UP     00:00:30   Ethernet2/9
fp-edge-4       N/A           1      UP     00:00:27   Ethernet2/11
```

After the adjacencies are formed, connectivity can be tested across the FabricPath core, as shown in Example 2-77.

Example 2-77 *Testing Connectivity Across the FabricPath Core*

```
fp-spine-1# ping 10.10.10.4
PING 10.10.10.4 (10.10.10.4): 56 data bytes
64 bytes from 10.10.10.4: icmp_seq=0 ttl=254 time=1.252 ms
64 bytes from 10.10.10.4: icmp_seq=1 ttl=254 time=0.744 ms
64 bytes from 10.10.10.4: icmp_seq=2 ttl=254 time=0.743 ms
64 bytes from 10.10.10.4: icmp_seq=3 ttl=254 time=0.796 ms
64 bytes from 10.10.10.4: icmp_seq=4 ttl=254 time=0.731 ms


--- 10.10.10.4 ping statistics ---
5 packets transmitted, 5 packets received, 0.00% packet loss
round-trip min/avg/max = 0.731/0.853/1.252 ms
```

To understand the FabricPath switching process, look at what is happening behind the scenes. First, the local switch is resolving the MAC address for 10.10.10.4, as shown in Example 2-78

Example 2-78 *ARP Resolution Verification*

```
fp-spine-1# show ip arp 10.10.10.4

Flags: * - Adjacencies learnt on non-active FHRP router
       + - Adjacencies synced via CFSoE
       # - Adjacencies Throttled for Glean
       D - Static Adjacencies attached to down interface
```

```
IP ARP Table
Total number of entries: 1
Address          Age       MAC Address      Interface
10.10.10.4       00:08:55  0026.982e.b044   Vlan10
```

By examining the MAC address table, you can see that rather than pointing to an egress interface on the switch, there is FabricPath reachability information provided. This is demonstrated in Example 2-79.

Example 2-79 *Verifying the MAC Address Table*

```
fp-spine-1# show mac address-table address 0026.982e.b044
Legend:
        * - primary entry, G - Gateway MAC, (R) - Routed MAC, O - Overlay MAC
        age - seconds since last seen,+ - primary entry using vPC Peer-Link
   VLAN     MAC Address      Type      age      Secure NTFY Ports/SWID.SSID.LID
---------+----------------+--------+---------+------+----+------------------
   10       0026.982e.b044   dynamic   30        F    F   4.0.1054
```

In Example 2-79 you can see that for traffic destined to 0026.982e.b044 it will be FabricPath encapsulated with information that directs this frame to SID 4, SSID 0, and LID 1054. To determine which interface the packet will be switched out of, the FabricPath routing table can be consulted, as shown in Example 2-80.

Example 2-80 *Displaying the FabricPath Routing Table*

```
fp-spine-1# show fabricpath route
FabricPath Unicast Route Table
'a/b/c' denotes ftag/switch-id/subswitch-id
'[x/y]' denotes [admin distance/metric]
ftag 0 is local ftag
subswitch-id 0 is default subswitch-id


FabricPath Unicast Route Table for Topology-Default

0/1/0, number of next-hops: 0
        via ---- , [60/0], 4 day/s 00:16:21, local
1/2/0, number of next-hops: 1
        via Po1, [115/20], 0 day/s 01:11:34, isis_fabricpath-default
1/3/0, number of next-hops: 1
        via Eth2/5, [115/40], 1 day/s 00:41:32, isis_fabricpath-default
1/4/0, number of next-hops: 1
        via Eth2/7, [115/40], 1 day/s 00:41:30, isis_fabricpath-default
```

You can see that to reach SID 4, traffic will be sent out Ethernet 2/7. This process would be repeated on all intermediate FabricPath switches, until the frame arrives at SID 4 or the TTL in the FabricPath header is decremented to zero.

vPC+

FabricPath is designed to interoperate with other Layer 2 technologies such as vPC. vPC+ provides extensions to vPC for connecting classical Ethernet devices to a FabricPath cloud. vPC+ enables the entire vPC domain to be seen as one virtual switch by the FabricPath network. vPC+ enables classical Ethernet devices such as hosts or STP domains to communicate with each other through the cloud. With vPC+, the FabricPath cloud is seen as a single L2 bridge for STP purposes.

vPC+ can also enables FabricPath nodes to combine as a single virtual switch for the purpose of creating active/active First Hop Redundancy Protocols (FHRPs) such as HSRP and GLBP to operate in an active/active fashion. These protocols are discussed in detail in Chapter 3, "Layer 3 Support and Configurations."

Caution   The following points should be kept in mind as they relate to vPC+:

■ The vPC Peer-Link and all vPC members must reside on F1, F2, or F2e linecards.

■ Peer-Switch is not recommended in a vPC+ domain configuration.

■ The vPC+ should be configured with STP priorities low enough to ensure that they become the root bridge of the connected L2 domain.

Configuring vPC+

Building upon the FabricPath topology and configuration used so far, now consider another device that can connect in via vPC+ configuration, as shown in Figure 2-11.

First, enable the vPC as done earlier in this chapter. The steps that must be completed follows:

■ Enable the vPC feature.

■ Define the vPC domain.

■ Configure the peer-keepalive.

■ Configure the peer-link.

These configuration tasks are outlined in Example 2-81.

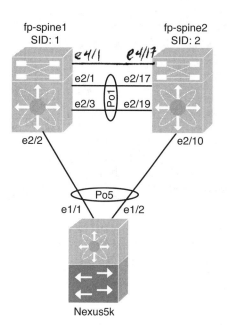

Figure 2-11   *νPC+ Topology*

Example 2-81   *Configuring νPC Domain*

```
Configuration for fp-spine-2
fp-spine-1(config)# feature vpc
fp-spine-1(config)# vrf context vpc-pkal
fp-spine-1(config-vrf)# interface ethernet 4/1
fp-spine-1(config-if)# vrf member vpc-pkal
% Deleted all L3 config on interface Ethernet4/1
fp-spine-1(config-if)# ip address 1.1.1.1/30
fp-spine-1(config-if)# vpc domain 1
fp-spine-1(config-vpc-domain)# peer-keepalive destination 1.1.1.2 source 1.1.1.1 vrf
vpc-pkal
fp-spine-1(config-vpc-domain)# interface port-channel 1
fp-spine-1(config-if)# vpc peer-link
fp-spine-1(config-if)# exit
fp-spine-1(config)# exit

Configuration for fp-spine-2
fp-spine-2(config)# feature vpc
fp-spine-2(config)# vrf context vpc-pkal
fp-spine-2(config-vrf)# interface ethernet 4/17
fp-spine-2(config-if)# vrf member vpc-pkal
% Deleted all L3 config on interface Ethernet4/17
fp-spine-2(config-if)# ip address 1.1.1.2/30
```

```
fp-spine-2(config-if)# vpc domain 1
fp-spine-2(config-vpc-domain)# peer-keepalive destination 1.1.1.1 source 1.1.1.2 vrf
vpc-pkal
fp-spine-2(config-vpc-domain)# interface port-channel 1
fp-spine-2(config-if)# vpc peer-link
fp-spine-2(config-if)# exit
```

Because Port-Channel 1 is running in FabricPath mode, the Peer-Link does not come up until the vPC+ configuration is in place. In Example 2-82 you can see the error message.

Example 2-82 *Error with Incomplete vPC+ Configuration*

```
fp-spine-1# show vpc
Legend:
                    (*) - local vPC is down, forwarding via vPC peer-link

vPC domain id                    : 1
vPC+ switch id                   : 12
Peer status                      : peer link is down
                                   (Peer-link is in mode fabricpath
                                   for vPC)
vPC keep-alive status            : peer is alive
vPC fabricpath status            : peer not found
Configuration consistency status : failed
Per-vlan consistency status      : success
Configuration inconsistency reason: Consistency Check Not Performed
Type-2 inconsistency reason      : Consistency Check Not Performed
vPC role                         : none established
Number of vPCs configured        : 0
Peer Gateway                     : Disabled
Dual-active excluded VLANs       : -
Graceful Consistency Check       : Disabled (due to peer configuration)
Auto-recovery status             : Disabled


vPC Peer-link status
---------------------------------------------------------------------
id   Port   Status Active vlans
--   ----   ------ -------------------------------------------------
1    Po1    down   -
```

To complete the vPC+ configuration, the Virtual Switch ID must be configured on both members of the vPC+ domain. This configuration is accomplished via the **fabricpath switch-id** command in the vPC domain configuration mode, as shown in Example 2-83.

Example 2-83   *Configuring vPC+ Virtual switch-id*

```
fp-spine-1(config)# vpc domain 1
fp-spine-1(config-vpc-domain)# fabricpath switch-id 12
Configuring fabricpath switch id will flap vPCs. Continue (yes/no)? [no] yes
Note:
 --------:: Re-init of peer-link and vPCs started  ::--------
fp-spine-1(config-vpc-domain)#


fp-spine-2(config)# vpc domain 1
fp-spine-2(config-vpc-domain)# fabricpath switch-id 12
Configuring fabricpath switch id will flap vPCs. Continue (yes/no)? [no] yes
Note:
 --------:: Re-init of peer-link and vPCs started  ::--------
fp-spine-2(config-vpc-domain)#
```

At this point the vPC+ domain should be operational, as shown in Example 2-84.

Example 2-84   *Operational vPC+ Domain*

```
fp-spine-1# show vpc
Legend:
                (*) - local vPC is down, forwarding via vPC peer-link

vPC domain id                    : 1
vPC+ switch id                   : 12
Peer status                      : peer adjacency formed ok
vPC keep-alive status            : peer is alive
vPC fabricpath status            : peer is reachable through fabricpath
Configuration consistency status : success
Per-vlan consistency status      : success
Type-2 consistency status        : success
vPC role                         : primary
Number of vPCs configured        : 0
Peer Gateway                     : Disabled
Dual-active excluded VLANs       : -
Graceful Consistency Check       : Enabled
Auto-recovery status             : Disabled


vPC Peer-link status
---------------------------------------------------------------------
id   Port   Status Active vlans
--   ----   ------ --------------------------------------------------
1    Po1    up     10-20
```

After the vPC+ domain is configured and operational, vPCs can be created to CE devices as described earlier in this chapter. For the purposes of the sample topology, the configuration would be as shown in Figure 2-12.

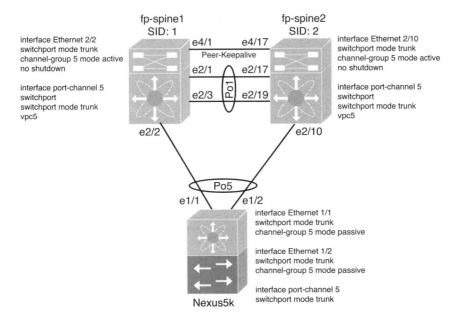

interface Ethernet 2/2
switchport mode trunk
channel-group 5 mode active
no shutdown

interface port-channel 5
switchport
switchport mode trunk
vpc5

interface Ethernet 2/10
switchport mode trunk
channel-group 5 mode active
no shutdown

interface port-channel 5
switchport
switchport mode trunk
vpc5

interface Ethernet 1/1
switchport mode trunk
channel-group 5 mode passive

interface Ethernet 1/2
switchport mode trunk
channel-group 5 mode passive

interface port-channel 5
switchport mode trunk

Figure 2-12   *vPC+ Interface Configuration*

The vPC+ configuration can be verified by using the **show vpc** command, as shown in Example 2-85.

Example 2-85   *Verifying vPC Configuration*

```
fp-spine-2# show vpc
Legend:
                (*) - local vPC is down, forwarding via vPC peer-link

vPC domain id                      : 1
vPC+ switch id                     : 12
Peer status                        : peer adjacency formed ok
vPC keep-alive status              : peer is alive
vPC fabricpath status              : peer is reachable through fabricpath
Configuration consistency status   : success
Per-vlan consistency status        : success
Type-2 consistency status          : success
vPC role                           : secondary
Number of vPCs configured          : 1
Peer Gateway                       : Disabled
```

```
Dual-active excluded VLANs      : -
Graceful Consistency Check      : Enabled
Auto-recovery status            : Disabled


vPC Peer-link status
-----------------------------------------------------------------------
id   Port   Status Active vlans
--   ----   ------ ------------------------------------------------------
1    Po1    up     10-20


vPC status
-----------------------------------------------------------------------
id   Port   Status Consistency Reason       Active vlans   vPC+ Attribute
--   ----   ------ ----------- ------        ------------   --------------
5    Po5    up     success     success       10-20          DF: Yes, FP
                                                            MAC: 12.11.0
fp-spine-2#
```

Comparing the output from Example 2-85 to previous (non-vPC+) outputs, you can see a new column has appeared that provides vPC+ attributes, including which device is the multicast designated forwarder (DF: Yes) and what the subswitch ID is for this particular vPC (MAC: 12.11.0). Other FabricPath devices now can reach devices downstream from the vPC attached device by encapsulating frames with an ODA of SID 12 and SSID 11, as shown in Example 2-86.

Example 2-86   *MAC Addresses Located on vPC+ Attached Switch as Shown on the FabricPath Edge Device*

```
fp-edge-3# show mac address-table
Legend:
        * - primary entry, G - Gateway MAC, (R) - Routed MAC, O - Overlay MAC
        age - seconds since last seen,+ - primary entry using vPC Peer-Link
   VLAN    MAC Address     Type      age     Secure NTFY Ports/SWID.SSID.LID
---------+-----------------+--------+---------+------+----+------------------
G    -     0026.982e.b043  static     -        F      F   sup-eth1(R)
G 10       0026.982e.b043  static     -        F      F   sup-eth1(R)
  10       0000.0c07.ac0a  dynamic    0        F      F   12.0.1054
  10       0005.73cd.6c81  dynamic    660      F      F   12.11.0
  10       0026.982e.b041  dynamic    630      F      F   1.0.1054
  10       0026.982e.b042  dynamic    0        F      F   2.0.1054
  10       0026.982e.b044  dynamic    660      F      F   4.0.1054
```

Summary

The Layer 2 switching capabilities of NX-OS provide a scalable, resilient foundation for your data center. This chapter covered the following topics:

■ VLANs segment traffic at Layer 2 to address security concerns or define failure domains.

■ PVLANs provide an additional level of security by enabling administrators to | subdivide VLANs.

■ Spanning Tree provides a mechanism to ensure that physically redundant networks are logically loop-free. You learned how to configure and tune Rapid-PVST+ and MST.

■ Enhancements are available for Spanning Tree such as BPDUGuard, BPDUFilter, RootGuard, and LoopGuard.

■ Links can be aggregated through the use of port-channels and vPCs to simplify Spanning Tree topologies while making additional bandwidth available for data traffic.

■ Cisco FabricPath represents a new way to build large Layer 2 networks, which optimizes bandwidth, latency, and system resources such as MAC address tables. FabricPath accomplishes this by taking the best characteristics from Layer 2 and Layer 3 technologies and combining them.

With NX-OS on the Nexus 7000 and 5000, Cisco provides a highly available implementation of standards-based Layer 2 technology and builds upon it with new innovation required to meet the specific demands within today's data centers.

## Chapter 3

Layer 3 Support and Configurations

The Nexus line of switches provides a robust Layer 3 feature set. This chapter features common implementations and syntax for Layer 3 features such as EIGRP, OSPF, IS-IS, and BGP and FHRPs such as HSRP, VRRP, and GLBP and covers the following topics:

- **EIGRP:** Describes the configuration and operations of EIGRP

- **OSPF:** Describes the configuration and operations of OSPF

- **IS-IS:** Describes the configuration and operations of IS-IS

- **BGP:** Describes the configuration and operations of BGP

- **HSRP:** Describes the configuration and operations of HSRP

- **VRRP:** Describes the configuration and operations of VRRP

- **GLBP:** Describes the configuration and operations of GLBP

EIGRP

Cisco NX-OS on the Nexus 7000 series switches support Layer 3 routing using dynamic routing protocols, static routing, and policy-based routing. The Nexus 5500 series switches support Layer 3 routing using dynamic routing protocols and static routing. NX-OS also provides advanced virtualization capabilities using Virtual Routing and Forwarding instances (VRF). Supporting industry-leading protocols such as Enhanced Interior Gateway Routing Protocol (EIGRP), Open Shortest Path First (OSPF), Border Gateway Protocol (BGP), Intermediate System-to-Intermediate System (IS-IS), Routing Information Protocol (RIP), and static routing, the Nexus 7000 enables significant flexibility and options to interconnect multiple topologies. The Route Policy Manager supports complex configurations, tight routing control, and migrations from one protocol to another. This chapter covers common implementations and syntax for EIGRP, OSPF, IS-IS, and BGP and First-Hop Redundancy Protocols (FHRP) such as Hot Standby Router Protocol

(HSRP), Virtual Router Redundancy Protocol (VRRP), and Gateway Load Balancing Protocol (GLBP).

EIGRP was developed by Cisco and runs only on Cisco devices. EIGRP is a highly scalable, flexible, and robust routing protocol considered a hybrid of distance vector and link-state protocols. Considered a hybrid routing protocol, EIGRP implements the best characteristics of both distance vector and link-state protocols such as the hello mechanism and incremental updates. EIGRP is supported on both the Nexus 7000 and 5500 series switches. The Nexus 5500 series switches must be configured with a Layer-3 daughtercard or module, dependent on the specific platform. The Nexus 5500 series also requires an Enterprise License for full EIGRP functionality. (The Base license includes EIGRP stub routing only.) The examples in this chapter focus on EIGRP configuration for the Nexus 7000.

EIGRP Operation

EIGRP calculates routes based on metrics received from neighbors and uses an algorithm called the Diffusing Update Algorithm (DUAL). The primary advantage that DUAL provides over other routing algorithms is the capability to provide loop-free topologies at every stage of network convergence. When joined with the other capabilities of EIGRP, such as its multiprotocol nature, WAN-friendly neighboring and updating capabilities, and flexible summarization and quick convergence, it makes a powerful routing protocol.

EIGRP forms adjacencies with its directly connected neighbors to exchange routing updates similar to a link state protocol. During the initial neighbor formation, attributes such as smooth round-trip time (SRTT), hold time, retry timeout, IP address, and interface on which the hello was received are negotiated and recorded in a neighbor table, as demonstrated in Example 3-1.

Example 3-1   *EIGRP Neighbors*

```
Congo# show ip eigrp ne
IP-EIGRP neighbors for process 100 VRF default
H   Address                 Interface      Hold  Uptime   SRTT   RTO  Q   Seq
                                           (sec)          (ms)        Cnt Num
1   10.10.10.3              Vlan10         11    01:42:49  44     264  0   128
0   192.168.1.38            Eth1/18        14    01:52:06  414    2484 0   221
```

The hellos between the EIGRP neighbors are the mechanism for maintaining the adjacency. Within the hello is a hold timer that tells EIGRP the maximum time before the next hello should be received. By default, the hold timer is three times the hello interval. If the hold timer is exceeded before another hello is received, EIGRP considers the neighbor unreachable and informs DUAL. The network's topology is recalculated and bounded, partial updates are sent to the remaining neighbors, and the network begins to converge.

Configuring EIGRP

EIGRP within NX-OS is compatible with EIGRP on IOS devices enabling a smooth integration of Nexus equipment with existing gear. Configuring EIGRP within NX-OS will be similar yet distinctly different in some aspects to traditional IOS configuration. These differences will be highlighted throughout the section.

Enabling EIGRP is a multistep process that will be covered in detail. The following is a quick listing of steps to enable a basic configuration of EIGRP:

1. Enable EIGRP.

2. Configure the EIGRP routing process with support for IPv4 or IPv6.

3. Assign interfaces to the instance tag.

4. Configure passive interfaces if necessary.

5. Configure network summarization.

6. Configure the redistribution of other protocols if necessary.

7. Verify EIGRP operation.

The first step to configure EIGRP is to enable it in global configuration mode using the **feature** command, as demonstrated in Example 3-2. With the modular nature of NX-OS, using the **feature** command loads the EIGRP modular code into memory for execution. Without the feature enabled, it would not be resident in memory.

Example 3-2 *Enabling EIGRP*

```
Congo# config t
Enter configuration commands, one per line. End with CNTL/Z.
Congo(config)# feature eigrp
Congo(config)# end
Congo# show run eigrp
!Command: show running-config eigrp
!Time: Tue Sep 29 16:03:10 2009
version 4.2(2a)
feature eigrp
```

As with IOS-based EIGRP configuration, the next step is to configure the EIGRP routing process, as demonstrated in Example 3-3. In NX-OS, you configure an instance tag for the process. Traditionally in IOS this would be the autonomous system (AS) number. In NX-OS the instance tag can be the AS, but in addition the instance tag can be up to 20 case-sensitive, alphanumeric characters.

Example 3-3   *Creating an EIGRP Instance with a Numeric Tag*

```
Congo# config t
Enter configuration commands, one per line. End with CNTL/Z.
Congo(config)# router eigrp 200
Congo(config-router)# exit
Congo(config)# show run eigrp
!Command: show running-config eigrp
!Time: Tue Sep 29 16:05:21 2009
version 4.2(2a)
feature eigrp
router eigrp 200
```

Example 3-4 shows an alphanumeric string for the tag.

Example 3-4   *Creating an EIGRP Instance with an Alphanumeric String*

```
Congo# config t
Enter configuration commands, one per line. End with CNTL/Z.
Congo(config)# router eigrp DataCenter1
Congo(config)# show run eigrp
!Command: show running-config eigrp
!Time: Tue Sep 29 16:11:05 2009
version 4.2(2a)
feature eigrp
router eigrp DataCenter1
```

When using an instance tag that cannot qualify as an AS number, use the **autonomous-system** *as-number* command to configure the AS; otherwise, EIGRP remains shut down.

Example 3-5 shows how to configure an AS number under an EIGRP process that uses an alphanumeric tag.

Example 3-5   *Configuring EIGRP with an Autonomous System Number*

```
Congo# config t
Enter configuration commands, one per line. End with CNTL/Z.
Congo(config)# router eigrp DataCenter1
Congo(config-router)# autonomous-system 100
Congo(config-router)# exit
Congo(config)# show run eigrp
!Command: show running-config eigrp
!Time: Tue Sep 29 16:11:05 2009
version 4.2(2a)
feature eigrp
```

```
router eigrp DataCenter1
  autonomous-system 100
```

NX-OS supports the ability to configure a single EIGRP routing process instance for IPv4 and IPv6 routing capabilities. This enables a more streamlined configuration approach. To distinguish between IPv4 and IPv6 under the EIGRP routing process, the **address-family** keyword is used. For backward compatibility, you can configure EIGRPv4 in route configuration mode or in IPv4 address family mode. You must configure EIGRP for IPv6 in address family mode.

EIGRP features can be configured using the **ip** keyword for IPv4 and **ipv6** keyword for IPv6, as shown in the remaining configuration examples; **show** commands follow this same methodology.

Example 3-6 shows options for both IPv4 and IPv6.

Example 3-6 *Configuring an Address-Family for IPv4 or IPv6*

```
Congo# config t
Enter configuration commands, one per line.  End with CNTL/Z.
Congo(config)# router eigrp DataCenter1
Congo(config-router)# address-family ?
  ipv4  Configure IPv4 address-family
  ipv6  Configure IPv6 address-family
Congo(config-router)# address-family ipv4 unicast
Congo(config-router)# address-family ipv6 unicast
```

With EIGRP configured as a feature and assigned an autonomous system ID, the next step is to assign interfaces to the instance tag, as shown in Example 3-7. This advertises the IP subnet in EIGRP and enables the capability for neighbor adjacencies to be formed.

This is different from a traditional IOS configuration where you configure a **network** statement under the routing process and then, in turn, any interface on the router that fell within that network range was advertised. The approach taken in NX-OS is more granular and enables additional levels of control over which networks are advertised.

Example 3-7 *Adding an SVI to EIGRP with a Numeric Tag*

```
Congo# config t
Enter configuration commands, one per line. End with CNTL/Z.
Congo(config)# int vlan 10
Congo(config-if)# ip router eigrp 200
Congo(config-if)# show ip eigrp int vlan 10
IP-EIGRP interfaces for process 200 VRF default

                      Xmit Queue   Mean   Pacing Time  Multicast   Pending
Interface      Peers  Un/Reliable  SRTT   Un/Reliable  Flow Timer  Routes
```

```
Vlan10              0         0/0         0       0/10       0        0
  Hello interval is 5 sec
  Holdtime interval is 15 sec
  Next xmit serial <none>
  Un/reliable mcasts: 0/0  Un/reliable ucasts: 0/0
  Mcast exceptions: 0  CR packets: 0  ACKs suppressed: 0
  Retransmissions sent: 0  Out-of-sequence rcvd: 0
  Authentication mode is not set
```

Example 3-8 shows how to add an SVI to EIGRP when using an alphanumeric tag.

Example 3-8   *Adding an SVI to EIGRP with an Alphanumeric Tag*

```
Congo# config t
Enter configuration commands, one per line. End with CNTL/Z.
Congo(config)# int vlan 10
Congo(config-if)# ip router eigrp DataCenter1
Congo(config-if)# show ip eigrp int vlan 10
IP-EIGRP interfaces for process 100 VRF default

                     Xmit Queue   Mean   Pacing Time   Multicast    Pending
Interface      Peers  Un/Reliable  SRTT   Un/Reliable   Flow Timer   Routes
Vlan10           1      0/0         44       0/10         208          0
  Hello interval is 5 sec
  Holdtime interval is 15 sec
  Next xmit serial <none>
  Un/reliable mcasts: 0/1  Un/reliable ucasts: 2/2
  Mcast exceptions: 0  CR packets: 0  ACKs suppressed: 1
  Retransmissions sent: 0  Out-of-sequence rcvd: 0
  Authentication mode is not set
```

Example 3-9 shows how to add an IPv6 SVI to EIGRP using an alphanumeric tag.

Example 3-9   *Adding an IPv6 SVI to EIGRP Using an Alphanumeric Tag*

```
Congo# config t
Enter configuration commands, one per line. End with CNTL/Z.
Congo(config)# int vlan 10
Congo(config-if)# ipv6 router eigrp DataCenter1
Congo(config-if)# show ipv6 eigrp interfaces vlan 10
IPv6-EIGRP interfaces for process 100 VRF default

                     Xmit Queue   Mean   Pacing Time   Multicast    Pending
Interface      Peers  Un/Reliable  SRTT   Un/Reliable   Flow Timer   Routes
Vlan10           1      0/0          2       0/1          0            0
  Hello interval is 5 sec
```

```
Holdtime interval is 15 sec
Next xmit serial <none>
Un/reliable mcasts: 0/0  Un/reliable ucasts: 0/3
Mcast exceptions: 0  CR packets: 0  ACKs suppressed: 1
Retransmissions sent: 1  Out-of-sequence rcvd: 0
Authentication mode is not set
Classic/wide metric peers: 1/0
```

Beginning in software version 5.2(1), NX-OS supports the capability to leverage wide (64-bit) metrics. This improves route selection on higher-speed interfaces or bundled interfaces. NX-OS defaults to supporting the classic metrics, and wide metrics can be configured under the **address-family** keyword. Devices leveraging wide metrics are backward compatible with ones not capable or configured of supporting them. EIGRP wide metrics introduce the following two new metric values represented as *k6* in the EIGRP metrics configuration, jitter and energy. Jitter is accumulated across all links in the route path and is measured in microseconds. Energy is also accumulated across all links in the route path and is measured in watts per kilobit.

Example 3-10 shows how to configure wide metrics for EIGRP.

Example 3-10 *Configuring Wide Metrics for EIGRP*

```
Congo# config t
Enter configuration commands, one per line.  End with CNTL/Z.
Congo(config)# router eigrp DataCenter1
Congo(config-router)# address-family ipv4 unicast
Congo(config-router-af)# metric version 64bit
```

Note Mixing standard and wide metrics in an EIGRP network with interface speeds of 1 Gigabit or greater may result in suboptimal routing.

In a data center's distribution or aggregation layer, it is common to have multiple VLAN interfaces that, in turn, need to be advertised to the network at large. By default, when EIGRP is enabled on the VLAN interface, it sends and receives hellos. If a neighbor is detected, EIGRP attempts to form an adjacency. Although this default setup is wanted, there might be designs in which forming multiple EIGRP adjacencies between the same pair of switches is not wanted due to the potential impact of network convergence time and unnecessary duplicate next hops. In configurations such as this, use the **passive-interface** command, as shown in Example 3-11. A passive interface accomplishes the requirement of advertising the subnet via EIGRP but also instructing the EIGRP process to not listen to hellos on the interfaces configured to be passive.

Example 3-11   *Configuring a Passive Interface in EIGRP with a Numeric Tag*

```
Congo# config t
Congo(config)# int vlan100
Congo(config-if)# ip passive-interface eigrp 200
Congo(config-if)# end
```

Example 3-12 shows how to configure a passive interface in EIGRP when using an alpha-numeric tag.

Example 3-12   *Configuring a Passive Interface in EIGRP with an Alphanumeric Tag*

```
Congo# config t
Congo(config)# int vlan100
Congo(config-if)# ip passive-interface eigrp DataCenter1
Congo(config-if)# exit
Congo(config)# show run int vlan 100
!Command: show running-config interface Vlan100
!Time: Tue Sep 29 16:30:02 2009
version 4.2(2a)
interface Vlan100
  no shutdown
  description Server Subnet1
  ip address 10.10.100.2/24
  ip router eigrp DataCenter1
  ip passive-interface eigrp DataCenter1
```

EIGRP Summarization

EIGRP has the capability to summarize routes in a flexible manner per interface. This enables network designers to summarize their networks for maximum efficiency without the constraints of specific borders or other topological designations. When a network is summarized, a single entry with a shorter prefix (commonly called a *supernet*) is created and added to the routing table as a representation of the longer prefix subnets. The examples that follow show how to create a summary for 192.168.128.0 /20 that is advertised out interface e1/18.

Note   With this summary, the following networks are represented: 192.168.128.0/24 through 192.168.143.0/24.

Example 3-13 shows EIGRP summarization between the Congo and Libya networks, as shown in Figure 3-1.

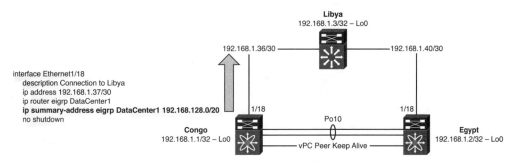

Figure 3-1 *EIGRP Summarization*

Example 3-13 *Summarizing Networks in EIGRP Using Numeric Tags*

```
Congo# config t
Congo(config)# interface e1/18
Congo(config-if)# ip summary-address eigrp 200 192.168.128.0/20
Congo(config-if)# end
```

Example 3-14 shows how to summarize a network when EIGRP uses an alphanumeric tag.

Example 3-14 *Summarizing Networks in EIGRP Using Alphanumeric Tags*

```
Congo# config t
Congo(config)# int e1/18
Congo(config-if)# ip summary-address eigrp DataCenter1 192.168.128.0/20
```

As highlighted in Example 3-15, you can see the resulting summary address in the routing table on Congo.

Example 3-15 *Reviewing the Network Summarization in NX-OS*

```
Congo(config-if)# show ip route
IP Route Table for VRF "default"
'*' denotes best ucast next-hop
'**' denotes best mcast next-hop
'[x/y]' denotes [preference/metric]
10.10.10.0/24, ubest/mbest: 1/0, attached
    *via 10.10.10.2, Vlan10, [0/0], 2d22h, direct
10.10.10.1/32, ubest/mbest: 1/0
    *via 10.10.10.1, Vlan10, [0/0], 2d22h, hsrp
10.10.10.2/32, ubest/mbest: 1/0, attached
    *via 10.10.10.2, Vlan10, [0/0], 2d22h, local
10.10.100.0/24, ubest/mbest: 1/0, attached
    *via 10.10.100.2, Vlan100, [0/0], 01:33:23, direct
```

```
10.10.100.1/32, ubest/mbest: 1/0
    *via 10.10.100.1, Vlan100, [0/0], 01:33:03, hsrp
10.10.100.2/32, ubest/mbest: 1/0, attached
    *via 10.10.100.2, Vlan100, [0/0], 01:33:23, local
192.168.1.1/32, ubest/mbest: 2/0, attached
    *via 192.168.1.1, Lo0, [0/0], 2d22h, local
    *via 192.168.1.1, Lo0, [0/0], 2d22h, direct
192.168.1.2/32, ubest/mbest: 1/0
    *via 192.168.1.38, Eth1/18, [90/128832], 02:22:00, eigrp-DataCenter1, internal
192.168.1.3/32, ubest/mbest: 1/0
    *via 192.168.1.38, Eth1/18, [90/128512], 02:29:54, eigrp-DataCenter1, internal
192.168.1.32/30, ubest/mbest: 1/0, attached
    *via 192.168.1.33, Vlan5, [0/0], 2d22h, direct
192.168.1.33/32, ubest/mbest: 1/0, attached
    *via 192.168.1.33, Vlan5, [0/0], 2d22h, local
192.168.1.36/30, ubest/mbest: 1/0, attached
        *via 192.168.1.37, Eth1/18, [0/0], 2d22h, direct
192.168.1.37/32, ubest/mbest: 1/0, attached
    *via 192.168.1.37, Eth1/18, [0/0], 2d22h, local
192.168.1.40/30, ubest/mbest: 1/0
    *via 192.168.1.38, Eth1/18, [90/768], 02:29:54, eigrp-DataCenter1, internal
192.168.128.0/20, ubest/mbest: 1/0
    *via Null0, [5/128320], 00:01:54, eigrp-DataCenter1, discard
192.168.128.1/32, ubest/mbest: 2/0, attached
    *via 192.168.128.1, Lo2, [0/0], 00:02:04, local
    *via 192.168.128.1, Lo2, [0/0], 00:02:04, direct
```

As Example 3-16 demonstrates, the summary address is propagated to an IOS-speaking EIGRP neighbor, Libya, and that it is summarizing the /32 route for Loopback2 as expected.

Example 3-16   *Reviewing the Network Summarization in IOS*

```
Libya#show ip route
Codes: C - connected, S - static, R - RIP, M - mobile, B - BGP
       D - EIGRP, EX - EIGRP external, O - OSPF, IA - OSPF inter area
       N1 - OSPF NSSA external type 1, N2 - OSPF NSSA external type 2
       E1 - OSPF external type 1, E2 - OSPF external type 2
       i - IS-IS, su - IS-IS summary, L1 - IS-IS level-1, L2 - IS-IS level-2
       ia - IS-IS inter area, * - candidate default, U - per-user static route
       o - ODR, P - periodic downloaded static route
```

```
Gateway of last resort is not set
     192.168.128.0/32 is subnetted, 1 subnets
D       192.168.128.1
           [90/131072] via 192.168.1.41, 00:05:38, TenGigabitEthernet1/49
     172.26.0.0/16 is variably subnetted, 2 subnets, 2 masks
S       172.26.2.0/23 [1/0] via 172.26.32.33
C       172.26.32.32/27 is directly connected, GigabitEthernet1/48
     10.0.0.0/24 is subnetted, 2 subnets
D       10.10.10.0
           [90/3072] via 192.168.1.41, 02:24:25, TenGigabitEthernet1/49
           [90/3072] via 192.168.1.37, 02:24:25, TenGigabitEthernet1/50
D       10.10.100.0
           [90/3072] via 192.168.1.41, 01:36:59, TenGigabitEthernet1/49
            [90/3072] via 192.168.1.37, 01:36:59, TenGigabitEthernet1/50
     192.168.1.0/24 is variably subnetted, 5 subnets, 2 masks
C       192.168.1.40/30 is directly connected, TenGigabitEthernet1/49
C       192.168.1.36/30 is directly connected, TenGigabitEthernet1/50
D       192.168.1.1/32
           [90/128576] via 192.168.1.37, 00:07:51, TenGigabitEthernet1/50
C       192.168.1.3/32 is directly connected, Loopback0
D       192.168.1.2/32
           [90/128576] via 192.168.1.41, 02:25:45, TenGigabitEthernet1/49
D    192.168.128.0/20
           [90/128576] via 192.168.1.37, 00:05:38, TenGigabitEthernet1/50
```

EIGRP Stub Routing

One of EIGRP's scalability features is stub routing. When EIGRP stub routing is enabled, the router advertises a smaller subset of networks dependent on the configuration. An EIGRP stub router informs its neighbors that it is a stub and responds to queries with **INACCESSIBLE**. Although not commonly deployed in the data center, there are use cases for the EIGRP stub. An example would be to define the data center as an EIGRP stub to minimize updates and queries from the WAN. Another example that could leverage the EIGRP stub would be when a merger or acquisition is made and complex routing can be simplified with the EIGRP stub.

Stub routing is configured under the address-family mode in the routing process, as shown in Example 3-17, for the network topology shown in Figure 3-2.

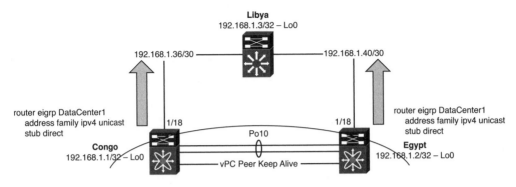

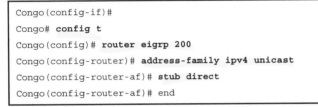

Figure 3-2 *EIGRP Stub Routing*

Example 3-17 *Configuring EIGRP Stub Routing with Numeric Tags*

```
Congo(config-if)#
Congo# config t
Congo(config)# router eigrp 200
Congo(config-router)# address-family ipv4 unicast
Congo(config-router-af)# stub direct
Congo(config-router-af)# end
```

Example 3-18 shows how to configure an EIGRP stub when using an alphanumeric tag.

Example 3-18 *Configuring EIGRP Stub Routing with Alphanumeric Tags*

```
Congo# config t
Congo(config)# router eigrp DataCenter1
Congo(config-router)# address-family ipv4 unicast
Congo(config-router-af)# stub
Congo(config-router-af)# end
```

The stub status of a neighbor can be identified in the detail output from **show ip eigrp neighbor detail**, as shown in Example 3-19.

Example 3-19 *Verification of EIGRP Stub Neighbor*

```
Congo# show ip eigrp neighbor detail
IP-EIGRP neighbors for process 100 VRF default
H   Address            Interface        Hold  Uptime   SRTT   RTO  Q   Seq
                                        (sec)          (ms)        Cnt Num
1   10.10.10.3         Vlan10           13   00:00:19  38    228   0   149
    Version 12.4/1.2, Retrans: 0, Retries: 0, Prefixes: 3
    Stub Peer Advertising ( CONNECTED/DIRECT SUMMARY ) Routes
    Suppressing queries
```

```
0    192.168.1.38              Eth1/18         12   02:40:32 36   216   0   245
     Restart time 00:14:10
     Version 12.2/3.0, Retrans: 0, Retries: 0, Prefixes: 3
```

Securing EIGRP

Securing EIGRP routing updates is also possible by using authentication between EIGRP neighbors. EIGRP authentication is enabled either at the routing process level or per-interface allowing for flexible deployment options.

Note   The interface-level authentication overrides the process-level configuration.

Configuring EIGRP authentication involves a multistep process. You must first define a keychain that contains attributes such as the password to be used to authenticate the connection and the lifetime of the keychain for both sending and receiving, as shown in the configuration in Example 3-20, for the network topology in Figure 3-3.

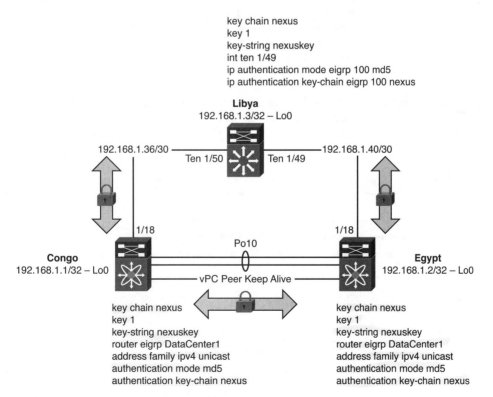

Figure 3-3   *EIGRP Authentication*

Example 3-20 *Configuring a Keychain*

```
Congo(config)# key chain nexus
Congo(config-keychain)# key 1
Congo(config-keychain-key)# key-string nexus
```

Now that a key exists, the next step is to configure the routing protocol, EIGRP in this case, to enable authentication and to use the keychain, as shown in Example 3-21. This step is completed under the address-family configuration. It is necessary to specify an encryption mechanism, MD5, and configure the keychain to use.

Note The use of **address-family** commands provides the ability to group protocol-specific attributes such as stub, authentication, and redistribution. This flexibility allows for complex routing scenarios with a fine level of control.

Example 3-21 *Configuring EIGRP Authentication*

```
Congo(config-router)# router eigrp DataCenter1
Congo(config-router)# address-family ipv4 unicast
Congo(config-router-af)# authentication mode md5
Congo(config-router-af)# authentication key-chain nexus
```

The values specified under the address-family configuration are for all EIGRP neighbors. These values can be overridden by an interface-specific configuration that might be helpful when multiple keys are used on different devices in the internetwork, as shown in Example 3-22.

Example 3-22 *Configuring EIGRP Authentication on an Interface*

```
Congo# config t
Congo(config)# interface e1/18
Congo(config-if)# ip authentication mode eigrp DataCenter1 md5
Congo(config-if)# ip authentication key-chain eigrp DataCenter1 newkey
```

Example 3-23 demonstrates how to verify the authentication configuration.

Example 3-23 *Verification of EIGRP Authentication*

```
Congo# show ip eigrp DataCenter1 vrf default
IP-EIGRP AS 100 ID 192.168.1.1 VRF default
  Process-tag: DataCenter1
  Status: running
  Authentication mode: md5
```

```
Authentication key-chain: nexus
Metric weights: K1=1 K2=0 K3=1 K4=0 K5=0
IP proto: 88 Multicast group: 224.0.0.10
Int distance: 90 Ext distance: 170
Max paths: 8
Number of EIGRP interfaces: 4 (2 loopbacks)
Number of EIGRP passive interfaces: 1
Number of EIGRP peers: 2
Graceful-Restat: Enabled
Stub-Routing: Disabled
NSF converge time limit/expiries: 120/0
NSF route-hold time limit/expiries: 240/7
NSF signal time limit/expiries: 20/0
Redistributed max-prefix: Disabled
```

EIGRP Redistribution

It is a common requirement to redistribute routes learned from other routing protocols or for directly connected interfaces into EIGRP. With the exception of the default route, this is accomplished in a similar manner to traditional IOS redistribution with a few minor differences that are highlighted in the sample configurations.

Starting with the default route, the methodology to redistribute it into the routing table uses the **default-information originate** command.

As shown in Example 3-24, the process begins by defining a prefix list, which is then used by a route map referenced by the **default-information originate** command (see Figure 3-4).

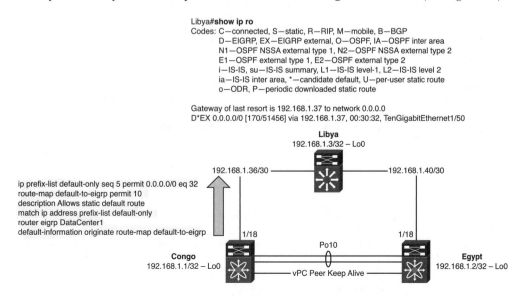

Figure 3-4 *EIGRP Redistribution of the Default Route*

> **Note** NX-OS does not have the capability to do "wide-open" or "uncontrolled" redistribution. NX-OS enforces the use of a route map to define routes that should be redistributed.

Example 3-24 *Defining a Prefix List*

```
Congo# config t
Enter configuration commands, one per line. End with CNTL/Z.
Congo(config)# ip prefix-list default-only seq 5 permit 0.0.0.0/0 eq 32
Congo(config)#
```

> **Note** Three operators can be used in a prefix list: **eq**, **le**, and **ge**. The **eq** operator is an *exact* match of the prefix. The **le** operator specifies less than or equal to the matching prefix. Finally, the **ge** operator specifies greater than or equal to the matching prefix.

The next step is to define a route map, called **default-to-eigrp**, which uses the prefix list named **default-only** to bring in only the 0/0 route, as shown in Example 3-25.

Example 3-25 *Defining a Route Map*

```
Congo(config)# route-map default-to-eigrp permit 10
Congo(config-route-map)# description Allows static default route
Congo(config-route-map)# match ip address prefix-list default-only
```

Finally, you configure EIGRP to use the route map **default-to-eigrp** as part of the **default-information originate** command, as shown in Example 3-26.

Example 3-26 *Redistribution of the Default Route into EIGRP*

```
Congo(config)# router eigrp DataCenter1
Congo(config-router)# default-information originate route-map default-to-eigrp
```

Now the default route shows up in the neighboring routers, as highlighted in Example 3-27.

Example 3-27 *Verification of the Redistribution of the Default Route into EIGRP in NX-OS*

```
Egypt# show ip route
IP Route Table for VRF "default"
'*' denotes best ucast next-hop
```

```
'**' denotes best mcast next-hop
'[x/y]' denotes [preference/metric]
0.0.0.0/0, ubest/mbest: 1/0
    *via 10.10.10.2, Vlan10, [170/51456], 00:28:57, eigrp-DataCenter1, external
```

On an IOS router, you see the default is learned as well but displayed a bit differently, as shown in Example 3-28.

Example 3-28   *Verification of the Redistribution of the Default Route into EIGRP in IOS*

```
Libya# show ip route
Codes: C - connected, S - static, R - RIP, M - mobile, B - BGP
       D - EIGRP, EX - EIGRP external, O - OSPF, IA - OSPF inter area
       N1 - OSPF NSSA external type 1, N2 - OSPF NSSA external type 2
       E1 - OSPF external type 1, E2 - OSPF external type 2
       i - IS-IS, su - IS-IS summary, L1 - IS-IS level-1, L2 - IS-IS level-2
       ia - IS-IS inter area, * - candidate default, U - per-user static route
       o - ODR, P - periodic downloaded static route
Gateway of last resort is 192.168.1.37 to network 0.0.0.0
     172.26.0.0/16 is variably subnetted, 2 subnets, 2 masks
S       172.26.2.0/23 [1/0] via 172.26.32.33
C       172.26.32.32/27 is directly connected, GigabitEthernet1/48
     10.0.0.0/24 is subnetted, 2 subnets
D       10.10.10.0
            [90/3072] via 192.168.1.41, 01:00:41, TenGigabitEthernet1/49
            [90/3072] via 192.168.1.37, 01:00:41, TenGigabitEthernet1/50
D       10.10.100.0
            [90/3072] via 192.168.1.41, 01:00:41, TenGigabitEthernet1/49
            [90/3072] via 192.168.1.37, 01:00:41, TenGigabitEthernet1/50
     192.168.1.0/24 is variably subnetted, 5 subnets, 2 masks
C       192.168.1.40/30 is directly connected, TenGigabitEthernet1/49
C       192.168.1.36/30 is directly connected, TenGigabitEthernet1/50
D       192.168.1.1/32
            [90/128576] via 192.168.1.37, 01:15:04, TenGigabitEthernet1/50
C       192.168.1.3/32 is directly connected, Loopback0
D       192.168.1.2/32
            [90/128576] via 192.168.1.41, 01:00:41, TenGigabitEthernet1/49
D*EX 0.0.0.0/0 [170/51456] via 192.168.1.37, 00:30:32, TenGigabitEthernet1/50
```

NX-OS also has a feature that enables network administrators to control the number of routes redistributed into EIGRP. You need to consider three options based on the specific requirement of the network:

- **Fixed Limit:** Enables network administrators to specify a number of routes between 1 and 65,535. This can be used as a safety mechanism to prevent a problem or misconfiguration elsewhere in the network where too many routes are flooded, preventing propagation into EIGRP. You can configure a warning threshold to create a syslog message as the number of routes redistributed approaches a percentage of the configured limit. When the maximum limit is reached, EIGRP no longer accepts additional routes.

- **Warning:** Creates a syslog warning when the maximum number of routes is exceeded. However, it is important to note that EIGRP continues to process and accept routes that exceed the maximum limit.

- **Withdraw:** Starts a timer and withdraws all redistributed routes when the maximum limit is exceeded. The number of routes must be brought below the maximum before they are redistributed back into EIGRP.

Example 3-29 specifies the maximum number of prefixes to a fixed limit of 100 routes to be redistributed into EIGRP with a warning message logged when the number of routes exceeds 75 percent.

Example 3-29 *Limiting the Number of Prefixes Redistributed into EIGRP*

```
Congo# config t
Enter configuration commands, one per line. End with CNTL/Z.
Congo(config)# router eigrp DataCenter1
Congo(config-router)# redistribute maximum-prefix 100 75
```

On IOS devices, network administrators are used to using the **show ip protocol** command to review system values for their routing protocols. Similarly in NX-OS, a concise source of information regarding the EIGRP configuration can be found using the syntax shown in Example 3-30.

Example 3-30 *EIGRP Routing Detail*

```
Congo# show ip eigrp DataCenter1 vrf default
IP-EIGRP AS 100 ID 192.168.1.1 VRF default
  Process-tag: DataCenter1
  Status: running
  Authentication mode: md5
  Authentication key-chain: nexus
  Metric weights: K1=1 K2=0 K3=1 K4=0 K5=0
  IP proto: 88 Multicast group: 224.0.0.10
  Int distance: 90 Ext distance: 170
  Max paths: 8
  Number of EIGRP interfaces: 4 (2 loopbacks)
  Number of EIGRP passive interfaces: 1
  Number of EIGRP peers: 2
```

```
    Graceful-Restart: Enabled
    Stub-Routing: Disabled
    NSF converge time limit/expiries: 120/0
    NSF route-hold time limit/expiries: 240/7
    NSF signal time limit/expiries: 20/0
    Redistributed max-prefix: Enabled
    Redistributed max-prefix mode: Not specified
    Redistributed prefix count/max: 1/100
    Redistributed max-prefix warning threshold: 75%
    Redistributed max-prefix retries attempted/allowed: 0/1
    Redistributed max-prefix timer left: 0.000000 (300s total)
```

With the output in Example 3-30, a network administrator can discern multiple key attributes about the configuration such as the number of interfaces configured in the routing protocol, how many interfaces are passive, authentication, and more. This information is extremely valuable when troubleshooting network issues.

With the modular nature of NX-OS, it is now possible to display the relevant EIGRP configuration by using the **show run eigrp** command, as shown in Example 3-31.

Example 3-31   *Reviewing the Entire EIGRP Configuration*

```
Congo# show run eigrp
!Command: show running-config eigrp
!Time: Tue Sep 29 19:06:34 2009
version 4.2(2a)
feature eigrp
router eigrp DataCenter1
  autonomous-system 100
  redistribute maximum-prefix 100 75
  default-information originate route-map default-to-eigrp
  address-family ipv4 unicast
    authentication mode md5
    authentication key-chain nexus
interface Vlan10
  ip router eigrp DataCenter1
interface Vlan100
  ip router eigrp DataCenter1
  ip passive-interface eigrp DataCenter1
interface loopback0
  ip router eigrp DataCenter1
interface loopback2
  ip router eigrp DataCenter1
interface Ethernet1/18
  ip router eigrp DataCenter1
  ip summary-address eigrp DataCenter1 192.168.128.0/20
```

With the output in Example 3-30, a network administrator can quickly review the entire EIGRP configuration and speed resolution of configuration issues. This information is extremely valuable when troubleshooting network issues.

OSPF

OSPF is a dynamic link-state routing protocol based on the Internet Engineering Task Force (IETF) Requests for Comments (RFCs). OSPF uses the concept of areas to provide scalability and administrative control for IP routes. Following are three versions of OSPF:

- OSPFv1, which has been replaced by OSPFv2

- OSPFv2, which routes IPv4

- OSPFv3, which introduces significant changes to OSPFv2 and is designed to route IPv6

OSPF is supported on both the Nexus 7000 and 5500 series switches. The Nexus 5500 series switches must be configured with a Layer 3 daughtercard or module, dependent on the specific platform. The Nexus 5500 series also requires an Enterprise License for full OSPF functionality. (The Base license is limited to 256 OSPF dynamically learned routes.) The examples in this chapter focus on OSPF configuration for the Nexus 7000.

OSPFv2 Configuration

OSPF within NX-OS is compatible with OSPF on IOS and other IETF-compliant devices enabling a smooth integration of Nexus equipment. Configuring OSPF within NX-OS will be similar, yet distinctly different in some aspects to traditional IOS configuration. These differences will be highlighted throughout the section.

Enabling OSPF is a multistep process that is covered in detail. The following is a quick listing of steps to enable a basic configuration of OSPF:

1. Enable OSPF.
2. Configure the OSPF routing process.
3. Assign interfaces to the OSPF instance.
4. Configure passive-interfaces if necessary.
5. Configure network summarization.
6. Configure redistribution of other protocols if necessary.
7. Verify the OSPF operation.

The first step to configure OSPF is to enable it in global configuration mode using the **feature** command, as shown in Example 3-31. With the modular nature of NX-OS, using the **feature** command loads the OSPF modular code into memory for execution. Without the feature enabled, it would not be resident in memory. Figure 3-5 illustrates the topology used in Example 3-32 through 3-41.

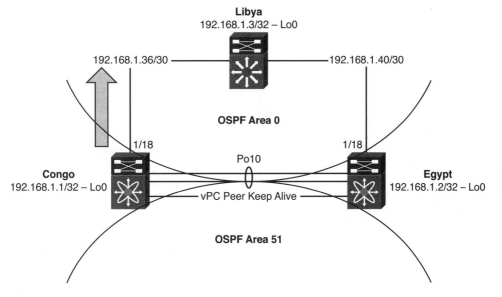

Figure 3-5 *Network Topology for OSPFv2 Configuration*

Example 3-32 *Enabling the OSPF Feature*

```
Congo# config t
Enter configuration commands, one per line. End with CNTL/Z.
Congo(config)# feature ospf
Congo(config)# end
Congo# show run ospf
!Command: show running-config ospf
!Time: Tue Sep 29 19:52:55 2009
version 4.2(2a)
feature ospf
```

As with IOS-based OSPF configuration, the next step is to configure the OSPF routing process, as demonstrated in Example 3-33. NX-OS requires an instance tag configured for the process. Traditionally, in IOS this would be a device-specific instance tag. The instance tag can be a device-specific tag, or the instance tag can be up to 20 case-sensitive, alphanumeric characters. This helps document the network configuration and can simplify device identification.

Example 3-33 *Configuring OSPF with a Numeric Process ID*

```
Congo# config t
Enter configuration commands, one per line. End with CNTL/Z.
Congo(config)# router ospf 100
```

```
Congo(config-router)# end
Congo# show run ospf
!Command: show running-config ospf
!Time: Tue Sep 29 20:04:59 2009
version 4.2(2a)
feature ospf
router ospf 100
```

Example 3-34 demonstrates how to configure an alphanumeric string for the tag.

Example 3-34 *Configuring OSPF with an Alphanumeric Process ID*

```
Congo# config t
Enter configuration commands, one per line. End with CNTL/Z.
Congo(config)# router ospf DataCenter1
Congo(config-router)# end
Congo# show run ospf
!Command: show running-config ospf
!Time: Tue Sep 29 20:05:46 2009
version 4.2(2a)
feature ospf
router ospf DataCenter1
```

Note The *preference* in IOS was to configure a router ID, whereas in NX-OS, it is a *requirement* for OSPF to obtain an IP address to use as a router ID, or a router ID must be configured, as demonstrated in Example 3-35. A router ID is used to uniquely identify an OSPF router on an internetwork and is included in every Hello packet.

Example 3-35 *Configuring an OSPF Router ID*

```
Congo# config t
Enter configuration commands, one per line. End with CNTL/Z.
Congo(config)# router ospf DataCenter1
Congo(config-router)# router-id 192.168.1.1
Congo(config-router)# end
Congo# show run ospf
!Command: show running-config ospf
!Time: Tue Sep 29 20:10:10 2009
version 4.2(2a)
feature ospf
router ospf DataCenter1
  router-id 192.168.1.1
```

With OSPF configured as a feature and assigned a router ID, the next step is to assign interfaces to the instance tag, as demonstrated in Example 3-36. This advertises the IP subnet in OSPF and enables the capability for neighbor adjacencies to be formed.

Note   This is different from traditional IOS configuration in which you configured a **network** and **area** statement under the routing process and then, in turn, any interface on the router that fell within that network range was advertised. The approach taken in NX-OS is much more granular and enables additional levels of control over which networks are advertised.

Example 3-36   *Advertising Networks in OSPF Using a Numeric Process ID*

```
Congo# config t
Enter configuration commands, one per line. End with CNTL/Z.
Congo(config)# int vlan 10
Congo(config-if)# ip router ospf 100 area 0
Congo(config-if)# show ip ospf int vlan 10
 Vlan10 is up, line protocol is up
    IP address 10.10.10.2/24, Process ID 100 VRF default, area 0.0.0.0
    Enabled by interface configuration
    State WAITING, Network type BROADCAST, cost 40
    Index 1, Transmit delay 1 sec, Router Priority 1
    No designated router on this network
    No backup designated router on this network
    0 Neighbors, flooding to 0, adjacent with 0
    Timer intervals: Hello 10, Dead 40, Wait 40, Retransmit 5
      Hello timer due in 00:00:05
      Wait timer due in 00:00:35
    No authentication
    Number of opaque link LSAs: 0, checksum sum 0
```

Example 3-37 demonstrates how to configure an alphanumeric process ID.

Example 3-37   *Advertising Networks in OSPF Using an Alphanumeric Process ID*

```
Congo# config t
Enter configuration commands, one per line. End with CNTL/Z.
Congo(config)# int vlan 10
Congo(config-if)# ip router ospf DataCenter1 area 0
Congo(config-if)# show ip ospf int vlan 10
 Vlan10 is up, line protocol is up
    IP address 10.10.10.2/24, Process ID DataCenter1 VRF default, area 0.0.0.0
    Enabled by interface configuration
```

```
State BDR, Network type BROADCAST, cost 40
Index 1, Transmit delay 1 sec, Router Priority 1
Designated Router ID: 192.168.1.2, address: 10.10.10.3
Backup Designated Router ID: 192.168.1.1, address: 10.10.10.2
1 Neighbors, flooding to 1, adjacent with 1
Timer intervals: Hello 10, Dead 40, Wait 40, Retransmit 5
  Hello timer due in 00:00:03
No authentication
Number of opaque link LSAs: 0, checksum sum 0
```

Another difference between IOS and NX-OS behavior can be seen in the way OSPF shows the area number. In the preceding examples, the area designator is entered as **area 0**; however, this shows up as area 0.0.0.0 in the output. As demonstrated in Example 3-38, this behavior does not impact the actual functionality of OSPF as shown between an OSPF router running IOS and a router running NX-OS.

Example 3-38   *OSPF Areas in IOS Compared to NX-OS*

```
Libya# show ip ospf neighbor detail
 Neighbor 192.168.1.2, interface address 192.168.1.41
    In the area 0 via interface TenGigabitEthernet1/49
    Neighbor priority is 1, State is FULL, 6 state changes
    DR is 192.168.1.42 BDR is 192.168.1.41
    Options is 0x42
    Dead timer due in 00:00:37
    Neighbor is up for 00:00:38
    Index 1/1, retransmission queue length 0, number of retransmission 1
    First 0x0(0)/0x0(0) Next 0x0(0)/0x0(0)
    Last retransmission scan length is 1, maximum is 1
    Last retransmission scan time is 0 msec, maximum is 0 msec
! The output from NX-OS shows that the area is area 0.0.0.0
Egypt# show ip ospf ne detail
 Neighbor 192.168.1.3, interface address 192.168.1.42
    Process ID DataCenter1 VRF default, in area 0.0.0.0 via interface Ethernet1/18
    State is FULL, 5 state changes, last change 00:05:49
    Neighbor priority is 1
    DR is 192.168.1.42 BDR is 192.168.1.41
    Hello options 0x12, dbd options 0x52
    Last non-hello packet received 00:01:46
      Dead timer due in 00:00:33
```

In a data center's distribution or aggregation layer, it is common to have multiple VLAN interfaces that, in turn, need to be advertised to the network at large. By default, when OSPF is enabled on the VLAN interface, it sends and receives hellos. If a neighbor is detected, OSPF attempts to form an adjacency. Although this default behavior is wanted, there might be designs where forming multiple OSPF adjacencies between the same pair of switches is not wanted because of the potential impact of network convergence time and unnecessary duplicate next hops. In configurations such as this, you can use the **passive-interface** command, as demonstrated in Example 3-39. A passive interface accomplishes the requirement of advertising the subnet via OSPF but also instructs the OSPF process to not listen to hellos on the interfaces configured to be passive.

Example 3-39   *OSPF Passive Interface with a Numeric Process ID*

```
Congo# config t
Congo(config)# int vlan100
Congo(config-if)# ip ospf passive-interface ospf 100
Congo(config-if)# end
```

Example 3-40 demonstrates how to configure an OSPF passive interface with an alphanumeric process ID.

Example 3-40   *OSPF Passive Interface with an Alphanumeric Process ID*

```
Congo# config t
Enter configuration commands, one per line. End with CNTL/Z.
Congo(config)# int vlan 100
Congo(config-if)# ip ospf passive-interface
Congo(config-if)# show ip ospf int vlan 100
 Vlan100 is up, line protocol is up
    IP address 10.10.100.2/24, Process ID DataCenter1 VRF default, area 0.0.0.51
    Enabled by interface configuration
    State DR, Network type BROADCAST, cost 40
    Index 2, Passive interface
Congo(config-if)# show run int vlan 100
!Command: show running-config interface Vlan100
!Time: Tue Sep 29 23:35:42 2009
version 4.2(2a)
interface Vlan100
  no shutdown
  description Server Subnet1
  ip address 10.10.100.2/24
  ip ospf passive-interface
  ip router ospf DataCenter1 area 0.0.0.51
```

NX-OS version 5.2(1) brings support for default passive interfaces, as outlined in Example 3-41. This sets all interfaces to passive by default, and enables you to manually configure a specific interface to listen to hellos and form neighbor adjacencies. This is accomplished via the **no ip ospf passive-interface** command under the interface subconfiguration.

Example 3-41   *OSPF Default Passive Interface Configuration*

```
Congo# config t
Enter configuration commands, one per line.  End with CNTL/Z.
Congo(config)# router ospf DataCenter1
Congo(config-router)# passive-interface default
Congo(config-router)#
Congo(config-router)# int vlan 10
Congo(config-if)# no ip ospf passive-interface
Congo(config-if)#
```

OSPF Summarization

The capability of OSPF to summarize routes is restricted to area boundary routers (ABRs) or autonomous system boundary routers (ASBRs). When a network is summarized, a single entry with a shorter prefix (commonly called a *supernet*) is created and added to the routing table as a representation of the longer prefix subnets. In Example 3-39, a summary for 192.168.128.0 /20 is created and advertised out interface e1/18 for the network topology illustrated in Figure 3-6.

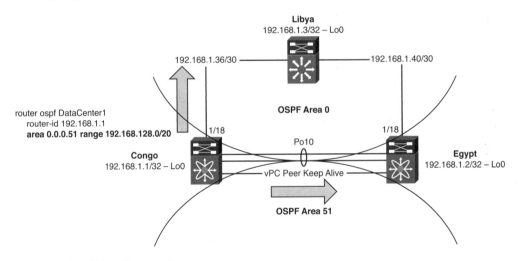

Figure 3-6   *OSPF Summarization*

Note   With this summary, the following networks are represented: 192.168.128.0/24 through 192.168.143.0/24.

Example 3-42 demonstrates how to configure OSPF summarization with a numeric process ID.

Example 3-42   *OSPF Summarization with a Numeric Process ID*

```
Congo(config)# router ospf 100
Congo(config-router)# area 52 range 192.168.128.0/20
Congo(config-router)# end
```

Example 3-43 demonstrates how to configure OSPF summarization with an alphanumeric process ID.

Example 3-43   *OSPF Summarization with an Alphanumeric Process ID*

```
config t
Congo(config)# router ospf DataCenter1
Congo(config-router)# area 52 range 192.168.128.0/20
Congo(config-router)# end
```

You can see the resulting summary address in the routing table on Congo, as highlighted in Example 3-44.

Example 3-44   *Verification of the OSPF Summary Address in NX-OS*

```
Congo# show ip route
IP Route Table for VRF "default"
'*' denotes best ucast next-hop
'**' denotes best mcast next-hop
'[x/y]' denotes [preference/metric]
0.0.0.0/0, ubest/mbest: 1/0
    *via 192.168.1.38, Eth1/18, [1/0], 00:20:40, static
10.10.10.0/24, ubest/mbest: 1/0, attached
    *via 10.10.10.2, Vlan10, [0/0], 01:02:21, direct
10.10.10.1/32, ubest/mbest: 1/0
    *via 10.10.10.1, Vlan10, [0/0], 01:02:21, hsrp
10.10.10.2/32, ubest/mbest: 1/0, attached
    *via 10.10.10.2, Vlan10, [0/0], 01:02:21, local
10.10.100.0/24, ubest/mbest: 1/0, attached
    *via 10.10.100.2, Vlan100, [0/0], 01:02:21, direct
10.10.100.1/32, ubest/mbest: 1/0
    *via 10.10.100.1, Vlan100, [0/0], 01:02:21, hsrp
10.10.100.2/32, ubest/mbest: 1/0, attached
    *via 10.10.100.2, Vlan100, [0/0], 01:02:21, local
192.168.1.1/32, ubest/mbest: 2/0, attached
    *via 192.168.1.1, Lo0, [0/0], 01:02:21, local
    *via 192.168.1.1, Lo0, [0/0], 01:02:21, direct
192.168.1.2/32, ubest/mbest: 1/0
    *via 192.168.1.38, Eth1/18, [110/6], 00:12:39, ospf-DataCenter1, intra
```

```
192.168.1.3/32, ubest/mbest: 1/0
    *via 192.168.1.38, Eth1/18, [110/5], 00:12:00, ospf-DataCenter1, intra
192.168.1.32/30, ubest/mbest: 1/0, attached
    *via 192.168.1.33, Vlan5, [0/0], 01:02:21, direct
192.168.1.33/32, ubest/mbest: 1/0, attached
    *via 192.168.1.33, Vlan5, [0/0], 01:02:21, local
192.168.1.36/30, ubest/mbest: 1/0, attached
    *via 192.168.1.37, Eth1/18, [0/0], 00:20:40, direct
192.168.1.37/32, ubest/mbest: 1/0, attached
    *via 192.168.1.37, Eth1/18, [0/0], 00:20:40, local
192.168.1.40/30, ubest/mbest: 1/0
    *via 192.168.1.38, Eth1/18, [110/5], 00:18:56, ospf-DataCenter1, intra
192.168.128.0/20, ubest/mbest: 1/0
    *via Null0, [220/1], 00:03:46, ospf-DataCenter1, discard
192.168.128.1/32, ubest/mbest: 2/0, attached
*via 192.168.128.1, Lo2, [0/0], 01:02:21, local
    *via 192.168.128.1, Lo2, [0/0], 01:02:21, direct
```

As Example 3-45 demonstrates, you also see that the summary address is propagated
to an IOS-speaking OSPF neighbor, Libya, and that it is summarizing the /32 route for
Loopback2 as expected.

Example 3-45   *Verification of the OSPF Summary Address in IOS*

```
Libya# show ip route
Codes: C - connected, S - static, R - RIP, M - mobile, B - BGP
       D - EIGRP, EX - EIGRP external, O - OSPF, IA - OSPF inter area
       N1 - OSPF NSSA external type 1, N2 - OSPF NSSA external type 2
       E1 - OSPF external type 1, E2 - OSPF external type 2
       i - IS-IS, su - IS-IS summary, L1 - IS-IS level-1, L2 - IS-IS level-2
       ia - IS-IS inter area, * - candidate default, U - per-user static route
       o - ODR, P - periodic downloaded static route
Gateway of last resort is not set
     172.26.0.0/16 is variably subnetted, 2 subnets, 2 masks
S       172.26.2.0/23 [1/0] via 172.26.32.33
C       172.26.32.32/27 is directly connected, GigabitEthernet1/48
     10.0.0.0/24 is subnetted, 2 subnets
O       10.10.10.0 [110/41] via 192.168.1.41, 00:07:23, TenGigabitEthernet1/49
                   [110/41] via 192.168.1.37, 00:07:23, TenGigabitEthernet1/50
O IA    10.10.100.0
```

```
                [110/41] via 192.168.1.41, 00:07:23, TenGigabitEthernet1/49
                [110/41] via 192.168.1.37, 00:07:23, TenGigabitEthernet1/50
       192.168.1.0/24 is variably subnetted, 5 subnets, 2 masks
C        192.168.1.40/30 is directly connected, TenGigabitEthernet1/49
C        192.168.1.36/30 is directly connected, TenGigabitEthernet1/50
O        192.168.1.1/32
                [110/2] via 192.168.1.37, 00:07:23, TenGigabitEthernet1/50
C        192.168.1.3/32 is directly connected, Loopback0
O        192.168.1.2/32
                [110/2] via 192.168.1.41, 00:07:23, TenGigabitEthernet1/49
O IA 192.168.128.0/20
                [110/2] via 192.168.1.37, 00:04:56, TenGigabitEthernet1/50
```

OSPF Stub Routing

One of OSPF's scalability features is stub routing. When OSPF stub routing is enabled, the ABR no longer floods Type 5 LSAs into the area, minimizing the routing table and SPF churn. Following are two forms of stub routing:

- **Not-so-stubby routing:** Permits external routes

- **Totally stub by routing:** Does not enable external routes

Stub routing enables intra-area routes to be learned and flooded throughout the area and all external routes. A not-so-stubby area (NSSA) behaves in much the same way as a stub area with the exception that you can configure the NSSA to allow redistribution of external routes as Type 7 LSAs. Although not commonly deployed in the data center, there are use cases for the OSPF stub. A common model for environments is where end-host systems such as servers or mainframes can route via multiple interfaces via OSPF benefit from stub routing to minimize the amount of routing table state maintained. Another example that could leverage the OSPF stub would be when a merger or acquisition is made and complex routing can be simplified with the OSPF stub.

Stub routing is configured under the main routing process, as demonstrated in Example 3-46 for the network topology illustrated in Figure 3-7.

Example 3-46 *OSPF Stub Routing Using a Numeric Process ID*

```
Congo# config t
Enter configuration commands, one per line. End with CNTL/Z.
Congo(config)# router ospf 100
Congo(config-router)# area 51 stub
```

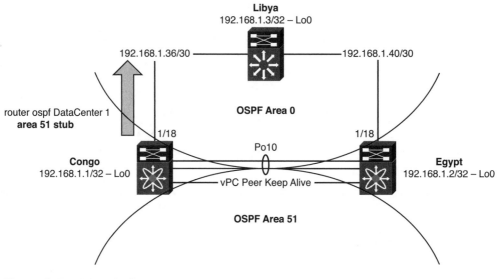

Figure 3-7 *OSPF Stub*

Example 3-47 demonstrates configuring OSPF stub routing using an alphanumeric tag.

Example 3-47 *OSPF Stub Routing Using an Alphanumeric Process ID*

```
Congo# config t
Enter configuration commands, one per line. End with CNTL/Z.
Congo(config)# router ospf DataCenter1
Congo(config-router)# area 51 stub
```

You can identify the stub status of a neighbor from the **show ip ospf detail** command output, as demonstrated in Example 3-48.

Example 3-48 *Verification of OSPF Stub Neighbor*

```
Congo# show ip ospf
 Routing Process DataCenter1 with ID 192.168.1.1 VRF default
 Stateful High Availability enabled
 Graceful-restart is configured
   Grace period: 60 state: Inactive
   Last graceful restart exit status: None
 Supports only single TOS(TOS0) routes
 Supports opaque LSA
 This router is an area border
 Administrative distance 110
 Reference Bandwidth is 40000 Mbps
 Initial SPF schedule delay 200.000 msecs,
   minimum inter SPF delay of 1000.000 msecs,
```

```
    maximum inter SPF delay of 5000.000 msecs
 Initial LSA generation delay 0.000 msecs,
    minimum inter LSA delay of 5000.000 msecs,
    maximum inter LSA delay of 5000.000 msecs
 Minimum LSA arrival 1000.000 msec
 Maximum paths to destination 8
Number of external LSAs 0, checksum sum 0
 Number of opaque AS LSAs 0, checksum sum 0
 Number of areas is 2, 1 normal, 1 stub, 0 nssa
 Number of active areas is 2, 1 normal, 1 stub, 0 nssa
    Area BACKBONE(0.0.0.0)
         Area has existed for 00:03:13
         Interfaces in this area: 2 Active interfaces: 2
         Passive interfaces: 0  Loopback interfaces: 0
         No authentication available
         SPF calculation has run 5 times
          Last SPF ran for 0.000502s
    Area ranges are
         Number of LSAs: 6, checksum sum 0x33cd3
    Area (0.0.0.51) (Inactive)
         Area has existed for 00:03:13
         Interfaces in this area: 1 Active interfaces: 1
         Passive interfaces: 1  Loopback interfaces: 0
         This area is a STUB area
         Generates stub default route with cost 1
         No authentication available
         SPF calculation has run 5 times
          Last SPF ran for 0.000076s
         Area ranges are
           192.168.128.0/20 Passive (Num nets: 0) Advertise
         Number of LSAs: 7, checksum sum 0x446f2
```

Example 3-49 demonstrates the syntax for configuring a totally stubby area.

Example 3-49   *Configuration of a Totally Stub by Area Using a Numeric Process ID*

```
Congo# config t
Enter configuration commands, one per line. End with CNTL/Z.
Congo(config)# router ospf 100
Congo(config-router)# area 51 stub no-summary
```

Example 3-50 demonstrates configuring a totally stubby area using an alphanumeric tag for the routing process ID.

Example 3-50   *Configuration of a Totally Stub Area Using an Alphanumeric Process ID*

```
Congo# config t
Enter configuration commands, one per line. End with CNTL/Z.
Congo(config)# router ospf DataCenter1
Congo(config-router)# area 51 stub no-summary
```

You can identify the stub status of a neighbor from the **show ip ospf detail** command output, as demonstrated in Example 3-51. You can notice an additional line that indicates **Summarization is disabled** to reflect the totally stub by area status.

Example 3-51   *Verification of Totally Stub by Status on a Neighbor*

```
Congo(config-router)# show ip ospf
 Routing Process DataCenter1 with ID 192.168.1.1 VRF default
 Stateful High Availability enabled
 Graceful-restart is configured
   Grace period: 60 state: Inactive
   Last graceful restart exit status: None
 Supports only single TOS(TOS0) routes
 Supports opaque LSA
 This router is an area border
 Administrative distance 110
 Reference Bandwidth is 40000 Mbps
 Initial SPF schedule delay 200.000 msecs,
   minimum inter SPF delay of 1000.000 msecs,
   maximum inter SPF delay of 5000.000 msecs
 Initial LSA generation delay 0.000 msecs,
   minimum inter LSA delay of 5000.000 msecs,
   maximum inter LSA delay of 5000.000 msecs
 Minimum LSA arrival 1000.000 msec
Maximum paths to destination 8
Number of external LSAs 0, checksum sum 0
 Number of opaque AS LSAs 0, checksum sum 0
 Number of areas is 2, 1 normal, 1 stub, 0 nssa
 Number of active areas is 2, 1 normal, 1 stub, 0 nssa
   Area BACKBONE(0.0.0.0)
        Area has existed for 00:15:47
        Interfaces in this area: 2 Active interfaces: 2
```

```
        Passive interfaces: 0  Loopback interfaces: 0
        No authentication available
        SPF calculation has run 7 times
         Last SPF ran for 0.000484s
        Area ranges are
        Number of LSAs: 6, checksum sum 0x33ad4
   Area (0.0.0.51) (Inactive)
        Area has existed for 00:15:47
        Interfaces in this area: 1 Active interfaces: 1
        Passive interfaces: 1  Loopback interfaces: 0
        This area is a STUB area
        Generates stub default route with cost 1
        Summarization is disabled
        No authentication available
        SPF calculation has run 7 times
         Last SPF ran for 0.000074s
        Area ranges are
           192.168.128.0/20 Passive (Num nets: 0) Advertise
        Number of LSAs: 2, checksum sum 0x17359
```

Securing OSPF

You can secure OSPF routing updates by using authentication between OSPF neighbors. OSPF authentication is enabled either at the routing process level or per-interface, allowing for flexible deployment options.

Note   Interface-level authentication overrides the process-level configuration.

Configuring OSPF authentication is a multistep process. You must first define a keychain that contains attributes such as the password to be used to authenticate the connection and the lifetime of the key chain for both sending and receiving, as demonstrated in Example 3-52, for the network topology illustrated in Figure 3-8.

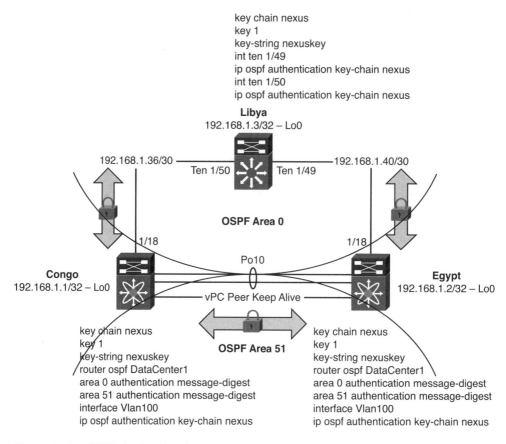

```
key chain nexus
key 1
key-string nexuskey
int ten 1/49
ip ospf authentication key-chain nexus
int ten 1/50
ip ospf authentication key-chain nexus
```

Libya
192.168.1.3/32 – Lo0

192.168.1.36/30 ——————— ——————— 192.168.1.40/30

Ten 1/50   Ten 1/49

OSPF Area 0

1/18   1/18

Po10

Congo   **Egypt**
192.168.1.1/32 – Lo0   vPC Peer Keep Alive   192.168.1.2/32 – Lo0

```
key chain nexus
key 1
key-string nexuskey
router ospf DataCenter1
area 0 authentication message-digest
area 51 authentication message-digest
interface Vlan100
ip ospf authentication key-chain nexus
```

OSPF Area 51

```
key chain nexus
key 1
key-string nexuskey
router ospf DataCenter1
area 0 authentication message-digest
area 51 authentication message-digest
interface Vlan100
ip ospf authentication key-chain nexus
```

Figure 3-8   *OSPF Authentication*

Example 3-52   *Configuring a Keychain*

```
Congo(config)# key chain nexus
Congo(config-keychain)# key 1
Congo(config-keychain-key)# key-string nexus
```

Now that a key exists, the next step is to configure the routing protocol, OSPF in this case, to enable authentication and configure the interface to use the key chain. This step is completed under the OSPF routing process configuration. It is necessary to specify an encryption mechanism, MD5, and configure the key chain to use it, as demonstrated in Example 3-53.

Example 3-53   *Configuring OSPF MD5 Authentication*

```
Congo# config t
Enter configuration commands, one per line. End with CNTL/Z.
Congo(config)# router ospf DataCenter1
```

```
Congo(config-router)# area 0 authentication message-digest
Congo(config-router)# int vlan 10
Congo(config-if)# ip ospf authentication key-chain nexus
```

The values specified under the address-family configuration are for all OSPF neighbors in the area configured for authentication, as demonstrated in Example 3-54. These values can be overridden by interface-specific configuration that can be helpful when multiple keys are used on different devices in the internetwork.

Example 3-54 *Configuration of OSPF Authentication on an SVI*

```
Congo#config t
Congo(config)# router ospf DataCenter1
Congo(config-router)# area 0 authentication message-digest
Congo(config-if)# int vlan 10
Congo(config-if)# ip ospf authentication-key 7 newkey
```

Example 3-55 demonstrates how to verify authentication configuration.

Example 3-55 *Verification of OSPF Authentication*

```
Congo# show ip ospf int vlan 10
 Vlan10 is up, line protocol is up
    IP address 10.10.10.2/24, Process ID DataCenter1 VRF default, area 0.0.0.0
    Enabled by interface configuration
    State BDR, Network type BROADCAST, cost 40
    Index 1, Transmit delay 1 sec, Router Priority 1
    Designated Router ID: 192.168.1.2, address: 10.10.10.3
    Backup Designated Router ID: 192.168.1.1, address: 10.10.10.2
    1 Neighbors, flooding to 1, adjacent with 1
    Timer intervals: Hello 10, Dead 40, Wait 40, Retransmit 5
      Hello timer due in 00:00:01
    Message-digest authentication, using keychain nexus (ready)
    Number of opaque link LSAs: 0, checksum sum 0
```

OSPF Redistribution

It is a common requirement to redistribute routes learned from other routing protocols or for directly connected interfaces into OSPF. With the exception of the default route, this is accomplished in a similar manner to traditional IOS redistribution with a few minor differences that are highlighted in the sample configurations.

Starting with the default route, the methodology to redistribute it into the routing table is similar to IOS in that the **default-information originate** command is used.

The process begins by defining a prefix list, as demonstrated in Example 3-56, which is then used by a route map referenced by the **default-information originate** command. Figure 3-9 illustrates the topology used for Examples 3-54 through 3-66.

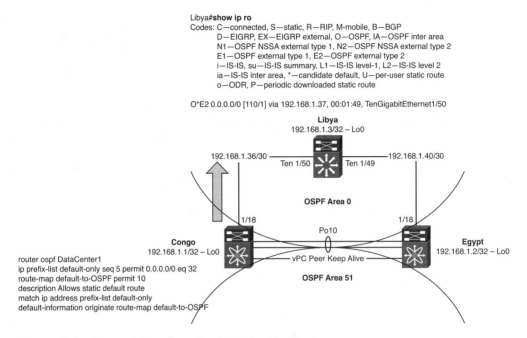

Figure 3-9   *Network Topology for OSPF Redistribution*

Example 3-56   *Defining a Prefix List for the Default Route*

```
Congo# config t
Enter configuration commands, one per line. End with CNTL/Z.
Congo(config)# ip prefix-list default-only seq 5 permit 0.0.0.0/0 eq 32
Congo(config)#
```

Next, you define a route map, called **default-to-ospf**, which uses the prefix list named **default-only**, to bring in only the 0/0 route, as demonstrated in Example 3-57.

Example 3-57   *Defining a Route Map for the Default Route*

```
Congo(config)# route-map default-to-OSPF permit 10
Congo(config-route-map)# description Allows static default route
Congo(config-route-map)# match ip address prefix-list default-only
```

Finally, configure OSPF to use the route map default-**to-ospf** as part of the **default-information originate** command, as demonstrated in Example 3-58.

Example 3-58 *Configuring OSPF to Redistribute the Default Route*

```
Congo(config)# router ospf DataCenter1
Congo(config-router)# default-information originate route-map default-to-OSPF
```

Now the default route shows up in the neighboring routers, as highlighted in
Example 3-59. In NX-OS, you see the 0/0 route as an OSPF route and know that
it is external because of the type-2 designation.

Example 3-59 *Verification of the Default Route in OSPF in NX-OS*

```
Egypt# show ip route
IP Route Table for VRF "default"
'*' denotes best ucast next-hop
 '**' denotes best mcast next-hop
'[x/y]' denotes [preference/metric]
0.0.0.0/0, ubest/mbest: 1/0
    *via 192.168.1.42, Eth1/18, [110/1], 00:00:19, ospf-DataCenter1, type-2
```

On an IOS router, you see the default is learned as well but displayed a bit differently. The
route is learned as an External Type 2 route, as demonstrated in Example 3-60.

Example 3-60 *Verification of the Default Route in OSPF in IOS*

```
Libya# show ip route
Codes: C - connected, S - static, R - RIP, M - mobile, B - BGP
       D - EIGRP, EX - EIGRP external, O - OSPF, IA - OSPF inter area
       N1 - OSPF NSSA external type 1, N2 - OSPF NSSA external type 2
       E1 - OSPF external type 1, E2 - OSPF external type 2
       i - IS-IS, su - IS-IS summary, L1 - IS-IS level-1, L2 - IS-IS level-2
       ia - IS-IS inter area, * - candidate default, U - per-user static route
       o - ODR, P - periodic downloaded static route
Gateway of last resort is 192.168.1.37 to network 0.0.0.0
     172.26.0.0/16 is variably subnetted, 2 subnets, 2 masks
S       172.26.2.0/23 [1/0] via 172.26.32.33
C       172.26.32.32/27 is directly connected, GigabitEthernet1/48
     10.0.0.0/24 is subnetted, 2 subnets
O       10.10.10.0 [110/41] via 192.168.1.41, 00:01:49, TenGigabitEthernet1/49
                   [110/41] via 192.168.1.37, 00:01:49, TenGigabitEthernet1/50
O IA    10.10.100.0
            [110/41] via 192.168.1.41, 00:01:49, TenGigabitEthernet1/49
            [110/41] via 192.168.1.37, 00:01:49, TenGigabitEthernet1/50
     192.168.1.0/24 is variably subnetted, 4 subnets, 2 masks
C       192.168.1.40/30 is directly connected, TenGigabitEthernet1/49
C       192.168.1.36/30 is directly connected, TenGigabitEthernet1/50
```

```
C       192.168.1.3/32 is directly connected, Loopback0
O       192.168.1.2/32
            [110/2] via 192.168.1.41, 00:01:49, TenGigabitEthernet1/49
O*E2 0.0.0.0/0 [110/1] via 192.168.1.37, 00:01:49, TenGigabitEthernet1/50
```

Redistribution of routes other than the default follows a similar sequence of steps in that you create a prefix list, use it in a route map, and then enable the redistribution.

NX-OS does not require a default metric to be specified on the **redistribution** command or under the routing protocol configuration as it sets the default metric to 0. This can be changed by using the **default-metric** command that applies a metric to any redistributed routes where a metric is not applied on the **redistribution** command as demonstrated here:

```
router ospf DataCenter1
    default-metric 100
```

The process begins by defining a prefix list, as demonstrated in Example 3-61, which is then used by a route map referenced by the **default-information originate** command.

Example 3-61   *Defining a Prefix List for Redistribution*

```
Egypt# config t
Enter configuration commands, one per line. End with CNTL/Z.
Egypt(config)# ip prefix-list connected-interfaces seq 15 permit 10.100.0.0/16 ge
17
Egypt(config)#
```

Next, define a route map, called **connected-to-OSPF**, which uses the prefix list named **connected-interfaces**, to bring in only the 10.100.0.0/16 or longer routes, as demonstrated in Example 3-62.

Example 3-62   *Defining a Route Map for Redistribution*

```
Egypt(config)# route-map connected-to-OSPF permit 10
Egypt(config-route-map)# description allows local interfaces
Egypt(config-route-map)# match ip address prefix-list connected-interfaces
```

Finally, configure OSPF to use the route map **connected-to-OSPF** as part of the **redistribute direct** command, as demonstrated in Example 3-63.

Example 3-63   *Configuring Redistribution into OSPF*

```
Egypt(config)# router ospf DataCenter1
Egypt(config-router)# redistribute direct route-map connected-to-OSPF
```

Now the new routes show up in the neighboring routers, as highlighted in Example 3-64. In NX-OS, you see the 10.100.0.0/16 routes as OSPF routes and know that they are external because of the type-2 designation.

Example 3-64   *Verification of the Redistributed Routes in NX-OS*

```
Congo# show ip route ospf
IP Route Table for VRF "default"
'*' denotes best ucast next-hop
'**' denotes best mcast next-hop
'[x/y]' denotes [preference/metric]
10.100.100.0/24, ubest/mbest: 1/0
    *via 192.168.1.38, Eth1/18, [110/20], 00:26:53, ospf-DataCenter1, type-2
10.100.200.0/24, ubest/mbest: 1/0
    *via 192.168.1.38, Eth1/18, [110/20], 00:26:53, ospf-DataCenter1, type-2
10.100.201.0/24, ubest/mbest: 1/0
    *via 192.168.1.38, Eth1/18, [110/20], 00:26:53, ospf-DataCenter1, type-2
10.100.202.0/24, ubest/mbest: 1/0
    *via 192.168.1.38, Eth1/18, [110/20], 00:26:53, ospf-DataCenter1, type-2
192.168.1.2/32, ubest/mbest: 1/0
    *via 192.168.1.38, Eth1/18, [110/6], 00:26:53, ospf-DataCenter1, intra
192.168.1.3/32, ubest/mbest: 1/0
    *via 192.168.1.38, Eth1/18, [110/5], 15:24:13, ospf-DataCenter1, intra
192.168.1.40/30, ubest/mbest: 1/0
    *via 192.168.1.38, Eth1/18, [110/5], 00:27:01, ospf-DataCenter1, intra
```

On an IOS router, you see the 10.100.0.0/16 routes are learned as well but displayed a bit differently. The routes are learned as an External Type 2 route, as demonstrated in Example 3-65.

Example 3-65   *Verification of the Redistributed Routes in IOS*

```
Libya# show ip route
Codes: C - connected, S - static, R - RIP, M - mobile, B - BGP
       D - EIGRP, EX - EIGRP external, O - OSPF, IA - OSPF inter area
       N1 - OSPF NSSA external type 1, N2 - OSPF NSSA external type 2
       E1 - OSPF external type 1, E2 - OSPF external type 2
       i - IS-IS, su - IS-IS summary, L1 - IS-IS level-1, L2 - IS-IS level-2
       ia - IS-IS inter area, * - candidate default, U - per-user static route
       o - ODR, P - periodic downloaded static route
Gateway of last resort is 192.168.1.37 to network 0.0.0.0
     172.26.0.0/16 is variably subnetted, 2 subnets, 2 masks
S       172.26.2.0/23 [1/0] via 172.26.32.33
C       172.26.32.32/27 is directly connected, GigabitEthernet1/48
     10.0.0.0/24 is subnetted, 6 subnets
```

```
O E2    10.100.100.0
            [110/20] via 192.168.1.41, 00:16:20, TenGigabitEthernet1/49
O           10.10.10.0 [110/41] via 192.168.1.41, 00:16:20, TenGigabitEthernet1/49
                        [110/41] via 192.168.1.37, 00:16:20, TenGigabitEthernet1/50
O IA    10.10.100.0
            [110/41] via 192.168.1.41, 00:16:20, TenGigabitEthernet1/49
            [110/41] via 192.168.1.37, 00:16:20, TenGigabitEthernet1/50
O E2    10.100.202.0
            [110/20] via 192.168.1.41, 00:16:20, TenGigabitEthernet1/49
O E2    10.100.200.0
            [110/20] via 192.168.1.41, 00:16:20, TenGigabitEthernet1/49
O E2    10.100.201.0
            [110/20] via 192.168.1.41, 00:16:20, TenGigabitEthernet1/49
        192.168.1.0/24 is variably subnetted, 5 subnets, 2 masks
C       192.168.1.40/30 is directly connected, TenGigabitEthernet1/49
O IA    192.168.1.32/30
            [110/41] via 192.168.1.41, 00:16:20, TenGigabitEthernet1/49
            [110/41] via 192.168.1.37, 00:16:20, TenGigabitEthernet1/50
C       192.168.1.36/30 is directly connected, TenGigabitEthernet1/50
C       192.168.1.3/32 is directly connected, Loopback0
O       192.168.1.2/32
            [110/2] via 192.168.1.41, 00:16:20, TenGigabitEthernet1/49
O*E2 0.0.0.0/0 [110/1] via 192.168.1.37, 00:16:20, TenGigabitEthernet1/50
```

NX-OS also has a feature that enables network administrators to control the number of routes redistributed into OSPF. Following are three options to consider based on the specific requirement of the network:

- **Fixed limit:** Enables network administrators to specify a number of routes between 1 and 65,535. This can be used as a safety mechanism to prevent a problem or misconfiguration elsewhere in the network where too many routes are flooded and prevent propagation into OSPF. A warning threshold can be configured to create a syslog message as the number of routes redistributed approaches a percentage of the configured limit. When the maximum limit is reached, OSPF no longer accepts additional routes.

- **Warning:** Creates a syslog warning when the maximum number of routes is exceeded. However, OSPF continues to process and accept routes that exceed the maximum limit.

- **Withdraw:** Starts a timer and withdraws all redistributed routes when the maximum limit is exceeded. The number of routes must be brought below the maximum before they are redistributed back into OSPF.

In Example 3-66, a fixed limit of 100 routes is specified to be redistributed into OSPF with a warning message logged when the number of routes exceeds 75 percent.

Example 3-66 *Limiting the Number of Redistributed Routes in OSPF*

```
Congo# config t
Enter configuration commands, one per line. End with CNTL/Z.
Congo(config)# router ospf DataCenter1
Congo(config-router)# redistribute maximum-prefix 100 75
```

On IOS devices, network administrators are accustomed to using the **show ip protocol** command to review system values for their routing protocols. Similarly in NX-OS, a concise source of information for the OSPF configuration can be found, as demonstrated in Example 3-67. This information is extremely valuable when troubleshooting network issues.

Example 3-67 *Reviewing Detailed OSPF Information*

```
Congo# show ip ospf
 Routing Process DataCenter1 with ID 192.168.1.1 VRF default
 Stateful High Availability enabled
 Graceful-restart is configured
   Grace period: 60 state: Inactive
   Last graceful restart exit status: None
 Supports only single TOS(TOS0) routes
 Supports opaque LSA
 This router is an area border and autonomous system boundary.
 Administrative distance 110
 Reference Bandwidth is 40000 Mbps
 Initial SPF schedule delay 200.000 msecs,
   minimum inter SPF delay of 1000.000 msecs,
   maximum inter SPF delay of 5000.000 msecs
Initial LSA generation delay 0.000 msecs,
   minimum inter LSA delay of 5000.000 msecs,
   maximum inter LSA delay of 5000.000 msecs
 Minimum LSA arrival 1000.000 msec
 Maximum paths to destination 8
 Number of external LSAs 1, checksum sum 0xd193
Number of opaque AS LSAs 0, checksum sum 0
 Number of areas is 2, 1 normal, 1 stub, 0 nssa
Number of active areas is 2, 1 normal, 1 stub, 0 nssa
   Area BACKBONE(0.0.0.0)
        Area has existed for 00:49:34
        Interfaces in this area: 2 Active interfaces: 2
        Passive interfaces: 0  Loopback interfaces: 0
        Message-digest authentication
        SPF calculation has run 15 times
         Last SPF ran for 0.000501s
```

```
        Area ranges are
        Number of LSAs: 6, checksum sum 0x31cde
  Area (0.0.0.51) (Inactive)
        Area has existed for 00:49:34
        Interfaces in this area: 1 Active interfaces: 1
        Passive interfaces: 1  Loopback interfaces: 0
        This area is a STUB area
        Generates stub default route with cost 1
        Summarization is disabled
        No authentication available
        SPF calculation has run 15 times
         Last SPF ran for 0.000074s
        Area ranges are
          192.168.128.0/20 Passive (Num nets: 0) Advertise
        Number of LSAs: 2, checksum sum 0x16f5b
```

With the modular nature of NX-OS, you can now display the relevant OSPF configuration by using the **show run ospf** command, as demonstrated in Example 3-68.

Example 3-68 *Viewing the OSPF-Only Configuration*

```
Congo# show run ospf
!Command: show running-config ospf
!Time: Wed Sep 30 01:25:45 2009
version 4.2(2a)
feature ospf
router ospf DataCenter1
  router-id 192.168.1.1
  area 0.0.0.51 stub no-summary
  default-information originate route-map default-to-OSPF
  area 0.0.0.51 range 192.168.128.0/20
  redistribute maximum-prefix 100 75
  area 0.0.0.0 authentication message-digest
  default-metric 100
interface Vlan10
  ip ospf authentication key-chain nexus
  ip router ospf DataCenter1 area 0.0.0.0
interface Vlan100
  ip ospf passive-interface
  ip router ospf DataCenter1 area 0.0.0.51
interface loopback0
  ip router ospf DataCenter area 0.0.0.0
interface loopback2
  ip router ospf DataCenter area 0.0.0.51
interface Ethernet1/18
```

```
ip ospf network point-to-point
ip router ospf DataCenter1 area 0.0.0.0
```

With the output in Example 3-68, a network administrator can quickly review the entire OSPF configuration and speed resolution of configuration issues. This information is extremely valuable when troubleshooting network issues.

OSPFv3 Configuration

OSPFv3 is a new version of OSPF based on RFC 5340, which brings support for IPv6. Unlike EIGRP, OSPFv3 requires a separate configuration stanza, **router ospfv3** for IPv6 configurations. OSPFv3 leverages a separate feature than OSPFv2, **feature ospfv3**. IPv6 configuration elements for OSPF features discussed earlier in this chapter, such as summarization and redistribution, follow similar configuration guidelines; however, they are outside the scope of this book. This section focuses on basic OSPFv3 configuration and verification.

Similar to OSPFv2, enabling OSPFv3 is a multistep process. The first step in OSPFv3 configuration is to enable the feature by executing the **feature ospfv3** command. The process of enabling this specific feature is the same as discussed earlier in this chapter for OSPFv2. After the feature is enabled, the next step in the process is to configure the OSPFv3 router process. It is also mandatory to configure a **router-id** as part of the configuration process, as shown in Example 3-69.

Example 3-69 *Configuring the OSPFv3 Process and Router-ID Using an Alphanumeric Process ID*

```
Congo# config t
Enter configuration commands, one per line. End with CNTL/Z.
Congo(config)# router ospfv3 DataCenter1
Congo(config-router)# router-id 192.168.1.1
```

Now that the feature, routing process, and router-id have been configured, the next step is to add IPv6-enabled interfaces to the OSPFv3 process.

Example 3-70 shows the addition of an SVI to the OSPFv3 DataCenter1 and verification that the configuration was successful.

Example 3-70 *Configuring an Interface for OSPFv3*

```
Congo(config)# int vlan 10
Congo(config-if)# ipv6 router ospfv3 DataCenter1 area 0

Congo(config-if)# sh ospfv3 interface vlan 10
 Vlan10 is up, line protocol is up
    IPv6 address 3000:ab8::1/64
```

```
Process ID DataCenter1 VRF default, Instance ID 0, area 0.0.0.0
Enabled by interface configuration
State DR, Network type BROADCAST, cost 40
Index 1, Transmit delay 1 sec, Router Priority 1
Designated Router ID: 192.168.205.1, address: fe80::21b:54ff:fec2:ab41
No backup designated router on this network
0 Neighbors, flooding to 0, adjacent with 0
Timer intervals: Hello 10, Dead 40, Wait 40, Retransmit 5
  Hello timer due in 00:00:05
Number of link LSAs: 1, checksum sum 0x3755
```

The last step is to configure optional summarization and redistribution. One important item to consider is that both summarization and redistribution for OSPFv3 must be configured for the **address-family ipv6 unicast** subconfiguration.

Note   Specific configuration is outside of the scope of this book; however, you can find more information in the "Configuring OSPFv3" section of the *Cisco Nexus 7000 Series NX-OS Unicast Routing Configuration Guide*, Release 5.x, which is available at http://tinyurl.com/cp7wlbh.

IS-IS

IS-IS is an Interior Gateway Protocol (IGP) based on Standardization (ISO)/International Engineering Consortium (IEC) 10589. Like OSPF, IS-IS is a link-state routing protocol that uses a link state database that describes the state of the network. It uses information from this database to calculate the best, loop-free path to other devices on the network. IS-IS also uses an area concept; however, IS-IS defines two area types: Level 1 (nonbackbone) or Level 2 (backbone). A Level 1 router establishes adjacencies with other Level 1 routers within a local area (intra-area routing), whereas a Level 2 router builds adjacencies to other Level 2 routers and routes between different Level 1 areas (interarea routing).

IS-IS Configuration

The Cisco Nexus 7000 series switches support using IS-IS as an IGP routing protocol. At the time of this writing, the Nexus 5500 series switches do not support using IS-IS as a routing protocol. Each IS-IS instance in Cisco NX-OS supports either a single Level 1 or Level 2 area, or one of each. By default, all IS-IS instances automatically support Level 1 and Level 2 routing. At the time of this writing, NX-OS for the Nexus 7000 supports IPv4 or IPv6 single topology routing.

Enabling IS-IS is a multistep process that is covered in detail. The following is a quick listing of steps to enable a basic configuration of IS-IS:

1. Enable IS-IS.

2. Configure the IS-IS instance.

3. Assign interfaces to the IS-IS instance.

4. Verify the IS-IS operation.

The first step to configure IS-IS is to enable it in global configuration mode using the **feature** command, as demonstrated in Example 3-71. With the modular nature of NX-OS, using the **feature** command loads the IS-IS modular code into memory for execution. Without the feature enabled, it would not be resident in memory.

Example 3-71   *Enabling the IS-IS Feature*

```
Congo# config t
Enter configuration commands, one per line.   End with CNTL/Z.
Congo(config)# feature isis
Congo(config)# show run isis

!Command: show running-config isis
!Time: Fri Sep 28 16:20:04 2012

version 5.2(3a)
feature isis
```

The next step is to configure the IS-IS routing instance, as demonstrated in Example 3-72. NX-OS requires an instance tag configured for the process. Traditionally in IOS this would be a device-specific instance tag. In NX-OS, the instance tag can be a device-specific tag, or the instance tag can be up to 20 case-sensitive, alphanumeric characters. This helps document the network configuration and can simplify device identification. The following example illustrates configuring IS-IS with an alphanumeric instance tag.

IS-IS also requires configuration of a Network Entity Title (NET) and an optionally defined Level type. The NET is composed of the IS-IS system ID, which uniquely identifies this IS-IS instance in the area and the area ID. For example, if the NET is 47.0004.004d.0001.0001.0c11.1111.00, the system ID is 0001.0c11.1111.00, and the area ID is 47.0004.004d.0001. The Level type defaults to **level-1-2** but can be configured specifically to **level-1** or **level-2**.

Example 3-72   *Configuring the IS-IS Instance*

```
Congo(config)# router isis Datacenter1
Congo(config-router)# is-type level-1-2
Congo(config-router)# net 47.0004.004d.0001.0001.0c11.1111.00
Congo(config-router)#
Congo(config)# show run isis
```

```
!Command: show running-config isis
!Time: Fri Sep 28 16:26:13 2012

version 5.2(3a)
feature isis

router isis Datacenter1
  net 47.0004.004d.0001.0001.0c11.1111.00
  is-type level-1-2
```

With IS-IS configured as a feature and an instance configured, the next step is to assign interfaces to the instance tag, as demonstrated in Example 3-73 for IPv4 and Example 3-74 for IPv6. You can optionally configure the interface medium type to either broadcast or point-to-point, using either the **medium broadcast** or the **medium p2p** keyword, respectively.

Example 3-73   *Add an IPv4-Enabled Interface to the IS-IS Instance*

```
Congo(config-if)# interface vlan100
Congo(config-if)# ip router isis Datacenter1
Congo(config-if)#
Congo(config-if)# show isis interface vlan 100
IS-IS process: Datacenter1 VRF: default
Vlan100, Interface status: protocol-up/link-up/admin-up
  IP address: 192.168.0.1, IP subnet: 192.168.0.0/27
  IPv6 routing is disabled
  Level1
    No auth type and keychain
    Auth check set
  Level2
    No auth type and keychain
    Auth check set
  Index: 0x0001, Local Circuit ID: 0x01, Circuit Type: L1-2
  BFD is disabled
  LSP interval: 33 ms, MTU: 1500
  Level-1 Designated IS: Congo
  Level-2 Designated IS: Congo
  Level      Metric    CSNP   Next CSNP   Hello    Multi    Next IIH
  1             40      10    00:00:08      3        3      00:00:02
  2             40      10    00:00:08      3        3      00:00:01
  Level  Adjs   AdjsUp Pri  Circuit ID           Since
  1       1        1   64   Congo.01           * 00:00:35
  2       1        1   64   Congo.01           * 00:00:35
```

Example 3-74 *Add an IPv6-Enabled Interface to the IS-IS Instance*

```
Congo(config-if)# interface vlan101
Congo(config-if)# ipv6 router isis Datacenter1
Congo(config-if)#
Congo(config)# show isis interface vlan 101
IS-IS process: Datacenter1 VRF: default
Vlan101, Interface status: protocol-up/link-up/admin-up
  IP address: none
  IPv6 address: 6000:ab8::3
  IPv6 subnet:  6000:ab8::/64
  IPv6 link-local address: fe80::21b:54ff:fec2:ca41
  Level1
    No auth type and keychain
    Auth check set
  Level2
    No auth type and keychain
    Auth check set
  Index: 0x0002, Local Circuit ID: 0x02, Circuit Type: L1-2
  BFD is disabled
  LSP interval: 33 ms, MTU: 1500
  Level-1 Designated IS: Congo
  Level-2 Designated IS: Congo
  Level      Metric   CSNP   Next CSNP  Hello   Multi   Next IIH
  1              40     10   00:00:05       3       3   0.991595
  2              40     10   00:00:05       3       3   0.012652
  Level  Adjs   AdjsUp Pri  Circuit ID          Since
  1         1        1  64  Congo.02          * 00:02:25
  2         1        1  64  Congo.02          * 00:02:25
```

On IOS devices, network administrators are accustomed to using the **show ip protocol** command to review system values for their routing protocols. Similarly in NX-OS, a concise source of information for the IS-IS configuration can be found, as demonstrated in Example 3-75. This information is extremely valuable when troubleshooting network issues.

Example 3-75 *Reviewing Detailed IS-IS Information*

```
Congo(config-if)# show isis

ISIS process : Datacenter1
VRF: default
  System ID : 0001.0c11.1111  IS-Type : L1-L2
  SAP : 412  Queue Handle : 14
  Maximum LSP MTU: 1492
```

```
          Stateful HA enabled
          Graceful Restart enabled. State: Inactive
          Last graceful restart status : none
          Start-Mode Complete
          BFD is disabled
          Metric-style : advertise(wide), accept(narrow, wide)
          Area address(es) :
            47.0004.004d.0001
          Process is up and running
          VRF ID: 1
          Stale routes during non-graceful controlled restart
          Interfaces supported by IS-IS :
            Vlan100
            Vlan101
          Address family IPv4 unicast :
            Number of interface : 1
            Distance : 115
          Address family IPv6 unicast :
            Number of interface : 1
            Distance : 115
          Level1
          No auth type and keychain
          Auth check set
          Level2
          No auth type and keychain
          Auth check set
          L1 Next SPF: Inactive
          L2 Next SPF: Inactive

Congo(config-if)# sh isis adj
IS-IS process: Datacenter1 VRF: default
IS-IS adjacency database:
System ID       SNPA           Level  State  Hold Time  Interface
Egypt           001b.54c2.ab41 1      UP     00:00:24   Vlan101
Egypt           001b.54c2.ab41 2      UP     00:00:24   Vlan101
```

With the modular nature of NX-OS, you can now display the relevant IS-IS configuration by using the **show run isis** command, as demonstrated in Example 3-76.

Example 3-76 *Viewing the IS-IS-Only Configuration*

```
Congo(config)# sh run isis

!Command: show running-config isis
!Time: Fri Sep 28 17:20:19 2012
```

```
version 5.2(3a)
feature isis

router isis Datacenter1
  net 47.0004.004d.0001.0001.0c11.1111.00
  is-type level-1-2

interface Vlan100
  ip router isis Datacenter1

interface Vlan101
  ipv6 router isis Datacenter1
```

With the output in Example 3-76, a network administrator can quickly review the entire IS-IS configuration and speed resolution of configuration issues. This information is extremely valuable when troubleshooting network issues.

BGP

The Border Gateway Protocol (BGP) is an Internet Engineering Task Force (IETF) standard protocol that traditionally has been used as the routing protocol of the Internet. BGP has attributes such as timers and administrative routing controls designed to meet the scale of large networks. NX-OS supports both IPv4 and IPv6 unicast and multicast address families, and VPNv6 (6VPE) and IPv6 labeled-unicast (6PE), which are both discussed in more detail in Chapter 12, "MPLS." Many network administrators choose to leverage BGP for scaling challenges as their IP networks grow. Another common option is for mergers and acquisitions in which disparate networks are required to interconnect and share routing information but lack a common administrative control.

BGP uses the concept of autonomous systems (AS) as delineation between networks. An AS is a collection of routers under a common administrative control. Neighbor relationships are manually configured between autonomous systems to exchange routing tables and apply routing policy.

BGP is supported on both the Nexus 7000 and 5500 series switches. The Nexus 5500 series switches must be configured with a Layer 3 daughtercard or module, dependent on the specific platform. The Nexus 5500 series also requires an Enterprise License for BGP. The examples in this chapter focus on BGP configuration for the Nexus 7000.

BGP Configuration

BGP within NX-OS is compatible with BGP on IOS and other IETF-compliant devices enabling a smooth integration of Nexus equipment. Configuring BGP within NX-OS will be similar, yet distinctly different in some aspects to traditional IOS configuration. These differences are highlighted throughout the section.

Enabling BGP is a multistep process covered in detail. The following is a quick listing of steps to enable a basic configuration of BGP:

1. Enable BGP.

2. Configure BGP routing process with the AS identification.

3. Configure address families.

4. Configure BGP neighbors.

5. Configure network routing policy.

6. Configure redistribution of other protocols if necessary.

7. Verify BGP operation.

The first step to configure BGP is to enable it on global configuration mode using the **feature** command, as demonstrated in Example 3-77. With the modular nature of NX-OS, using the **feature** command loads the BGP modular code into memory for execution. Without the feature enabled, it would not be resident in memory. Figure 3-10 illustrates the topology used for Examples 3-77 through 3-99.

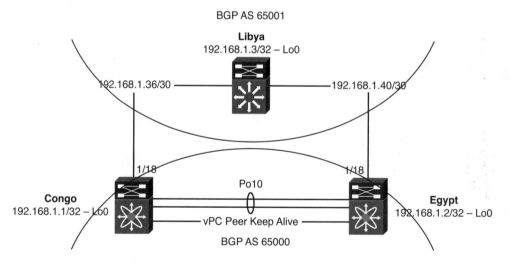

Figure 3-10 *Network Topology for Basic BGP Configuration*

Example 3-77 *Enabling the BGP Feature*

```
Congo# config t
Enter configuration commands, one per line. End with CNTL/Z.
Congo(config)# feature bgp
Congo(config)# end
Congo# show run bgp
```

```
!Command: show running-config bgp
!Time: Wed Sep 30 18:47:51 2009

version 4.2(2a)

feature bgp
```

Similar to IOS-based BGP configuration, the next step is to configure the BGP routing process with the AS identification, as demonstrated in Example 3-78.

Note   NX-OS does not support the use of an alphanumeric tag for BGP like it does for IGPs such as EIGRP and OSPF.

Example 3-78   *Configuring the BGP Process*

```
Congo# config t
Enter configuration commands, one per line. End with CNTL/Z.
Congo(config)# router bgp 65000
Congo# show run bgp
!Command: show running-config bgp
!Time: Wed Sep 30 18:51:45 2009

version 4.2(2a)

feature bgp
router bgp 65000
```

NX-OS also supports the capability to use 4-byte AS numbers. This 4-byte support can be configured using either plain-text notation or dotted-decimal notation. This is important for companies with newer Internet AS number registrations that can use the new 4-byte AS assignments.

Example 3-79 demonstrates the use of plain-text notation.

Example 3-79   *Configuring BGP with 4-Byte AS Numbers Using Plain Text*

```
Congo# config t
Congo(config)# router bgp 4200000088
Congo# show run bgp
!Command: show running-config bgp
!Time: Sun Oct 11 15:32:42 2009

version 4.2(2a)

feature bgp
router bgp 4200000088
```

Example 3-80 demonstrates the use of dotted-decimal notation.

Example 3-80   *Configuring BGP with 4-Byte AS Numbers Using Dotted-Decimal Notation*

```
Congo# config t
Congo(config)# router bgp 65000.65088
Congo# show run bgp
!Command: show running-config bgp
!Time: Sun Oct 11 15:31:05 2009
version 4.2(2a)
feature bgp
router bgp 65000.65088
```

In IOS, it was *preferred* to configure a router ID, whereas in NX-OS it is a *requirement* that BGP obtain an IP address to use as a router ID or one must be configured, as demonstrated in Example 3-81.

Example 3-81   *Configuring the BGP Router ID*

```
Congo# config t
Enter configuration commands, one per line. End with CNTL/Z.
Congo(config)# router bgp 65000
Congo(config-router)# router-id 192.168.1.1
Congo# show run bgp
!Command: show running-config bgp
!Time: Wed Sep 30 19:17:36 2009
version 4.2(2a)
feature bgp
router bgp 65000
  router-id 192.168.1.1
```

With BGP configured as a feature and assigned a router ID, the next step is to configure address families, as demonstrated in Example 3-82. Address families are subcomponents of the global BGP configuration, and although not mandatory for basic BGP configurations, address families are required for use with advanced features such as route redistribution, load balancing, and route aggregation. As mentioned earlier in this chapter, NX-OS supports both IPv4 and IPv6 unicast and multicast address families.

Example 3-82   *Configuring BGP Address Families*

```
Congo# config t
Congo(config)# router bgp 65000
Congo(config-router)# address-family ipv4 unicast
Congo(config-router-af)# exit
Congo(config-router)# address-family ipv6 unicast
Congo(config-router-af)# end
```

```
Congo# sh run bgp

!Command: show running-config bgp
!Time: Thu Sep 27 16:10:10 2012

version 5.2(3a)
feature bgp

router bgp 65000
  router-id 192.168.1.1
  address-family ipv4 unicast
  address-family ipv6 unicast
```

BGP Neighbors

After the address family is configured, the next step would be to configure the iBGP and eBGP peers using the **neighbor** commands. iBGP is used between BGP speakers in the same autonomous system, whereas eBGP is used between BGP speakers in different autonomous systems. Example 3-83 notes the update source as Loopback 0 to make peering simpler by using the loopback 0 IP address as the source IP for a peering session.

Example 3-83   *Configuring an IPv4 iBGP Neighbor*

```
Congo# config t
Enter configuration commands, one per line. End with CNTL/Z.
Congo(config)# router bgp 65000
Congo(config-router-af)# neighbor 192.168.1.2 remote-as 65000
Congo(config-router-neighbor)# description Egypt
Congo(config-router-neighbor)# update-source loopback0
Congo(config-router-neighbor)# address-family ipv4 unicast
Congo(config-router-neighbor-af)# end
```

You can verify the peering session by looking at the output from the **show ip bgp neighbor 192.168.1.2** command, as demonstrated in Example 3-84.

Example 3-84   *Verification of an IPv4 iBGP Neighbor*

```
Congo# show ip bgp neighbors 192.168.1.2
BGP neighbor is 192.168.1.2,  remote AS 65000, ibgp link,  Peer index 1
  Description: Egypt
  BGP version 4, remote router ID 192.168.1.2
  BGP state = Established, up for 4d14h
  Using loopback0 as update source for this peer
  Last read 00:00:31, hold time = 180, keepalive interval is 60 seconds
```

```
Last written 00:00:32, keepalive timer expiry due 00:00:27
Received 6610 messages, 0 notifications, 0 bytes in queue
Sent 6628 messages, 0 notifications, 0 bytes in queue
Connections established 1, dropped 0
Last reset by us 4d14h, due to session closed
Last reset by peer never, due to process restart

Neighbor capabilities:
Dynamic capability: advertised (mp, refresh, gr) received (mp, refresh, gr)
Dynamic capability (old): advertised received
Route refresh capability (new): advertised received
Route refresh capability (old): advertised received
4-Byte AS capability: advertised received
Address family IPv4 Unicast: advertised received
Graceful Restart capability: advertised received
Graceful Restart Parameters:
Address families advertised to peer:
  IPv4 Unicast
Address families received from peer:
  IPv4 Unicast
Forwarding state preserved by peer for:
Restart time advertised to peer: 120 seconds
Stale time for routes advertised by peer: 300 seconds
Restart time advertised by peer: 120 seconds
Message statistics:
                          Sent           Rcvd
Opens:                     19              1
Notifications:             0              0
Updates:                   1              1
Keepalives:              6608           6608
Route Refresh:             0              0
Capability:                0              0
Total:                   6628           6610
Total bytes:            125556         125556
Bytes in queue:            0              0
For address family: IPv4 Unicast
BGP table version 3, neighbor version 3
0 accepted paths consume 0 bytes of memory
0 sent paths
Third-party Nexthop will not be computed.
Local host: 192.168.1.1, Local port: 58042
Foreign host: 192.168.1.2, Foreign port: 179
fd = 37
```

Establishing an external BGP (eBGP) session is similar to an internal BGP (iBGP) session with the primary difference being the remote-as number used. For an iBGP session, the AS number is the same as the AS number used on the BGP process, whereas with eBGP it is a different AS number. Example 3-85 demonstrates the configuration of an eBGP session.

Example 3-85 *Configuring an IPv4 eBGP Neighbor*

```
Congo# config t
Enter configuration commands, one per line. End with CNTL/Z.
Congo(config)# router bgp 65000
Congo(config-router)#
Congo(config-router)# neighbor 192.168.1.38 remote-as 65001
Congo(config-router-neighbor)# description Libya
Congo(config-router-neighbor)# address-family ipv4 unicast
Congo(config-router-neighbor-af)# end
```

You can verify the peering session by looking at the output from **show ip bgp neighbor 192.168.1.38**, as demonstrated in Example 3-86.

Example 3-86 *Verification of an IPv4 eBGP Neighbor*

```
Congo# show ip bgp neighbor 192.168.1.38
BGP neighbor is 192.168.1.38,  remote AS 65001, ebgp link,  Peer index 2
  Description: Libya
  BGP version 4, remote router ID 192.168.1.3
  BGP state = Established, up for 00:01:13
  Peer is directly attached, interface Ethernet1/18
  Last read 00:00:11, hold time = 180, keepalive interval is 60 seconds
  Last written 00:00:12, keepalive timer expiry due 00:00:47
  Received 4 messages, 0 notifications, 0 bytes in queue
  Sent 5 messages, 0 notifications, 0 bytes in queue
  Connections established 1, dropped 0
  Last reset by us never, due to process restart
  Last reset by peer never, due to process restart
  Neighbor capabilities:
  Dynamic capability: advertised (mp, refresh, gr)
  Dynamic capability (old): advertised
  Route refresh capability (new): advertised received
  Route refresh capability (old): advertised received
  4-Byte AS capability: advertised
  Address family IPv4 Unicast: advertised received
  Graceful Restart capability: advertised
  Graceful Restart Parameters:
  Address families advertised to peer:
    IPv4 Unicast
```

```
Address families received from peer:
Forwarding state preserved by peer for:
Restart time advertised to peer: 120 seconds
Stale time for routes advertised by peer: 300 seconds
Message statistics:
                             Sent              Rcvd
Opens:                        1                 1
Notifications:                0                 0
Updates:                      1                 0
Keepalives:                   3                 3
Route Refresh:                0                 0
Capability:                   0                 0
Total:                        5                 4
Total bytes:                 61                38
Bytes in queue:               0                 0
For address family: IPv4 Unicast
BGP table version 4, neighbor version 4
0 accepted paths consume 0 bytes of memory
0 sent paths
Local host: 192.168.1.37, Local port: 179
Foreign host: 192.168.1.38, Foreign port: 38354
fd = 42
```

Securing BGP

You can secure BGP routing updates through authentication between BGP neighbors. BGP authentication is enabled on a per-neighbor basis and uses MD5 hashing.

Note   The BGP password *must* match on both BGP peers to establish a session. This is particularly important when peering with external organizations, such as an ISP in which the peering router might not be under your direct control.

Configuring BGP authentication simply requires the password to be enabled on the neighbor, as shown in Example 3-87.

Example 3-87   *Configuring BGP Authentication*

```
Congo# config t
Enter configuration commands, one per line. End with CNTL/Z.
Congo(config)# router bgp 65000
Congo(config-router)# neighbor 192.168.1.38
Congo(config-router-neighbor)# password bgppassword
Congo(config-router-neighbor)# end
```

You can verify the authentication on the peer session by using the **show ip bgp neighbor** command, as demonstrated in Example 3-88.

Example 3-88 *Verification of BGP Authentication*

```
Congo# show ip bgp neighbor 192.168.1.38
BGP neighbor is 192.168.1.38,  remote AS 65001, ebgp link,  Peer index 2
  Description: Libya
  BGP version 4, remote router ID 192.168.1.3
  BGP state = Established, up for 00:05:16
  Peer is directly attached, interface Ethernet1/18
  TCP MD5 authentication is enabled
  Last read 00:00:14, hold time = 180, keepalive interval is 60 seconds
  Last written 00:00:15, keepalive timer expiry due 00:00:44
  Received 31 messages, 0 notifications, 0 bytes in queue
  Sent 37 messages, 1 notifications, 0 bytes in queue
  Connections established 2, dropped 1
  Last reset by us 00:05:36, due to holdtimer expired error
  Last reset by peer never, due to process restart
  Neighbor capabilities:
  Dynamic capability: advertised (mp, refresh, gr)
  Dynamic capability (old): advertised
  Route refresh capability (new): advertised received
  Route refresh capability (old): advertised received
  4-Byte AS capability: advertised
  Address family IPv4 Unicast: advertised received
  Graceful Restart capability: advertised
  Graceful Restart Parameters:
  Address families advertised to peer:
    IPv4 Unicast
  Address families received from peer:
  Forwarding state preserved by peer for:
  Restart time advertised to peer: 120 seconds
  Stale time for routes advertised by peer: 300 seconds
  Message statistics:
                          Sent               Rcvd
  Opens:                     2                  2
  Notifications:             1                  0
  Updates:                   2                  0
  Keepalives:               32                 29
  Route Refresh:             0                  0
  Capability:                0                  0
  Total:                    37                 31
  Total bytes:             637                513
  Bytes in queue:            0                  0
```

```
For address family: IPv4 Unicast
BGP table version 6, neighbor version 6
0 accepted paths consume 0 bytes of memory
0 sent paths
Local host: 192.168.1.37, Local port: 60095
Foreign host: 192.168.1.38, Foreign port: 179
fd = 42
```

BGP Peer Templates

When configuring BGP, it is common to find that many of the commands required to establish a baseline for consistent network policy are repetitive. NX-OS features a capability for creating BGP peering templates that are convenient time-saving tools. These templates enable the network administrator to configure attributes that will be used among multiple peers once and apply them when a new peer is configured.

BGP peer templates support multiple attributes including multihop Time-To-Live (TTL), timers, next-hop-self, password, remote-as, and maximum prefix. In Example 3-89, a BGP peer template named iBGP-Peers is created and applied to an iBGP session.

Note   You can find a full listing of template options on Cisco.com: http://tinyurl.com/ a96dcbg.

Example 3-89   *Configuring BGP Peer Templates*

```
Egypt# config t
Enter configuration commands, one per line. End with CNTL/Z.
Egypt(config)# router bgp 65000
Egypt(config-router)# template peer iBGP-Peers
Egypt(config-router-neighbor)# remote-as 65000
Egypt(config-router-neighbor)# password 3 cd87a249cfe3fb9aefc4f7f321a18044
Egypt(config-router-neighbor)# update-source loopback0
Egypt(config-router-neighbor)# timers 45 120
Egypt(config-router-neighbor)# neighbor 192.168.1.1
Egypt(config-router-neighbor)# inherit peer iBGP-Peers
Egypt(config-router-neighbor)# end
```

You can verify the peer using the peer template, as demonstrated in Example 3-90.

Example 3-90 *Verification of BGP Peer Using the Peer Template*

```
Egypt# show ip bgp neighbor 192.168.1.1
BGP neighbor is 192.168.1.1,  remote AS 65000, ibgp link,  Peer index 1
  Inherits peer configuration from peer-template iBGP-Peers
  Description: Congo
  BGP version 4, remote router ID 192.168.1.1
  BGP state = Established, up for 00:02:05
  Using loopback0 as update source for this peer
  TCP MD5 authentication is enabled
  Last read 00:00:04, hold time = 120, keepalive interval is 45 seconds
  Last written 00:00:34, keepalive timer expiry due 00:00:10
  Received 6672 messages, 1 notifications, 0 bytes in queue
  Sent 6689 messages, 1 notifications, 0 bytes in queue
  Connections established 3, dropped 2
  Last reset by us 00:02:23, due to session cleared
  Last reset by peer 00:24:09, due to administratively shutdown
  Neighbor capabilities:
  Dynamic capability: advertised (mp, refresh, gr) received (mp, refresh, gr)
  Dynamic capability (old): advertised received
  Route refresh capability (new): advertised received
  Route refresh capability (old): advertised received
  4-Byte AS capability: advertised received
  Address family IPv4 Unicast: advertised received
  Graceful Restart capability: advertised received
  Graceful Restart Parameters:
  Address families advertised to peer:
    IPv4 Unicast
  Address families received from peer:
    IPv4 Unicast
  Forwarding state preserved by peer for:
    IPv4 Unicast
  Restart time advertised to peer: 120 seconds
  Stale time for routes advertised by peer: 300 seconds
  Restart time advertised by peer: 120 seconds
  Message statistics:
                       Sent              Rcvd
  Opens:                 21                 3
  Notifications:          1                 1
  Updates:                3                 3
  Keepalives:          6664              6665
  Route Refresh:          0                 0
  Capability:             0                 0
  Total:               6689              6672
  Total bytes:       126649            126668
```

```
Bytes in queue:                 0                0
For address family: IPv4 Unicast
BGP table version 8, neighbor version 8
0 accepted paths consume 0 bytes of memory
0 sent paths
Third-party Nexthop will not be computed.
Local host: 192.168.1.2, Local port: 54942
Foreign host: 192.168.1.1, Foreign port: 179
fd = 42
```

Advertising BGP Networks

When BGP neighbor relationships are defined, secured, and simplified using templates, the next step is to advertise networks. The NX-OS implementation of BGP is flexible and enables entries to be added to the routing table through multiple mechanisms. The two most common are **network** statements and redistribution from an IGP.

In Example 3-91, the network 10.100.100.0/24 is advertised via BGP to Libya using the **network** command.

Example 3-91   *Advertising Networks in BGP*

```
Congo# config t
Enter configuration commands, one per line. End with CNTL/Z.
Congo(config)# router bgp 65000
Congo(config-router)# address-family ipv4 unicast
Congo(config-router-af)# network 10.100.100.0 mask 255.255.255.0
```

On the IOS router Libya, the route shows as an eBGP route with an administrative distance of 20, as demonstrated in Example 3-92.

Example 3-92   *Verification of Advertised Network in IOS*

```
Libya# show ip route
Codes: C - connected, S - static, R - RIP, M - mobile, B - BGP
       D - EIGRP, EX - EIGRP external, O - OSPF, IA - OSPF inter area
       N1 - OSPF NSSA external type 1, N2 - OSPF NSSA external type 2
       E1 - OSPF external type 1, E2 - OSPF external type 2
       i - IS-IS, su - IS-IS summary, L1 - IS-IS level-1, L2 - IS-IS level-2
       ia - IS-IS inter area, * - candidate default, U - per-user static route
       o - ODR, P - periodic downloaded static route
Gateway of last resort is not set
     172.26.0.0/16 is variably subnetted, 2 subnets, 2 masks
S       172.26.2.0/23 [1/0] via 172.26.32.33
C       172.26.32.32/27 is directly connected, GigabitEthernet1/48
```

```
C    192.168.200.0/24 is directly connected, Loopback10
C    192.168.201.0/24 is directly connected, Loopback11
     10.0.0.0/24 is subnetted, 1 subnets
B       10.100.100.0 [20/0] via 192.168.1.37, 00:10:20
     192.168.1.0/24 is variably subnetted, 3 subnets, 2 masks
C       192.168.1.40/30 is directly connected, TenGigabitEthernet1/49
C       192.168.1.36/30 is directly connected, TenGigabitEthernet1/50
C       192.168.1.3/32 is directly connected, Loopback0
```

Advertising routes via the **network** command might not be wanted for all situations or designs. With this in mind, NX-OS supports the redistribution of routes into BGP from other protocols or topologies such as directly connected or static routes.

In Example 3-93, the OSPF process DataCenter1 will be redistributed into BGP. Any subnets that are in the 192.168.0.0/16 range and the 10.100.0.0/16 range will be advertised into BGP.

Note   By default, a prefix list is designed to make an exact match. With the addition of the **le** (less than or equal to) argument, you can instruct the prefix list to match subnets less than or equal to 192.168.0.0/16 and 10.100.0.0/16.

The process begins by defining a prefix list to define subnets you either want to permit or deny into BGP.

Example 3-93   *Defining a Prefix List for BGP Redistribution*

```
Congo(config)# ip prefix-list OSPFtoBGP description Defines routes from OSPF to be
redistributed into BGP
Congo(config)# ip prefix-list OSPFtoBGP permit 192.168.0.0/16 le 32
Congo(config)# ip prefix-list OSPFtoBGP permit 10.100.0.0/16 le 32
```

Next, you define a route map, called **OSPFtoBGP**, which uses the prefix list named **OSPFtoBGP**, to bring in only the 192.168.0.0/16 10.100.0.0/16 or longer routes, as demonstrated in Example 3-94.

Example 3-94   *Defining a Route Map for BGP Redistribution*

```
Congo(config)# route-map OSPFtoBGP permit
Congo(config-route-map)# match ip address prefix-list OSPFtoBGP
```

Finally, you configure BGP to use the route map **OSPFtoBGP** as part of the **redistribute bgp** command, as demonstrated in Example 3-95.

Example 3-95   *Configuring BGP Redistribution*

```
Congo(config-route-map)# router bgp 65000
Congo(config-router)# address-family ipv4 unicast
Congo(config-router-af)# redistribute ospf DataCenter1 route-map OSPFtoBGP
```

On a neighboring IOS router, the subnets have been added to the routing table via BGP and display an administrative distance of 20, which is one of the metrics used by the router to determine a route's viability in the routing table, as shown in Example 3-96.

Example 3-96   *Verification of Redistribution in IOS*

```
Libya# show ip route
Codes: C - connected, S - static, R - RIP, M - mobile, B - BGP
       D - EIGRP, EX - EIGRP external, O - OSPF, IA - OSPF inter area
       N1 - OSPF NSSA external type 1, N2 - OSPF NSSA external type 2
       E1 - OSPF external type 1, E2 - OSPF external type 2
       i - IS-IS, su - IS-IS summary, L1 - IS-IS level-1, L2 - IS-IS level-2
       ia - IS-IS inter area, * - candidate default, U - per-user static route
       o - ODR, P - periodic downloaded static route
Gateway of last resort is not set
     172.26.0.0/16 is variably subnetted, 2 subnets, 2 masks
S       172.26.2.0/23 [1/0] via 172.26.32.33
C       172.26.32.32/27 is directly connected, GigabitEthernet1/48
C    192.168.200.0/24 is directly connected, Loopback10
C    192.168.201.0/24 is directly connected, Loopback11
     10.0.0.0/24 is subnetted, 4 subnets
B       10.100.100.0 [20/0] via 192.168.1.37, 6d01h
B       10.100.202.0 [20/100] via 192.168.1.37, 00:33:43
B       10.100.200.0 [20/100] via 192.168.1.37, 00:33:43
B       10.100.201.0 [20/100] via 192.168.1.37, 00:33:43
     192.168.1.0/24 is variably subnetted, 4 subnets, 2 masks
C       192.168.1.40/30 is directly connected, TenGigabitEthernet1/49
C       192.168.1.36/30 is directly connected, TenGigabitEthernet1/50
C       192.168.1.3/32 is directly connected, Loopback0
B       192.168.1.2/32 [20/41] via 192.168.1.37, 00:34:37
```

Note   NX-OS does not have the capability to do "wide-open" or "uncontrolled" redistribution. NX-OS enforces the use of a route-map to define routes that should be redistributed.

Modifying BGP Routing Metrics

BGP administrators frequently require flexibility in the manipulation of the multitude of BGP metrics that can influence routing policy. NX-OS supports administration of metrics such as AS-Path, weight, local preference, and more. These metrics can be applied in a granular nature using prefix lists to define the wanted metric.

Example 3-97 shows the weight and local preference set to nondefault values.

Example 3-97 *Changing Weight and Local Preference in BGP*

```
Congo# config t
Enter configuration commands, one per line. End with CNTL/Z.
Congo(config)# route-map OSPFtoBGP permit 10
Congo(config-route-map)# match ip address prefix-list OSPFtoBGP
Congo(config-route-map)# set weight 200
Congo(config-route-map)# set local-preference 2500
```

You can verify the changes to the weight and local preference through the **show ip bgp** command, as demonstrated in Example 3-98.

Example 3-98 *Verification of Weight and Local Preference in BGP*

```
Congo# config t
Enter configuration commands, one per line. End with CNTL/Z.
Congo(config)# route-map OSPFtoBGP permit 10
Congo(config-route-map)# match ip address prefix-list OSPFtoBGP
Congo(config-route-map)# set weight 200
Congo(config-route-map)# set local-preference 2500
Congo# show ip bgp
BGP routing table information for VRF default, address family IPv4 Unicast
BGP table version is 12, local router ID is 192.168.1.1
Status: s-suppressed, x-deleted, S-stale, d-dampened, h-history, *-valid, >-best
Path type: i-internal, e-external, c-confed, l-local, a-aggregate, r-redist
Origin codes: i - IGP, e - EGP, ? - incomplete, | - multipath
  Network            Next Hop          Metric      LocPrf      Weight Path
* r10.100.100.0/24   0.0.0.0              100        2500         200 ?
*>l                  0.0.0.0                         100       32768 i
*>r10.100.200.0/24   0.0.0.0              100        2500         200 ?
*>r10.100.201.0/24   0.0.0.0              100        2500         200 ?
*>r10.100.202.0/24   0.0.0.0              100        2500         200 ?
*>r192.168.1.2/32    0.0.0.0               41        2500         200 ?
*>r192.168.1.40/30   0.0.0.0               44        2500         200 ?
```

Verifying BGP-Specific Configuration

With the modular nature of NX-OS, you can now show the relevant BGP configuration by using the **show run bgp** command, as demonstrated in Example 3-99.

Example 3-99   *Viewing the BGP-Only Configuration*

```
Congo# show run bgp
!Command: show running-config bgp
!Time: Sun Oct 11 15:18:30 2009
version 4.2(2a)
feature bgp
router bgp 65000
  router-id 192.168.1.1
  address-family ipv4 unicast
    network 10.100.100.0/24
    redistribute ospf DataCenter1 route-map OSPFtoBGP
  address-family ipv6 unicast
  template peer iBGP-Peers
    remote-as 65000
    password 3 cd87a249cfe3fb9aefc4f7f321a18044
    update-source loopback0
    timers 45 120
  neighbor 192.168.1.2 remote-as 65000
    inherit peer iBGP-Peers
    description Egypt
    address-family ipv4 unicast
  neighbor 192.168.1.38 remote-as 65001
    description Libya
    password 3 cd87a249cfe3fb9aefc4f7f321a18044
    address-family ipv4 unicast
```

First Hop Redundancy Protocols

Data center network designs frequently call for maximum redundancy to support the 24x7x365 operation mode called for in high-availability environments. A component of these designs is the use of a First-Hop Redundancy Protocol (FHRP). FHRPs provide a mechanism for maintaining an active default IP gateway at all times. This section covers three FHRPs and their associated configurations, including the following:

- Hot Standby Router Protocol (HSRP)

- Virtual Router Redundancy Protocol (VRRP)

- Gateway Load Balancing Protocol (GLBP)

HSRP

HSRP is a Cisco innovation introduced to the networking world in 1998 and described in RFC 2281. HSRP enables two or more routers to provide first-hop redundancy services for IP traffic. In HSRP, a virtual IP address is configured and is "owned" by one of the routers participating in the HSRP group to represent the default gateway for a given sub-net. If that router fails or is taken out of service, the second router assumes the role of the default gateway using the same Media Access Control (MAC) address. This prevents the hosts on the network from needing to send an Address Resolution Protocol (ARP) for the new gateway's MAC address, and traffic is passed with minimal to no disruption.

HSRP is supported on both the Nexus 7000 and 5500 series switches. The examples in this chapter focus on HSRP configuration for the Nexus 7000.

HSRP Configuration

The first step to configure HSRP is to enable it in global configuration mode using the **feature** command, as demonstrated in Example 3-88. With the modular nature of NX-OS, using the **feature** command loads the HSRP modular code into memory for execution. Without the feature enabled, it would not be resident in memory.

Figure 3-11 illustrates the topology used in Examples 3-100 through 3-110.

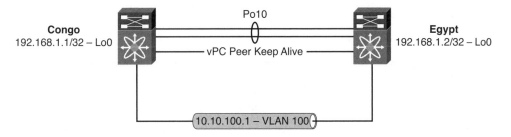

Figure 3-11 *Network Topology for HSRP Configuration*

Example 3-100 *Enabling the HSRP Feature*

```
Congo# config t
Enter configuration commands, one per line. End with CNTL/Z.
Congo(config)# feature hsrp
Congo(config)# end
Congo# show run hsrp
!Command: show running-config hsrp
!Time: Sun Oct 11 21:44:42 2009
version 4.2(2a)
feature hsrp
```

Similar to IOS-based HSRP configuration, the next step is to configure the HSRP process under a VLAN interface, as demonstrated in Example 3-101.

Note Recommended practice dictates that you should configure all HSRP options such as priority, preempt, authentication, and so on prior to adding the IP address to the group. This minimizes disruption and state change on the network.

Example 3-101 *Configuring HSRP on an SVI*

```
Congo# config t
Enter configuration commands, one per line. End with CNTL/Z.
Congo(config)# int vlan 100
Congo(config-if)# hsrp 100
Congo(config-if-hsrp)# ip 10.10.100.1
Congo# show run hsrp
!Command: show running-config hsrp
!Time: Sun Oct 11 21:57:16 2009
version 4.2(2a)
feature hsrp

interface Vlan100
  hsrp 100
    ip 10.10.100.1
```

HSRP Priority and Preempt

NX-OS supports the capability to configure different HSRP priorities to help the network administrator define deterministic switching through the network. Similar to the HSRP implementation in IOS, a device with a higher priority will become the active gateway and the lower-priority device will become the standby. The default HSRP priority is 100, and it might be preferable to change the default to another value to align HSRP priorities with spanning tree configuration to optimize traffic flows and provide deterministic switching. When two HSRP devices have the same priority, HSRP selects the device with the highest IP address to be active.

In addition, when a priority is configured, it is typical to configure a **preempt** command to ensure that the active router is consistent after a network change. In Example 3-102, a priority of 200 is configured in addition to a preempt that uses the capability to wait a specified amount of time before preempting. This is preferable to minimize the potential of a flapping link or other inconsistent state in the network forcing HSRP changes.

Example 3-102 *Configuring HSRP Priority and Preemption*

```
Congo# config t
Enter configuration commands, one per line. End with CNTL/Z.
Congo(config)# int vlan 100
Congo(config-if)# hsrp 100
Congo(config-if-hsrp)# priority 200
Congo(config-if-hsrp)# preempt delay minimum 60
Congo(config-if-hsrp)# end
Congo# show run hsrp
!Command: show running-config hsrp
!Time: Sun Oct 11 22:07:18 2009
version 4.2(2a)
feature hsrp


interface Vlan100
  hsrp 100
    preempt delay minimum 60
    priority 200
    ip 10.10.100.1
```

Verifying the HSRP Configuration

A quick method to use to see the current state of the HSRP configuration is to use the **show hsrp** command, as demonstrated in Example 3-101. All the parameters configured in Example 3-103 are reflected in the output such as priority, preempt, and IP address.

Example 3-103 *Verification of HSRP Status*

```
Congo# show hsrp
Vlan100 - Group 100 (HSRP-V1) (IPv4)
  Local state is Active, priority 200 (Cfged 200), may preempt
    Forwarding threshold(for VPC), lower: 1 upper: 200
  Preemption Delay (Seconds) Minimum:60
  Hellotime 3 sec, holdtime 10 sec
  Next hello sent in 2.539000 sec(s)
  Virtual IP address is 10.10.100.1 (Cfged)
  Active router is local
  Standby router is 10.10.100.3
  Virtual mac address is 0000.0c07.ac64 (Default MAC)
  2 state changes, last state change 00:01:00
  IP redundancy name is hsrp-Vlan100-100 (default)
```

Securing HSRP

Securing HSRP is important in many environments to avoid a new router or device being added to the network and incorrectly assuming the role of the default gateway on a subnet. HSRP authentication can be configured to prevent such a situation. The implementation of HSRP authentication in NX-OS provides two forms of authentication:

- **Plain text:** Has the password used for authentication in clear text and passes it as such on the network

- **MD5:** Uses the MD5 algorithm to hash the password before it is passed across the network

Example 3-104 shows the configuration of plain-text authentication.

Example 3-104   *Configuring HSRP Plain-Text Authentication*

```
Congo# config t
Enter configuration commands, one per line. End with CNTL/Z.
Congo(config)# int vlan100
Congo(config-if)# hsrp 100
Congo(config-if-hsrp)# authentication text hsrp
```

You can see the addition of authentication to the HSRP configuration in the output of **show hsrp**, as illustrated in Example 3-105.

Example 3-105   *Verification of HSRP Plain-Text Authentication*

```
Congo# show hsrp
Vlan100 - Group 100 (HSRP-V1) (IPv4)
  Local state is Active, priority 200 (Cfged 200), may preempt
    Forwarding threshold(for VPC), lower: 1 upper: 200
  Preemption Delay (Seconds) Minimum:60
  Hellotime 3 sec, holdtime 10 sec
  Next hello sent in 0.069000 sec(s)
  Virtual IP address is 10.10.100.1 (Cfged)
  Active router is local
  Standby router is 10.10.100.3
  Authentication text "hsrp"
  Virtual mac address is 0000.0c07.ac64 (Default MAC)
  2 state changes, last state change 00:15:24
  IP redundancy name is hsrp-Vlan100-100 (default)
```

Configuration of MD5 authentication is a multistep process. You must first define a keychain that contains attributes such as the password to be used to authenticate the connection and the lifetime of the keychain for both sending and receiving, as demonstrated in Example 3-106.

Example 3-106 *Configuring a Keychain*

```
Congo(config)# key chain nexus
Congo(config-keychain)# key 1
Congo(config-keychain-key)# key-string nexus
```

The next step is to enable authentication under the HSRP process, as illustrated in Example 3-107, and reference the keychain created in the previous step.

Example 3-107 *Configuring HSRP MD5 Authentication*

```
Congo# config t
Enter configuration commands, one per line. End with CNTL/Z.
Congo(config)# int vlan 100
Congo(config-if)# hsrp 100
Congo(config-if-hsrp)# authentication md5 key-chain nexus
```

You can verify that the MD5 authentication is in place from the output of the **show hsrp** command, as demonstrated in Example 3-108.

Example 3-108 *Verification of HSRP MD5 Authentication*

```
Congo(config-if-hsrp)# show hsrp
Vlan100 - Group 100 (HSRP-V1) (IPv4)
  Local state is Active, priority 200 (Cfged 200), may preempt
    Forwarding threshold(for VPC), lower: 1 upper: 200
  Preemption Delay (Seconds) Minimum:60
  Hellotime 3 sec, holdtime 10 sec
  Next hello sent in 1.059000 sec(s)
  Virtual IP address is 10.10.100.1 (Cfged)
  Active router is local
  Standby router is 10.10.100.3
  Authentication MD5, key-chain nexus
  Virtual mac address is 0000.0c07.ac64 (Default MAC)
  2 state changes, last state change 00:23:03
  IP redundancy name is hsrp-Vlan100-100 (default)
```

HSRP Secondary Support

The implementation of HSRP in NX-OS also supports secondary IP addressing. Secondary IP addresses are typically found in environments under transition to a new IP addressing scheme and are usually temporary.

Example 3-109 shows HSRP configured to provide services to a secondary IP subnet, 172.16.1.0/24.

Example 3-109 *Configuring HSRP for Secondary Subnets*

```
Congo# config t
Enter configuration commands, one per line. End with CNTL/Z.
Congo(config)# int vlan 100
Congo(config-if)# ip address 172.16.1.2/24 secondary
Congo(config-if)# hsrp 100
Congo(config-if-hsrp)# ip 172.16.1.1 secondary
Congo(config-if-hsrp)# end
Congo# show hsrp
Vlan100 - Group 100 (HSRP-V1) (IPv4)
  Local state is Active, priority 200 (Cfged 200), may preempt
    Forwarding threshold(for VPC), lower: 1 upper: 200
  Preemption Delay (Seconds) Minimum:60
  Hellotime 3 sec, holdtime 10 sec
  Next hello sent in 0.489000 sec(s)
  Virtual IP address is 10.10.100.1 (Cfged)
    Secondary Virtual IP address is 172.16.1.1
  Active router is local
  Standby router is 10.10.100.3
  Authentication MD5, key-chain nexus
  Virtual mac address is 0000.0c07.ac64 (Default MAC)
  2 state changes, last state change 00:40:20
  IP redundancy name is hsrp-Vlan100-100 (default)
```

HSRP Support for IPv6

NX-OS supports both HSRP version 1 (HSRPv1) and HSRP version 2 (HSRPv2). HSRPv2 brings certain enhancements to HSRPv1, including expanded group number support, IPv6 support, and improved management and troubleshooting. At the time of this writing, HSRPv2 is the only FHRP available for NX-OS that provides support for IPv6. The IPv6 neighbor discovery (ND) process relies on periodic multicasting of available IPv6 routers via router advertisement (RA). A failover could take as long as 30 seconds. HSRPv2 provides a much faster, millisecond failover alternative to the traditional IPv6 ND process.

Example 3-110 shows the process of configuring basic HSRPv2 for IPv6.

Example 3-110 *Configuring HSRPv2 for IPv6*

```
Congo# config t
Enter configuration commands, one per line. End with CNTL/Z.
Congo(config-if)# int vlan100
Congo(config-if)# ipv6 address 6000:ab8::3/64
Congo(config-if)# hsrp version 2
Congo(config-if)# hsrp 100 ipv6
```

```
Congo(config-if-hsrp)# ip 6000:ab8::1
Congo(config-if-hsrp)# ip autoconfig
Congo(config-if-hsrp)# no shut
Congo(config)# sh hsrp group 101 ipv6
Vlan101 - Group 101 (HSRP-V2) (IPv6)
  Local state is Active, priority 100 (Cfged 100)
    Forwarding threshold(for vPC), lower: 1 upper: 100
  Hellotime 3 sec, holdtime 10 sec
  Next hello sent in 2.629000 sec(s)
  Virtual IP address is fe80::5:73ff:fea0:65 (Auto)
  Active router is local
  Standby router is fe80::21b:54ff:fec2:ca41 , priority 100 expires in 5.865000
sec(s)
  Authentication text "cisco"
  Virtual mac address is 0005.73a0.0065 (Default MAC)
  2 state changes, last state change 00:00:39
  IP redundancy name is hsrp-Vlan101-101-V6 (default)
  Secondary VIP(s):
                    6000:ab8::1
```

VRRP

Virtual Router Redundancy Protocol (VRRP) is an industry standard introduced to the networking world in 2004 and described in RFC 3768. VRRP enables two or more routers to provide first-hop redundancy services for IP traffic. In VRRP, a virtual IP address is configured and is "owned" by one of the routers participating in the VRRP group to represent the default gateway for a given subnet. If that router fails or is taken out of service, the second router assumes the role of the default gateway using the same MAC address. This prevents the hosts on the network from needing to send an ARP request for the new gateway's MAC address, and traffic is passed with minimal to no disruption.

VRRP is supported on both the Nexus 7000 and 5500 series switches. The examples in this chapter focus on VRRP configuration for the Nexus 7000.

VRRP Configuration

The first step to configure VRRP is to enable it in global configuration mode using the **feature** command, as demonstrated in Example 3-111. With the modular nature of NX-OS, using the **feature** command loads the VRRP modular code into memory for execution. Without the feature enabled, it would not be resident in memory.

Figure 3-12 illustrates the topology used in Examples 3-111 through 3-118.

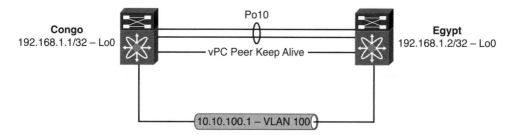

Figure 3-12 *Network Topology for VRRP Configuration*

Example 3-111 *Enabling the VRRP Feature*

```
Congo# config t
Enter configuration commands, one per line. End with CNTL/Z.
Congo(config)# feature vrrp
Congo(config)# end
Congo# show run vrrp
!Command: show running-config vrrp
!Time: Sun Oct 11 23:01:46 2009

version 4.2(2a)
feature vrrp
```

Similar to IOS-based VRRP configuration, the next step is to configure the VRRP process under a VLAN interface, as demonstrated in Example 3-112.

Caution Recommended practice dictates that you should configure all VRRP options such as priority, preempt, authentication, and so on prior to adding the IP address to the group. This minimizes disruption and state change on the network.

Example 3-112 *Configuring VRRP on an SVI*

```
Congo# config t
Enter configuration commands, one per line. End with CNTL/Z.
Congo(config)# int vlan 100
Congo(config-if)# vrrp 100
Congo(config-if-vrrp)# address 10.10.100.1
Congo(config-if-vrrp)# end
Congo# show run vrrp
!Command: show running-config vrrp
!Time: Sun Oct 11 23:04:13 2009

version 4.2(2a)
feature vrrp
```

```
interface Vlan100
  vrrp 100
    address 10.10.100.1
    no shutdown
```

> **Caution**   Unlike HSRP, VRRP groups must be manually enabled before they begin operation.

VRRP Priority and Preempt

NX-OS supports the capability to configure different VRRP priorities to help the network administrator define deterministic switching through the network. Similar to the VRRP implementation in IOS, a device with a higher priority becomes the active gateway and the lower-priority device becomes the standby. The default VRRP priority is 100.

In addition, when a priority is configured, it is typical to configure a **preempt** command to ensure that the active router is consistent after a network change. In Example 3-113, a priority of 200 is configured in addition to a preempt.

> **Caution**   Preempt in VRRP does not support a delay mechanism similar to HSRP and also is enabled by default.

Example 3-113   *Configuring VRRP Priority*

```
Congo# config t
Enter configuration commands, one per line. End with CNTL/Z.
Congo(config)# int vlan 100
Congo(config-if)# vrrp 100
Congo(config-if-vrrp)# priority 200
Congo(config-if-vrrp)# end
Congo# show run vrrp
!Command: show running-config vrrp
!Time: Sun Oct 11 23:10:55 2009

version 4.2(2a)
feature vrrp

interface Vlan100
  vrrp 100
    priority 200
    address 10.10.100.1
    no shutdown
```

Verifying VRRP Configuration

A quick method to use to see the current state of the VRRP configuration is to use the **show vrrp** command, as demonstrated in Example 3-114. The output displays all the parameters configured in Example 3-113, such as priority, preempt, and IP address.

Example 3-114   *Viewing VRRP Status*

```
Congo# show vrrp
      Interface  VR IpVersion Pri   Time Pre State    VR IP addr
_____--

         Vlan100 100    IPV4    200   1 s  Y  Master  10.10.100.1
```

You can display additional details by reviewing the output from the **show vrrp detail** command, as demonstrated in Example 3-115.

Example 3-115   *Viewing VRRP Detail*

```
Congo# show vrrp detail
Vlan100 - Group 100 (IPV4)
    State is Master
    Virtual IP address is 10.10.100.1
    Priority 200, Configured 200
    Forwarding threshold(for VPC), lower: 1 upper: 200
    Advertisement interval 1
    Preemption enabled
    Virtual MAC address is 0000.5e00.0164
    Master router is 10.10.100.2
```

Securing VRRP

Securing VRRP is important in many environments to avoid a new router or device that is added to the network from incorrectly assuming the role of the default gateway on a subnet. VRRP authentication can be configured to prevent such a situation. The current implementation of VRRP authentication in NX-OS provides one form of authentication: plain text. Plain text, as its name implies, has the password used for authentication in clear text and passes it as such on the network.

Example 3-116 shows the use of plaintext authentication.

Example 3-116   *Configuring VRRP Authentication*

```
Congo# config t
Enter configuration commands, one per line. End with CNTL/Z.
Congo(config)# int vlan 100
Congo(config-if)# vrrp 100
Congo(config-if-vrrp)# authentication text vrrp
```

You can see the addition of authentication to the VRRP configuration in the output of **show vrrp detailed,** as demonstrated in Example 3-117.

Example 3-117   *Verification of VRRP Authentication*

```
Egypt# show vrrp det
Vlan100 - Group 100 (IPV4)
    State is Backup
    Virtual IP address is 10.10.100.1
    Priority 100, Configured 100
    Forwarding threshold(for VPC), lower: 1 upper: 100
    Advertisement interval 1
    Preemption disabled
    Authentication text "vrrp"
    Virtual MAC address is 0000.5e00.0164
    Master router is 10.10.100.2
```

VRRP Secondary Support

The implementation of VRRP in NX-OS also supports secondary IP addressing. Secondary IP addresses are typically found in environments under transition to a new IP addressing scheme and are usually temporary.

Example 3-118 shows VRRP configured to provide services to a secondary IP subnet, 172.16.1.0/24.

Example 3-118   *Configuring VRRP for Secondary Subnets*

```
Congo# config t
Enter configuration commands, one per line. End with CNTL/Z.
Congo(config)# int vlan 100
Congo(config-if)# vrrp 100
Congo(config-if-vrrp)# address 172.16.1.1 secondary
Congo(config-if-vrrp)# end
Congo# show vrrp det
Vlan100 - Group 100 (IPV4)
    State is Master
    Virtual IP address is 10.10.100.1
    Secondary Virtual IP address(es):
        172.16.1.1
    Priority 200, Configured 200
    Forwarding threshold(for VPC), lower: 1 upper: 200
    Advertisement interval 1
    Preemption enabled
    Authentication text "vrrp"
    Virtual MAC address is 0000.5e00.0164
    Master router is 10.10.100.2
```

HSRP, VRRP, and vPC Interactions

Both HSRP and VRRP are tightly integrated with vPC, which enables both HSRP and VRRP to operate in an active/active scenario from the data plane via the addition of a G (gateway) flag programmed into the MAC table of both systems for the HSRP MAC address, while the control plane remains active/standby, as illustrated in Figure 3-13. This means that in a vPC topology, both routers are actively forwarding traffic for the HSRP/VRRP VIP but only the active HSRP device responds to ARP requests. No additional configuration is required for this functionality, and it is activated by default. General HSRP and VRRP configuration best practices apply; however, in a vPC environment there is no need to configure nondefault HSRP or VRRP priority and preemption values for load-balancing purposes because this is now a function of vPC. Furthermore, it is highly advised to use default timers to reduce control-plane load because both devices are actively forwarding.

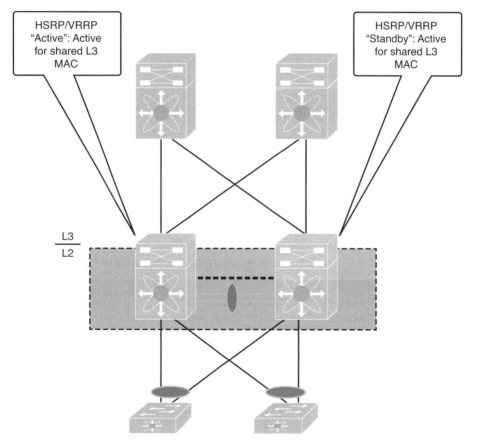

Figure 3-13 *HSRP/VRRP Interaction with vPC*

It is also recommended to configure a method to protect against complete uplink and local Layer 3 failures in a vPC environment. Because vPC employs loop prevention in hardware, it is recommended to implement IGP routing across either a dedicated router link between the vPC peers or via an SVI across the peer-link. Figure 3-14 illustrates a dedicated routed link between the two vPC peers to be used for IGP routing. Using traditional methods such as object-tracking for HSRP/VRRP might lead to a black-hole scenario for traffic being forwarded across two different vPC interfaces. This occurs because a complete local Layer 3 failure on one of the switches would lead to all traffic being forced across the peer-link, triggering vPC to drop any traffic received from the peer-link destined for another vPC interface. IGP routing between vPC peers enables traffic to be properly forwarded if an uplink or local Layer 3 failure occurs.

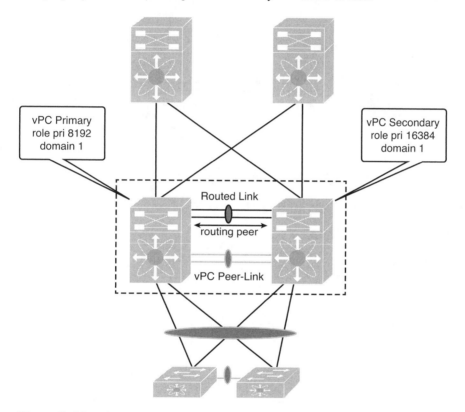

Figure 3-14 *IGP Routing with vPC*

GLBP

Gateway Load Balancing Protocol (GLBP) is a Cisco innovation that, although similar to HSRP and VRRP, provides basic load-balancing capabilities. GLBP enables two or more routers to provide first-hop redundancy services for IP traffic. In GLBP, a virtual IP address is configured and is "owned" by one of the routers participating in the GLBP group to represent the default gateway for a given subnet. The owning router or active virtual gateway (AVG) in a GLBP environment responds to the sender with a unique MAC address to enable the distribution of traffic.

GLBP uses different load-balancing mechanisms to determine the distribution of traffic between the routers participating in the GLBP group.

At the time of this writing, GLBP is supported on the Nexus 7000 series switches.

GLBP Configuration

The first step to configure GLBP is to enable it in global configuration mode using the **feature** command, as demonstrated in Example 3-119. With the modular nature of NX-OS, using the **feature** command loads the GLBP modular code into memory for execution. Without the feature enabled, it would not be resident in memory.

Figure 3-15 illustrates the topology used in Examples 3-119 through 3-128.

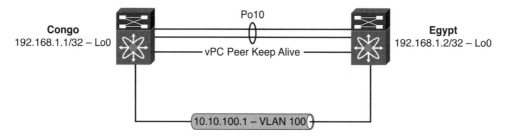

Figure 3-15 *Network Topology for GLBP Configuration*

Example 3-119 *Enabling the GLBP Feature*

```
Congo# config t
Enter configuration commands, one per line. End with CNTL/Z.
Congo(config)# feature glbp
Congo(config)# end
Congo# show run glbp
!Command: show running-config glbp
!Time: Sun Oct 11 23:36:24 2009
version 4.2(2a)
feature glbp
```

Similar to IOS-based GLBP configuration, the next step is to configure the GLBP process under a VLAN interface, as demonstrated in Example 3-120.

Caution Recommended practice dictates that you should configure all GLBP options such as priority, preempt, authentication, and so on prior to adding the IP address to the group. This minimizes disruption and state change on the network.

Example 3-120 *Configuring GLBP on an SVI*

```
Congo# config t
Enter configuration commands, one per line. End with CNTL/Z.
Congo(config)# int vlan 100
Congo(config-if)# glbp 100
Congo(config-if-glbp)# ip 10.10.100.1
Congo# show run glbp
!Command: show running-config glbp
!Time: Sun Oct 11 23:38:42 2009
version 4.2(2a)
feature glbp

interface Vlan100
  glbp 100
    ip 10.10.100.1
```

GLBP Priority and Preempt

NX-OS supports the capability to configure different GLBP priorities. In GLBP, the priority determines the AVG for each group. The AVG is responsible for assigning virtual MAC addresses to each member of the GLBP group including itself. This enables each router to have an AVF that is responsible for forwarding traffic directed to its virtual MAC address. The default priority is 100.

In Example 3-121, a priority of 200 is configured in addition to a preempt that uses the capability to wait a specified amount of time before preempting for the AVG role.

Example 3-121 *Configuring GLBP Priority and Preemption*

```
Congo# config t
Enter configuration commands, one per line. End with CNTL/Z.
Congo(config)# int vlan 100
Congo(config-if)# glbp 100
Congo(config-if-glbp)# priority 200
Congo(config-if-glbp)# preempt
Congo(config-if-glbp)# end
Congo# show run glbp
!Command: show running-config glbp
!Time: Sun Oct 11 23:49:01 2009
version 4.2(2a)
feature glbp

interface Vlan100
  glbp 100
```

```
ip 10.10.100.1
priority 200
preempt
```

Verifying GLBP Configuration

A quick method to use to see the current state of the GLBP configuration is to use the **show glbp** command, as demonstrated in Example 3-122. The output displays all the parameters configured in Example 3-122, such as priority, preempt, and IP address.

Example 3-122   *Verification of GLBP Priority and Preemption*

```
Congo# show glbp
Vlan100 - Group 100
   State is Active
     4 state change(s), last state change(s) 00:11:13
   Virtual IP address is 10.10.100.1
   Hello time 3 sec, hold time 10 sec
     Next hello sent in 2.480 sec
   Redirect time 600 sec, forwarder time-out 14400 sec
   Preemption enabled, min delay 0 sec
   Active is local
   Standby is 10.10.100.3, priority 100 (expires in 7.221 sec)
   Priority 200 (configured)
   Weighting 100 (default 100), thresholds: lower 1, upper 100
   Load balancing: round-robin
   Group members:
     001B.54C2.7641 (10.10.100.2) local
     001B.54C2.78C1 (10.10.100.3)
   There are 2 forwarders (1 active)
   Forwarder 1
    State is Active
       2 state change(s), last state change 00:11:03
    MAC address is 0007.B400.6401 (default)
    Owner ID is 001B.54C2.7641
    Preemption enabled, min delay 30 sec
    Active is local, weighting 100
   Forwarder 2
    State is Listen
       1 state change(s), last state change 00:03:10
    MAC address is 0007.B400.6402 (learnt)
    Owner ID is 001B.54C2.78C1
    Redirection enabled, 597.221 sec remaining (maximum 600 sec)
    Time to live: 14397.221 sec (maximum 14400 sec)
    Preemption enabled, min delay 30 sec
    Active is 10.10.100.3 (primary), weighting 100 (expires in 7.221 sec)
```

Securing GLBP

Securing GLBP is important in many environments to avoid a new router or device that is added to the network from incorrectly assuming the role of the default gateway on a subnet. GLBP authentication can be configured to prevent such a situation. The implementation of GLBP authentication in NX-OS provides two forms of authentication:

■ **Plain text:** Has the password used for authentication in clear text and passes it as such on the network

■ **MD5:** Uses the MD5 algorithm to hash the password before it is passed across the network

Example 3-123 shows the configuration of plain-text authentication.

Example 3-123 *Configuring GLBP Clear-Text Authentication*

```
Congo# config t
Enter configuration commands, one per line. End with CNTL/Z.
Congo(config)# int vlan100
Congo(config-if)# glbp 100
Congo(config-if-hsrp)# authentication text glbp
```

You can confirm the addition of authentication to the GLBP configuration from the output of the **show glbp** command, as demonstrated in Example 3-124.

Example 3-124 *Verification of GLBP Clear-Text Authentication*

```
Congo# show glbp
Vlan100 - Group 100
  State is Active
    4 state change(s), last state change(s) 00:19:40
  Virtual IP address is 10.10.100.1
  Hello time 3 sec, hold time 10 sec
    Next hello sent in 2.890 sec
  Redirect time 600 sec, forwarder time-out 14400 sec
  Authentication text "glbp"
  Preemption enabled, min delay 0 sec
  Active is local
  Standby is 10.10.100.3, priority 100 (expires in 7.827 sec)
  Priority 200 (configured)
  Weighting 100 (default 100), thresholds: lower 1, upper 100
  Load balancing: round-robin
  Group members:
    001B.54C2.7641 (10.10.100.2) local
    001B.54C2.78C1 (10.10.100.3)
  There are 2 forwarders (1 active)
```

```
Forwarder 1
  State is Active
     2 state change(s), last state change 00:19:30
  MAC address is 0007.B400.6401 (default)
  Owner ID is 001B.54C2.7641
  Preemption enabled, min delay 30 sec
  Active is local, weighting 100
Forwarder 2
  State is Listen
     3 state change(s), last state change 00:00:54
  MAC address is 0007.B400.6402 (learnt)
  Owner ID is 001B.54C2.78C1
  Redirection enabled, 597.827 sec remaining (maximum 600 sec)
  Time to live: 14397.827 sec (maximum 14400 sec)
  Preemption enabled, min delay 30 sec
  Active is 10.10.100.3 (primary), weighting 100 (expires in 7.827 sec)
```

Configuring MD5 authentication is a multistep process. You must first define a keychain that contains attributes like the password to be used to authenticate the connection and lifetime of the key chain for both sending and receiving, as demonstrated in Example 3-125.

Example 3-125   *Configuring a Keychain*

```
Congo(config)# key chain nexus
Congo(config-keychain)# key 1
Congo(config-keychain-key)# key-string nexus
```

The next step is to enable authentication under the GLBP process, as demonstrated in Example 3-126, and reference the keychain created in Example 3-125.

Example 3-126   *Configuring GLBP MD5 Authentication*

```
Congo# config t
Enter configuration commands, one per line. End with CNTL/Z.
Congo(config)# int vlan 100
Congo(config-if)# glbp 100
Congo(config-if-glbp)# authentication md5 key-chain nexus
```

You can verify that the MD5 authentication is in place via the **show glbp** command, as demonstrated in Example 3-127.

Example 3-127 *Verification of GLBP MD5 Authentication*

```
Congo# show glbp
Vlan100 - Group 100
   State is Active
      4 state change(s), last state change(s) 00:21:30
   Virtual IP address is 10.10.100.1
   Hello time 3 sec, hold time 10 sec
     Next hello sent in 2.500 sec
   Redirect time 600 sec, forwarder time-out 14400 sec
   Authentication MD5, key-chain "nexus"
   Preemption enabled, min delay 0 sec
   Active is local
   Standby is 10.10.100.3, priority 100 (expires in 7.458 sec)
   Priority 200 (configured)
   Weighting 100 (default 100), thresholds: lower 1, upper 100
   Load balancing: round-robin
   Group members:
     001B.54C2.7641 (10.10.100.2) local
     001B.54C2.78C1 (10.10.100.3) authenticated
   There are 2 forwarders (1 active)
   Forwarder 1
    State is Active
       2 state change(s), last state change 00:21:20
    MAC address is 0007.B400.6401 (default)
    Owner ID is 001B.54C2.7641
    Preemption enabled, min delay 30 sec (00:00:08 secs remaining)
    Active is local, weighting 100
   Forwarder 2
    State is Listen
       5 state change(s), last state change 00:00:21
    MAC address is 0007.B400.6402 (learnt)
    Owner ID is 001B.54C2.78C1
    Redirection enabled, 597.458 sec remaining (maximum 600 sec)
    Time to live: 14397.458 sec (maximum 14400 sec)
    Preemption enabled, min delay 30 sec
    Active is 10.10.100.3 (primary), weighting 100 (expires in 7.458 sec)
```

GLBP Secondary Support

The implementation of GLBP in NX-OS also supports secondary IP addressing. Secondary IP addresses are typically found in environments that are under transition to a new IP addressing scheme and are usually temporary.

Example 3-128 shows GLBP configured to provide services to a secondary IP subnet, 172.16.1.0/24.

Example 3-128   *Configuring GLBP for Secondary Subnets*

```
Congo# config t
Enter configuration commands, one per line. End with CNTL/Z.
Congo(config)# int vlan 100
Congo(config-if)# ip address 172.16.1.2/24 secondary
Congo(config-if)# glbp 100
Congo(config-if-glbp)# ip 172.16.1.1 secondary
Congo(config-if-glbp)# show glbp
Vlan100 - Group 100
  State is Active
    4 state change(s), last state change(s) 00:23:27
  Virtual IP address is 10.10.100.1
    Secondary virtual IP address 172.16.1.1
  Hello time 3 sec, hold time 10 sec
    Next hello sent in 190 msec
  Redirect time 600 sec, forwarder time-out 14400 sec
  Authentication MD5, key-chain "nexus"
  Preemption enabled, min delay 0 sec
  Active is local
  Standby is 10.10.100.3, priority 100 (expires in 7.980 sec)
  Priority 200 (configured)
  Weighting 100 (default 100), thresholds: lower 1, upper 100
  Load balancing: round-robin
  Group members:
    001B.54C2.7641 (10.10.100.2) local
    001B.54C2.78C1 (10.10.100.3) authenticated
  There are 2 forwarders (1 active)
  Forwarder 1
   State is Active
     2 state change(s), last state change 00:23:17
   MAC address is 0007.B400.6401 (default)
   Owner ID is 001B.54C2.7641
   Preemption enabled, min delay 30 sec
   Active is local, weighting 100
  Forwarder 2
   State is Listen
     5 state change(s), last state change 00:02:18
   MAC address is 0007.B400.6402 (learnt)
   Owner ID is 001B.54C2.78C1
```

```
Redirection enabled, 597.980 sec remaining (maximum 600 sec)
Time to live: 14397.980 sec (maximum 14400 sec)
Preemption enabled, min delay 30 sec
Active is 10.10.100.3 (primary), weighting 100 (expires in 7.980 sec)
```

Summary

The Layer 3 routing capabilities of NX-OS are flexible and incorporate a wide range of IGPs in addition to BGP with support for both IPv4 and IPv6. Combining an underlying architecture focused on high availability with years of routing experience makes a compelling operating system. With VRF-aware features as a standard offering, along with support for both Cisco-innovated and industry-standard protocols, the network administrator can easily develop and deploy flexible, scalable, and resilient data center architectures.

Chapter 4

IP Multicast Configuration

This chapter covers the following topics:

- Multicast operation

- PIM configuration on Nexus 7000 and Nexus 5500

- IGMP operation

- IGMP configuration on Nexus 7000

- IGMP configuration on Nexus 5x00

- IGMP configuration on Nexus 1000V

- MSDP configuration on Nexus 7000 and Nexus 5500

- Administrative scoping of multicast RPs in PIM

- PIM prune and join policies

Cisco NX-OS was designed to be a data center-class operating system. A component of such an operating system includes support for a rich set of IP multicast features, including key capabilities such as Internet Group Management Protocol (IGMP), Protocol Independent Multicast (PIM) sparse mode, Source Specific Multicast (SSM), Multicast Source Discovery Protocol (MSDP), and Multiprotocol Border Gateway Protocol (MBGP).

Multicast Operation

As a technology, IP multicast enables a single flow of traffic to be received by multiple destinations in an efficient manner. This provides an optimal use of network bandwidth wherein destinations that do not want to receive the traffic do not have it sent to them. There are multiple methodologies used to provide this functionality that cover aspects such as discovery of sources and receivers and delivery mechanisms. Multicast is a network-centric technology and as such, the network equipment between the sender of multicast traffic and the receivers must be multicast-aware and understand the services and addressing used by multicast. In IPv4, multicast uses a block of addresses that has been set aside by the Internet Assigned Number Authority (IANA). This range of addresses is the Class D block 224.0.0.0 through 239.255.255.255, and within this block a range has been set aside for private intranet usage, similar to Request for Comments (RFC) 1918 addressing for unicast. RFC 2365, "Administratively Scoped IP Multicast," documents this usage and allocates addresses in the 239.0.0.0 through 239.255.255.255 range for private use. Each individual multicast address can represent a group that the receivers then request to join.

The network listens for receivers to signal their requirement to join a group. The network then begins to forward and replicate the data from the source to the receivers that join the group. This is significantly more efficient than generally flooding the traffic to all systems on a network to only have the traffic discarded.

Multicast Distribution Trees

Multiple methods can be used to control and optimize the learning and forwarding of multicast traffic through the network. A key concept to understand is a *distribution tree*, which represents the path that multicast data takes across the network between the sources of traffic and the receivers. NX-OS can build different multicast distribution trees to support different multicast technologies such as Source Specific Multicast (SSM), Any Source Multicast (ASM), and Bi-Directional (BiDir).

The first multicast distribution tree is the source tree, which represents the shortest path that multicast traffic follows through the network from the source transmitting to a group address and the receivers that request the traffic from the group, which is the Shortest Path Tree (SPT).

Figure 4-1 depicts a source tree for group 239.0.0.1 with a source on Host A and receivers on Hosts B and C.

The next multicast distribution tree is the *shared tree*. The shared tree represents a shared distribution path that multicast traffic follows through the network from a network-centric function called the *Rendezvous Point (RP)* to the receivers that request the traffic from the group. The RP creates a source tree, or SPT, to the source. The shared tree can also be referred to as the RP tree or RPT.

Figure 4-2 depicts a shared tree, or RPT, for group 239.0.0.10 with a source on Host A. Router C is the RP, and the receivers are Hosts B and C.

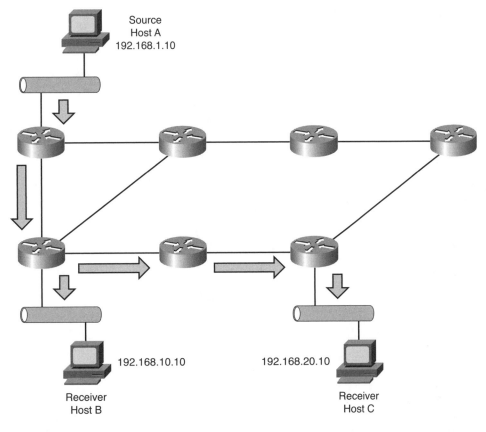

Figure 4-1   *Source Tree or SPT for 239.0.0.1*

The final multicast distribution tree is the Bi-Directional shared tree or *BiDir*, which represents a shared distribution path that multicast traffic follows through the network from the RP or a shared root to the receivers that request the traffic from the group. The capability to send multicast traffic from the shared root can provide a more efficient method of traffic delivery and optimize the amount of state the network must maintain.

> **Note**   One of the primary scalability considerations in a multicast design is the amount of information the network needs to maintain for the multicast traffic to work. This information is referred to as *state* and contains the multicast routing table, information on senders and receivers, and other metrics on the traffic.

Figure 4-3 depicts a shared tree, or RPT, for group 239.0.0.10 with a source on Host A. Router D is the RP, and the receivers are Hosts B and C.

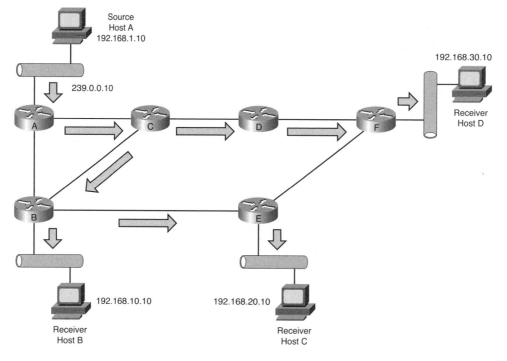

Figure 4-2 *Shared Tree or RPT for 239.0.0.10*

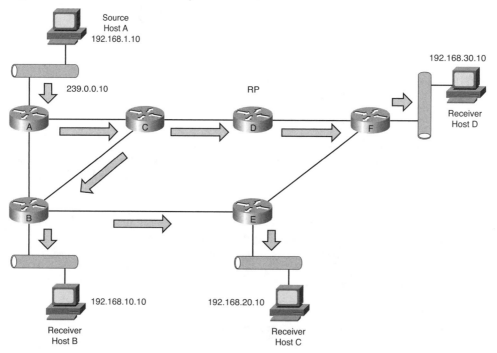

Figure 4-3 *Bidirectional Shared Tree for 239.0.0.25*

Reverse Path Forwarding

An additional concept beyond multicast distribution trees that is important for multicast is that of Reverse Path Forwarding (RPF). Multicast, by design, is traffic not intended for every system on a network but rather sent only to receivers that request it. Routers in the network must form a path toward the source or RP. The path from the source to the receivers flows in the reverse direction from which the path was created when the receiver requested to join the group. Each incoming multicast packet undergoes an RPF check to verify it was received on an interface leading to the source. If the packet passes the RPF check, it is forwarded; if not, the packet is discarded. The RPF check is done to minimize the potential for duplicated packets and maintain source integrity.

Protocol Independent Multicast (PIM)

With a solid understanding of the multicast distribution tree modes and the RPF, the next concept is Protocol Independent Multicast (PIM), which is an industry-standard protocol developed to leverage any existing underlying Interior Gateway Routing (IGP) protocol, such as Enhanced Interior Gateway Routing Protocol (EIGRP), Open Shortest Path First (OSPF), or Routing Information Protocol (RIP), to determine the path of multicast packets in the network. PIM does not maintain its own routing table and as such has a much lower overhead when compared with other multicast routing technologies.

In general, PIM can operate in two modes: dense mode and sparse mode. NX-OS supports only sparse mode because most dense mode applications have been depreciated from networks, and the flood and prune behavior of dense mode is not efficient for modern data centers.

PIM sparse mode mechanics entail neighbor relationships between PIM-enabled devices. These neighbor relationships determine PIM-enabled paths in a network and enable the building of distribution trees through the network. As mentioned, PIM leverages the existing unicast routing table for path selection. This gives PIM a dynamic capability to adapt the multicast topology to match the unicast topology as the network changes because of link failures, system maintenance, or administrative policy.

NX-OS implementation of PIM supports three modes:

- **Any Source Multicast (ASM):** Uses RPs with a shared tree to discover sources and receivers. ASM also supports the capability for traffic to be switched from the shared tree to an SPT between the source and receiver if signaled to do so. ASM is the default mode when an RP is configured.

- **Source Specific Multicast (SSM):** Unlike ASM or BiDir, does not use RPs and instead builds SPTs between the source and receivers. SSM sends an immediate join to the source and reduces state in the network. SSM is also frequently used to facilitate communication between PIM domains where sources are not dynamically learned via MSDP or other mechanisms. SSM relies on the receivers to use IGMPv3, as discussed in the next section.

■ **Bidirectional shared tree (BiDir):** Similar to ASM in that it builds a shared tree between receivers and the RP, but unlike ASM does not support switching over to an SPT. With BiDir, the routers closest to the receivers take on a role called *Designated Forwarder (DF)*. This enables the source to send traffic directly to the DF without passing through the RP and may be a significant benefit in some environments.

A final option would be to configure static RPF routes that would force multicast traffic to not follow the unicast table. As with most static routes, the opportunity for dynamic failover and changes to the multicast routing might be compromised, so you should give careful consideration when employing this option.

The ASM, BiDir, SSM, and static RPF modes are typically deployed within a single PIM domain. In cases where multicast traffic needs to cross multiple PIM domains and Border Gateway Protocol (BGP) is used to interconnect the networks, the Multicast Source Discovery Protocol (MSDP) is typically used. MSDP is used to advertise sources in each domain without needing to share domain-specific state and scales well.

RPs

Rendezvous Points are key to the successful forwarding of multicast traffic for ASM and BiDir configurations. Given this importance, there are multiple methods to configure RPs and learn about them in the network. RPs are routers that the network administrator selects to perform this role and are the shared root for RPTs. A network can have multiple RPs designated to service particular groups or have a single RP that services all groups.

Following are four primary methods to configure RPs in NX-OS:

■ **Static RPs:** As their name implies, Static RPs are statically configured on every router in the PIM domain. This is the simplest method for RP configuration, although it requires configuration on every PIM device.

■ **Bootstrap Routers (BSRs):** Distribute the same RP cache information to every router in the PIM domain. This is done by the BSR when it sends BSR messages out all PIM-enabled interfaces. These messages are flooded hop-by-hop to all routers in the network. The BSR candidate role is configured on the router, and an election is performed to determine the single BSR for the domain.

When the BSR is elected, messages from candidate RPs are received, via unicast, for each multicast group. The BSR sends these candidate RPs out in BSR messages, and every router in the PIM domain runs the same algorithm against the list of candidate RPs. Because each router has the same list of candidate RPs and each router runs the same algorithm to determine the RP, every router selects the same RP.

Note   BSR is described in RFC 5059 and provides a nonproprietary method for RP definition.

Caution   Do not configure both Auto-RP and BSR protocols in the same network. Auto-RP is the Cisco proprietary implementation of what was standardized as BSR, and they serve the same purpose. As such, only one is needed. Inconsistent multicast routing can be observed if both are configured.

- **Auto-RP:** A Cisco proprietary protocol to define RPs in a network. Auto-RP was developed before BSR was standardized. Auto-RP uses candidate mapping agents and RPs to determine the RP for a group. A primary difference between Auto-RP and BSR is that Auto-RP uses multicast to deliver the candidate-RP group messages on multicast group 224.0.1.39. The mapping agent sends the group to the RP mapping table on multicast group 224.0.1.40.

- **Anycast-RP:** Another methodology to advertise RPs in a network. There are two implementations of Anycast-RP. One uses MSDP and the other is based on RFC 4610, PIM Anycast-RP. With Anycast-RP, the same IP address is configured on multiple routers, typically a loopback interface. Because PIM uses the underlying unicast routing table, the closest RP will be used. Anycast is the only RP method that enables more than one RP to be active, which enables load-balancing and additional fault tolerance options.

Note   Anycast-RP doesn't advertise the RP to the multicast table but rather the unicast table. Due to this behavior, it is not necessary to configure the Anycast-RP loopback with PIM. The RP still needs to be dynamically discovered using technologies such as BSR or Auto-RP or statically defined to make a complete and working configuration.

PIM Configuration on Nexus 7000 and Nexus 5500

PIM within NX-OS is compatible with PIM on IOS devices enabling a smooth integration of Nexus equipment with existing gear.

Note   PIM is a Layer 3 protocol and as such does not work on Nexus 5000, 2000, and 1000V switches because they are Layer 2-only. The Nexus 5500 can be equipped with a Layer 3 module, which provides support for the PIM configurations illustrated.

The first step to configure PIM is to enable it on global configuration mode using the **feature** command. With the modular nature of NX-OS, using the **feature** command loads the PIM modular code into memory for execution. Without the feature enabled, it would not be resident in memory. In Example 4-1, PIM is enabled as a feature on Router N7K-1-Core and sparse mode is configured on interfaces e4/1 and e4/7 per the topology depicted in Figure 4-4, which serves as the topology for all the following PIM configuration examples.

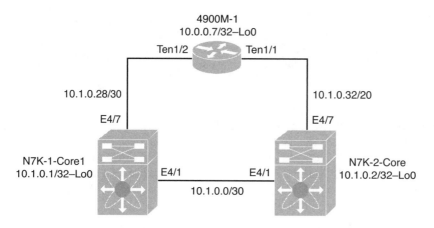

Figure 4-4 *Basic Multicast Topology*

Example 4-1 *Enabling the PIM Feature and Basic Interface Configuration*

```
N7K-1-Core1# config
Enter configuration commands, one per line.   End with CNTL/Z.
N7K-1-Core1(config)# feature pim
N7K-1-Core1(config)# int e4/1
N7K-1-Core1(config-if)# ip pim sparse-mode
N7K-1-Core1(config-if)# int e4/7
N7K-1-Core1(config-if)# ip pim sparse-mode
N7K-1-Core1(config)# end
N7K-1-Core1# show run pim


!Command: show running-config pim
!Time: Mon Jul  9 13:01:20 2012


version 6.1(1)
feature pim


ip pim ssm range 232.0.0.0/8



interface Ethernet4/1
  ip pim sparse-mode


interface Ethernet4/7
  ip pim sparse-mode


N7K-1-Core1#
```

> **Note**   To add PIM to the configuration on an interface, it must be an L3 port. If L2 were selected as a default during initial setup, the **no switchport** command must be used before PIM can be configured.

With PIM sparse mode enabled, more options can be configured per interface including authentication, priority, hello interval border, and neighbor policy.

> **Note**   You can find additional information about these options at Cisco.com at http://www.cisco.com/en/US/docs/switches/datacenter/sw/nx-os/multicast/configuration/guide/b_multicast.html.

In Example 4-2, authentication is enabled on the PIM hellos for interface e4/1.

Example 4-2   *Configuration of PIM Hello Authentication*

```
N7K-1-Core1# config
Enter configuration commands, one per line.  End with CNTL/Z.
N7K-1-Core1(config)# interface e4/1
N7K-1-Core1(config-if)# ip pim hello-authentication ah-md5 cisco
N7K-1-Core1(config-if)# end

N7K-1-Core1# show ip pim neighbor
PIM Neighbor Status for VRF "default"
Neighbor         Interface            Uptime    Expires   DR        Bidir-  BFD
                                                          Priority  Capable State
10.1.0.2         Ethernet4/1          00:00:16  00:01:32  1         yes     n/a
N7K-1-Core1# show ip pim interface e4/1
PIM Interface Status for VRF "default"
Ethernet4/1, Interface status: protocol-up/link-up/admin-up
  IP address: 10.1.0.1, IP subnet: 10.1.0.0/30
  PIM DR: 10.1.0.2, DR's priority: 1
  PIM neighbor count: 1
  PIM hello interval: 30 secs, next hello sent in: 00:00:01
  PIM neighbor holdtime: 105 secs
  PIM configured DR priority: 1
  PIM border interface: no
  PIM GenID sent in Hellos: 0x1b66fb55
  PIM Hello MD5-AH Authentication: enabled
  PIM Neighbor policy: none configured
  PIM Join-Prune inbound policy: none configured
  PIM Join-Prune outbound policy: none configured
  PIM Join-Prune interval: 1 minutes
  PIM Join-Prune next sending: 1 minutes
```

```
    PIM BFD enabled: no
    PIM Interface Statistics, last reset: never
      General (sent/received):
        Hellos: 15/10, JPs: 0/0, Asserts: 0/0
        Grafts: 0/0, Graft-Acks: 0/0
        DF-Offers: 0/0, DF-Winners: 0/0, DF-Backoffs: 0/0, DF-Passes: 0/0
      Errors:
        Checksum errors: 0, Invalid packet types/DF subtypes: 0/0
        Authentication failed: 4
        Packet length errors: 0, Bad version packets: 0, Packets from self: 0
        Packets from non-neighbors: 0
        JPs received on RPF-interface: 0
        (*,G) Joins received with no/wrong RP: 0/0
        (*,G)/(S,G) JPs received for SSM/Bidir groups: 0/0
        JPs filtered by inbound policy: 0
        JPs filtered by outbound policy: 0
N7K-1-Core1#
```

When PIM sparse mode is enabled on all interfaces that need to participate in multicast, the next step is to configure the RPs. As previously discussed, multiple methods of RP configuration exist.

Configuring Static RPs

The first configuration methodology for RPs is static RP. Example 4-3 illustrates the steps required to configure a static RP on Router N7K-1-Core1.

Example 4-3   *Configuration of a Static RP*

```
N7K-1-Core1# show ip pim rp
PIM RP Status Information for VRF "default"
BSR disabled
Auto-RP disabled
BSR RP Candidate policy: None
BSR RP policy: None
Auto-RP Announce policy: None
Auto-RP Discovery policy: None

N7K-1-Core1# config
Enter configuration commands, one per line.  End with CNTL/Z.
N7K-1-Core1(config)# ip pim rp-address 10.1.0.1
N7K-1-Core1(config)# end
N7K-1-Core1# show ip pim rp
PIM RP Status Information for VRF "default"
BSR disabled
```

```
Auto-RP disabled

BSR RP Candidate policy: None

BSR RP policy: None

Auto-RP Announce policy: None

Auto-RP Discovery policy: None


RP: 10.1.0.1*, (0), uptime: 00:00:02, expires: never,
  priority: 0, RP-source: (local), group ranges:
      224.0.0.0/4
N7K-1-Core1#
```

In the output in Example 4-3, the static RP configured supports all multicast traffic for 224.0.0.0/4. NX-OS enables the configuration of multiple RP addresses to service different group ranges. In Example 4-4, N7K-1-Core1's configuration is modified to use N7K-2-Core as the RP for 239.0.0.0/8.

Example 4-4   *Configuring a Group Range Per RP*

```
N7K-1-Core1# show ip pim rp
PIM RP Status Information for VRF "default"
BSR disabled
Auto-RP disabled
BSR RP Candidate policy: None
BSR RP policy: None
Auto-RP Announce policy: None
Auto-RP Discovery policy: None


RP: 10.1.0.1*, (0), uptime: 00:03:07, expires: never,
  priority: 0, RP-source: (local), group ranges:
      224.0.0.0/4
N7K-1-Core1# config
Enter configuration commands, one per line.  End with CNTL/Z.
N7K-1-Core1(config)# ip pim rp-address 10.1.0.2 group-list 238.0.0.0/8
N7K-1-Core1(config)# end
N7K-1-Core1# show ip pim rp
PIM RP Status Information for VRF "default"
BSR disabled
Auto-RP disabled
BSR RP Candidate policy: None
BSR RP policy: None
Auto-RP Announce policy: None
Auto-RP Discovery policy: None


RP: 10.1.0.1*, (0), uptime: 00:03:07, expires: never,
  priority: 0, RP-source: (local), group ranges:
```

```
    224.0.0.0/4
RP: 10.1.0.2, (0), uptime: 0.016089, expires: never,
  priority: 0, RP-source: (local), group ranges:
      238.0.0.0/8
N7K-1-Core1#
```

Configuring BSRs

The next RP configuration methodology is Bootstrap Router (BSR). In Example 4-5, N7K-1-Core1 is configured with both a bsr-candidate and bsr rp-candidate policy for groups in the 239.0.0.0/8 range. This enables N7K-1-Core1 to participate in BSR elections and, if elected as a RP, apply a policy determining which routes will be advertised. N7K-1-Core1 is configured to listen to BSR messages as well.

Example 4-5 *BSR Base Configuration*

```
N7K-1-Core1# show ip pim rp
PIM RP Status Information for VRF "default"
BSR disabled
Auto-RP disabled
BSR RP Candidate policy: None
BSR RP policy: None
Auto-RP Announce policy: None
Auto-RP Discovery policy: None

RP: 10.1.0.1*, (0), uptime: 00:05:04, expires: never,
  priority: 0, RP-source: (local), group ranges:
      224.0.0.0/4
RP: 10.1.0.2, (0), uptime: 00:01:57, expires: never,
  priority: 0, RP-source: (local), group ranges:
      238.0.0.0/8
N7K-1-Core1#
N7K-1-Core1# config
Enter configuration commands, one per line.  End with CNTL/Z.
N7K-1-Core1(config)# ip pim bsr bsr-candidate e4/1
N7K-1-Core1(config)# ip pim bsr rp-candidate e4/1 group-list 239.0.0.0/8
N7K-1-Core1(config)# end
N7K-1-Core1# show ip pim rp
PIM RP Status Information for VRF "default"
BSR: 10.1.0.1*, next Bootstrap message in: 00:00:55,
    priority: 64, hash-length: 30
Auto-RP disabled
BSR RP Candidate policy: None
BSR RP policy: None
```

```
Auto-RP Announce policy: None
Auto-RP Discovery policy: None


RP: 10.1.0.1*, (0), uptime: 00:05:06, expires: 00:02:27 (B),
  priority: 192, RP-source: 10.1.0.1 (B), (local), group ranges:
      239.0.0.0/8   224.0.0.0/4
RP: 10.1.0.2, (0), uptime: 00:01:59, expires: never,
  priority: 0, RP-source: (local), group ranges:
      238.0.0.0/8
N7K-1-Core1#


N7K-2-Core# show ip pim rp
PIM RP Status Information for VRF "default"
BSR disabled
Auto-RP disabled
BSR RP Candidate policy: None
BSR RP policy: None
Auto-RP Announce policy: None
Auto-RP Discovery policy: None


N7K-2-Core# config
N7K-2-Core(config)# ip pim bsr listen
N7K-2-Core(config)# end
N7K-2-Core# show ip pim rp
PIM RP Status Information for VRF "default"
BSR listen-only mode
BSR: 10.1.0.1, uptime: 00:00:16, expires: 00:01:53,
     priority: 64, hash-length: 30
Auto-RP disabled
BSR RP Candidate policy: None
BSR RP policy: None
Auto-RP Announce policy: None
Auto-RP Discovery policy: None


RP: 10.1.0.1, (0), uptime: 00:00:16, expires: 00:02:13,
  priority: 192, RP-source: 10.1.0.1 (B), group ranges:
      239.0.0.0/8
N7K-2-Core#
```

Configuring BSR for BiDir is simply a matter of adding **bidir** to the **rp-candidate** command. Example 4-6 illustrates this, and you can see the change on N7K-1-Core1.

Example 4-6   *Configuring BSR and BiDir*

```
N7K-1-Core1# show ip pim rp
PIM RP Status Information for VRF "default"
BSR disabled
Auto-RP disabled
BSR RP Candidate policy: None
BSR RP policy: None
Auto-RP Announce policy: None
Auto-RP Discovery policy: None


N7K-1-Core1# show ip pim group
PIM Group-Range Configuration for VRF "default"
Group-range        Mode      RP-address         Shared-tree-only range
232.0.0.0/8        SSM       -                  -
N7K-1-Core1#
N7K-1-Core1# config
Enter configuration commands, one per line.  End with CNTL/Z.
N7K-1-Core1(config)# ip pim bsr bsr-candidate e4/1
N7K-1-Core1(config)# ip pim bsr rp-candidate e4/1 group-list 239.0.0.0/8 bidir
N7K-1-Core1(config)# end
N7K-1-Core1# show ip pim rp
PIM RP Status Information for VRF "default"
BSR: 10.1.0.1*, next Bootstrap message in: 00:00:59,
     priority: 64, hash-length: 30
Auto-RP disabled
BSR RP Candidate policy: None
BSR RP policy: None
Auto-RP Announce policy: None
Auto-RP Discovery policy: None


RP: 10.1.0.1*, (1), uptime: 0.007167, expires: 00:02:29,
  priority: 192, RP-source: 10.1.0.1 (B), group ranges:
     239.0.0.0/8  (bidir)
N7K-1-Core1# show ip pim group
PIM Group-Range Configuration for VRF "default"
Group-range        Mode      RP-address         Shared-tree-only range
232.0.0.0/8        SSM       -                  -
239.0.0.0/8        Bidir     10.1.0.1           -
N7K-1-Core1#


N7K-2-Core# config
Enter configuration commands, one per line.  End with CNTL/Z.
N7K-2-Core(config)# ip pim bsr listen
N7K-2-Core(config)# end
```

```
N7K-2-Core# show ip pim rp
PIM RP Status Information for VRF "default"
BSR listen-only mode
BSR: 10.1.0.1, uptime: 00:00:18, expires: 00:01:51,
     priority: 64, hash-length: 30
Auto-RP disabled
BSR RP Candidate policy: None
BSR RP policy: None
Auto-RP Announce policy: None
Auto-RP Discovery policy: None

RP: 10.1.0.1, (1), uptime: 00:00:18, expires: 00:02:11,
  priority: 192, RP-source: 10.1.0.1 (B), group ranges:
      239.0.0.0/8  (bidir)
N7K-2-Core# show ip pim group
PIM Group-Range Configuration for VRF "default"
Group-range       Mode      RP-address       Shared-tree-only range
232.0.0.0/8       SSM       -                -
239.0.0.0/8       Bidir     10.1.0.1         -
N7K-2-Core#
```

Configuring Auto-RP

NX-OS also supports Auto-RP, a Cisco-specific precursor to BSR. In Example 4-7, N7K-1-Core1 is configured as both a mapping agent and candidate RP. A mapping agent is a role a router can take in an Auto-RP network responsible for RP elections based on information sent from candidate RPs. A candidate RP in an Auto-RP network advertises its capability to serve as an RP to the mapping agent. This can be useful to help scale networks as they grow. N7K-2-Core is configured to listen and forward Auto-RP messages.

Example 4-7 *Configuring an Auto-RP Mapping Agent and Candidate RP*

```
N7K-1-Core1#show ip pim rp
PIM RP Status Information for VRF "default"
BSR disabled
Auto-RP disabled
BSR RP Candidate policy: None
BSR RP policy: None
Auto-RP Announce policy: None
Auto-RP Discovery policy: None

N7K-1-Core1#config
Enter configuration commands, one per line.  End with CNTL/Z.
N7K-1-Core1(config)# ip pim auto-rp forward listen
```

```
N7K-1-Core1(config)# ip pim auto-rp rp-candidate e4/1 group-list 239.0.0.0/8
N7K-1-Core1(config)# ip pim auto-rp mapping-agent e4/1
N7K-1-Core1(config)# end
N7K-1-Core1# show ip pim rp
PIM RP Status Information for VRF "default"
BSR disabled
Auto-RP RPA: 10.1.0.1*, next Discovery message in: 00:00:53
BSR RP Candidate policy: None
BSR RP policy: None
Auto-RP Announce policy: None
Auto-RP Discovery policy: None


RP: 10.1.0.1*, (0), uptime: 00:03:19, expires: 00:02:31,
  priority: 0, RP-source: 10.1.0.1 (A), group ranges:
      239.0.0.0/8


N7K-1-Core1#


N7K-2-Core# show ip pim rp
PIM RP Status Information for VRF "default"
BSR disabled
Auto-RP disabled
BSR RP Candidate policy: None
BSR RP policy: None
Auto-RP Announce policy: None
Auto-RP Discovery policy: None


N7K-2-Core# config
Enter configuration commands, one per line.  End with CNTL/Z.
N7K-2-Core(config)# ip pim auto-rp forward listen
N7K-2-Core(config)# end
N7K-2-Core# show ip pim rp
PIM RP Status Information for VRF "default"
BSR disabled
Auto-RP RPA: 10.1.0.1, uptime: 00:04:00, expires: 00:02:42
BSR RP Candidate policy: None
BSR RP policy: None
Auto-RP Announce policy: None
Auto-RP Discovery policy: None


RP: 10.1.0.1, (0), uptime: 00:03:59, expires: 00:02:42,
  priority: 0, RP-source: 10.1.0.1 (A), group ranges:
      239.0.0.0/8
N7K-2-Core#
```

> **Note**   The commands **ip pim send-rp-announce** and **ip pim auto-rp rp-candidate**
> perform the same function and can be used as alternatives for each other with no impact
> to functionality.

Configuring Auto-RP for BiDir is simply a matter of adding **bidir** to the **rp-candidate**
command. Example 4-8 illustrates this, and the change can be observed on N7K-1-Core1.

Example 4-8   *Configuring Auto-RP and BiDir*

```
N7K-1-Core1# show ip pim group
PIM Group-Range Configuration for VRF "default"

Group-range       Mode      RP-address      Shared-tree-only range
232.0.0.0/8       SSM       -               -
239.0.0.0/8       ASM       10.1.0.1        -
N7K-1-Core1# config
Enter configuration commands, one per line.  End with CNTL/Z.
N7K-1-Core1(config)# ip pim auto-rp forward listen
N7K-1-Core1(config)# ip pim auto-rp rp-candidate e4/1 group-list 239.0.0.0/8 bidir
N7K-1-Core1(config)# ip pim auto-rp mapping-agent e4/1
N7K-1-Core1(config)# end
N7K-1-Core1# show ip pim group
PIM Group-Range Configuration for VRF "default"

Group-range       Mode      RP-address      Shared-tree-only range
232.0.0.0/8       SSM       -               -
239.0.0.0/8       Bidir     10.1.0.1        -
N7K-1-Core1#
```

Configuring Anycast-RP

An alternative configuration is PIM Anycast-RP in which the same IP address is configured on multiple devices. This capability enables receivers to follow the unicast routing
table to find the best path to the RP. It is commonly used in large environments where the
preference is to minimize the impact of being an RP on a device and provide rudimentary
load-balancing. In Example 4-9, both N7K-1-Core1 and N7K-2-Core have Loopback1
added to their configuration and defined as the PIM Anycast-RP for the network, as
shown in Figure 4-5. This additional loopback is added to ease troubleshooting in the
network and easily identify anycast traffic.

Example 4-9   *Configuring PIM Anycast-RP*

```
N7K-1-Core1# show ip pim rp
PIM RP Status Information for VRF "default"
BSR disabled
Auto-RP disabled
```

```
BSR RP Candidate policy: None
BSR RP policy: None
Auto-RP Announce policy: None
Auto-RP Discovery policy: None


N7K-1-Core1# config
Enter configuration commands, one per line.  End with CNTL/Z.
N7K-1-Core1(config)# int lo1
N7K-1-Core1(config-if)# Desc Loopback or PIM Anycast-RP
N7K-1-Core1(config-if)# ip address 10.1.0.10/32
% 10.1.0.10/32 overlaps with address configured on Ethernet4/3
N7K-1-Core1(config-if)# ip router ospf 100 area 0
N7K-1-Core1(config-if)# no shut
N7K-1-Core1(config-if)# exit
N7K-1-Core1(config)# ip pim anycast-rp 10.1.0.10 10.1.0.1
N7K-1-Core1(config)# ip pim anycast-rp 10.1.0.10 10.1.0.2
N7K-1-Core1(config)# end
N7K-1-Core1#
N7K-1-Core1# show ip pim rp
PIM RP Status Information for VRF "default"
BSR disabled
Auto-RP disabled
BSR RP Candidate policy: None
BSR RP policy: None
Auto-RP Announce policy: None
Auto-RP Discovery policy: None


Anycast-RP 10.1.0.10 members:
  10.1.0.1*  10.1.0.2


N7K-1-Core1#


N7K-2-Core# show ip pim rp
PIM RP Status Information for VRF "default"
BSR disabled
Auto-RP disabled
BSR RP Candidate policy: None
BSR RP policy: None
Auto-RP Announce policy: None
Auto-RP Discovery policy: None


N7K-2-Core# config
Enter configuration commands, one per line.  End with CNTL/Z.
N7K-2-Core(config)# int lo1
N7K-2-Core(config-if)# Desc Loopback or PIM Anycast-RP
```

```
N7K-2-Core(config-if)# ip address 10.1.0.10/32
N7K-2-Core(config-if)# ip router ospf 100 area 0
N7K-2-Core(config-if)# no shut
N7K-2-Core(config-if)# exit
N7K-2-Core(config)# ip pim anycast-rp 10.1.0.10 10.1.0.2
N7K-2-Core(config)# ip pim anycast-rp 10.1.0.10 10.1.0.1
N7K-2-Core(config)# end
N7K-2-Core# show ip pim rp
PIM RP Status Information for VRF "default"
BSR disabled
Auto-RP disabled
BSR RP Candidate policy: None
BSR RP policy: None
Auto-RP Announce policy: None
Auto-RP Discovery policy: None

Anycast-RP 10.1.0.10 members:
  10.1.0.2*  10.1.0.1

N7K-2-Core#
```

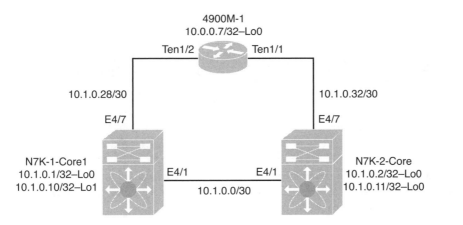

Figure 4-5   *PIM Anycast-RP Topology*

Configuring SSM and Static RPF

Two methods for configuring support of multicast traffic do not rely on an RP: Source
Specific Multicast (SSM) and Static RPF entries. In Example 4-10, N7K-1-Core1 is configured to support SSM on the 239.0.0.0/8 range of multicast addresses.

SSM has the advantage to not require an RP to function, and in some topologies this can
lend itself to more efficient routing through the network. The main considerations for

using SSM include the requirement for the receivers to use IGMPv3 and support for SSM by the internetworking equipment.

Static RPF, similar to static routing in unicast traffic, might be preferable where the topology is simple or lacks multiple paths where a dynamic routing protocol would be advantageous.

Example 4-10   *Configuration of SSM*

```
N7K-1-Core1# show ip pim group
PIM Group-Range Configuration for VRF "default"
Group-range        Mode      RP-address       Shared-tree-only range
232.0.0.0/8        SSM       -                -
N7K-1-Core1# config
Enter configuration commands, one per line.  End with CNTL/Z.
N7K-1-Core1(config)# ip pim ssm range 239.0.0.0/8
This command overwrites default SSM route
N7K-1-Core1(config)# end
N7K-1-Core1# show ip pim group
PIM Group-Range Configuration for VRF "default"
Group-range        Mode      RP-address       Shared-tree-only range
239.0.0.0/8        SSM       -                -
N7K-1-Core1#
```

Note   NX-OS displays a warning about changing the default SSM configuration. NX-OS supports SSM on 232.0.0.0/8 by default.

Finally, configuration of static RPF entries enables the network administrator to define multicast routes through the network that do not follow the unicast routing table via PIM. In Example 4-11, a static RPF entry is created on N7K-1-Core1 to send 10.1.0.2/32 traffic through 4900,M-1 via 10.1.0.30. Using static RPF entries can be preferable in networks where per usage fees are associated or where extremely high latency might be masked by the unicast routing protocol, such as satellite networks.

Example 4-11   *Configuring a Static RPF Entry*

```
N7K-1-Core1# show ip route 10.1.0.2
IP Route Table for VRF "default"
'*' denotes best ucast next-hop
'**' denotes best mcast next-hop
'[x/y]' denotes [preference/metric]
'%<string>' in via output denotes VRF <string>

10.1.0.2/32, ubest/mbest: 1/0, attached
```

```
     *via 10.1.0.2, Eth4/1, [250/0], 04:11:21, am
N7K-1-Core1# config
Enter configuration commands, one per line.  End with CNTL/Z.
N7K-1-Core1(config)# ip mroute 10.1.0.2/32 10.1.0.30
N7K-1-Core1(config)# end
N7K-1-Core1# show ip route 10.1.0.2
IP Route Table for VRF "default"
'*' denotes best ucast next-hop
'**' denotes best mcast next-hop
'[x/y]' denotes [preference/metric]
'%<string>' in via output denotes VRF <string>

10.1.0.2/32, ubest/mbest: 1/0, attached
    *via 10.1.0.2, Eth4/1, [250/0], 04:11:21, am
N7K-1-Core1# show ip route 10.1.0.2
IP Route Table for VRF "default"
'*' denotes best ucast next-hop
'**' denotes best mcast next-hop
'[x/y]' denotes [preference/metric]
'%<string>' in via output denotes VRF <string>

10.1.0.2/32, ubest/mbest: 1/1, attached
    *via 10.1.0.2, Eth4/1, [250/0], 04:12:54, am
    **via 10.1.0.30, [1/0], 00:01:32, mstatic
N7K-1-Core1#
```

IGMP Operation

Internet Group Management Protocol (IGMP) is an important component of a multicast network. IGMP is the protocol used by a host to signal it wants to join a specific multicast group. The router that sees the IGMP join message begins to send the multicast traffic requested by the host to the receiver. IGMP has matured over time, and there currently are three versions specified, named appropriately enough: IGMPv1, IGMPv2, and IGMPv3. IGMPv1 is defined in the Internet Engineering Task Force (IETF) RFC 1112, IGMPv2 is defined in RFC 2236, and IGMPv3 is defined in RFC 3376.

Note   Most modern operating systems use IGMPv3, although there are legacy systems that do not yet support it.

IGMP works through membership reports, and at its most simple process, routers on a network receive an unsolicited membership report from hosts that want to receive multicast traffic. The router processes these requests and begins to send the multicast traffic to the host until either a timeout value or a leave message is received.

IGMPv3 adds support for SSM, previously described in the chapter. In addition, IGMPv3 hosts do not perform report suppression like IGMPv1 and IGMPv2 hosts. IGMP report suppression is a methodology in which the switch sends only one IGMP report per multicast router query to avoid duplicate IGMP reports and preserve CPU resources.

IGMP works on routers that understand multicast traffic. For switches that might operate only at Layer 2, a technology called *IGMP snooping* enables intelligent forwarding of multicast traffic without broadcast or flooding behaviors. IGMP snooping enables a Layer 2 switch to examine, or snoop, IGMP membership reports and send multicast traffic only to ports with hosts that ask for the specific groups. Without IGMP snooping, a typical Layer 2 switch would flood all multicast traffic to every port. This can be quite a lot of traffic and negatively impact network performance.

IGMP Configuration on Nexus 7000

The Nexus 7000 is a Layer 3 switch and as such can do both full IGMP processing and IGMP snooping. By default, IGMP is enabled on an interface when the following conditions are met:

- PIM is enabled on the interface.

- A local multicast group is statically bound.

- Link-local reports are enabled.

Note   IGMPv2 is enabled by default, although IGMPv3 can be specified to change the default.

In Example 4-12, PIM is configured on interface VLAN10 and IGMP in turn is enabled for the network, as shown in Figure 4-6.

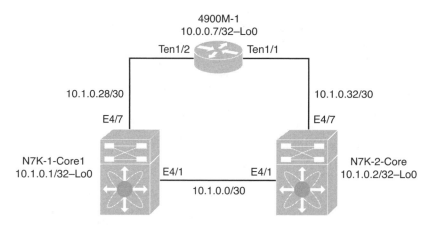

Figure 4-6   *IGMP Topology*

Example 4-12 *Enabling IGMP on an Interface*

```
N7K-1-Core1# show ip igmp int vlan 100
IGMP Interfaces for VRF "default"
Vlan100, Interface status: protocol-up/link-up/admin-up
  IP address: 10.100.1.2, IP subnet: 10.100.1.0/24
  Active querier: 10.100.1.2, version: 2, next query sent in: 00:01:56
  Membership count: 0
  Old Membership count 0
  Route-queue depth: 0
  IGMP version: 2, host version: 2
  IGMP query interval: 125 secs, configured value: 125 secs
  IGMP max response time: 10 secs, configured value: 10 secs
  IGMP startup query interval: 31 secs, configured value: 31 secs
  IGMP startup query count: 2
  IGMP last member mrt: 1 secs
  IGMP last member query count: 2
  IGMP group timeout: 260 secs, configured value: 260 secs
  IGMP querier timeout: 255 secs, configured value: 255 secs
  IGMP unsolicited report interval: 10 secs
  IGMP robustness variable: 2, configured value: 2
  IGMP reporting for link-local groups: disabled
  IGMP interface enable refcount: 1
  IGMP interface immediate leave: disabled
  IGMP VRF name default (id 1)
  IGMP Report Policy: None
  IGMP State Limit: None
  IGMP interface statistics: (only non-zero values displayed)
    General (sent/received):
      v2-queries: 2468/2468, v2-reports: 0/14797, v2-leaves: 0/1
    Errors:
  Interface PIM DR: No
  Interface vPC CFS statistics:
N7K-1-Core1#
```

In Example 4-13, the version of IGMP is changed from IGMPv2 to IGMPv3 to enable support for SSM.

Example 4-13 *Changing the IGMP Version*

```
N7K-1-Core11# config
Enter configuration commands, one per line.  End with CNTL/Z.
N7K-1-Core1(config)# int vlan 100
N7K-1-Core1(config-if)# ip igmp version 3
N7K-1-Core1(config-if)# end
```

```
N7K-1-Core1# show ip igmp interface vlan 100
IGMP Interfaces for VRF "default"
Vlan100, Interface status: protocol-up/link-up/admin-up
  IP address: 10.100.1.2, IP subnet: 10.100.1.0/24
  Active querier: 10.100.1.2, version: 3, next query sent in: 00:01:55
  Membership count: 0
  Old Membership count 0
  Route-queue depth: 0
  IGMP version: 3, host version: 3
  IGMP query interval: 125 secs, configured value: 125 secs
  IGMP max response time: 10 secs, configured value: 10 secs
  IGMP startup query interval: 31 secs, configured value: 31 secs
  IGMP startup query count: 2
  IGMP last member mrt: 1 secs
  IGMP last member query count: 2
  IGMP group timeout: 260 secs, configured value: 260 secs
  IGMP querier timeout: 255 secs, configured value: 255 secs
  IGMP unsolicited report interval: 10 secs
  IGMP robustness variable: 2, configured value: 2
  IGMP reporting for link-local groups: disabled
  IGMP interface enable refcount: 1
  IGMP interface immediate leave: disabled
  IGMP VRF name default (id 1)
  IGMP Report Policy: None
  IGMP State Limit: None
  IGMP interface statistics: (only non-zero values displayed)
    General (sent/received):
      v2-queries: 2469/2469, v2-reports: 0/14807, v2-leaves: 0/1
      v3-queries: 1/1, v3-reports: 0/0
    Errors:
  Interface PIM DR: No
  Interface vPC CFS statistics:
N7K-1-Core1#
```

In Example 4-14, IGMP snooping is enabled and the configuration displays.

Example 4-14 *IGMP Snooping on Nexus 7000 and 5500*

```
N7K-1-Core1# show ip igmp snooping vlan 100
IGMP Snooping information for vlan 100
  IGMP snooping enabled
  Lookup mode: IP
  Optimised Multicast Flood (OMF) enabled
  IGMP querier present, address: 10.100.1.2, version: 3, i/f Vlan100
  Querier interval: 125 secs
```

```
    Querier last member query interval: 1 secs
    Querier robustness: 2
    Switch-querier disabled
    IGMPv3 Explicit tracking enabled
    IGMPv2 Fast leave disabled
    IGMPv1/v2 Report suppression enabled
    IGMPv3 Report suppression disabled
    Link Local Groups suppression enabled
    Router port detection using PIM Hellos, IGMP Queries
    Number of router-ports: 2
    Number of groups: 0
    VLAN vPC function enabled
    Active ports:
      Po1 Po10
N7K-1-Core1#
```

Note   By default, IGMP snooping is enabled. Network administrators should carefully examine any requirements to disable IGMP snooping and the detrimental performance that might be experienced.

IGMP Configuration on Nexus 5000

The Nexus 5000 is a Layer 2 switch and fully supports IGMP snooping. By default, IGMP snooping is enabled, so no direct configuration is required for this feature to work. Example 4-15 reviews the IGMP snooping configuration for the network, as illustrated in Figure 4-7.

Example 4-15   *IGMP Snooping on Nexus 5000*

```
CMHLAB-N5K1# show ip igmp snooping vlan 100
IGMP Snooping information for vlan 100
  IGMP snooping enabled
  IGMP querier present, address: 10.2.1.1, version: 2, interface port-channel30
  Switch-querier disabled
  IGMPv3 Explicit tracking enabled
  IGMPv2 Fast leave disabled
  IGMPv1/v2 Report suppression enabled
  IGMPv3 Report suppression disabled
  Link Local Groups suppression enabled
  Router port detection using PIM Hellos, IGMP Queries
  Number of router-ports: 2
  Number of groups: 2
  VLAN vPC function enabled
CMHLAB-N5K1#
```

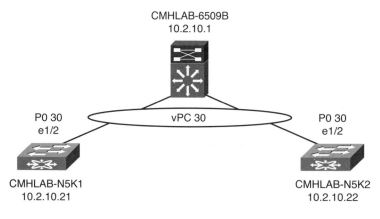

Figure 4-7   *IGMP Snooping Topology on Nexus 5000*

IGMP Configuration on Nexus 1000V

The Nexus 1000V is a Layer 2 switch and fully supports IGMP snooping. By default, IGMP snooping is enabled, so no direct configuration is required for this feature to work. Example 4-16 reviews the IGMP snooping configuration, as depicted in Figure 4-8.

Example 4-16   *IGMP Snooping on Nexus 1000V*

```
CMHLAB-DC2-VSM1# show ip igmp snooping vlan 100
IGMP Snooping information for vlan 100
  IGMP snooping enabled
  IGMP querier present, address: 10.2.1.1, version: 2, interface Ethernet4/2
  Switch-querier disabled
  IGMPv3 Explicit tracking enabled
  IGMPv2 Fast leave disabled
  IGMPv1/v2 Report suppression enabled
  IGMPv3 Report suppression disabled
  Router port detection using PIM Hellos, IGMP Queries
  Number of router-ports: 3
  Number of groups: 3
CMHLAB-DC2-VSM1#
```

The Nexus 1000V also supports IGMP snooping on vEthernet ports created for Guest Virtual Machines (VMs). This provides the capability to better control IP multicast traffic in a VMware virtualized network to improve performance and reduce CPU load. Example 4-17 shows the IGMP snooping on vEthernet1 that maps to a Guest VM called CMHLAB-TestSrv3.

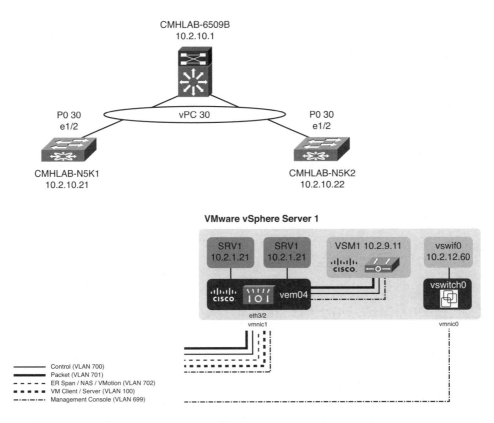

Figure 4-8 *Network Topology for IGMP Snooping Configuration*

Example 4-17 *IGMP Snooping on vEthernet1*

```
CMHLAB-DC2-VSM1# show ip igmp snooping groups vlan 100
Type: S - Static, D - Dynamic, R - Router port


Vlan  Group Address      Ver   Type   Port list
100   */*                v2    R      Eth6/2 Eth5/1 Eth4/2
100   224.0.1.24         v2    D      Veth8
100   239.0.0.10         v2    D      Veth1
100   239.255.255.254    v2    D      Veth8
CMHLAB-DC2-VSM1#
CMHLAB-DC2-VSM1# show int vether1
Vethernet1 is up
    Port description is CMHLAB-Testsrv3, Network Adapter 1
    Hardware is Virtual, address is 0050.5686.0a8d
    Owner is VM "CMHLAB-Testsrv3", adapter is Network Adapter 1
    Active on module 4
    VMware DVS port 66
```

```
Port-Profile is DC2-N1K-VLAN100
Port mode is access
5 minute input rate 112 bits/second, 0 packets/second
5 minute output rate 930872 bits/second, 818 packets/second
Rx
144716 Input Packets 128048 Unicast Packets
19 Multicast Packets 16649 Broadcast Packets
26634502 Bytes
Tx
1857975 Output Packets 158259 Unicast Packets
540565 Multicast Packets 1159151 Broadcast Packets 529325 Flood Packets
257965170 Bytes
100 Input Packet Drops 0 Output Packet Drops

CMHLAB-DC2-VSM1#
```

MSDP Configuration on Nexus 7000

NX-OS on the Nexus 7000 supports MSDP to provide interdomain multicast capabilities. MSDP enables for multicast source information to be shared between PIM domains.

Note   MSDP does not require BGP to be configured and working prior to successful implementation.

The first step to configure MSDP is to enable it in global configuration mode using the **feature** command. With the modular nature of NX-OS, using the **feature** command loads the MSDP modular code into memory for execution. The MSDP feature will not be resident in memory without first being enabled. This is advantageous because it preserves memory resources in the router when a feature is not used. In Example 4-18, MSDP is enabled as a feature on Router N7K-1-Core1, as depicted in Figure 4-9.

Example 4-18   *Enabling the MSDP Feature on the N7k-1-Core Router*

```
N7K-1-Core1# config
Enter configuration commands, one per line.  End with CNTL/Z.
N7K-1-Core1(config)# feature msdp
N7K-1-Core1(config)# end
N7K-1-Core1# show run msdp

!Command: show running-config msdp
!Time: Mon Jul  9 21:46:10 2012
```

```
version 6.1(1)

feature msdp


N7K-1-Core1#
```

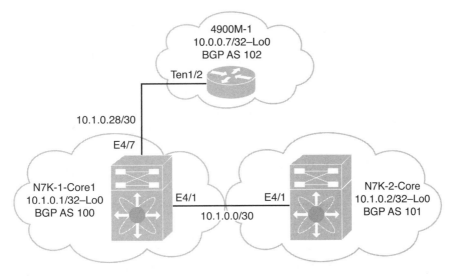

Figure 4-9   *Network Topology for MSDP Configuration*

In Example 4-19, MSDP is configured on N7K-1-Core1 (AS 100) to provide an interdo-main multicast connection between N7K-2-Core(AS 101) and 4900M-1 (AS 102).

Example 4-19   *MSDP Peer Configuration*

```
N7K-1-Core1# config
Enter configuration commands, one per line.  End with CNTL/Z.
N7K-1-Core1(config)# ip msdp peer 10.0.0.2 connect-source lo0 remote-as 101
N7K-1-Core1(config)# ip msdp description 10.0.0.2 MSDP Peer to N7K-2-Core
N7K-1-Core1(config)# ip msdp peer 10.0.0.7 connect-source lo0 remote-as 102
N7K-1-Core1(config)# ip msdp description 10.0.0.7 MSDP Peer to 400M-1
N7K-1-Core1(config)# end
N7K-1-Core1# show ip msdp sum
MSDP Peer Status Summary for VRF "default"
Local ASN: 0, originator-id: 0.0.0.0

Number of configured peers:  2
Number of established peers: 2
Number of shutdown peers:    0
```

```
Peer            Peer        Connection      Uptime/     Last msg   (S,G)s
Address         ASN         State           Downtime    Received   Received
10.0.0.2        101         Established     00:00:12    00:00:11   0
10.0.0.7        102         Established     00:00:12    00:00:11   0
N7K-1-Core1#
```

Administrative Scoping of Multicast RPs in PIM

NX-OS offers two methods (inline scoping and route maps) for network administrators to control multicast scoping for RPs. This is a common capability used because it enables granular control of traffic and flexibility in RP placement and usage.

The first methodology, referred to as *inline scoping* is to configure each group or use of simple ACLs to specify the group to RP mapping. This is easy to do if you have a few groups or if they are contiguous groups. Example 4-20 illustrates this where N7K-1-Core1 has multiple RPs configured for multiple groups.

Example 4-20 *Inline Scoping of RPs*

```
N7K-1-Core1# config
Enter configuration commands, one per line.  End with CNTL/Z.
N7K-1-Core1(config)# ip pim rp-address 10.1.0.2 group-list 238.1.1.1/32
N7K-1-Core1(config)# ip pim rp-address 10.1.0.2 group-list 238.1.2.1/32
N7K-1-Core1(config)# ip pim rp-address 10.1.0.2 group-list 238.1.2.1/32
N7K-1-Core1(config)# ip pim rp-address 10.1.0.2 group-list 238.1.3.1/32
N7K-1-Core1(config)# ip pim rp-address 10.1.0.7 group-list 238.100.1.1/32
N7K-1-Core1(config)# ip pim rp-address 10.1.0.7 group-list 238.100.1.1/32
N7K-1-Core1(config)# ip pim rp-address 10.1.0.7 group-list 238.101.1.1/32
N7K-1-Core1(config)# ip pim rp-address 10.1.0.7 group-list 238.102.1.1/32
N7K-1-Core1(config)# ip pim rp-address 10.1.0.7 group-list 238.102.1.1/32
N7K-1-Core1(config)# end
N7K-1-Core1# show ip pim rp
PIM RP Status Information for VRF "default"
BSR disabled
Auto-RP disabled
BSR RP Candidate policy: None
BSR RP policy: None
Auto-RP Announce policy: None
Auto-RP Discovery policy: None

Anycast-RP 10.1.0.10 members:
  10.1.0.1*  10.1.0.2

RP: 10.1.0.2, (0), uptime: 0.227006, expires: never,
  priority: 0, RP-source: (local), group ranges:
```

```
        238.1.3.1/32    238.1.2.1/32
        238.1.1.1/32
RP: 10.1.0.7, (0), uptime: 0.177876, expires: never,
  priority: 0, RP-source: (local), group ranges:
        238.102.1.1/32    238.101.1.1/32
        238.100.1.1/32
N7K-1-Core1#
```

The next methodology uses route maps to define traffic that is to be dropped. This is accomplished by creating a blackhole RP and matching unwanted traffic to the blackhole. This provides the functionality many networks require because NX-OS doesn't support deny semantics with RP scoping route-maps. Example 4-21 shows this process step-by-step where a static route to null0 is created and a route map is configured to match the unwanted traffic and then applied to the RP configuration. At the same time a route map is created for the wanted traffic and applied to the RP configuration.

Example 4-21   *Using Route-Maps with a Blackhole RP for Administrative Scoping*

```
N7K-1-Core1# config
N7K-1-Core1(config)# ip route 255.255.255.254/32 Null0
N7K-1-Core1(config)# route-map blackhole-rp permit 10
N7K-1-Core1(config-route-map)# match ip multicast group 239.100.110.1/32
N7K-1-Core1(config-route-map)# route-map blackhole-rp permit 20
N7K-1-Core1(config-route-map)# match ip multicast group 239.100.112.1/32
N7K-1-Core1(config-route-map)# route-map real-rp permit 10
N7K-1-Core1(config-route-map)# match ip multicast group 239.100.0.0/16
N7K-1-Core1(config-route-map)#
N7K-1-Core1(config-route-map)# ip pim rp-address 10.1.0.1 route-map real-rp
N7K-1-Core1(config)# ip pim rp-address 255.255.255.254 route-map blackhole-rp
N7K-1-Core1# show ip pim rp
PIM RP Status Information for VRF "default"
BSR disabled
Auto-RP disabled
BSR RP Candidate policy: None
BSR RP policy: None
Auto-RP Announce policy: None
Auto-RP Discovery policy: None

RP: 10.1.0.1*, (0), uptime: 0.175350, expires: never,
  priority: 0, RP-source: (local), group-map: real-rp, group ranges:
        239.100.0.0/16
RP: 255.255.255.254, (0), uptime: 0.059510, expires: never,
  priority: 0, RP-source: (local), group-map: blackhole-rp, group ranges:
        239.100.112.1/32    239.100.110.1/32
N7K-1-Core1(config)#
```

Configuring PIM Join and Prune Policies

NX-OS enables the network administrator to specify-interface level PIM join and prune policies that provide a means to controlling traffic in a granular method. By either permitting or denying PIM join and prune messages, the network administrator can develop a specific topology and pathing through a network for multicast. In Example 4-22, a simple policy is applied to Ethernet 4/7 on N7K-1-Core1 to filter PIM join and prune messages for 239.100.10.1/32 and permit all others.

Example 4-22   *Configuring PIM Join and Prune Policies*

```
N7K-1-Core1# config
Enter configuration commands, one per line.  End with CNTL/Z.
N7K-1-Core1(config)# route-map pim-policy deny 10
N7K-1-Core1(config-route-map)# match ip multicast group 239.100.10.1/32
N7K-1-Core1(config-route-map)# route-map pim-policy permit 20
N7K-1-Core1(config-route-map)# match ip multicast group 224.0.0.0/4
N7K-1-Core1(config-route-map)# int e4/7
N7K-1-Core1(config-if)# ip pim jp-policy pim-policy in
N7K-1-Core1(config-if)# end
N7K-1-Core1# show ip pim interface e4/7
PIM Interface Status for VRF "default"
Ethernet4/7, Interface status: protocol-up/link-up/admin-up
  IP address: 10.1.0.29, IP subnet: 10.1.0.28/30
  PIM DR: 10.1.0.30, DR's priority: 1
  PIM neighbor count: 1
  PIM hello interval: 30 secs, next hello sent in: 00:00:18
  PIM neighbor holdtime: 105 secs
  PIM configured DR priority: 1
  PIM border interface: no
  PIM GenID sent in Hellos: 0x26fb3a1b
  PIM Hello MD5-AH Authentication: disabled
  PIM Neighbor policy: none configured
  PIM Join-Prune inbound policy: pim-policy
  PIM Join-Prune outbound policy: none configured
  PIM Join-Prune interval: 1 minutes
  PIM Join-Prune next sending: 1 minutes
  PIM BFD enabled: no
  PIM Interface Statistics, last reset: never
    General (sent/received):
      Hellos: 128/121, JPs: 0/61, Asserts: 0/0
      Grafts: 0/0, Graft-Acks: 0/0
      DF-Offers: 0/0, DF-Winners: 0/0, DF-Backoffs: 0/0, DF-Passes: 0/0
    Errors:
      Checksum errors: 0, Invalid packet types/DF subtypes: 0/0
      Authentication failed: 0
```

```
        Packet length errors: 0, Bad version packets: 0, Packets from self: 0
        Packets from non-neighbors: 0
        JPs received on RPF-interface: 0
        (*,G) Joins received with no/wrong RP: 0/0
        (*,G)/(S,G) JPs received for SSM/Bidir groups: 0/0
        JPs filtered by inbound policy: 0
        JPs filtered by outbound policy: 0
N7K-1-Core1#
```

Multicast and Control Plane Policing (CoPP)

Both the Nexus 7000 and Nexus 5x00 series of switches support a feature called Control Plane Policing (CoPP), which is considered a security mechanism, but also can have a direct impact to a successful multicast deployment. CoPP is covered in detail in Chapter 5, "Security," but you must be aware of its interaction with multicast. In a properly functioning multicast network, a number of control plane protocols determine IGMP membership, the type of multicast network (ASM, SSM, BiDir, and so on), and PIM joins and prunes. In most multicast networks the default values for CoPP are sufficient; in a multicast-heavy network, it may require modification to accommodate larger amounts of multicast control traffic. The process to monitor, tune, and optimize CoPP configurations is detailed in Chapter 6, "High Availability."

Summary

NX-OS has a rich set of multicast features embedded that the administrator requires. Support for PIM and its myriad of choices such as ASM, SSM, BiDir, and static RPF provide the capability to integrate into networks of almost any size and topology.

Supporting key technologies such as IGMP and IGMP snooping empower NX-OS to scale to meet the demands of a modern multicast network. These tools also enable the network administrator to filter and control the flow of multicast at Layer 2 with a comprehensive set of options in the Nexus 7000, 5500, 5000, and 1000V.

Next, providing support for interdomain multicast through the use of MSDP enables network administrators to scale their networks with the use of BGP and still retain the ability to implement multicast. MSDP also enables multicast to be facilitated between autonomous systems and between PIM domains for significant flexibility and control.

NX-OS also provides the capability to perform administrative scoping of IP multicast through two methodologies: static scoping and the use of blackhole-rp configurations. These provide granular capabilities for traffic control. Finally, when coupled with flexible PIM join and prune policies, network administrators can meet the demands and controls required in a modern network.

Chapter 5

Security

This chapter covers the following topics:

- Configuring RADIUS
- Configuring TACACS+
- Configuring SSH
- Configuring Cisco TrustSec
- Configuring IP ACLs
- Configuring MAC ACLs
- Configuring VLAN ACLs
- Configuring Port Security
- Configuring DHCP Snooping
- Configuring Dynamic ARP Inspection
- Configuring IP Source Guard
- Configuring Keychain Management
- Configuring Traffic Storm Control
- Configuring Unicast RPF
- Configuring Control Plane policing
- Configuring Rate Limits
- SNMPv3

Security is a common discussion and concern. Cisco NX-OS Software supports a pervasive security feature set that protects NX-OS switches, protects the network against network degradation, protects the network against failure, and protects against data loss or compromise resulting from intentional attacks. This chapter discusses several security features to address a defense in-depth approach to provide a scaleable, robust, and secure data center solution set.

Configuring RADIUS

Authentication, Authorization, and Accounting (AAA) services enable verification of identity, granting of access, and tracking the actions of users managing a Cisco NX-OS device. Cisco NX-OS devices support Remote Access Dial-In User Service (RADIUS) and Terminal Access Controller Access Control device Plus (TACACS+) protocols.

Based on the user ID and password combination provided, Cisco NX-OS devices perform local authentication or authorization using the local database or remote authentication or authorization using one or more AAA servers. A preshared secret key provides security for communication between the Cisco NX-OS device and AAA servers. A common secret key can be configured for all AAA servers or for a specific AAA server.

AAA security provides the following services:

- **Authentication:** Identifies users, including login and password dialog; challenge and response; messaging support; and, depending on the security protocol selected, encryption.

  Authentication is the process of verifying the identity of the person or device accessing the Cisco NX-OS device, which is based on the user ID and password combination provided by the entity trying to access the Cisco NX-OS device. Cisco NX-OS devices enable local authentication (using the local lookup database) or remote authentication (using one or more RADIUS or TACACS+ servers).

- **Authorization:** Provides access control. AAA authorization is the process of assembling a set of attributes that describe what the user is authorized to perform. Authorization in the Cisco NX-OS Software is provided by attributes downloaded from AAA servers. Remote security servers, such as RADIUS and TACACS+, authorize users for specific rights by associating attribute-value (AV) pairs, which define those rights with the appropriate user.

- **Accounting:** Provides the method for collecting information; logging the information locally; and sending the information to the AAA server for billing, auditing, and reporting.

The accounting feature tracks and maintains a log of every management session used to access the Cisco NX-OS device. The logs can be used to generate reports for troubleshooting and auditing purposes. The accounting log can be stored locally or sent to remote AAA servers.

AAA services provide several benefits such as flexibility and control of access configuration; scalability; and centralized or distributed authentication methods, such as RADIUS and TACACS+.

Successful deployment of AAA services includes several prerequisites:

- Verification that the RADIUS or TACACS+ server is reachable through IP, such as a simple ping test.

- Verification that the Cisco NX-OS device is configured as a client of the AAA servers.

- Configuration of a secret key on the Cisco NX-OS device and the remote AAA servers.

- Verification that the remote server responds to AAA requests from the Cisco NX-OS device by specifying the correct source interface.

The TACACS+ protocol provides centralized validation of users attempting to gain access to a Cisco NX-OS device. TACACS+ services are maintained in a database on a TACACS+ daemon running on a Cisco ACS Linux appliance. TACACS+ provides for separate authentication, authorization, and accounting facilities. The TACACS+ protocol uses TCP port 49 for transport communication.

RADIUS is a client/server protocol through which remote access servers communicate with a central server to authenticate users and authorize their access to the requested system or service. RADIUS maintains user profiles in a central database that all remote servers can share. This model provides security, and the company can use it to set up a policy that is applied at a single administered network point. Cisco Secure ACS 5.0 accepts authentication requests on port 1645 and port 1812. For RADIUS accounting, Cisco Secure ACS accepts accounting packets on ports 1646 and 1813.

Example 5-1 shows how to configure the authentication methods for the console login with RADIUS authentication, based on the network topology shown in Figure 5-1.

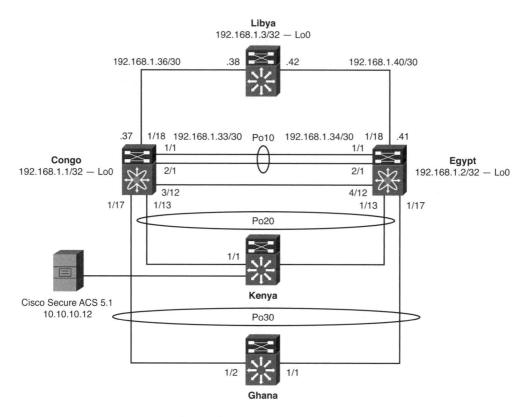

Figure 5-1 *Security Network Topology Used Throughout the Chapter*

Note Unless otherwise noted, refer to the network topology illustrated in Figure 5-1 for all remaining configuration examples throughout the chapter.

Example 5-1 *AAA RADIUS Configuration for Console Authentication*

```
Egypt#
Egypt# conf t
Egypt (config)# interface loopback0
Egypt (config-if)# ip address 192.168.1.2/32
Egypt (config)# ip radius source-interface loopback0
Egypt (config)# radius-server host 10.10.10.12 key 7 "QTSX123" authentication
accounting
Egypt (config)# aaa authentication login console group radius
Egypt (config)# exit
Egypt# copy running-config startup-config
```

Example 5-2 shows the configuration of default login authentication methods.

Example 5-2   *AAA RADIUS Configuration for Default Telnet SSH Authentication*

```
Egypt#
Egypt (config)# interface loopback0
Egypt (config-if)# ip address 192.168.1.2/32
Egypt (config)# ip radius source-interface loopback0
Egypt (config)# radius-server host 10.10.10.12 key 7 "QTSX123" authentication
accounting
Egypt (config)# aaa authentication login console group radius
Egypt (config)# exit
Egypt# copy running-config startup-config
```

Note   AAA configuration and operations are local to the Virtual Device Context (VDC), except the default console methods and the AAA accounting log. The configuration and operation of the AAA authentication methods for the console login apply only to the default VDC.

RADIUS Configuration Distribution

Cisco Fabric Services (CFS) enables the Cisco NX-OS device to distribute the RADIUS configuration to other Cisco NX-OS devices in the network. When you enable CFS distribution for a feature on your device, the device belongs to a CFS region containing other devices in the network that you have also enabled for CFS distribution for the feature.

RADIUS CFS distribution is disabled by default. To enable RADIUS configuration distribution, use the following command:

```
Egypt (config)# radius distribute
```

To apply the RADIUS configuration changes in the temporary database to the running configuration and distribute RADIUS, use the following command:

```
Egypt (config)# radius commit
```

Note   Because RADIUS server and global keys are unique, they are not distributed through the CFS sessions. Also, CFS does not distribute the RADIUS server group or AAA commands.

Example 5-3 verifies that there is not any RADIUS configuration on Congo; this example demonstrates that CFS distributes the RADIUS configuration.

Example 5-3 *Verifying No RADIUS Configuration on Congo*

```
Congo#
before cfs:
Congo# show running-config radius
!Command: show running-config radius
!Time: Thu Oct  8 18:01:04 2009
version 5.2(3a)
Congo#
```

Example 5-4 verifies that there is not any RADIUS configuration on Egypt; this example demonstrates that CFS distributes the RADIUS configuration.

Example 5-4 *Verifying No RADIUS Configuration on Egypt*

```
Egypt# show running-config radius
!Command: show running-config radius
!Time: Thu Oct  8 18:00:24 2009
version 5.2(3a)
```

Example 5-5 shows how to configure RADIUS on Egypt.

Example 5-5 *Configuring RADIUS on Egypt*

```
Egypt#
Egypt# conf t
Egypt(config)# ip radius source-interface  loopback 0
Source-interface configuration is exempted from CFS distribution
Egypt(config)# radius-server host 10.10.10.12 key NXOS123
Egypt(config)# aaa authentication login console group radius
Egypt(config)# radius commit
```

Example 5-6 verifies the RADIUS configuration delivered via CFS distribution.

Example 5-6 *Verifying RADIUS CFS Distribution on Egypt*

```
Egypt(config)# show running-config radius
!Command: show running-config radius
!Time: Thu Oct  8 18:09:31 2009
version 5.2(3a)
radius distribute
radius-server retransmit 0
```

```
radius-server host 10.10.10.12 authentication accounting
radius commit
Egypt(config)#
```

Example 5-7 shows how to verify the RADIUS CFS configuration.

Example 5-7 *Verifying RADIUS CFS Configuration*

```
Egypt# show radius-cfs
distribution : enabled
session ongoing: no
session db: does not exist
merge protocol status: merge activation done
Egypt#

Egypt# show radius-server
retransmission count:1
timeout value:5
deadtime value:0
source interface:loopback0
total number of servers:1

following RADIUS servers are configured:
        10.10.10.12:
                available for authentication on port:1812
                available for accounting on port:1813
Egypt#

Egypt# show cfs peers

Physical Fabric
Switch WWN               IP Address
--------------------------------------------------------------------------------
20:00:00:1b:54:c2:78:c1 172.26.32.39                              [Local]
20:00:00:1b:54:c2:76:41 172.26.32.37
Total number of entries = 2

Egypt# show cfs status
Distribution : Enabled
Distribution over IP : Enabled - mode IPv4
IPv4 multicast address : 239.255.70.83
IPv6 multicast address : ff15::efff:4653
Distribution over Ethernet : Enabled

Egypt# show cfs merge status
```

```
Application        Scope            Vsan        Status
radius             Physical-fc-ip    -          Success
Egypt# copy running-config startup-config
```

Note   If the RADIUS server becomes unavailable, the default behavior is to fall back to local NX-OS authentication.

Example 5-8 demonstrates the loss of communication to the Cisco Secure ACS 5.0 Virtual Machine. Manually shut down the interface to the Cisco Secure ACS 5.0 Linux Server, as shown in the example. Cisco Secure ACS provides centralized management of access policies for device administration, access control management, and compliance.

Example 5-8   *Administratively Shut Down Interface Gigabit Ethernet1/1 Connected to Cisco ACS RADIUS Server*

```
Kenya# config t
Kenya(config)#int gi1/1
Kenya(config-if)#shutdown
Kenya(config-if)# exit
Kenya(config)# exit

Kenya# show interfaces gigabitEthernet 1/1
GigabitEthernet1/1 is administratively down, line protocol is down (disabled)
  Hardware is Gigabit Ethernet Port, address is 0018.73b1.e280 (bia 0018.73b1.e280)
  MTU 1500 bytes, BW 1000000 Kbit, DLY 10 usec,
      reliability 255/255, txload 1/255, rxload 1/255
  Encapsulation ARPA, loopback not set
  Keepalive set (10 sec)
  Auto-duplex, Auto-speed, link type is auto, media type is 10/100/1000-TX
  input flow-control is off, output flow-control is off
  ARP type: ARPA, ARP Timeout 04:00:00
  Last input 00:01:09, output never, output hang never
  Last clearing of "show interface" counters never
  Input queue: 0/2000/0/0 (size/max/drops/flushes); Total output drops: 0
  Queueing strategy: fifo
  Output queue: 0/40 (size/max)
  5 minute input rate 0 bits/sec, 0 packets/sec
  5 minute output rate 0 bits/sec, 0 packets/sec
     114119 packets input, 73777471 bytes, 0 no buffer
     Received 59680 broadcasts (48762 multicasts)
     0 runts, 0 giants, 0 throttles
     0 input errors, 0 CRC, 0 frame, 0 overrun, 0 ignored
     0 input packets with dribble condition detected
```

```
    3453776 packets output, 281211243 bytes, 0 underruns
    0 output errors, 0 collisions, 0 interface resets
    0 babbles, 0 late collision, 0 deferred
    0 lost carrier, 0 no carrier
    0 output buffer failures, 0 output buffers swapped out
Kenya#
```

Telnet to the Nexus 7000 NX-OS device and log in as admin, as shown in Example 5-9.

Example 5-9 *Local Authentication in the Event the RADIUS Server Is Not Available or Offline*

```
[hk@hk ~]$ telnet congo
Trying 172.26.32.37...
Connected to congo.
Escape character is '^]'.
User Access Verification
login: admin
Password:

Remote AAA servers unreachable; local authentication done

Cisco Nexus Operating System (NX-OS) Software
TAC support: http://www.cisco.com/tac
Copyright (c) 2002-2009, Cisco Systems, Inc. All rights reserved.
The copyrights to certain works contained in this software are
owned by other third parties and used and distributed under
license. Certain components of this software are licensed under
the GNU General Public License (GPL) version 2.0 or the GNU
Lesser General Public License (LGPL) Version 2.1. A copy of each
such license is available at
http://www.opensource.org/licenses/gpl-2.0.php and
http://www.opensource.org/licenses/lgpl-2.1.php
Congo# ping 10.10.10.12
PING 10.10.10.12 (10.10.10.12): 56 data bytes
Request 0 timed out
Request 1 timed out
Request 2 timed out
Request 3 timed out
Request 4 timed out
--- 10.10.10.12 ping statistics ---
5 packets transmitted, 0 packets received, 100.00% packet loss
Congo#
```

To finish the configuration, the Cisco Secure ACS 5.0 Server needs configuration as well. Figures 5-2 through 5-5 provide a series of screenshots to show the configuration steps from the Cisco Secure ACS GUI.

Figure 5-2 shows the Cisco Secure ACS RADIUS configuration that defines the loopback of the NX-OS device and the shared secret key that needs to match between both the NX-OS device and the Cisco Secure ACS Server.

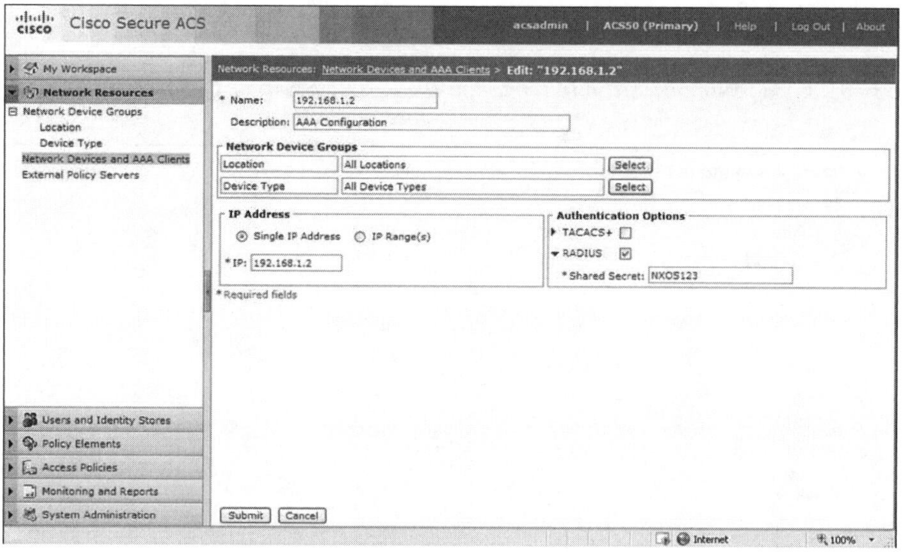

Figure 5-2 *Displaying the Specific Cisco Secure ACS RADIUS Configuration*

Figure 5-3 shows how to add a user to the Cisco Secure Database; user **console1** is added to demonstrate console AAA RADIUS authentication.

Figure 5-4 demonstrates a successful authentication and login with user console1 via the Async console interface of the NX-OS device.

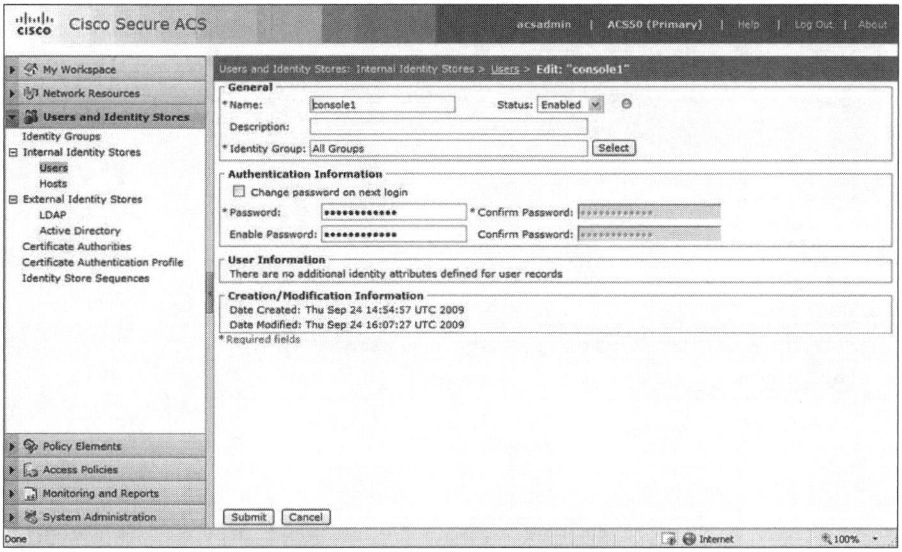

Figure 5-3 *Adding a User to the Cisco Secure RADIUS Database*

Figure 5-4 *A Successful Authentication for User console1 via the Console Interface*

Figure 5-5 verifies the successful RADIUS Authentication report on the Cisco Secure ACS server.

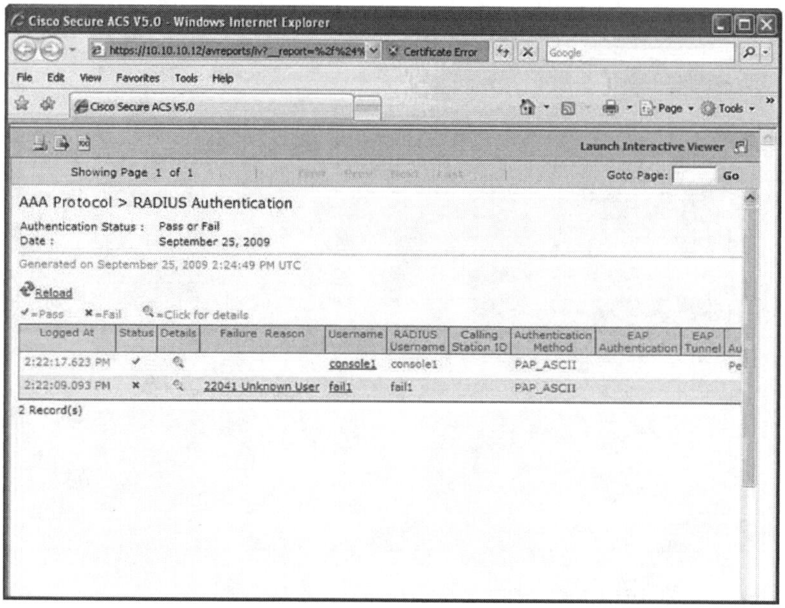

Figure 5-5 *Confirming That User console1 Successfully Authenticates via the RADIUS Protocol*

Configuring TACACS+

The TACACS+ protocol provides centralized validation of users attempting to gain access to a Cisco NX-OS device. TACACS+ services are maintained in a database on a TACACS+ daemon running on a Cisco ACS Linux appliance. TACACS+ provides for separate authentication, authorization, and accounting facilities. The TACACS+ protocol uses TCP port 49 for transport communication.

Enabling TACACS+

The TACACS+ feature is disabled by default. TACACS+ must explicitly enable the TACACS+ feature to access the configuration and verification commands for authentication.

To verify the default TACACS+ feature status, use the following command:

```
Egypt# show feature | i tacacs
tacacs              1         disabled
```

To enable the TACACS+ feature, enter the configuration demonstrated in Example 5-10.

Example 5-10 *Enabling TACACS+ Feature/Process*

```
Egypt#
Egypt# conf t
Enter configuration commands, one per line. End with CNTL/Z.
Egypt(config)# feature tacacs+
Egypt(config)# show feature | i tacacs
tacacs                 1          enabled
Egypt(config)# exit
Egypt# copy running-configuration startup=configuration
```

To verify that the TACACS+ feature is enabled, enter the following command:

```
Egypt# show feature | i tacacs+
tacacs                 1          enabled
Egypt#
```

TACACS+ Configuration Distribution

CFS enables the Cisco NX-OS device to distribute the TACACS+ configuration to other Cisco NX-OS devices in the network. When you enable CFS distribution for a feature on your device, the device belongs to a CFS region containing other devices in the network that you have also enabled for CFS distribution for the feature. CFS distribution for TACACS+ is disabled by default.

To enable TACACS+ CFS distribution, enter the following command:

```
Egypt(config)# tacacs+ distribute
```

To verify TACACS+ CFS distribution, enter the **show tacacs+ status** command, as demonstrated in Example 5-11.

Example 5-11 *Verifying TACACS+ CFS Distribution*

```
Egypt(config)# show tacacs+ status
distribution : enabled
session ongoing: no
session db: does not exist
merge protocol status: not yet initiated after enable

last operation: enable
last operation status: success
Egypt(config)#
```

Configuring the Global TACACS+ Keys

TACACS+ secret keys can be configured at the global level for all servers used by the NX-OS device. The secret key is a shared secret text string between the Cisco NX-OS device and the TACACS+ server hosts.

Note   Because TACACS+ server and global keys are unique, they are not distributed through the CFS sessions. Also, CFS does not distribute the RADIUS server group or aaa commands.

Example 5-12 shows how to configure the TACACS+ server keys.

Example 5-12   *Configuring the TACACS+ Server Keys*

```
Egypt(config)# tacacs-server key 0 NXOS123
Global key configuration is exempted from CFS distribution
Egypt(config)# show tacacs-server
Global TACACS+ shared secret:********
timeout value:5
deadtime value:0
source interface:any available
total number of servers:0
Egypt(config)#
```

Configuring the TACACS+ Server Hosts

To access a remote TACACS+ server, you must configure the IP address or the hostname for the TACACS+ server; in this example the TACACS+ server is 10.10.10.12.

Note   Sixty-four TACACS+ servers can be defined or configured.

Example 5-13 shows how to configure the TACACS+ server host; this is the IP address of the Cisco Secure ACS TACACS+ Server.

Example 5-13   *Configuring the TACACS Server Host*

```
Egypt(config)# tacacs-server host 10.10.10.12
Egypt(config)# show tacacs+ pend
pending          pending-diff
Egypt(config)# show tacacs+ pending
tacacs-server key 7 QTSX123
tacacs-server host 10.10.10.12
Egypt(config)# tacacs+ commit
```

```
Egypt(config)# show tacacs-server
Global TACACS+ shared secret:********
timeout value:5
deadtime value:0
source interface:any available
total number of servers:1

following TACACS+ servers are configured:
        10.10.10.12:
                available on port:49
Egypt(config)# show tacacs+ pending
No active CFS distribution session exist for TACACS+
Egypt(config)# copy running-config startup-config
[########################################] 100%
Egypt(config)#
```

Note The **tacacs+ commit** command changes the temporary database configuration to the running configuration.

Configuring TACACS+ Server Groups

With NX-OS, you can specify one or more remote AAA servers to authenticate users using server groups; members of a group must belong to the TACACS+ protocol. The TACACS+ servers are tried in the same order in which they are configured.

Example 5-14 shows how to configure TACACS+ server groups.

Example 5-14 *Configuring the TACACS+ Server Group of TACACS+Server*

```
Egypt(config)# aaa group server tacacs+ TACACS+Server
Egypt(config-tacacs+)# server 10.10.10.12
Egypt(config-tacacs+)# show tacacs-server groups
total number of groups:1

following TACACS+ server groups are configured:
        group TACACS+Server:
                server 10.10.10.12 on port 49
                deadtime is 0
Egypt(config-tacacs+)#
```

Example 5-15 shows how to configure the default TACACS+ authentication method for Telnet and SSH.

Example 5-15   *Configuring the Default TACACS+ Authentication Method for Telnet and SSH*

```
Egypt(config)# aaa authentication login default group TACACS+Server
Egypt(config)# show tacacs-server
Global TACACS+ shared secret:********
timeout value:5
deadtime value:0
source interface:loopback0
total number of servers:1
following TACACS+ servers are configured:
        10.10.10.12:
                available on port:49
Egypt(config)#
Egypt#
```

Configuring TACACS+ Source Interface

Because you can have multiple Layer 3 interfaces, you can specify the global source interface for TACACS+ server groups to use when accessing TACACS+ because IP reachability is required between the NX-OS device and the Cisco Secure ACS Server:

```
Egypt(config)# ip tacacs source-interface loopback 0
```

Note   Different source interfaces can be specified for specific TACACS+ server groups; by default the NX-OS device picks the IP address of the egress interface used to reach the TACACS+ server based on the routing table.

Note   With TACACS+ CFS enabled, the source-interface configuration is exempted from CFS distribution.

Example 5-16 verifies TACACS+ CFS configuration distribution on the second switch.

Example 5-16   *Verifying TACACS+ CFS Configuration Distribution on the Second Switch*

```
Congo(config)# ip tacacs source-interface loopback 0
Source-interface configuration is exempted from CFS distribution
Congo(config)#
Congo#

CFS on the second Switch
```

```
Congo(config)# show feature | i tacacs+
tacacs                 1             disabled
Congo(config)# feature tacacs+
Congo(config)# show feature | i tacacs+
tacacs                 1             enabled
Congo(config)# tacacs+ distribute
Congo(config)# show tacacs+ status
distribution : disabled
session ongoing: no
session db: does not exist
merge protocol status:

last operation: none
last operation status: none
Congo(config)# show running-config tacacs+
!Command: show running-config tacacs+
!Time: Thu Oct  1 14:15:42 2009
version 5.2(3a)
feature tacacs+
Congo(config)# tacacs+ distribute
Congo(config)# show tacacs+ status
distribution : enabled
session ongoing: no
session db: does not exist
merge protocol status: merge activation done

last operation: enable
last operation status: success
Congo(config)# show running-config tacacs+

!Command: show running-config tacacs+
!Time: Thu Oct  1 14:16:02 2009

version 5.2(3a)
feature tacacs+

tacacs+ distribute
tacacs-server host 10.10.10.12
tacacs+ commit

Congo(config)#
```

Example 5-17 shows successful Telnet authentication using TACACS+.

Example 5-17   *Verifying Successful Telnet Authentication Using TACACS+*

```
[hk@hk ~]$ telnet egypt
Trying 172.26.32.39...
Connected to egypt.
Escape character is '^]'.
User Access Verification
login: admin
Password:
Cisco Nexus Operating System (NX-OS) Software
TAC support: http://www.cisco.com/tac
Copyright (c) 2002-2009, Cisco Systems, Inc. All rights reserved.
The copyrights to certain works contained in this software are
owned by other third parties and used and distributed under
license. Certain components of this software are licensed under
the GNU General Public License (GPL) version 2.0 or the GNU
Lesser General Public License (LGPL) Version 2.1. A copy of each
such license is available at
http://www.opensource.org/licenses/gpl-2.0.php and
http://www.opensource.org/licenses/lgpl-2.1.php
Egypt#
```

In Example 5-18, NX-OS shows the default local fallback behavior, administratively shut-ting down interface gigabit ethernet 1/1 connected to the Cisco Secure ACS TACACS+ Server. The ping test demonstrates loss of connectivity to the TACACS+ server. The local fallback is required in the event that the AAA server is unreachable; there is no additional configuration required in NX-OS.

Example 5-18   *Default Local Fallback Behavior, Administratively Shutting Down Interface Gigabit Ethernet 1/1 Connected to Cisco Secure ACS TACACS+ Server*

```
Kenya(config)#int gi1/1
Kenya(config-if)#shut
Kenya(config-if)#
---------------------------------------------------------------------------
Egypt# ping 10.10.10.12
PING 10.10.10.12 (10.10.10.12): 56 data bytes
Request 0 timed out
```

```
Request 1 timed out
Request 2 timed out
Request 3 timed out
Request 4 timed out
--- 10.10.10.12 ping statistics ---

5 packets transmitted, 0 packets received, 100.00% packet loss
Egypt#
[hk@hk ~]$ telnet egypt
Trying 172.26.32.39...
Connected to egypt.
Escape character is '^]'.
User Access Verification
login: admin
Password:
Cisco Nexus Operating System (NX-OS) Software
TAC support: http://www.cisco.com/tac
Copyright (c) 2002-2009, Cisco Systems, Inc. All rights reserved.
The copyrights to certain works contained in this software are
owned by other third parties and used and distributed under
license. Certain components of this software are licensed under
the GNU General Public License (GPL) version 2.0 or the GNU
Lesser General Public License (LGPL) Version 2.1. A copy of each
such license is available at
http://www.opensource.org/licenses/gpl-2.0.php and
http://www.opensource.org/licenses/lgpl-2.1.php
Egypt#
2009 Oct  1 15:59:05 Egypt %TACACS-3-TACACS_ERROR_MESSAGE: All servers failed to
respond
2009 Oct  1 16:00:31 Egypt %TACACS-3-TACACS_ERROR_MESSAGE: All servers failed to
respond
Egypt#
```

Figure 5-6 shows the configuration of the Cisco Secure ACS TACACS+ configuration, which defines the loopback of the NX-OS device and shared secret key that needs to match between both the NX-OS device and the Cisco Secure ACS Server.

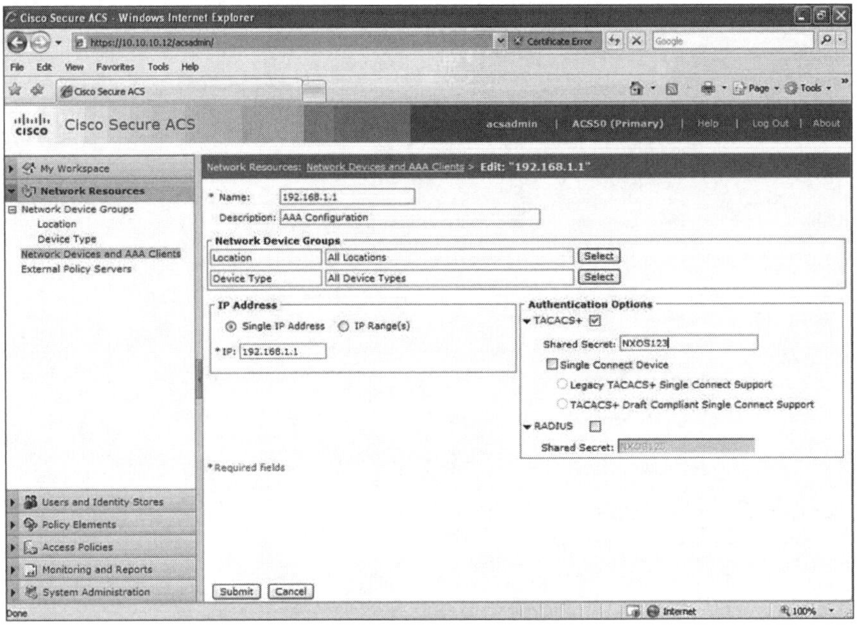

Figure 5-6 *Specific Cisco Secure ACS TACACS+ Configuration*

Figure 5-7 shows the configuration of the redundant NX-OS devices, both of which need to be defined.

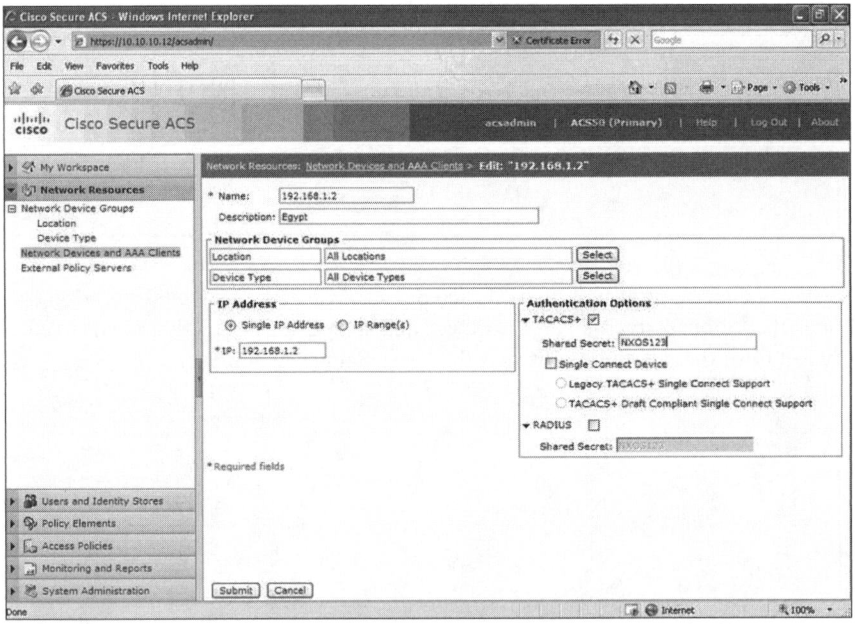

Figure 5-7 *Adding Redundant NX-OS Devices to the Cisco Secure ACS Database*

Figure 5-8 show successful TACACS+ authentication of user **admin** for SSH access to the NX-OS device.

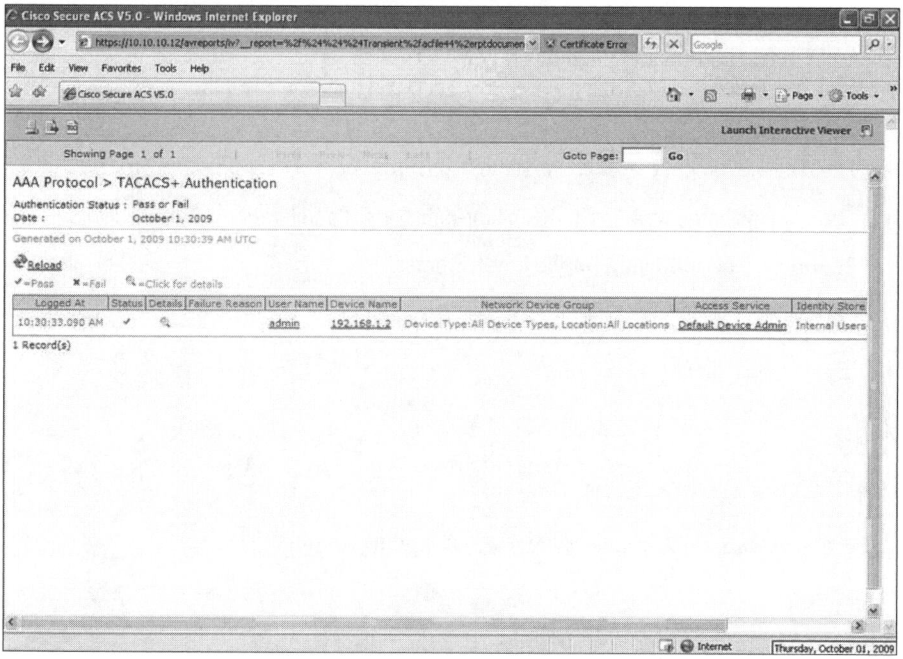

Figure 5-8   *Successful Authentication via TACACS+ for User "admin"*

Configuring SSH

Secure Shell (SSH) is composed of an SSH server, SSH client, and SSH server keys. SSH server is enabled on the NX-OS devices and a SSH client to make a secure, encrypted connection to a Cisco NX-OS device. SSH uses strong encryption for authentication; SSH user authentication mechanisms supported for SSH are RADIUS, TACACS+, and the default locally stored usernames and passwords.

The SSH client application runs over the SSH protocol to provide device authentication and encryption. The SSH client enables a Cisco NX-OS device to make a secure, encrypted connection to another Cisco NX-OS device or to any other device that runs the SSH server.

The NX-OS SSH server and SSH client implementation enables interoperability with publicly and commercially available implementations.

Cisco NX-OS supports the following SSH server keys:

- SSH requires server keys for secure communications to the Cisco NX-OS device. You can use SSH server keys for the following SSH options:

- SSH version 2 using Rivest, Shamir, and Adelman (RSA) public-key cryptography

- SSH version 2 using the Digital System Algorithm (DSA)

- Be sure to have an SSH Server key-pair with the appropriate version before enabling the SSH service. You can generate the SSH server key-pair according to the SSH Client version used. The SSH service accepts two types of key-pairs for use by SSH version 2:

  - The **dsa** option generates the DSA key-pair for the SSH version 2 protocol.

  - The **rsa** option generates the RSA key-pair for the SSH version 2 protocol.

- SSH supports the following public key formats:

  - OpenSSH

  - IETF Secure Shell (SECSH)

Note Ensure that you are in the correct VDC (or use the **switchto vdc** command).

To enable the SSH modular process, enter the following commands:

```
Congo# conf t
Enter configuration commands, one per line. End with CNTL/Z.
Congo(config)# feature ssh
```

Example 5-19 shows how to generate SSH Server keys. The default SSH Server key is an RSA key generated using 2048 per the code in Example 5-19 bits.

Example 5-19 *Generating a 2048-Bit SSH RSA Server Key*

```
Congo# conf t
Enter configuration commands, one per line. End with CNTL/Z.
Congo(config)# ssh key rsa 2048
rsa keys already present, use force option to overwrite them
Congo(config)# ssh key rsa 2048 force
deleting old rsa key.....
generating rsa key(2048 bits).....

generated rsa key
Congo(config)# feature ssh
Congo(config)# exit
```

Example 5-20 shows how to verify the SSH Server keys that were generated on the NX-OS device.

Example 5-20   *Verifying the SSH Server Keys That Were Generated on the NX-OS Device*

```
Congo# show ssh key
****************************************
rsa Keys generated:Wed Sep 30 14:38:37 2009

ssh-rsa AAAAB3NzaC1yc2EAAAABIwAAAQEAsxCDzRe9HzqwzWXSp5kQab2NlX9my68RdmFFsM0M+fAB
GNdwd5q01g5AKfuqvnrkAl7DR9n0d2v2Zde7JbZx2HCUjQFGEVAlK2a7I6pfCBschiRUf6j/7DBcCdHf
1SQrTTvQLhwEhFkbginXqlhuNjSbJj5uxMZYEInenxLswNe7Kc/Ovdw3lBbxdgHCKOSTrVs47PKshwST
PBcoqX/7Df5oCW8Um8ipJ0U3/7lnZlEE9Uz+ttT1zYf1ApqfsErAGT4wZo973Iza0Ub3lyWBnChQBN6n
ScxvYk/1wuqF4P0nS4ujnW9X+pxvBE1JedQDf6f0rj+Txt9L5AfqYnI+bQ==

bitcount:2048
fingerprint:
15:63:01:fc:9f:f7:66:35:3c:90:d3:f8:ed:f8:bb:16
****************************************
```

Example 5-21 shows how to verify SSH server communication to the NX-OS device.

Example 5-21   *Verifying SSH Server Communication to the NX-OS Device*

```
Congo# show int mgmt 0
mgmt0 is up
  Hardware: GigabitEthernet, address: 001b.54c1.b448 (bia 001b.54c1.b448)
  Internet Address is 172.26.32.37/27
  MTU 1500 bytes, BW 1000000 Kbit, DLY 10 usec,
      reliability 255/255, txload 1/255, rxload 1/255
  Encapsulation ARPA
  full-duplex, 1000 Mb/s
  Auto-Negotiation is turned on
  1 minute input rate 952 bits/sec, 1 packets/sec
  1 minute output rate 648 bits/sec, 0 packets/sec
  Rx
    12649 input packets 11178 unicast packets 951 multicast packets
    520 broadcast packets 1423807 bytes
  Tx
    7653 output packets 6642 unicast packets 953 multicast packets
    58 broadcast packets 943612 bytes

[hk@hk .ssh]$ ssh admin@172.26.32.37
User Access Verification
Password:
Cisco Nexus Operating System (NX-OS) Software
TAC support: http://www.cisco.com/tac
```

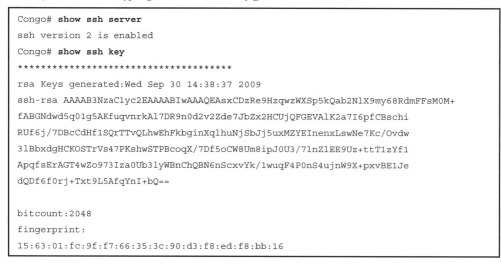

```
Copyright (c) 2002-2009, Cisco Systems, Inc. All rights reserved.
The copyrights to certain works contained in this software are
owned by other third parties and used and distributed under
license. Certain components of this software are licensed under
the GNU General Public License (GPL) version 2.0 or the GNU
Lesser General Public License (LGPL) Version 2.1. A copy of each
such license is available at
http://www.opensource.org/licenses/gpl-2.0.php and
http://www.opensource.org/licenses/lgpl-2.1.php
```

Example 5-22 shows how to verify SSH Server configuration on the NX-OS device.

Example 5-22 *Verifying SSH Server Configuration on the NX-OS Device*

```
Congo# show ssh server
ssh version 2 is enabled
Congo# show ssh key
**************************************
rsa Keys generated:Wed Sep 30 14:38:37 2009
ssh-rsa AAAAB3NzaC1yc2EAAAABIwAAAQEAsxCDzRe9HzqwzWXSp5kQab2NlX9my68RdmFFsM0M+
fABGNdwd5q01g5AKfuqvnrkAl7DR9n0d2v2Zde7JbZx2HCUjQFGEVAlK2a7I6pfCBschi
RUf6j/7DBcCdHf1SQrTTvQLhwEhFkbginXqlhuNjSbJj5uxMZYEInenxLswNe7Kc/Ovdw
3lBbxdgHCKOSTrVs47PKshwSTPBcoqX/7Df5oCW8Um8ipJ0U3/7lnZlEE9Uz+ttT1zYf1
ApqfsErAGT4wZo973Iza0Ub3lyWBnChQBN6nScxvYk/1wuqF4P0nS4ujnW9X+pxvBE1Je
dQDf6f0rj+Txt9L5AfqYnI+bQ==

bitcount:2048
fingerprint:
15:63:01:fc:9f:f7:66:35:3c:90:d3:f8:ed:f8:bb:16
```

Cisco TrustSec

Cisco TrustSec is a security architecture that builds upon policy, identity, and security into the network infrastructure. TrustSec security architecture creates secure networks by establishing a trusted set of network devices. Cisco TrustSec security architecture can control and identify the type of devices allowed, location, resources, and what resources are allowed access. This security architecture decouples the access control list (ACL) management of defining IP addresses to ACLs on a distributed enterprise network while having employees, guests, and contractors on the network fabric.

Cisco TrustSec can provide audit events, provide authentication information and history, and provide access control to enable enterprises to adhere to regulatory and compliance guidelines. TrustSec includes dynamic virtual local area networks (VLANs), downloadable access control lists (dACLs) or named ACLs. The packet classification is maintained by tagging packets on ingress to the Cisco TrustSec network so that they can be properly identified for the purpose of applying security and other policy enforcement criteria along the data path. The tag, also called the *security group tag (SGT)*, enables the network to enforce the access control policy by enabling the egress device to act upon the SGT to filter traffic.

MACsec (IEEE 802.1AE) encryption provides secure data transmission combined with hop-by-hop encrypted data inspection. It builds upon existing identity-aware infrastructure while helping to ensure complete data confidentiality between network devices.

The Cisco TrustSec architecture enables a more scalable network access control with authentication, classification, and authorization.

Authentication methods follows:

- 802.1X-based endpoint authentication
- MAC Authentication Bypass

After authentication, TrustSec can classify and apply a specific policy for the authenticated endpoint. This enforcement method is Authorization.

TrustSec supports the following Authorization methods:

- Dynamic VLAN Assignment
- Downloadable ACL from ISE
- Security Group Tag/Security Group ACL (SGTACL)

Figure 5-9 illustrates the Cisco TrustSec reference topology for the Cisco TrustSec example throughout the section.

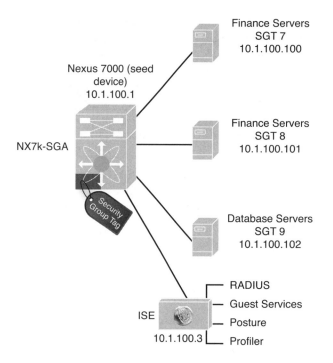

Figure 5-9   *Cisco TrustSec Example*

To enable 802.1x and CTS features on the NX-OS device for CTS support, enter the following commands:

```
NX7k-SGA# conf t
NX7k-SGA (config)# feature dot1x
NX7k-SGA (config)# feature cts
```

To verify that 802.1x and CTS features are enabled, enter the following command:

```
NX7k-SGA # show run cts
feature dot1x
feature cts
```

Note   The CTS unique device ID and password can have a maximum length of 32 characters and are case-sensitive.

Example 5-23 shows how to configure the CTS unique device ID.

Example 5-23 *Configuring the CTS Unique Device ID*

```
NX7k-SGA(config)# cts device-id NX7k-SGA password CTS_TrustSec123
```

To enable 802.1x and CTS features on the NX-OS device for CTS support on NX7k-SGA, enter the following commands:

```
NX7k-SGA# conf t
NX7k-SGA (config)# feature dot1x
NX7k-SGA (config)# feature cts
```

To verify that 802.1x and CTS features are enabled, enter the following command:

```
NX7k-SGA # show run cts
feature dot1x
feature cts
```

Configuring AAA for Cisco TrustSec

You can use Cisco Secure ACS for Cisco TrustSec authentication. You must configure RADIUS server groups and specify the default AAA authentication and authorization methods on one of the Cisco TrustSec-enabled Cisco NX-OS devices in your network cloud. Because Cisco TrustSec supports RADIUS relay, you need to configure AAA only on a seed Cisco NX-OS device that is directly connected to a Cisco Secure ACS. For all the other Cisco TrustSec-enabled Cisco NX-OS devices, Cisco TrustSec automatically provides a private AAA server group, aaa-private-sg. The seed devices use the management VRF to communicate with the Cisco Secure ACS.

Note   Only the Cisco Secure ACS or the Cisco Identity Services Engine (ISE) supports Cisco TrustSec.

Example 5-24 shows how to configure a RADIUS server host with a key and proxy auto-config (PAC) file on NX7k-SGA.

Example 5-24 *Configuring the RADIUS Server Host with a Key and PAC on NX7k-SGA*

```
NX7k-SGA # conf t
NX7k-SGA (config)# radius-server host 10.1.100.3 key TrustSec123 pac
! Specifying the RADIUS server group and enter RADIUS server group configuration
mode on NX7k-SGA
NX7k-SGA # conf t
NX7k-SGA (config)# aaa group server radius CTS1
NX7k-SGA (config-radius)#
! Specify  the RADIUS server host address. on NX7k-SGA
NX7k-SGA # conf t
NX7k-SGA (config)# aaa group server radius CTS1
NX7k-SGA (config-radius)#
! Specify  the management VRF for the AAA server group on NX7k-SGA
NX7k-SGA (config-radius)# use-vrf management
! Exit RADIUS server group configuration mode on NX7k-SGA
NX7k-SGA (config-radius)# exit
NX7k-SGA (config)#
! Specify the RADIUS server groups to use for 802.1X Authentication on NX7k-SGA
NX7k-SGA (config)# aaa authentication dot1x default group CTS1
! Specify the RADIUS server groups to use for TrustSec authorization on NX7k-SGA
NX7k-SGA (config)# aaa authentication cts default group CTS1
```

The following SGT example uses the Cisco ISE platform. As many servers are in the data center, this example demonstrates how to use SGTs to tag each server and use SGACLs to enforce traffic between them. The Security Group Access (SGA) enables dynamic control for server-to-server communication. The dynamic control enables operational excellence; it also, for example, reduces the administrative overhead by not defining static access lists on each switch. This example is going to demonstrate SGT enforcement between the servers on the same Layer 2 VLAN. The SGT enforcement could also leverage servers on different subnets. SGACLs can be used to filter traffic between them.

Defining Network Device Admission Control

Network Device Admission Control (NDAC) is a key component of TrustSec because it creates a trusted network by enabling only authenticated switches into the network. The following list that explains the steps for defining NDAC:

1. As illustrated in Figure 5-10, in ISE, navigate to **Administration > Network Resources > Network Devices**.

2. Click **Add**.

3. Enter the name **Nx7k-SGA** and an IP address of **10.1.100.1**.

4. Click **Submit.**

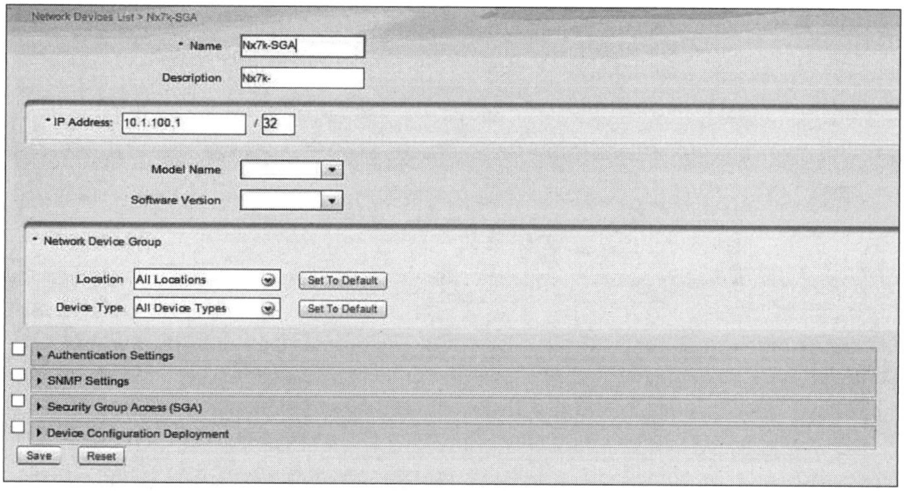

Figure 5-10 *Creating Network Devices in ISE*

5. Under **Network Device Group**, click the "+" to create a new device group, as illustrated in Figure 5-11.

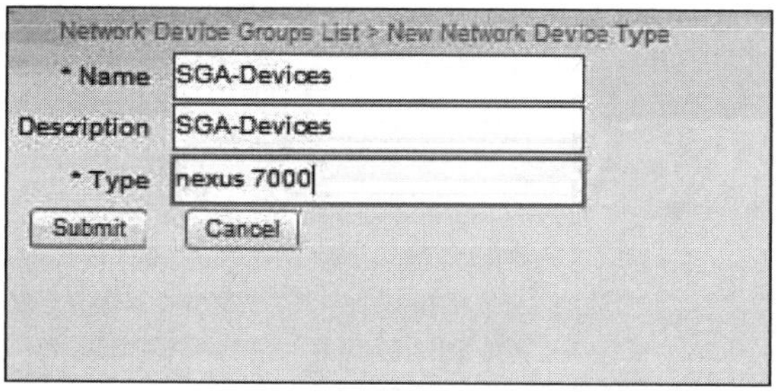

Figure 5-11 *Creating a Device Group in ISE*

6. Now that you have created the SGA Device Group, select it as the Device Type.

7. Scroll down and check the box for **Authentication Settings.** Configure the secret as "cisco123".

8. Scroll down and check the box for **Security Group Access (SGA).** Fill in the resulting fields and check boxes, as shown in Figure 5-12.

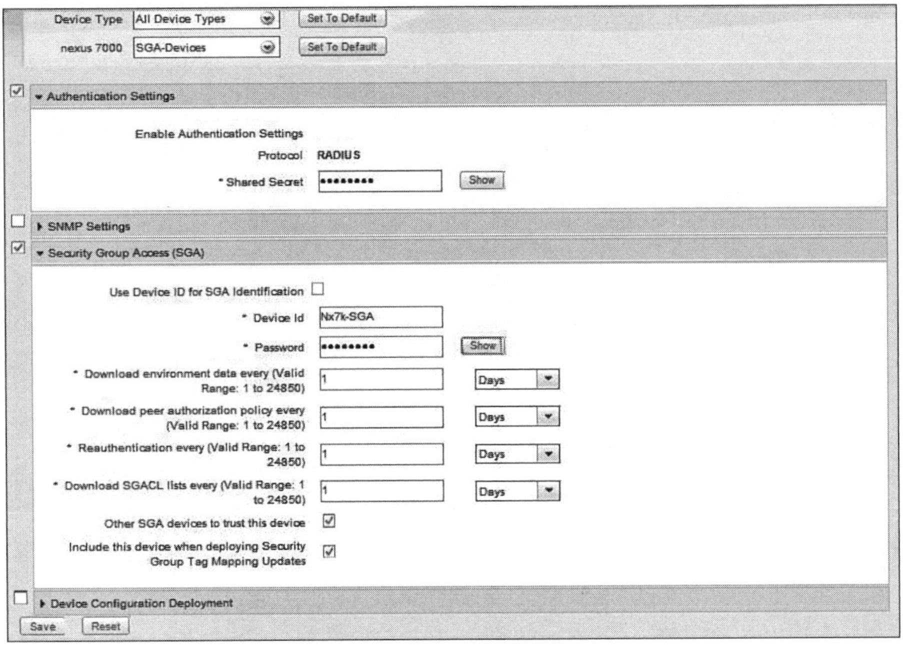

Figure 5-12 *The Required Fields to Enter the Specific Attributes for the Devices Being Added*

9. To create the security group in ISE, navigate to **Policy > Policy Elements > Results > Security Group Access >Security Groups**. Click **Add**.

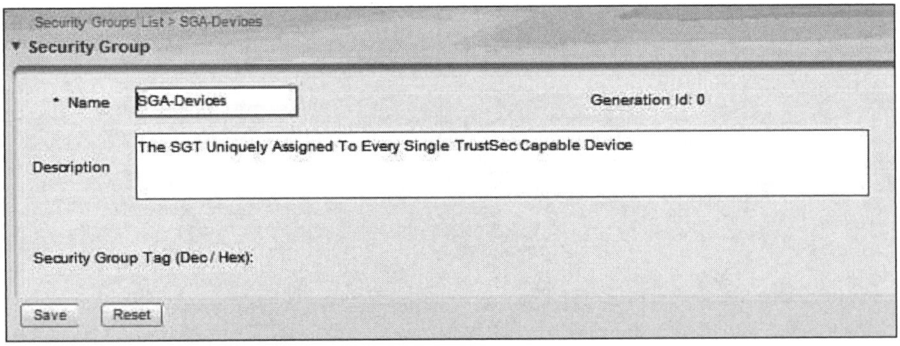

Figure 5-13 *Creating the Security Group in ISE*

10. Next create a policy rule by navigating to **Policy > Security Group Access > Network Device Authorization**. On the far right, click the **Actions** button, as shown in Figure 5-14, and choose **Insert New Row Above**.

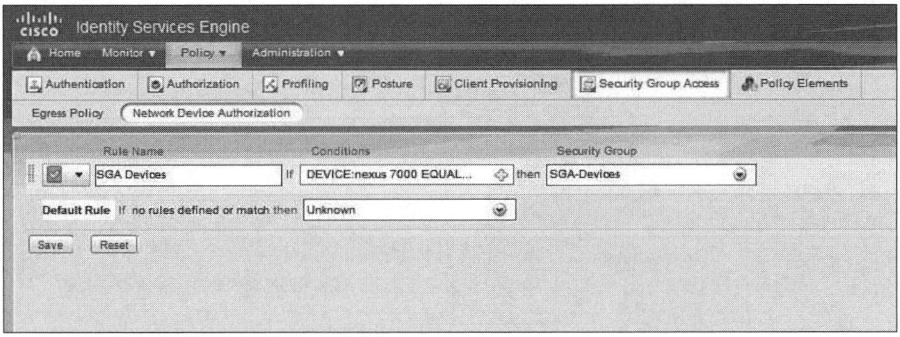

Figure 5-14 *Creating a Policy Rule in ISE*

You have now created an NDAC policy to assign the SGT-Device-SGT to all switches that are part of the SGA Device Group grouping.

Configuring the Nexus 7000 for 802.1x and SGA Features

Example 5-25 shows how to enable 802.1x and CTS features on the Nexus 7000 device.

Example 5-25 *Enabling 802.1x and CTS Features on a Nexus 7000 Device*

```
NX7K-SGA# conf t
Enter configuration commands, one per line.   End with CNTL/Z.
NX7K-SGA(config)# feature dot1x
NX7K-SGA(config)# feature cts
NX7K-SGA(config)# end
```

Example 5-26 shows how to verify the 802.1x feature is properly enabled.

Example 5-26 *Verifying 802.1x Is Properly Enabled*

```
NX7K-SGA# show dot1x
Sysauthcontrol Enabled
Dot1x Protocol Version 2
NX7K-SGA#
```

Example 5-27 shows how to verify that 802.1x and SGA are enabled on the Nexus 7000 device.

Example 5-27   *Verifying 802.1x and SGA Are Enabled on the Nexus 7000*

```
NX7K-SGA# show cts
CTS Global Configuration
==============================
CTS support          : enabled
CTS device identity  : not configured
SGT                  : 0
CTS caching support  : disabled
Number of CTS interfaces in
DOT1X mode : 0
Manual mode : 0
```

Next, configure the Nexus 7000 to join the TrustSec domain, as demonstrated in Example 5-28.

Example 5-28   *Configuring the Trustsec Domain on the Nexus 7000 Device*

```
NX7K-SGA(config)# cts device-id Nx7k-SGA password C!sco123
NX7K-SGA(config)#
```

Note   The device ID must match the name entry in ISE.

Example 5-29 shows how to verify the device identity has been configured for the TrustSec domain on the Nexus 7000 device.

Example 5-29   *Verifying Device Identity Configuration*

```
Nx7k-SGA# show cts
CTS Global Configuration
==============================
  CTS support          : enabled
  CTS device identity  : Nx7k-SGA
  SGT                  : 0
  CTS caching support  : disabled

  Number of CTS interfaces in
    DOT1X mode : 0
    Manual mode : 0

NX7K-SGA#
```

Example 5-30 shows how to configure the AAA commands that are required for 802.1x authentication with ISE.

Example 5-30 *Configuring AAA Commands Required for 802.1x Authentication with ISE*

```
NX7K-SGA# conf t
Enter configuration commands, one per line.  End with CNTL/Z.
NX7K-SGA(config)# radius-server host 10.1.100.3 key Cisco123 pac
NX7K-SGA(config)# aaa group server radius ise-radius
NX7K-SGA(config-radius)# server 10.1.100.3
NX7K-SGA(config-radius)# use-vrf default
NX7K-SGA(config-radius)#
```

Example 5-31 shows how to configure AAA for communication with ISE and for 802.1x authentication.

Example 5-31 *Configuring AAA for ISE Communication and 802.1x Authentication*

```
NX7K-SGA# conf t
Enter configuration commands, one per line.  End with CNTL/Z.
NX7K-SGA(config)# aaa authentication dot1x default group ise-radius
NX7K-SGA(config)# aaa accounting dot1x default group ise-radius
NX7K-SGA(config)# aaa authorization cts default group ise-radius
NX7K-SGA(config)# cts device-id NX7k-SGA password C!sco123
```

Note   The last command, **cts device-id NX7k-SGA password C!sco123**, invokes device registration with ISE and forces a PAC download.

Example 5-32 shows the successful download of the PAC file to the Nexus 7000 device.

Example 5-32 *Confirming PAC File Download Success to the Nexus 7000*

```
NX7K-SGA(config)# show cts pac
PAC Info :
==============================
  PAC Type            : Trustsec
  AID                 : f0d01f8a0e202a0525da1f9f7ec4f4bd
  I-ID                : NX7K-SGA
  AID Info            : ise
  Credential Lifetime : Tue Feb  7 12:19:08 2012

  PAC Opaque          : 000200b00003000100040010f0d01f8a0e202a0525da1f9f7ec4f4bd
```

```
00060094000301006005c57a476fc548351719db92a342c2000000134e37fc8101dfe2008a499eed
04f29035429b72cabdfcfdf5648dd6fb79a2ee971dd6e55159c01a3214e9f6eeaab4b1b2ba20eca7
c5c23621d1f292b56ecd70525c3c03a4d58b02ce393f1c97c4148f34ce864637f4cd2da2eebd6a3b
85cfdc4769ddc2e5d27ebe14a242f2b20935d9aa3b3281ea1324687aa8038857


NX7K-SGA(config)#
```

Example 5-33 shows the CTS environmental data.

Example 5-33 *Displaying CTS Environmental Data*

```
NX7K-SGA# show cts environment-data
CTS Environment Data
==============================
  Current State         : CTS_ENV_DNLD_ST_ENV_DOWNLOAD_DONE
  Last Status           : CTS_ENV_SUCCESS
  Local Device SGT      : 0x0006
  Transport Type        : CTS_ENV_TRANSPORT_DIRECT
  Data loaded from cache : FALSE
  Env Data Lifetime     : 86400 seconds after last update
  Last Update Time      : Wed Nov  9 19:08:16 2011


  Server List           : CTSServerList1
    AID:f0d01f8a0e202a0525da1f9f7ec4f4bd IP:10.1.100.3 Port:1812
```

SGT Assignment via ISE Server

This example demonstrates SGT assignment via the ISE server; the policy component creates SGT for the resources attached to the TrustSec domain.

For SGT creation, go to **Policy > Policy Elements > Results > Security Group Access > Security Groups**, and click **Add**.

Create the SGT values for the following user and server groups: FinanceServers, PublicServers, and DatabaseServers.

Figure 5-15 shows the information for the FinanceServers server group. Repeat the same actions for the other two server groups.

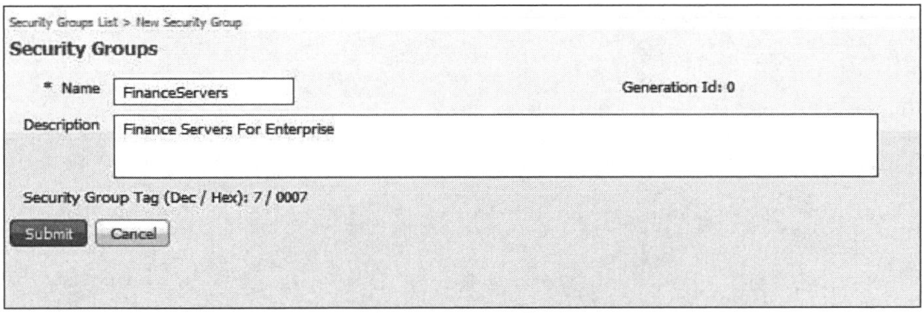

Figure 5-15 *Creating the Security Group for FinanceServers in ISE*

Figure 5-16 shows all the security groups created and the associated SGT in ISE.

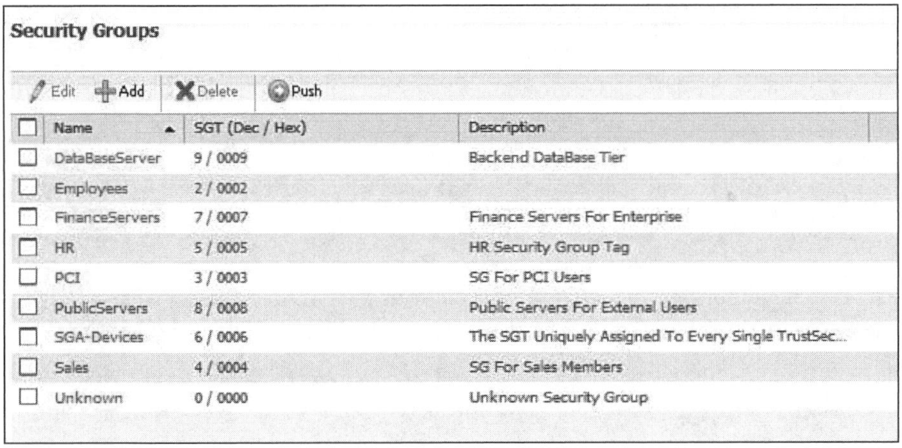

Figure 5-16 *Displaying All the Created Security Groups and the Associated SGT in ISE*

The following SGTs have been assigned to the following resources:

- Employees 2 (decimal) / 0002 (hex)

- PCI 3 (decimal) / 0003 (hex)

- Sales 4 (decimal)/ 0004 (hex)

- HR 5 (decimal) / 0005 (hex)

- SGA-Devices 6 (decimal) / 0006 (hex)

- FinanceServers 7 (decimal) / 0007 (hex)

- PublicServers 8 (decimal) / 0008 (hex)

- DataBaseServer 9 (decimal) / 0009 (hex)

Note SGT values are determined by the order in which the tag is created on the ISE server. SGT tags are assigned sequentially based on the order created in the tool. For example, Employees was entered first followed by PCI, Sales, and so on.

Policy Component: IP to SGT Mapping

This section demonstrates IP to SGT mapping on ISE. After the mappings are defined in ISE, the ISE deploys these mappings to the N7K.

Note IP addresses are typically statically defined. This solution simplifies the data center use case to define SGT to IP mappings.

1. Go to **Policy> Policy Elements > Results > Security Group Access > Security Group Mappings.** Add the IP to SGT mappings illustrated in Figure 5-17 through Figure 5-19.

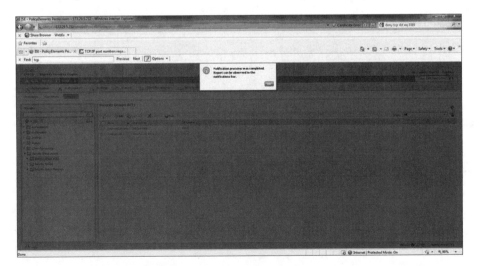

Figure 5-17 *Adding the IP to SGT Mappings in ISE*

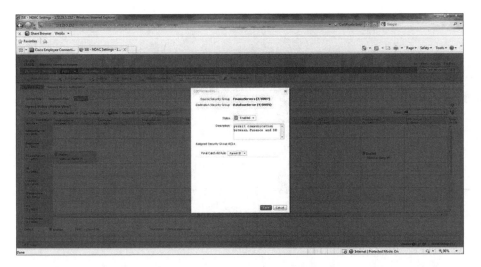

Figure 5-18 *Adding Permissions Between Security Groups Defined in ISE*

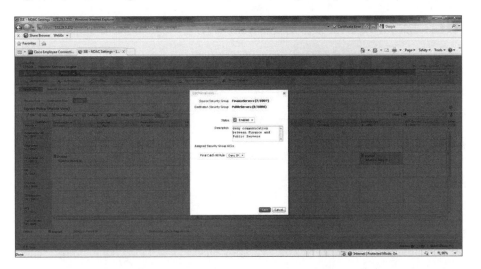

Figure 5-19 *Adding Permissions Between Security Groups Defined in ISE*

2. Click the **Check Status** icon. ISE compares its SGT mapping to what is configured on the N7K, as illustrated in Figure 5-20. Currently, there is no configuration on the N7K; therefore, the result will be "Not Up to Date".

> **Note** Make sure you have configured the Device Configuration Deployment with the proper credentials to authenticate to the network devices; without this, you receive a Device Not Reachable error message.

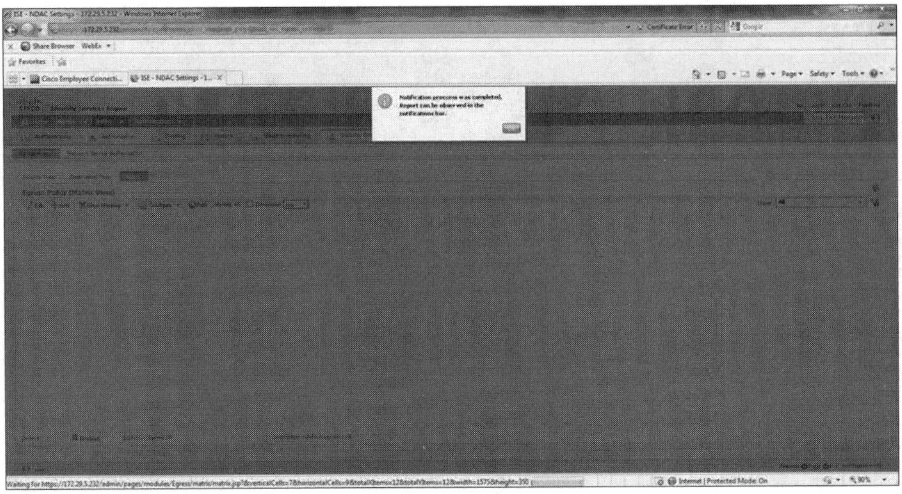

Figure 5-20 *The ISE Compares Its SGT Mapping to What Is Configured on the Nexus 7000*

3. Click **Deploy** to push the SGT mappings to the N7K.

4. Verify on Nexus 7000 SGT to IP Mappings, as demonstrated in Example 5-34.

Example 5-34 *Verifying the SGT to IP Mappings Deployed to the Nexus 7000 from the ISE*

```
NX7K-SGA# show cts role-based sgt-map
IP ADDRESS          SGT          VRF/VLAN       SGT CONFIGURATION
10.1.100.100        7            vrf:1          CLI Configured
10.1.100.101        8            vrf:1          CLI Configured
10.1.100.102        9            vrf:1          CLI Configured
NX7K-SGA#
```

The next thing to do is to create Security Group Access Control Lists (SGACL) that will be used to create security policy.

Policy Component: SGACL Creation

1. Go to **Policy** >**Policy Elements** >**Results** >**Security Group Access** > **Security Group ACLs.**

2. Enter **WebServers** for the name and then the SGACL to permit http, https, dns, icmp (ping), and deny RDP traffic (3389), as demonstrated in Example 5-35.

Example 5-35 *Policy Created for Web and Database Servers*

```
WebServers
permit tcp dst eq 80
permit tcp dst eq 443
permit udp dst eq 53
permit icmp
deny tcp dst eq 3389


Database Servers
permit tcp dst eq 1433
```

3. Click **Push** to deploy the security group ACLs.

Now that you have SGT and SGACLs defined, you need to construct the Egress policy:

1. Go to **Policy > Security Group Access > Egress Policy**.

2. Click **Add Security Group ACL Mapping**.

3. Select Source Security Group as **IT_Servers** and Destination Security Group as **Finance_Servers**.

For the Assigned Security Group ACLs, you need to enforce the SGACL policy created on ISE, as demonstrated in Example 5-36.

Example 5-36 *Enforcing the SGACL Policy on the Nexus 7000*

```
NX7K-SGA# conf t
Enter configuration commands, one per line.  End with CNTL/Z.
NX7K-SGA(config)# cts role-based enforcement
NX7K-SGA(config)# cts role-based counters enable
Note: Clearing previously collected counters...
NX7K-SGA(config)# cts refresh role-based-policy
NX7K-SGA(config)#


Push the following the devices
NX7K-SGA# sho cts role-based policy
sgt:7
dgt:9    rbacl:Permit IP
        permit ip


sgt:7
dgt:8    rbacl:Deny IP
        deny ip


sgt:any
```

```
dgt:any rbacl:Permit IP
        permit ip
```

Example 5-37 verifies the downloaded SGACL policy on the Nexus 7000 from the ISE.

Example 5-37   *Verifying the Downloaded SGACL Policy*

```
NX7K-SGA# show cts role-based policy
sgt:7
dgt:9    rbacl:Permit IP
        permit ip

sgt:7
dgt:8    rbacl:Deny IP
        deny ip

sgt:any
dgt:any rbacl:Permit IP
        permit ip
```

Note   The output from Example 5-36 and Example 5-37 verify the policy defined on the ISE. The policy for the source group-tag of 7 (Finance Servers) and a destination group-tag of 9 (Database Servers) will permit traffic; the policy for source group-tag of 7 (Finance Servers) and the destination group-tag of 8 (Public Servers) deny traffic. The last statement is the default egress policy of permit any.

Configuring Cisco TrustSec: IEEE 802.1AE LinkSec

With the Cisco TrustSec security suite, Cisco NX-OS provides data confidentiality and integrity, supporting standard IEEE 802.1AE link-layer cryptography with 128-bit Advanced Encryption Standard (AES) cryptography. Link-layer cryptography helps ensure end-to-end data privacy while enabling the insertion of security service devices along the encrypted path. Today, the IEEE 802.1AE link-layer encryption is point-to-point. The Cisco TrustSec security architecture builds secure networks by establishing trusted network devices. Each device is authenticated by its neighbors. Communication on the links between devices in the cloud is secured with a combination of encryption, message integrity checks, and data-path replay protection mechanisms.

Refer to the network topology in Figure 5-21 for the configurations in this section.

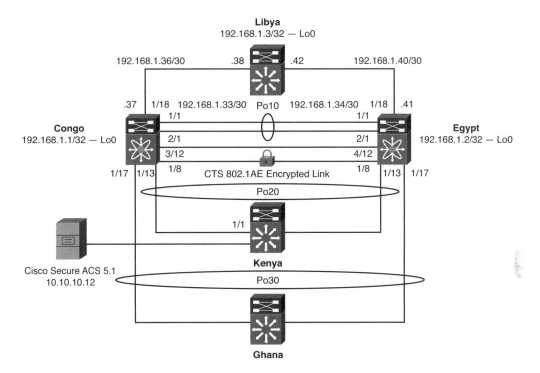

Figure 5-21   *Cisco CTS 802.1AE Topology*

To enable 802.1x and CTS features on the NX-OS device for CTS support, enter the following commands:

```
Egypt# conf t
Egypt (config)# feature dot1x
Egypt (config)# feature cts
```

To verify that 802.1x and CTS features are enabled, enter the following command:

```
Egypt# show run cts
feature dot1x
feature cts
```

Note   The CTS unique device ID and password can have a maximum length of 32 characters and are case-sensitive.

Example 5-38 shows how to configure the CTS unique device ID.

Example 5-38   *Configuring the CTS Unique Device ID*

```
Egypt(config)# cts device-id egypt-cts password CTS_TrustSec123

Egypt(config) # interface Ethernet1/8
Egypt(config-if)# description to Congo
Egypt(config-if)# switchport
Egypt(config-if)# switchport access vlan 500
Egypt(config-if)# cts manual
Egypt(config-if-cts-manual)# sap pmk deadbeef modelist gcm-encrypt
(config-if-cts-manual)# mtu 9216
Egypt(config-if)# no shutdown

Egypt(config)# interface Vlan500
Egypt(config-if)# no shutdown
Egypt(config-if)# ip address 1.1.1.1/24
```

To enable 802.1x and CTS features on the NX-OS device for CTS support on Congo, enter the following commands:

```
Congo# conf t
Congo (config)# feature dot1x
Congo (config)# feature cts
```

To verify that 802.1x and CTS features are enabled, enter the following command:

```
Egypt# show run cts
feature dot1x
feature cts
```

Example 5-39 shows how to configure the CTS unique device ID on Congo.

Example 5-39   *Configuring the CTS Unique Device ID on Congo*

```
Congo(config)# cts device-id congo-cts password CTS_TrustSec123

Congo(config)# interface Ethernet1/8
Congo(config-if)# description to Egypt
Congo(config-if)# switchport
Congo(config-if)# switchport access vlan 500
Congo(config-if)# cts manual
Congo(config-if-cts-manual)# sap pmk deadbeef modelist gcm-encrypt
Congo(config-if-cts-manual)# mtu 9216
Congo(config-if)# no shutdown
Congo(config)# interface Vlan500
```

```
Congo(config-if)# no shutdown
Congo(config-if)# ip address 1.1.1.2/24
--------------------------------------------------------------------
Egypt# show runn int e1/8

!Command: show running-config interface Ethernet1/8
!Time: Wed Sep 30 18:25:19 2009

version 5.2(3a)

interface Ethernet1/8
  description to Congo
  cts manual
    sap pmk deadbeef0000000000000000000000000000000000000000000000000000000000
  switchport
  switchport access vlan 500
  mtu 9216
  no shutdown
```

Example 5-40 demonstrates how to verify the CTS configuration on Egypt.

Example 5-40   *Verifying the CTS Configuration on Egypt*

```
Egypt# show runn cts

!Command: show running-config cts
!Time: Wed Sep 30 18:25:27 2009

version 5.2(3a)
feature cts
cts device-id egypt-cts password 7 FPW_LrpxlVoh123

interface Ethernet1/8
  cts manual
    sap pmk deadbeef0000000000000000000000000000000000000000000000000000000000

Egypt# show cts interface e1/8
CTS Information for Interface Ethernet1/8:
    CTS is enabled, mode:       CTS_MODE_MANUAL
    IFC state:                  CTS_IFC_ST_CTS_OPEN_STATE
    Authentication Status:      CTS_AUTHC_SKIPPED_CONFIG
      Peer Identity:
      Peer is:                  Unknown in manual mode
      802.1X role:              CTS_ROLE_UNKNOWN
      Last Re-Authentication:
```

```
      Authorization Status:    CTS_AUTHZ_SKIPPED_CONFIG
        PEER SGT:              0
        Peer SGT assignment:   Not Trusted
      SAP Status:              CTS_SAP_SUCCESS
        Configured pairwise ciphers: GCM_ENCRYPT
        Replay protection: Enabled
        Replay protection mode: Strict
        Selected cipher: GCM_ENCRYPT
        Current receive SPI: sci:23ac65020c0000 an:2
        Current transmit SPI: sci:23ac6409d80000 an:2
Egypt#
```

Example 5-41 demonstrates verifying the CTS configuration on Congo.

Example 5-41 *Verify the CTS Configuration on Congo*

```
Congo# show runn int e1/8

!Command: show running-config interface Ethernet1/8
!Time: Wed Sep 30 18:24:39 2009

version 5.2(3a)

interface Ethernet1/8
  description to Egypt
  cts manual
    sap pmk deadbeef00000000000000000000000000000000000000000000000000000000
  switchport
  switchport access vlan 500
  mtu 9216
  no shutdown

Congo# show runn cts

!Command: show running-config cts
!Time: Wed Sep 30 18:24:48 2009

version 5.2(3a)
feature cts
cts device-id congo-cts password 7 FPW_LrpxlVoh123
interface Ethernet1/8
  cts manual
    sap pmk deadbeef00000000000000000000000000000000000000000000000000000000
Congo# show cts interface e1/8
CTS Information for Interface Ethernet1/8:
```

```
    CTS is enabled, mode:    CTS_MODE_MANUAL
    IFC state:               CTS_IFC_ST_CTS_OPEN_STATE
    Authentication Status:   CTS_AUTHC_SKIPPED_CONFIG
      Peer Identity:
      Peer is:               Unknown in manual mode
      802.1X role:           CTS_ROLE_UNKNOWN
      Last Re-Authentication:
    Authorization Status:    CTS_AUTHZ_SKIPPED_CONFIG
      PEER SGT:              0
      Peer SGT assignment:   Not Trusted
    SAP Status:              CTS_SAP_SUCCESS
      Configured pairwise ciphers: GCM_ENCRYPT
      Replay protection: Enabled
      Replay protection mode: Strict
      Selected cipher: GCM_ENCRYPT
      Current receive SPI: sci:23ac6409d80000 an:1
      Current transmit SPI: sci:23ac65020c0000 an:1

Congo#
```

Example 5-42 confirms the VLAN used for CTS to verify correct configuration.

Example 5-42   *Confirming the VLAN Used for CTS*

```
Congo# show vlan

VLAN Name                        Status    Ports
-------------------------------------------------------------------------------
1    default                     active    Po10
5    Congo_Egypt_Transit         active    Po10
10   Secure_Subnet               active    Po10, Po20, Po30
100  Server_Subnet1              active    Po10, Po30
500  CTS_TrustSec                active    Po10, Eth1/8

VLAN Type
---- -----
1    enet
5    enet
10   enet
100  enet
500  enet
```

Example 5-43 demonstrates a ping test between Congo and Egypt (the two Nexus 7000 switches), showing an encrypted ping frame is captured on the receiving Nexus 7000

through the embedded WireShark application running in NX-OS on Egypt. The ping test
verifies that traffic is making it through the encrypted CTS 802.1AE session between
Congo and Egypt.

Example 5-43   *Ping Test Between Congo and Egypt*

```
Started ping from Congo:
Congo# ping 1.1.1.1
PING 1.1.1.1 (1.1.1.1): 56 data bytes
64 bytes from 1.1.1.1: icmp_seq=0 ttl=254 time=1.189 ms
64 bytes from 1.1.1.1: icmp_seq=1 ttl=254 time=0.702 ms
64 bytes from 1.1.1.1: icmp_seq=2 ttl=254 time=0.718 ms
64 bytes from 1.1.1.1: icmp_seq=3 ttl=254 time=0.601 ms
64 bytes from 1.1.1.1: icmp_seq=4 ttl=254 time=0.604 ms


Egypt# ethanalyzer local interface inband detail limit-captured-frames 200


Frame 4 (98 bytes on wire, 98 bytes captured)
    Arrival Time: Sep 30, 2009 18:39:12.837070000
    [Time delta from previous captured frame: 0.255613000 seconds]
    [Time delta from previous displayed frame: 0.255613000 seconds]
    [Time since reference or first frame: 0.256374000 seconds]
    Frame Number: 4
    Frame Length: 98 bytes
    Capture Length: 98 bytes
    [Frame is marked: False]
    [Protocols in frame: eth:ip:icmp:data]
Ethernet II, Src: 00:1b:54:c2:76:41 (00:1b:54:c2:76:41), Dst: 00:1b:54:c2:78:c1
(00:1b:54:c2:78:c1)
    Destination: 00:1b:54:c2:78:c1 (00:1b:54:c2:78:c1)
        Address: 00:1b:54:c2:78:c1 (00:1b:54:c2:78:c1)
        .... ...0 .... .... .... .... = IG bit: Individual address (unicast)
        .... ..0. .... .... .... .... = LG bit: Globally unique address (factory
default)
    Source: 00:1b:54:c2:76:41 (00:1b:54:c2:76:41)
        Address: 00:1b:54:c2:76:41 (00:1b:54:c2:76:41)
        .... ...0 .... .... .... .... = IG bit: Individual address (unicast)
        .... ..0. .... .... .... .... = LG bit: Globally unique address (factory
 default)
    Type: IP (0x0800)
Internet Protocol, Src: 1.1.1.2 (1.1.1.2), Dst: 1.1.1.1 (1.1.1.1)
    Version: 4
    Header length: 20 bytes
    Differentiated Services Field: 0x00 (DSCP 0x00: Default; ECN: 0x00)
        0000 00.. = Differentiated Services Codepoint: Default (0x00)
```

```
        .... ..0. = ECN-Capable Transport (ECT): 0
        .... ...0 = ECN-CE: 0
    Total Length: 84
    Identification: 0x43b2 (17330)
    Flags: 0x00
        0... = Reserved bit: Not set
        .0.. = Don't fragment: Not set
        ..0. = More fragments: Not set
    Fragment offset: 0
    Time to live: 255
    Protocol: ICMP (0x01)
    Header checksum: 0x73f2 [correct]
        [Good: True]
        [Bad : False]
    Source: 1.1.1.2 (1.1.1.2)
    Destination: 1.1.1.1 (1.1.1.1)
Internet Control Message Protocol
    Type: 8 (Echo (ping) request)
    Code: 0 ()
    Checksum: 0x5573 [correct]
    Identifier: 0x572d
    Sequence number: 0 (0x0000)
    Data (56 bytes)

0000  e1 a5 c3 4a cd e7 03 00 cd ab 00 00 cd ab 00 00   ...J............
0010  cd ab 00 00 cd ab 00 00 cd ab 00 00 cd ab 00 00   ................
0020  cd ab 00 00 cd ab 00 00 cd ab 00 00 cd ab 00 00
................
0030  30 31 32 33 34 35 36 37                           01234567
        Data: E1A5C34ACDE70300CDAB0000CDAB0000CDAB0000CDAB0000...
```

Note   Ethanalyzer is available only in the default Virtual Device Context (VDC). Ethanalyzer can capture traffic received by the Supervisor from both the out-of-band management port (mgmt0) and the I/O modules.

Layer 2 Solutions Between Data Centers

A top customer request is to have Layer 2 connectivity between data centers to accommodate the clustering and server virtualization applications. With the Layer 2 requirement often follows the need for encryption whether driven by regulatory and compliance regulations or other factors. The Nexus 7000 supports 802.1AE point-to-point LinkSec encryption on all M-series and some F2e-series interfaces in hardware. Refer to

Figure 5-8 if you have a Multiprotocol Label Switching (MPLS) environment; you can front-end the Nexus 7000 switches with an ASR1000 or a Catalyst 6500 running port-mode Ethernet over MPLS (EoMPLS). Port-mode EoMPLS looks like a wire to the Nexus 7000; this is important because you need to make sure that the control-plane SAP messages (Security Association Protocol EAPOL frames) for CTS Encryption are forwarded through the EoMPLS pseudo-wire (PW). Also, Virtual port-channel (vPC) on the Nexus 7000 enables for a loop-free spanning-tree environment and STP isolation so that you can have an STP root in each data center.

If MPLS is not required, the Nexus 7000 TrustSec can secure data across a remote data center if Layer 2 and BPDU transparency is ensured through dark fiber or dense wavelength division multiplexing (DWDM) transport.

If the Cisco ASR1000 is used for the port-mode EoMPLS connectivity, it provides remote-port shutdown where communication of link status to a CE and traffic from the Customer Edge (CE) can be stopped if MPLS or the PW is down. Remote port shutdown enables subsecond failover and restoration to local/remote links/nodes end-to-end signaled through LDP.

Figure 5-22 illustrates Data Center Interconnect, which provides P2P interconnect with encryption through the MPLS cloud. The Nexus 7000s and ASR1002s are configured with Cisco TrustSec and port-mode EoMPLS PW, respectively.

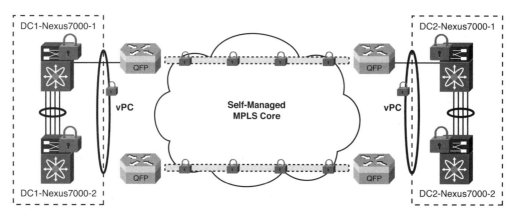

Figure 5-22   *Data Center Interconnects Across an MPLS Cloud Leveraging Cisco TrustSec on the Nexus 7000*

Configuring IP ACLs

ACLs are ordered sets of rules that you can use to filter traffic; each rule specifies a set of conditions that a packet must satisfy to match the rule. The first matching rule determines whether the packet is permitted or denied. ACLs protect networks and specific hosts from unnecessary or unwanted traffic. NX-OS supports IPv4 and IPv6 IP ACLs to be created and applied to interfaces, VLAN interfaces, and port-channels.

To improve the scalability of ACL management, using Session Manager is recommended to perform ACL configuration, verify ACL configuration, and confirm that the resources required by the configuration are available prior to committing them to the running configuration. Session Manager supports the following benefits for ACL management:

- **Configuration session:** Creates a list of commands that you want to implement in Session Manager mode.

- **Validation:** Provides a basic semantic check on your configuration.

- **Verification:** Verifies the configuration as a whole, based on the existing hardware and software configuration and resources.

- **Commit:** Cisco NX-OS verifies the complete configuration and applies the changes to the device.

- **Session termination:** Session Manager enables termination of a configuration session without committing the changes. Session Manager enables session configurations to be saved. Session configurations can be saved to bootflash:, slot0:, or volatile:.

Example 5-44 shows how to create a configuration session and enter session configuration mode.

Example 5-44 *Creating a Configuration Session and Entering Session Configuration Mode*

```
Congo# conf t
Enter configuration commands, one per line. End with CNTL/Z.
Congo(config)# configure session ACL-TCP-IN
Config Session started, Session ID is 3
```

Example 5-45 shows how to create an ACL to enable TCP.

Example 5-45 *Creating an ACL*

```
Congo(config-s)# ip access-list TCP1
Congo(config-s-acl)# permit tcp any any
Congo(config-s-acl)# exit
Congo(config-s)# save bootflash:SessionMgrTCPIn
Congo(config-s)# interface ethernet 1/1
```

Example 5-46 shows how to apply the ACL to the interface and specify the direction to apply the access group.

Example 5-46   *Applying the ACL to the Interface and Specifying the Direction to Apply the Access Group*

```
Congo(config-s-if)# ip access-group TCP1 in
```

Example 5-47 shows how to verify the configuration as a whole, based on the existing hardware and software configuration and resources. The NX-OS device returns errors if the configuration does not pass this verification.

Example 5-47   *Verifying the Configuration as a Whole, Based on the Existing Hardware and Software Configuration and Resources*

```
Congo(config-s-if)# verify
Verification Successful
```

Example 5-48 validates the configuration changes made in the current session and applies the changes to the device. If the validation fails, the NX-OS device reverts to the original configuration.

Example 5-48   *Validating the Configuration Changes Made in the Current Session and Applying the Changes to the Device*

```
Congo(config-s)# commit
Commit Successful
```

Example 5-49 shows how to verify the Session Manager and the ACL.

Example 5-49   *Verifying the Session Manager and the ACL*

```
Congo# conf t
Congo(config)# configure session ACL-TCP-IN
Config Session started, Session ID is 3
Congo(config-s)# ip access-list TCP1
Congo(config-s-acl)# permit tcp any any
Congo(config-s-acl)# interface e1/1
Congo(config-s-if)# ip access-group TCP1 in
Congo(config-s-if)# show configuration session
config session IP-ACL1

config session ACL-TCP-IN
0001  ip access-list TCP1
0002  permit tcp any any
0003  interface Ethernet1/1
0004  ip access-group TCP1 in
```

```
Number of active configuration sessions = 3
Congo(config-s-if)# save  bootflash:SessionMgrTCPIn
Congo(config-s)# verify
Verification Successful
Congo(config-s)# commit
Commit Successful

Congo# show access-lists TCP1

IP access list TCP1
      10 permit tcp any any
Congo# show running-config interface e1/1

!Command: show running-config interface Ethernet1/1
!Time: Sat Oct 10 12:10:55 2009

version 5.2(3a)

interface Ethernet1/1
  description to Egypt
  ip access-group TCP1 in
  switchport
  switchport access vlan 500
  mtu 9216
  no shutdown

Congo#
```

Configuring MAC ACLs

MAC ACLs match traffic information in the Layer 2 header of packets to filter traffic. MAC packet classification enables you to control whether a MAC ACL on a Layer 2 interface applies to all traffic entering the interface, including IP traffic, or to non-IP traffic only.

Note   MAC ACLs can be applied to ingress traffic only.

Example 5-50 shows how to create a MAC ACL and enter ACL configuration.

Example 5-50   *Creating a MAC ACL and Entering ACL Configuration*

```
Egypt# conf t
Enter configuration commands, one per line. End with CNTL/Z.
Egypt(config)# mac access-list mac-acl
Egypt(config-mac-acl)# permit 0050.561f.73d3 0050.56bc.48dd any
```

Example 5-51 shows how to maintain global statistics and a counter for packets that match the ACL rules. The switch maintains global statistics for packets that match the rules in the ACL.

Example 5-51   *Maintaining Global Statistics and Counter for Packets That Match the ACL Rules*

```
Egypt(config-mac-acl)# statistics per-entry
```

Example 5-52 shows how to verify the MAC ACL configuration.

Example 5-52   *Verifying the MAC ACL Configuration*

```
Egypt(config-mac-acl)# show mac access-lists mac-acl

MAC access list mac-acl
        statistics per-entry
        10 permit 0050.561f.73d3 0050.56bc.48dd any
Egypt(config-mac-acl)# exit
Egypt(config)# exit

Egypt(config)# mac access-list mac-acl
Egypt(config-mac-acl)# 100 permit  0050.561f.73d3 0000.00ff.ffff any
Egypt# show mac access-lists mac-acl

MAC access list mac-acl
        statistics per-entry
        10 permit 0050.561f.73d3 0050.56bc.48dd any
        100 permit 0050.561f.73d3 0000.00ff.ffff any
```

Example 5-53 shows how to change the ACL sequence numbers assigned to rules in a MAC ACL. Resequencing is useful when you need to insert rules into an ACL. The first rule receives the number specified, and each subsequent rule receives a number larger than the preceding rule. The difference in numbers is determined by the increment number that you specify.

Example 5-53   *Changing the ACL Sequence Numbers Assigned to Rules in a MAC ACL*

```
Egypt(config)# resequence mac access-list mac-acl 200 10
Egypt(config)# exit
Egypt# show mac access-lists mac-acl

MAC access list mac-acl
        statistics per-entry
        200 permit 0050.561f.73d3 0050.56bc.48dd any
        210 permit 0050.561f.73d3 0000.00ff.ffff any
Egypt#
```

Configuring VLAN ACLs

A VLAN ACL (VACL) is an application of a MAC ACL or IP ACL. You can configure VACLs to apply to all packets routed into or out of a VLAN or bridged within a VLAN. VACLs are deployed for security packet filtering and redirecting traffic to specific physical interfaces.

Note   VACLs are not defined by direction (ingress or egress).

Example 5-54 shows how to configure a VACL to forward traffic permitted by a MAC ACL named acl-mac-map.

Example 5-54   *Creating a VACL or Adding a VACL Entry*

```
Egypt# conf t
Enter configuration commands, one per line. End with CNTL/Z.
Egypt(config)# vlan access-map acl-mac-map
Egypt(config-access-map)# match mac address mac-acl
Egypt(config-access-map)# action forward
Egypt(config-access-map)# statistics per-entry
Egypt(config-access-map)# exit
Egypt(config)# exit
Egypt# show runn aclmgr

!Command: show running-config aclmgr
!Time: Thu Oct  1 17:19:24 2009

version 5.2(3a)
mac access-list mac-acl
  statistics per-entry
  200 permit 0050.561f.73d3 0050.56bc.48dd any
```

```
    210 permit 0050.561f.73d3 0000.00ff.ffff any
vlan access-map acl-mac-map 10
        match mac address mac-acl
        action forward
        statistics per-entry
Egypt#
```

Example 5-55 shows how to apply the VACL to the VLAN list.

Example 5-55   *Applying the VACL to the VLAN List*

```
Egypt(config)# vlan filter acl-mac-map vlan-list 10
Egypt(config)# show running-config aclmgr


!Command: show running-config aclmgr
!Time: Thu Oct  1 17:24:17 2009
version 5.2(3a)
mac access-list mac-acl
  statistics per-entry

  200 permit 0050.561f.73d3 0050.56bc.48dd any
  210 permit 0050.561f.73d3 0000.00ff.ffff any
vlan access-map acl-mac-map 10
        match mac address mac-acl
        action forward
        statistics per-entry
vlan filter acl-mac-map vlan-list 10
Egypt(config)#
```

Configuring Port Security

Port security enables you to configure Layer 2 physical interfaces and Layer 2 port-channel interfaces that enable inbound traffic from only a restricted set of MAC address-es. The MAC addresses in the restricted set are called *secure MAC addresses*. In addition, the device does not enable traffic from these MAC addresses on another interface within the same VLAN. The number of MAC addresses that the device can secure is configurable per interface.

Example 5-56 shows how to verify the port security feature and enable it if it is currently disabled.

Example 5-56 *Verifying and Enabling the Port Security Feature Is Enabled Globally*

```
Egypt(config)# show feature | i port
eth_port_sec          1           disabled
Egypt(config)# feature port-security
Egypt(config)# show feature | i port
eth_port_sec          1           enabled
Egypt(config)#
```

Example 5-57 shows how to enable port security on Layer 2 interfaces.

Example 5-57 *Enabling Port Security on Layer 2 Interfaces*

```
Egypt# conf t
Enter configuration commands, one per line. End with CNTL/Z.
Egypt(config)# int e1/1
Egypt(config-if)# switchport port-security
Egypt(config-if)#
Egypt# show running-config port-security
!Command: show running-config port-security
!Time: Thu Oct  1 17:41:20 2009

version 5.2(3a)


feature port-security


interface Ethernet1/1
  switchport port-security


Egypt#
```

Note When port security is disabled on an interface, all port security configuration for the interface is lost, including any secure MAC addresses learned on the interface.

Example 5-58 shows how to enable sticky MAC address learning. When you enable sticky learning on an interface, the switch does not perform dynamic learning and performs sticky learning instead; the switch does not age sticky secure MAC addresses.

Example 5-58   *Enabling Sticky MAC Address Learning*

```
Egypt# conf t
Enter configuration commands, one per line. End with CNTL/Z.
Egypt(config)# int e1/1
Egypt(config-if)# switchport port-security mac-address sticky
Egypt(config-if)# exit
Egypt# show running-config port-security


!Command: show running-config port-security
!Time: Thu Oct  1 17:43:06 2009


version 5.2(3a)
feature port-security


interface Ethernet1/1
  switchport port-security
  switchport port-security mac-address sticky


Egypt#
```

Note   If sticky learning is disabled on an interface, the interface reverts back to the default state of dynamic MAC address learning.

Example 5-59 shows how to add a static secure MAC address to Interface Ethernet 1/1. The static MAC is useful for "misbehaving" applications with MAC addresses (for example, cluster servers and load balancers).

Example 5-59   *Add a Static Secure MAC Address to an Interface*

```
Egypt# conf t
Enter configuration commands, one per line. End with CNTL/Z.
Egypt(config)# int e1/1
Egypt(config-if)# switchport port-security mac-address 0050.561f.73d3
Egypt(config-if)# exit
Egypt# show running-config port-security


!Command: show running-config port-security
!Time: Thu Oct  1 17:46:20 2009


version 5.2(3a)
feature port-security
```

```
interface Ethernet1/1
  switchport port-security
  switchport port-security mac-address 0050.561F.73D3

Egypt# show port-security

Total Secured Mac Addresses in System (excluding one mac per port)    : 0
Max Addresses limit in System (excluding one mac per port) : 8192
-----------------------------------------------------------------------

Secure Port  MaxSecureAddr  CurrentAddr  SecurityViolation  Security Action
             (Count)        (Count)      (Count)
-----------------------------------------------------------------------
Ethernet1/1       1              1            0              Shutdown
=======================================================================
Egypt#
```

Security Violations and Actions

When a security violation occurs, a violation action is configurable on each interface enabled with port security. The configurable violation actions are as follows:

- **shutdown:** Shuts down the interface that received the packet that triggered the violation; the interface is error-disabled. Reenabling the interface, it retains its port security configuration, including its secure MAC addresses.

- **errdisable:** Global configuration command to configure the device to reenable the interface automatically if a shutdown occurs, or you can manually reenable the interface by entering the **shutdown** and **no shutdown** interface configuration commands.

- **restrict:** After 100 security violations occur, the device disables learning on the interface and drops all ingress traffic from nonsecure MAC addresses. In addition, the device generates an SNMP notification for each security violation. The address that triggered the security violation is learned, but any traffic from the address is dropped.

- **protect:** Prevents further violations from occurring. The address that triggered the security violation is learned, but any traffic from the address is dropped.

Note The default security action is to shut down the port on which the security violation occurs.

Example 5-60 shows how to configure the specific port security violations on interface Ethernet 1/1.

Example 5-60   *Configuring the Specific Port Security Violations on Interface Ethernet 1/1*

```
Egypt# conf t
Enter configuration commands, one per line. End with CNTL/Z.
Egypt(config)# interface ethernet 1/1
Egypt(config-if)# switchport port-security violation ?
  protect    Security violation protect mode
  restrict   Security violation restrict mode
  shutdown   Security violation shutdown mode

Egypt(config-if)# switchport port-security violation
```

Example 5-61 shows how to configure a maximum number of MAC addresses on Interface Ethernet 1/1. Depending on what connects to the interface, such as a virtualized server, you need to increase the number of MAC addresses, based on the number of virtual machines and virtual interfaces.

Note   A maximum number of MAC addresses can be learned or statically configured on a Layer 2 interface. By default, an interface has a maximum of one secure MAC address; VLANs have no default maximum.

Example 5-61   *Configuring a Maximum Number of MAC Addresses on Interface Ethernet 1/1*

```
Egypt(config)# int e1/1
Egypt(config-if)# switchport port-security maximum 51
Egypt(config-if)# show port-security

Total Secured Mac Addresses in System (excluding one mac per port)   : 0
Max Addresses limit in System (excluding one mac per port) : 8192
------------------------------------------------------------------

Secure Port  MaxSecureAddr  CurrentAddr  SecurityViolation  Security Action
             (Count)        (Count)      (Count)
------------------------------------------------------------------
Ethernet1/1      51             0            0              Shutdown
==================================================================
Egypt(config-if)#

Egypt# show port-security int e1/1
Port Security          : Enabled
Port Status            : Secure UP
```

```
Violation Mode            : Shutdown
Aging Time                : 0 mins
Aging Type                : Absolute
Maximum MAC Addresses     : 51
Total MAC Addresses       : 0
Configured MAC Addresses  : 0
Sticky MAC Addresses      : 0
Security violation count  : 0
Egypt#
```

Configuring DHCP Snooping

DHCP snooping is the traffic cop between untrusted hosts and trusted DHCP servers. DHCP snooping performs the following responsibilities:

- Validates DHCP messages received from untrusted sources and filters out invalid messages

- Builds and maintains the DHCP snooping binding database, which contains information about untrusted hosts with leased IP addresses

- Uses the DHCP snooping binding database to validate subsequent requests from untrusted hosts

Note   By default, the feature is inactive on all VLANs; DHCP snooping is enabled on a per-VLAN basis.

Example 5-62 shows how to enable and verify the DHCP snooping process/feature.

Example 5-62   *Enabling the DHCP Snooping Process/Feature*

```
Egypt# show feature | i dhcp-snooping
dhcp-snooping       1          disabled
Egypt# conf t
Enter configuration commands, one per line. End with CNTL/Z.
Egypt(config)# feature dhcp
Egypt(config)# show feature | i dhcp-snooping
dhcp-snooping       1          enabled
Egypt(config)#


Egypt(config)# show running-config dhcp


!Command: show running-config dhcp
!Time: Thu Oct  1 18:08:40 2009
```

```
version 5.2(3a)
feature dhcp

service dhcp
ip dhcp relay

Egypt(config)#
```

Note   Enable DHCP snooping globally on the switch. Globally disabling DHCP snooping stops the device from performing any DHCP snooping or relaying DHCP messages.

Example 5-63 shows how to enable DHCP snooping globally.

Example 5-63   *Enabling DHCP Snooping Globally*

```
Egypt# conf t
Enter configuration commands, one per line. End with CNTL/Z.
Egypt(config)# ip dhcp snooping
Egypt(config)# show running-config dhcp

!Command: show running-config dhcp
!Time: Thu Oct  1 18:11:05 2009

version 5.2(3a)
feature dhcp

ip dhcp snooping
service dhcp
ip dhcp relay

Egypt(config)#
```

Example 5-64 shows how to enable DHCP snooping on a per-VLAN basis, allowing granularity of configuration.

Example 5-64   *Enabling DHCP Snooping on a Per-VLAN Basis*

```
Egypt(config)# ip dhcp snooping vlan 5,10,100,500
Egypt(config)# show runn dhcp

!Command: show running-config dhcp
!Time: Thu Oct  1 18:12:28 2009
```

```
version 5.2(3a)
feature dhcp

ip dhcp snooping
ip dhcp snooping vlan 5,10,100,500
service dhcp
ip dhcp relay

Egypt(config)#
```

If the device receives a packet on an untrusted interface and the source MAC address and the DHCP client hardware address do not match, address verification causes the device to drop the packet.

Example 5-65 shows how to enable DHCP Snooping MAC Address verification.

Example 5-65   *Enabling DHCP Snooping MAC Address Verification*

```
Egypt(config)# ip dhcp snooping verify mac-address
```

Example 5-66 shows how to configure interface Ethernet 1/1 trusted source of DHCP messages. The trusted interface is an interface configured to receive only messages from within the network.

Example 5-66   *Configuring Interface Ethernet 1/1 Trusted Source of DHCP Messages*

```
Egypt# conf t
Enter configuration commands, one per line. End with CNTL/Z.
Egypt(config)# int e1/1
Egypt(config-if)# ip dhcp snooping trust
Egypt(config-if)# exit
Egypt# show running-config dhcp

!Command: show running-config dhcp
!Time: Thu Oct  1 18:16:13 2009

version 5.2(3a)
feature dhcp

interface Ethernet1/1
  ip dhcp snooping trust
ip dhcp snooping
ip dhcp snooping vlan 5,10,100,500
service dhcp
```

```
ip dhcp relay

Egypt#
```

Example 5-67 shows how to verify the DHCP Snooping configuration.

Example 5-67   *Verifying the DHCP Snooping Configuration*

```
Egypt# show ip dhcp snooping
DHCP snooping service is enabled
Switch DHCP snooping is enabled
DHCP snooping is configured on the following VLANs:
5,10,100,500
DHCP snooping is operational on the following VLANs:
5,10,100,500
Insertion of Option 82 is disabled
Verification of MAC address is enabled
DHCP snooping trust is configured on the following interfaces:
Interface          Trusted
------------       -------
Ethernet1/1        Yes
Egypt#


Egypt# show ip dhcp snooping binding
MacAddress         IpAddress        LeaseSec  Type        VLAN  Interface
0050.561f.73d3     10.10.10.211     1600      dynamic     100   ethernet4/1
----------------   --------------   --------  ----------  ----  -------------
Egypt#
```

The DHCP binding table shows the client MAC address; client IP address assigned from
the DHCP server; IP address lease time; binding type, statically configured from the CLI
or dynamically learned; VLAN number of the client interface; and the interface that connects to the DHCP client host.

Configuring Dynamic ARP Inspection

Address Resolution Protocol (ARP) provides IP communication within a Layer 2 broadcast domain by mapping an IP address to a MAC address. There are known security
issues with ARP, such as ARP spoofing attacks. ARP spoofing attacks affect hosts,
switches, and routers connected to your Layer 2 network by sending false information to
the ARP caches of the devices connected to the subnet.

Dynamic ARP Inspection (DAI) ensures that only valid ARP requests and responses are
relayed. When DAI is enabled and properly configured, an NX-OS device performs the
following activities:

- Intercepts all ARP requests and responses on untrusted ports

- Verifies that each of these intercepted packets has a valid IP-to-MAC address binding before updating the local ARP cache or before forwarding the packet to the appropriate destination

- Drops invalid ARP packets

DAI can determine the validity of an ARP packet based on valid IP-to-MAC address bindings stored in a DHCP snooping binding database. This database is built by DHCP snooping if DHCP snooping is enabled on the VLANs and on the device. It can also contain static entries that you create. If the ARP packet is received on a trusted interface, the device forwards the packet without any checks. On untrusted interfaces, the device forwards the packet only if it is valid.

Example 5-68 shows how to enable DAI for VLAN 10.

Example 5-68   *Enabling DAI for a VLAN 10*

```
Egypt# conf t
Enter configuration commands, one per line. End with CNTL/Z.
Egypt(config)# ip arp inspection vlan 10
Egypt(config)# show ip arp inspection vlan 10


Source Mac Validation     : Disabled
Destination Mac Validation : Disabled
IP Address Validation     : Disabled


Vlan : 10
-----------
Configuration    : Enabled
Operation State  : Active
Egypt(config)#
```

Dynamic ARP Inspection Trust State

A device forwards ARP packets that it receives on a trusted Layer 2 interface but does not check them. On untrusted interfaces, the device intercepts all ARP requests and responses and verifies that the intercepted packets have valid IP-MAC address bindings before updating the local cache and forwarding the packet to the appropriate destination.

Example 5-69 shows how to configure DAI trust state of a Layer 2 interface.

Note   By default, all interfaces are untrusted.

Example 5-69   *Configuring DAI Trust State of a Layer 2 Interface*

```
Egypt(config)# int e1/1
Egypt(config-if)# ip arp inspection trust
Egypt(config-if)# show ip arp inspection int e1/1


 Interface        Trust State
 ------------     -----------
 Ethernet1/1        Trusted


Egypt(config-if)#
```

Example 5-70 shows how to apply ACLs to VLANs for DAI filtering. The NX-OS device permits only packets that the ACL permits. In this case, the ACL creates a rule that permits any ARP message with IP address 10.10.10.12 and MAC address of 0050.561f.73d3.

Example 5-70   *Applying ACLs to VLANs for DAI Filtering*

```
Egypt(config)# arp access-list arp-list
Egypt(config-arp-acl)# 10 permit request ip 10.10.10.12 0.0.0.0 mac 0050.561f.73d3
EEEE.EEEE.EEEE
Egypt(config-arp-acl)# exit
Egypt(config)# ip arp inspection filter arp-list vlan 10
Egypt(config)# show ip arp inspection vlan 10


Source Mac Validation      : Disabled
Destination Mac Validation : Disabled
IP Address Validation      : Disabled


Vlan : 10
-----------
Configuration     : Enabled
Operation State   : Active
ACL Match         : arp-list
Egypt(config)#
```

Example 5-71 shows how to enable additional DAI validation including DAI intercepts, logs, and the discard of ARP packets with invalid IP-to-MAC address bindings. You can enable additional validation on the destination MAC address, the sender and target IP addresses, and the source MAC address.

Example 5-71 *Enabling Additional DAI Validation*

```
Egypt(config)# ip arp inspection validate src-mac dst-mac ip
Egypt(config)# show running-config dhcp

!Command: show running-config dhcp
!Time: Thu Oct  1 18:42:12 2009

version 5.2(3a)
feature dhcp


interface Ethernet1/1
  ip dhcp snooping trust
  ip arp inspection trust
ip dhcp snooping
ip dhcp snooping vlan 5,10,100,500
service dhcp
ip dhcp relay
ip arp inspection validate src-mac dst-mac ip
ip arp inspection vlan 10
ip arp inspection filter arp-list vlan 10

Egypt(config)#
```

Example 5-72 shows how to verify the DAI configuration.

Example 5-72 *Verifying the DAI Configuration on Egypt*

```
Egypt# show ip arp inspection

Source Mac Validation      : Enabled
Destination Mac Validation : Enabled
IP Address Validation      : Enabled


Vlan : 1
-----------
Configuration     : Disabled
Operation State   : Inactive


Vlan : 5
-----------
Configuration     : Disabled
Operation State   : Inactive
Vlan : 10
```

```
-----------
Configuration    : Enabled
Operation State  : Active
ACL Match        : arp-list

ARP Req Forwarded  = 0
ARP Res Forwarded  = 0
ARP Req Dropped    = 2
ARP Res Dropped    = 6
DHCP Drops         = 8
DHCP Permits       = 0
SMAC Fails-ARP Req = 0
SMAC Fails-ARP Res = 0
DMAC Fails-ARP Res = 0
IP Fails-ARP Req   = 0
IP Fails-ARP Res   = 0


Vlan : 100
-----------
Configuration    : Disabled
Operation State  : Inactive


Vlan : 500
-----------
Configuration    : Disabled
Operation State  : Inactive
Egypt# show ip arp inspection interface ethernet 1/1

 Interface        Trust State
 ------------     -----------
 Ethernet1/1        Trusted
Egypt# show ip arp inspection vlan 10
Source Mac Validation      : Enabled
Destination Mac Validation : Enabled
IP Address Validation      : Enabled


Vlan : 10
-----------
Configuration    : Enabled
Operation State  : Active
ACL Match        : arp-list
Egypt# show arp access-lists
ARP access list arp-list
10 permit request ip 10.10.10.12 255.255.255.0 mac 0050.561f.73d3 eeee.eeee
Egypt#
```

Configuring IP Source Guard

IP Source Guard is configured on a per-interface traffic filter that permits IP traffic only when the IP address and MAC address of each packet matches one of two sources of IP and MAC address bindings:

- Entries in the DHCP Snooping binding table

- Static IP source entries

Filtering on trusted IP and MAC address bindings helps prevent spoofing attacks, in which an attacker uses the IP address of a valid host to gain unauthorized network access. To circumvent IP Source Guard, an attacker would have to spoof both the IP address and the MAC address of a valid host.

You can enable IP Source Guard on Layer 2 interfaces that are not trusted by DHCP Snooping. IP Source Guard supports interfaces that are configured to operate in access mode and trunk mode. When you initially enable IP Source Guard, all inbound IP traffic on the interface is blocked except for the following:

- DHCP packets, which DHCP Snooping inspects and then forwards or drops, depending upon the results of inspecting the packet

- IP traffic from static IP source entries that you have configured in the Cisco NX-OS device

Example 5-73 demonstrates how to enable IP Source Guard on Layer 2 interface Ethernet 1/1.

Example 5-73   *Enabling IP Source Guard on a Layer 2 Interface*

```
Egypt# conf t
Enter configuration commands, one per line. End with CNTL/Z.
Egypt(config)# interface ethernet 1/1
Egypt(config-if)# ip verify source dhcp-snooping-vlan
Egypt(config-if)# show running-config dhcp


!Command: show running-config dhcp
!Time: Thu Oct  1 18:47:28 2009
version 5.2(3a)
feature dhcp
interface Ethernet1/1
  ip dhcp snooping trust
  ip arp inspection trust
  ip verify source dhcp-snooping-vlan
ip dhcp snooping
ip dhcp snooping vlan 5,10,100,500
```

```
service dhcp
ip dhcp relay
ip arp inspection validate src-mac dst-mac ip
ip arp inspection vlan 10
ip arp inspection filter arp-list vlan 10

Egypt(config-if)#
```

Example 5-74 demonstrates how to add a static IP source entry on interface Ethernet 1/1.

Example 5-74   *Adding a Static IP Source Entry on Interface Ethernet 1/1*

```
Egypt(config)# ip source binding 10.10.10.12 0050.561f.73d3 vlan 10 interface e1
Egypt(config)# show ip dhcp snooping binding
MacAddress          IpAddress        LeaseSec  Type      VLAN  Interface
-------------------------------------------------------------------
00:50:56:1f:73:d3  10.10.10.12      infinite  static    10    Ethernet1/1
Egypt(config)#
```

Configuring Keychain Management

Keychain management includes the creation and maintenance of keychains, which are sequences of keys or shared secrets. Keychains can be used with features such as routing protocols for secure, authenticated communication with other devices.

Example 5-75 demonstrates how to configure keychain management and create a keychain.

Example 5-75   *Configuring Keychain Management and Creating a Keychain*

```
Egypt(config)# key chain nexus
Egypt(config-keychain)#
```

Example 5-76 demonstrates how to configure the key for the keychain; the default accept and send lifetime for a new key are infinite.

Example 5-76   *Configuring the Key for the Keychain*

```
Egypt(config-keychain)# key 7010
Egypt(config-keychain)#
```

Example 5-77 demonstrates how to associate the keychain. This example shows associating the keychain nexus with OSPF authentication.

Example 5-77 *Associating the Keychain*

```
ip ospf authentication key-chain nexus
```

Example 5-78 verifies the keychain association and management.

Example 5-78 *Verifying the Keychain Association and Management*

```
Egypt# show key chain nexus
Key-Chain nexus
  Key 1 -- text 7 070124545b1a12000e
    accept lifetime (always valid) [active]
    send lifetime (always valid) [active]
Egypt# show ip ospf
Area BACKBONE(0.0.0.0)
      Area has existed for 1d00h
      Interfaces in this area: 3 Active interfaces: 3
      Passive interfaces: 0  Loopback interfaces: 1
      Message-digest authentication
      SPF calculation has run 15 times
       Last SPF ran for 0.000527s
      Area ranges are
      Number of LSAs: 8, checksum sum 0x3c6ce
```

Configuring Traffic Storm Control

Traffic storms occur when packets flood the LAN, creating excessive traffic and degrading network performance. The traffic storm control feature in NX-OS prevents disruptions on Layer 2 ports by a broadcast, multicast, or unknown unicast traffic storm on physical interfaces. Within NX-OS, the administrator is allowed to monitor the levels of the incoming broadcast, multicast, and unicast traffic over a 1-second interval. During the 1-second interval, the traffic level is compared with the traffic storm control level configured. The storm control levels are configured as a percentage of the total available bandwidth of the port. If the ingress traffic reaches the traffic storm control level configured as a percentage of bandwidth of the port, storm control drops the traffic until the interval ends.

Example 5-79 shows how to configure broadcast traffic storm control on interface Ethernet 1/1.

Example 5-79 *Configuring Broadcast Traffic Storm Control*

```
Egypt(config)# interface ethernet 1/1
Egypt(config-if)# storm-control broadcast level 20
```

Example 5-80 verifies the broadcast storm control percentage of bandwidth on interface Ethernet 1/1.

Example 5-80 *Verifying Broadcast Storm Control Percentage of Bandwidth*

```
Egypt# show interface ethernet 1/1 counters storm-control


Port        UcastSupp %    McastSupp %    BcastSupp %    TotalSuppDiscards
--------------------------------------------------------------------
Eth1/1        100.00         100.00         20.00            0
Egypt#
Egypt# show interface ethernet 1/1 counters storm-control
--------------------------------------------------------------------


Port        UcastSupp %    McastSupp %    BcastSupp %    TotalSuppDiscards
--------------------------------------------------------------------
Eth1/1        100.00         100.00         20.00            0
Egypt#
```

Example 5-81 shows how to configure multicast traffic storm control on interface Ethernet 1/1.

Example 5-81 *Configuring Multicast Traffic Storm Control on an Interface*

```
Egypt# conf t
Enter configuration commands, one per line. End with CNTL/Z.
Egypt(config)# interface ethernet 1/1
Egypt(config-if)# storm-control multicast level 20
```

Example 5-82 verifies the multicast storm control percentage of bandwidth on interface Ethernet 1/1.

Example 5-82 *Verifying the Multicast Storm Control Percentage of Bandwidth on Interface Ethernet 1/1*

```
Egypt# show interface ethernet 1/1 counters storm-control
--------------------------------------------------------------------


Port        UcastSupp %    McastSupp %    BcastSupp %    TotalSuppDiscar
--------------------------------------------------------------
Eth1/1        100.00          20.00          20.00
Egypt#
```

Example 5-83 shows how to configure unicast traffic storm control on interface Ethernet 1/1.

Example 5-83 *Configuring Unicast Traffic Storm Control on Interface Ethernet 1/1*

```
Egypt# conf t
Enter configuration commands, one per line. End with CNTL/Z.
Egypt(config)# interface ethernet 1/1
Egypt(config-if)# storm-control unicast level 20
Egypt(config-if)#
```

Example 5-84 verifies the unicast storm control percentage of bandwidth on interface Ethernet 1/1.

Example 5-84 *Verifying the Unicast Storm Control Percentage of Bandwidth on Interface Ethernet 1/1*

```
Egypt# show interface ethernet 1/1 counters storm-control
--------------------------------------------------------------------

Port        UcastSupp %    McastSupp %    BcastSupp %    TotalSuppDiscar
--------------------------------------------------------------------
Eth1/1         20.00          20.00          20.00
Egypt#
```

Configuring Unicast RPF

Unicast Reverse Path Forwarding (RPF) reduces the chances of malformed or forged (spoofed) IPv4 or IPv6 source addresses into a network by discarding IPv4 or IPv6 packets that are not valid IP source addresses. Several security threats or types of attacks such as denial-of-service (DoS) attacks, Smurf attacks, and Tribal Flood Network (TFN) attacks take advantage of forged or rapidly changing source IPv4 or IPv6 addresses. Unicast RPF deflects attacks by forwarding only the packets that have source addresses that are valid and consistent with the IP routing table. When Unicast RPF is enabled on an interface, the NX-OS device examines all ingress packets received on that interface to ensure that the source address and source interface appear in the routing table and match the interface on which the packet was received.

Unicast RFP can be configured in two different modes on the ingress interface:

- **Strict Unicast RPF mode:** Strict mode check is successful when Unicast RFP finds a match in the Forwarding Information Base (FIB) for the packet source address and the ingress interface through which the packet is received matches one of the Unicast RPF interfaces in the FIB match. If this check fails, the packet is discarded. You can use this type of Unicast RPF check where packet flows are expected to be symmetrical.

■ **Loose Unicast RPF mode:** Loose mode check is successful when a lookup of a packet source address in the FIB returns a match and the FIB result indicates that the source is reachable through at least one real interface. The ingress interface through which the packet is received is not required to match any of the interfaces in the FIB result.

Note   Unicast RFP is applied only on the ingress interface of a device. The **any** keyword specifies loose Unicast RPF; the **rx** keyword specifies strict Unicast RPF.

Example 5-85 shows how to configure Unicast RPF on interface Ethernet1/1 for IPv4.

Example 5-85   *Configuring Unicast RPF on Interface Ethernet1/1 for IPv4*

```
Egypt(config)# interface ethernet 1/1
Egypt(config-if)# ip address 20.20.20.20 255.0.0.0
Egypt(config-if)# ip verify unicast source reachable-via any
Egypt(config-if)# exit
```

Example 5-86 verifies the Unicast RPF on interface ethernet1/1 for IPv4.

Example 5-86   *Verifying the Unicast RPF on Interface Ethernet1/1 for IPv4*

```
Egypt(config)# show ip interface ethernet 1/1
IP Interface Status for VRF "default"(1)
Ethernet1/1, Interface status: protocol-up/link-up/admin-up, iod: 99,
  IP address: 20.20.20.20, IP subnet: 20.0.0.0/8
  IP broadcast address: 255.255.255.255
  IP multicast groups locally joined: none
  IP MTU: 9216 bytes (using link MTU)
  IP primary address route-preference: 0, tag: 0
  IP proxy ARP : disabled
  IP Local Proxy ARP : disabled
  IP multicast routing: disabled
  IP icmp redirects: enabled
  IP directed-broadcast: disabled
  IP icmp unreachables (except port): disabled
  IP icmp port-unreachable: enabled
  IP unicast reverse path forwarding: loose
  IP interface statistics last reset: never
  IP interface software stats: (sent/received/forwarded/originated/consume
    Unicast packets    : 0/0/0/0/0
    Unicast bytes      : 0/0/0/0/0
    Multicast packets  : 0/0/0/0/0
    Multicast bytes    : 0/0/0/0/0
```

```
    Broadcast packets   : 0/0/0/0/0
    Broadcast bytes     : 0/0/0/0/0
    Labeled packets     : 0/0/0/0/0
    Labeled bytes       : 0/0/0/0/0
Egypt(config)# exit


Egypt # show running-config interface ethernet 1/1
!Command: show running-config interface Ethernet1/1
!Time: Thu Oct  1 20:06:53 2009


version 5.2(3a)


interface Ethernet1/1
  description to Congo
  mtu 9216
  ip address 20.20.20.20/8
  ip verify unicast source reachable-via any
  no shutdown
```

Configuring Control Plane Policing

Control Plan Policing (CoPP) protects the supervisor engine against one class of traffic hitting too heavily on the Supervisor CPU, causing too many CPU resources being consumed by one class of traffic. This enables the resources for other processes to stay available. Packets not destined for the switch (transit packets) are handled by the data plane of the switch, consisting of the forwarding engines on the linecards.

The Supervisor CPU is responsible for the control plane (L2 and L3 network protocols), switch software data plane (transit packets and software-based processing), management plane (for example, SSH, SNMP, Telnet, ICMP), and hardware management.

The Cisco NX-OS device provides CoPP to prevent DoS attacks from impacting performance.

The supervisor module divides the traffic that it manages into three functional planes:

- **Data plane:** Forwards packets from one interface to another; the packets are not destined to the switch.

- **Control plane:** Controls packets between devices, the packets are destined to router addresses.

- **Management plane:** Supervisor module has both the management plane and control plane and is critical to the operation of the network.

By default, when booting up the Cisco NX-OS device for the first time, the Cisco NX-OS Software installs the default copp-system-policy policy to protect the Supervisor module from DoS attacks. You can set the level of protection by choosing one of the following CoPP policy options from the initial setup utility:

- Strict

- Moderate

- Lenient

- None

If the setup script is run at initial setup, the CoPP policy can be selected; the default CoPP policy is strict policing. If the administrator would like to change the default CoPP policy, this can also be done at the CLI.

Note   You can find additional information about the default CoPP policies at http://tinyurl.com/d3ywvsy.

To change the default CoPP policy through the initial setup script, enter the following:

```
Configure best practices CoPP profile
(strict/moderate/lenient/none) [strict]:
```

Example 5-87 shows the default, strict, copp-system-policy, which can be changed based on specific requirements.

Example 5-87   *Default, Strict, Copp-System-Policy*

```
congo# show copp profile strict
ip access-list copp-system-p-acl-bgp
  permit tcp any gt 1024 any eq bgp
  permit tcp any eq bgp any gt 1024
ipv6 access-list copp-system-p-acl-bgp6
  permit tcp any gt 1024 any eq bgp
  permit tcp any eq bgp any gt 1024
ip access-list copp-system-p-acl-cts
  permit tcp any any eq 64999
  permit tcp any eq 64999 any
ip access-list copp-system-p-acl-dhcp
  permit udp any eq bootpc any
  permit udp any neq bootps any eq bootps
ip access-list copp-system-p-acl-dhcp-relay-response
  permit udp any eq bootps any
  permit udp any any eq bootpc
ip access-list copp-system-p-acl-eigrp
  permit eigrp any any
```

```
ipv6 access-list copp-system-p-acl-eigrp6
  permit eigrp any any
ip access-list copp-system-p-acl-ftp
  permit tcp any any eq ftp-data
  permit tcp any any eq ftp
  permit tcp any eq ftp-data any
  permit tcp any eq ftp any
ip access-list copp-system-p-acl-glbp
  permit udp any eq 3222 224.0.0.0/24 eq 3222
ip access-list copp-system-p-acl-hsrp
  permit udp any 224.0.0.0/24 eq 1985
ipv6 access-list copp-system-p-acl-hsrp6
  permit udp any ff02::66/128 eq 2029
ip access-list copp-system-p-acl-icmp
  permit icmp any any echo
  permit icmp any any echo-reply
ipv6 access-list copp-system-p-acl-icmp6
  permit icmp any any echo-request
  permit icmp any any echo-reply
ipv6 access-list copp-system-p-acl-icmp6-msgs
  permit icmp any any router-advertisement
[7m--More--[27m
  permit icmp any any router-solicitation
  permit icmp any any nd-na
  permit icmp any any nd-ns
  permit icmp any any mld-query
  permit icmp any any mld-report
  permit icmp any any mld-reduction
ip access-list copp-system-p-acl-igmp
  permit igmp any 224.0.0.0/3
mac access-list copp-system-p-acl-mac-cdp-udld-vtp
  permit any 0100.0ccc.cccc 0000.0000.0000
mac access-list copp-system-p-acl-mac-cfsoe
  permit any 0180.c200.000e 0000.0000.0000 0x8843
mac access-list copp-system-p-acl-mac-dot1x
  permit any 0180.c200.0003 0000.0000.0000 0x888e
mac access-list copp-system-p-acl-mac-fabricpath-isis
  permit any 0180.c200.0015 0000.0000.0000
  permit any 0180.c200.0014 0000.0000.0000
mac access-list copp-system-p-acl-mac-flow-control
  permit any 0180.c200.0001 0000.0000.0000 0x8808
mac access-list copp-system-p-acl-mac-gold
  permit any any 0x3737
mac access-list copp-system-p-acl-mac-l2pt
  permit any 0100.0ccd.cdd0 0000.0000.0000
```

```
mac access-list copp-system-p-acl-mac-lacp
  permit any 0180.c200.0002 0000.0000.0000 0x8809
mac access-list copp-system-p-acl-mac-lldp
  permit any 0180.c200.000c 0000.0000.0000 0x88cc
mac access-list copp-system-p-acl-mac-otv-isis
  permit any 0100.0cdf.dfdf 0000.0000.0000
mac access-list copp-system-p-acl-mac-sdp-srp
  permit any 0180.c200.000e 0000.0000.0000 0x3401
mac access-list copp-system-p-acl-mac-stp
  permit any 0100.0ccc.cccd 0000.0000.0000
  permit any 0180.c200.0000 0000.0000.0000
mac access-list copp-system-p-acl-mac-undesirable
  permit any any
ip access-list copp-system-p-acl-mpls-ldp
  permit udp any eq 646 any eq 646
  permit tcp any any eq 646
[7m--More--[27m
  permit tcp any eq 646 any
ip access-list copp-system-p-acl-mpls-oam
  permit udp any eq 3503 any
ip access-list copp-system-p-acl-mpls-rsvp
  permit 46 any any
ip access-list copp-system-p-acl-msdp
  permit tcp any gt 1024 any eq 639
  permit tcp any eq 639 any gt 1024
ip access-list copp-system-p-acl-ntp
  permit udp any any eq ntp
  permit udp any eq ntp any
ipv6 access-list copp-system-p-acl-ntp6
  permit udp any any eq ntp
  permit udp any eq ntp any
ip access-list copp-system-p-acl-ospf
  permit ospf any any
ipv6 access-list copp-system-p-acl-ospf6
  permit ospf any any
ip access-list copp-system-p-acl-otv-as
  permit udp any any eq 8472
ip access-list copp-system-p-acl-pim
  permit pim any 224.0.0.0/24
  permit udp any any eq 496
  permit ip any 224.0.0.13/32
ip access-list copp-system-p-acl-pim-mdt-join
  permit udp any 224.0.0.13/32
ip access-list copp-system-p-acl-pim-reg
  permit pim any any
```

```
ipv6 access-list copp-system-p-acl-pim6
  permit pim any ff02::d/128
  permit udp any any eq 496
ipv6 access-list copp-system-p-acl-pim6-reg
  permit pim any any
ip access-list copp-system-p-acl-radius
  permit udp any any eq 1812
  permit udp any any eq 1813
  permit udp any any eq 1645
  permit udp any any eq 1646
  permit udp any eq 1812 any
[7m--More--[27m
  permit udp any eq 1813 any
  permit udp any eq 1645 any
  permit udp any eq 1646 any
ipv6 access-list copp-system-p-acl-radius6
  permit udp any any eq 1812
  permit udp any any eq 1813
  permit udp any any eq 1645
  permit udp any any eq 1646
  permit udp any eq 1812 any
  permit udp any eq 1813 any
  permit udp any eq 1645 any
  permit udp any eq 1646 any
ip access-list copp-system-p-acl-rip
  permit udp any 224.0.0.0/24 eq 520
ipv6 access-list copp-system-p-acl-rip6
  permit udp any ff02::9/64 eq 521
ip access-list copp-system-p-acl-sftp
  permit tcp any any eq 115
  permit tcp any eq 115 any
ip access-list copp-system-p-acl-snmp
  permit udp any any eq snmp
  permit udp any any eq snmptrap
ip access-list copp-system-p-acl-ssh
  permit tcp any any eq ssh
  permit tcp any eq ssh any
ipv6 access-list copp-system-p-acl-ssh6
  permit tcp any any eq ssh
  permit tcp any eq ssh any
ip access-list copp-system-p-acl-tacacs
  permit tcp any any eq tacacs
  permit tcp any eq tacacs any
ipv6 access-list copp-system-p-acl-tacacs6
  permit tcp any any eq tacacs
```

```
    permit tcp any eq tacacs any
ip access-list copp-system-p-acl-telnet
    permit tcp any any eq telnet
    permit tcp any any eq 107
    permit tcp any eq telnet any
    permit tcp any eq 107 any
[7m--More--[27m
ipv6 access-list copp-system-p-acl-telnet6
    permit tcp any any eq telnet
    permit tcp any any eq 107
    permit tcp any eq telnet any
    permit tcp any eq 107 any
ip access-list copp-system-p-acl-tftp
    permit udp any any eq tftp
    permit udp any any eq 1758
    permit udp any eq tftp any
    permit udp any eq 1758 any
ipv6 access-list copp-system-p-acl-tftp6
    permit udp any any eq tftp
    permit udp any any eq 1758
    permit udp any eq tftp any
    permit udp any eq 1758 any
ip access-list copp-system-p-acl-traceroute
    permit icmp any any ttl-exceeded
    permit icmp any any port-unreachable
    permit udp any any range 33434 33534
ip access-list copp-system-p-acl-undesirable
    permit udp any any eq 1434
ip access-list copp-system-p-acl-vpc
    permit udp any any eq 3200
ip access-list copp-system-p-acl-vrrp
    permit ip any 224.0.0.18/32
ip access-list copp-system-p-acl-wccp
    permit udp any eq 2048 any eq 2048

class-map type control-plane match-any copp-system-p-class-critical
    match access-group name copp-system-p-acl-bgp
    match access-group name copp-system-p-acl-pim
    match access-group name copp-system-p-acl-rip
    match access-group name copp-system-p-acl-vpc
    match access-group name copp-system-p-acl-bgp6
    match access-group name copp-system-p-acl-igmp
    match access-group name copp-system-p-acl-msdp
    match access-group name copp-system-p-acl-ospf
    match access-group name copp-system-p-acl-pim6
```

```
    match access-group name copp-system-p-acl-rip6
[7m--More--[27m
  match access-group name copp-system-p-acl-eigrp
  match access-group name copp-system-p-acl-ospf6
  match access-group name copp-system-p-acl-eigrp6
  match access-group name copp-system-p-acl-otv-as
  match access-group name copp-system-p-acl-mac-l2pt
  match access-group name copp-system-p-acl-mpls-ldp
  match access-group name copp-system-p-acl-mpls-oam
  match access-group name copp-system-p-acl-mpls-rsvp
  match access-group name copp-system-p-acl-mac-otv-isis
  match access-group name copp-system-p-acl-mac-fabricpath-isis
  match protocol mpls router-alert
  match protocol mpls exp 6
class-map type control-plane match-any copp-system-p-class-exception
  match exception ip option
  match exception ip icmp unreachable
  match exception ipv6 option
  match exception ipv6 icmp unreachable
class-map type control-plane match-any copp-system-p-class-important
  match access-group name copp-system-p-acl-cts
  match access-group name copp-system-p-acl-glbp
  match access-group name copp-system-p-acl-hsrp
  match access-group name copp-system-p-acl-vrrp
  match access-group name copp-system-p-acl-wccp
  match access-group name copp-system-p-acl-hsrp6
  match access-group name copp-system-p-acl-pim-reg
  match access-group name copp-system-p-acl-mac-lldp
  match access-group name copp-system-p-acl-pim6-reg
  match access-group name copp-system-p-acl-icmp6-msgs
  match access-group name copp-system-p-acl-pim-mdt-join
  match access-group name copp-system-p-acl-mac-flow-control
 class-map type control-plane match-any copp-system-p-class-l2-default
  match access-group name copp-system-p-acl-mac-undesirable
  match protocol mpls
class-map type control-plane match-any copp-system-p-class-l2-unpoliced
  match access-group name copp-system-p-acl-mac-stp
  match access-group name copp-system-p-acl-mac-gold
  match access-group name copp-system-p-acl-mac-lacp
  match access-group name copp-system-p-acl-mac-cfsoe
  match access-group name copp-system-p-acl-mac-sdp-srp
[7m--More--[27m
  match access-group name copp-system-p-acl-mac-cdp-udld-vtp
class-map type control-plane match-any copp-system-p-class-management
  match access-group name copp-system-p-acl-ftp
```

```
    match access-group name copp-system-p-acl-ntp
    match access-group name copp-system-p-acl-ssh
    match access-group name copp-system-p-acl-ntp6
    match access-group name copp-system-p-acl-sftp
    match access-group name copp-system-p-acl-snmp
    match access-group name copp-system-p-acl-ssh6
    match access-group name copp-system-p-acl-tftp
    match access-group name copp-system-p-acl-tftp6
    match access-group name copp-system-p-acl-radius
    match access-group name copp-system-p-acl-tacacs
    match access-group name copp-system-p-acl-telnet
    match access-group name copp-system-p-acl-radius6
    match access-group name copp-system-p-acl-tacacs6
    match access-group name copp-system-p-acl-telnet6
class-map type control-plane match-any copp-system-p-class-monitoring
    match access-group name copp-system-p-acl-icmp
    match access-group name copp-system-p-acl-icmp6
    match access-group name copp-system-p-acl-traceroute
class-map type control-plane match-any copp-system-p-class-normal
    match access-group name copp-system-p-acl-mac-dot1x
    match protocol arp
class-map type control-plane match-any copp-system-p-class-normal-dhcp
    match access-group name copp-system-p-acl-dhcp
    match redirect dhcp-snoop
class-map type control-plane match-any copp-system-p-class-normal-dhcp-relay-resp
onse
    match access-group name copp-system-p-acl-dhcp-relay-response
class-map type control-plane match-any copp-system-p-class-redirect
    match redirect arp-inspect
class-map type control-plane match-any copp-system-p-class-undesirable
    match access-group name copp-system-p-acl-undesirable

policy-map type control-plane copp-system-p-policy-strict
    class copp-system-p-class-critical
      set cos 7
      police cir 39600 kbps bc 250 ms conform transmit violate drop
[7m--More--[27m
    class copp-system-p-class-important
      set cos 6
      police cir 1060 kbps bc 1000 ms conform transmit violate drop
    class copp-system-p-class-management
      set cos 2
      police cir 10000 kbps bc 250 ms conform transmit violate drop
    class copp-system-p-class-normal
      set cos 1
```

```
    police cir 680 kbps bc 250 ms conform transmit violate drop
class copp-system-p-class-normal-dhcp
  set cos 1
  police cir 680 kbps bc 250 ms conform transmit violate drop
class copp-system-p-class-normal-dhcp-relay-response
  set cos 1
  police cir 900 kbps bc 500 ms conform transmit violate drop
class copp-system-p-class-redirect
  set cos 1
  police cir 280 kbps bc 250 ms conform transmit violate drop
class copp-system-p-class-exception
  set cos 1
  police cir 360 kbps bc 250 ms conform transmit violate drop
class copp-system-p-class-monitoring
  set cos 1
  police cir 130 kbps bc 1000 ms conform transmit violate drop
class copp-system-p-class-l2-unpoliced
  police cir 8 gbps bc 5 mbytes conform transmit violate transmit
class copp-system-p-class-undesirable
  set cos 0
  police cir 32 kbps bc 250 ms conform drop violate drop
class copp-system-p-class-l2-default
  police cir 100 kbps bc 250 ms conform transmit violate drop
class class-default
  set cos 0
  police cir 100 kbps bc 250 ms conform transmit violate drop


congo#
```

Note   If you upgrade NX-OS Software by not using ISSU (non-ISSU), the system will not be updated with the new "best practice CoPP" policy. The old CoPP policy will be retained, which means the new CoPP policy and best practices will not be implemented. You need to run the following command to update the CoPP policy to be updated to the new best practices. The customer must manually run the copp copy command and update the CoPP policy: **copp copy profile** {**strict** | **moderate** | **lenient**} {**prefix** | **suffix**} *string*.

Configuring Rate Limits

Rate limits can prevent redirected packets for egress exceptions from overwhelming the supervisor module on a Cisco NX-OS device. Rate limits are configured in packets per second for the following types of redirected packets:

- Access list logging packets

- Data and control packets copied to the Supervisor module

- Layer 2 storm control packets

- Layer 2 port security packets

- Layer 3 glean packets

- Layer 3 maximum transmission unit (MTU) check failure packets

- Layer 3 multicast directly connected packets

- Layer 3 multicast local group packets

- Layer 3 multicast Reverse Path Forwarding (RPF) leak packets

- Layer 3 Time-To-Live (TTL) check failure packets

- Layer 3 control packets

- Receive packets

The general command syntax for configuring rate limiting follows:

```
Switch(config)# hardware rate-limit {access-list-log | copy |
layer-2 {port-security | storm-control} | layer-3 {control | glean
| mtu | multicast {directly-connect | local-groups | rpf-leak} |
ttl} | receive} packets
```

Note Rate limits are applied only to egress traffic. If you need to apply ingress rate limits, use CoPP.

Example 5-88 verifies the default rate limit settings.

Example 5-88 *Verifying the Default Rate Limit Settings*

```
Egypt# show hardware rate-limiter

Units for Config: packets per second
Allowed, Dropped & Total: aggregated since last clear counters
Rate Limiter Class                    Parameters
-----------------------------------------------------------------------
layer-3 mtu                           Config    : 500
                                      Allowed   : 0
                                      Dropped   : 0


layer-3 multicast directly-connected  Config    : 3000
```

```
                                       Allowed    : 0
                                       Dropped    : 0
                                       Total      : 0

layer-3 multicast local-groups         Config     : 3000
                                       Allowed    : 0
                                       Dropped    : 0
                                       Total      : 0

layer-3 multicast rpf-leak             Config     : 500
                                       Allowed    : 0
                                       Dropped    : 0
                                       Total      : 0

layer-2 storm-control                  Config     : Disabled
access-list-log                        Config     : 100
                                       Allowed    : 0
                                       Dropped    : 0
                                       Total      : 0

copy                                   Config     : 30000
                                       Allowed    : 197080
                                       Dropped    : 0
                                       Total      : 197080

receive                                Config     : 30000
                                       Allowed    : 905484
                                       Dropped    : 0
                                       Total      : 905484

layer-2 port-security                  Config     : Disabled

layer-2 mcast-snooping                 Config     : 10000
                                       Allowed    : 21
                                       Dropped    : 0
                                       Total      : 21

Egypt#
```

Example 5-89 shows how to configure rate limits on Layer 3 control packets. Rate limits are in packets per second for Layer 3 control packets.

Example 5-89 *Configuring Rate Limits on Layer 3 Control Packets*

```
Congo(config)# hardware rate-limiter layer-3 control 50000
```

Example 5-90 shows how to configure rate limits for Layer 3 glean packets. Rate limits are in packets per second for Layer 3 glean packets.

Note Glean packets are IP packets to a directly connected network host for which there is no ARP entry yet on the switch, and are punted to the CPU to trigger an ARP response.

Example 5-90 *Configuring Rate Limits for Layer 3 Glean Packets*

```
Congo(config)# hardware rate-limiter layer-3 glean 500
```

Example 5-91 shows how to configure rate limits for Layer 2 storm control limits (in packets per seconds).

Example 5-91 *Configuring Rate Limits for Layer 2 Storm Control Limits in Packets per Second*

```
Congo(config)# hardware rate-limiter layer-2 storm-control 60000
```

Example 5-92 shows how to verify rate limit configuration changes and settings.

Example 5-92 *Verifying Rate Limit Configuration Changes and Settings*

```
                                        Dropped   : 0
                                        Total     : 3
Congo# show hardware rate-limiter layer-2 storm-control

Units for Config: packets per second
Allowed, Dropped & Total: aggregated since last clear counters


Rate Limiter Class                      Parameters
-------------------------------------------------------------------
layer-2 storm-control                   Config    : 60000
                                        Allowed   : 113
                                        Dropped   : 1
                                        Total     : 114
Congo# show hardware rate-limiter

Units for Config: packets per second
Allowed, Dropped & Total: aggregated since last clear counters


Rate Limiter Class                      Parameters
-------------------------------------------------------------------
```

```
layer-3 mtu                             Config    : 500
                                        Allowed   : 0
                                        Dropped   : 0
                                        Total     : 0

layer-3 ttl                             Config    : 500
                                        Allowed   : 7771
                                        Dropped   : 0
                                        Total     : 7771

layer-3 control                         Config    : 50000
                                        Allowed   : 1042557
                                        Dropped   : 0
                                        Total     : 1042557

layer-3 glean                           Config    : 500
                                        Allowed   : 3
                                        Dropped   : 0
                                        Total     : 3

layer-3 multicast directly-connected    Config    : 3000
                                        Allowed   : 0
                                        Dropped   : 0
                                        Total     : 0

layer-3 multicast local-groups          Config    : 3000
                                        Allowed   : 0
                                        Dropped   : 0
                                        Total     : 0

layer-3 multicast rpf-leak              Config    : 500
                                        Allowed   : 0
                                        Dropped   : 0
                                        Total     : 0

layer-2 storm-control                   Config    : 60000
                                        Allowed   : 126
                                        Dropped   : 1
                                        Total     : 127

access-list-log                         Config    : 100
                                        Allowed   : 0
                                        Dropped   : 0
                                        Total     : 0

copy                                    Config    : 30000
                                        Allowed   : 2634651
```

```
                               Dropped    : 0
                               Total      : 2634651
receive                        Config     : 30000
                               Allowed    : 8275085
                               Dropped    : 0
                               Total      : 8275085


layer-2 port-security          Config     : Disabled


layer-2 mcast-snooping         Config     : 10000
                               Allowed    : 0
                               Dropped    : 0
                               Total      : 0

Congo#
```

SNMPv3

The section covers SNMPv3 only. SNMPv3 provides secure access to devices by a combination of authenticating and encrypting frames over the network. The security features
provided in SNMPv3 follows:

- **Message integrity:** Ensures that a packet has not been tampered.

- **Authentication:** The message is from a valid source.

- **Encryption:** Prevent it from being seen by unauthorized sources.

SNMPv3 provides for both security models and security levels. A security model is an
authentication strategy set up for a user and the role in which the user resides. A security
level is the permitted level of security within a security model. A combination of a security model and a security level determines which security mechanism is employed when
handling an SNMP packet.

Example 5-93 shows how to configure SNMP users with authentication and privacy configuration.

Example 5-93 *Configuring SNMP Users with Authentication and Privacy
Configuration*

```
Egypt(config)# snmp-server user manager auth sha MGTUser123 priv MGTUser
Egypt(config)# show snmp user
                SNMP USERS


User                      Auth   Priv(enforce) Groups
____                      ____   _____  _____
admin                     md5    des(no)       network-admin
```

```
manager                     sha  des(no)      network-operator

NOTIFICATION TARGET USERS (configured  for sending V3 Inform)
_____


User                        Auth Priv
____                        ____ ____
Egypt(config)#
```

Example 5-94 shows how to enforce SNMP message encryption on a per-user basis.

Example 5-94   *Enforcing SNMP Message Encryption on a Per-User Basis*

```
Egypt(config)# snmp-server user manager enforcePriv
Egypt(config)# show snmp user
                  SNMP USERS
-------------------------------------------------------------------

User                        Auth  Priv(enforce) Groups
____                        ____  _____  _____
admin                       md5   des(no)       network-admin

manager                     sha   des(no)       network-operator
                                                enforcePriv
-----------------------------------------------------------

NOTIFICATION TARGET USERS (configured  for sending V3 Inform)

User                        Auth  Priv
____                        ____ ____
```

Example 5-95 shows how to enforce message encryption for all users.

Example 5-95   *Enforcing Message Encryption for All Users*

```
Egypt(config)# snmp-server globalEnforcePriv
Egypt(config)# show snmp user
                  SNMP USERS [global privacy flag enabled]
-------------------------------------------------------------------

User                        Auth  Priv(enforce) Groups
____                        ____  _____  _____
admin                       md5   des(no)       network-admin

manager                     sha   des(no)       network-operator
```

```
                                          enforcePriv
----------------------------------------------------------------------


NOTIFICATION TARGET USERS (configured  for sending V3 Inform)


User                        Auth  Priv

____                        ____  ____
Egypt(config)#
```

Example 5-96 shows how to assign SNMPv3 users to multiple roles.

Example 5-96 *Assigning SNMPv3 Users to Multiple Roles*

```
Egypt(config)# snmp-server user manager network-admin
Egypt(config)# show snmp user
                    SNMP USERS [global privacy flag enabled]
----------------------------------------------------------------------


User                        Auth  Priv(enforce) Groups

____                        ____  _____  _____
admin                       md5   des(no)       network-admin

manager                     sha   des(no)       network-operator
                                                 enforcePriv
                                                 network-admin

----------------------------------------------------------------------


NOTIFICATION TARGET USERS (configured  for sending V3 Inform)


User                        Auth  Priv

____                        ____  ____
Egypt(config)# show role

Role: network-admin
  Description: Predefined network admin role has access to all commands
  on the switch
  Rule   Perm   Type     Scope            Entity
---------------------------------------------------------------------- 1       per-
mit   read-write


Role: network-operator
  Description: Predefined network operator role has access to all read
  commands on the switch
  Rule   Perm   Type     Scope            Entity
  1      permit read
```

```
Role: vdc-admin
  Description: Predefined vdc admin role has access to all commands with
  a VDC instance
  Rule    Perm    Type      Scope                 Entity
  --------------------------------------------------------------------
  1       permit  read-write

Role: vdc-operator
  Description: Predefined vdc operator role has access to all read comm
  within a VDC instance
  Rule    Perm    Type      Scope                 Entity
  --------------------------------------------------------------------
  1       permit  read

Role: enforcePriv
  Description: new role
  Vlan policy: permit (default)
  Interface policy: permit (default)
  Vrf policy: permit (default)
Egypt(config)#
```

Example 5-97 shows how to create SNMP communities. The SNMP community is a collection of hosts grouped together for administrative purposes.

Example 5-97 *Creating SNMP Communities*

```
Egypt(config)# snmp-server community public ro
Egypt(config)# snmp-server community private rw
Egypt(config)# show snmp community
Community           Group / Access      context    acl_filter
---------           --------------      -------    ----------
public              network-operator
private             network-admin
Egypt(config)#
```

Example 5-98 shows how to configure notification receivers. For example, the notification receiver can determine whether a syslog message notification contained the structured data elements of a syslog message.

Example 5-98 *Configuring Notification Receivers*

```
Egypt(config)# snmp-server host 10.10.10.12 informs version 3 priv private
Egypt(config)# show snmp host
--------------------------------------------------------------------
```

```
Host                            Port Version Level  Type   SecName
------------------------------------------------------------------
10.10.10.12                     162  v3      priv   inform private
Egypt(config)#


Configuring a Source Interface for SNMP Notifications


Egypt(config)# show snmp source-interface
Notification                    source-interface
------------------------------------------------------------------
trap                            -
inform                          -
```

Example 5-99 shows how to configure the SNMP source interface. The source interface specifies the source IP address of the SMTP messages, trap messages, for example.

Example 5-99   *Configuring the SNMP Source Interface*

```
Egypt(config)# snmp-server source-interface traps loopback 0
Egypt(config)# show snmp source-interface
Notification                    source-interface
------------------------------------------------------------------
trap                            loopback0
inform                          -
------------------------------------------------------------------
Egypt(config)# snmp-server source-interface informs loopback 0
Egypt(config)# show snmp source-interface
Notification                    source-interface
------------------------------------------------------------------
trap                            loopback0
inform                          loopback0
------------------------------------------------------------------
Egypt(config)#
```

Example 5-100 shows how to disable LinkUp/LinkDown SNMP notifications globally.

Example 5-100   *Disabling LinkUp/LinkDown SNMP Notifications Globally*

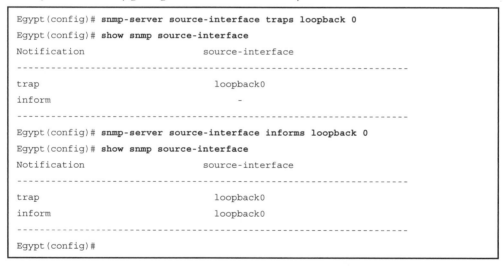

```
Egypt# show snmp trap
Trap type                                                     Enabled
------------------------------------------------------------------
entity            : entity_mib_change                         Yes
entity            : entity_module_status_change               Yes
entity            : entity_power_status_change                Yes
entity            : entity_module_inserted                    Yes
```

```
entity            : entity_module_removed            Yes
entity            : entity_unrecognised_module       Yes
entity            : entity_fan_status_change         Yes
entity            : entity_power_out_change          Yes
link              : linkDown                         Yes
link              : linkUp                           Yes
link              : extended-linkDown                Yes
link              : extended-linkUp                  Yes
link              : cieLinkDown                      Yes
link              : cieLinkUp                        Yes
callhome          : event-notify                     No
callhome          : smtp-send-fail                   No
cfs               : state-change-notif               No
cfs               : merge-failure                    No
rf                : redundancy_framework             Yes
port-security     : access-secure-mac-violation      No
port-security     : trunk-secure-mac-violation       No
aaa               : server-state-change              No
license           : notify-license-expiry            Yes
license           : notify-no-license-for-feature    Yes
license           : notify-licensefile-missing       Yes
license           : notify-license-expiry-warning    Yes
hsrp              : state-change                      No
upgrade           : UpgradeOpNotifyOnCompletion       No
upgrade           : UpgradeJobStatusNotify            No
feature-control   : FeatureOpStatusChange             No
snmp              : authentication                    No
Egypt# conf t
Enter configuration commands, one per line. End with CNTL/Z.
Egypt(config)# no snmp-server enable traps link linkup
Egypt(config)# no snmp-server enable traps link linkdown
Egypt(config)# show snmp trap
Trap type                                            Enabled
--------------------------------------------------------------------
entity            : entity_mib_change                Yes
entity            : entity_module_status_change      Yes
entity            : entity_power_status_change       Yes
entity            : entity_module_inserted           Yes
entity            : entity_module_removed            Yes
entity            : entity_unrecognised_module       Yes
entity            : entity_fan_status_change         Yes
entity            : entity_power_out_change          Yes
link              : linkDown                         No
link              : linkUp                           No
link              : extended-linkDown                Yes
```

```
link               : extended-linkUp                   Yes
link               : cieLinkDown                       Yes
link               : cieLinkUp                         Yes
callhome           : event-notify                      No
callhome           : smtp-send-fail                    No
cfs                : state-change-notif                No
cfs                : merge-failure                     No
rf                 : redundancy_framework              Yes
port-security      : access-secure-mac-violation       No
port-security      : trunk-secure-mac-violation        No
aaa                : server-state-change               No
license            : notify-license-expiry             Yes
license            : notify-no-license-for-feature     Yes
license            : notify-licensefile-missing        Yes
license            : notify-license-expiry-warning     Yes
hsrp               : state-change                      No
upgrade            : UpgradeOpNotifyOnCompletion       No
upgrade            : UpgradeJobStatusNotify            No
feature-control    : FeatureOpStatusChange             No
snmp               : authentication                    No
Egypt(config)#
```

Example 5-101 shows how to disable LinkUp/LinkDown SNMP notifications on a specific interface.

Example 5-101   *Disabling LinkUp/LinkDown SNMP Notifications on Interface Ethernet 1/1*

```
Egypt(config)# int e1/1
Egypt(config-if)# no snmp trap link-status
```

Example 5-102 shows how to enable SNMP notifications.

Example 5-102   *Enabling SNMP Notifications*

```
Egypt# conf t
Enter configuration commands, one per line. End with CNTL/Z.
Egypt(config)# snmp-server enable traps
Egypt(config)# show snmp trap
Trap type                                             Enabled
--------------------------------------------------------------------
entity             : entity_mib_change                 Yes
entity             : entity_module_status_change       Yes
entity             : entity_power_status_change        Yes
entity             : entity_module_inserted            Yes
```

```
entity              : entity_module_removed              Yes
entity              : entity_unrecognised_module         Yes
entity              : entity_fan_status_change           Yes
entity              : entity_power_out_change            Yes
link                : linkDown                           Yes
link                : linkUp                             Yes
link                : extended-linkDown                  Yes
link                : extended-linkUp                    Yes
link                : cieLinkDown                        Yes
link                : cieLinkUp                          Yes
callhome            : event-notify                       Yes
callhome            : smtp-send-fail                     Yes
cfs                 : state-change-notif                 Yes
cfs                 : merge-failure                      Yes
rf                  : redundancy_framework               Yes
port-security       : access-secure-mac-violation        Yes
port-security       : trunk-secure-mac-violation         Yes
aaa                 : server-state-change                Yes
license             : notify-license-expiry              Yes
license             : notify-no-license-for-feature      Yes
license             : notify-licensefile-missing         Yes
license             : notify-license-expiry-warning      Yes
hsrp                : state-change                       Yes
upgrade             : UpgradeOpNotifyOnCompletion        Yes
upgrade             : UpgradeJobStatusNotify             Yes
feature-control     : FeatureOpStatusChange              Yes
snmp                : authentication                     Yes
Egypt(config)#
```

Summary

NX-OS security capabilities are scalable and flexible and support a wide range of solutions and protocols. Combining an underlying architecture focused on high availability with years of security features experience makes for a secure and robust platform. VRF-aware features enable the network administrator to develop and deploy flexible, scalable, and resilient secure data center architectures.

## Chapter 6

High Availability

This chapter covers the following topics focused on high availability:

- Physical redundancy

- Generic online diagnostics

- NX-OS high-availability architecture

- Process modularity

- Process restart

- Stateful switchover

- Nonstop forwarding

- In-Service Software Upgrades (ISSU)

Requirements in the data center are rapidly changing—where there were once generous maintenance windows, now there are none. Best effort delivery of service has been replaced with strict service-level agreements (SLAs), sometimes with financial penalties incurred to lines of business or customers. This chapter introduces various hardware and software components that make the Nexus 7000 a highly available platform to meet these changing data center requirements. Furthermore, as chassis-based solutions provide the highest levels of high availability, this chapter focuses primarily on the Nexus 7000 series switch.

Physical Redundancy

Redundancy within the Nexus 7000 begins at the physical chassis and extends into the software and operational characteristics of the system. To provide a redundant hardware platform from which to build on, the Nexus 7000 provides the following hardware components:

- Redundant power supplies

- Cooling system

- Redundant supervisors

- Redundant Ethernet Out-of-Band (EOBC)

- Redundant fabric modules

The Nexus 5500, 3000, and 2000 series also provide various redundant hardware components:

- Redundant power supplies

- Cooling system

The following sections describe the highly available components of the Nexus series switches in greater detail.

Redundant Power Supplies

Several power supply options exist for the Nexus 7000 series. The Nexus 7009 provides the ability to install two 6 KW or 7.5 KW AC power supplies, or two 6 KW DC power supplies, whereas the Nexus 7010, which has a larger footprint, can support up to three power supplies. To account for the additional line cards in the system, the Nexus 7018 provides the ability to install up to four power supplies. The Nexus 7004 uses a smaller 3 KW form factor power supply, available in AC at the time of this writing. The 6 and 7.5 KW power supplies have redundant inputs that feed completely independent power units that feed two redundant power buses within the chassis. The mode in which redundancy is achieved is user configurable to one of four modes; these power redundancy schemes are consistent between the 4-slot, 9-slot, and 10-slot and 18-slot versions of the Nexus 7000:

- **Nonredundant (combined):** All available power from all available power supplies and inputs is made available for the system to draw from. This mode is available but not recommended unless extraordinary circumstances exist.

- **N+1 (ps-redundant):** The default mode that protects against the failure of one power supply. When operating in this mode, the power made available to the system is the sum of all the power supplies minus the largest.

- **Grid redundancy (insrc-redundant):** Also called input source redundancy. Most data centers today are equipped with redundant power feeds to the data center and redundant distribution systems within the data center. In the Nexus 7009, 7010, and 7018 grid redundancy, each input of the installed power supplies connects to different power grids. In the Nexus 7004, each grid powers half of the power supplies because each power supply has only a single input. If a total loss of power occurs on either side, the system remains powered on. In this mode, the power made available to the system is the sum of all the power supplies installed in the system. This number is then cut in half to create the power budget for modules.

■ **Full redundancy (redundant):** The combination of input source redundancy and power supply redundancy. This provides the least amount of power available for line cards and crossbars but ensures that no failure, whether internal or external, compromises the availability of the system.

Example 6-1 shows how to configure the power redundancy mode and verify the operating mode.

Example 6-1   *Configuring and Verifying Power Redundancy*

```
N7k-1(config)# power redundancy-mode ?
  combined         Configure power supply redundancy mode as combined
  insrc-redundant  Configure power supply redundancy mode as grid/AC input source
redundant
  ps-redundant     Configure power supply redundancy mode as PS redundant
  redundant        Configure power supply redundancy mode as InSrc and PS redundant

N7k-1(config)# power redundancy-mode redundant

N7k-1# show environment power
Power Supply:
Voltage: 50 Volts
Power                        Actual        Total
Supply    Model              Output       Capacity     Status
                             (Watts )     (Watts )
-------   -----------------  -----------  -----------  --------------
1         N7K-AC-6.0KW       1019 W       3000 W       Ok
2         N7K-AC-6.0KW       955 W        3000 W       Ok
3         N7K-AC-6.0KW       0 W          0 W          Shutdown


                             Actual        Power
Module    Model              Draw         Allocated    Status
                             (Watts )     (Watts )
-------   -----------------  -----------  -----------  --------------
1         N7K-M132XP-12      N/A          750 W        Powered-Up
2         N7K-M148GT-11      N/A          400 W        Powered-Up
5         N7K-SUP1           N/A          210 W        Powered-Up
6         N7K-SUP1           N/A          210 W        Powered-Up
10        N7K-M132XP-12L     554 W        750 W        Powered-Up
Xb1       N7K-C7010-FAB-1    N/A          60 W         Powered-Up
Xb2       N7K-C7010-FAB-1    N/A          60 W         Powered-Up
Xb3       N7K-C7010-FAB-1    N/A          60 W         Powered-Up
Xb4       N7K-C7010-FAB-1    N/A          60 W         Powered-Up
```

```
Xb5        N7K-C7010-FAB-1           N/A           60 W    Powered-Up
fan1       N7K-C7010-FAN-S            76 W        720 W    Powered-Up
fan2       N7K-C7010-FAN-S            76 W        720 W    Powered-Up
fan3       N7K-C7010-FAN-F             8 W        120 W    Powered-Up
fan4       N7K-C7010-FAN-F             8 W        120 W    Powered-Up


N/A - Per module power not available



Power Usage Summary:
--------------------
Power Supply redundancy mode (configured)          PS-Redundant
Power Supply redundancy mode (operational)         Non-Redundant


Total Power Capacity (based on configured mode)        6000 W
Total Power of all Inputs (cumulative)                 6000 W
Total Power Output (actual draw)                       1974 W
Total Power Allocated (budget)                         4300 W
Total Power Available for additional modules           1700 W
```

Redundant Cooling System

The Nexus 7010 has two redundant fans for line cards and two redundant fans for fabric modules located in the rear of the chassis. For the Nexus 7009 and 7018, the system I/O and fabric fans are located within the same field replaceable unit (FRU). Because the 7004 doesn't contain fabric modules, it has only one fan tray for the system I/O. Placing the fan trays in the rear of the Nexus 7009, 7010, and 7018 chassis makes the system extremely serviceable and ensures that cabling does not get in the way of removal or replacement of the fan tray. All the fans in the system are hot-swappable. Each chassis has unique characteristics for the fan operation:

- **Cisco Nexus 7004 Series fan tray:** The switch can function without a fan tray for up to 3 minutes by which time you must replace the missing fan tray.

- **Cisco Nexus 7009 Series fan tray:** The switch can function without a fan tray for up to 3 minutes by which time you must replace the missing fan tray.

- **Cisco Nexus 7010 Series system fan tray:** The fans in the remaining system fan tray increase their speeds as needed for the current temperature until you replace the missing fan tray.

- **Cisco Nexus 7010 Series fabric fan tray:** The fan in the remaining fabric fan tray increases its speed to the maximum speed until you replace the missing fabric fan tray.

- **Cisco Nexus 7018 Series fan tray:** If you do not replace the fan tray within 3 minutes, the system shuts down the modules cooled by the removed fan tray. For the top fan tray, that means that the system would shut down the supervisor in slot 9, the I/O modules in slots 1 through 8, and the fabric modules. For the bottom fan tray, that means that the system would shut down the supervisor in slot 10 and the I/O modules in slots 11 through 18.

Example 6-2 shows how to verify the status of the fans installed in the system.

Example 6-2   *Verifying System and I/O Fans*

```
N7k-1# show environment fan
Fan:
-----------------------------------------------------
Fan            Model            Hw         Status
-----------------------------------------------------
Fan1(sys_fan1)  N7K-C7010-FAN-S  1.1        Ok
Fan2(sys_fan2)  N7K-C7010-FAN-S  1.1        Ok
Fan3(fab_fan1)  N7K-C7010-FAN-F  1.0        Ok
Fan4(fab_fan2)  N7K-C7010-FAN-F  1.1        Ok
Fan_in_PS1      --               --         Ok
Fan_in_PS2      --               --         Ok
Fan_in_PS3      --               --         Shutdown
Fan Air Filter : Absent
```

A status of **Ok** should be in all installed fans; anything other than this status would require attention from the administrator, ensuring that the appropriate fan tray is properly seated, which is a good first step. If one or more fans fail within a tray, the Nexus 7000 switch can adjust the speed of the remaining fans to compensate for the failed fans. A fan failure could also lead to temperature alarms if not corrected in a timely manner.

Temperature sensors are located throughout the system to monitor temperature and adjust fan speeds as necessary to ensure all components are within their appropriate operational range. Each module is equipped with intake, outlet, and on-board sensors. Two temperature thresholds are tracked for each sensor:

■ **Minor temperature threshold:** When a minor threshold is exceeded, a system message will be logged; call home and SNMP notifications are sent if configured.

■ **Major temperature threshold:** A major temperature threshold being exceeded would cause the same actions as a minor threshold, unless the intake sensor experiences a major threshold violation. In this scenario, the module is powered down. If the intake module of the active supervisor experiences a major threshold violation and an HA-standby supervisor is present, the module shuts down. If no standby supervisor is present, the system monitors the temperature every 5 seconds for 2 minutes and then shuts down the module.

Example 6-3 shows how to monitor the temperature at various points within the system.

Example 6-3   *Verifying System Temperature*

```
N7k-1# show environment temperature
Temperature:
-------------------------------------------------------------------
Module   Sensor        MajorThresh  MinorThres   CurTemp      Status
                       (Celsius)    (Celsius)    (Celsius)
-------------------------------------------------------------------
1        Crossbar(s5)  105          95           61           Ok
1        QEng1Sn1(s12) 115          110          72           Ok
1        QEng1Sn2(s13) 115          110          70           Ok
1        QEng1Sn3(s14) 115          110          68           Ok
1        QEng1Sn4(s15) 115          110          69           Ok
1        QEng2Sn1(s16) 115          110          72           Ok
1        QEng2Sn2(s17) 115          110          70           Ok
1        QEng2Sn3(s18) 115          110          68           Ok
1        QEng2Sn4(s19) 115          110          69           Ok
1        L2Lookup(s27) 115          105          52           Ok
1        L3Lookup(s28) 120          110          61           Ok
2        Crossbar(s5)  105          95           43           Ok
2        CTSdev4 (s9)  115          105          52           Ok
2        CTSdev5 (s10) 115          105          51           Ok
2        CTSdev7 (s12) 115          105          51           Ok
2        CTSdev9 (s14) 115          105          49           Ok
2        CTSdev10(s15) 115          105          49           Ok
2        CTSdev11(s16) 115          105          47           Ok
2        CTSdev12(s17) 115          105          47           Ok
2        QEng1Sn1(s18) 115          105          48           Ok
2        QEng1Sn2(s19) 115          105          47           Ok
2        QEng1Sn3(s20) 115          105          46           Ok
2        QEng1Sn4(s21) 115          105          46           Ok
2        L2Lookup(s22) 120          110          43           Ok
2        L3Lookup(s23) 120          110          50           Ok
5        Intake  (s3)  60           42           21           Ok
5        EOBC_MAC(s4)  105          95           39           Ok
5        CPU     (s5)  105          95           33           Ok
5        Crossbar(s6)  105          95           49           Ok
5        Arbiter (s7)  110          100          54           Ok
5        CTSdev1 (s8)  115          105          43           Ok
5        InbFPGA (s9)  105          95           40           Ok
5        QEng1Sn1(s10) 115          105          45           Ok
5        QEng1Sn2(s11) 115          105          44           Ok
5        QEng1Sn3(s12) 115          105          41           Ok
5        QEng1Sn4(s13) 115          105          42           Ok
6        Intake  (s3)  60           42           21           Ok
```

6	EOBC_MAC(s4)	105	95	36	Ok
6	CPU (s5)	105	95	32	Ok
6	Crossbar(s6)	105	95	47	Ok
6	Arbiter (s7)	110	100	50	Ok
6	CTSdev1 (s8)	115	105	39	Ok
6	InbFPGA (s9)	105	95	40	Ok
6	QEng1Sn1(s10)	115	105	44	Ok
6	QEng1Sn2(s11)	115	105	43	Ok
6	QEng1Sn3(s12)	115	105	40	Ok
6	QEng1Sn4(s13)	115	105	42	Ok
10	Crossbar(s5)	105	95	48	Ok
10	QEng1Sn1(s12)	115	110	72	Ok
10	QEng1Sn2(s13)	115	110	69	Ok
10	QEng1Sn3(s14)	115	110	72	Ok
10	QEng1Sn4(s15)	115	110	73	Ok
10	QEng2Sn1(s16)	115	110	71	Ok
10	QEng2Sn2(s17)	115	110	69	Ok
10	QEng2Sn3(s18)	115	110	72	Ok
10	QEng2Sn4(s19)	115	110	73	Ok
10	L2Lookup(s27)	115	105	50	Ok
10	L3Lookup(s28)	120	110	65	Ok
xbar-1	Intake (s2)	60	42	30	Ok
xbar-1	Crossbar(s3)	105	95	66	Ok
xbar-2	Intake (s2)	60	42	30	Ok
xbar-2	Crossbar(s3)	105	95	62	Ok
xbar-3	Intake (s2)	60	42	30	Ok
xbar-3	Crossbar(s3)	105	95	77	Ok
xbar-4	Intake (s2)	60	42	30	Ok
xbar-4	Crossbar(s3)	105	95	70	Ok
xbar-5	Intake (s2)	60	42	30	Ok
xbar-5	Crossbar(s3)	105	95	68	Ok

In this example, all current temperature values are well below any threshold violation. Each environment might be slightly different; therefore, it is considered good practice to baseline these temperatures in your environment and trend these over time.

Redundant Supervisors

Supervisor modules provide the control plane operations for the system. These functions include building forwarding tables, maintaining protocol adjacencies, and providing management interfaces to the system. In the Nexus 7004 and 7009, slots 1 and 2 are reserved for supervisor modules. In the Nexus 7010, slots 5 and 6 are reserved for supervisor modules. In the Nexus 7018, slots 9 and 10 are reserved for supervisor modules. Supervisor modules have a slightly different form factor, so I/O modules *cannot* be installed in these slots. Redundant supervisor modules provide a completely redundant control plane and redundant management interfaces for the platform. Redundant supervisors behave in an active/standby configuration where only one supervisor is active at any time. This level of control plane redundancy provides protection against hardware failure and provides a foundation for advanced features such as Stateful Switchover (SSO) and In-Service Software Upgrades (ISSU). From a management standpoint, each supervisor provides an out-of-band Connectivity Management Processor (CMP) and an in-band management (mgmt0) interface. These interfaces were covered in detail in the previous chapter.

The CMP provides a standalone network stack that is always available as long as power is applied to the system. This type of technology is analogous to the "lights out" capabilities of most modern server offerings. When comparing this to legacy networking applications, the CMP functionality can be used to replace terminal servers that provide console connectivity if the system has experienced major issues causing normal connectivity to be lost. From the CMP, a network operator can monitor log files and console ports and power cycle the entire system. The CMP is completely independent of NX-OS and guarantees that any outages will not be prolonged because of the inability to access the device remotely. The management interfaces operate in active/standby just as the supervisors do. Whichever supervisor is active is where connectivity for the mgmt0 interface is derived.

Note The CMP is currently only available on the Nexus 7000 supervisor Module-1X (N7K-SUP1). Later revisions of the supervisor Module including supervisor Module-2 and supervisor Module-2E (N7K-SUP2 and N7K-SUP2E) *do not* include the CMP.

Note Because of the active/standby nature of the mgmt0 interface, it is recommended that the management interfaces of both supervisors are physically connected to an external switching infrastructure at all times.

Example 6-4 shows how to verify supervisor redundancy.

Example 6-4 *Verifying Supervisor Redundancy*

```
N7k-1# show system redundancy status
Redundancy mode
---------------
       administrative:   HA
          operational:   HA


This supervisor (sup-1)
----------------------
    Redundancy state:   Active
```

```
    Supervisor state:    Active
      Internal state:    Active with HA standby


Other supervisor (sup-2)
-----------------------
    Redundancy state:    Standby
    Supervisor state:    HA standby
      Internal state:    HA standby
```

Redundant Ethernet Out-of-Band (EOBC)

Various forms of communication between line cards, fabric modules, and supervisors are required within a normal system operation. This communication occurs over an internal switching infrastructure called the Ethernet Out-of-Band Channel (EOBC). Each supervisor contains a 24-port Gigabit switch that connects to line cards and fabric modules within the system. In addition, each line card contains a small switch with ports connecting to both supervisors and the local processor. The components that make up the EOBC bus provide a redundant infrastructure for management and control traffic local to the system.

Redundant Fabric Modules

The Nexus 7009, 7010, and 7018 switches provide the ability to install up to five fabric modules per system. The fabric modules are installed to meet the capacity and redundancy requirements of the system. Each line card load balances data plane traffic across all the available fabric modules within the system. If one of the fabric modules should fail, traffic rebalances across the remaining fabrics. When the failed fabric is replaced, traffic is automatically redistributed again. The Nexus 7004 switch contains integrated fabrics, which have a capacity of 480 Gbps.

To date, two versions of the fabric modules for the Nexus 7000 have been released. The first-generation fabric modules, the Fabric1, provide each line card with 46 Gbps of forwarding capacity. With all five fabric modules installed, each line card has 230 Gbps of forwarding capacity. The latest fabric module, the Fabric2, provides each line card with 110 Gbps of forwarding capacity. With all five fabric modules installed, each line card has 550 Gbps of forwarding capacity. Migration from Fabric1 to Fabric2 to can be done nondisruptively; however, Fabric1 and Fabric2 modules cannot be mixed in the same chassis for any period of time outside of the migration.

You can monitor fabric module status and utilization, as demonstrated in Example 6-5.

Example 6-5 *Verifying Fabric Module Status and Utilization*

```
N7k-1# show module xbar
Xbar Ports  Module-Type                               Model              Status
---  -----  ----------------------------------------  -----------------  ----------
```

```
1    0       Fabric Module 1              N7K-C7010-FAB-1    ok
2    0       Fabric Module 1              N7K-C7010-FAB-1    ok
3    0       Fabric Module 1              N7K-C7010-FAB-1    ok
4    0       Fabric Module 1              N7K-C7010-FAB-1    ok
5    0       Fabric Module 1              N7K-C7010-FAB-1    ok


Xbar Sw              Hw
---  --------------  ------
1    NA              1.0
2    NA              1.0
3    NA              1.0
4    NA              1.1
5    NA              1.1



Xbar MAC-Address(es)                         Serial-Num
---  -------------------------------------   ----------
1    NA                                      JAB122400PW
2    NA                                      JAB122400Q4
3    NA                                      JAB122400P7
4    NA                                      JAF1504ACTQ
5    NA                                      JAF1504BJPL


* this terminal session

N7k-1# show hardware fabric-utilization
-------------------------------------------------
Slot       Total Fabric       Utilization
           Bandwidth      Ingress % Egress %
-------------------------------------------------
1             230 Gbps       0.00      0.00
2             230 Gbps       0.00      0.00
5             115 Gbps       0.00      0.00
6             115 Gbps       0.00      0.00
10            230 Gbps       0.00      0.00
```

Generic Online Diagnostics

There is a strong interest within data centers today to move operations from reactive to proactive. As part of this operational shift, it becomes necessary to identify hardware failures before they happen and to take preventative action prior to their failure. NX-OS follows the tradition of the widely deployed Catalyst line of switches with its implementation of Generic Online Diagnostics (GOLD), which provides the mechanisms necessary to test and verify the functionality of a particular component at various times during the operation of the component. As the name implies, GOLD provides these mechanisms in a fashion that can usually be done on a device that is connected to the network with minimal or no disruption to the operation of the device. This section provides an overview of the capabilities, operation, and configuration of GOLD.

Note GOLD provides a robust suite of diagnostic tests; many of them are executed in the background with no disruption to the system. Some of the tests, however, are disruptive and should be used with caution within a production environment.

GOLD verifies functionality using a variety of techniques; the full suite of diagnostic utilities is broken down into the following categories:

- Bootup diagnostics

- Runtime diagnostics

- On-demand diagnostics

Within each of these categories, specific tests are also classified as disruptive or nondisruptive.

Bootup Diagnostics

Prior to a module coming online within NX-OS, several checks are run on the hardware depending on the type. By default, a complete set of tests are run prior to placing the module in service. It is not recommended to alter this behavior, but if necessary to decrease boot time, these tests can be bypassed, as shown in Example 6-6.

Example 6-6 *Bypassing Bootup Diagnostics*

```
Congo# show diagnostic bootup level

        Current bootup diagnostic level: complete

Congo# conf t
Enter configuration commands, one per line. End with CNTL/Z.
Congo(config)# diagnostic bootup level bypass
Congo(config)# sho diagnostic bootup level

        Current bootup diagnostic level: bypass

Congo(config)#
```

Runtime Diagnostics

Although bootup diagnostics prevent a module from coming online without exhaustively testing the hardware functionality, it is not uncommon for modules or entire systems to run for months or years without rebooting. It is therefore necessary to run periodic checks on the hardware during the normal operation of the device. These checks are referred to as runtime diagnostics and can be viewed from the command-line interface (CLI).

Example 6-7 shows the runtime diagnostics performed on a supervisor module.

Example 6-7   *Supervisor Runtime Diagnostics*

```
Congo# show diagnostic description module 5 test all
ManagementPortLoopback :
        A bootup test that tests loopback on the management port of
        the module

EOBCPortLoopback :
        A bootup test that tests loopback on the EOBC

ASICRegisterCheck :
        A health monitoring test, enabled by default that checks read/write
        access to scratch registers on ASICs on the module.

USB :
        A bootup test that checks the USB controller initialization
        on the module.

CryptoDevice :
        A bootup test that checks the CTS device initialization on
        the module.

NVRAM :
        A health monitoring test, enabled by default that checks the
        sanity of the NVRAM device on the module.

RealTimeClock :
        A health monitoring test, enabled by default that verifies
        the real time clock on the module.

PrimaryBootROM :
        A health monitoring test that verifies the primary BootROM
        on the module.

SecondaryBootROM :
```

```
        A health monitoring test that verifies the secondary BootROM
        on the module.

CompactFlash :
        A Health monitoring test, enabled by default, that verifies
        access to the internal compactflash devices.

ExternalCompactFlash :
        A Health monitoring test, enabled by default, that verifies
        access to the external compactflash devices.

PwrMgmtBus :
        A Health monitoring test, enabled by default, that verifies
        the standby Power Management Control Bus.

SpineControlBus :
        A Health monitoring, enabled by default, test that verifies
        the standby Spine Card Control Bus.

SystemMgmtBus :
        A Health monitoring test, enabled by default, that verifies
        the standby System Bus.

StatusBus :
        A Health monitoring test, enabled by default, that verifies
        status transmitted along Status Bus.

StandbyFabricLoopback :
        A Health monitoring test, enabled by default, that verifies
        packet path from the Standby supervisor to the Fabric
```

Example 6-8 shows the runtime diagnostics performed on a line card.

Example 6-8 *Line Card Runtime Diagnostics*

```
Congo# show diagnostic description module 2 test all
EOBCPortLoopback :
        A bootup test that tests loopback on the EOBC

ASICRegisterCheck :
        A health monitoring test, enabled by default that checks read/write
        access to scratch registers on ASICs on the module.

PrimaryBootROM :
        A health monitoring test that verifies the primary BootROM
```

```
             state.

SecondaryBootROM :
             A health monitoring test that verifies the secondary BootROM
             state.

PortLoopback :
             A health monitoring test that will test the packet path from
             the Supervisor card to the physical port in ADMIN DOWN state
             on Line cards.

RewriteEngineLoopback :
             A health monitoring test, enabled by default, that does non
             disruptive loopback for all LC ports upto the Rewrite Engine
             ASIC (i.e. Metro) device.
```

Each of these tests has a default run interval that can be verified, as shown in Example 6-9.

Example 6-9 *Default Runtime Diagnostics Schedule*

```
Congo# show diagnostic content module 2


Module 2: 10/100/1000 Mbps Ethernet Module


Diagnostics test suite attributes:
B/C/* - Bypass bootup level test / Complete bootup level test / NA
P/*   - Per port test / NA
M/S/* - Only applicable to active / standby unit / NA
D/N/* - Disruptive test / Non-disruptive test / NA
H/*   - Always enabled monitoring test / NA
F/*   - Fixed monitoring interval test / NA
X/*   - Not a health monitoring test / NA
E/*   - Sup to line card test / NA
L/*   - Exclusively run this test / NA
T/*   - Not an ondemand test / NA
A/I/* - Monitoring is active / Monitoring is inactive / NA


                                                  Testing Interval
ID      Name                          Attributes  (hh:mm:ss)
--------------------------------------------------------------------------------
  1)    EOBCPortLoopback-------------->   C**N**X**T*   -NA-
  2)    ASICRegisterCheck------------->   ***N******A   00:01:00
  3)    PrimaryBootROM--------------->    ***N******A   00:30:00
  4)    SecondaryBootROM------------->    ***N******A   00:30:00
```

```
     5)     PortLoopback------------------->     CP*N***E**A     00:15:00

     6)     RewriteEngineLoopback--------->      *P*N***E**A     00:01:00



Congo# show diagnostic content module 5


Module 5: Supervisor module-1X (Active)


Diagnostics test suite attributes:
B/C/* - Bypass bootup level test / Complete bootup level test / NA
P/*   - Per port test / NA
M/S/* - Only applicable to active / standby unit / NA
D/N/* - Disruptive test / Non-disruptive test / NA
H/*   - Always enabled monitoring test / NA
F/*   - Fixed monitoring interval test / NA
X/*   - Not a health monitoring test / NA
E/*   - Sup to line card test / NA
L/*   - Exclusively run this test / NA
T/*   - Not an ondemand test / NA
A/I/* - Monitoring is active / Monitoring is inactive / NA


                                                Testing Interval
ID      Name                            Attributes    (hh:mm:ss)
--------------------------------------------------------------------------------

    1)     ManagementPortLoopback-------->     C**D**X**T*     -NA-

    2)     EOBCPortLoopback-------------->     C**D**X**T*     -NA-

    3)     ASICRegisterCheck------------->     ***N******A     00:00:20

    4)     USB-------------------------->      C**N**X**T*     -NA-

    5)     CryptoDevice----------------->      C**N**X**T*     -NA-

    6)     NVRAM------------------------>      ***N******A     00:00:30

    7)     RealTimeClock---------------->      ***N******A     00:05:00

    8)     PrimaryBootROM--------------->      ***N******A     00:30:00

    9)     SecondaryBootROM------------->      ***N******A     00:30:00

   10)     CompactFlash----------------->      ***N******A     00:30:00

   11)     ExternalCompactFlash--------->      ***N******A     00:30:00

   12)     PwrMgmtBus------------------->      **MN******A     00:00:30

   13)     SpineControlBus-------------->      **MN******A     00:00:30

   14)     SystemMgmtBus---------------->      **MN******A     00:00:30

   15)     StatusBus-------------------->      **MN******A     00:00:30

   16)     StandbyFabricLoopback-------->      **SN******A     00:00:30
```

In certain configurations, these tests might not be applicable and can be disabled. If performance issues are experienced and a hardware failure is suspected, it might be preferable to change the runtime interval. Example 6-10 shows how to disable or change the runtime interval of these tests.

Example 6-10 *Manipulating Runtime Diagnostic Parameters*

```
Congo(config)# no diagnostic monitor module 5 test 9
Congo(config)# diagnostic monitor interval module 5 test 3 hour 00 min 00 second 45
Congo(config)# show diagnostic content module 5


Module 5: Supervisor module-1X (Active)


Diagnostics test suite attributes:
B/C/* - Bypass bootup level test / Complete bootup level test / NA
P/*   - Per port test / NA
M/S/* - Only applicable to active / standby unit / NA
D/N/* - Disruptive test / Non-disruptive test / NA
H/*   - Always enabled monitoring test / NA
F/*   - Fixed monitoring interval test / NA
X/*   - Not a health monitoring test / NA
E/*   - Sup to line card test / NA
L/*   - Exclusively run this test / NA
T/*   - Not an ondemand test / NA
A/I/* - Monitoring is active / Monitoring is inactive / NA


                                              Testing Interval
ID     Name                        Attributes  (hh:mm:ss)
  1)   ManagementPortLoopback-------->   C**D**X**T*   -NA-
  2)   EOBCPortLoopback-------------->   C**D**X**T*   -NA-
  3)   ASICRegisterCheck------------->   ***N******A   00:00:45
  4)   USB-------------------------->   C**N**X**T*   -NA-
  5)   CryptoDevice----------------->   C**N**X**T*   -NA-
  6)   NVRAM------------------------>   ***N******A   00:00:30
  7)   RealTimeClock---------------->   ***N******A   00:05:00
  8)   PrimaryBootROM--------------->   ***N******A   00:30:00
  9)   SecondaryBootROM------------->   ***N******I   00:30:00
 10)   CompactFlash----------------->   ***N******A   00:30:00
 11)   ExternalCompactFlash--------->   ***N******A   00:30:00
 12)   PwrMgmtBus------------------->   **MN******A   00:00:30
 13)   SpineControlBus-------------->   **MN******A   00:00:30
 14)   SystemMgmtBus---------------->   **MN******A   00:00:30
 15)   StatusBus-------------------->   **MN******A   00:00:30
 16)   StandbyFabricLoopback-------->   **SN******A   00:00:30


Congo(config)#
```

On-Demand Diagnostics

Problems that are intermittent are sometimes attributed to failing hardware. As a trouble-shooting step, you should test a particular component to verify that the hardware is operating properly and thus eliminate hardware as a potential cause. In NX-OS, you can do this by using *on-demand tests*.

Example 6-11 shows how to manually initiate a diagnostic test and view the results.

Example 6-11   *On-Demand Diagnostics*

```
Congo# diagnostic start module 5 test non-disruptive
Congo# show diagnostic result module 5

Current bootup diagnostic level: complete
Module 5: Supervisor module-1X  (Active)

        Test results: (. = Pass, F = Fail, I = Incomplete,
        U = Untested, A = Abort, E = Error disabled)

         1) ManagementPortLoopback--------> .
         2) EOBCPortLoopback-------------> .
         3) ASICRegisterCheck------------> .
         4) USB-------------------------> .
         5) CryptoDevice-----------------> .
         6) NVRAM-----------------------> .
         7) RealTimeClock----------------> .
         8) PrimaryBootROM---------------> .
         9) SecondaryBootROM-------------> .
        10) CompactFlash-----------------> .
        11) ExternalCompactFlash----------> .
        12) PwrMgmtBus-------------------> .
        13) SpineControlBus--------------> .
        14) SystemMgmtBus----------------> .
        15) StatusBus--------------------> .
        16) StandbyFabricLoopback--------> U

Congo#
```

Referring to the output of Example 6-11, all tests that were run against the module in question passed diagnostics as denoted with a period. Should a particular test fail, further investigation might be required. The Cisco Technical Assistance Center (TAC) can use this information to replace modules that are covered under support agreements.

NX-OS High-Availability Architecture

The high-availability features of NX-OS are managed by several system-level processes:

- **System Manager:** At the highest level, the System Manager is responsible for the overall state of the system. The System Manager monitors the health of the system and the various services that are running based on the configured high-availability policies. The System Manager manages the starting, stopping, monitoring, and restarting of services. Along with these high-level tasks, the System Manager also ensures that state is synchronized between supervisors and coordinates the switchover of supervisors if necessary. To verify the health of the System Manager process, there is a hardware watchdog timer located on the supervisor. Periodically, the System Manager resets the watchdog timer with a keepalive indicator. If the hardware watchdog timer expires, with no keepalives from the System Manager, a supervisor switchover occurs.

- **Persistent Storage Service (PSS):** Where state information for the various services are stored. PSS provides a database of state and runtime information. Services within NX-OS dump information to the PSS at various intervals and after restart glean this information from the PSS to restore the service to prefailure state.

- **Message and transaction services (MTS):** An interprocess communication (IPC) broker that handles message routing and queuing between services and hardware within the system. The function of the MTS ensures that processes can be restarted independently and that messages from the other processes are received after a restart has occurred.

These software features combine to create operational benefits, which are discussed throughout the remainder of this chapter.

Process Modularity

To achieve the highest levels of redundancy, NX-OS represents a complete modular software architecture. Each modular component within NX-OS must be enabled by the network administrator prior to the feature being configured, or even loaded into memory. Most services within NX-OS are represented as loadable modules or features that must be enabled. If one of these processes experiences errors, the service can be restarted independently of other features or services. This level of modularity exists primarily where high availability (HA) cannot be achieved by mechanisms within the protocol itself—for example, Graceful Restart for Border Gateway Protocol (BGP). Processes can be enabled using the **feature** command or disabled using the **no feature** command.

Certain software features are grouped into feature sets. A feature set is a collection of components that performs a specific set of functions. A particular feature set must be installed in the default Virtual Device Context (VDC) by using the **install feature-set** command and then enabled in any VDC using the **feature-set** command before you can configure the components that make up the feature set. A feature set can be disabled and uninstalled by first using the **no feature-set** command followed by the **no install feature-set** command in the default VDC.

Example 6-12 shows the modular processes that can be enabled.

Example 6-12   *Modular Features*

```
N7k-1(config)# feature ?
  bfd             Bfd
  bgp             Enable/Disable Border Gateway Protocol (BGP)
  cts             Enable/Disable CTS
  dhcp            Enable/Disable DHCP Manager
  dot1x           Enable/Disable dot1x
  eigrp           Enable/Disable Enhanced Interior Gateway Routing Protocol (EIGRP)
  eou             Enable/Disables feature l2nac(eou)
  glbp            Enable/Disable Gateway Load Balancing Protocol (GLBP)
  hsrp            Enable/Disable Hot Standby Router Protocol (HSRP)
  interface-vlan  Enable/Disable interface vlan
  isis            Enable/Disable IS-IS Unicast Routing Protocol (IS-IS)
  lacp            Enable/Disable LACP
  ldap            Enable/Disable ldap
  lisp            Enable/Disable Locator/ID Separation Protocol (LISP)
  lldp            Enable/Disable LLDP
  mpls            Enable/Disable MPLS Services
  msdp            Enable/Disable Multicast Source Discovery Protocol (MSDP)
  mvpn            Multicast Virtual Private Networks
  netflow         Enable/Disable NetFlow
  ntp             Enable/Disable NTP
  ospf            Enable/Disable Open Shortest Path First Protocol (OSPF)
  ospfv3          Enable/Disable Open Shortest Path First Version 3 Protocol (OSPFv3)
  otv             Enable/Disable Overlay Transport Virtualization (OTV)
  password        Credential(s) for the user(s)/device(s)
  pbr             Enable/Disable Policy Based Routing(PBR)
  pim             Enable/Disable Protocol Independent Multicast (PIM)
  pim6            Enable/Disable Protocol Independent Multicast (PIM) for IPv6
  pong            Enable/Disable Pong
  port-security   Enable/Disable port-security
  private-vlan    Enable/Disable private-vlan
  privilege       Enable/Disable IOS type privilege level support
  ptp             Enable/Disable PTP
  rip             Enable/Disable Routing Information Protocol (RIP)
  scheduler       Enable/Disable scheduler
  scp-server      Enable/Disable SCP server
  sftp-server     Enable/Disable SFTP server
  ssh             Enable/Disable ssh
  tacacs+         Enable/Disable tacacs+
```

```
    telnet          Enable/Disable telnet
    tunnel          Enable/Disable Tunnel Manager
    udld            Enable/Disable UDLD
    vpc             Enable/Disable VPC (Virtual Port Channel)
    vrrp            Enable/Disable Virtual Router Redundancy Protocol (VRRP)
    vtp             Enable/Disable VTP
    wccp            Enable/Disable Web Cache Communication Protocol (WCCP)


N7k-1(config)# install feature-set ?
  fabricpath  FABRICPATH
  fcoe        FCOE
  fex         FEX
  mpls        MPLS
```

In addition to selectively enabling or disabling particular features, software modularity provides a mechanism in which software can be patched to address security vulnerabilities or apply hot fixes without requiring a complete upgrade of the system.

Process Restart

Services within NX-OS can be restarted if they experience errors or failures. These restarts can be initiated by a network operator or by the System Manager upon detecting an error condition. Each NX-OS service has an associated set of HA policies.

HA policies define how the system reacts to a failed service. Following are actions performed by the System Manager:

- **Stateful process restart:** While in a running state, restartable processes checkpoint their runtime state information to the PSS. If a service fails to respond to heartbeats from the System Manager, that process is restarted. When the process has been restarted, all the state information is gleaned from the PSS.

- **Stateless process restart:** The service is restarted, and all runtime information is rebuilt from the configuration or by reestablishing adjacencies.

- **Supervisor switchover:** In a dual supervisor configuration, the active supervisor is rebooted, and the standby immediately takes over as the active supervisor.

Following are a few variables associated with the progression of possible System Manager actions:

- **Maximum retries:** Specifies the number of times the System Manager attempts to perform a specific action before declaring the attempt failed. For example, the system might try to perform a stateful restart three times before attempting a stateless restart three times, and finally initiating a supervisor switchover.

- **Minimum lifetime:** Specifies the time that a service must run after a restart before declaring the restart a success. This value is configurable but must be greater than 4 minutes.

Stateful Switchover

The combination of the NX-OS Software architecture and redundant supervisors provides the capability to seamlessly switch over to the redundant supervisor. This switchover can occur for a number of reasons, the most common of which are user-initiated, System Manager-initiated, or as part of an ISSU.

Example 6-13 shows how to verify the supervisor status of the system and initiate a manual switchover from the active to the standby supervisor.

Example 6-13   *Supervisor Redundancy*

```
N7k-1# show redundancy status
Redundancy mode
---------------
       administrative:   HA
          operational:   HA


This supervisor (sup-5)
-----------------------
    Redundancy state:   Active
    Supervisor state:   Active
      Internal state:   Active with HA standby


Other supervisor (sup-6)
------------------------
    Redundancy state:   Standby

    Supervisor state:   HA standby
      Internal state:   HA standby


System start time:          Fri May  4 07:42:43 2012

System uptime:              128 days, 9 hours, 12 minutes, 35 seconds
Kernel uptime:              128 days, 9 hours, 17 minutes, 12 seconds
Active supervisor uptime:   128 days, 9 hours, 12 minutes, 35 seconds


N7k-1# system switchover


N7k-1# show system redundancy status
Redundancy mode
---------------
```

```
        administrative:   HA
           operational:   HA

This supervisor (sup-6)
----------------------
     Redundancy state:   Active
     Supervisor state:   Active
       Internal state:   Active with HA standby

Other supervisor (sup-5)
----------------------
     Redundancy state:   Standby

     Supervisor state:   HA standby
       Internal state:   HA standby

System start time:          Fri May  4 07:42:43 2012

System uptime:              128 days, 9 hours, 21 minutes, 1 seconds
Kernel uptime:              128 days, 9 hours, 25 minutes, 42 seconds
Active supervisor uptime:   0 days, 0 hours, 7 minutes, 39 seconds
```

Nonstop Forwarding

Most modern protocols understand that while a control plane switchover might be occurring on an adjacent node, the data plane can still forward traffic. The most common implementations of this functionality are with OSPF, EIGRP, and BGP. These mechanisms are sometimes referred to as a *graceful restart*. This should not be confused with a stateless restart; a stateful restart requires no interaction with peers, whereas a graceful restart involves notification of peers.

If a stateful restart of the routing process fails, or is not possible, nonstop forwarding (NSF) specifies a mechanism to notify neighbors that the control plane is undergoing a restart, but the data plane can still forward traffic. All routing updates from this neighbor are held in their current states until the adjacency is restored or a hold timer expires. When the adjacency is reestablished, updates to the routing topology are then updated in the hardware forwarding tables. For NSF to work properly, the adjacent network devices must process the notification, in which case they are said to be *NSF-Aware*. Most modern networking devices, including IOS and NX-OS, are NSF-Aware.

In-Service Software Upgrades

With the combination of the distributing forwarding nature of the Nexus platform and the high-availability features described within this chapter, one of the most immediate and practical benefits of the approach is the capability to upgrade software without requiring a reload of the system or disruption to traffic flows through the system. This capability is referred to as In-Service Software Upgrades (ISSU), which is supported across both minor and major NX-OS versions and enables customers to quickly take advantage of new features, protect their infrastructure against security vulnerabilities, and provide a more proactive software upgrade cycle, all while not having to wait for extended maintenance windows or costly downtime. Prior to initiating a software upgrade, an administrator should verify that the features and functionality configured on the system are compatible with the new image and determine whether the upgrade process will have any impact on traffic flows. NX-OS release notes should be reviewed to ensure the target code version is supported for an ISSU operation based on the current running version.

During an ISSU operation, all components of the system are upgraded. This includes the NX-OS image running on the supervisor modules and line cards. ISSU leverages Stateful Switchover to upgrade the supervisor modules without disruption, and line cards are upgraded by default in a serial fashion. Beginning in NX-OS 5.2(1), line cards can now be upgraded in *parallel*. This option significantly reduces the overall time for the upgrade to complete.

Example 6-14 shows how to check for image compatibility based on the running configuration and any impact associated with the upgrade.

Example 6-14 *Verify System Image Compatibility and Impact*

```
! The following image is an older version of NX-OS which doesn't
support vPC and therefore would be incompatible with the running
configuration.
N7k-1# show incompatibility system bootflash:///n7000-s1-dk9.4.1.2.bin
The following configurations on active are incompatible with the system image
1) Service : vpc , Capability : CAP_FEATURE_VPC_ENABLED
Description : vPC feature is enabled
Capability requirement : STRICT
Disable command : Disable vPC using "no feature vpc"


2) Service : ascii-cfg , Capability : CAP_FEATURE_ASCII_CFG_SYSTEM_CHECKPOINT
Description : System checkpoints were created
Capability requirement : STRICT
Disable command : Remove all the system checkpoints


! The following shows an upgrade to a compatible software image


N7k-1# show incompatibility system bootflash:///n7000-s1-dk9.6.0.2.bin
No incompatible configurations


! The impact of the software upgrade can also be assessed as shown below
```

```
N7k-1# show install all impact kickstart bootflash:///n7000-s1-kickstart.6.0.2.bin
system bootflash:///n7000-s1-dk9.6.0.2.bin

Verifying image bootflash:/n7000-s1-kickstart.6.0.2.bin for boot variable "kick-
start".
[####################] 100% -- SUCCESS


Verifying image bootflash:/n7000-s1-dk9.6.0.2.bin for boot variable "system".
[####################] 100% -- SUCCESS


Verifying image type.
[####################] 100% -- SUCCESS


Extracting "lc-m1-n7k" version from image bootflash:/n7000-s1-dk9.6.0.2.bin.
[####################] 100% -- SUCCESS


Extracting "bios" version from image bootflash:/n7000-s1-dk9.6.0.2.bin.
[####################] 100% -- SUCCESS


Extracting "lc-m1-n7k" version from image bootflash:/n7000-s1-dk9.6.0.2.bin.
[####################] 100% -- SUCCESS


Extracting "system" version from image bootflash:/n7000-s1-dk9.6.0.2.bin.
[####################] 100% -- SUCCESS


Extracting "kickstart" version from image bootflash:/n7000-s1-kickstart.6.0.2.bin.
[####################] 100% -- SUCCESS


Extracting "lc-m1-n7k" version from image bootflash:/n7000-s1-dk9.6.0.2.bin.
[####################] 100% -- SUCCESS


Extracting "cmp" version from image bootflash:/n7000-s1-dk9.6.0.2.bin.
[####################] 100% -- SUCCESS


Extracting "cmp-bios" version from image bootflash:/n7000-s1-dk9.6.0.2.bin.
[####################] 100% -- SUCCESS


Performing module support checks.
[####################] 100% -- SUCCESS


Notifying services about system upgrade.
[####################] 100% -- SUCCESS
```

```
Compatibility check is done:
Module  bootable          Impact  Install-type  Reason
------  --------  --------------  ------------  ------
     1       yes  non-disruptive       rolling
     2       yes  non-disruptive       rolling
     5       yes  non-disruptive         reset
     6       yes  non-disruptive         reset
    10       yes  non-disruptive       rolling



Images will be upgraded according to following table:
Module       Image            Running-Version(pri:alt)        New-Version
Upg-Required
------  ----------  ------------------------------------------  ---------------------
------------
     1  lc-m1-n7k                                5.2(3a)                    6.0(2)
yes
     1        bios  v1.10.17(04/25/11):  v1.10.17(04/25/11)   v1.10.17(04/25/11)
no
     2  lc-m1-n7k                                5.2(3a)                    6.0(2)
yes
     2        bios  v1.10.17(04/25/11):  v1.10.17(04/25/11)   v1.10.17(04/25/11)
no
     5      system                                5.2(3a)                    6.0(2)
yes
     5    kickstart                               5.2(3a)                    6.0(2)
yes
     5        bios  v3.22.0(02/20/10):  v3.22.0(02/20/10)   v3.22.0(02/20/10)
no
     5         cmp                                 5.2(1)                    6.0(1)
yes
     5    cmp-bios                                02.01.05                  02.01.05
no
     6      system                                5.2(3a)                    6.0(2)
yes
     6    kickstart                               5.2(3a)                    6.0(2)
yes
     6        bios  v3.22.0(02/20/10):  v3.22.0(02/20/10)   v3.22.0(02/20/10)
no
     6         cmp                                 5.2(1)                    6.0(1)
yes
     6    cmp-bios                                02.01.05                  02.01.05
no
    10  lc-m1-n7k                                 5.2(3a)                    6.0(2)
yes
    10        bios  v1.10.17(04/25/11):  v1.10.17(04/25/11)   v1.10.17(04/25/11)
no
```

When an upgrade is initiated, the system goes through the following process to achieve a nondisruptive upgrade:

1. BIOS software is upgraded on the active and standby supervisors and all line cards.

2. The standby supervisor is upgraded and rebooted.

3. When the standby supervisor is online with the new version of NX-OS, a stateful switchover is initiated. At this point, the control plane is now operating on the new version.

4. The standby supervisor (previously Active) is then upgraded to the new version.

5. Line cards are upgraded one at a time and reloaded. (This reload is only of the CPU, not any of the data plane components and is nondisruptive to traffic flows.)

6. The CMP on both supervisors are upgraded.

Example 6-15 demonstrates the entire ISSU process.

Example 6-15 *ISSU Procedure*

```
! Verify the current image
N7k-1# sh ver
Cisco Nexus Operating System (NX-OS) Software
TAC support: http://www.cisco.com/tac
Documents: http://www.cisco.com/en/US/products/ps9372/tsd_products_support_series_
home.html
Copyright (c) 2002-2011, Cisco Systems, Inc. All rights reserved.
The copyrights to certain works contained in this software are
owned by other third parties and used and distributed under
license. Certain components of this software are licensed under
the GNU General Public License (GPL) version 2.0 or the GNU
Lesser General Public License (LGPL) Version 2.1. A copy of each
such license is available at
http://www.opensource.org/licenses/gpl-2.0.php and
http://www.opensource.org/licenses/lgpl-2.1.php


Software
  BIOS:      version 3.22.0
  kickstart: version 5.2(3a)
  system:    version 5.2(3a)
  BIOS compile time:      02/20/10
  kickstart image file is: bootflash:///n7000-s1-kickstart.5.2.3a.bin
  kickstart compile time:  12/25/2020 12:00:00 [12/16/2011 03:04:59]
  system image file is:    bootflash:///n7000-s1-dk9.5.2.3a.bin
  system compile time:     12/15/2011 12:00:00 [12/16/2011 04:15:48]
```

```
Hardware
  cisco Nexus7000 C7010 (10 Slot) Chassis ("Supervisor module-1X")
  Intel(R) Xeon(R) CPU         with 8254672 kB of memory.
  Processor Board ID JAB1223011V


  Device name: N7k-1
  bootflash:     2000880 kB
  slot0:         2044854 kB (expansion flash)

Kernel uptime is 128 day(s), 7 hour(s), 42 minute(s), 5 second(s)


Last reset at 196119 usecs after  Fri May  4 07:37:44 2012


  Reason: Reset Requested by CLI command reload
  System version: 5.2(3a)
  Service:

plugin
  Core Plugin, Ethernet Plugin



CMP (Module 5) ok
 CMP Software
  CMP BIOS version:         02.01.05
  CMP Image version:        5.2(1) [build 5.0(0.66)]
  CMP BIOS compile time:    7/13/2008 19:44:27
  CMP Image compile time:   12/15/2011 12:00:00


CMP (Module 6) ok
 CMP Software
  CMP BIOS version:         02.01.05
  CMP Image version:        5.2(1) [build 5.0(0.66)]
  CMP BIOS compile time:    7/13/2008 19:44:27
  CMP Image compile time:   6/7/2011 13:00:00


! Initiate the install process
N7k-1# install all kickstart bootflash:/// n7000-s1-kickstart.6.0.2.bin system boot-
flash:///n7000-s1-dk9.6.0.2.bin [parallel]



Verifying image bootflash:/n7000-s1-kickstart.6.0.2.bin for boot variable "kick-
start".
  -- SUCCESS
```

```
Verifying image bootflash:/n7000-s1-dk9.6.0.2.bin for boot variable "system".
 -- SUCCESS

Verifying image type.
 -- SUCCESS

Extracting "lc-m1-n7k" version from image bootflash:/n7000-s1-dk9.6.0.2.bin.
 -- SUCCESS

Extracting "bios" version from image bootflash:/n7000-s1-dk9.6.0.2.bin.
 -- SUCCESS

Extracting "lc-m1-n7k" version from image bootflash:/n7000-s1-dk9.6.0.2.bin.
 -- SUCCESS

Extracting "system" version from image bootflash:/n7000-s1-dk9.6.0.2.bin.
 -- SUCCESS

Extracting "kickstart" version from image bootflash:/n7000-s1-kickstart.6.0.2.bin.
 -- SUCCESS

Extracting "lc-f1-n7k" version from image bootflash:/n7000-s1-dk9.6.0.2.bin.
 -- SUCCESS

Extracting "lc-m1-n7k" version from image bootflash:/n7000-s1-dk9.6.0.2.bin.
 -- SUCCESS

Extracting "cmp" version from image bootflash:/n7000-s1-dk9.6.0.2.bin.
 -- SUCCESS

Extracting "cmp-bios" version from image bootflash:/n7000-s1-dk9.6.0.2.bin.
 -- SUCCESS

Performing module support checks.
 -- SUCCESS

Notifying services about system upgrade.
 -- SUCCESS




Compatibility check is done:
Module  bootable          Impact  Install-type  Reason
------  --------  --------------  ------------  ------
     1       yes  non-disruptive       rolling
```

```
     2        yes  non-disruptive       rolling
     5        yes  non-disruptive        reset
     6        yes  non-disruptive        reset
     7        yes  non-disruptive       rolling
    10        yes  non-disruptive       rolling




Images will be upgraded according to following table:
Module        Image             Running-Version(pri:alt)           New-Version
Upg-Required
------    ----------    ----------------------------------------    --------------------
-----------
     1    lc-m1-n7k                                  5.2(3a)                  6.0(2)
yes
     1         bios    v1.10.17(04/25/11):  v1.10.17(04/25/11)    v1.10.17(04/25/11)
no
     2    lc-m1-n7k                                  5.2(3a)                  6.0(2)
yes
     2         bios    v1.10.17(04/25/11):  v1.10.17(04/25/11)    v1.10.17(04/25/11)
no
     5       system                                  5.2(3a)                  6.0(2)
yes
     5     kickstart                                 5.2(3a)                  6.0(2)
yes
     5         bios     v3.22.0(02/20/10):  v3.22.0(02/20/10)    v3.22.0(02/20/10)
no
     5          cmp                                   5.2(1)                  6.0(1)
yes
     5     cmp-bios                                  02.01.05                02.01.05
no
     6       system                                  5.2(3a)                  6.0(2)
yes
     6     kickstart                                 5.2(3a)                  6.0(2)
yes
     6         bios     v3.22.0(02/20/10):  v3.22.0(02/20/10)    v3.22.0(02/20/10)
no
     6          cmp                                   5.2(1)                  6.0(1)
yes
     6     cmp-bios                                  02.01.05                02.01.05
no
     7    lc-f1-n7k                                  5.2(3a)                  6.0(2)
yes
     7         bios    v1.10.17(04/25/11):  v1.10.17(04/25/11)    v1.10.17(04/25/11)
no
    10    lc-m1-n7k                                  5.2(3a)                  6.0(2)
yes
    10         bios    v1.10.17(04/25/11):  v1.10.17(04/25/11)    v1.10.17(04/25/11)
no
```

```
Do you want to continue with the installation (y/n)?  [n] y


! Step 1 & 2: The BIOS is upgraded, followed by the standby supervisor which is
upgraded and rebooted


Install is in progress, please wait.

Performing runtime checks.
[####################] 100% -- SUCCESS

Syncing image bootflash:/n7000-s1-kickstart.6.0.2.bin to standby.
[####################] 100% -- SUCCESS

Syncing image bootflash:/n7000-s1-dk9.6.0.2.bin to standby.
[####################] 100% -- SUCCESS

Setting boot variables.
[####################] 100% -- SUCCESS

Performing configuration copy.
[####################] 100% -- SUCCESS

Module 1: Refreshing compact flash and upgrading bios/loader/bootrom.
Warning: please do not remove or power off the module at this time.
[####################] 100% -- SUCCESS

Module 2: Refreshing compact flash and upgrading bios/loader/bootrom.
Warning: please do not remove or power off the module at this time.
[####################] 100% -- SUCCESS

Module 5: Refreshing compact flash and upgrading bios/loader/bootrom.
Warning: please do not remove or power off the module at this time.
[####################] 100% -- SUCCESS

Module 6: Refreshing compact flash and upgrading bios/loader/bootrom.
Warning: please do not remove or power off the module at this time.
[####################] 100% -- SUCCESS

Module 7: Refreshing compact flash and upgrading bios/loader/bootrom.
Warning: please do not remove or power off the module at this time.
[####################] 100% -- SUCCESS

Module 10: Refreshing compact flash and upgrading bios/loader/bootrom.
Warning: please do not remove or power off the module at this time.
[####################] 100% -- SUCCESS
```

```
Module 6: Waiting for module online.
 -- SUCCESS


Notifying services about the switchover.
[####################] 100% -- SUCCESS


"Switching over onto standby".

! Step 3: The standby supervisor is online with the new version of
NX-OS, and a stateful switchover is initiated. "Switching over onto
standby".

! At this point the telnet session to the box is lost, as a result of
the supervisor switchover. The device is immediately available to
service sessions from the newly active supervisor which is now
running the updated software.


User Access Verification
Password:
Cisco Nexus Operating System (NX-OS) Software
TAC support: http://www.cisco.com/tac
Copyright (c) 2002-2011, Cisco Systems, Inc. All rights reserved.
The copyrights to certain works contained in this software are
owned by other third parties and used and distributed under
license. Certain components of this software are licensed under
the GNU General Public License (GPL) version 2.0 or the GNU
Lesser General Public License (LGPL) Version 2.1. A copy of each
such license is available at
http://www.opensource.org/licenses/gpl-2.0.php and
http://www.opensource.org/licenses/lgpl-2.1.php


N7k-1# sh ver
Cisco Nexus Operating System (NX-OS) Software
TAC support: http://www.cisco.com/tac
Documents: http://www.cisco.com/en/US/products/ps9372/tsd_products_support_series_
home.html
Copyright (c) 2002-2011, Cisco Systems, Inc. All rights reserved.
The copyrights to certain works contained in this software are
owned by other third parties and used and distributed under
license. Certain components of this software are licensed under
the GNU General Public License (GPL) version 2.0 or the GNU
Lesser General Public License (LGPL) Version 2.1. A copy of each
```

```
such license is available at
http://www.opensource.org/licenses/gpl-2.0.php and
http://www.opensource.org/licenses/lgpl-2.1.php

Software
  BIOS:       version 3.22.0
  kickstart: version 6.0(2)
  system:     version 6.0(2)
  BIOS compile time:       02/20/10
  kickstart image file is: bootflash:///n7000-s1-kickstart.6.0.2.bin
  kickstart compile time:  12/25/2020 12:00:00 [12/22/2011 06:56:22]
  system image file is:    bootflash:///n7000-s1-dk9.6.0.2.bin
  system compile time:     11/15/2011 12:00:00 [12/22/2011 08:46:28]


Hardware
  cisco Nexus7000 C7010 (10 Slot) Chassis ("Supervisor module-1X")
  Intel(R) Xeon(R) CPU       with 8245320 kB of memory.
  Processor Board ID JAB12230114

  Device name: N7k-1
  bootflash:    2000880 kB
  slot0:        2044854 kB (expansion flash)

Kernel uptime is 0 day(s), 0 hour(s), 9 minute(s), 47 second(s)

Last reset
  Reason: Unknown
  System version: 5.2(3a)
  Service:

plugin
  Core Plugin, Ethernet Plugin


CMP (Module 6) ok
 CMP Software
  CMP BIOS version:       02.01.05
  CMP Image version:      5.2(1) [build 5.0(0.66)]
  CMP BIOS compile time:  7/13/2008 19:44:27
  CMP Image compile time: 12/15/2011 12:00:00


! The interactive installer session can be resumed
N7k-1# sh install all status
There is an on-going installation...
```

```
Enter Ctrl-C to go back to the prompt.

Continuing with installation, please wait
Trying to start the installer...
! Step 4: The standby supervisor (previously active) is now being upgraded and
Rebooted
Module 6: Waiting for module online.
 -- SUCCESS


! Step 5: Line cards are upgraded,  non-disruptively.

Module 1: Non-disruptive upgrading.
 -- SUCCESS


Module 2: Non-disruptive upgrading.
 -- SUCCESS


Module 7: Non-disruptive upgrading.
 -- SUCCESS


Module 10: Non-disruptive upgrading.
 -- SUCCESS
! Step 6: Upgrade the CMP on both supervisors (This one's after the Module 2 line
below).
Module 6: Upgrading CMP image.
Warning: please do not reload or power cycle CMP module at this time.
-- SUCCESS

Module 5: Upgrading CMP image.
Warning: please do not reload or power cycle CMP module at this time.
-- SUCCESS

Recommended action::
"Please reload CMP(s) manually to have it run in the newer version.".

Install has been successful.
```

In addition to the NX-OS operating system, the Nexus 7000 switches include electronic programmable logic devices (EPLDs) that enable for additional hardware functionality or fixes without having to upgrade or replace the module. If new features or fixes are released that can be implemented in hardware through the use of EPLDs, this process must be done outside of the ISSU and might be disruptive to flowing traffic. The EPLD process is done on one module at a time, and therefore configurations that have module redundancy for port-channels or Layer 3 peering on multiple modules can make this process less disruptive. NX-OS release notes should be reviewed to determine if an EPLD upgrade is required.

Example 6-16 demonstrates the EPLD upgrade process.

Example 6-16   *EPLD Upgrade*

```
N7k-1# install module 3 epld bootflash:n7000-s1-epld.6.0.2.img
Copy complete, now saving to disk (please wait)...
Retrieving EPLD versions... Please wait.

Images will be upgraded according to following table:
Module  Type         EPLD      Running-Version  New-Version  Upg-Required
------  ----  -------------   ---------------  -----------  ------------
     3   LC  Power Manager         4.008           4.008         No
     3   LC  IO                    1.016           1.016         No
     3   LC  Forwarding Engine     1.006           1.006         No
     3   LC  FE Bridge(1)        186.006         186.008        Yes
     3   LC  FE Bridge(2)        186.006         186.008        Yes
     3   LC  Linksec Engine(1)     2.007           2.007         No
     3   LC  Linksec Engine(2)     2.007           2.007         No
     3   LC  Linksec Engine(3)     2.007           2.007         No
     3   LC  Linksec Engine(4)     2.007           2.007         No
     3   LC  Linksec Engine(5)     2.007           2.007         No
     3   LC  Linksec Engine(6)     2.007           2.007         No
     3   LC  Linksec Engine(7)     2.007           2.007         No
     3   LC  Linksec Engine(8)     2.007           2.007         No


Module 3 will be powered down.
Do you want to continue (y/n) ?  [n] y


2012 Aug  2 08:10:57 N7k-1 %$ VDC-1 %$ %PLATFORM-2-MOD_PWRDN: Module
3 powered down (Serial number JAF1623AHMN)
2012 Aug  2 08:11:10 N7k-1 %$ VDC-1 %$ %PLATFORM-2-MOD_DETECT: Module
3 detected (Serial number JAF1623AHMN) Module-Type 10 Gbps Ethernet
XL Module Model N7K-M132XP-12L
2012 Aug  2 08:11:10 N7k-1 %$ VDC-1 %$ %PLATFORM-2-MOD_PWRUP: Module
3 powered up (Serial number JAF1623AHMN)


Module 3 : FE Bridge [Programming ] : 100.00% (6466638 of 6466638 total bytes)


Waiting for Module to come online.
2012 Aug  2 08:15:15 N7k-1 %$ VDC-1 %$ %PLATFORM-2-MOD_PWRDN: Module
3 powered down (Serial number JAF1623AHMN)
2012 Aug  2 08:15:26 N7k-1 %$ VDC-1 %$ %PLATFORM-2-MOD_DETECT: Module
3 detected (Serial number JAF1623AHMN) Module-Type 10 Gbps Ethernet
```

```
XL Module Model N7K-M132XP-12L

2012 Aug  2 08:15:26 N7k-1 %$ VDC-1 %$ %PLATFORM-2-MOD_PWRUP: Module
3 powered up (Serial number JAF1623AHMN)


Module 3 EPLD upgrade is successful.
```

Summary

NX-OS was built for the high-availability requirements in the data center. High availability is achieved through the combination of resilient hardware and software architectures within the Nexus 7000. The Nexus 7000 hardware platform represents the highest levels of system redundancy within the control plane, fabric forwarding, power, and cooling systems. Building upon this foundation, NX-OS represents a modular software architecture with features such as stateful process restart, Nonstop Forwarding, and In-Service Software upgrades. This combination of hardware and software can provide administrators peace of mind in knowing that they have a system built to achieve the highest levels of availability for mission-critical data center environments.

## Chapter 7

Embedded Serviceability Features

The Nexus line of switches provides a robust embedded serviceability feature set. This chapter covers:

- **SPAN:** Describes the configuration and operations of SPAN on Nexus 7000, 5x00, and 1000V series switches

- **ERSPAN:** Describes the configuration and operations of ERSPAN on Nexus 7000, 5x00, and 1000V series switches

- **Embedded Analyzer:** Describes the configuration and operations of Embedded Analyzer on Nexus 7000 and 5x00 series switches

- **Smart Call Home:** Describes the configuration and operations of Smart Call Home on Nexus 7000 series switches

- **Configuration Checkpoint and Rollback:** Describes the configuration and operations of Configuration Checkpoint and Rollback on Nexus 7000 and 5x00 series switches

- **Netflow:** Describes the configuration and operations of Netflow on Nexus 7000 and 1000V series switches

- **NTP:** Describes the configuration and operations of Network Time Protocol on the Nexus 7000, 5x00, and 1000V series switches

- **PTP:** Describes the configuration and operations of Precision Time Protocol on the Nexus 7000 and 5500 series switches

- **IEEE 802.3az:** Describes the configuration and operations of Energy Efficient Ethernet on the Nexus 7000 F2e copper module.

- **Power On Auto-Provisioning:** Describes the configuration and operations of Power On Auto-Provisioning on the Nexus 7000 and 5500 series switches

- **Python:** Describes the configuration and operations of Python on the Nexus 7000 and 5500 series switches

SPAN

Cisco NX-OS was designed from the beginning to be a data center class operating system. A component of such an operating system includes support for a rich set of embedded serviceability features. These features should enable the network administrator and operator to have unprecedented access to tools to support and troubleshoot the network. This chapter covers many of the key features such as Switched Port Analyzer (SPAN), Encapsulated Remote Switch Port Analyzer (ERSPAN), Smart Call Home, Configuration Rollback, NetFlow, Network Time Protocol (NTP), Precision Time Protocol (PTP), IEEE 802.3az, and Power On Auto-Provisioning (POAP).

The SPAN feature is one of the most frequently used troubleshooting components in a network. It is not uncommon for the network team to be approached to provide packet level analysis of the traffic on the network as part of routine analysis, security compliance, or break/fix troubleshooting. SPAN creates a copy or mirror of the source traffic and delivers it to the destination. SPANning traffic does not have an impact on the delivery of the original traffic providing a nonintrusive method to perform high-speed traffic analysis. NX-OS provides the ability to configure SPAN across all three currently available platforms: Nexus 7000, Nexus 5x00, and Nexus 1000V series switches. In addition, the Nexus 1000V supports ERSPAN to provide additional flexibility for network administrators. The following sections cover the various aspects of SPAN for all three platforms.

SPAN on Nexus 7000

The Nexus 7000 series switches have the capability to configure traditional SPAN sessions in addition to Virtual SPAN. SPAN enables the network administrator flexible configuration options using the concepts of source ports and destination ports. Source ports, as their name implies, are the source of the traffic to be sent via SPAN to the destination ports. Source ports have the following requirements:

- Can be a physical Ethernet port.

- Can be a virtual local area network (VLAN); when a VLAN is used as a SPAN source, all ports that belong to the VLAN are considered as part of the SPAN source.

- Can be a Remote SPAN (RSPAN) VLAN.

- Can be configured with a direction (ingress, egress, or both) to monitor.

- Can be the inband interface to the switch's supervisor engine control plane.

> **Note**   If you use Virtual Device Contexts (VDCs), only the default VDC can SPAN the inband interface, and all control plane traffic from each VDC will be monitored from the default VDC.

- A source port cannot be a SPAN destination port.

SPAN destinations, as their name implies, define where traffic copied from the SPAN source will be sent. Destination ports have the following requirements:

■ Can include Ethernet or port channel interfaces in either access or trunk mode.

■ Can be configured in only one SPAN session at a time.

■ Do not participate in a spanning-tree instance; however, SPAN output includes STP hello packets.

■ Can be configured to support Intrusion Detection Systems/Intrusion Prevention Systems (IDS/IPS) applications where the need to have the forwarding engine learn the MAC address of the IDS/IPS is required.

■ Can be configured to inject packets enabling IDS/IPS to disrupt traffic.

In addition, SPAN destinations have the following restrictions:

■ SPAN destinations cannot be SPAN sources.

■ SPAN destinations cannot be an RSPAN VLAN.

SPAN on the Nexus 7000 supports the capability to configure up to 48 SPAN sessions with any two active simultaneously. The Nexus 7000 provides support for a feature called Virtual SPAN. Virtual SPAN enables the network administrator to SPAN multiple VLAN sources and selectively determine where the SPAN traffic is sent on multiple destination VLAN ports. This provides the ability to monitor a trunk, for example, and have the output from different VLANs sent to specific destinations or network analyzers without the need for multiple SPAN sessions. Table 7-1 lists the SPAN session limits on the Nexus 7000.

Table 7-1 *Nexus 7000 SPAN Session Limits*

Session Characteristic	Limit
Configured SPAN sessions	48
Simultaneously running SPAN sessions	2
Source interfaces per session	128
Source VLANs per session	32
Destination interfaces per session	32

Configuring SPAN on Nexus 7000

Configuration of SPAN on Nexus 7000 is a multistep process in which the SPAN source, destination, and monitoring ports are defined. The first step is to define the monitor port connection where the network analysis, IDS/IPS, or other device collects the SPAN traffic, as shown in Example 7-1. Figure 7-1 illustrates the topology used in this example.

Figure 7-1 *Network Topology for Configuring a SPAN Session*

Note The monitor port must be in switchport mode: either in access or trunk mode. SPAN monitor ports cannot be routed ports.

Example 7-1 *Configuring a SPAN Monitor Port*

```
Jealousy# config t
Enter configuration commands, one per line.   End with CNTL/Z.
Jealousy(config)# int e1/26
Jealousy(config-if)# switchport
Jealousy(config-if)# switchport monitor
Jealousy(config-if)# end
Jealousy#
```

If the device is an IDS/IPS, it might be required to have it participate in the network where the switch must learn the MAC address of the device and where the IDS/IPS might need to inject traffic, as shown in Example 7-2. Typically, IPS actively participate in the network to inject traffic to thwart an attack. In these cases, the ingress and the learning configuration parameters will be wanted.

Example 7-2 *Configuring a SPAN Monitor Port for IDS/IPS*

```
Jealousy# config t
Enter configuration commands, one per line.   End with CNTL/Z.
Jealousy(config)# int e1/26
Jealousy(config-if)# switchport
Jealousy(config-if)# switchport monitor ingress learning
Jealousy(config-if)# end
Jealousy#
```

After the monitor port is configured, the next step is to configure the SPAN monitor session. Source and destination interfaces are configured under the SPAN monitor session in addition to VLAN filters. Finally, the state of the SPAN session, shut or no shut, is configured in SPAN monitor session mode as well. In Example 7-3, a monitor session is configured that will SPAN traffic from VLANs 100, 101, and 102 to destination port e1/26. This SPAN monitors traffic that ingresses (rx) VLAN 100, traffic that egresses (tx) VLAN 101, and both on VLAN 102.

Note The default direction for SPAN monitoring is both. Use of tx or rx direction narrows the traffic monitored.

Example 7-3 *Configuring a SPAN Monitor Session*

```
Jealousy# config t

Enter configuration commands, one per line.  End with CNTL/Z.
Jealousy(config)# monitor session 1
Jealousy(config-monitor)# source vlan 100 rx
Jealousy(config-monitor)# source vlan 101 tx
Jealousy(config-monitor)# source vlan 102
Jealousy(config-monitor)# description SPAN Session 1
Jealousy(config-monitor)# destination interface e1/26
Jealousy(config-monitor)# no shut
Jealousy(config-monitor)# end
```

Tip Don't forget to **no shut** the monitor session!

The monitor session's status can be reviewed through the use of the **show monitor** command, as demonstrated in Example 7-4. This information is helpful when verifying the SPAN session's configuration and status.

Example 7-4 *Displaying a Monitor Session's Configuration*

```
Jealousy# show monitor session 1
   session 1
--------------
description      : SPAN Session 1
type             : local
state            : down (No operational src/dst)
source intf      :
    rx           :
    tx           :
    both         :
source VLANs     :
    rx           : 100,102
    tx           : 101-102
    both         : 102
filter VLANs     : filter not specified
destination ports : Eth1/26


Legend: f = forwarding enabled, l = learning enabled
```

When the **ingress** and **learning** keywords are present on the monitor port configuration—for example, to support an IDS/IPS—the destination port's status reflects this, as shown in Example 7-5.

Example 7-5 *Displaying a Monitor Session Configuration with Ingress and Learning*

```
Jealousy# conf t
Enter configuration commands, one per line.  End with CNTL/Z.
Jealousy(config)# int e1/26
Jealousy(config-if)# switchport monitor ingress learning
Jealousy(config-if)# end
Jealousy# show monitor session 1
   session 1
---------------
description      : SPAN Session 1
type            : local
state           : down (No operational src/dst)
source intf     :
    rx          :
    tx          :
    both        :
source VLANs    :
    rx          : 100,102
    tx          : 101-102
    both        : 102
filter VLANs    : filter not specified
destination ports : Eth1/26 (f+l)

Legend: f = forwarding enabled, l = learning enabled
```

Configuration of a virtual SPAN session is the same as a normal SPAN session with the difference residing in the configuration of the destination ports. A virtual SPAN session enables the network administrator to use a single SPAN session on an 802.1Q trunk and direct traffic from specific VLANs to the appropriate network analyzers, as demonstrated in Example 7-6 for the network in Figure 7-2.

Example 7-6 *Configuring a Virtual SPAN Session*

```
Jealousy# config t
Enter configuration commands, one per line.  End with CNTL/Z.
Jealousy(config)# int e1/25
Jealousy(config-if)# switchport
Jealousy(config-if)# switch mode trunk
Jealousy(config-if)# switchport trunk allowed vlan 100-105
Jealousy(config-if)# no shut
```

```
Jealousy(config-if)# int e1/26
Jealousy(config-if)# desc Connection to Network Analyzer for VLAN 100
Jealousy(config-if)# switchport
Jealousy(config-if)# switchport monitor
Jealousy(config-if)# switchport mode trunk
Jealousy(config-if)# switchport trunk allowed vlan 100
Jealousy(config-if)# int e1/27
Jealousy(config-if)# desc Connection to Network Analyzer for VLAN 101
Jealousy(config-if)# switchport
Jealousy(config-if)# switchport monitor
Jealousy(config-if)# switchport mode trunk
Jealousy(config-if)# switchport trunk allowed vlan 101
Jealousy(config-if)# monitor session 2
Jealousy(config-monitor)# desc Virtual SPAN Session
Jealousy(config-monitor)# source int e1/25
Jealousy(config-monitor)# destination in e1/26,e1/27
Jealousy(config-monitor)# no shut
Jealousy(config-monitor)# end
```

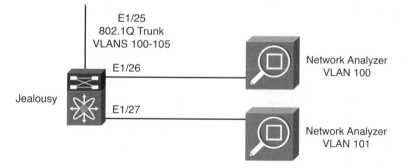

Figure 7-2 *Network Topology for Configuring a Virtual SPAN Session*

Note   It is necessary for a virtual SPAN session destination port to be a trunk. VLAN member ports can be used for traditional SPAN destinations.

The virtual SPAN session is verified using the same syntax as a normal SPAN session, as demonstrated in Example 7-7.

Example 7-7   *Displaying a Virtual SPAN Session*

```
Jealousy# show monitor session 2
   session 2
---------------
description       : Virtual SPAN Session
```

```
type               : local
state              : down (No operational src/dst)
source intf        :
    rx             : Eth1/25
    tx             : Eth1/25
    both           : Eth1/25
source VLANs       :
    rx             :
    tx             :
    both           :
filter VLANs       : filter not specified
destination ports : Eth1/26       Eth1/27

Legend: f = forwarding enabled, l = learning enabled
```

Note   Virtual SPAN copies all source frames to all destinations, whether the frames are required at the destination. Frames are filtered on a per-VLAN basis at the egress destination port level.

SPAN on Nexus 5x00

The Nexus 5x00 series switches have the capability to configure traditional SPAN sessions for Ethernet traffic in addition to Fibre Channel and Fibre Channel over Ethernet (FCoE) traffic. SPAN enables the network administrator to configure SPAN using the concepts of source ports and destination ports. Source ports, as their name implies, are the source of the traffic to be sent via SPAN to the destination ports. Source ports have the following requirements:

- Can be any port type including Ethernet, Fibre Channel, port channel, SAN port channel, VLAN, and virtual storage area network (VSAN).

- Can be a VLAN or VSAN. When a VLAN or VSAN is used as the SPAN source, all ports that belong to the VLAN or VSAN are considered as part of the SPAN source.

- Can be configured with a direction (ingress, egress, or both) to monitor on Ethernet and Fibre Channel ports. In the case of VLAN, VSAN, Ethernet port channel, and SAN port channel sources, the monitored direction can be only ingress.

- Cannot be a SPAN destination port.

SPAN destinations, as their name implies, define where traffic copied from the SPAN source will be sent. Destination ports have the following requirements:

- Can include any physical port including Ethernet or Fibre Channel

> **Note**   Logical interfaces such as virtual Fibre Channel, Ethernet port channel, and SAN
> port channel interfaces cannot be SPAN destinations.

- Can be configured in only one SPAN session at a time

- Do not participate in a spanning-tree instance

- Can be configured to support IDS/IPS applications where the need to have the for-warding engine learn the MAC address of the IDS/IPS is required

- Can be configured to inject packets enabling IDS/IPS to disrupt traffic

In addition, SPAN destinations have the following restrictions:

- Cannot be SPAN sources

- Cannot be Virtual Fibre Channel, Ethernet port channel, and SAN port channel interfaces

SPAN on the Nexus 5x00 supports the capability to configure up to 18 SPAN sessions with any two active simultaneously. Table 7-2 lists the SPAN session limits for the Nexus 5x00.

Table 7-2   *Nexus 5x00 SPAN Session Limits*

Session Characteristic	Limit
Configured SPAN sessions	18
Simultaneously running SPAN sessions	2
Source interfaces per session	128
Source VLANs per session	32
Destination interfaces per session	32

Configuring SPAN on Nexus 5x00

Configuring SPAN on a Nexus 5x00 is a multistep process in which the SPAN source, SPAN destination, and monitoring ports are defined. The first step is to define the moni-tor port connection where the network analysis, IDS/IPS, or other device collects the SPAN traffic, as demonstrated in Example 7-8. Figure 7-3 illustrates the topology used in Examples 7-8 through 7-14.

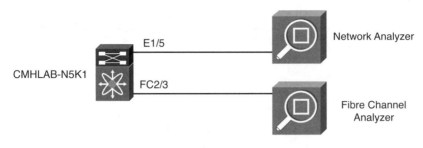

Figure 7-3   *Nexus 5x00 SPAN Topology*

Example 7-8   *Configuring a SPAN Monitor Port*

```
CMHLAB-N5K1# config t
Enter configuration commands, one per line.  End with CNTL/Z.
CMHLAB-N5K1(config)# int e1/5
CMHLAB-N5K1(config-if)# desc Connection to Network Analyzer
CMHLAB-N5K1(config-if)# switchport
CMHLAB-N5K1(config-if)# switchport monitor
CMHLAB-N5K1(config-if)# no shut
CMHLAB-N5K1(config-if)# end
CMHLAB-N5K1#
```

If the device is an IDS/IPS, it might be required to have it participate in the network where the switch must learn the MAC address of the device and where the IDS/IPS might need to inject traffic, as demonstrated in the configuration in Example 7-9. Typically, IPS actively participate in the network to inject traffic to thwart an attack. In these cases, the ingress and the learning configuration parameters will be wanted.

Example 7-9   *Configuring a SPAN Monitor Port for IDS/IPS*

```
CMHLAB-N5K1# config t
Enter configuration commands, one per line.  End with CNTL/Z.
CMHLAB-N5K1(config)# int e1/5
CMHLAB-N5K1(config-if)# desc Connection to Network Analyzer
CMHLAB-N5K1(config-if)# switchport
CMHLAB-N5K1(config-if)# switchport monitor ingress learning
CMHLAB-N5K1(config-if)# end
CMHLAB-N5K1#
```

After the monitor port is configured, the next step is to configure the SPAN monitor session. Source and destination interfaces are configured under the SPAN monitor session. Finally, the state of the SPAN session, shut or no shut, is configured in SPAN monitor session mode as well. In Example 7-10, a monitor session is configured that will SPAN traffic from interface e1/28, e1/29, and e1/30 to destination port e1/5. This SPAN monitors traffic that ingresses (rx) e1/28, traffic that egresses (tx) e1/29, and both on e1/30.

Note   The default direction for SPAN monitoring is both. Use of tx or rx direction narrows the traffic monitored.

Example 7-10   *Configuring a SPAN Monitor Session*

```
CMHLAB-N5K1# config t
Enter configuration commands, one per line.  End with CNTL/Z.
CMHLAB-N5K1(config)# monitor session 1
CMHLAB-N5K1(config-monitor)# source int e1/28 rx
CMHLAB-N5K1(config-monitor)# source int e1/29 tx
CMHLAB-N5K1(config-monitor)# source int e1/30
CMHLAB-N5K1(config-monitor)# desc SPAN Session 1
CMHLAB-N5K1(config-monitor)# destination interface e1/5
CMHLAB-N5K1(config-monitor)# no shut
CMHLAB-N5K1(config-monitor)# end
CMHLAB-N5K1#
```

Note   Don't forget to **no shut** the monitor session.

You can review the monitor session's status through the use of the **show monitor** command, as demonstrated in Example 7-11. This information is helpful when verifying the SPAN session's configuration and status.

Example 7-11   *Displaying a Monitor Session's Configuration*

```
CMHLAB-N5K1# show monitor session 1
   session 1
--------------
description       : SPAN Session 1
type              : local
state             : down (No operational src/dst)
source intf       :
    rx            : Eth1/28       Eth1/30
    tx            : Eth1/29       Eth1/30
    both          : Eth1/30
source VLANs      :
    rx            :
destination ports : Eth1/5
```

```
Legend: f = forwarding enabled, l = learning enabled
source VSANs      :
   rx           :     rx         :


Legend: f = forwarding enabled, l = learning enabled
```

When the **ingress** and **learning** keywords are present on the monitor port configuration (for example, to support an IDS/IPS), the destination port's status reflects this, as shown in Example 7-12.

Example 7-12 *Displaying a Monitor Session Configuration with Ingress and Learning*

```
CMHLAB-N5K1(config)# int e1/5
CMHLAB-N5K1(config-if)# switchport
CMHLAB-N5K1(config-if)# switchport monitor ingress learning
CMHLAB-N5K1# show monitor session 1
   session 1
---------------
description       : SPAN Session 1
type             : local
state            : down (No operational src/dst)
source intf      :
   rx            : Eth1/28      Eth1/30
   tx            : Eth1/29      Eth1/30
   both          : Eth1/30
source VLANs     :
   rx            :
destination ports : Eth1/5  (f+l)

Legend: f = forwarding enabled, l = learning enabled
source VSANs      :
   rx           :     rx         :
```

Configuration of Fibre Channel SPAN is similar to a typical Ethernet SPAN configuration. If the destination port is a Fibre Channel interface, it must be configured as a SPAN Destination (SD) port under the interface configuration, as demonstrated in Example 7-13.

Example 7-13 *Configuring a SPAN Session with a Fibre Channel Destination Port*

```
CMHLAB-N5K1# config t
Enter configuration commands, one per line.  End with CNTL/Z.
CMHLAB-N5K1(config)# int fc2/3
CMHLAB-N5K1(config-if)# switchport speed 2000
CMHLAB-N5K1(config-if)# switchport mode sd
```

```
CMHLAB-N5K1(config-if)# no shut
CMHLAB-N5K1(config)# monitor session 2
CMHLAB-N5K1(config-monitor)# desc SPAN Session for Fibre Channel
CMHLAB-N5K1(config-monitor)# source interface vfc10
CMHLAB-N5K1(config-monitor)# destination int fc2/3
CMHLAB-N5K1(config-monitor)# no shut
CMHLAB-N5K1(config-monitor)# end
CMHLAB-N5K1#
```

The session's configuration can be verified by using the **show monitor session** command, as demonstrated in Example 7-14.

Example 7-14   *Displaying a Fibre Channel Monitor Session*

```
CMHLAB-N5K1# show mon sess 2
   session 2
---------------
description      : SPAN Session for Fibre Channel
type             : local
state            : up
source intf      :
   rx            : vfc10
   tx            : vfc10
   both          : vfc10
source VLANs     :
   rx            :
destination ports : fc2/3


Legend: f = forwarding enabled, l = learning enabled
source VSANs     :
   rx            :      rx              :
```

SPAN on Nexus 1000V

The Nexus 1000V series switches have the capability to configure traditional SPAN sessions, referred to as local SPAN sessions, for Ethernet traffic in addition to ERSPAN. SPAN enables the network administrator to configure SPAN using the concepts of source ports and destination ports. Source ports, as their name implies, are the source of the traffic to be sent via SPAN to the destination ports. Source ports have the following requirements:

■ Can be any port type including Ethernet, virtual Ethernet, port channel, or VLAN.

■ Can be a VLAN. When a VLAN is used as a SPAN source, all ports that belong to the VLAN are considered as part of the SPAN source.

■ Can be configured with a direction (ingress, egress, or both) to monitor.

■ Cannot be a SPAN destination port.

■ A local SPAN session must be on the same host Virtual Ethernet Module (VEM) as the destination port.

SPAN destinations, as their name implies, define where traffic copied from the SPAN source will be sent. As the Nexus 1000V supports local SPAN and ERSPAN, the destination ports have distinctly different requirements and configuration.

Local SPAN destination ports have the following requirements:

■ Can be any Ethernet or virtual Ethernet port

■ Must be on the same host VEM as the source port

In addition, SPAN destinations have the following restrictions:

■ Cannot be SPAN sources

ERSPAN destinations have the following characteristics:

■ IP addresses rather than ports or VLANs.

■ Generic Routing Encapsulation (GRE) will be used to encapsulate the ERSPAN traffic enabling it to traverse an IP network.

SPAN on the Nexus 1000V supports the capability to configure up to 64 SPAN and 64 ERSPAN sessions. Table 7-3 lists the SPAN and ERSPAN session limits for the Nexus 1000V.

Table 7-3   *Nexus 1000V SPAN and ERSPAN Session Limits*

Session Characteristic	Limit
Configured SPAN and ERSPAN sessions	64
Simultaneously running SPAN and ERSPAN sessions	64
Source interfaces per session	128
Source VLANs per session	32

Configuring SPAN on Nexus 1000V

Configuration of SPAN on Nexus 1000V is a multistep process in which the SPAN source, SPAN destination, and monitoring ports are defined. The first step is to define the monitor port connection where the network analysis, IDS/IPS, or other device collects the SPAN traffic, as demonstrated in Example 7-15. Figure 7-4 illustrates the topology used in Examples 7-15 through 7-17.

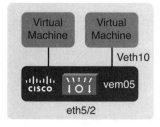

Figure 7-4 *Network Topology for Nexus 1000V SPAN Configuration*

Example 7-15 *Configuring a SPAN Monitor Port*

```
CMHLAB-DC2-VSM1# config t
CMHLAB-DC2-VSM1(config)# int e5/1
CMHLAB-DC2-VSM1 (config-if)# desc Connection to Network Analyzer
CMHLAB-DC2-VSM1 (config-if)# switchport
CMHLAB-DC2-VSM1(config-if)# switchport monitor
CMHLAB-DC2-VSM1 (config-if)# no shut
CMHLAB-DC2-VSM1 (config-if)# end
CMHLAB-DC2-VSM1#
```

Note The Nexus 1000V does not support the ingress and learning configuration parameters at this time.

After the monitor port is configured, the next step is to configure the SPAN monitor session. Source and destination interfaces are configured under the SPAN monitor session. Finally, the state of the SPAN session, shut or no shut, is configured in SPAN monitor session mode as well. In Example 7-16, a monitor session is configured that will SPAN traffic from interface vEthernet10 to destination port e5/1.

Note The default direction for SPAN monitoring is both. Use of tx or rx direction narrows the traffic monitored.

Example 7-16 *Configuring a SPAN Monitor Session*

```
CMHLAB-DC2-VSM1# config t
CMHLAB-DC2-VSM1(config)# monitor session 1
CMHLAB-DC2-VSM1(config-monitor)# desc Local SPAN Session 1
```

```
CMHLAB-DC2-VSM1(config-monitor)# source int vethernet10
CMHLAB-DC2-VSM1(config-monitor)# destination int e5/1
CMHLAB-DC2-VSM1(config-monitor)# no shut
CMHLAB-DC2-VSM1(config-monitor)# end
```

Note   Don't forget to **no shut** the monitor session.

The monitor session's status can be reviewed through the use of the **show monitor** command, as demonstrated in Example 7-17. This information is helpful when verifying the SPAN session's configuration and status.

Example 7-17   *Displaying a Monitor Session's Configuration*

```
CMHLAB-DC2-VSM1# show monitor session 1
   session 1
---------------
description       : Local SPAN Session 1
type              : local
state             : up
source intf       :
    rx            : Veth10
    tx            : Veth10
    both          : Veth10
source VLANs      :
    rx            :
    tx            :
    both          :
filter VLANs      : filter not specified
destination ports : Eth5/1
```

ERSPAN on Nexus 1000V

The Nexus 1000V series switches have the capability to configure traditional SPAN sessions, referred to as local SPAN sessions, for Ethernet traffic in addition to ERSPAN. ERSPAN differs from traditional SPAN in that ERSPAN enables the monitored traffic to be encapsulated in a GRE packet and routed across an IP network. With ERSPAN, network administrators can centralize network analysis tools and route the monitored traffic.

ERSPAN builds on the concepts of source ports and destination ports. Source ports, as their name implies, are the source of the traffic to be sent via ERSPAN to the destination ports. Source ports have the following requirements:

- Can be any port type including Ethernet, virtual Ethernet, port channel, or VLAN.

- Can be a VLAN. When a VLAN is used as SPAN source, all ports that belong to the VLAN are considered as part of the SPAN source.

- Can be configured with a direction (ingress, egress or both) to monitor.

- Cannot be a SPAN destination port.

ERSPAN destinations define where traffic copied from the ERSPAN source will be sent. ERSPAN destination ports are specified by an IP address.

In addition, ERSPAN destinations have the following restrictions:

- Cannot be ERSPAN sources

SPAN on the Nexus 1000V supports the ability to configure up to 64 SPAN and ERSPAN sessions.

Configuration of ERSPAN on Nexus 1000V is a multistep process in which the ERSPAN source and ERSPAN destination are defined. The first step is to configure the ERSPAN port profile. Refer to Chapter 9, "Nexus 1000V," for additional details on port profile configuration. Example 7-18 illustrates a port profile that will be used for ERSPAN.

Example 7-18   *ERSPAN Port Profile Configuration*

```
CMHLAB-DC2-VSM1# config t
CMHLAB-DC2-VSM1(config-port-prof)# port-profile DC2-N1K-ERSPAN
CMHLAB-DC2-VSM1(config-port-prof)# capability l3control
CMHLAB-DC2-VSM1(config-port-prof)# vmware port-group
CMHLAB-DC2-VSM1(config-port-prof)# switchport mode access
CMHLAB-DC2-VSM1(config-port-prof)# switchport access vlan 702
CMHLAB-DC2-VSM1(config-port-prof)# no shutdown
CMHLAB-DC2-VSM1(config-port-prof)# system vlan 702
CMHLAB-DC2-VSM1(config-port-prof)# state enabled
CMHLAB-DC2-VSM1(config-port-prof)# end
```

The two differences between the ERSPAN port profile and a port profile that would be used directly by a guest machine are the following commands:

```
CMHLAB-DC2-VSM1(config-port-prof)# capability l3control
CMHLAB-DC2-VSM1(config-port-prof)# system vlan 702
```

The **capability l3control** command indicates that the interface created will use Layer 3 (IP) control functions. In this case, ERSPAN will encapsulate traffic in GRE for transport across an IP network.

The **system vlan 702** command indicates a VLAN that will be brought up before communication between the VEM and Virtual Supervisor Module (VSM) is established. Use of the system VLAN is recommended for all VMware Kernel Port (vmk) ports because the vmk ports are used for system functions such as IP-based network attached storage connectivity, VEM to VSM communication, service consoles, and more.

Next, use the ERSPAN port profile to create a new vmk port on the host from which traffic will be sourced. A typical cluster configuration will have a vmk port configured on each cluster member server that uses the ERSPAN port profile. Figure 7-5 demonstrates how to do this. You can find details on adding a vmk port in Chapter 9.

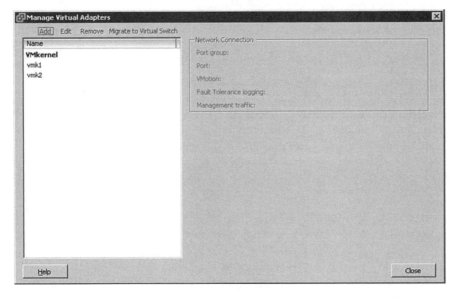

Figure 7-5   *Create a vmk Port Using the ERSPAN Port Profile: Step 1*

Click **Add** in the upper-left corner. The screen in Figure 7-6 displays.

Select **New virtual adapter** and then click **Next**. The screen in Figure 7-7 displays.

Select the ERSPAN port group from the drop-down list, and click **Next**. The screen in Figure 7-8 displays.

Configure a unique IP address for the ERSPAN vmk to use, the subnet mask, and default gateway, and then click **Next**. The screen in Figure 7-9 displays.

Review the configuration and click **Finish**.

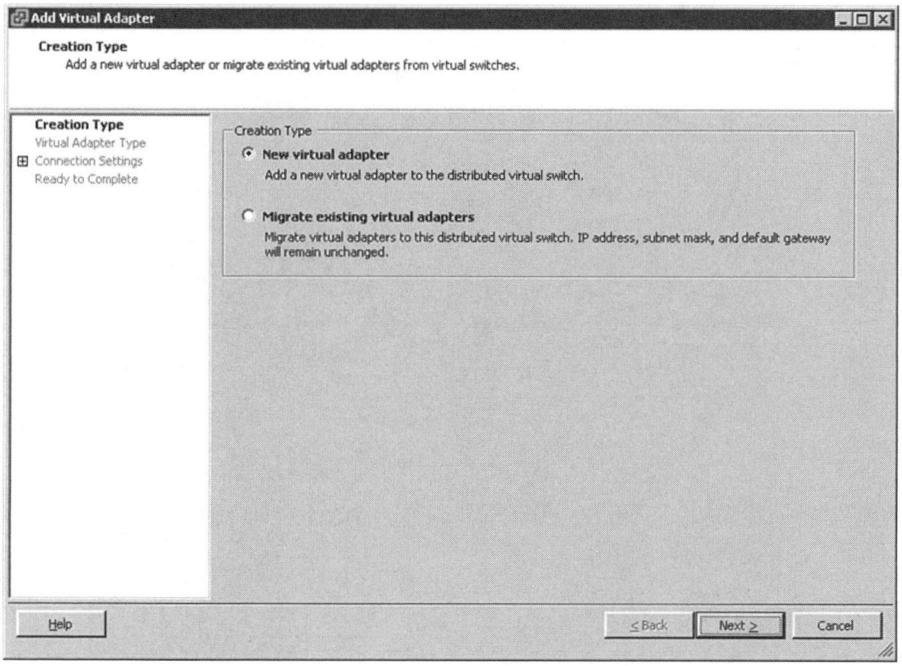

Figure 7-6   *Create a vmk Port Using the ERSPAN Port Profile: Step 2*

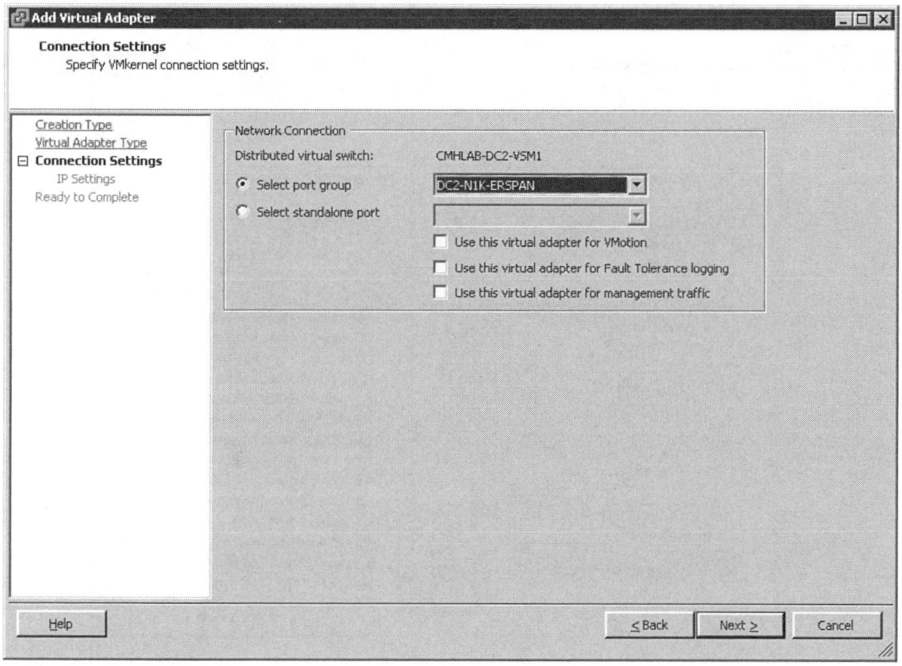

Figure 7-7   *Create a vmk Port Using the ERSPAN Port Profile: Step 3*

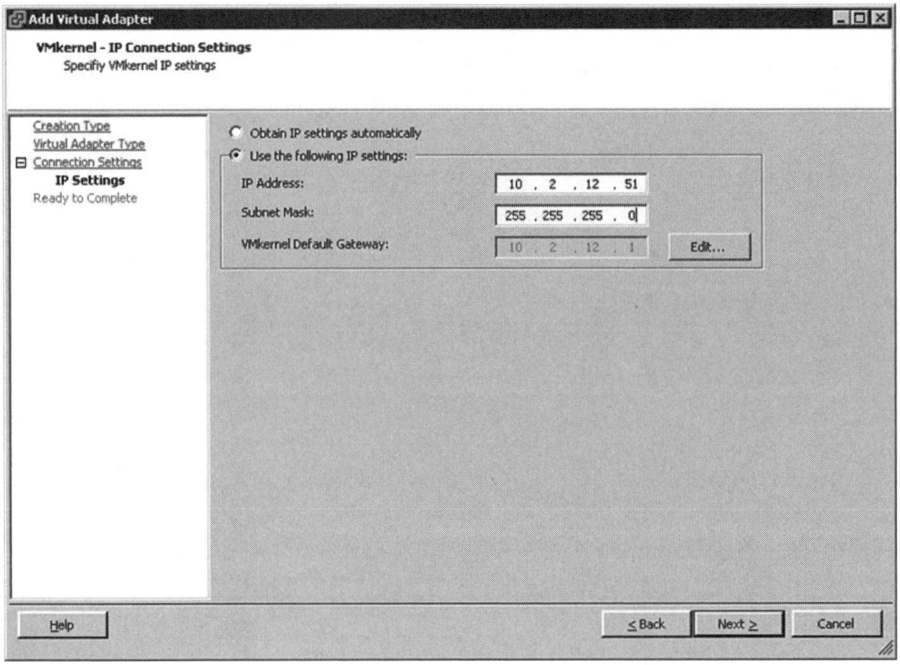

Figure 7-8   *Create a vmk Port Using the ERSPAN Port Profile: Step 4*

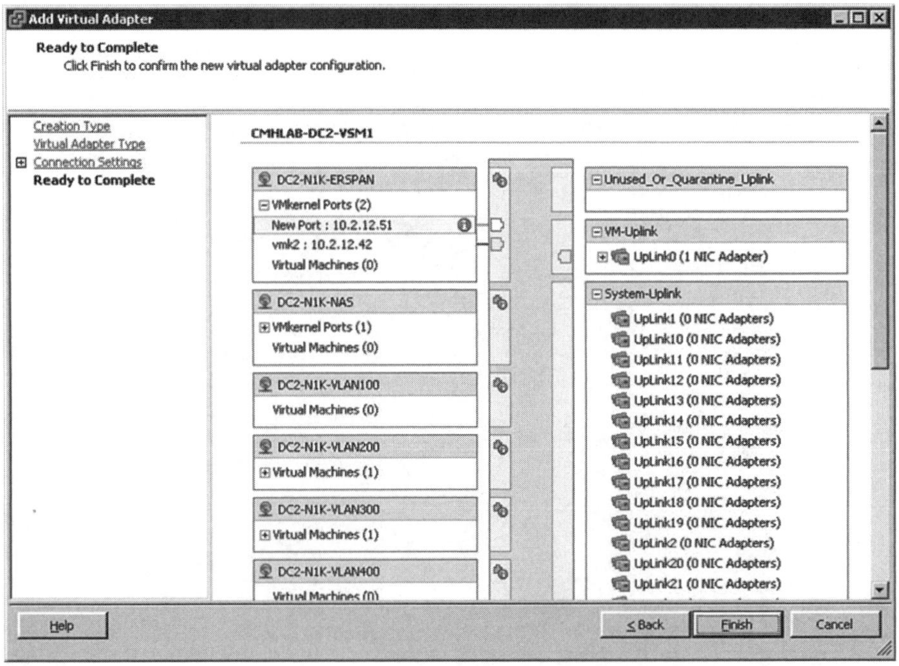

Figure 7-9   *Create a vmk Port Using the ERSPAN Port Profile: Step 5*

Source and destination IP addresses are configured under the ERSPAN monitor session along with the ERSPAN ID. ERSPAN IDs perform an important role in that they uniquely identify an ERSPAN session and can be used to differentiate between multiple ERSPAN sessions at the destination. This is particularly helpful in a centralized model where there might be many ERSPAN sessions aggregated. Finally, the state of the ERSPAN session, shut or no shut, is configured in ERSPAN monitor session mode as well. In Example 7-19, a monitor session is configured that will SPAN traffic from interface vEthernet27 to the destination IP address of 10.1.1.100 and an ERSPAN-ID of 1000.

Example 7-19 *Configuring an ERSPAN Monitor Session*

```
CMHLAB-DC2-VSM1# config t
CMHLAB-DC2-VSM1(config)# monitor session 1 type erspan-source
CMHLAB-DC2-VSM1(config-erspan-src)# desc ERSPAN Session 1
CMHLAB-DC2-VSM1(config-erspan-src)# source interface vethernet27
CMHLAB-DC2-VSM1(config-erspan-src)# destination ip 10.1.1.100
CMHLAB-DC2-VSM1(config-erspan-src)# erspan-id 1000
CMHLAB-DC2-VSM1(config-erspan-src)# no shut
CMHLAB-DC2-VSM1(config-erspan-src)# end
```

Note Don't forget to **no shut** the monitor session.

The monitor session's status can be reviewed through the use of the **show monitor** command, as shown in Example 7-20. This information is helpful when verifying the ERSPAN session's configuration and status.

Example 7-20 *Displaying a Monitor Session's Configuration*

```
CMHLAB-DC2-VSM1(config-erspan-src)# show monitor session 1
   session 1
---------------
description       : ERSPAN Session
type              : erspan-source
state             : up
source intf       :
    rx            : Veth27
    tx            : Veth27
    both          : Veth27
source VLANs      :
    rx            :
    tx            :
    both          :
filter VLANs      : filter not specified
```

```
destination IP      : 10.1.1.100
ERSPAN ID           : 1000
ERSPAN TTL          : 64
ERSPAN IP Prec.     : 0
ERSPAN DSCP         : 0
ERSPAN MTU          : 1500
```

ERSPAN on Nexus 7000

The Nexus 7000 series switches have the capability to configure traditional SPAN sessions, referred to as local SPAN sessions, for Ethernet traffic in addition toERSPAN. ERSPAN differs from traditional SPAN in that ERSPAN enables the monitored traffic to be encapsulated in a GRE packet and routed across an IP network. With ERSPAN, network administrators can centralize network analysis tools and route the monitored traffic.

ERSPAN builds on the concepts of source ports and destination ports. Source ports, as their name implies, are the source of the traffic to be sent via ERSPAN to the destination ports. Source ports have the following requirements:

■ Can be any port type including Ethernet, virtual Ethernet, port channel, or VLAN.

■ Can be a VLAN. When a VLAN is used as SPAN source, all ports that belong to the VLAN are considered as part of the SPAN source.

■ Can be configured with a direction (ingress, egress or both) to monitor.

■ Cannot be a SPAN destination port.

ERSPAN destinations define where traffic copied from the ERSPAN source will be sent. ERSPAN destination ports are specified by an IP address.

In addition, ERSPAN destinations have the following restriction: They cannot be ERSPAN sources.

ERSPAN on the Nexus 7000 supports the capability to configure up to 48 ERSPAN sessions, though only 2 SPAN and ERSPAN sessions can be running simultaneously.

Configuration of ERSPAN on Nexus 7000 is a multistep process in which the ERSPAN source and ERSPAN destination are defined. One difference between SPAN and ERSPAN configuration is that with ERSPAN you must first specify an IP address that is used as the source IP of all GRE packets. This is done in the default VDC or the admin VDC and used across all VDCs. Example 7-21 illustrates an ERSPAN source session.

Example 7-21   *ERSPAN Source Configuration for Nexus 7000*

```
N7K-2# config
Enter configuration commands, one per line.  End with CNTL/Z.
N7K-2(config)# monitor erspan origin ip-address 10.20.20.20
```

```
N7K-2(config)# monitor session 1 type erspan-source
N7K-2(config-erspan-src)#  description ERSPAN Source of traffic
N7K-2(config-erspan-src)#  erspan-id 100
N7K-2(config-erspan-src)#  vrf default
N7K-2(config-erspan-src)#  destination ip 10.10.10.1
N7K-2(config-erspan-src)#  source interface Ethernet7/1 both
N7K-2(config-erspan-src)#  no shut
N7K-2(config-erspan-src)# show monitor session 1
   session 1
---------------
description      : ERSPAN Source of traffic
type             : erspan-source
state            : up
erspan-id        : 100
vrf-name         : default
acl-name         : acl-name not specified
ip-ttl           : 255
ip-dscp          : 0
destination-ip   : 10.10.10.1
origin-ip        : 10.20.20.20 (global)
source intf      :
    rx           : Eth7/1
    tx           : Eth7/1
    both         : Eth7/1
source VLANs     :
    rx           :
    tx           :
    both         :
filter VLANs     : filter not specified


Feature        Enabled  Value  Modules Supported     Modules Not-Supported
------------------------------------------------------------------------------
Rate-limiter   No
MTU-Trunc      No
MCBE           No
L3-TX          -        -      3  4  7  8            -


Legend:
  l = learning enabled
  f = forwarding enabled
  MCBE  = multicast best effort
  L3-TX = L3 Multicast Egress SPAN
```

The volume of an ERSPAN session can be significant depending on the amount of traffic in the network and the configuration of the session. In many cases, the most useful information is the in the header of the packet or frame, not necessarily in the payload. To facilitate a reduction in volume of data sent, you can specify only a certain number of bytes be sent out the session. This is referred to as *MTU truncation* and can be enabled only on F1 and F2 modules. Example 7-22 illustrates MTU truncation for ERSPAN.

Example 7-22   *MTU truncation for ERSPAN*

```
N7K-2# config
Enter configuration commands, one per line.  End with CNTL/Z.
N7K-2(config)# monitor session 1 type erspan-source
N7K-2(config-erspan-src)# mtu 192
N7K-2(config-erspan-src)# show monitor session 1
   session 1
---------------
description      : ERSPAN Source of traffic
type            : erspan-source
state           : up
erspan-id       : 100
vrf-name        : default
acl-name        : acl-name not specified
ip-ttl          : 255
ip-dscp         : 0
destination-ip  : 10.10.10.1
origin-ip       : 10.20.20.20 (global)
source intf     :
    rx          : Eth7/1
    tx          : Eth7/1
    both        : Eth7/1
source VLANs    :
    rx          :
    tx          :
    both        :
filter VLANs    : filter not specified


Feature         Enabled   Value   Modules Supported       Modules Not-Supported
-------------------------------------------------------------------------------
Rate-limiter    No
MTU-Trunc       Yes       192     3                       4   7   8
MCBE            No
L3-TX           -         -       3   4   7   8           -
```

```
Legend:
  l = learning enabled
  f = forwarding enabled
  MCBE  = multicast best effort
  L3-TX = L3 Multicast Egress SPAN



N7K-2(config-erspan-src)# show mod
Mod  Ports  Module-Type                          Model              Status
---  -----  ------------------------------------ ------------------ ----------
3    32     1/10 Gbps Ethernet Module            N7K-F132XP-15      ok
4    8      10 Gbps Ethernet XL Module           N7K-M108X2-12L     ok
5    0      Supervisor module-1X                 N7K-SUP1           active *
6    0      Supervisor module-1X                                    powered-up
7    48     10/100/1000 Mbps Ethernet XL Module  N7K-M148GT-11L     ok
8    48     1000 Mbps Optical Ethernet Module    N7K-M148GS-11      ok
9    48     1/10 Gbps Ethernet Module            N7K-F248XP-25      ok
```

Another mechanism that network administrators can use to minimize the amount of traffic sent is to use the **rate-limit** command on the F1 and F2 modules. This command can limit the amount of traffic sent and help prevent the destination port from becoming overloaded, which could cause data traffic to be dropped. There are two options for the **rate limit** command: **auto** and **manual**.

In auto mode, the rate limiter is calculated using the following formula:

destination bandwidth / aggregate input bandwidth.

For example, if the destination is a 10-G interface, only 5 G of traffic will be sent.

In manual mode, the network administrator can specify the percentage used for the rate limiter.

Note   If both MTU truncation and rate limiting are configured on a session, only rate limiting takes effect.

Example 7-23 illustrates an ERSPAN session with rate limiting and MTU truncation.

Example 7-23   *MTU Truncation for ERSPAN*

```
N7K-2# config
Enter configuration commands, one per line.  End with CNTL/Z.
N7K-2(config)# monitor session 1 type erspan-source
N7K-2(config-erspan-src)# rate-limit 50
N7K-2(config-erspan-src)# show monitor sess 1
```

```
     session 1
---------------
description       : ERSPAN Source of traffic
type              : erspan-source
state             : up
erspan-id         : 100
vrf-name          : default
acl-name          : acl-name not specified
ip-ttl            : 255
ip-dscp           : 0
destination-ip    : 10.10.10.1
origin-ip         : 10.20.20.20 (global)
source intf       :
   rx             : Eth7/1
   tx             : Eth7/1
   both           : Eth7/1
source VLANs      :
   rx             :
   tx             :
   both           :
filter VLANs      : filter not specified


Feature           Enabled   Value   Modules Supported      Modules Not-Supported
------------------------------------------------------------------------------
Rate-limiter      Yes       50%     3                      4   7   8
MTU-Trunc         Yes       192     -                      3   4   7   8
MCBE              No
L3-TX             -         -       3   4   7   8          -


Legend:
 l = learning enabled
 f = forwarding enabled
  MCBE  = multicast best effort
  L3-TX = L3 Multicast Egress SPAN


N7K-2(config-erspan-src)#
```

Finally, ERSPAN enables the network administrator to filter traffic using an access control list (ACL) or list of VLANs to provide granular control of the traffic sent. There are two options for the filter command:

■ The first option is the **access-group** command that enables a standard ACL to specify traffic sent via the session.

■ The second option is the **vlan** command that enables the network administrator to specify a list of VLANs where traffic will be limited to.

Example 7-24 shows using ERSPAN with an access list.

Example 7-24   *Filtering ERSPAN with an Access List*

```
N7K-2# config
Enter configuration commands, one per line.  End with CNTL/Z.
N7K-2(config)# ip access-list erspan-filter
N7K-2(config-acl)# permit ip 10.100.100.0/24 any
N7K-2(config-acl)# monitor session 1 type erspan-source
N7K-2(config-erspan-src)#
N7K-2(config-erspan-src)# filter access-group erspan-filter
N7K-2(config-erspan-src)# show monitor session 1
   session 1
---------------
description     : ERSPAN Source of traffic
type            : erspan-source
state           : up
erspan-id       : 100
vrf-name        : default
acl-name        : erspan-filter
ip-ttl          : 255
ip-dscp         : 0
destination-ip  : 10.10.10.1
origin-ip       : 10.20.20.20 (global)
source intf     :
   rx           : Eth7/1
   tx           : Eth7/1
   both         : Eth7/1
source VLANs    :
   rx           :
   tx           :
   both         :
filter VLANs    : filter not specified


Feature         Enabled  Value  Modules Supported     Modules Not-Supported
-------------------------------------------------------------------------------
Rate-limiter    Yes      50%    3                     4  7  8
MTU-Trunc       No
MCBE            No
```

```
L3-TX           -            -      3  4  7  8            -



Legend:
 l = learning enabled
 f = forwarding enabled
 MCBE  = multicast best effort
 L3-TX = L3 Multicast Egress SPAN



N7K-2(config-erspan-src)#
```

ERSPAN on Nexus 5x00

The Nexus 5x00 series switches have the capability to configure traditional SPAN sessions, referred to as *local SPAN sessions*, for Ethernet traffic in addition to ERSPAN. ERSPAN differs from traditional SPAN in that ERSPAN enables the monitored traffic to be encapsulated in a GRE packet and routed across an IP network. With ERSPAN, network administrators can centralize network analysis tools and route the monitored traffic.

ERSPAN builds on the concepts of source ports and destination ports. Source ports, as their name implies, are the source of the traffic to be sent via ERSPAN to the destination ports. Source ports have the following requirements:

■ Can be any port type including Ethernet, virtual Ethernet, port channel, VLAN, or VSAN.

Note   The Nexus 5500 series switches do not support a VSAN as a source interface for ERSPAN.

■ Can be a VLAN. When a VLAN is used as SPAN source, all ports that belong to the VLAN are considered as part of the SPAN source.

■ Can be configured with a direction (ingress, egress or both) to monitor.

■ Cannot be a SPAN destination port.

ERSPAN destinations define where traffic copied from the ERSPAN source will be sent. ERSPAN destination ports are specified by an IP address.

In addition, ERSPAN destinations have the following restriction:

■ Cannot be ERSPAN sources

Note The Nexus 5000 and 5500 series switches do not support rate limiting or ACL filtering for ERSPAN.

ESPAN on the Nexus 5x00 supports the capability to configure up to 18 ERSPAN sessions. The Nexus 5010 and 5020 supports 2 ERSPAN sessions configured simultaneously, while the Nexus 5500 supports 4 ERSPAN sessions configured simultaneously.

Configuration of ERSPAN on Nexus 5x00 is a multistep process in which the ERSPAN source and ERSPAN destination are defined. One difference between SPAN and ERSPAN configuration is that you must first specify a IP address that is used as the source IP of all GRE packets.

Example 7-25 illustrates an ERSPAN source session.

Example 7-25 *ERSPAN Source Configuration for Nexus 5x00*

```
cmhlab-dc2-tor2# config
Enter configuration commands, one per line.  End with CNTL/Z.
cmhlab-dc2-tor2(config)#
cmhlab-dc2-tor2(config)#
cmhlab-dc2-tor2(config)# monitor erspan origin ip-address 10.20.20.20 global
cmhlab-dc2-tor2(config)#
cmhlab-dc2-tor2(config)# monitor session 1 type erspan-source
cmhlab-dc2-tor2(config-erspan-src)#   description ERSPAN Source of traffic
cmhlab-dc2-tor2(config-erspan-src)#   erspan-id 100
cmhlab-dc2-tor2(config-erspan-src)#   vrf default
cmhlab-dc2-tor2(config-erspan-src)#   destination ip 10.10.10.1
cmhlab-dc2-tor2(config-erspan-src)#   source vlan 502
cmhlab-dc2-tor2(config-erspan-src)#   no shut
cmhlab-dc2-tor2(config-erspan-src)# show monitor session 1
   session 1
---------------
description     : ERSPAN Source of traffic
type            : erspan-source
state           : up
erspan-id       : 100
vrf-name        : default
destination-ip  : 10.10.10.1
ip-ttl          : 255
ip-dscp         : 0
origin-ip       : 10.20.20.20 (global)
source intf     :
    rx          :
    tx          :
    both        :
```

```
source VLANs      :
   rx             : 502


cmhlab-dc2-tor2(config-erspan-src
```

The volume of an ERSPAN session can be significant depending on the amount of traffic in the network and the configuration of the session. In many cases, the most useful information is the int header of the packet or frame, not necessarily in the payload. To facilitate a reduction in the volume of data sent, you can specify only a certain number of bytes be sent out the session. This is referred to as MTU truncation. Example 7-26 illustrates MTU truncation for ERSPAN.

Example 7-26   *MTU Truncation for ERSPAN*

```
cmhlab-dc2-tor2# config
Enter configuration commands, one per line.  End with CNTL/Z.
cmhlab-dc2-tor2(config)# monitor session 1 type erspan-source
cmhlab-dc2-tor2(config-erspan-src)# mtu 192
cmhlab-dc2-tor2(config-erspan-src)# show monitor session 1
   session 1
---------------
description       : ERSPAN Source of traffic
type              : erspan-source
state             : up
erspan-id         : 100
vrf-name          : default
destination-ip    : 10.10.10.1
ip-ttl            : 255
ip-dscp           : 0
mtu               : 192
origin-ip         : 10.20.20.20 (global)
source intf       :
   rx             :
   tx             :
   both           :
source VLANs      :
   rx             : 502
cmhlab-dc2-tor2(config-erspan-src)#
```

Embedded Analyzer

NX-OS on the Nexus 7000 and 5x00 series switches has the capability to perform detailed protocol-level analysis of traffic from the network destined for the control plane of the switch. This capability is extremely valuable when troubleshooting issues with control plane protocols such as STP, OSPF, SNMP, CDP, and more. The embedded analyzer is based on Wireshark, which is open source code that provides a multitude of filtering options and a familiar interface. Output from the embedded analyzer is saved in a format readable in many packet analysis tools for easy decoding.

Note   The embedded analyzer feature cannot be used to capture and analyze data plane traffic. Traffic traversing through the switch is not handled by the control plane and therefore cannot be processed by the embedded analyzer. Data plane traffic analysis can be performed by using SPAN or ERSPAN and an external network analyzer.

The embedded analyzer can be configured to filter traffic based on filters defined in TCPdump and Wireshark. The comprehensive list of filters can be found here:

■ **Capture filters:** http://www.tcpdump.org/tcpdump_man.html

■ **Display filters:** http://wiki.wireshark.org/DisplayFilters

Example 7-27 illustrates using the embedded analyzer feature to review IGMP traffic.

Example 7-27   *Using the Embedded Analyzer for IGMP Traffic Analysis*

```
CMHLAB-N5K1# ethanalyzer local interface inbound-hi display-filter "stp" write
bootflash:stp.pcap
Capturing on eth4
Frame 1 (68 bytes on wire, 68 bytes captured)
    Arrival Time: Mar  1, 2010 11:16:21.875330000
    [Time delta from previous captured frame: 1267442181.875330000 seconds]
    [Time delta from previous displayed frame: 1267442181.875330000 seconds]
    [Time since reference or first frame: 1267442181.875330000 seconds]
    Frame Number: 1
    Frame Length: 68 bytes
    Capture Length: 68 bytes
    [Frame is marked: False]
    [Protocols in frame: eth:vlan:llc:stp]
Ethernet II, Src: 00:0d:ec:d3:86:30 (00:0d:ec:d3:86:30), Dst: 01:00:0c:cc:cc:cd
(01:00:0c:cc:cc:cd)
    Destination: 01:00:0c:cc:cc:cd (01:00:0c:cc:cc:cd)
        Address: 01:00:0c:cc:cc:cd (01:00:0c:cc:cc:cd)
        .... ...1 .... .... .... .... = IG bit: Group address (multicast/broadcast)
        .... ..0. .... .... .... .... = LG bit: Globally unique address (factory
default)
    Source: 00:0d:ec:d3:86:30 (00:0d:ec:d3:86:30)
        Address: 00:0d:ec:d3:86:30 (00:0d:ec:d3:86:30)
        .... ...0 .... .... .... .... = IG bit: Individual addres   .... ..0. ....
.... .... .... = LG bit: Globally unique address (factory default)
    Source: 00:50:56:86:09:eb (00:50:56:86:09:eb)
```

```
        Address: 00:50:56:86:09:eb (00:50:56:86:09:eb)
            .... ...0 .... .... .... .... = IG bit: Individual address (unicast)
            .... ..0. .... .... .... .... = LG bit: Globally unique address (factory
default)
        Type: 802.1Q Virtual LAN (0x8100)
802.1Q Virtual LAN
        000. .... .... .... = Priority: 0
        ...0 .... .... .... = CFI: 0
        .... 0000 0000 1001 = ID: 9
        Type: IP (0x0800)
        Trailer: 1164EE9B00000000000900017CE0
Internet Protocol, Src: 10.2.1.20 (10.2.1.20), Dst: 224.0.1.24 (224.0.1.24)
        Version: 4
        Header length: 24 bytes
        Differentiated Services Field: 0x00 (DSCP 0x00: Default; ECN: 0x00)
            0000 00.. = Differentiated Services Codepoint: Default (0x00)
            .... ..0. = ECN-Capable Transport (ECT): 0
            .... ...0 = ECN-CE: 0
        Total Length: 32
        Identification: 0x4f70 (20336)
        Flags: 0x00
            0... = Reserved bit: Not set
            .0.. = Don't fragment: Not set
            ..0. = More fragments: Not set
        Fragment offset: 0
 (unicast)
            .... ..0. .... .... .... .... = LG bit: Globally unique address (factory
default)
        Type: 802.1Q Virtual LAN (0x8100)
802.1Q Virtual LAN
        111. .... .... .... = Priority: 7
        ...0 .... .... .... = CFI: 0
        .... 0010 0000 0001 = ID: 513
        Length: 50
Logical-Link Control
        DSAP: SNAP (0xaa)
        IG Bit: Individual
        SSAP: SNAP (0xaa)
        CR Bit: Command
        Control field: U, func=UI (0x03)
            000. 00.. = Command: Unnumbered Information (0x00)
            .... ..11 = Frame type: Unnumbered frame (0x03)
        Organization Code: Cisco (0x00000c)
        PID: PVSTP+ (0x010b)
Spanning Tree Protocol
```

```
    Protocol Identifier: Spanning Tree Protocol (0x0000)
    Protocol Version Identifier: Rapid Spanning Tree (2)
        Address: 00:0d:ec:d3:86:30 (00:0d:ec:d3:86:30)
        .... ...0 .... .... .... .... = IG bit: Individual address (unicast)
        .... ..0. .... .... .... .... = LG bit: Globally unique address (factory
default)
    Type: 802.1Q Virtual LAN (0x8100)
802.1Q Virtual LAN
    111. .... .... .... = Priority: 7
    ...0 .... .... .... = CFI: 0
    .... 0010 0000 0001 = ID: 513
    Length: 50
Logical-Link Control
    DSAP: SNAP (0xaa)
    IG Bit: Individual
    SSAP: SNAP (0xaa)
    CR Bit: Command
    Control field: U, func=UI (0x03)
        000. 00.. = Command: Unnumbered Information (0x00)
        .... ..11 = Frame type: Unnumbered frame (0x03)
    Organization Code: Cisco (0x00000c)
    PID: PVSTP+ (0x010b)
Spanning Tree Protocol
    Protocol Identifier: Spanning Tree Protoco        Address: 00:0d:ec:d3:86:30
(00:0d:ec:d3:86:30)
        .... ...0 .... .... .... .... = IG bit: Individual address (unicast)
        .... ..0. .... .... .... .... = LG bit: Globally unique address (factory
default)
    Type: 802.1Q Virtual LAN (0x8100)
802.1Q Virtual LAN
    111. .... .... .... = Priority: 7
    ...0 .... .... .... = CFI: 0
    .... 0010 0000 000d Information (0x00)
Spanning Tree Protocol
    Protocol Identifier: Spanning Tree Protocol (0x0000)
    Protocol Version Identifier: Rapid Spanning Tree (2)
    BPDU Type: Rapid/Multiple Spanning Tree (0x02)
    BPDU flags: 0x78 (Agreement, Forwarding, Learning, Port Role: Root)
        0... .... = Topology Change Acknowledgment: No
        .1.. .... = Agreement: Yes
        ..1. .... = Forwarding: Yes
        ...1 .... = Learning: Yes
        .... 10.. = Port Role: Root (2)
        .... ..0. = Proposal: No
        .... ...0 = Topology Change: No
    Root Identifier: 24676 / 00:d0:04:57:c0:00
```

```
        Root Path Cost: 2
        Bridge Identifier: 32868 / 00:0d:ec:d3:86:3c
        Port identifier: 0x9063
        Message Age: 1
        Max Age: 20
        Hello Time: 2
        Forward Delay: 15
        Version 1 Length: 0
..............output truncated
Frame 111 (57 bytes on wire, 57 bytes captured)
     Arrival Time: Mar  1, 2010 11:16:23.973683000
     [Time delta from previous captured frame: 0.000012000 seconds]    [Time delta
from previous displayed frame: 0.000012000 seconds]
     [Time since reference or first frame: 1267442183.973683000 seconds]
     Frame Number: 111
     Frame Length: 57 bytes
     Capture Length: 57 bytes
     [Frame is marked: False]
     [Protocols in frame: eth:vlan:llc:stp]
Ethernet II, Src: 00:0d:ec:a3:0d:30 (00:0d:ec:a3:0d:30), Dst: 01:80:c2:00:00:00
(01:80:c2:00:00:00)
     Destination: 01:80:c2:00:00:00 (01:80:c2:00:00:00)
        Address: 01:80:c2:00:00:00 (01:80:c2:00:00:00)
        .... ...1 .... .... .... .... = IG bit: Group address (multicast/broadcast)
        .... ..0. .... .... .... .... = LG bit: Globally unique address (factory
default)
     Source: 00:0d:ec:a3:0d:30 (00:0d:ec:a3:0d:30)
        Address: 00:0d:ec:a3:0d:30 (00:0d:ec:a3:0d:30)
        .... ...0 .... .... .... .... = IG bit: Individual address (ungment: No
        .0.. .... = Agreement: No
        ..1. .... = Forwarding: Yes
        ...1 .... = Learning: Yes
        .... 11.. = Port Role: Designated (3)
        .... ..0. = Proposal: No
        .... ...0 = Topology Change: No
     Root Identifier: 32769 / 00:0d:ec:a3:0d:3c
     Root Path Cost: 0
     Bridge Identifier: 32769 / 00:0d:ec:a3:0d:3c
     Port identifier: 0x9063
     Message Age: 0
     Max Age: 20
     Hello Time: 2
     Forward Delay: 15
     Version 1 Length: 0

100 packets captured
```

```
CMHLAB-N5K1# dir bootflash:
        47      Dec 17 13:53:06 2009   ..tmp-kickstart
        37      Dec 17 13:53:07 2009   ..tmp-system
  22315520      Dec 17 13:53:06 2009   .tmp-kickstart
 136327913      Dec 17 13:53:07 2009   .tmp-system
       575      Jan 06 21:35:12 2009   N5K1SS.lic
     49152      Dec      Protocol Version Identifier: Rapid Spanning Tree (2)
    BPDU Type: Rapid/Multiple Spanning Tree (0x02)
    BPDU flags: 0x78 (Agreement, Forwarding, Learning, Port Role: Root)
        0... .... = Topology Change Acknowledgment: No
        .1.. .... = Agreement: Yes
        ..1. .... = Forwarding: Yes
        ...1 .... = Learning: Yes
        .... 10.. = Port Role: Root (2)
        .... ..0. = Proposal: No
        .... ...0 = Topology Change: No
    Root Identifier: 24676 / 00:d0:04:57:c0:00
    Root Path Cost: 2
    Bridge Identifier: 32868 / 00:0d:ec:d3:86:3c
    Port identifier: 0x9063
    Message Age: 1
    Max Age: 20
    Hello Time: 2
    Forward Delay: 15
    Version 1 Length: 0
.............output truncated
Frame 111 (57 bytes on wire, 57 bytes captured)
    Arrival Time: Mar  1, 2010 11:16:23.973683000
    [Time delta from previous captured frame: 0.000012000 seconds]    [Time delta
from previous displayed frame: 0.000012000 seconds]
    [Time since reference or first frame: 1267442183.973683000 seconds]
    Frame Number: 111
    Frame Length: 57 bytes
    Capture Length: 57 bytes
    [Frame is marked: False]
    [Protocols in frame: eth:vlan:llc:stp]
Ethernet II, Src: 00:0d:ec:a3:0d:30 (00:0d:ec:a3:0d:30), Dst: 01:80:c2:00:00:00
(01:80:c2:00:00:00)
    Destination: 01:80:c2:00:00:00 (01:80:c2:00:00:00)
        Address: 01:80:c2:00:00:00 (01:80:c2:00:00:00)
        .... ...1 .... .... .... .... = IG bit: Group address (multicast/broadcast)
        .... ..0. .... .... .... .... = LG bit: Globally unique address (factory
default)
    Source: 00:0d:ec:a3:0d:30 (00:0d:ec:a3:0d:30)
        Address: 00:0d:ec:a3:0d:30 (00:0d:ec:a3:0d:30)
        .... ...0 .... .... .... .... = IG bit: Individual address (unicast)
```

```
        .... ..0. .... .... .... .... = LG bit: Globally unique address (factory
default)
    Type: 802.1Q Virtual LAN (0x8100)
802.1Q Virtual LAN
17 13:53:06 2009  lost+found/
        3066     Feb 23 19:54:03 2010  mts.log
    21680640     Nov 16 18:31:06 2009  n5000-uk9-kickstart.4.1.3.N2.1.bin
    22315520     Dec 17 13:34:13 2009  n5000-uk9-kickstart.4.1.3.N2.1a.bin
   136255825     Nov 16 18:32:57 2009  n5000-uk9.4.1.3.N2.1.bin
   136327913     Dec 17 13:33:43 2009  n5000-uk9.4.1.3.N2.1a.bin
       12463     Feb 23 14:22:59 2010  pre-demo.txt
        8331     Mar 01 11:16:23 2010  stp.pcap
        4096     Jul 31 15:07:28 2009  vdc_2/
        4096     Jul 31 15:07:28 2009  vdc_3/
        4096     Jul 31 15:07:28 2009  vdc_4/
Usage for bootflash://sup-local
  537387008 bytes used
  343097344 bytes free
  880484352 bytes total
CMHLAB-N5K1#
```

In Example 7-28, 100 packets were captured and placed in a file named *stp.pcap* on the switch's bootflash. This file could then be copied off of the switch for analysis.

The embedded analyzer defaults to capturing 100 frames, but this can be changed by using the **limit-captured-frames** command (refer to Example 7-28).

Example 7-28 *Limiting the Number of Captured Frames*

```
CMHLAB-N5K1# ethanalyzer local interface inbound-hi display-filter "stp" limit-cap-
tured-frames 20 write bootflash:stp1.pcap
Capturing on eth4
Frame 2 (68 bytes on wire, 68 bytes captured)
    Arrival Time: Mar  1, 2010 11:21:39.881854000
    [Time delta from previous captured frame: 0.075555000 seconds]
    [Time delta from previous displayed frame: 1267442499.881854000 seconds]
    [Time since reference or first frame: 1267442499.881854000 seconds]
    Frame Number: 2
    Frame Length: 68 bytes
    Capture Length: 68 bytes
    [Frame is marked: False]
    [Protocols in frame: eth:vlan:llc:stp]
Ethernet II, Src: 00:0d:ec:d3:86:30 (00:0d:ec:d3:86:30), Dst: 01:00:0c:cc:cc:cd
(01:00:0c:cc:cc:cd)
    Destination: 01:00:0c:cc:cc:cd (01:00:0c:cc:cc:cd)
        Address: 01:00:0c:cc:cc:cd (01:00:0c:cc:cc:cd)
```

```
            .... ...1 .... .... .... .... = IG bit: Group address (multicast/broadcast)
            .... ..0. .... .... .... .... = LG bit: Globally unique address (factory
default)
    Source: 00:0d:ec:d3:86:30 (00:0d:ec:d3:86:30)
        Address: 00:0d:ec:d3:86:30 (00:0d:ec:d3:86:30)
            .... ...0 .... .... .... .... = IG bit: Individual address (unicast)
            .... ..0. .... .... .... .... = LG bit: Globally unique address (factory
default)
    Type: 802.1Q Virtual LAN (0x8100)
802.1Q Virtual LAN
    111. .... .... .... = Priority: 7
    ...0 .... .... .... = CFI: 0
    .... 0010 0000 0001 = ID: 513
    Length: 50
Logical-Link Control
    DSAP: SNAP (0xaa)
    IG Bit: Individual
    SSAP: SNAP (0xaa)
    CR Bit: Command
    Control field: U, func=UI (0x03)
        000. 00.. = Command: Unnumbered Information (0x00)
        .... ..11 = Frame type: Unnumbered frame (0x03)
    Organization Code: Cisco (0x00000c)
    PID: PVSTP+ (0x010b)
Spanning Tree Protocol
    Protocol Identifier: Spanning Tree Protocol (0x0000)
    BPDU Type: Rapid/Multiple Spanning Tree (0x02)
    BPDU flags: 0x78 (Agreement, Forwarding, Learning, Port Role: Root)
        0... .... = Topology Change Acknowledgment: No
        .1.. .... = Agreement: Yes
        ..1. .... = Forwarding: Yes
        ...1 .... = Learning: Yes
        .... 10.. = Port Role: Root (2)
        .... ..0. = Proposal: No
        .... ...0 = Topology Change: No
    Root Identifier: 24676 / 00:d0:04:57:c0:00
    Root Path Cost: 2
    Bridge Identifier: 32868 / 00:0d:ec:d3:86:3c
    Port identifier: 0x9063
    Message Age: 1
    Max Age: 20
    Hello Time: 2
    Forward Delay: 15
    Version 1 Length: 0
```

```
.............output truncated

Frame 21 (68 bytes on wire, 68 bytes captured)
    Arrival Time: Mar  1, 2010 11:21:39.977388000
    [Time delta from previous captured frame: 0.000005000 seconds]
    [Time delta from previous displayed frame: 0.000005000 seconds]
    [Time since reference or first frame: 1267442499.977388000 seconds]
    Frame Number: 21
    Frame Length: 68 bytes
    Capture Length: 68 bytes
    [Frame is marked: False]
    [Protocols in frame: eth:vlan:llc:stp]
Ethernet II, Src: 00:0d:ec:a3:0d:0c (00:0d:ec:a3:0d:0c), Dst: 01:00:0c:cc:cc:cd
(01:00:0c:cc:cc:cd)
    Destination: 01:00:0c:cc:cc:cd (01:00:0c:cc:cc:cd)
        Address: 01:00:0c:cc:cc:cd (01:00:0c:cc:cc:cd)
        .... ...1 .... .... .... .... = IG bit: Group address (multicast/broadcast)
        .... ..0. .... .... .... .... = LG bit: Globally unique address (factory
default)
    Source: 00:0d:ec:a3:0d:0c (00:0d:ec:a3:0d:0c)
        Address: 00:0d:ec:a3:0d:0c (00:0d:ec:a3:0d:0c)
        .... ...0 .... .... .... .... = IG bit: Individual address (unicast)
        .... ..0. .... .... .... .... = LG bit: Globally unique address (factory
default)
    Type: 802.1Q Virtual LAN (0x8100)
802.1Q Virtual LAN
    111. .... .... .... = Priority: 7
    ...0 .... .... .... = CFI: 0
    .... 0000 0001 0011 = ID: 19
    Length: 50
Logical-Link Control
    DSAP: SNAP (0xaa)
    IG Bit: Individual
    SSAP: SNAP (0xaa)
    CR Bit: Command
    Control field: U, func=UI (0x03)
        000. 00.. = Command: Unnumbered Information (0x00)
        .... ..11 = Frame type: Unnumbered frame (0x03)
    Organization Code: Cisco (0x00000c)
    PID: PVSTP+ (0x010b)
Spanning Tree Protocol
    Protocol Identifier: Spanning Tree Protocol (0x0000)
    Protocol Version Identifier: Rapid Spanning Tree (2)
    BPDU Type: Rapid/Multiple Spanning Tree (0x02)
    BPDU flags: 0x3c (Forwarding, Learning, Port Role: Designated)
        0... .... = Topology Change Acknowledgment: No
```

```
            .0.. .... = Agreement: No

            ..1. .... = Forwarding: Yes
            ...1 .... = Learning: Yes
            .... 11.. = Port Role: Designated (3)
            .... ..0. = Proposal: No
            .... ...0 = Topology Change: No
      Root Identifier: 32778 / 00:0d:ec:a3:0d:3c
      Root Path Cost: 0
      Bridge Identifier: 32778 / 00:0d:ec:a3:0d:3c
      Port identifier: 0x8085
      Message Age: 0
      Max Age: 20
      Hello Time: 2
      Forward Delay: 15
      Version 1 Length: 0

20 packets captured
CMHLAB-N5K1# dir
          47     Dec 17 13:53:06 2009  ..tmp-kickstart
          37     Dec 17 13:53:07 2009  ..tmp-system
    22315520     Dec 17 13:53:06 2009  .tmp-kickstart
   136327913     Dec 17 13:53:07 2009  .tmp-system
         575     Jan 06 21:35:12 2009  N5K1SS.lic
       49152     Dec 17 13:53:06 2009  lost+found/
        3066     Feb 23 19:54:03 2010  mts.log
    22315520     Dec 17 13:34:13 2009  n5000-uk9-kickstart.4.1.3.N2.1a.bin
   136255825     Nov 16 18:32:57 2009  n5000-uk9.4.1.3.N2.1.bin
   136327913     Dec 17 13:33:43 2009  n5000-uk9.4.1.3.N2.1a.bin
       12463     Feb 23 14:22:59 2010  pre-demo.txt
        8331     Mar 01 11:16:23 2010  stp.pcap
        1696     Mar 01 11:21:39 2010  stp1.pcap
        4096     Jul 31 15:07:28 2009  vdc_2/
        4096     Jul 31 15:07:28 2009  vdc_3/
        4096     Jul 31 15:07:28 2009  vdc_4/

Usage for bootflash://
  537391104 bytes used
  343093248 bytes free
  880484352 bytes total
CMHLAB-N5K1#
```

Referring to the output in Example 7-28, you see that 20 frames were captured rather than the default of 100, and they were saved to a file named *stp1.pcap* on the switch's bootflash.

Smart Call Home

Smart Call Home is an embedded feature for NX-OS platforms with a distinct hardware component, currently the Nexus 7000 and the Nexus 5x00/2000 combination. As the Nexus 1000V does not have a distinct hardware component because it leverages the server hardware running VMware vSphere, it does not use Smart Call Home. Smart Call Home provides an automated notification system for policies the network administrator defines. For example, Smart Call Home can automate the process of opening a case with the Cisco Technical Assistance Center (TAC) for a hardware failure and attach the appropriate supporting CLI output. This helps customers simplify their support needs and maintain the integrity of their environments through automation.

Smart Call Home is email-based and supports multiple message formats including Short Text, Long Text, and Extensible Markup Language (XML). This enables the network administrator to configure profiles that are the best use case in their environment. Short-text format is good for pagers and printed reports, whereas full text is formatted for ease of reading. The XML format is a machine-readable format and is the format used when NX-OS communicates with Cisco TAC.

Smart Call Home uses multiple configuration elements to provide a customizable utility that can meet many different configuration scenarios. Smart Call Home has destination profiles that define who and with what message format is the recipient of a Smart Call Home message. The destination profile also determines the alert group that is used to trigger specific Smart Call Home messages.

NX-OS provides preconfigured alert groups that can be modified to add or remove specific commands to collect. Table 7-4 displays the predefined alert groups and their executed commands.

Table 7-4 *Nexus 7000 Smart Call Home Alert Groups and Executed Commands*

Alert Group	Description	Executed Command
Cisco-TAC	All critical alerts from the other alert groups destined for Smart Call Home.	Execute commands based on the alert group that originates the alert.
Configuration	Periodic events related to configuration.	show module show running-configuration vdc-all all show startup-configuration vdc-all show vdc current show vdc membership show version

Alert Group	Description	Executed Command
Diagnostic	Events generated by diagnostics.	show diagnostic result module all detail show diagnostic result module number detail show hardware show logging last 200 show module show sprom all show tech-support gold show tech-support platform show tech-support sysmgr show vdc current show vdc membership show version
EEM	Events generated by EEM.	show diagnostic result module all detail show diagnostic result module number detail show module show tech-support gold show tech-support platform show tech-support sysmgr show vdc current show vdc membership
Environmental	Events related to power, fan, and environment-sensing elements such as temperature alarms.	show environment show logging last 200 show module show vdc current show vdc membership show version
Inventory	Inventory status that is provided whenever a unit is cold booted, or when FRUs are inserted or removed. This alert is considered a noncritical event, and the information is used for status and entitlement.	show inventory show license usage show module show system uptime show sprom all show vdc current show vdc membership show version
License	Events related to licensing and license violations.	show license usage vdc all show logging last 200 show vdc current show vdc membership

Alert Group	Description	Executed Command
Linemodule hardware	Events related to standard or intelligent switching modules.	show diagnostic result module all detail show diagnostic result module number detail show hardware show logging last 200 show module show sprom all| show tech-support ethpm show tech-support gold show tech-support platform show tech-support sysmgr show vdc current show vdc membership show version
Supervisor hardware	Events related to supervisor modules.	show diagnostic result module all detail show hardware show logging last 200 show module show sprom all show tech-support ethpm show tech-support gold show tech-support platform show tech-support sysmgr show vdc current show vdc membership show version
Syslog port group	Events generated by the syslog PORT facility.	show license usage show logging last 200 show vdc current show vdc membership
System	Events generated by a failure of a software system that is critical to unit operation.	show diagnostic result module all detail show hardware show logging last 200 show module show sprom all show tech-support ethpm show tech-support gold show tech-support platform show tech-support sysmgr show vdc current show vdc membership

Alert Group	Description	Executed Command
Test	User-generated test message.	show module show vdc current show vdc membership show version

Note   You can add more **show** commands only to full text and XML destination profiles. Short text profiles enable only 128 bytes of text.

Smart Call Home provides the ability to filter messages based on urgency. This allows the network administrator to have flexibility in defining which messages are critical by defining the urgency level in the destination profile.

Note   Smart Call Home does not change the syslog message level.

Table 7-5 shows the default Smart Call Home Severity and Syslog Level.

Smart Call Home configuration can be distributed among NX-OS switches that participate in a Cisco Fabric Services (CFS) domain. When CFS is leveraged for this function, all Smart Call Home parameters except SNMP sysContact and the device priority are distributed. Chapter 8, "Unified Fabric," provides additional information on CFS.

Table 7-5   *Nexus 7000 and 5x00 Smart Call Home Severity and Syslog Level Mapping*

Call Home Level	Keyword	Syslog Level	Description
9	Catastrophic	N/A	Networkwide catastrophic failure.
8	Disaster	N/A	Significant network impact.
7	Fatal	Emergency (0)	System is unusable.
6	Critical	Alert (1)	Critical conditions that indicate that immediate attention is needed.
5	Major	Critical (2)	Major conditions.
4	Minor	Error (3)	Minor conditions.
3	Warning	Warning (4)	Warning conditions.

Call Home Level	Keyword	Syslog Level	Description
2	Notification	Notice (5)	Basic notification and informational messages. Possibly independently insignificant.
1	Normal	Information (6)	Normal event signifying return to normal state.
0	Debugging	Debug (7)	Debugging messages.

Smart Call Home Configuration

Smart Call Home configuration begins with defining a system contact; contract number; and other key attributes such as site address, phone number, and email address. Example 7-29 shows this initial step.

Example 7-29   *Defining Key Attributes for Smart Call Home*

```
Jealousy# config t
Enter configuration commands, one per line.  End with CNTL/Z.
Jealousy(config)# snmp-server contact Cisco
Jealousy(config)# callhome
Jealousy(config-callhome)# email-contact smartcallhome@cisco.com
Jealousy(config-callhome)# phone-contact +1-800-123-4567
Jealousy(config-callhome)# streetaddress 123 Main Street Data Center
Jealousy(config-callhome)# contract-id 1
Jealousy(config-callhome)# exit
Jealousy(config)# exit
Jealousy# show callhome
callhome disabled
Callhome Information:
contact person name(sysContact):Cisco
contact person's email:smartcallhome@cisco.com
contact person's phone number:+1-800-123-4567
street addr:123 Main Street Data Center
site id:
customer id:
contract id:1
switch priority:7
duplicate message throttling : enabled
periodic inventory : enabled
periodic inventory time-period : 7 days
```

```
periodic inventory timeofday : 08:00 (HH:MM)
Distribution : Disabled
```

The next step in Smart Call Home configuration is to define a destination profile. The destination profile is where key elements such as message format, message urgency level, destination email address, or URL for alerts and the message transport are defined. Example 7-30 illustrates a destination profile for a Network Operations Center (NOC) team that will receive full-text messages via email for all major conditions.

Example 7-30 *Creation of a Smart Call Home Destination Profile for an NOC*

```
Jealousy# config t
Enter configuration commands, one per line.  End with CNTL/Z.
Jealousy(config)# callhome
Jealousy(config-callhome)# destination-profile NOC-email
Jealousy(config-callhome)# destination-profile NOC-email email-addr noc@whereiwork.
com
Jealousy(config-callhome)# destination-profile NOC-email format full-txt
Jealousy(config-callhome)# destination-profile NOC-email message-level 5
Jealousy(config-callhome)# destination-profile NOC-e-mail transport-method e-mail
Jealousy(config-callhome)# destination-profile NOC-e-mail alert-group All
```

The new destination profile can be verified by using the command shown in Example 7-31.

Example 7-31 *Displaying a Smart Call Home Destination Profile*

```
Jealousy# show callhome destination-profile profile NOC-e-mail
NOC-e-mail destination profile information
maximum message size:2500000
message format:full-txt
message-level:5
transport-method:email
email addresses configured:
noc@whereiwork.com

url addresses configured:

alert groups configured:
all
```

Smart Call Home enables network administrators to customize the output collected by adding commands to be executed through an Alert group. Example 7-32 illustrates this by adding the CLI command **show cdp neigh**bors to the Linecard-Hardware Alert group.

Example 7-32   *Modification of an Existing Alert Group to Collect Additional Output*

```
Jealousy# config t
Enter configuration commands, one per line.  End with CNTL/Z.
Jealousy(config)# callhome
Jealousy(config-callhome)# alert-group Linecard-Hardware user-def-cmd show cdp
neighbor
Jealousy(config-callhome)# end
Jealousy# show callhome user-def-cmds
User configured commands for alert groups :
alert-group linecard-hardware user-def-cmd show cdp neighbor
```

If the email transport option is selected, Smart Call Home requires additional information about the email server it is to use to send its messages through. In Example 7-33, an email server is added to the configuration.

Example 7-33   *Adding an Email Server for Smart Call Home to Use*

```
Jealousy# config t
Enter configuration commands, one per line.  End with CNTL/Z.
Jealousy(config)# callhome
Jealousy(config-callhome)# transport email smtp-server 10.100.10.1 port 25 use-vrf
management
Jealousy(config-callhome)# transport email from Jealousy-Nexus@whereiwork.com
Jealousy(config-callhome)# transport email reply-to noc@whereiwork.com
Jealousy(config-callhome)# end

Jealousy# show callhome transport-email
from email addr:Jealousy-Nexus@whereiwork.com
reply to email addr:noc@whereiwork.com
smtp server:10.100.10.1
smtp server port:25
```

Smart Call Home supports CFS configuration distribution across CFS-enabled platforms in a CFS domain. Example 7-34 illustrates how to configure Smart Call Home to use CFS.

Example 7-34   *Configuring Smart Call Home to Use CFS*

```
Jealousy# config t
Enter configuration commands, one per line.  End with CNTL/Z.
Jealousy(config)# callhome
Jealousy(config-callhome)# distribute
Jealousy(config-callhome)# commit
Jealousy(config-callhome)# end
```

```
Jealousy# show cfs application
-----------------------------------------------

 Application    Enabled    Scope
-----------------------------------------------

ntp             No         Physical-fc-ip
 stp            Yes        Physical-eth
 l2fm           Yes        Physical-eth
 role           No         Physical-fc-ip
 radius         No         Physical-fc-ip
 callhome       Yes        Physical-fc-ip


Total number of entries = 6

Jealousy#
```

Configuration Checkpoint and Rollback on Nexus 7000

NX-OS on the Nexus 7000 provides the capability for a network administrator to capture the configuration of the switch in a snapshot or checkpoint. The checkpoint can then be re-applied to the switch via rollback to facilitate the restoration of the original configuration captured in the checkpoint. Checkpoint enables the network administrator to implement changes in the devices, configuration and back those changes out if required in a fast and reliable manner.

When checkpoints are created by a network administrator, they are stored on the switch rather than an external server or device. Checkpoints can also be reviewed prior to application on the switch, and their execution is configurable in three modes:

■ **Atomic:** Implements a rollback only if no errors occur

■ **Best-Effort:** Implements a rollback and skips any errors

■ **Stop-at-First-Failure:** Implements a rollback that stops if an error occurs

Note   Atomic is the default rollback mode.

NX-OS can generate checkpoints automatically when specific events happen. The intent for the automatic checkpoints is to minimize network downtime because of disabling key features or when a license expires. Specific triggers for these automated checkpoints include

■ Disabling a feature with the **no feature** command

■ Removing an instance of a Layer 3 protocol, such as Enhanced Interior Gateway Routing Protocol (EIGRP or PIM)

■ License expiration of a feature

The system-generated checkpoint names begin with **system-** and includes the feature name. Example 7-35 shows the system-generated checkpoints.

Example 7-35 *System-Generated Checkpoints*

```
Jealousy(config)# feature eigrp
Jealousy(config)# router eigrp 1
Jealousy(config-router)# autonomous-system 100
Jealousy(config-router)# exit
Jealousy(config)# no feature eigrp
Jealousy(config)# show check all
Name: system-fm-__inst_1__eigrp
```

Checkpoint Creation and Rollback

The creation of a checkpoint is done on per-VDC basis, and the switch can store up to 10 user-defined checkpoints.

Note   System checkpoints do not reduce the number of user-defined checkpoints.

Checkpoints can be given a name and description and can be redirected to a file. Example 7-36 shows the creation of a checkpoint named **one**.

Example 7-36 *Creation of a Checkpoint*

```
Jealousy # checkpoint one
.....................Done
Jealousy #
Jealousy # show checkpoint summary
User Checkpoint Summary
1) one:
Created by admin
Created at Wed, 07:54:07 16 Dec 2009
Size is 16,350 bytes
Description: None
```

Note Checkpoints are not preserved after the execution of **write erase** and **reload.** The **clear checkpoint database** also removes all checkpoints.

NX-OS provides context-sensitive help for checkpoint filenames and displays them when you use the **?** on the **show checkpoint** command. Example 7-37 demonstrates this behavior and shows all user- and system-created checkpoints.

Example 7-37 *Checkpoint Context-Sensitive Help*

```
Jealousy# show checkpoint ?
  <CR>
  >                           Redirect it to a file
  >>                          Redirect it to a file in append mode
  all (no abbrev)             Show default config
  five                        Checkpoint name
  four                        Checkpoint name
  one                         Checkpoint name
  summary (no abbrev)         Show configuration rollback checkpoints summary
  system (no abbrev)          Show only system configuration rollback checkpoints
  system-fm-__inst_1__eigrp   Checkpoint name
  three                       Checkpoint name
  two                         Checkpoint name
  user (no abbrev)            Show only user configuration rollback checkpoints
  |                           Pipe command output to filter
```

When checkpoints are established, the need to perform a rollback might arise. Before a rollback is performed, it might be prudent to review the differences in the checkpoint to the running configuration. Example 7-38 shows the creation of a checkpoint named **six**. In the time since the checkpoint was made, EIGRP has been added to the running configuration. NX-OS displays the differences in the configuration.

Example 7-38 *Comparing a Checkpoint to the Running Configuration*

```
Jealousy# show diff rollback-patch checkpoint six running-config
Collecting Running-Config
Generating Rollback Patch
..
!!
!
feature eigrp
!
router eigrp 1
 autonomous-system 100
```

After a review of the differences, rolling the system back to the checkpoint named **six** is illustrated in Example 7-39.

Example 7-39   *Rollback of the Configuration from a Checkpoint*

```
Jealousy# rollback running-config checkpoint six
Note: Applying config parallelly may fail Rollback verification
Collecting Running-Config
Generating Rollback Patch
Executing Rollback Patch
Generating Running-config for verification
Generating Patch for verification
Jealousy# show run eigrp
                     ^
% Invalid command at '^' marker.
```

Configuration Checkpoint and Rollback on Nexus 5x00

NX-OS on the Nexus 5x00 provides the capability for a network administrator to capture the configuration of the switch in a snapshot or checkpoint. The checkpoint can then be re-applied to the switch via rollback to facilitate the restoration of the original configuration captured in the checkpoint. The checkpoint enables the network administrator to implement changes in the devices, configuration and back those changes out if required in a fast and reliable manner.

When checkpoints are created by a network administrator, they are stored on the switch rather than an external server or device. Checkpoints can also be reviewed prior to application on the switch, and their execution is configurable in three modes:

- **Atomic:** Implements a rollback only if no errors occur
- **Best-Effort:** Implements a rollback and skips any errors
- **Stop-at-First-Failure:** Implements a rollback that stops if an error occurs

Note   Atomic is the default rollback mode.

NX-OS can generate checkpoints automatically when specific events happen. The intent for the automatic checkpoints is to minimize network downtime because of disabling key features or when a license expires. Specific triggers for these automated checkpoints include

- Disabling a feature with the **no** feature command
- License expiration of a feature

> **Note** Rollback does not operate if FCoE is enabled on the switch.

The system-generated checkpoint names begin with **system-** and includes the feature name. Example 7-40 shows the system-generated checkpoints.

Example 7-40 *System-Generated Checkpoints*

```
cmhlab-dc2-tor2(config)# feature-set fabricpath
cmhlab-dc2-tor2(config)# show check
cmhlab-dc2-tor2(config)# no feature-set fabricpath
Feature-set Operation may take up to 30 minutes depending on the size of configura-
tion.


2012 May  5 20:35:29 cmhlab-dc2-tor2 %FEATURE-MGR-2-FM_AUTOCKPT_IN_PROGRESS:
AutoCheckpoint system-fm-fabricpath's creation in progress...
2012 May  5 20:35:34 cmhlab-dc2-tor2 %FEATURE-MGR-2-FM_AUTOCKPT_SUCCEEDED:
AutoCheckpoint  created successfully
cmhlab-dc2-tor2(config)# show check summary
System Checkpoint Summary
-----------------------------------------------------------------------------
1) system-fm-fabricpath:
Created by admin
Created at Sat, 20:35:34 05 May 2012
Size is 18,249 bytes
Description: Created by Feature Manager.
cmhlab-dc2-tor2(config)#
```

Checkpoint Creation and Rollback

The creation of a checkpoint is done on per-switch basis, and the switch can store up to 10 user-defined checkpoints.

> **Note** System checkpoints do not reduce the number of user-defined checkpoints.

Checkpoints can be given a name and description and can be redirected to a file. Example 7-41 shows the creation of a checkpoint named **before-big-change**.

Example 7-41 *Creation of a Checkpoint*

```
cmhlab-dc2-tor2# checkpoint before-big-change
...Done
cmhlab-dc2-tor2# show check summary
User Checkpoint Summary
```

```
-------------------------------------------------------------------------------
1) before-big-change:
Created by admin
Created at Sat, 20:39:47 05 May 2012
Size is 18,200 bytes
Description: None

System Checkpoint Summary
```

Note   Checkpoints are not preserved after execution of **write erase** and **reload**. The **clear checkpoint database** also removes all checkpoints.

NX-OS provides context-sensitive help for checkpoint filenames and displays them when you use the **?** on the **show checkpoint** command. Example 7-42 demonstrates this behavior and shows all user- and system-created checkpoints.

Example 7-42   *Checkpoint Context-Sensitive Help*

```
cmhlab-dc2-tor2# show checkpoint ?
  <CR>
  >                     Redirect it to a file
  >>                    Redirect it to a file in append mode
  all (no abbrev)       Show default config
  before-big-change
  summary (no abbrev)   Show configuration rollback checkpoints summary
  system (no abbrev)    Show only system configuration rollback checkpoints
  system-fm-fabricpath
  user (no abbrev)      Show only user configuration rollback checkpoints
  |                     Pipe command output to filter

cmhlab-dc2-tor2#
```

When checkpoints are established, the need to perform a rollback might arise. Before a rollback is performed, it might be prudent to review the differences in the checkpoint to the running configuration. Example 7-43 shows the creation of a checkpoint named **before-big-change**. In the time since the checkpoint was made, FabricPath has been added to the running configuration. NX-OS displays the differences in the configuration.

Example 7-43   *Comparing a Checkpoint to the Running Configuration*

```
cmhlab-dc2-tor2# show diff rollback-patch checkpoint before-big-change running-con-
fig
Collecting Running-Config
```

```
#Generating Rollback Patch

!!
!
feature-set fabricpath
!
fabricpath domain default
!
fabricpath switch-id 100
cmhlab-dc2-tor2#
```

After a review of the differences, rolling the system back to the checkpoint named **before-big-change** is illustrated in Example 7-44.

Example 7-44 *Rollback of the Configuration from a Checkpoint*

```
cmhlab-dc2-tor2# rollback running-config checkpoint before-big-change
Collecting Running-Config
Generating Rollback patch for switch profile
Rollback Patch is Empty
Note: Applying config parallelly may fail Rollback verification
Collecting Running-Config
#Generating Rollback Patch
Executing Rollback Patch
Generating Running-config for verification
Generating Patch for verification

Rollback completed successfully.

cmhlab-dc2-tor2# show run fabricpath
                          ^
% Invalid command at '^' marker.
cmhlab-dc2-tor2#
```

NetFlow

NX-OS on the Nexus 7000 and Nexus 1000V provides a powerful tool for collecting network statistics, NetFlow. Network administrators use NetFlow to provide statistics for network monitoring, planning, and accounting. An ecosystem of NetFlow analysis tools and packages exists that enables network administrators to parse, report, and audit the NetFlow records to suit their needs.

NX-OS defines a *flow* as a unidirectional stream of packets that arrive on a source interface or VLAN and has the same values for the keys that are an identified value for a field or fields within a packet. The network administrator creates a flow though a flow record that defines the keys that will be unique to the flow.

NetFlow needs to be exported for analysis, and NX-OS uses the concept of an exporter to do this task. NetFlow exports the flow data using UDP and supports both Version 5 and Version 9 formats.

Note Cisco recommends that you use the Version 9 export format for the following reasons:

- Variable field specification format
- Support for IPv6, Layer 2, and MPLS fields
- More efficient network utilization

For information about the Version 9 export format, see RFC 3954.

The Version 5 export format has these limitations:

- Fixed field specifications
- A 16-bit representation of the 32-bit interface index used in Cisco NX-OS
- No support for IPv6, Layer 2, or MPLS fields

NetFlow on NX-OS can operate in one of two modes:

- **Full mode:** NX-OS analyzes all packets on the interface.
- **Sampled mode:** NX-OS uses a user-defined sampling algorithm and rate to analyze packets on interfaces with NetFlow configured.

NX-OS uses the concept of a monitor that, in turn, references a flow record and flow exporter. The monitor is applied to an interface and is the mechanism that enables NetFlow on the interface.

Configuring NetFlow on Nexus 7000

The first step to configure NetFlow is to enable it in global configuration mode using the **feature** command. With the modular nature of NX-OS, using the **feature** command loads the NetFlow modular code into memory for execution. Without the feature enabled, it would not be resident in memory. Example 7-45 demonstrates enabling NetFlow.

Example 7-45 *Enabling NetFlow*

```
Jealousy# config t
Enter configuration commands, one per line.  End with CNTL/Z.
Jealousy(config)# feature NetFlow
Jealousy(config)# end
Jealousy# show feature | include NetFlow
NetFlow              1          enabled
```

The next step is to define a flow record that determines the keys that will be used to define the flow. Example 7-46 shows the creation of a flow that matches on source and destination interfaces and collects both byte and packet counters.

Example 7-46 *Creating a Flow Record*

```
Jealousy# config t
Enter configuration commands, one per line.  End with CNTL/Z.
Jealousy(config)# flow record inbound
Jealousy(config-flow-record)# match ipv4 source address
Jealousy(config-flow-record)# match ipv4 destination address
Jealousy(config-flow-record)# collect counter packets
Jealousy(config-flow-record)# collect counter bytes
Jealousy(config-flow-record)# end

Jealousy# show flow record
Flow record inbound:
    No. of users: 0
    Template ID: 0
    Fields:
        match ipv4 source address
        match ipv4 destination address
        match interface input
        match interface output
        match flow direction
        collect counter bytes
        collect counter packets
```

Now that a flow record is defined, the next step is to configure a flow exporter. The flow exporter is the destination for NetFlow data for further analysis. Example 7-47 demonstrates the process for defining a flow exporter.

Example 7-47 *Defining a Flow Exporter*

```
Jealousy# config t
Enter configuration commands, one per line.  End with CNTL/Z.
Jealousy(config)# flow exporter NetFlowcollector
Jealousy(config-flow-exporter)# destination 10.100.100.235
Jealousy(config-flow-exporter)# source loopback 0
Jealousy(config-flow-exporter)# version 9
Jealousy(config-flow-exporter-version-9)# exit
Jealousy(config-flow-exporter)# end

Jealousy# show flow exporter
Flow exporter NetFlowcollector:
```

```
Destination: 10.100.100.235
VRF: default (1)
Source Interface loopback0 (192.168.1.1)
Export Version 9
Exporter Statistics
    Number of Flow Records Exported 0
    Number of Templates Exported 0
    Number of Export Packets Sent 0
    Number of Export Bytes Sent 0
    Number of Destination Unreachable Events 0
    Number of No Buffer Events 0
    Number of Packets Dropped (No Route to Host) 0
    Number of Packets Dropped (other) 0
    Number of Packets Dropped (LC to RP Error) 0
    Number of Packets Dropped (Output Drops) 0
    Time statistics were last cleared: Never
```

With both a flow and an exporter defined, the last step is to define a flow monitor,
which then is applied to interfaces to begin matching and exporting flows. Example 7-48
defines a flow monitor and applies it to interface Ethernet 1/9.

Example 7-48   *Definition and Application of a Flow Monitor*

```
Jealousy# config t
Enter configuration commands, one per line.  End with CNTL/Z.
Jealousy(config)# flow monitor NetFlowmonitor
Jealousy(config-flow-monitor)# exporter NetFlowcollector
Jealousy(config-flow-monitor)# record inbound
Jealousy(config-flow-monitor)# exit
Jealousy(config)# int e1/9
Jealousy(config-if)# ip flow monitor NetFlowmonitor in

Jealousy# show flow interface e1/9
Interface Ethernet1/9:
    Monitor: NetFlowmonitor
    Direction: Input

Jealousy# show flow monitor
Flow Monitor NetFlowmonitor:
    Use count: 1
    Flow Record: inbound
    Flow Exporter: NetFlowcollector
```

The Nexus 7000 supports the collection of NetFlow at Layer 2 in addition to the rich set of attributes that can be collected at Layer 3. With the NetFlow modular configuration, enabling Layer 2 NetFlow is a matter of defining a flow record to match on Layer 2 attributes. Example 7-49 defines a Layer 2 NetFlow flow record.

Note   Layer 2 NetFlow cannot be applied to Layer 3 interfaces such as routed ports and VLAN interfaces.

Layer 2 NetFlow cannot be applied in the egress direction; it is an ingress-only feature.

Example 7-49   *Defining a Flow Record for Layer 2 NetFlow*

```
Jealousy# config t
Enter configuration commands, one per line.  End with CNTL/Z.
Jealousy(config)# flow record l2NetFlow
Jealousy(config-flow-record)# match datalink mac destination-address
Jealousy(config-flow-record)# match datalink mac source-address
Jealousy(config-flow-record)# collect counter bytes
Jealousy(config-flow-record)# collect counter packets
Jealousy(config-flow-record)# end

Jealousy# show flow record l2NetFlow
Flow record l2NetFlow:
    No. of users: 0
    Template ID: 0
    Fields:
        match interface input
        match interface output
        match datalink mac source-address
        match datalink mac destination-address
        match flow direction
        collect counter bytes
        collect counter packets
Jealousy#
```

NX-OS enables the network administrator to be granular with the amount of NetFlow data collected. One of the mechanisms available to facilitate this granularity is sampled NetFlow.

Note   As of NX-OS 6.1(2) F2 and F2e modules support sampled NetFlow.

Example 7-50 shows the configuration of a sampler and subsequent application to an interface monitor.

Example 7-50   *Defining a NetFlow Sampler*

```
Jealousy# config t
Enter configuration commands, one per line.  End with CNTL/Z.
Jealousy(config)# sampler netflowsampler
Jealousy(config-flow-sampler)# desc Netflow Sampler 1 out of 100
Jealousy(config-flow-sampler)# mode 1 out-of 100
Jealousy(config-flow-sampler)# exit
Jealousy(config)# interface e1/9
Jealousy(config-if)# ip flow monitor netflowmonitor input sampler netflowsampler
Jealousy(config-if)# end

Jealousy# show sampler
Sampler: netflowsampler
    Description: Netflow Sampler 1 out of 100
    ID: 65537
    mode 1 out-of 100
```

Configuring NetFlow on Nexus 1000V

The first step to enable NetFlow on the Nexus 1000V is to define a flow record that determines the keys that will be used to define the flow. Example 7-51 shows the creation of a flow that matches on source and destination interfaces and collects both byte and packet counters.

Example 7-51   *Creating a Flow Record*

```
CMHLAB-DC2-VSM1# config t
CMHLAB-DC2-VSM1(config)# flow record inbound
CMHLAB-DC2-VSM1(config-flow-record)# match ipv4 source address
CMHLAB-DC2-VSM1(config-flow-record)# match ipv4 destination address
CMHLAB-DC2-VSM1(config-flow-record)# match transport source-port
CMHLAB-DC2-VSM1(config-flow-record)# match transport destination-port
CMHLAB-DC2-VSM1(config-flow-record)# collect counter bytes
CMHLAB-DC2-VSM1(config-flow-record)# collect counter packets
CMHLAB-DC2-VSM1(config-flow-record)# end
CMHLAB-DC2-VSM1# show flow record inbound
Flow record inbound:
    No. of users: 0
    Template ID: 0
    Fields:
        match ipv4 source address
```

```
        match ipv4 destination address
        match transport source-port
        match transport destination-port
        match interface input
        match interface output
        match flow direction
        collect counter bytes
        collect counter packets          collect counter bytes
        collect counter packets
```

Now that a flow record is defined, the next step is to configure a flow exporter. The flow exporter is the destination for NetFlow data for further analysis. Example 7-52 demonstrates the process for defining a flow exporter.

Example 7-52 *Defining a Flow Exporter*

```
CMHLAB-DC2-VSM1# config t
CMHLAB-DC2-VSM1(config)# flow exporter NetFlowcollector
CMHLAB-DC2-VSM1(config-flow-exporter)# destination 10.100.100.235
CMHLAB-DC2-VSM1(config-flow-exporter)# source mgmt0
CMHLAB-DC2-VSM1(config-flow-exporter)# version 9
CMHLAB-DC2-VSM1(config-flow-exporter-version-9)# end
CMHLAB-DC2-VSM1# show flow exporter NetFlowcollector
Flow exporter NetFlowcollector:
    Destination: 10.100.100.235
    VRF: default (1)
    Source Interface mgmt0 (10.2.9.10)
    Export Version 9
        Data template timeout 0 seconds
    Exporter Statistics
        Number of Flow Records Exported 0
        Number of Templates Exported 0
        Number of Export Packets Sent 0
        Number of Export Bytes Sent 0
        Number of No Buffer Events 0
        Number of Packets Dropped (other) 0
        Number of Packets Dropped (LC to RP Error) 0
        Number of Packets Dropped (Output Drops) 0
        Time statistics were last cleared: Never
```

With both a flow and an exporter defined, the last step is to define a flow monitor, which then is applied to interfaces to begin matching and exporting flows. Example 7-53 defines a flow monitor and applies it to port profile DC2-N1K-VLAN100.

Example 7-53 *Definition and Application of a Flow Monitor*

```
CMHLAB-DC2-VSM1# config t
CMHLAB-DC2-VSM1(config)# flow monitor netflowmonitor
CMHLAB-DC2-VSM1(config-flow-monitor)# record inbound
CMHLAB-DC2-VSM1(config-flow-monitor)# exporter NetFlowcollector
CMHLAB-DC2-VSM1(config-flow-monitor)# exit
CMHLAB-DC2-VSM1(config)# port-profile DC2-N1K-VLAN100
CMHLAB-DC2-VSM1(config-port-prof)# ip flow monitor netflowmonitor in
CMHLAB-DC2-VSM1(config-port-prof)# end

CMHLAB-DC2-VSM1# show flow monitor
Flow Monitor netflowmonitor:
    Use count: 3
    Flow Record: inbound
    Flow Exporter: NetFlowcollector
    Inactive timeout: 15
    Active timeout: 1800
    Cache Size: 4096
CMHLAB-DC2-VSM1#
```

Network Time Protocol

NTP is a widely used protocol to synchronize time on networks. Having a consistent, synchronized time in a network facilitates operations as accurate event correlation and logging analysis are easier when time is reported properly. Imagine trying to determine the root cause of a network issue when every device has a different timestamp in their logs.

NX-OS supports NTP and the configuration is consistent across the platforms. There is an exception for the Nexus 7000 where NTP can be run in multiple VDCs. In an environment where NTP runs in multiple VDCs, the network administrator can select which VDC owns the system clock on the supervisor. This VDC then updates the system clock and synchronizes time on all linecards in the chassis. Example 7-54 illustrates specifying a specific VDC that will control the system clock.

Example 7-54 *Configuration of a Specific VDC to Own the System Clock*

```
N7K-2# config
Enter configuration commands, one per line.  End with CNTL/Z.
N7K-2(config)# clock protocol ntp vdc 1
N7K-2(config)# end
N7K-2#
```

A typical NTP configuration in NX-OS consists of specifying the IP address of the NTP servers and the source interface the device will use for the source IP of all NTP packets. If no source interface is specified, the device uses the IP address of the interface that is used to egress toward the NTP server. Example 7-55 illustrates a typical NTP configuration.

Example 7-55 *NTP Configuration in NX-OS*

```
N7K-2# config
Enter configuration commands, one per line.  End with CNTL/Z.
N7K-2(config)# ntp server 10.89.64.1 use-vrf management
N7K-2(config)# ntp source-interface  mgmt0
N7K-2(config)# end
N7K-2# show ntp peer-status
Total peers : 1
* - selected for sync, + -  peer mode(active),
- - peer mode(passive), = - polled in client mode
    remote               local              st  poll   reach delay   vrf
    -----------------------------------------------------------------------
*10.89.64.1           172.26.251.21         2   64     377   0.04861 management
N7K-2#
```

Precision Time Protocol

PTP is based on IEEE 1588 and is becoming an emerging technology in applications where submicrosecond accuracy is needed. Commonly found in financial networks and research and scientific networks, PTP is more common than ever. PTP has some significant differences from a protocol like NTP beyond clock accuracy. PTP networks are typically smaller in diameter with fewer nodes per domain. With NTP it's not uncommon to have hundreds of devices across the world using the same clock source. NTP scales well, and the extra distance and latency don't have significant impact on accuracy. PTP, on the other hand, usually spans a handful of network devices and has a much smaller diameter. Distance and latency significantly impact the accuracy of the clock, so PTP is deployed in smaller pockets. Typically, a GPS or cellular device takes a role called *grandmaster* and is the top of the PTP domain's hierarchy.

PTP networks have multiple types of clocks including ordinary, boundary, and transparent clocks, each with its own set of function and capabilities. NX-OS devices operate in boundary clock mode where each port can decide which state it is in regarding synchronization.

Configuring PTP is a multistep process where the feature is enabled and the PTP domain and clocks are specified. Example 7-56 illustrates enabling PTP, and setting the domain and clocks.

Example 7-56   *PTP Enablement, Domain Configuration, and PTP Source Configuration*

```
N7K-1-Agg1# config
Enter configuration commands, one per line.  End with CNTL/Z.
N7K-1-Agg1(config)# feature ptp
N7K-1-Agg1(config)# ptp domain 100
N7K-1-Agg1(config)# ptp source 10.89.64.1
N7K-1-Agg1(config)# end
N7K-1-Agg1# show ptp clock
PTP Device Type: Boundary clock
Clock Identity :  00:26:98:ff:fe:0f:d9:c2
Clock Domain: 100
Number of PTP ports: 0
Priority1 : 255
Priority2 : 255
Clock Quality:
        Class : 248
        Accuracy : 254
        Offset (log variance) : 65535
Offset From Master : 0
Mean Path Delay : 0
Steps removed : 0
Local clock time:Sun May  6 03:21:16 2012
N7K-1-Agg1#
```

The next step would be to enable PTP on specific interfaces where devices configured to use PTP reside.

Note   On the Nexus 7000, only F1, F2, F2e, and M2 interfaces can be configured with PTP. Only the Nexus 5500 series switches support PTP.

Example 7-57 illustrates enabling PTP on an interface.

Example 7-57   *Enabling PTP on an Interface*

```
N7K-1(config)# int e4/24
N7K-1(config-if)# ptp
N7K-1(config-if)# show ptp port int e4/24
PTP Port Dataset: Eth4/24
Port identity: clock identity:   00:26:98:ff:fe:0f:d9:c2
Port identity: port number: 791
PTP version: 2
Port state: Disabled
Delay request interval(log mean): 2
```

```
Announce receipt time out: 3

Peer mean path delay: 0

Announce interval(log mean): 1

Sync interval(log mean): 2

Delay Mechanism: End to End

Peer delay request interval(log mean): 0

N7K-1(config-if)#
```

IEEE 802.3az (Energy Efficient Ethernet)

With the increasing focus on energy usage in data centers, the IEEE has created a new standard that enables devices to negotiate lower power consumption during idle periods. This is specified in the IEEE 802.3az standard and is referred to as Energy Efficient Ethernet (EEE). EEE enables end stations to signal in-band via Link Pulse Idle (LPI) frames when there is no traffic to be sent. When EEE devices receive this LPI, they know they can reduce the amount of power used by the port. If traffic needs to be sent across the link, the devices send a wakeup signal and buffer data until the link is ready to traffic. Using EEE can significantly reduce the power required during idle periods by up to 18 percent.

The Nexus 7000 switch has support for IEEE 802.3az on the F2e copper module (N7K-F248XT-25E) today. The F2e module is described in more detail in Chapter 1, "Introduction to NX-OS." By default IEEE EEE is disabled and can be enabled by following Example 7-58.

Example 7-58   *Enabling IEEE Energy Efficient Ethernet*

```
N7K-1-EEE# show int e5/45
Ethernet5/45 is down (Link not connected)
admin state is up, Dedicated Interface
<snip>
  EEE (efficient-ethernet) : Disabled
N7K-1-EEE# config
Enter configuration commands, one per line.  End with CNTL/Z.
N7K-1-EEE(config)# int e5/45
N7K-1-EEE(config-if)# power efficient-ethernet auto
N7K-1-EEE(config-if)# end
N7K-1-EEE# show int e5/45
Ethernet5/45 is up
admin state is up, Dedicated Interface
<snip>
EEE (efficient-ethernet) : Enabled
N7K-1-EEE#
```

Note Enabling IEEE EEE is disruptive as the link is flapped to allow the end points to negotiate EEE parameters.

Power On Auto-Provisioning

As of NX-OS 6.1(2) on the Nexus 7000 and NX-OS 5.1(3)N2, a feature named Power on Auto Provisioning has been added to the capabilities of NX-OS. POAP provides the foundation to automate the provisioning of Nexus switches in a data center through the use of automation tools and Python scripting. To use POAP, a few infrastructure services are needed as Dynamic Host Configuration Protocol (DHCP) and Trivial File Transfer Protocol (TFTP) are used during the process. When a new switch boots up for the first time with no configuration, a DHCP server supplies the IP address of a TFTP server with a Python script, which can be configured to tell the switch how to configure itself on the network with parameters such as IP address, NX-OS version, switchname, and more. Following are the steps performed during a switch booting up in a POAP environment.

1. Switch powers on and starts the POAP process.

2. A DHCP request is sent and replied to with attributes such as IP address, default gateway, script server, and script filename via Client Identifier option 61. DHCP option 61 contains the serial number of the unit, which is used to determine which attributes to provide via the script.

3. Switch downloads the script from the script server using FTP or other supported mechanism, and the switch begins script execution.

4. Script instructs the device on how to download the configuration, NX-OS files, license files, and other attributes.

5. The switch reloads if needed and joins the network per the downloaded configuration.

POAP is designed to be flexible and provides a foundation for customers to minimize the amount of time needed to deploy devices. POAP is leveraged in Enterprise and cloud and service provider data centers.

Note POAP is enabled by default and does not require any NX-OS configuration to use.

Sample POAP scripts can be found on Cisco.com.

Python

Python is a popular scripting language that has been embedded in NX-OS as of 6.1(2) on the Nexus 7000 and 5.1(3)N2 on the Nexus 5500.

Note   Python is not supported on the Nexus 5010 and 5020.

Integrating Python into NX-OS provides a foundation to simplify network operations through the ability to run Python scripts directly on the switch, as shown in Example 7-59. These scripts can be used to run both configuration and show commands, parse CLI output, call other scripts, provide POAP services, and more.

Example 7-59   *Entering the Python Scripting Shell*

```
N7K-1-Core1# python
Copyright (c) 2001-2012 Python Software Foundation; All Rights Reserved


N7K-1-Core1# >>>
```

A sample Python script that has been helpful for customers is illustrated next. The script defines variables for network services, and when the script is run it pings them, creates a log file, and copies the log file to another device for analysis:

```
#!/usr/local/bin/python
DHCP_IP="192.168.1.100"
FTP_IP="192.168.1.100"
SSH_IP="192.168.1.100"
#FTP_IP="192.168.1.100"
#SSH_IP="192.168.1.100"

VRF="management"

import pexpect
from cisco import *
from datetime import datetime

strTime = datetime.now().strftime("%Y.%m.%d.%H.%M")
scLogFileName = "sanitycheck." + strTime + ".log"
scLogDestFileName = "/home/admin/sanitycheck." + strTime + ".log"
scLogFile = open("/bootflash/" + scLogFileName, 'w')

def ping(serverName, IP, VRF="default"):
        oCli = CLI('ping ' + IP + ' vrf ' + VRF, False)
        pingStatus = oCli.get_output()[8].split(' ')[6]
```

```
            if pingStatus == "0.00%":
                    pingStatus = serverName + "(" + IP + ") is reachable"
            elif pingStatus == "100.00%":
                    pingStatus = serverName + "(" + IP + ") is not responding to pin
g"
            else:
                    pingStatus = "Connection to " + serverName + "(" + IP + ") may n
ot be stable"
            scLogFile.write("%s\n" % pingStatus)
            scLogFile.write("%s" % oCli.get_raw_output())
            scLogFile.write("=========================================================
=======================\n")
        print pingStatus

def connect(protocol = "", host = "", username = "", password = "", vrf = "manag
ement", login_timeout=10):
        if protocol == "telnet":
                c = "/isan/bin/vsh -c 'telnet " + host + " vrf " + vrf + "'"
        else:
                c = "/isan/bin/vsh -c 'ssh " + username + "@" + host + " vrf " +
vrf+ "'"
        cmd = pexpect.spawn(c)

        expect_list = [ \
        "(?i)re you sure you want to continue connecting", \
        "(?i)ogin:", \
        "(?i)assword:", \
        "(?i)(?:permission denied)|(?:login incorrect)", \
        "(?i)onnection refused", \
        pexpect.TIMEOUT, \
        "[#|$]", \
        pexpect.EOF
        ]

        i = cmd.expect(expect_list, timeout=login_timeout)

        while i != None:
                if i == 0:
                        cmd.sendline("yes")
                        i = cmd.expect(expect_list, timeout=login_timeout)
                elif i == 1:
                        cmd.sendline(username)
                        i = cmd.expect(expect_list, timeout=login_timeout)
                elif i == 2:
                        cmd.sendline(password)
```

```
                             i = cmd.expect(expect_list, timeout=login_timeout)
                 elif i == 3:
                         raise pexpect.ExceptionPexpect("Password was bad. Permis
sion Denied")
                         i = None
                 elif i == 4:
                         raise pexpect.ExceptionPexpect("Could not connect to the
 host")
                         i = None
                 elif i == 5:
                         raise pexpect.ExceptionPexpect("Your request timed out")
                         i = None
                 elif i == 6:
                         conStatus = "Successfully connected to " + host + " over
 " + protocol
                         scLogFile.write("%s\n" % conStatus)
                         scLogFile.write("======================================
======================================\n")
                         print conStatus
                         cmd.sendline("exit")
                         cmd.close()
                         i = None
             else:
                         raise pexpect.ExceptionPexpect("Unexpected login respons
e")
                         i = None


def transferOut (protocol = "", host = "", source = "", dest = "", vrf = "manage
ment", login_timeout=10, user = "", password = ""):
        if protocol == "tftp":
                c = "/isan/bin/vsh -c 'copy " + source + " " + protocol + "://"
+ host + "/" + dest + " vrf " + vrf + "'"
        else:
                c = "/isan/bin/vsh -c 'copy " + source + " " + protocol + "://"
+ user + "@" + host + "/" + dest + " vrf " + vrf + "'"
        cmd = pexpect.spawn(c)
        split_src = source.split("/")
        fname = split_src[len(split_src)-1]
        expect_list = [ \
        "(?i)re you sure you want to continue connecting", \
        "(?i)here is already a file existing with this name. do you want to over
write", \
        "(?i)(?:password)|(?:passphrase for key)", \
        "(?i)(?:permission denied)|(?:login incorrect)", \
```

```
            "(?i)onnection refused", \
            scLogFileName + ".*100%", \
            pexpect.TIMEOUT, \
            "(?i)(?:ile not found)|(?:no such file or directory)", \
            "(?i)(?:et operation was successful)|(?:transfer of file completed succe
ssfully)", \
            "(?i)cmd exec error", \
            "[#.*]", \
            pexpect.EOF
            ]

        i = cmd.expect(expect_list, timeout=login_timeout)

        while i != None:
            if i==0:
                    cmd.sendline("yes")
                    i = cmd.expect(expect_list, timeout=login_timeout)
            elif i==1:
                    cmd.sendline("yes")
                    i = cmd.expect(expect_list, timeout=login_timeout)
            elif i==2:
                    cmd.sendline(password)
                    i = cmd.expect(expect_list, timeout=login_timeout)
            elif (i==3):
                    raise pexpect.ExceptionPexpect("Password was bad. Permis
sion Denied")
                    i = None
            elif i==4:
                    raise pexpect.ExceptionPexpect("Could not connect to the
 host")
                    i = None
            elif (i==5 or i==8):
                    tOutStatus = "Log file stored locally on bootflash://" +
 scLogFileName + "\n"
                    tOutStatus = tOutStatus + "Copied log file " + scLogFile
Name + " to server " + host + " over " + protocol + "\n"
                    tOutStatus = tOutStatus + "Destination Location: " + scL
ogDestFileName
                    print tOutStatus
                    i = None
                    return True
            elif i==6:
                    raise pexpect.ExceptionPexpect("Your request timed out")
                    i = None
            elif (i==7):
```

```
                              raise pexpect.ExceptionPexpect("Check source path. File
not found")
                              i = None
                  elif (i==10):
                              i = cmd.expect(expect_list, timeout=login_timeout)
                  else:
                              raise pexpect.ExceptionPexpect("Unexpected login respons
e")
                              i = None

# Check availablity via ping

ping("DHCP Server", DHCP_IP, VRF)
ping("FTP Server", FTP_IP, VRF)
ping("SSH Server", SSH_IP, VRF)

# Check connectivity by actually connecting

protocol="telnet"
host="192.168.1.2"
username="admin"
password="cisco123"

try:
        connect(protocol, host, username, password)
except Exception as inst:
        print "Failed connecting to " + host + " over " + protocol

protocol="ssh"
host="192.168.1.100"
try:
        connect(protocol, host, username, password)
except Exception as inst:
        print "Failed connecting to " + host + " over " + protocol

# Turn on beacon
# oCli = CLI('locator-led chassis', False)


scLogFile.close()

# Copy log file to some location -
try:
        transferOut("scp", "192.168.1.100", "bootflash:" + scLogFileName, scLogD
estFileName, "management", 10, "admin", "cisco123")
```

```
except Exception as inst:
        print("Copy Failed: %s" % inst)
```

Summary

NX-OS has a rich set of serviceability features embedded into the operating system to simplify the day-to-day operations and maintenance tasks of the network administrator. Ubiquitous capabilities such as SPAN and ERSPAN cross all three Nexus platforms.

Smart Call Home provides opportunities for organizations to streamline their processes and enable automation of TAC case creation for different issues that might arise in the network. Layering configuration checkpoints and rollback on the Nexus 7000 and 5x00 equates to a platform that is scalable and takes operational considerations into account.

Leveraging features such as NetFlow on the Nexus 7000 and Nexus 1000V provide insight to traffic on the network and empowers network administrators to project growth, defend the network, and provide accounting information.

Finally, support for well-established technologies such as NTP and an eye for the future with support for technologies such as PTP, IEEE 802.3az, Power On Auto-Provisioning, and Python scripting establish Nexus switches as valuable components of a modern network.

## Chapter 8

Unified Fabric

This chapter covers the following topics:

- Unified Fabric overview

- Enabling technologies

- Nexus 5x00 Unified Fabric configuration

- Nexus 7000 Unified Fabric configuration

- Cisco MDS Unified Fabric configuration

The Nexus family of switches represents a revolutionary approach to I/O within the data center referred to as Unified Fabric.

Unified Fabric Overview

One of the biggest trends in data centers today is consolidation, which can mean many different things. In some cases, consolidation refers to a physical consolidation of data centers where dozens or even hundreds of data centers are geographically dispersed and consolidated into a smaller number of large data centers. Consolidation can also exist within a data center where a large number of underutilized physical servers are consolidated, usually by leveraging some type of virtualization technology, into a smaller number of physical servers. Although virtualization offers many benefits, including consolidation of processors, memory, and storage, little is done to consolidate the amount of adapters, cables, and ports within the data center. In most virtualization implementations, there is actually a requirement for more adapters, cables, and ports to achieve the dense I/O requirements associated with virtualization. Data centers today contain multiple network fabrics that require discreet connectivity components to each fabric.

I/O consolidation is a trend within data centers that refers to the capability to aggregate connectivity to multiple fabrics into a single or redundant pair of adapters, cables, and port. Although new technologies have emerged to enable this consolidation to occur, the concept is not new. Fibre Channel, iSCSI, Infiniband, and others were all introduced in an attempt to consolidate I/O. Although the merits or consolidation capabilities of each of these technologies might be open to debate, for one reason or another, all failed to reach mainstream adoption as the single fabric for all I/O requirements.

As a consolidation technology, Unified Fabric offers several benefits to customers, including

- **Lower capital expenditures:** Through the reduction of adapters, cables, and ports required within the infrastructure.

- **Lower operational expenses:** Through the reduction of adapters, cables, and ports drawing power within the data center.

- **Reduced deployment cycles:** Unified Fabric provides a wire-once model, in which all LAN, SAN, IPC, and management traffic is available to every server without requiring additional connectivity components.

- **Higher availability:** Quite simply, fewer adapters and ports means fewer components that could fail.

Enabling Technologies

Ethernet represents an ideal candidate for I/O consolidation. Ethernet is a well-understood and widely deployed medium that has taken on many consolidation efforts already. Ethernet has been used to consolidate other transport technologies such as FDDI, Token Ring, ATM, and Frame Relay networking technologies. It is agnostic from an upper layer perspective in that IP, IPX, AppleTalk, and others have used Ethernet as transport. More recently, Ethernet and IP have been used to consolidate voice and data networks. From a financial aspect, there is a tremendous investment in Ethernet that also must be taken into account.

For all the positive characteristics of Ethernet, there are several drawbacks of looking to Ethernet as an I/O consolidation technology. Ethernet has traditionally not been a lossless transport and relied on other protocols to guarantee delivery. In addition, a large portion of Ethernet networks range in speed from 100 Mbps to 1 Gbps and are not equipped to deal with the higher-bandwidth applications such as storage.

New hardware and technology standards are emerging that will enable Ethernet to overcome these limitations and become the leading candidate for consolidation.

10-Gigabit Ethernet

10-Gigabit Ethernet (10GbE) represents the next major speed transition for Ethernet technology. Like earlier transitions, 10GbE started as a technology reserved for backbone applications in the core of the network. New advances in optic and cabling technologies have made the price points for 10GbE attractive as a server access technology as well.

The desire for 10GbE as a server access technology is driven by advances in computer technology in the way of multisocket/multicore, larger memory capacity, and virtualization technology. In some cases, 10GbE is a requirement simply for the amount of network throughput required for a device. In other cases, however, the economics associated with multiple 1-G ports versus a single 10GbE port might drive the consolidation alone. In addition, 10GbE becoming the de facto standard for LAN-on-motherboard implementations is driving this adoption.

In addition to enabling higher transmission speeds, current 10GbE offerings provide a suite of extensions to traditional Ethernet. These extensions are standardized within IEEE 802.1 Data Center Bridging. Data Center Bridging is an umbrella referring to a collection of specific standards within IEEE 802.1, which are as follows:

- **Priority-based flow control (PFC; IEEE 802.1Qbb):** One of the basic challenges associated with I/O consolidation is that different protocols place different requirements on the underlying transport. IP traffic is designed to operate in large wide area network (WAN) environments that are global in scale, and as such applies mechanisms at higher layers to account for packet loss, for example, Transmission Control Protocol (TCP). Because of the capabilities of the upper layer protocols, underlying transports can experience packet loss and in some cases even require some loss to operate in the most efficient manner. Storage area networks (SANs), on the other hand, are typically smaller in scale than WAN environments. These protocols typically provide no guaranteed delivery mechanisms within the protocol and instead rely solely on the underlying transport to be completely lossless. Ethernet networks traditionally do not provide this lossless behavior for a number of reasons including collisions, link errors, or most commonly congestion. Congestion can be avoided with the implementation of *pause* frames. When a receiving node begins to experience congestion, it transmits a pause frame to the transmitting station, notifying it to stop sending frames for a period of time. Although this link-level pause creates a lossless link, it does so at the expense of performance for protocols equipped to deal with it in a more elegant manner. PFC solves this problem by enabling a pause frame to be sent only for a given Class of Service (CoS) value. This per-priority pause enables LAN and SAN traffic to coexist on a single link between two devices.

- **Enhanced transmission selection (ETS; IEEE 802.1Qaz):** The move to multiple 1-Gbps connections is done primarily for two reasons:

  - The aggregate throughput for a given connection exceeds 1 Gbps; this is straightforward but is not always the only reason that multiple 1-Gbps links are used.

  - To provide a separation of traffic, guaranteeing that one class of traffic will not interfere with the functionality of other classes. ETS provides a way to allocate bandwidth for each traffic class across a shared link. Each class of traffic can be guaranteed some portion of the link, and if a particular class doesn't use all the allocated bandwidth, that bandwidth can be shared with other classes.

- **Congestion notification (IEEE 802.1Qau):** Although PFC provides a mechanism for Ethernet to behave in a lossless manner, it is implemented on a hop-by-hop basis and provides no way for multihop implementations. 802.1Qau is currently proposed as a mechanism to provide end-to-end congestion management. Through the use of backward congestion notification (BCN) and quantized congestion notification (QCN), Ethernet networks can provide dynamic rate limiting similar to what TCP provides only at Layer 2.

- **Data Center Bridging Capability Exchange Protocol extensions to LLDP (IEEE 802.1AB):** To negotiate the extensions to Ethernet on a specific connection and to ensure backward compatibility with legacy Ethernet networks, a negotiation protocol is required. Data Center Bridging Capability Exchange (DCBX) represents an extension to the industry standard Link Layer Discovery Protocol (LLDP). Using DCBX, two network devices can negotiate the support for PFC, ETS, and Congestion Management.

Fibre Channel over Ethernet

Fibre Channel over Ethernet (FCoE) represents the latest in standards-based I/O consolidation technologies. FCoE was approved within the FC-BB-5 working group of INCITS (formerly ANSI) T11. The beauty of FCoE is in its simplicity. As the name implies, FCoE is a mechanism that takes Fibre Channel (FC) frames and encapsulates them into an Ethernet. This simplicity enables for the existing skillsets and tools to be leveraged while reaping the benefits of a Unified I/O for LAN and SAN traffic.

FCoE provides two protocols to achieve Unified I/O:

- **FCoE:** The data plane protocol that encapsulates FC frames into an Ethernet header.

- **FCoE Initialization Protocol (FIP):** A control plane protocol that manages the login/logout process to the FC fabric.

Figure 8-1 provides a visual representation of FCoE.

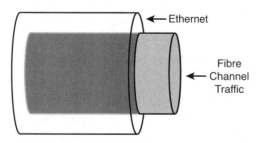

← Ethernet

Fibre
← Channel
Traffic

Figure 8-1   *Fibre Channel over Ethernet*

When Fibre Channel frames are encapsulated in an Ethernet, the entire Fibre Channel frame, including the original Fibre Channel header, payload, and CRC are encapsulated in an Ethernet. Figure 8-2 depicts this.

Normal ethernet frame, ethertype = FCoE
Same as a physical FC frame
Ethernet Header
FCoE Header
FC Header
FC Payload
CRC
EOF
FCS
Control information: version, ordered sets (SOF, EOF)

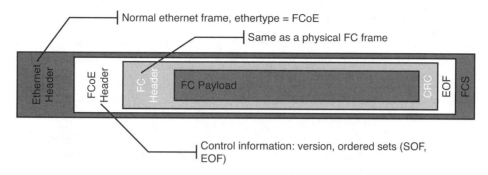

Figure 8-2 *Fibre Channel Frame Encapsulated in an Ethernet*

The ANSI T11 specifies the frame format for FCoE. It is a standard Ethernet frame with a new EtherType of 0x8906. Also note that the new Ethernet frame has a new Frame Check Sequence (FCS) created rather than using the FCS from the Fibre Channel frame. Figure 8-3 illustrates the FCoE frame format.

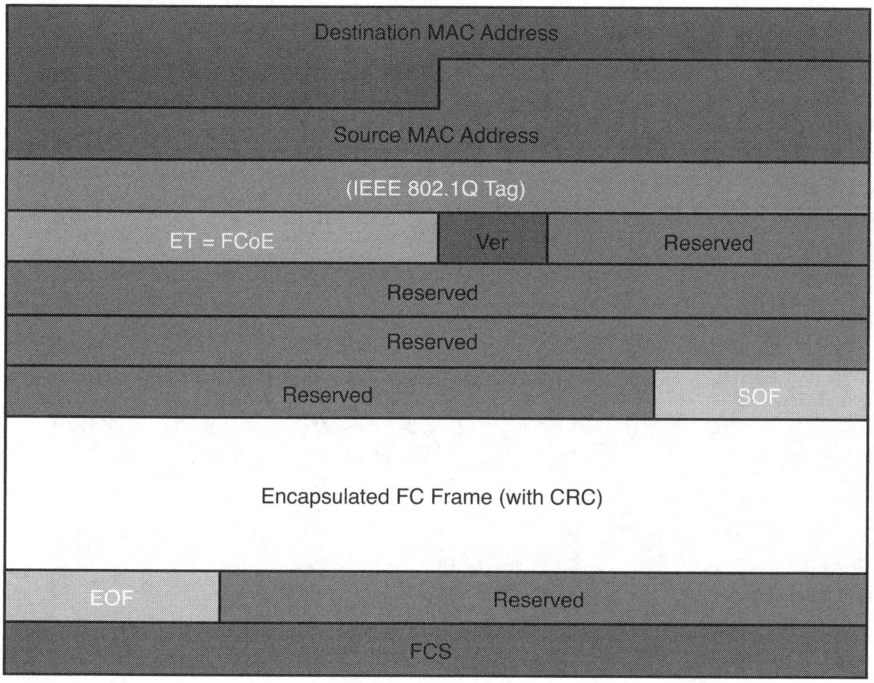

Destination MAC Address
Source MAC Address
(IEEE 802.1Q Tag)
ET = FCoE
Ver
Reserved
Reserved
Reserved
Reserved
SOF
Encapsulated FC Frame (with CRC)
EOF
Reserved
FCS

Figure 8-3 *FcoE Frame Format*

FCoE standards also define several new port types:

- **Virtual N_Port (VN_Port):** An N_Port that operates over an Ethernet link. N_Ports, also referred to as Node Ports, are the ports on hosts or storage arrays used to connect to the FC fabric.

- **Virtual F_Port (VF_Port):** An F_port that operates over an Ethernet link. F_Ports are switch or director ports that connect to a node.

- **Virtual E_Port (VE_Port):** An E_Port that operates over an Ethernet link. E_Ports or Expansion ports are used to connect Fibre Channel switches together; when two E_Ports are connected the link, it is an interswitch link (ISL).

To facilitate using FCoE an additional control plane protocol was needed and thus FCoE Initialization Protocol (FIP) was developed. FIP helps the FCoE perform VLAN discovery, assists the device in login (FLOGI) to the fabric, and finds key resources such as Fibre Channel Forwarders (FCFs). FIP is its own Ethertype (0x8914), which makes it easier to identify on a network and helps FIP Snooping devices identify FCoE traffic. Figure 8-4 depicts where FIP starts and ends and where FCoE takes over.

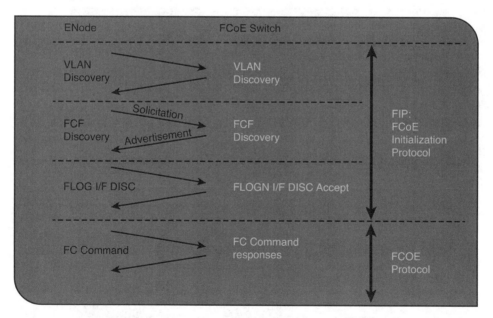

Figure 8-4 *FIP Process*

FIP can be leveraged by native FCoE-aware devices to help provide security against concerns such as spoofing MAC addresses of end nodes and helps simpler switches, such as FIP Snooping devices, learn about FCoE traffic. This awareness can provide security and QoS mechanisms that protect FCoE traffic from other Ethernet traffic and can help ensure a good experience with FCoE without the need to have a full FCoE stack on the switch. Currently the Nexus 4000 is the only Nexus device that supports FIP snooping.

Single-Hop Fibre Channel over Ethernet

Single-hop FCoE refers to an environment in which FCoE is enabled on one part of the network, frequently at the edge between the server and the directly connected network switch or fabric extender. In a single-hop topology the directly connected switch usually has native Fibre Channel ports which in turn uplink into an existing SAN, although you can have a complete network without any other fibre channel switches. Single-hop FCoE is the most commonly deployed FCoE model because of its double benefit of seamless interoperability into an existing SAN and the cost savings with a reduction in adapters, cabling, and optics to servers.

This reduction in cabling and adapters is accomplished through the use of a new adapter: Converged Network Adapter (CNA). CNAs have the capability to encapsulate Fibre Channel frames into Ethernet and use a 10GbE Ethernet interface to transmit both native Ethernet/IP traffic and storage traffic to the directly connected network switch or fabric extender. The CNA's drivers dictate how it appears to the underlying operating system, but in most cases it appears as a separate Ethernet card and separate Fibre Channel Host Bus Adapter (HBA).

Figure 8-5 shows how a CNA appears in Device Manager of a Microsoft Windows Server.

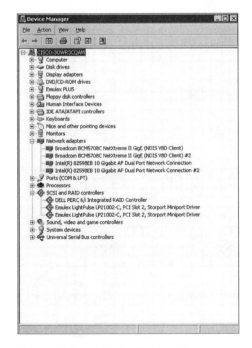

Figure 8-5   *CNA in Device Manager*

Using CNAs in a server, a typical single-hop FCoE topology would look like Figure 8-6 where a server is connected to Nexus 5x00 switches via Ethernet interfaces. The Nexus

5x00 switches have both Ethernet and native Fibre Channel interfaces for connectivity to the rest of the network topology. The fibre channel interfaces connect to native fibre channel ports on the Cisco MDS switches, and the Ethernet interfaces connect to the Ethernet interfaces on the Nexus 7000 switches. The FCoE traffic is transported only across the first or single hop from the server to the network switch. The current implementation of the Cisco Unified Computing System (UCS) uses single-hop FCoE between the UCS blade servers and the UCS Fabric Interconnects.

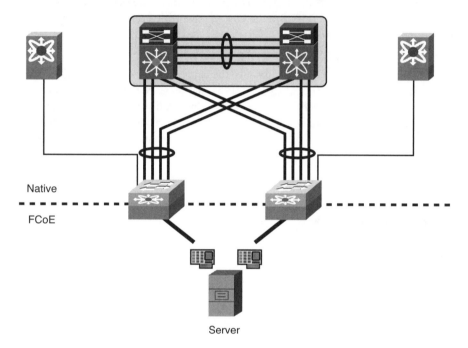

Native

FCoE

Server

Figure 8-6   *Single-Hop FCoE Network Topology*

Multhop Fibre Channel over Ethernet

Building on the implementations of single-hop FCoE, multihop FCoE topologies can be created. As illustrated in Figure 8-6, native fibre channel links exist between the Nexus 5x00 and the Cisco MDS Fibre Channel switches, whereas separate Ethernet links interconnect the Nexus 5x00 and Nexus 7000. With multihop FCoE, topologies can be created where the native fibre channel links are not needed, and both fibre channel and Ethernet traffic use Ethernet interfaces.

The benefit of multihop FCoE is to simplify the topology and reduce the number of native fibre channel ports required in the network as a whole. Multihop FCoE takes the same principles of encapsulating fibre channel frames in Ethernet and uses it for switch-to-switch connections, referred to as Inter-Switch Links (ISL) in the Fibre Channel world, and uses the VE port capability in the switches.

Figure 8-7 shows a multihop FCoE topology where the server connects via CNAs to Nexus 5x00s, which in turn connect to Nexus 7000 series switches via the Ethernet carrying FCoE. The storage array is directly connected to the Nexus 7000 via FCoE as well.

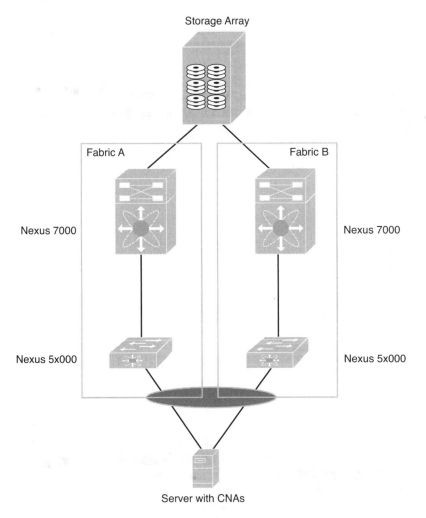

Figure 8-7 *Multihop FCoE Topology*

Storage VDC on Nexus 7000

One of the building blocks in a multihop FCoE topology is the storage Virtual Device Context (VDC) on the Nexus 7000. VDCs are discussed in detail in Chapter 1, "Introduction to Cisco NX-OS," and the focus in this chapter is on the Storage VDC and its use in a multihop FCoE topology. VDC is a capability of the Nexus 7000 series switches that enables a network administrator to logically virtualize the Nexus 7000 into multiple logical devices. The storage VDC is a special VDC that enables the virtualization of storage resources on the switch. This enables in essence a "virtual MDS" inside the Nexus 7000 that participates fully in the FCoE network as a full fibre channel forwarder (FCF).

With a Storage VDC network, administrators can provide the storage team a context that allows the storage team to manage their own interfaces; configurations; and fibre channel-specific attributes such as zones, zonesets, and aliases. Figure 8-8 shows how a storage VDC can be implanted in an existing topology where single-hop FCoE was initially deployed and then multihop FCoE was added. The storage VDC was created with VE ports connecting downstream to the Nexus 7000 and VE port to the Cisco MDS fibre channel director.

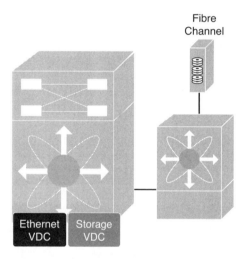

Figure 8-8   *Storage VDC on the Nexus 7000*

The storage VDC has some requirements that are unique to this type of VDC as storage traffic is traversing it. The first requirement is that the storage VDC can support only interfaces hosted on the F1 or F2/F2e series of modules. These modules support the capability to provide lossless Ethernet and as such are only suitable for doing FCoE. The VDC allocation process in NX-OS does not allow for other types of modules to have interfaces in a VDC that has been defined as a storage VDC.

Note   To use FCoE with the F2/F2e series module, the switch must have a Supervisor 2 or Supervisor 2E installed. FCoE on F2/F2e is not supported with the Supervisor 1 module.

In addition to requiring F1 or F2/F2e series modules, the storage VDC cannot run non-storage related protocols. You cannot enable features such as OSPF, vPC, PIM, or other Ethernet/IP protocols in the storage VDC. The only features allowed are directly related to storage. Finally, the default VDC cannot be configured as a storage VDC.

N-Port Virtualization

The fibre channel module of the Nexus 5x00 series switch can operate in two modes:

- Fabric

- NPV (N-Port Virtualization)

When in fabric mode, the switch module operates as any switch in a fibre channel network does.

Fabric mode switches have the following characteristics:

- Unique domain ID per virtual storage area network (VSAN)

- Participation in all domain services (zoning, fabric security, Fibre Channel Identification [FCID] allocation, and so on)

- Support for interoperability modes

When the fibre channel module is configured in NPV mode, it does not operate as a typical fibre channel switch; instead leveraging a service, NPIV, on the upstream or core fibre channel switch for domain services. The switch operates in a similar fashion as an NPIV-enabled host on the fabric. The advantage NPV provides the network administrator is the control of domain IDs and points of management on a fibre channel network as it scales.

Note   The fibre channel specification supports 239 domain IDs per VSAN; however, the reality is that many SAN vendors recommend and support a much lower number. Consult your storage vendor (Original Storage Manufacturer [OSM]) for specific scalability numbers.

Additional benefits of NPV include the capability to manage the fibre channel switch as a discrete entity for tasks such as software management and debugging the fibre channel network. NPV also enables network administrators to connect FCoE hosts to non–FCoE-enabled SANs and simplifies third-party interoperability concerns because the NPV enabled fibre channel module does not participate in domain operations or perform local switching. This enables multivendor topologies to be implemented without the restrictions the interoperability mode requires.

The fibre channel module in the Nexus 5x00 creates a new port type to the fibre channel network when in NPV mode: the NP-port. The NP-port proxies fabric login (FLOGI) requests from end stations and converts them to Fabric Discoveries (FDISC) dynamically and transparently to the end device. The result is that end systems see the NPV-enabled switch as a Fabric Port (F-port) and the upstream/core switch sees the NPV-enabled switch as an F-port as well. Figure 8-9 illustrates the port roles used in an NPV-enabled network.

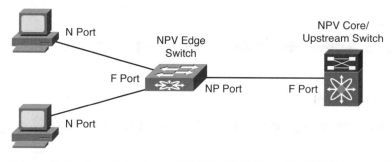

Figure 8-9   *Port Roles in an NPV-Enabled Network*

Note   Enabling NPV mode can cause the current configuration to be erased and the device rebooted. It is therefore recommended that NPV be enabled prior to completing any additional configuration.

N-Port Identification Virtualization

A key component to enable the proper operation of NPV is the need for N-Port Identification Virtualization (NPIV) on the core/upstream fibre channel switch. NPIV is an industry-standard technology defined by the T11 committee as part of the Fibre Channel Link Services (FC-LS) specification and enables multiple N Port IDs or FCIDs to share a single physical N Port. Prior to NPIV, it was not possible to have a system that used multiple logins per physical port—it was a one-login-to-one-port mapping. With the increasing adoption of technologies such as virtualization, the need to allow multiple logins was created. NPIV operates by using Fabric Discovery (FDISC) requests to obtain additional FCIDs.

FCoE NPV Mode

Building on Fibre Channel NPV mode, the Nexus 5x00 supports running in FCoE-NPV mode as well. FCoE-NPV brings similar benefits as the Fibre Channel NPV mode to a pure FCoE implementation. The switch still uses FIP snooping to determine FCoE traffic and to maintain separation and provide security with the benefits of minimized domain sprawl, simplified management, and fewer FCoE devices to manage. FCoE NPV also creates a new port type for the VNP (Virtual NPV Port). Figure 8-10 illustrates where the VNP port resides in an FCoE NPV topology.

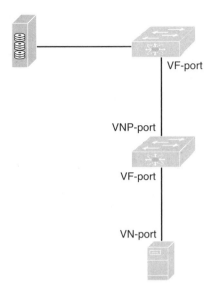

Figure 8-10   *FCoE NPV Topology*

Nexus 5x00 Unified Fabric Configuration

The Nexus 5x00 switches provide multiple options for using FCoE and have evolved since the platform was introduced in 2008. With the majority of Nexus 5x00 implementations used in the access layer of data center networks, it stands to reason that FCoE is predominant in the access layer. Nexus 5x00s can be used in single hop, multihop, and Fabric Extender (FEX)-based topologies using both native fibre channel interfaces, pure FCoE, or any combination. In addition, new features such as FCoE NPV and Enhanced vPC provide even more options for network administrators to choose from.

With the Nexus 5x00 switch, FCoE functionality is a licensed feature. After the license is installed, FCoE configuration can be completed.

Example 8-1 shows how to verify the installed licenses.

Example 8-1   *Verifying FCoE License*

```
N5K-1# show lic usa
Feature                   Ins  Lic   Status Expiry Date Comments
                               Count
----------------------------------------------------------------------
FCOE_NPV_PKG              No    -    Unused             -
FM_SERVER_PKG            No    -    Unused             -
ENTERPRISE_PKG          Yes   -    Unused Never      -
```

```
FC_FEATURES_PKG              Yes    -   Unused Never      -
VMFEX_FEATURE_PKG            No     -   Unused            -
ENHANCED_LAYER2_PKG          No     -   Unused            -
--------------------------------------------------------------------
N5K-1#
```

Example 8-2 shows how to enable the FCoE feature.

Example 8-2 *Enabling FCoE*

```
N5K-1# config
Enter configuration commands, one per line.  End with CNTL/Z.
N5K-1(config)# feature fcoe
FC license checked out successfully
fc_plugin extracted successfully
FC plugin loaded successfully
FCoE manager enabled successfully
N5K-1(config)#
N5K-1(config)# show license usage
Feature                     Ins  Lic   Status Expiry Date Comments
                                 Count
--------------------------------------------------------------------
FCOE_NPV_PKG                 No     -   Unused            -
FM_SERVER_PKG                No     -   Unused            -
ENTERPRISE_PKG              Yes    -   Unused Never      -
FC_FEATURES_PKG             Yes    -   In use Never      -
VMFEX_FEATURE_PKG            No     -   Unused            -
ENHANCED_LAYER2_PKG          No     -   Unused            -
--------------------------------------------------------------------
N5K-1(config)#
```

Enabling NPV mode requires a write erase and reboot, as demonstrated in Example 8-3.

Example 8-3 *Enabling NPV Mode*

```
N5K-1# config
Enter configuration commands, one per line.  End with CNTL/Z.
N5K-1(config)# show license usage
Feature                     Ins  Lic   Status Expiry Date Comments
                                 Count
--------------------------------------------------------------------
FCOE_NPV_PKG                 No     -   Unused            -
FM_SERVER_PKG                No     -   Unused            -
ENTERPRISE_PKG              Yes    -   Unused Never      -
FC_FEATURES_PKG             Yes    -   In use Never      -
```

```
VMFEX_FEATURE_PKG                   No    -   Unused               -
ENHANCED_LAYER2_PKG                 No    -   Unused               -

-------------------------------------------------------------------


N5K-1(config)# feature npv
Verify that boot variables are set and the changes are saved.
Changing to npv mode erases the current configuration and reboots the
switch in npv mode. Do you want to continue? (y/n):y
Shutdown Ports..
 writing reset reason 90,
2012 Jul 30 00:32:39 N5K-1 %$ VDC-1 %$ Jul 30 00:32:39 %KERN-0-
SYSTEM_MSG: Shutdown Ports.. - kernel
2012 Jul 30 00:32:39 N5K-1 %$ VDC-1 %$ Jul 30 00:32:39 %KERN-0-
SYSTEM_MSG:  writINIT: Sending processes the TERM signal
Sending all processes the TERM signal...
Sending all processes the KILL signal...
Unmounting filesystems...
Restarting system.
```

Single-Hop FCoE Configuration: Nexus 5x00

Now that the switches are configured for FCoE and have NPV configured, the next step is to configure the interconnection between the upstream Fibre Channel switch and the Nexus 5x00. In this example, a Nexus 5010 is connected to a Cisco MDS 9500 Fibre Channel directory via a 4-Gb native Fibre Channel port.

The first step is to configure the MDS to use NPIV, configure the port, and add it to the correct VSAN. This enables the MDS to support multiple FLOGI on a physical interface (NPIV), and for good documentation a description is added to the physical interface before being enabled. Finally, the port is added to the correct VSAN, 10 in this example. Figure 8-11 shows the topology for this environment.

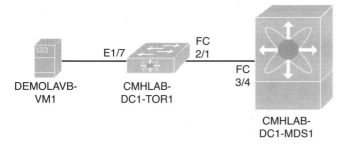

Figure 8-11 *Single-Hop FCoE with Nexus 5x00*

Example 8-4 shows how to configure the ISL between the MDS and the Nexus 5000.

Example 8-4 *Configuring the MDS Port*

```
CMHLAB-DC1-MDS1# config
CMHLAB-DC1-MDS1(config)# feature npiv
CMHLAB-DC1-MDS1(config)# interface fc3/4
CMHLAB-DC1-MDS1(config)# switchport description Connection to CMHLAB-DC1-TOR1 2/1
CMHLAB-DC1-MDS1(config)# switchport trunk mode off
CMHLAB-DC1-MDS1(config)# no shutdown
CMHLAB-DC1-MDS1(config)# vsan database
CMHLAB-DC1-MDS1(config-vsan-db)# vsan 10 interface fc3/4
CMHLAB-DC1-MDS1(config)# end
CMHLAB-DC1-MDS1#
CMHLAB-DC1-MDS1# show vsan membership interface fc3/4
fc3/4
        vsan:10
        allowed list:1-4078,4080-4093
CMHLAB-DC1-MDS1#
```

Next, the Nexus 5x00 needs to have a port configured for the connection to the MDS. The port is configured for the NP mode and added to the appropriate VSAN, 10 to match with the MDS configuration.

Example 8-5 shows how to configure the fibre channel uplink to the SAN core.

Example 8-5 *Configuring FC Uplink*

```
CMHLAB-DC1-TOR1# config
Enter configuration commands, one per line.  End with CNTL/Z.
CMHLAB-DC1-TOR1(config)# int fc2/1
CMHLAB-DC1-TOR1(config-if)# switchport mode NP
CMHLAB-DC1-TOR1(config-if)# switchport description Connection to CMHLAB-DC1-MDS1
fc3/4
CMHLAB-DC1-TOR1(config-if)# no shutdown
CMHLAB-DC1-TOR1(config-if)# end
CMHLAB-DC1-TOR1#


CMHLAB-DC1-TOR1# show int fc2/1
fc2/1 is up
    Port description is Connection to CMHLAB-DC1-MDS1 fc3/4
    Hardware is Fibre Channel, SFP is short wave laser w/o OFC (SN)
    Port WWN is 20:41:00:0d:ec:a3:0d:00
    Admin port mode is NP, trunk mode is off
    snmp link state traps are enabled
    Port mode is NP
    Port vsan is 10
    Speed is 4 Gbps
```

```
        Transmit B2B Credit is 16
        Receive B2B Credit is 16
        Receive data field Size is 2112
        Beacon is turned off
        1 minute input rate 0 bits/sec, 0 bytes/sec, 0 frames/sec
        1 minute output rate 0 bits/sec, 0 bytes/sec, 0 frames/sec
          10055 frames input, 5625012 bytes
            0 discards, 0 errors
            0 CRC,  0 unknown class
            0 too long, 0 too short
          10054 frames output, 523260 bytes
            0 discards, 0 errors
          1 input OLS, 1 LRR, 0 NOS, 0 loop inits
          1 output OLS, 1 LRR, 0 NOS, 0 loop inits
        last clearing of "show interface" counters never
          16 receive B2B credit remaining
          16 transmit B2B credit remaining
          0 low priority transmit B2B credit remaining
        Interface last changed at Mon May 21 20:09:15 2012


CMHLAB-DC1-TOR1# show npv sta

npiv is enabled

disruptive load balancing is disabled

External Interfaces:
====================
  Interface:  fc2/1, VSAN:   10, FCID: 0x7c0020, State: Up

  Number of External Interfaces: 1

Server Interfaces:
==================

  Number of Server Interfaces: 0

CMHLAB-DC1-TOR1#
```

After the connection between the MDS and Nexus 5x00 is configured, the next task is to configure the FCoE VLAN to VSAN mapping, configure the Ethernet interface that connects to the server, and finally configure the Virtual Fibre Channel (VFC) interface. This process is shown in Example 8-6 and Example 8-7.

Example 8-6 *Configuring FCoE VLAN to VSAN Mapping*

```
CMHLAB-DC1-TOR1# config
Enter configuration commands, one per line.  End with CNTL/Z.
CMHLAB-DC1-TOR1(config)# vlan 10
CMHLAB-DC1-TOR1(config-vlan)# fcoe vsan 10
CMHLAB-DC1-TOR1(config-vlan)# name FCOE-FabA
CMHLAB-DC1-TOR1(config-vlan)# end
CMHLAB-DC1-TOR1# show vlan fcoe


Original VLAN ID       Translated VSAN ID      Association State
---------------        ------------------      ----------------


    10                      10                  Operational


CMHLAB-DC1-TOR1#
```

After the FCoE VLAN is configured and mapped to a fibre channel VSAN, the Ethernet
port that connects to the server should be configured (refer to Example 8-7).

Example 8-7 *Configuring the Physical and VFC Interface for FCoE*

```
CMHLAB-DC1-TOR1# config
Enter configuration commands, one per line.  End with CNTL/Z.
CMHLAB-DC1-TOR1(config)# interface Ethernet1/7
CMHLAB-DC1-TOR1(config-if)# description Connection to DEMOLAB-VM1 - Emulex CNA
CMHLAB-DC1-TOR1(config-if)# switchport mode trunk
CMHLAB-DC1-TOR1(config-if)# switchport trunk allowed vlan 10,101,301,401,701,801
CMHLAB-DC1-TOR1(config-if)# interface vfc17
CMHLAB-DC1-TOR1(config-if)# bind interface Ethernet1/7
CMHLAB-DC1-TOR1(config-if)# switchport description FCoE Interface for DEMOLAB-VM1
CMHLAB-DC1-TOR1(config-if)# no shutdown
CMHLAB-DC1-TOR1(config-if)# end
CMHLAB-DC1-TOR1# CMHLAB-DC1-TOR1# show int e1/7 trunk


--------------------------------------------------------------------------------
Port          Native  Status      Port
              Vlan                Channel
--------------------------------------------------------------------------------
Eth1/7        1       trunking      --


--------------------------------------------------------------------------------
Port          Vlans Allowed on Trunk
--------------------------------------------------------------------------------
Eth1/7        10,101,301,401,701,801
```

```
-------------------------------------------------------------------------------
Port          Vlans Err-disabled on Trunk
-------------------------------------------------------------------------------
Eth1/7        none


-------------------------------------------------------------------------------
Port          STP Forwarding
-------------------------------------------------------------------------------
Eth1/7        10,101,301,401,701,801


-------------------------------------------------------------------------------
Port          Vlans in spanning tree forwarding state and not pruned
-------------------------------------------------------------------------------
Eth1/7        --


-------------------------------------------------------------------------------
Port          Vlans Forwarding on FabricPath
-------------------------------------------------------------------------------
CMHLAB-DC1-TOR1# show int vfc17
vfc17 is up
    Bound interface is Ethernet1/7
    Port description is FCoE Interface for DEMOLAB-VM1
    Hardware is Ethernet
    Port WWN is 20:10:00:0d:ec:a3:0d:3f
    Admin port mode is F, trunk mode is on
    snmp link state traps are enabled
    Port vsan is 10
    1 minute input rate 0 bits/sec, 0 bytes/sec, 0 frames/sec
    1 minute output rate 0 bits/sec, 0 bytes/sec, 0 frames/sec
      0 frames input, 0 bytes
        0 discards, 0 errors
      0 frames output, 0 bytes
        0 discards, 0 errors
    last clearing of "show interface" counters never

CMHLAB-DC1-TOR1#
```

FCoE-NPV on Nexus 5x00

Configuration of the FCoE NPV mode on a Nexus 5x00 switch is similar to the configuration for the Fibre Channel NPV mode. The main difference is the configuration of an Ethernet port for the ISL and the VNP port. Figure 8-12 shows the topology used for the FCoE-NPV examples.

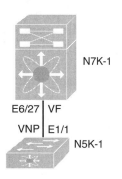

Figure 8-12 *FCoE NPV Configuration Between a Nexus 5000 and Nexus 7000*

First, the FCoE NPV feature must be enabled, as shown in Example 8-8.

> **Note**   FCoE-NPV cannot be enabled if FCoE is already enabled; otherwise, the following message displays: ERROR: Cannot enable feature fcoe-npv because feature fcoe is enabled. Disable feature fcoe, reload the system, and try again.

Example 8-8   *FCOE-NPV Feature Installation*

```
N5K-1# config
Enter configuration commands, one per line.  End with CNTL/Z.
N5K-1(config)# feature fcoe-npv
FCoE NPV license checked out successfully
fc_plugin extracted successfully
FC plugin loaded successfully
FCoE manager enabled successfully
FCoE NPV enabled on all modules successfully
N5K-1(config)# end
N5K-1#
```

After the feature is installed, the switch needs to be configured for the VSAN and VLAN mapping to associate traffic in a VLAN to a VSAN, as shown in Example 8-9.

Example 8-9   *VLAN to VSAN Mapping*

```
N5K-1# config
Enter configuration commands, one per line.  End with CNTL/Z.
N5K-1(config)# vsan database
N5K-1(config-vsan-db)# vsan 2000 name FCOE
N5K-1(config-vsan-db)# vlan 2000
N5K-1(config-vlan)# fcoe vsan 2000
N5K-1(config-vlan)# end
```

```
N5K-1# show vlan fcoe

Original VLAN ID        Translated VSAN ID      Association State
----------------        ------------------      -----------------

     2000                    2000               Operational
N5K-1#
```

Next, the Ethernet interface and VFC interface need to be configured to carry the
Ethernet VLAN and VNP mode. Example 8-10 reflects this process.

Example 8-10 *VNP Port Configuration on the Nexus 5000*

```
N5K-1# config
Enter configuration commands, one per line.  End with CNTL/Z.
N5K-1(config)# int e1/1
N5K-1(config-if)# switchport mode trunk
N5K-1(config-if)# switchport trunk allowed vlan 2000
N5K-1(config-if)# no shut
N5K-1(config-if)# desc FCoE-NPV Connection to N7K-1 E6/27
N5K-1(config-if)# interface vfc11
N5K-1(config-if)# desc FCoE-NPV Connection to N7K-1 vfc11
N5K-1(config-if)# switchport mode np
N5K-1(config-if)# bind interface e1/1
N5K-1(config-if)# switchport trunk allowed vsan 2000
N5K-1(config-if)# no shut
N5K-1(config-if)# end
N5K-1#N5K-1# show int vfc11
vfc11 is trunking
    Bound interface is Ethernet1/1
    Port description is FCoE-NPV Connection to N7K-1 vfc11
    Hardware is Ethernet
    Port WWN is 20:0a:00:05:73:d3:14:7f
    Admin port mode is NP, trunk mode is on
    snmp link state traps are enabled
    Port mode is TNP
    Port vsan is 1
    Trunk vsans (admin allowed and active) (2000)
    Trunk vsans (up)                        (2000)
    Trunk vsans (isolated)                  ()
    Trunk vsans (initializing)              ()
    1 minute input rate 0 bits/sec, 0 bytes/sec, 0 frames/sec
    1 minute output rate 0 bits/sec, 0 bytes/sec, 0 frames/sec
      10 frames input, 1140 bytes
        0 discards, 0 errors
```

```
     7 frames output, 980 bytes
       0 discards, 0 errors
    last clearing of "show interface" counters Mon Jul 30 17:21:52 2012


    Interface last changed at Mon Jul 30 17:21:52 2012



N5K-1#
```

A similar configuration must be applied on the Nexus 7000 side of the link. The primary difference is that the VFC is configured for the VF mode and NPIV is enabled. Example 8-11 shows the commands used for the configuration and the commands to verify the correct operation.

Example 8-11   *VFC and Ethernet Port Configuration on the Nexus 7000*

```
N7K-1-FCoE# config
Enter configuration commands, one per line.  End with CNTL/Z.
N7K-1-FCoE(config)# feature npiv
N7K-1-FCoE(config)# interface Ethernet6/27
N7K-1-FCoE(config-if)# description FCoE-NPV Connection to N5K-1 e1/1
N7K-1-FCoE(config-if)# switchport
N7K-1-FCoE(config-if)# switchport mode trunk
N7K-1-FCoE(config-if)# switchport trunk allowed vlan 2000
N7K-1-FCoE(config-if)# no shutdown
N7K-1-FCoE(config-if)#
N7K-1-FCoE(config-if)#interface vfc11
N7K-1-FCoE(config-if)#bind interface Ethernet6/27
N7K-1-FCoE(config-if)# switchport trunk allowed vsan 2000
N7K-1-FCoE(config-if)# no shutdown
N7K-1-FCoE(config-if)#end
N7K-1-FCoE#N7K09-FCoE# show int vfc11
vfc11 is trunking
    Bound interface is Ethernet6/27
    Hardware is Ethernet
    Port WWN is 20:0a:00:26:98:0f:d9:bf
    Admin port mode is F, trunk mode is on
    snmp link state traps are enabled
    Port mode is TF
    Port vsan is 1
    Speed is auto
    Trunk vsans (admin allowed and active) (2000)
    Trunk vsans (up)                       (2000)
    Trunk vsans (isolated)                 ()
    Trunk vsans (initializing)             ()
```

```
      7 fcoe in packets
      868 fcoe in octets
      11 fcoe out packets
      1324 fcoe out octets
      Interface last changed at Mon Jul 30 17:44:30 2012


N7K01-FCoE# show fcns data


VSAN 2000:

-----------------------------------------------------------------------
FCID        TYPE  PWWN                    (VENDOR)        FC4-TYPE:FEATURE
-----------------------------------------------------------------------

0x010000    N     20:0a:00:05:73:d3:14:7f (Cisco)        npv


Total number of entries = 1
N7K-1-FCoE#
```

Nexus 7000 Unified Fabric Configuration

The Nexus 7000 provides director class support for FCoE solutions and can be used in both core and edge topologies. The platforms provides the high-availability features and capabilities such as redundant supervisors, redundant hardware components, and the inherent availability components of NX-OS, such as Storage VDCs. In-Service Software Upgrade (ISSU), Stateful Switch Over (SSO) and stateful process restart make for a solid foundation.

FCoE on the Nexus 7000 is available on the F1 (N7K-F132XP-15) and F2/F2e (N7K-F248XP-25) modules. When using FCoE on the F2/F2e module, a Supervisor 2 or Supervisor 2E must be used. FCoE on F2/F2e cannot work with a Supervisor 1 module. FCoE is also a licensed feature, and the license is bound to a module, so if FCoE will be used across multiple modules in a chassis, there must be an FCoE license installed per module.

With these requirements met, FCoE can be installed on the Nexus 7000. FCoE installation requires the system QoS policy is configured to a template that provides a no-drop class. This is configured in either the default VDC or the admin VDC if running NX_OS 6.1(1) or later. The default QoS policy uses eight drop classes and is named **default-np-8e-policy**. Example 8-12 shows the QoS classes available to be selected and shows the change to a single no-drop class. This policy matches FCoE traffic in CoS 3 and provides a lossless Ethernet transport (no drop).

Example 8-12   *Setting the System QoS Policy*

```
N7K-1# config
Enter configuration commands, one per line.  End with CNTL/Z.
N7K-1(config)# system qos
```

```
N7K-1(config-sys-qos)# service-policy type network-qos ?
  default-nq-4e-policy  Default 4-ethernet policy (4-drop 4-nodrop CoS)
  default-nq-6e-policy  Default 6-ethernet policy (6-drop 2-nodrop CoS)
  default-nq-7e-policy  Default 7-ethernet policy (7-drop 1-nodrop CoS)
  default-nq-8e-policy  Default 8-ethernet policy (8-drop CoS)
N7K-1(config-sys-qos)# service-policy type network-qos default-nq-7e-policy
N7K-1(config-sys-qos)# end
N7K-1# show policy-map system type network-qos

  Type network-qos policy-maps
  ============================
  policy-map type network-qos default-nq-7e-policy
    class type network-qos c-nq-7e-drop
      match cos 0-2,4-7
      congestion-control tail-drop
      mtu 1500
    class type network-qos c-nq-7e-ndrop-fcoe
      match cos 3
      match protocol fcoe
      pause
      mtu 2112

N7K-1#
```

With the QoS policy mapped to a no-drop policy, the next step is to install the FCoE feature set and configure a Storage VDC. This enables FCoE across the entire chassis and then creates a VDC to be used for storage functions. Example 8-13 describes this process.

Example 8-13   *Installing FCoE Feature Set and Creating a Storage VDC*

```
N7K-1# config
Enter configuration commands, one per line.  End with CNTL/Z.
N7K-1(config)# install feature-set fcoe
N7K-1(config)# vdc FCoE type storage
Note:  Creating VDC, one moment please ...
N7K-1(config-vdc)# show vdc

vdc_id  vdc_name   state   mac                 type       lc
-------  --------  -----   ---                 ----       --
1       N7K-1     active  00:26:98:0f:d9:c1   Admin      None
2       Agg1      active  00:26:98:0f:d9:c2   Ethernet   f2
3       Core1     active  00:26:98:0f:d9:c3   Ethernet   m1 f1 m1xl m2xl
4       Access1   active  00:26:98:0f:d9:c4   Ethernet   m1 f1 m1xl m2xl
5       FCoE      active  00:26:98:0f:d9:c5   Storage    f1 f2
```

```
N7K-1(config-vdc)# show vdc FCoE detail

vdc id: 5
vdc name: FCoE
vdc state: active
vdc mac address: 00:26:98:0f:d9:c5
vdc ha policy: RESTART
vdc dual-sup ha policy: SWITCHOVER
vdc boot Order: 1
CPU Share: 5
CPU Share Percentage: 16%
vdc create time: Tue Jul 31 00:15:39 2012
vdc reload count: 0
vdc restart count: 0
vdc type: Storage
vdc supported linecards: f1 f2

N7K-1(config-vdc)#
```

The next step is to configure the storage VDC by allocating ports from modules, allocating a range of VLANs for use with FCoE, and then setting up the VDC for FCoE usage. Because this VDC is new, the switch prompts for a few items such as system password strength, password, and to run the setup script. When completed, basic FCoE configuration can begin. Example 8-14 walks through this process.

Example 8-14 *Allocation of Ports and Initial VDC Configuration*

```
N7K-1# config
Enter configuration commands, one per line.  End with CNTL/Z.
N7K-1(config)# vdc fcoe
N7K-1(config-vdc)# allocate interface e6/17,e6/27,e6/29-32
Entire port-group is not present in the command. Missing ports will be included
automatically
Moving ports will cause all config associated to them in source vdc to be removed.
Are you sure you want to move the ports (y/n)?  [yes] yes
N7K-1(config-vdc)# allocate fcoe-vlan-range 2000 from vdc Access1
N7K-1(config-vdc)# end
N7K-1#
N7K-1# switchto vdc fcoe
```

```
            ---- System Admin Account Setup ----


Do you want to enforce secure password standard (yes/no) [y]: n

   Enter the password for "admin":
   Confirm the password for "admin":

            ---- Basic System Configuration Dialog VDC: 5 ----

This setup utility will guide you through the basic configuration of
the system. Setup configures only enough connectivity for management
of the system.

Please register Cisco Nexus7000 Family devices promptly with your
supplier. Failure to register may affect response times for initial
service calls. Nexus7000 devices must be registered to receive
entitled support services.

Press Enter at anytime to skip a dialog. Use ctrl-c at anytime
to skip the remaining dialogs.

Would you like to enter the basic configuration dialog (yes/no): no
Cisco Nexus Operating System (NX-OS) Software
TAC support: http://www.cisco.com/tac
Copyright (c) 2002-2012, Cisco Systems, Inc. All rights reserved.
The copyrights to certain works contained in this software are
owned by other third parties and used and distributed under
license. Certain components of this software are licensed under
the GNU General Public License (GPL) version 2.0 or the GNU
Lesser General Public License (LGPL) Version 2.1. A copy of each
such license is available at
http://www.opensource.org/licenses/gpl-2.0.php and
http://www.opensource.org/licenses/lgpl-2.1.php
N7K-1-FCoE#
N7K-1-FCoE# config
Enter configuration commands, one per line.  End with CNTL/Z.
N7K-1-FCoE(config)# feature-set fcoe
N7K-1-FCoE(config)# feature npiv
N7K-1-FCoE(config)# feature lldp
N7K-1-FCoE(config)# vsan database
N7K-1-FCoE(config-vsan-db)# vsan 2000
N7K-1-FCoE(config-vsan-db)# vlan 2000
```

```
N7K-1-FCoE(config-vlan)# fcoe
N7K-1-FCoE(config-vlan)# end
N7K-1-FCoE(config)# end
N7K-1-FCoE#
N7K-1-FCoE# show vlan fcoe


Original VLAN ID          Translated VSAN ID        Association State
----------------          ------------------        -----------------


     2000                        2000               Operational
N7K-1-FCoE#
N7K-1-FCoE(config)# end
N7K-1-FCoE#
```

With the foundation for FCoE configured, the next step is to provision connectivity. Figure 8-13 shows the topology the following examples use.

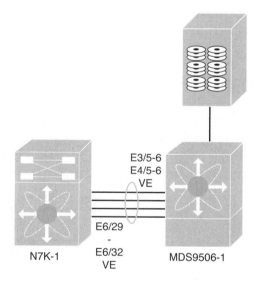

Figure 8-13 *FCoE Topology Between Nexus 7000 and MDS*

The first step is to configure the Ethernet interfaces, add them to a port channel for additional bandwidth on the ISL and redundancy, and then configure the VFC, as shown in Example 8-15.

Example 8-15 *Nexus 7000 to MDS Interconnection*

```
N7K-1-FCoE# config
Enter configuration commands, one per line.  End with CNTL/Z.
N7K-1-FCoE(config)# feature lacp
N7K-1-FCoE(config)# int e6/29-32
N7K-1-FCoE(config-if-range)# channel-group 258 mode active
N7K-1-FCoE(config-if-range)# int po258
N7K-1-FCoE(config-if)# desc Port Channel to MDS9506-1
N7K-1-FCoE(config-if)# switchport mode trunk
N7K-1-FCoE(config-if)# switchport trunk allowed vlan 2000
N7K-1-FCoE(config-if)# no shut
N7K-1-FCoE(config-if)# int vfc 101
N7K-1-FCoE(config-if)# switchport desc VE Port Channel to MDS9506-1
N7K-1-FCoE(config-if)# switch mode e
N7K-1-FCoE(config-if)# switch trunk allowed vsan 2000
N7K-1-FCoE(config-if)# bind interface po258
N7K-1-FCoE(config-if)# no shut
N7K-1-FCoE(config-if)# end
N7K-1-FCoE# show int vfc101
vfc101 is trunking
    Bound interface is port-channel258
    Port description is VE Port Channel to MDS9506-1
    Hardware is Ethernet
    Port WWN is 20:64:00:26:98:0f:d9:bf
    Admin port mode is E, trunk mode is on
    snmp link state traps are enabled
    Port mode is TE
    Port vsan is 1
    Speed is 40 Gbps
    Trunk vsans (admin allowed and active) (2000)
    Trunk vsans (up)                       (2000)
    Trunk vsans (isolated)                 ()
    Trunk vsans (initializing)             ()
    120677 fcoe in packets
    13910628 fcoe in octets
    120679 fcoe out packets
    10352660 fcoe out octets
    Interface last changed at Tue Jul 31 01:21:17 2012


N7K-1-FCoE#
```

For reference, Example 8-16 shows the corresponding configuration on the MDS.

Example 8-16 *MDS FCoE Configuration*

```
MDS9506-1# show run int Eth3/5, Eth3/6, Eth4/5, Eth4/6

!Command: show running-config interface Ethernet3/5-6, Ethernet4/5-6
!Time: Tue Jul 31 01:30:57 2012

version 5.2(2a)

interface Ethernet3/5
  switchport mode trunk
  switchport trunk allowed vlan 2000
  channel-group 258 mode active
  no shutdown

interface Ethernet3/6
  switchport mode trunk
  switchport trunk allowed vlan 2000
  channel-group 258 mode active
  no shutdown

interface Ethernet4/5
  switchport mode trunk
  switchport trunk allowed vlan 2000
  channel-group 258 mode active
  no shutdown

interface Ethernet4/6
  switchport mode trunk
  switchport trunk allowed vlan 2000
  channel-group 258 mode active
  no shutdown

MDS9506-1#
MDS9506-1# show run int epo258

!Command: show running-config interface ethernet-port-channel258
!Time: Tue Jul 31 01:31:42 2012

version 5.2(2a)

interface ethernet-port-channel258
  switchport mode trunk
  switchport trunk allowed vlan 2000
```

```
Invalid interface format at '^' marker.
MDS9506-1# show run int vfc101

!Command: show running-config interface vfc101
!Time: Tue Jul 31 01:31:52 2012

version 5.2(2a)

interface vfc101
  bind interface ethernet-port-channel258
  switchport mode E
  switchport trunk allowed vsan 2000
  no shutdown

MDS9506-1# MDS9506-1# show int vfc101
vfc101 is trunking
    Bound interface is ethernet-port-channel258
    Hardware is Ethernet
    Port WWN is 20:64:00:0d:ec:35:1e:ff
    Admin port mode is E, trunk mode is on
    snmp link state traps are enabled
    Port mode is TE
    Port vsan is 1
    Speed is 40 Gbps
    Trunk vsans (admin allowed and active) (2000)
    Trunk vsans (up)                       (2000)
    Trunk vsans (isolated)                 ()
    Trunk vsans (initializing)             ()
    117696 fcoe in packets
    10091312 fcoe in octets
    117695 fcoe out packets
    13575440 fcoe out octets
    Interface last changed at Tue Jul 31 01:17:09 2012

MDS9506-1#
```

FCoE on the Nexus 7000 also supports a unique capability that enables interfaces to be shared between two VDCs. This enables the Nexus 7000 to be used in the access layer of networks where servers connect to the switch and use FCoE. A shared interface enables FCoE traffic to be segmented into the Storage VDC at the edge of the network. When an interface is shared between two VDCs, a few rules must be followed:

- Interfaces can be shared only between one Ethernet VDC and one Storage VDC.

- Interfaces to be shared must be configured as 802.1Q trunks in the Ethernet VDC.

- Interfaces may be shared only from the Ethernet VDC that allocated VLANs to the Storage VDC.

- The Ethernet VDC "owns" the physical interface. If the interface is admin down in the Ethernet VDC, it will be admin down in the Storage VDC.

- All ports that have a common ASIC must be allocated as shared interfaces. This is done in groups of two on the F1 modules and groups of four on F2/F2e modules.

Note   If all the shared ASIC ports are not configured as trunks, allocation as shared interfaces will fail.

In Example 8-17, four ports are configured as trunks in the Ethernet VDC and then configured for shared interfaces in the Storage VDC.

Example 8-17   *Nexus 7000 Shared Interface Allocation*

```
N7K-1# config
Enter configuration commands, one per line.  End with CNTL/Z.
N7K-1(config)# vdc fcoe
N7K-1(config-vdc)# allocate shared interface e6/17
Entire port-group is not present in the command. Missing ports will be included
automatically
Ports that share the port group of the interfaces you have specified will be affected
as well. Continue (y/n)? [yes] yes
N7K-1(config-vdc)# end
N7K-1# fcoe
Cisco Nexus Operating System (NX-OS) Software
TAC support: http://www.cisco.com/tac
Copyright (c) 2002-2012, Cisco Systems, Inc. All rights reserved.
The copyrights to certain works contained in this software are
owned by other third parties and used and distributed under
license. Certain components of this software are licensed under
the GNU General Public License (GPL) version 2.0 or the GNU
Lesser General Public License (LGPL) Version 2.1. A copy of each
such license is available at
http://www.opensource.org/licenses/gpl-2.0.php and
http://www.opensource.org/licenses/lgpl-2.1.php
N7K-1-FCoE# show int brief

--------------------------------------------------------------------------------

Interface              Status                          Speed
```

```
                                                         (Gbps)
-------------------------------------------------------------------------------
sup-fc0                    up                            1


-------------------------------------------------------------------------------
Ethernet      VLAN   Type Mode   Status  Reason                  Speed     Por
t
Interface                                                                  Ch
#
-------------------------------------------------------------------------------
Eth6/17       1      eth  trunk  down    Administratively down   auto(D)   --
Eth6/18       1      eth  trunk  down    Administratively down   auto(D)   --
Eth6/19       1      eth  trunk  down    Administratively down   auto(D)   --
Eth6/20       1      eth  trunk  down    Administratively down   auto(D)   --
Eth6/25       --     eth  routed down    Administratively down   auto(D)   --
Eth6/26       --     eth  routed down    Administratively down   auto(D)   --
Eth6/27       --     eth  routed down    Administratively down   auto(D)   --
Eth6/28       --     eth  routed down    SFP not inserted        auto(D)   --
Eth6/29       1      eth  trunk  up      none                    10G(D)    258
Eth6/30       1      eth  trunk  up      none                    10G(D)    258
N7K-1-FCoE#
```

The next step required is to create the VFC interface for the host and specify the shared interface as the binding. This is the same syntax used on the Nexus 5x00 earlier in the chapter. Example 8-18 shows the process for the topology shown in Figure 8-14.

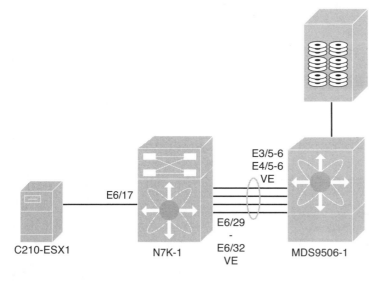

Figure 8-14 *FCoE Topology*

Example 8-18 *Nexus 7000 VFC Interface Creation*

```
N7K-1-FCoE# config
Enter configuration commands, one per line.  End with CNTL/Z.
N7K-1-FCoE(config)# int vfc617
N7K-1-FCoE(config-if)# bind interface ethernet 6/17
N7K-1-FCoE(config-if)# no shut
N7K-1-FCoE(config-if)# end
N7K-1-FCoE#
```

With the VFCs created and bound, VEs created to the MDS, and both storage and hosts connected to the fabric, the last step would be to configure zoning and device aliasing for the FC network. The Nexus switches can participate in zoning with a Fibre Channel network.

Note   Nexus 5x00 when configured in the NPV or FCoE-NPV mode do not participate in zoning and aliasing because they rely on the upstream device to perform those functions.

Example 8-19 shows a device-alias, zone and zoneset creation, and activation.

Example 8-19 *Device alias, zone, and zoneset Creation and Activation*

```
N7K-1-FCoE# config
Enter configuration commands, one per line.  End with CNTL/Z.
N7K-1-FCoE(config)# device-alias mode enhanced
N7K-1-FCoE(config)# device-alias database
N7K-1-FCoE(config-device-alias-db)#    device-alias name C210-ESX1 pwwn
20:00:e8:b7:48:4d:74:22
N7K-1-FCoE(config-device-alias-db)#    device-alias name NetApp_FAS270 pwwn
50:0a:09:81:85:75:90:88
N7K-1-FCoE(config-device-alias-db)# device-alias commit
N7K-1-FCoE(config-device-alias-db)# exit
N7K-1-FCoE(config)#zone name NetappArray vsan 2000
N7K-1-FCoE(config-zone)# member device-alias NetApp_FAS270
N7K-1-FCoE(config-zone)# member device-alias C210-ESX1
N7K-1-FCoE(config-zone)# zone name C210-ESX1 vsan 2000
N7K-1-FCoE(config-zone)# member device-alias C210-ESX1
N7K-1-FCoE(config-zone)# zoneset name VSAN2000_ZS vsan 2000
N7K-1-FCoE(config-zoneset)# member NetappArray
N7K-1-FCoE(config-zoneset)# member C210-ESX1
N7K-1-FCoE(config-zoneset)# exit
N7K-1-FCoE(config)# zoneset activate name VSAN2000_ZS vsan 2000
N7K-1-FCoE(config)# end
N7K-1-FCoE#
```

Summary

Unified Fabric offers several benefits to customers, including

- **Lower capital expenditures:** Through the reduction of adapters, cables, and ports required within the infrastructure.

- **Lower operational expenses:** Through the reduction of adapters, cables, and ports drawing power within the data center.

- **Reduced deployment cycles:** Provides a wire-once model, where all LAN, SAN, IPC, and management traffic is available to every server without requiring additional connectivity components.

- **Higher availability:** Few adapters and fewer ports means fewer components that could fail.

By taking advantage of enhancements to traditional Ethernet technologies, and the emergence of technologies such as FCoE, customers can realize these benefits with minimal disruption to operational models. This chapter showed the basic Nexus 5x00 and Nexus 7000 configurations necessary to provide a Unified access method for LAN data traffic and SAN storage traffic. The multiple technologies that can be used with Unified Fabric such as NPV, NPIV FCOE-NPV, Storage VDCs, and shared interfaces were illustrated, and various use cases were discussed.

## Chapter 9

Nexus 1000V

This chapter covers the following topics:

- Hypervisor and vSphere introduction
- Nexus 1000V system overview
- Nexus 1000V switching
- Nexus 1000V installation
- Nexus 1000V port profiles
- Virtual Network Management Center (VNMC)
- Virtual Security Gateway (VSG)
- Virtual Extensible LAN VXLAN
- Nexus 1000V port profiles
- Network Analysys Module (NAM)

Hypervisor and vSphere Introduction

A hypervisor, also called a *virtual machine manager*, is a program that enables multiple operating systems to share a single hardware host. Each operating system appears to have the host's processor, memory, and other resources. The hypervisor controls the host processor, memory, and other resources and allocates what is needed to each operating system. Each operating system is called a *guest operating system* or *virtual machine* running on top of the hypervisor.

The Cisco Nexus 1000V Series Switch is a software-based Cisco NX-OS switch with intelligent features designed specifically for integration with VMware vSphere environments. As more organizations move toward cloud services, VMware vSphere manages collections of CPU(s), storage, and networking as a seamless and dynamic operating environment. The Nexus 1000V operates inside the VMware ESX hypervisor. The Cisco Nexus 1000V Series supports Cisco VN-Link server virtualization technology to provide

- Policy-based virtual machine (VM) connectivity

- Mobile VM security

- Network policy

- Nondisruptive operational model for your server virtualization and networking teams

With the Nexus 1000V, virtual servers have the same network configuration, security policy, diagnostic tools, and operational models as physical servers. The Cisco Nexus 1000V Series is certified by VMware to be compatible with VMware vSphere, vCenter, ESX, and ESXi. VMware vCenter provides a single point of management for VMware virtual environments providing access control, performance monitoring, and configuration. The main difference between ESX and ESXi is that ESXi does not contain the service console. The Virtual Supervisor Module (VSM) can be deployed in high-availability mode; each VSM in an active-standby pair; and the active and standby should run on separate VMware ESX hosts. This requirement helps ensure high availability if one of the VMware ESX servers fails. An alternative option, the Nexus 1010/1010X, is now available as of this writing.

In addition to VMware support, Nexus 1000v supports KVM, XEN, and Microsoft Hyper-V. The Microsoft Hyper-V solution (1HCY13) requires Windows Server 2012 and System Center Virtual Machine Manager (SCVMM) 2012 Service Park 1 (SP1). This enables organizations to deploy Cisco Nexus 1000v across multiple hypervisor to have common services such as vPath across multiple hypervisors.

Nexus 1000V System Overview

The Cisco Nexus 1000V Series switch has two major components:

- **Virtual Ethernet Module (VEM):** Executes inside the hypervisor

- **External Virtual Supervisor Module (VSM):** Manages the VEMs

Figure 9-1 shows the Cisco Nexus 1000V Architecture.

The Distributed Virtual Switch (DVS) is a generic concept, the Nexus 1000v is the Cisco Distributed Virtual Switch implementation. The Cisco Nexus 1000V Virtual Ethernet Module (VEM) executes as part of the VMware ESX or ESXi kernel. The VEM uses the VMware vNetwork Distributed Switch (vDS) application programming interface (API). The API is used to provide advanced networking capability to virtual machines; enabling integration with VMware VMotion and Distributed Resource Scheduler (DRS). The VEM takes configuration information from the VSM and performs Layer 2 switching and advanced networking functions:

Cisco Nexus 1000V Architecture

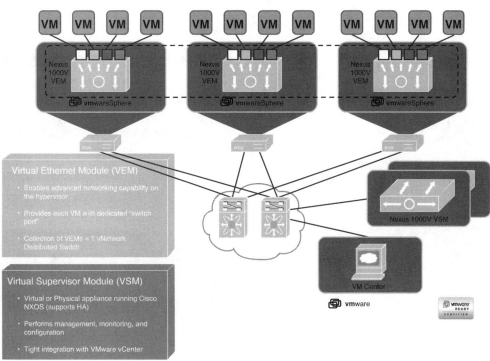

Figure 9-1 *Cisco Nexus 1000V Series Architecture*

- Port-channels
- Quality of service (QoS)
- Security, including Private VLAN (PVLAN), access control lists, and port security
- Monitoring, including NetFlow, Switch Port Analyzer (SPAN), and Encapsulated Remote SPAN (ERSPAN)
- vPath support for traffic steering and service chaining
- Access control list (ACL)

Note For more details on VMWare DRA and HA, visit the following links:

http://www.vmware.com/products/drs/

http://www.vmware.com/products/vmotion/

Figure 9-2 shows the Nexus 1000V topology used throughout the chapter.

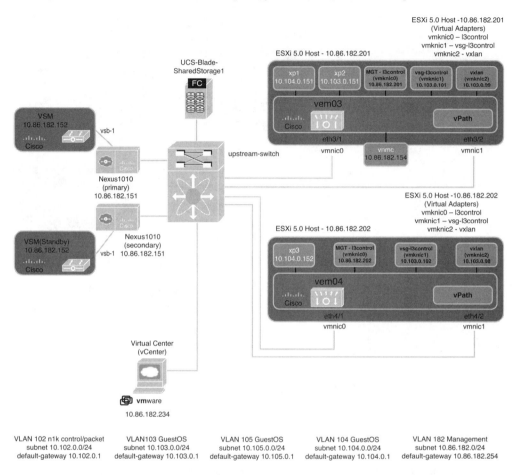

Figure 9-2 *Nexus 1000V Topology*

The Cisco Nexus 1000V Series VSM controls multiple VEMs as one logical modular switch. The VSM supports multiple VEMs running in software inside of the physical servers. Configuration is performed through the VSM and is automatically propagated to the VEMs. Instead of configuring soft switches inside the hypervisor on a host-by-host basis, administrators can define configurations for immediate use on all VEMs being managed by the VSM from a single interface.

There are two distinct VLAN interfaces used for communication between the VSM and VEM: the Control VLAN and the Packet VLAN. These two VLANs need L2 Adjacency between the VSM and VEM. The Control VLAN is used for

- Extended management communication between the VEM and VSM similar to control communication of chassis-based solutions Nexus 7000, Catalyst 6500

- Carrying low-level messages to ensure proper configuration of the VEM

- Maintaining a 2-second heartbeat with the VSM to the VEM (timeout 6 seconds)

- Maintaining synchronization between primary and secondary VSMs

The Packet VLAN is used for carrying network packets from the VEM to the VSM, such as Cisco Discovery Protocol (CDP) and Interior Gateway Management Protocol (IGMP).

By using the capabilities of Cisco NX-OS, the Cisco Nexus 1000V Series provides the following benefits:

- **Flexibility and scalability:** Port profiles provide configuration of ports by category, enabling the solution to scale to a large number of ports.

- **High availability:** Synchronized, redundant VSMs enable rapid, stateful failover and ensure an always-available virtual machine network.

- **Manageability:** The Cisco Nexus 1000V Series can be accessed through the XML Management interface, Cisco command-line interface (CLI), Simple Network Management Protocol (SNMP), and CiscoWorks LAN Management Solution (LMS).

Note With the release of the Nexus 1000V software 4.0(4)SV1(2), Layer 3 Control between the VSM and the VSM is supported. With Layer 3 Control, the spanning of the Control and Packets VLANs is no longer required; this is covered in more detail in the Layer 3 Control section.

The VSM is also integrated with VMware vCenter Server so that the virtualization administrator can take advantage of the network configuration in the Cisco Nexus 1000V. The Cisco Nexus 1000V includes the port profile feature to address the dynamic nature of server virtualization. Port profiles enable you to define VM network policies for different types or classes of VMs from the Cisco Nexus 1000V VSM. The port profiles are applied to individual VM virtual network interface cards (NICs) through VMware's vCenter GUI for transparent provisioning of network resources. Port profiles are a scalable mechanism to configure networks with large numbers of VMs.

Network and security policies defined in the port profile follow the VM throughout its life cycle, whether it is being migrated from one server to another, suspended, hibernated, or restarted. In addition to migrating the policy, the Cisco Nexus 1000V VSM also moves the VM's network state, such as the port counters and flow statistics. VMs participating in traffic monitoring activities, such as Cisco NetFlow or Encapsulated Remote Switched Port Analyzer (ERSPAN), can continue these activities uninterrupted by VMotion/migration operations. When a specific port profile is updated, the Cisco Nexus 1000V automatically provides live updates to all the virtual ports using that same port profile. With the capability to migrate network and security policies through VMotion, regulatory compliance is much easier to enforce with the Cisco Nexus 1000V because the security policy is defined in the same way as physical servers and constantly enforced by the switch.

Nexus 1000V Switching Overview

The VEM differentiates between the following interface types: VEM Virtual Ports and VEM Physical Ports.

The Nexus 1000V supports the following scalability numbers:

- 2 VSMs in a High Availability (HA) pair; active/standby relationship.

- 64 VEMs

- 2048 Active VLANs

- 2048 ports (Eth + vEth)

- 256 port channels

- 2048 port-profiles

Each VEM supports

- 216 ports (vEths)

- 32 physical NICs

- 8 port channels

Note You can find additional scale information in Table 2 of the "Cisco Nexus 1000V Release Notes, Release 4.2(1)SV1(5.1)" document at Cisco.com, which you can find at the following URL: http://tinyurl.com/ayudk8r.

VEM virtual ports are classified into the six port types:

- **Virtual NIC:** There are three types of virtual NIC in VMware:

    - **virtual NIC (vnic):** Part of the VM and represents the physical port of the host plugged into the switch.

    - **virtual kernel NIC (vmknic):** Used by the hypervisor for management, VMotion, iSCSI, NFS, and other network access needed by the kernel. This interface would carry the IP address of the hypervisor and is also bound to a virtual Ethernet port.

    - **vswif:** The VMWare Service Console network interface, the Service Console network interface. The first Service Console/vswif interface is always referenced as vwsif0. The vswif interface is used as the VMware management port; these interface types map to a vEth port within Nexus 1000V.

- **Virtual Ethernet (vEth) port:** Represents a port on the Cisco Nexus 1000V Distributed Virtual Switch. These vEth ports are what the virtual "cable" plugs into and are moved to the host that the VM runs on; Virtual Ethernet ports are assigned to port groups.

■ **Local Virtual Ethernet (lvEth) port:** Dynamically selected for vEth ports needed on the host.

Note   Local vEths do not move and are addressable by the module/port number.

VEM physical ports are classified into the three port types:

■ VMware NIC

■ Uplink port

■ Ethernet port

Each physical NIC in VMware is represented by an interface called a VMNIC. The VMNIC number is allocated during VMware installation, or when a new physical NIC is installed, and remains the same for the life of the host. Each uplink port on the host represents a physical interface. It acts like an lvEth port; however, because physical ports do not move between hosts, the mapping is 1:1 between an uplink port and a VMNIC. Each physical port added to Cisco Nexus 1000V appears as a physical Ethernet port, just as it would on a hardware-based switch.

Note   For more information on interface relationship mapping, read the Overview section from the *Cisco Nexus 1000V Installation and Upgrade Guide, Release 4.2(1)SV1(5.1)* at Cisco.com: http://tinyurl.com/bc6ujq5.

The Nexus 1000V does not run Spanning Tree Protocol (STP); the Nexus 1000V adheres to the following rules to obtain loop prevention without STP:

■ STP BDPUs are dropped.

■ No switching from physical NIC to NIC.

■ Layer 2 local MAC address packets are dropped on ingress.

Figure 9-3 shows how the VEM achieves loop prevention without running STP.

Each VEM learns independently and maintains a separate MAC table. The virtual machine MAC addresses are statically mapped including vEthernet interfaces, vmknics, and vswifs; devices external to the VEM are learned dynamically.

Note   While the interfaces are up, there is no aging.

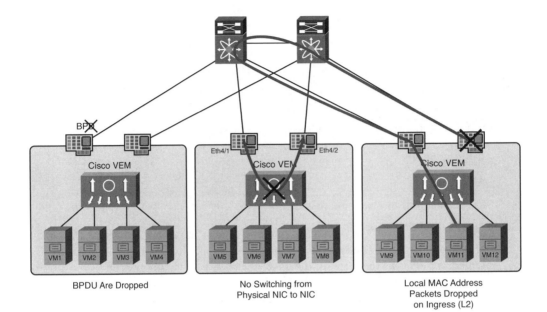

Figure 9-3 *VEM Loop Prevention*

Nexus 1000V VSM Installation

The Nexus 1000V VSM installation will be shown using the Nexus 1000v Installation Management Center as a Virtual Machine running on an ESX/ESXi host and the Nexus 1000v Installation Virtual Services Blade on the Nexus 1010 dedicated appliance. The two modes of installation are

■ Nexus 1000v Installation on a dedicated appliance running on the Nexus 1010 appliance

■ Nexus 1000v Installation Management Center virtual machine running as a virtual machine running on an ESX/ESXi host

Both methods of installation will be demonstrated throughout this section.

Note To use an ISO image to create a 1000V virtual machine (VM), use the following attributes when creating the VM:

■ VMType: Other 64-bit Linux

■ 1 processor

■ CPU speed 1500 MHZ

■ Configured 2 GB RAM for the VSM VM

- 3 NICs
- SCSI Hard Disk, 3 GB with LSI Logic Parallel adapter
- Reserve 2 GB RAM for the VSM VM
- Configure VM network adapters and attach ISO to VM and power on.

The Nexus 1000V virtual appliance has two different modes of installation with the 4.0(4) SV1(2) software release. The next section covers the manual installation of the VSM virtual appliance. The section, "Nexus 1000V GUI Installation" covers the GUI installation. Refer back to the topology in Figure 9-1 for the configuration that follows.

Nexus 1000V Deployed on Nexus 1010 Virtual Services Blade

The Nexus 1010 offers a dedicated hardware solution to deploy virtual network services. The following services can be deployed on the Nexus 1010 and Nexus 1010-X:

- Nexus 1000V Virtual Supervisor Module (VSM)
- Nexus 1000V Virtual Security Gateway
- Nexus 1000V Network Analysis Module
- Data Center Network Manager

The Nexus 1010(s) can be deployed in a HA pair. The HA pair offers stateful failover between active and standby Cisco Nexus 1010 appliances. The HA pairs need to be the same hardware platforms, meaning a pair to consist of Nexus 1010 and Nexus 1010 or a pair consisting of Nexus-1010-X and Nexus-1010-X; they cannot be mixed.

Providing a dedicated appliance for the virtualized services enables network administrators to easily install and configure virtual access switches similar to the way they install and configure physical switches. Dedicating a hardware appliance simplifies deployment, upgrades, and configuration because there is not a dependency on finding server resources for these resources.

The Nexus 1010 has different deployment options. These options vary depending on topology; the options are documented in the *Cisco Nexus 1010 Virtual Services Appliance Deployment Guide*, which you can find at Cisco.com or from this URL: http://tinyurl.com/ccwoyq2.

The Nexus-1010 and Nexus 1010-X have different scale and feature sets; refer to the *Cisco Nexus 1010 and 1010-X Virtual Services Appliances Data Sheet* for specifics (http://tinyurl.com/462udl8).

The Nexus 1000v Installation Management Center installs only the VSM on an ESX; it does not install the VSM on a Nexus 1010. For VSM on Nexus 1000V Virtual Supervisor Module on the Nexus 1010 dedicated appliance, perform the following steps:

1. SSH to the Nexus 1010 Appliance Management IP Address:

```
login as: admin
Nexus 1010
Using keyboard-interactive authentication.
Password:
Cisco Nexus Operating System (NX-OS) Software
TAC support: http://www.cisco.com/tac
Copyright (c) 2002-2012, Cisco Systems, Inc. All rights reserved.
The copyrights to certain works contained in this software are
owned by other third parties and used and distributed under
license. Certain components of this software are licensed under the GNU
General Public License (GPL) version 2.0 or the GNU
Lesser General Public License (LGPL) Version 2.1. A copy of each such license
is available at
http://www.opensource.org/licenses/gpl-2.0.php and http://www.opensource.org/
licenses/lgpl-2.1.php
```

2. TFTP the VSM ISO image to the bootflash:/repository directory:

```
Nexus1010# copy tftp: bootflash:/repository
Enter source filename: nexus-1000v.4.2.1.SV1.5.1a.iso
Enter vrf (If no input, current vrf 'default' is considered):
Enter hostname for the tftp server: 10.86.182.234
Trying to connect to tftp server......
Connection to Server Established.
TFTP get operation was successful
```

3. Verify the iso image is in bootflash:/repository:

```
Nexus1010(config-vsb-config)# cd repository
Nexus1010(config-vsb-config)# dir
   139923456    Aug 22 23:45:31 2012  nexus-1000v.4.2.1.SV1.5.1a.iso
Usage for bootflash://
   521699328 bytes used
  3469680640 bytes free
  3991379968 bytes total
Nexus1010(config-vsb-config)#
```

4. Create the virtual blade name, vsm, on the Nexus 1010:

```
Nexus1010(config)# virtual-service-blade vsm
```

5. Specify the Nexus 1000V VSM iso image:

```
Nexus1010(config-vsb-config)# virtual-service-blade-type new nexus-
1000v.4.2.1.SV1.5.1a.iso
Nexus1010(config-vsb-config)# show virtual-service-blade summary
```

6. Verify the VSM was created. Notice that the primary and secondary VSMs created as the Nexus 1010 are an HA pair:

```
Nexus1010(config-vsb-config)# show virtual-service-blade summary
-------------------------------------------------------------------------------
Name                HA-Role      HA-Status    Status                Location
-------------------------------------------------------------------------------
vsm                 PRIMARY      NONE         VSB NOT PRESENT       PRIMARY
vsm                 SECONDARY    NONE         VSB NOT PRESENT       SECONDARY
virtual-service-blade vsm
  Description:
  Slot id:        1
  Host Name:
  Management IP:
  VSB Type Name :  VSM-1.1
  vCPU:           1
  Ramsize:        2048
  Disksize:       3
  Heartbeat:      0
       ---------------------------------------------------------------------
       Interface         Type  VLAN       State          Uplink-Interface
                                      Primary  Secondary   Oper   Admin
       ---------------------------------------------------------------------
  VsbEthernet1/1    control    0        up          up      Po2    Po2
  VsbEthernet1/2    management 182      up          up      Po1    Po1
  VsbEthernet1/3    packet     0        up          up      Po2    Po2
       internal              NA   NA      up          up
  HA Role: Primary
    HA Status: NONE
    Status:       VSB NOT PRESENT
    Location:     PRIMARY
    SW version:
  HA Role: Secondary
    HA Status: NONE
    Status:       VSB NOT PRESENT
    Location:     SECONDARY
    SW version:
  VSB Info:
Nexus1010(config-vsb-config)#
```

7. Specify the control and packet VLANs for the VSM Virtual Service Blade (VSB).

```
Nexus1010(config-vsb-config)# interface control vlan 102
Nexus1010(config-vsb-config)# interface packet vlan 102
```

8. Configure the VSM VSB specific information:

```
Nexus1010(config-vsb-config)# enable
Enter vsb image: [nexus-1000v.4.2.1.SV1.5.1a.iso]
Enter domain id[1-4095]: 989
Management IP version [V4/V6]: [V4]
Enter Management IP address: 10.86.182.152
Enter Management subnet mask: 255.255.255.0
IPv4 address of the default gateway: 10.86.182.254
Enter HostName: vsm
Enter the password for 'admin': Cisco123
```

Note VSB installation is in progress; please use **show virtual-service-blade** commands to check the installation status:

```
Nexus1010(config-vsb-config)#
```

9. Verify the VSM VSB status and HA information:

```
Nexus1010# show virtual-service-blade name vsm
virtual-service-blade vsm
  Description:
  Slot id:        1
  Host Name:      vsm
  Management IP:  10.86.182.152
  VSB Type Name : VSM-1.1
  vCPU:           1
  Ramsize:        2048
  Disksize:       3
  Heartbeat:      183
  --------------------------------------------------------------------
```

Interface	Type	VLAN	State		Uplink-Interface	
			Primary	Secondary	Oper	Admin
VsbEthernet1/1	control	102	up	up	Po2	Po2
VsbEthernet1/2	management	182	up	up	Po1	Po1
VsbEthernet1/3	packet	102	up	up	Po2	Po2
internal		NA	NA	up	up	

```
HA Role: Primary
```

```
   HA Status: ACTIVE
   Status:      VSB POWERED ON
   Location:    PRIMARY
   SW version:  4.2(1)SV1(5.1a)
 HA Role: Secondary
   HA Status: STANDBY
   Status:      VSB POWERED ON
   Location:    SECONDARY
   SW version:  4.2(1)SV1(5.1a)
 VSB Info:
   Domain ID : 989
Nexus1010#
```

10. Log in to the VSM Nexux 1010 VSB:

```
Nexus1010# login virtual-service-blade vsm
Telnet escape character is '^\'.
Trying 127.1.0.18...
Connected to 127.1.0.18.
Escape character is '^\'.

Nexus 1000v Switch
vsm login: admin
Password:
Cisco Nexus Operating System (NX-OS) Software
TAC support: http://www.cisco.com/tac
Copyright (c) 2002-2012, Cisco Systems, Inc. All rights reserved.
The copyrights to certain works contained in this software are
owned by other third parties and used and distributed under
license. Certain components of this software are licensed under
the GNU General Public License (GPL) version 2.0 or the GNU
Lesser General Public License (LGPL) Version 2.1. A copy of each
such license is available at
http://www.opensource.org/licenses/gpl-2.0.php and
http://www.opensource.org/licenses/lgpl-2.1.php
vsm#
```

11. Verify management 0 interface status:

```
vsm# show int mgmt 0
mgmt0 is up
   Hardware: Ethernet, address: 0002.3d72.2b02 (bia 0002.3d72.2b02)
   Internet Address is 10.86.182.152/24
   MTU 1500 bytes, BW 1000000 Kbit, DLY 10 usec,
      reliability 255/255, txload 1/255, rxload 1/255
```

```
Encapsulation ARPA
full-duplex, 1000 Mb/s
Auto-Negotiation is turned on
1 minute input rate 8088 bits/sec, 9 packets/sec
1 minute output rate 4344 bits/sec, 1 packets/sec
Rx
    3239 input packets 312 unicast packets 264 multicast packets
    2663 broadcast packets 338778 bytes
Tx
    325 output packets 310 unicast packets 7 multicast packets
    8 broadcast packets 26312 bytes
```

12. Verify the svs domain:

```
vsm# show svs domain
SVS domain config:
  Domain id:    989
  Control vlan: 102
  Packet vlan:  102
  L2/L3 Control mode: L2
  L3 control interface:  NA
  Status: Config not pushed to VC.
vsm#
```

Note   The configuration has not been pushed to virtual center as the status is "Config not pushed to VC," so the configuration needs to be completed.

Registering the Nexus 1000V Plug-In to VMware Virtual Center Management Application

The VSM maintains a communication link to VMware vCenter Server. The communication link is used to maintain definitions and propagate port profiles to the VMware virtual center. The Cisco Nexus 1000V uses a VMware vCenter Server plug-in to properly display a representation of the Cisco Nexus 1000V. The Cisco Nexus 1000V plug-in is an XML file that is downloaded from the VSM's management IP address using a web browser; the XML plug-in must be installed before the VSM can communicate to the VMware vCenter Server. A common question is, "What if the connection between the VSM and VMware virtual center goes down?" If the connection between the VSM and VMware vCenter Server is disrupted, changes made on the VSM will not be propagated to VMware Virtual Center; the VEMs will still continue to forward traffic on the data plane. The VSM ensures that any configuration changes have been made during this period of disruption; the changes will be propagated when the communication link is restored.

1. Obtain the IP address/DNS information of the Virtual Center Server. The following example shows how to verify IP Address/DNS host information on the VMWare vCenter server:

```
C:\Documents and Settings\Administrator>ipconfig
Windows IP Configuration


Ethernet adapter vCenter Server:

    Connection-specific DNS Suffix  . :
    IP Address. . . . . . . . . . . : 10.86.182.234
    Subnet Mask . . . . . . . . . . : 255.255.255.0
    Default Gateway . . . . . . . . : 10.1.4.1
```

2. Verify IP connectivity between the VMware virtual center management station and the Cisco 1000V, as demonstrated in the following example:

```
vsm# ping 10.86.182.234
PING 10.86.182.234 (10.86.182.234): 56 data bytes
64 bytes from 10.86.182.234: icmp_seq=0 ttl=124 time=1.201 ms
64 bytes from 10.86.182.234: icmp_seq=1 ttl=124 time=1.196 ms
64 bytes from 10.86.182.234: icmp_seq=2 ttl=124 time=0.914 ms
64 bytes from 10.86.182.234: icmp_seq=3 ttl=124 time=0.917 ms
64 bytes from 10.86.182.234: icmp_seq=4 ttl=124 time=0.958 ms

--- 10.86.182.234 ping statistics ---
5 packets transmitted, 5 packets received, 0.00% packet loss
round-trip min/avg/max = 0.914/1.037/1.201 ms
vsm#
```

3. From the virtual center desktop, launch your web browser, and point to the management interface of the Nexus 1000V VSM, as demonstrated in Figure 9-4.

4. Under the section "Cisco Nexus 1000V Extension," right mouse-click and save the file named *cisco_nexus_1000v_extension.xml* to your desktop, as demonstrated in Figure 9-5.

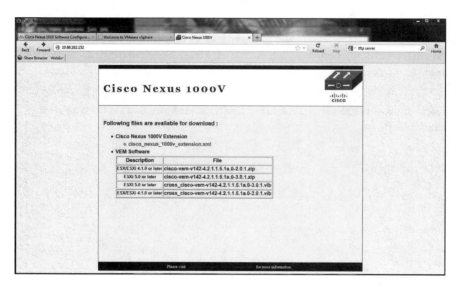

Figure 9-4 *Launching the Web Browser on the vCenter Server and Pointing to the mgmt0 Interface of the VSM*

Figure 9-5 *Saving the cisco_nexus_1000v_extension.xml File from the VSM*

5. Go back to VMware Virtual Center management application and select **Plug-ins > Manage Plug-Ins**, as shown in Figure 9-6.

6. Right-click under **Available Plug-ins** and select **New Plug-In**, as demonstrated in Figure 9-7.

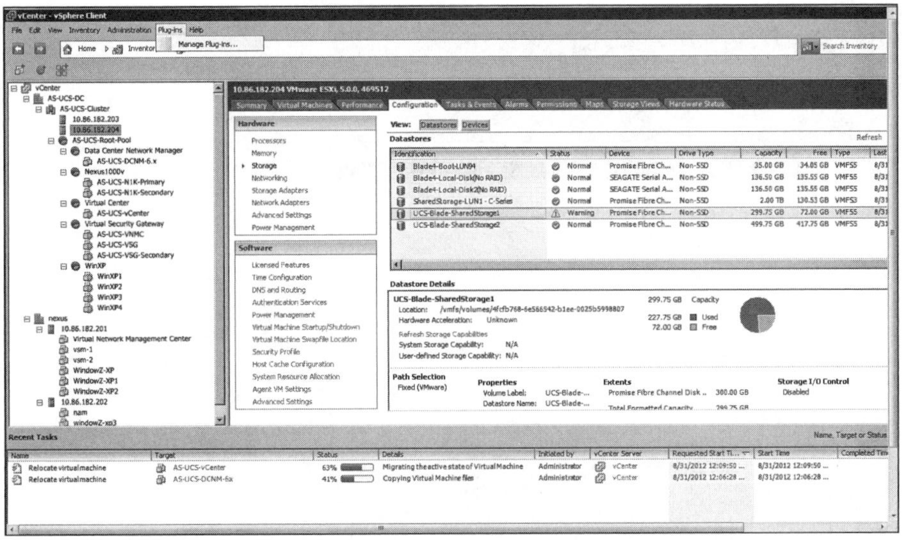

Figure 9-6   *Selecting the Plug-Ins Menu Option from vCenter*

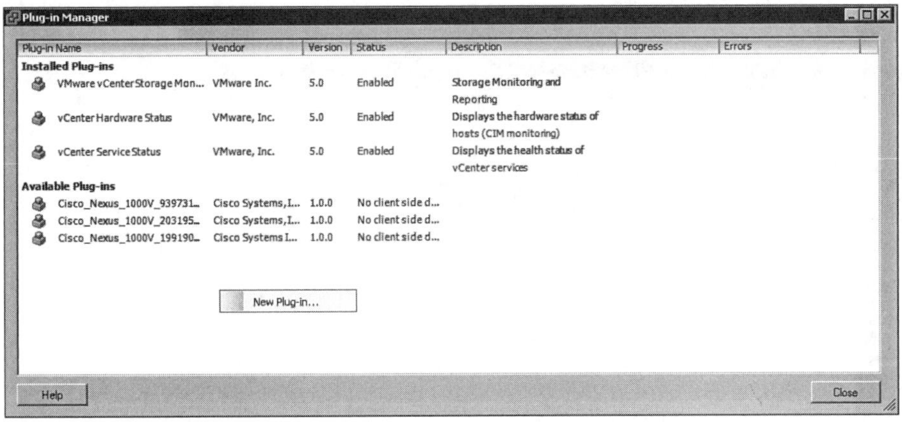

Figure 9-7   *Creating a New Managed Plug-In from vCenter*

7. The Register Plug-In window appears. As shown in Figure 9-8, select the browse button and find the file downloaded in step 4, cisco_nexus_1000v_extension.xml.

8. The Register Plug-In window appears. Click the **Register Plug-In** button, as shown in Figure 9-9.

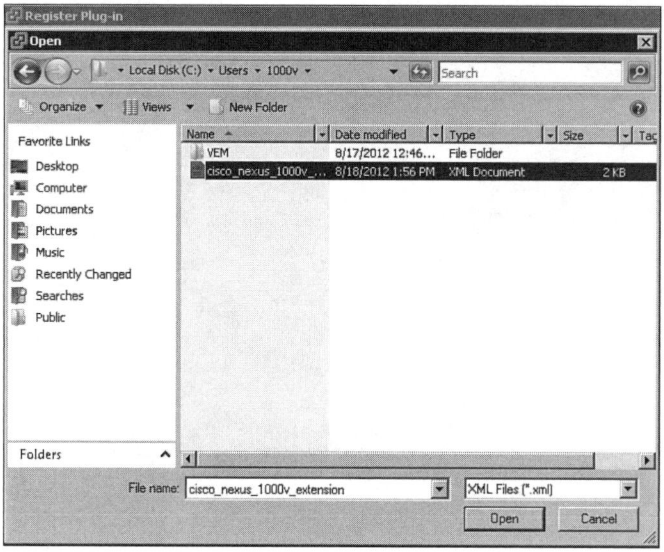

Figure 9-8   *Browsing for the cisco_nexus_1000v_extension.xml File That Was Downloaded to the Desktop in Step 4*

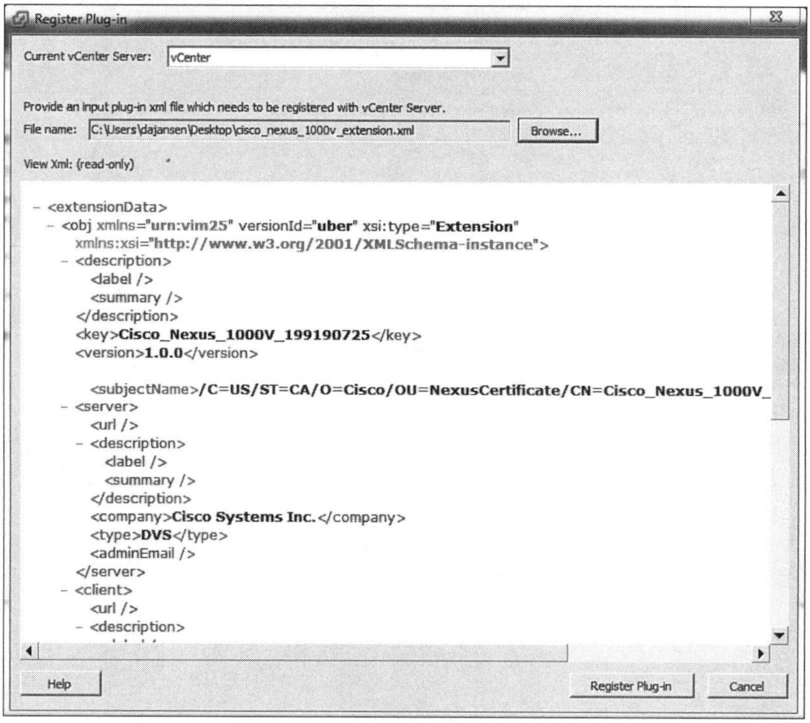

Figure 9-9   *Registering the Plug-In*

9. The Security Warning dialog box appears, as there is a new SSL cert being installed. Click the **Ignore** button. Figure 9-10 shows the certificate Security Warning dialog box.

10. You should receive a successful Register Plug-In window, as shown in Figure 9-11. Click **OK** to close this window.

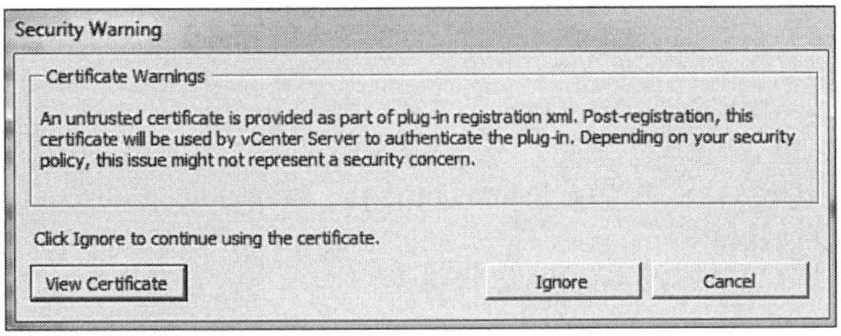

Figure 9-10   *Certificate Security Warning Dialog Box*

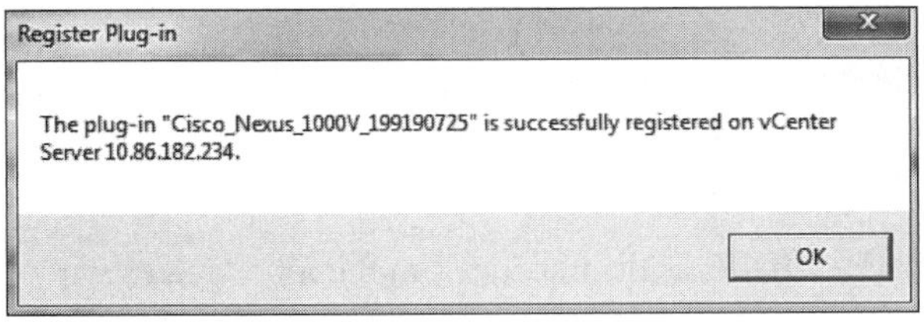

Figure 9-11   *Successful Register Plug-In Dialog Box*

Configuring the SVS Domain and Networking Characteristics

A domain ID is a parameter of the Cisco Nexus 1000V Series that is used to identify a VSM and VEM. The domain ID of the Cisco Nexus 1000V is defined when the VSM is first installed and becomes part of the opaque data that is transmitted to VMware vCenter Server. Each command sent by the VSM to any associated VEMs is tagged with this domain ID. When a VSM and VEM share the same domain ID, the VEM accepts and responds to requests and commands from the VSM. If the VEM receives a command or configuration request that is not tagged with the proper domain ID, that request is ignored. Similarly, if the VSM receives a packet from a VEM that is tagged with the wrong domain ID, it will be ignored.

1. Open the Nexus 1000V VSM Virtual Machine Console window or Telnet to the VSM MGMT0 Interface. The following example shows how to Telnet to the IP address of the mgmt0 interface:

```
vsm login: admin
Password:
Cisco Nexus Operating System (NX-OS) Software
TAC support: http://www.cisco.com/tac
Copyright (c) 2002-2009, Cisco Systems, Inc. All rights reserved.
```

```
The copyrights to certain works contained in this software are
owned by other third parties and used and distributed under
license. Certain components of this software are licensed under
the GNU General Public License (GPL) version 2.0 or the GNU
Lesser General Public License (LGPL) Version 2.1. A copy of each
such license is available at
http://www.opensource.org/licenses/gpl-2.0.php and
http://www.opensource.org/licenses/lgpl-2.1.php
vsm#
```

2. Configure the SVS domain ID on the VSM as demonstrated in the following example (in this case, the domain ID is 100):

```
vsm# conf t
vsm(config)# svs-domain
vsm(config-svs-domain)#  domain id 100
vsm(config)# exit
vsm# copy running-config startup-config
[#######################################] 100%
vsm#
```

3. Configure the Control and Packet VLANs as demonstrated in the following example:

```
vsm# conf t
vsm(config)# svs-domain
vsm(config-svs-domain)#  control vlan 700
vsm(config-svs-domain)#  packet vlan 701
vsm(config-svs-domain)#  svs mode L2
vsm(config-svs-domain)# exit
vsm(config)# exit
vsm# copy running-config startup-config
[#######################################] 100%
vsm#
```

Connecting the Nexus 1000V VSM to the vCenter Server

After the plug-in is installed, the network administrator can define the SVS connection. The SVS connection defines the link between the VSM and VMware vCenter Server. The connection contains the following parameters:

- VMware vCenter Server IP address

- Communication protocol (always VMware VIM over HTTPS)

- Name of the VMware data center in which the VMware ESX hosts reside

The Nexus 1000V plug-in must be registered before you connect it to the vCenter server.

1. SSH Telnet to the VSM mgmt0 interface, as demonstrated in the following example:

```
vsm login: admin
Password:
Cisco Nexus Operating System (NX-OS) Software
TAC support: http://www.cisco.com/tac
Copyright (c) 2002-2009, Cisco Systems, Inc. All rights reserved.
The copyrights to certain works contained in this software are
owned by other third parties and used and distributed under
license. Certain components of this software are licensed under
the GNU General Public License (GPL) version 2.0 or the GNU
Lesser General Public License (LGPL) Version 2.1. A copy of each
such license is available at
http://www.opensource.org/licenses/gpl-2.0.php and
http://www.opensource.org/licenses/lgpl-2.1.php
vsm#
```

2. Configure the connection on the Nexus 1000V VSM:

```
vsm#config t
vsm (confgi)# svs connection nexus
vsm(config-svs-conn)# protocol vmware-vim
vsm(config-svs-conn)# remote ip address 10.86.182.234
vsm(config-svs-conn)# vmware dvs datacenter-name nexus
vsm(config-svs-conn)# connect
```

3. After issuing the **connect** command, verify output on the vCenter server as demonstrated in the following example:

```
vsm# show svs connections
connection nexus:
    ip address: 10.86.182.234
    remote port: 80
    protocol: vmware-vim https
    certificate: default
    datacenter name: nexus
    admin:
    max-ports: 8192
    DVS uuid: ed 5d 0b 50 26 85 42 50-73 78 8e 28 b9 e6 36 dd
    config status: Enabled
    operational status: Connected
    sync status: Complete
    version: VMware vCenter Server 5.0.0 build-623373
    vc-uuid: 726028B9-F168-404A-B038-41CBFC66F3A6
vsm#.
```

Nexus 1000V Installation Management Center

Nexus 1000V software release 4.2.1.SV1.5.1a introduces a standalone Management Center application to reduce the installation and configuration time. The Nexus 1000V installation management center provides initial configuration for the following operations:

- Creating the SVS connection between the VSM and vCenter

- Creating VMware port groups for Control, Packet, and Management

- Creating the Control, Packet, and Management VLANs including Layer 2 or Layer 3 control between the VEM and the VSM

- Instaling HA pair of VSMs

- Enabling SSH and configuring the SSH connection

- Enabling the option to Telnet on the VSM

- Creating a Cisco Nexus 1000V plug-in and registering it on the vCenter server

- Migrating the host and network interfaces to the Cisco VEM

- VEM installation

- Installing VEM

During the Nexus 1000V OVF/OVA deployment, select **Nexus 1000V Installer**; all other steps are the same as described in the manual installation process.

Figure 9-12 shows how to launch the Nexus1000V-launchPad.jar file that was extracted from the Nexus1000v.4.2.1.SV1.5.2.zip downloaded from www.cisco.com; Nexus1000v.4.2.1.SV1.5.2.zip\Nexus1000v.4.2.1.SV1.5.2\VSM\Installer_App/Nexus1000V-launchPad.jar to start the application.

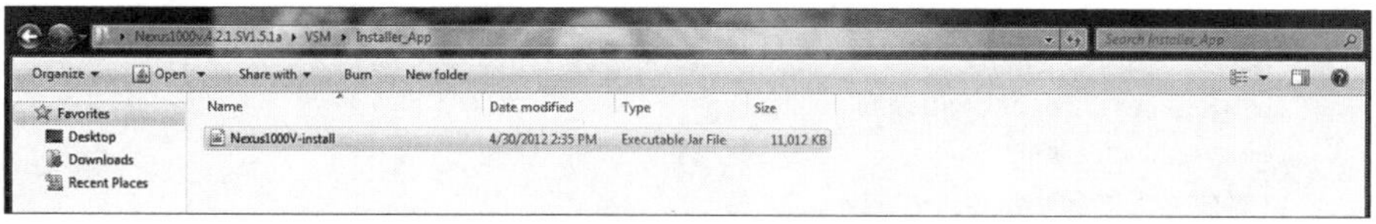

Figure 9-12 *How to Start the Nexus1000V-launchPad.jar Application to Install the VSM*

After the application download completes, the Nexus 1000V Management Center Application window appears and prompts for three options:

- VSM (Virtual Supervisor Module) Installation

- VEM (Virtual Ethernet Module) Installation

- VC (VMWare Virtual Center) Installation

Select VSM Installation, as shown in Figure 9-13.

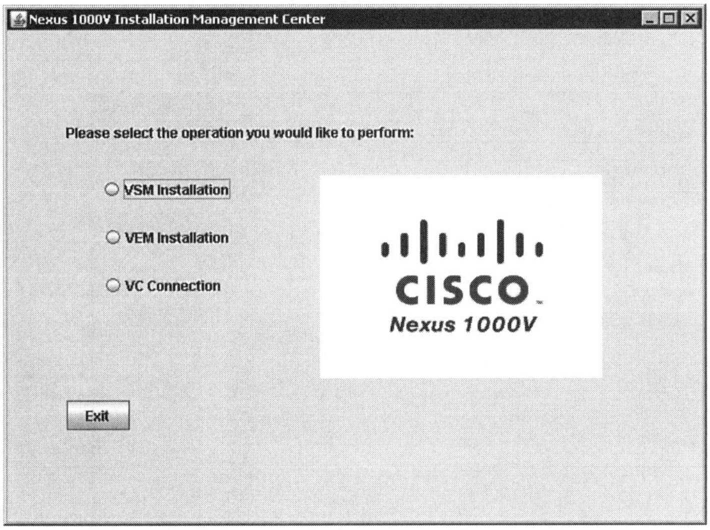

Figure 9-13   *VSM Installation Option to Install the VSM on an ESX Host*

Figure 9-14 shows how to enter the VMWare vCenter IP Address information, vCenter administrator username, and password.

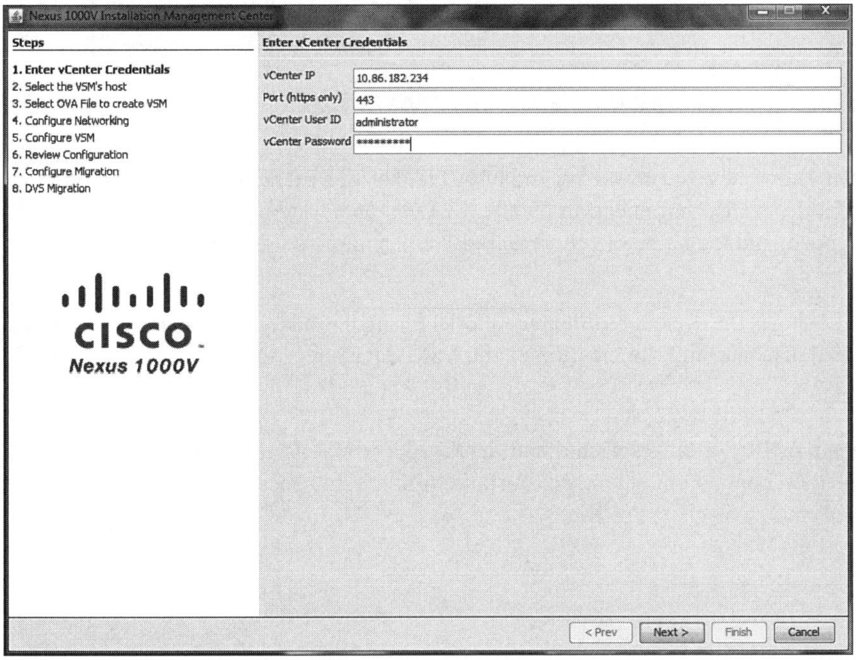

Figure 9-14   *Entering the VMWare vCenter IP Address Information, vCenter Administrator Username, and Password*

As shown in Figure 9-15, select the ESX host from vCenter inventory to install the Nexus 1000v VSM.

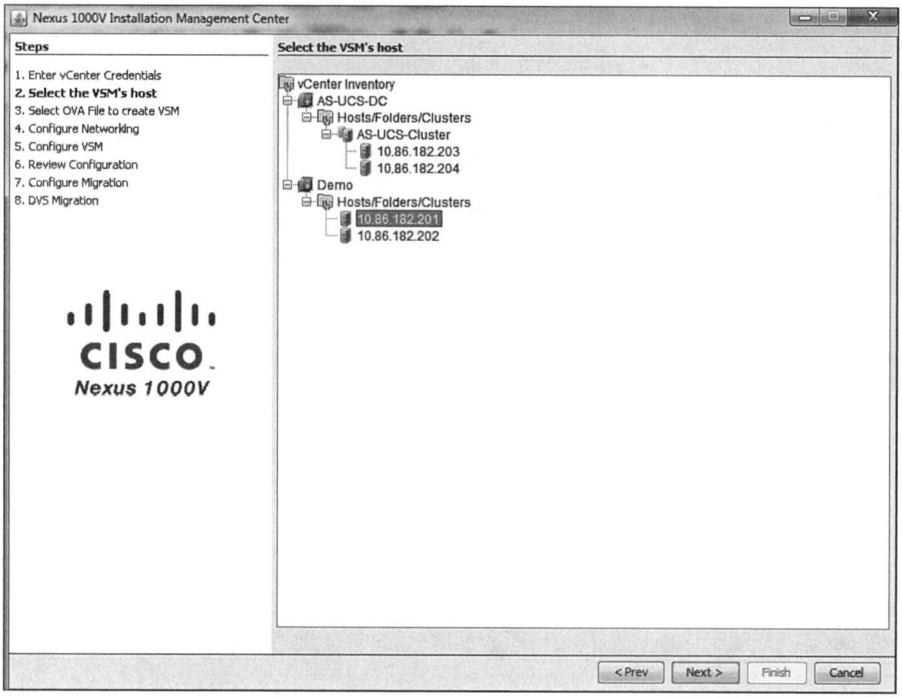

Figure 9-15   *Selecting the ESX Host to Install the Nexus 1000v VSM*

Figure 9-16 shows how to browse for the OVA file that was extracted from the Zip file downloaded from Cisco Connection Online (CCO); select system redundancy mode (HA Recommended) and the name of the virtual machine and the datastore for the virtual machine.

Figure 9-17 shows the system redundancy model for high availability, the name of the VSM virtual machine, and the location of the VSM datastore.

Note   When the HA option is selected and deployed, the Nexus 1000V Management Center Installation application will install both the primary and secondary VSM(s) on the same ESX selected.

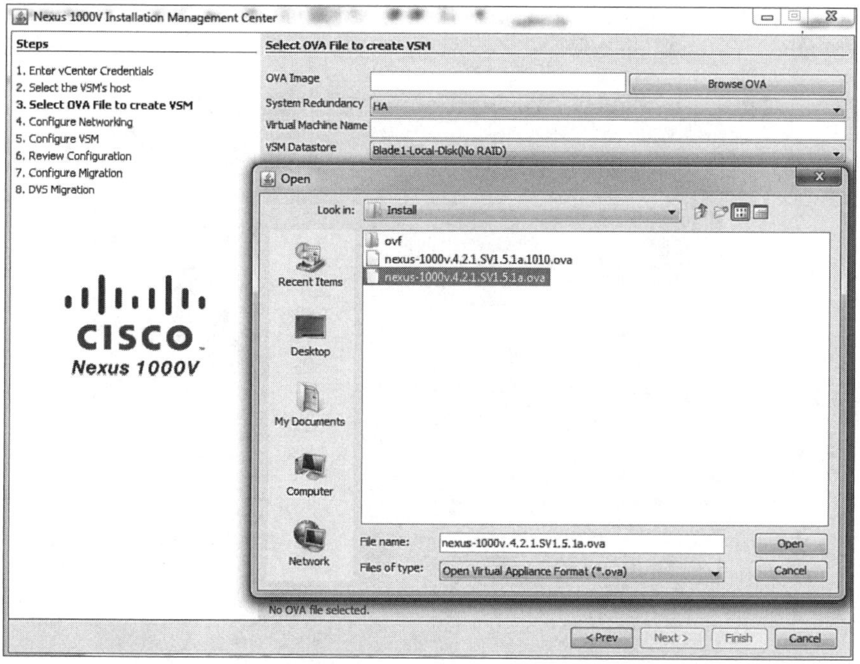

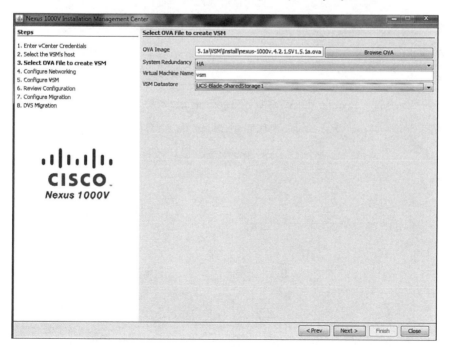

Figure 9-16 *The OVA File and VSM Role of HA for Deployment*

Figure 9-17 *System Redundancy Model for High Availability, the Name of the VSM VM, and VSM Datastore Location*

Figure 9-18 shows how to configure the networking VLANs and Layer 2 or Layer 3 control between the VEMs and the VSM.

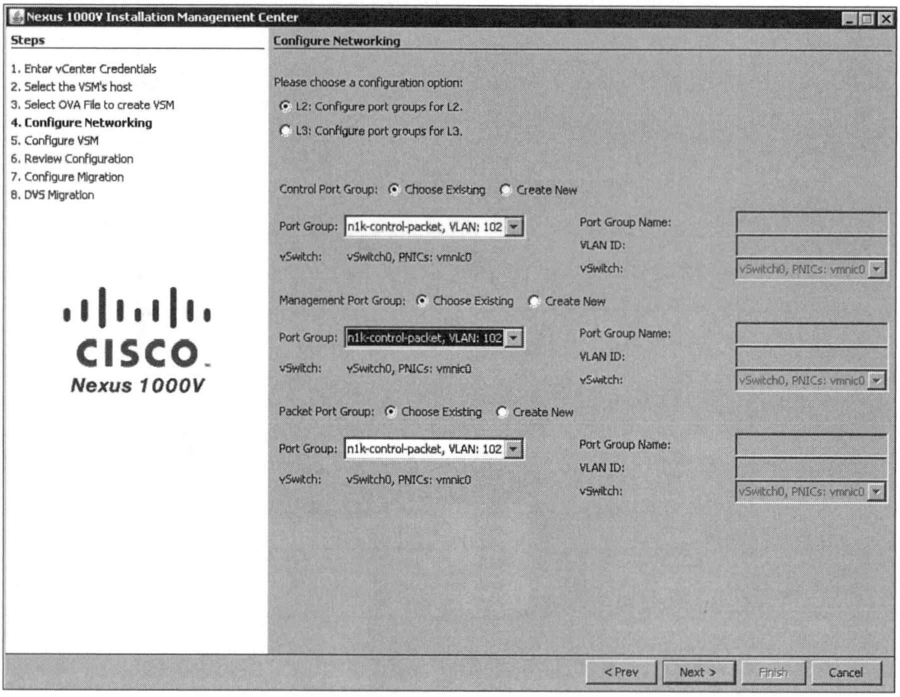

Figure 9-18   *Configuring the Networking VLANs and Layer 2 or Layer 3 Control Between the VEMs and the VSM*

Figure 9-19 shows how to enter the VSM configuration attributes for deployment.

Figure 9-20 shows all the VSM configuration attributes that will be deployed for this VSM.

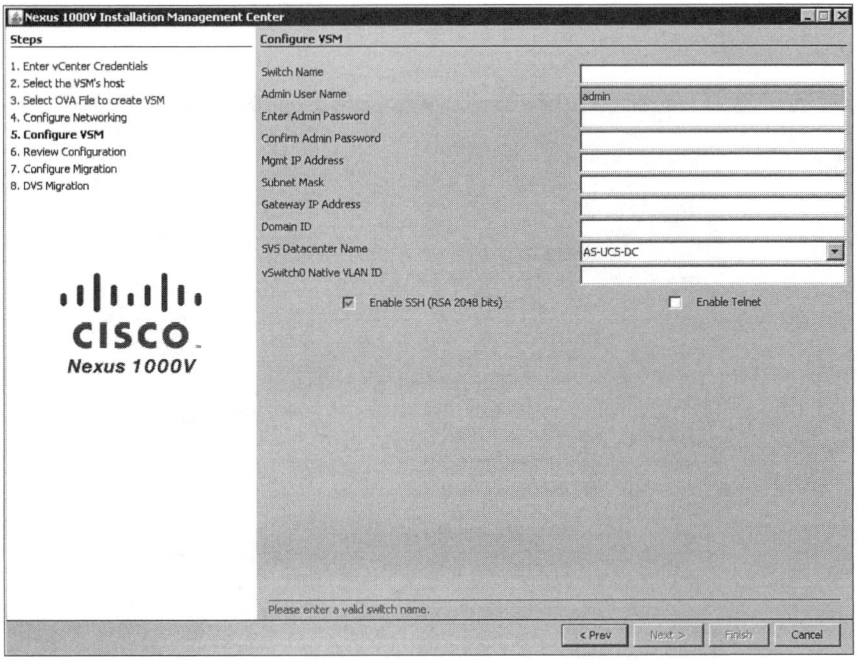

Figure 9-19 *Entering the VSM Configuration Attributes for Deployment*

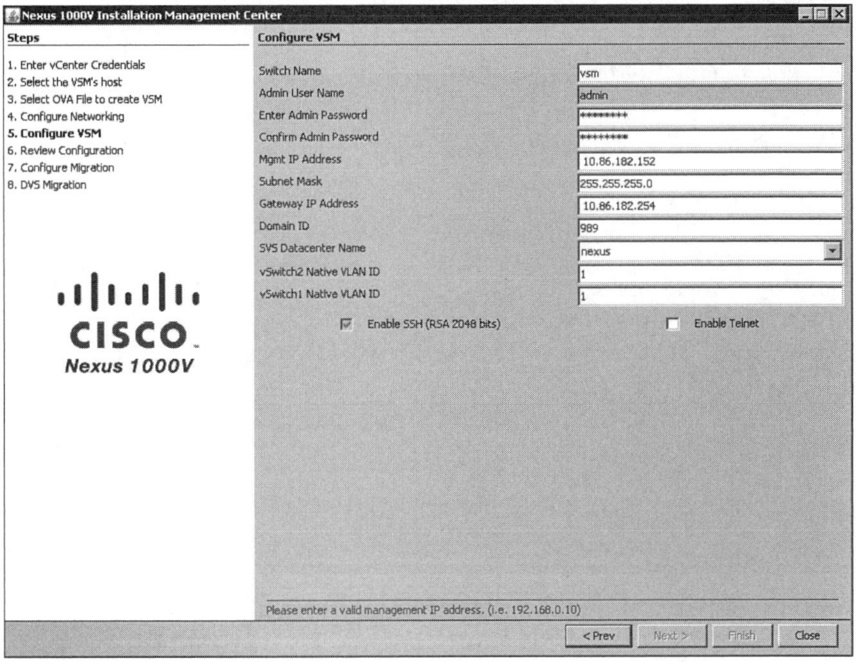

Figure 9-20 *VSM Configuration Attributes*

Figure 9-21 shows the configuration summary to review before deployment and creation on the virtual machine.

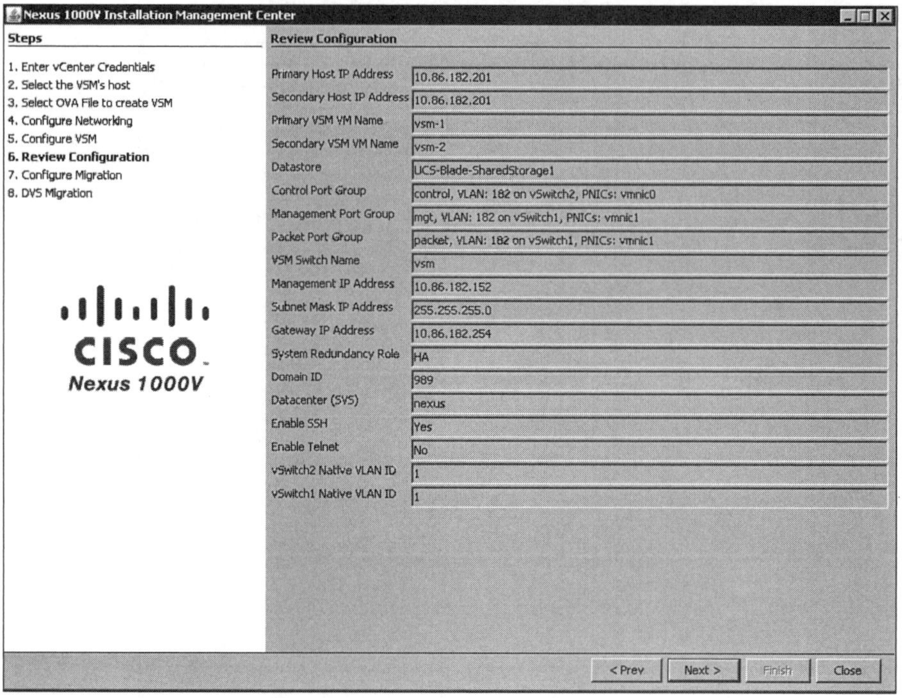

Figure 9-21   *Reviewing the VSM Configuration Summary*

Figure 9-22 shows the VSM installation progress.

Figure 9-23 shows the configuration host migration to the Cisco 1000V DVS.

Note   The question, "Would you like to migrate this host and its networks to the DVS?" was answered **No**. This will be performed manually later in this section. If you want to migrate interfaces during the installation, click **Yes**; you will be prompted to enter IP Address and subnet mask for the vmknic interface.

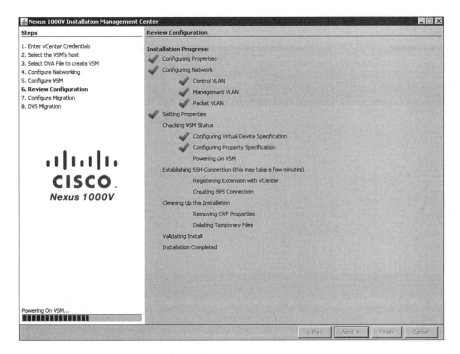

Figure 9-22 *VSM Installation Process*

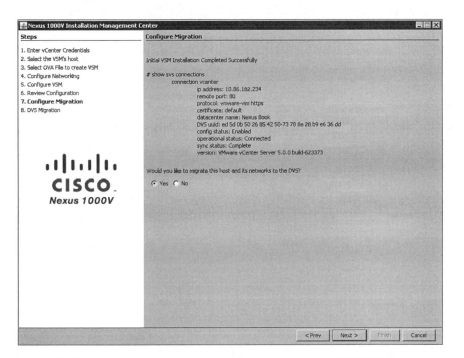

Figure 9-23 *Configuration Host Migration to the Cisco 1000V DVS*

Figure 9-24 shows the installation summary.

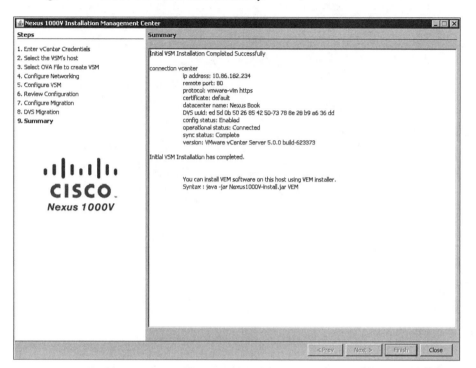

Figure 9-24   *VSM Installation Summary*

The Nexus 1000V Installation Management Center application significantly reduces the installation time. The application includes HA deployment, and Layer 3 Control configuration.

To verify the Virtual Supervisor Module (VSM) High Availability State, issue the commands in Example 9-1.

Example 9-1 displays the HA VSM pair deployed on the ESX host.

Example 9-1   *Displaying the HA VSM Pair Deployed on the ESX Host*

```
vsm# show system redundancy status
Redundancy role
---------------
        administrative:   primary
          operational:   primary


Redundancy mode
--------------
        administrative:   HA
```

```
        operational:   HA

This supervisor (sup-1)
-----------------------

    Redundancy state:   Active
    Supervisor state:   Active
      Internal state:   Active with HA standby


Other supervisor (sup-2)
-----------------------

    Redundancy state:   Standby
    Supervisor state:   HA standby
      Internal state:   HA standby
vsm#
```

Figure 9-25 shows the VSM HA pair deployed on the ESX selected during the Installation Wizard.

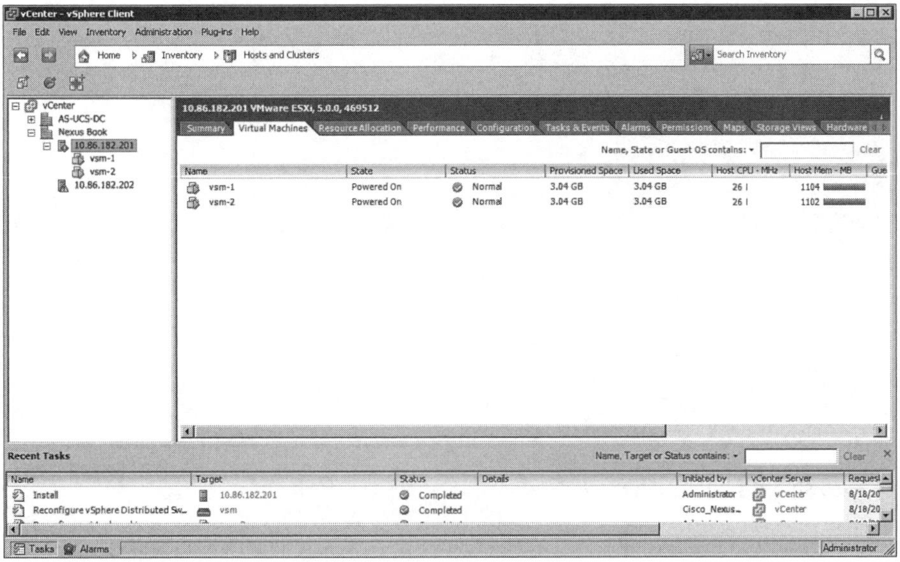

Figure 9-25   *Displaying the VSM HA Pair Deployed on the ESX*

VEM Installation Option on the Nexus 1000V Management Installation Center

The following process will copy the VEM bits to the ESX hosts selected during the Nexus 1000v Management Center.

> **Note** For the ESX host that the VSM was installed on, the VEM software was installed on the host during the VSM installation. In addition, only select the ESX hosts in VMWare vCenter Data Center container to install the VEM bits to.

The Nexus 1000V Management Installation Center Application VEM Installation option assumes that the ESX host does not have any pre-installed VEM bits on the host.

Figure 9-26 shows the Nexus 1000V Installation Management Center start page to select the VEM installation.

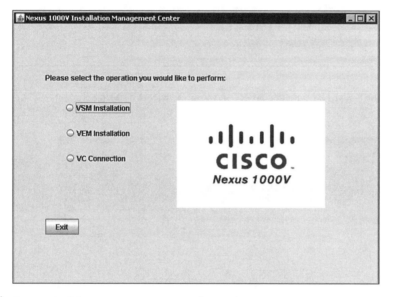

Figure 9-26 *Nexus 1000V Installation Management Center Start Page to Select the VEM Installation*

Figure 9-27 shows how to enter the vCenter information and user ID information.

Figure 9-28 shows how to enter the Nexus 1000V VSM information.

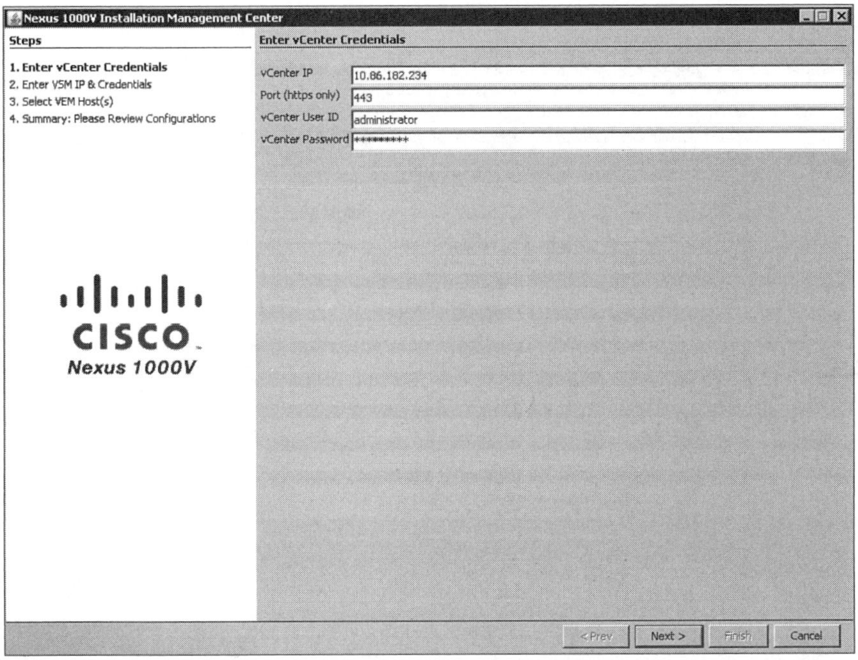

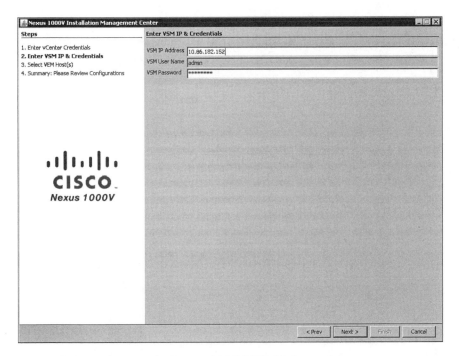

Figure 9-27 *Entering the vCenter Information and User ID Information*

Figure 9-28 *Entering the Nexus 1000V VSM Information*

Next, select the ESX host to install the VEM, as shown in Figure 9-29.

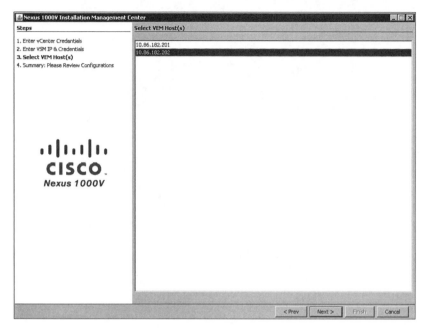

Figure 9-29   *Selecting the ESX Host to Install the VEM*

Figure 9-30 shows the summary configuration.

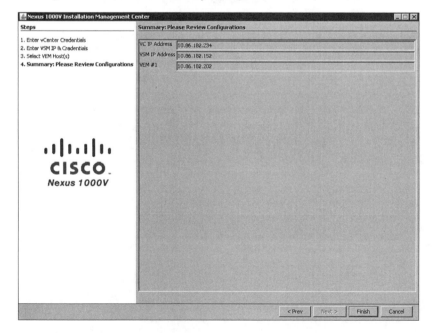

Figure 9-30   *VEM Configuration Summary*

vCenter Connection Option on the Nexus 1000V Management Installation Center

Figure 9-31 shows how to enter the vCenter information for the plug-in installation.

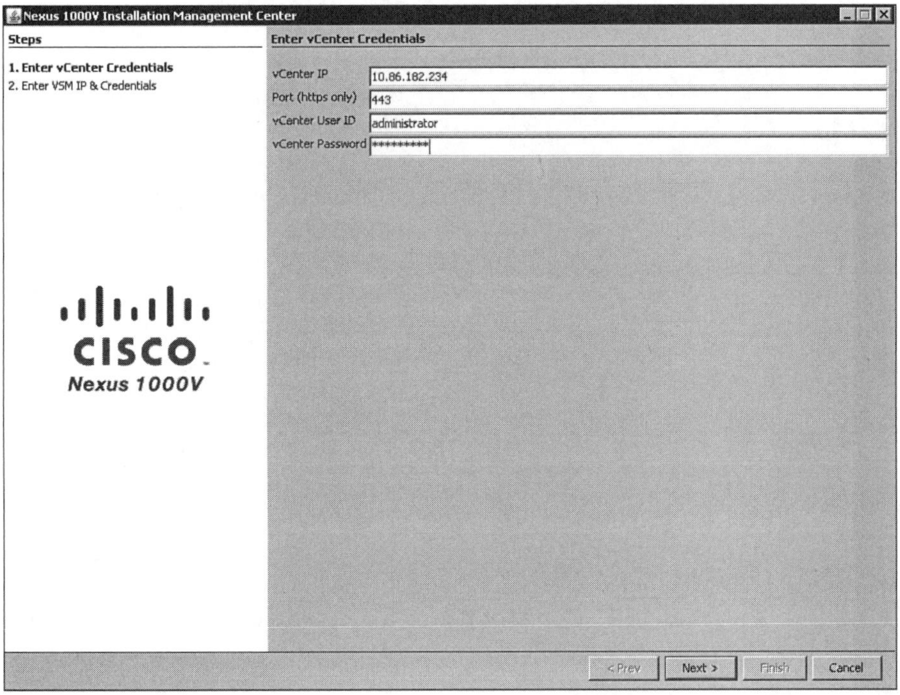

Figure 9-31   *Entering the vCenter Information for the Plug-In Installation*

Figure 9-32 shows how to configure the Nexus 1000V VSM information.

The administrator can also manually copy the VEM bits from the VSM to the ESX host with the following procedure:

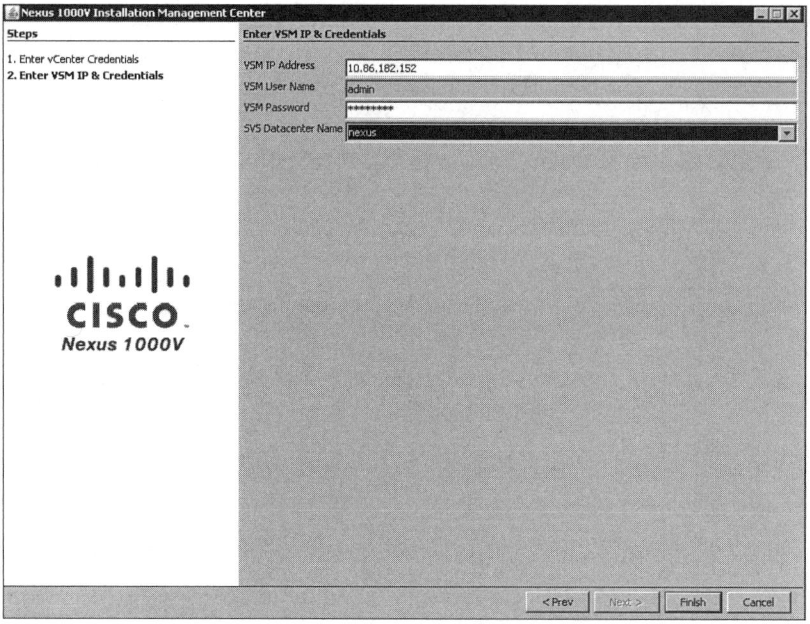

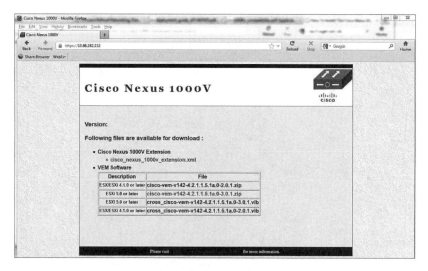

Figure 9-32 *Configuring the Nexus 1000V VSM Information*

Obtain the VEM VIB bits from the VSM for the ESX version you are running. You can point your web browser to the IP address of the VSM and download it that way or from the ESX CLI:

■ Browse the VSM to download the image, as shown in Figure 9-33. The VEM bits need to be copied to the following location on the ESC host: /var/log/vmware.

Figure 9-33 *Nexus 1000v VSM Main Page*

■ Use the ESX command line to get the image from the VSM to the ESX host. The VEM bits need to be copied to the following location on the ESX host: /var/log/ vmware

```
/var/log/vmware # wget http://10.86.182.152/cisco/vibs/VEM/4.1.0/VEM-4.1.0-patch01/
cross_cisco-vem-v142-4.2.1.1.5.1a.0-3.0.1.vib

Connecting to 10.86.182.152 (10.86.182.152:80)

cross_cisco-vem-v142 100% |*********************************************************
**********|  3627k --:--:-- ETA
```

```
/var/log/vmware # ls
cross_cisco-vem-v142-4.2.1.1.5.1a.0-3.0.1.vib
```

```
/var/log/vmware # esxcli software vib install -v /var/log/vmware/cross_cisco-vem-
v142-4.2.1.1.5.1a.0-3.0.1.vib
Installation Result
Message: Operation finished successfully.
Reboot Required: false
VIBs Installed: Cisco_bootbank_cisco-vem-v142-esx_4.2.1.1.5.1a.0-3.0.1
VIBs Removed:
VIBs Skipped:
```

```
/var/log/vmware # vem status -v
Package vssnet-esxmn-ga-release
Version 4.2.1.1.5.1a.0-3.0.1
Build 1
Date Wed Apr 25 21:31:48 PDT 2012

Number of PassThru NICs are 0
VEM modules are loaded

Switch Name     Num Ports    Used Ports   Configured Ports   MTU     Uplinks
vSwitch0        128          2            128                1500    vmnic1
DVS Name        Num Ports    Used Ports   Configured Ports   MTU     Uplinks
vsm             256          15           256                1500    vmnic0

Number of PassThru NICs are 0
VEM Agent (vemdpa) is running
```

Creating the Uplink Profile

VMWare has a vNetwork Distributed Switch (DVS) switch. The Cisco VEM plugs directly into the VMWare DVS. The DVS functionality spans many ESX/ESXi hosts. The DVS reduces network maintenance, increases network capacity, and enables virtual machines to maintain consistent network configuration. Before you can add a host to the DVS on vCenter Server, you must first create an uplink port profile. This will enable a VEM to be added to the VSM. Example 9-2 shows the Layer 2 communication mode between the VSM and the VEMs via the Control and Packet VLANs.

Note   You can find a feature comparison of the virtual networking features of the VMware vNetwork Distributed Switch and Cisco Nexus 1000V Switches at Cisco.com in the following document: http://tinyurl.com/cpfot2.

Example 9-2   *Verifying Control and Packet System VLANs, Which Are Used for VEM-to-VSM Communication*

```
vsm
vsm# show vlan
VLAN Name                             Status    Ports
---- -------------------------------- --------- ------------------------------
1    default                          active
102  control-packet                   active
103  GuestOS                          active
104  DB                               active
105  App                              active
182  mgt-vmk                          active


VLAN Type
---- -----
1    enet
102  enet
103  enet
104  enet
105  enet
182  enet


Remote SPAN VLANs
-------------------------------------------------------------------------------


Primary  Secondary  Type             Ports
-------  ---------  ---------------  -----------------------------------------

vsm#
```

Example 9-3 shows how to create the uplink profile on the Nexus 1000V VSM, the port-profile will be named "uplink" in this example.

Example 9-3 *Creating the Uplink Profile on the Nexus 1000V VSM*

```
vsm# conf t
vsm(config)# port-profile uplink
vsm(config-port-prof)# capability uplink
vsm(config-port-prof)# switchport mode trunk
vsm(config-port-prof)# switchport trunk allowed vlan 100, 699, 700, 701, 702
vsm(config-port-prof)# no shutdown
vsm(config-port-prof)# system vlan 700, 701
vsm(config-port-prof)# VMware port-group
vsm(config-port-prof)# state enabled
vsm# conf t
vsm (config)# port-profile type ethernet uplink
vsm (config-port-prof)# vmware port-group
vsm (config-port-prof)# switchport mode trunk
vsm (config-port-prof)# switchport trunk allowed vlan 102-105,182
vsm (config-port-prof)# mtu 9000
vsm (config-port-prof)# no shutdown
vsm (config-port-prof)# system vlan 102-103,182
vsm (config-port-prof)# state enabled
```

The output in Example 9-4 verifies the port-profile "uplink" configuration.

Example 9-4 *Verifying Port-Profile "Uplink" Configuration*

```
vsm# show port-profile name uplink

port-profile uplink
 type: Ethernet
 description:
 status: enabled
 max-ports: 32
 min-ports: 1
 inherit:
 config attributes:
  switchport mode trunk
  switchport trunk allowed vlan 102-105,182
  mtu 9000
  no shutdown
 evaluated config attributes:
  switchport mode trunk
  switchport trunk allowed vlan 102-105,182
```

```
   mtu 9000
   no shutdown
  assigned interfaces:
port-group: uplink
  system vlans: 102-103,182
  capability l3control: no
  capability iscsi-multipath: no
  capability vxlan: no
  capability l3-vn-service: no
  port-profile role: none
  port-binding: static

vsm# copy running-config startup-config
[#######################################] 100%
vsm#
```

Note   In the previous example, if the optional **VMware port-group uplink** *name* command was used in the port-profile configuration, the *name* parameter would specify the name that is displayed in the vCenter Server. If the command is not used, the port-profile name will be used.

Adding the VEM to a ESX vSphere Host

The VEM provides the Cisco Nexus 1000V Series with network connectivity and for-warding capabilities, and each VEM acts as an independent switch from a forwarding perspective. The VEM is tightly integrated with VMware ESX and is installed on each. To add the VEM within vCenter, browse to **Inventory > Networking** and select the **Cisco Nexus 1000V switch**. Right-click, and select **Add Host**, as shown in Figure 9-34.

Note   VMware update manager was installed prior to this configure; the manual VEM installation will not be shown.

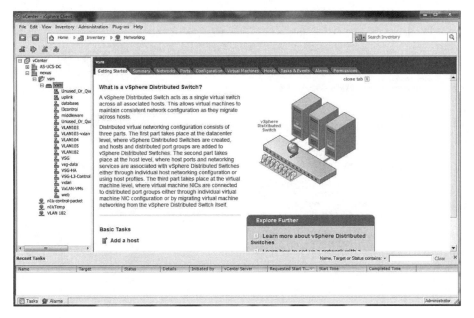

Figure 9-34   *Adding the VEM Through vCenter*

The following list outlines the steps to add an ESX host:

   1. Right mouse-click the vNetwork Distributed Switch named **vsm** and select **Add Host**, as shown in Figure 9-35.

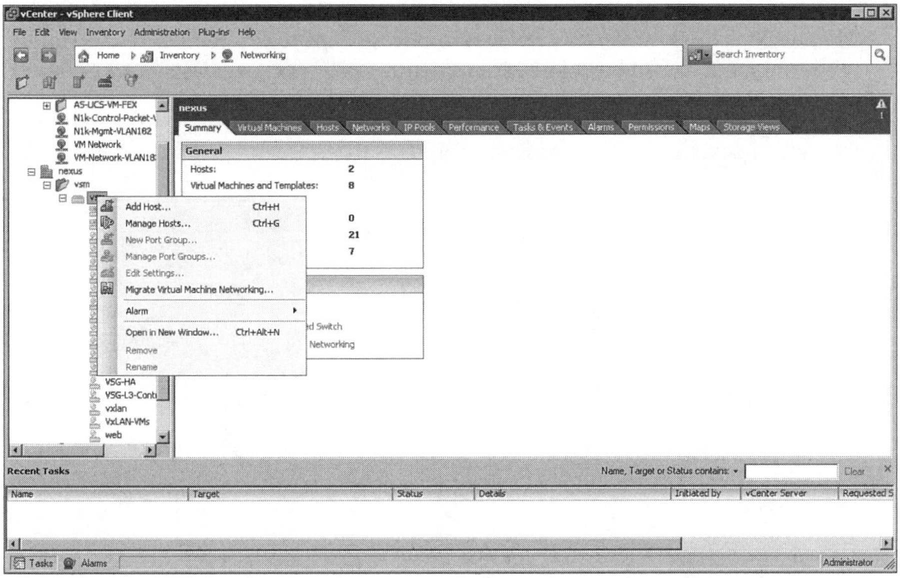

Figure 9-35   *Starting the Process of Adding a VEM to the ESX Host in Virtual Center*

2. Select the ESX host and the physical network adapters; make sure you have **uplink** profile selected in the DVUplink port group column, as shown in Figure 9-36.

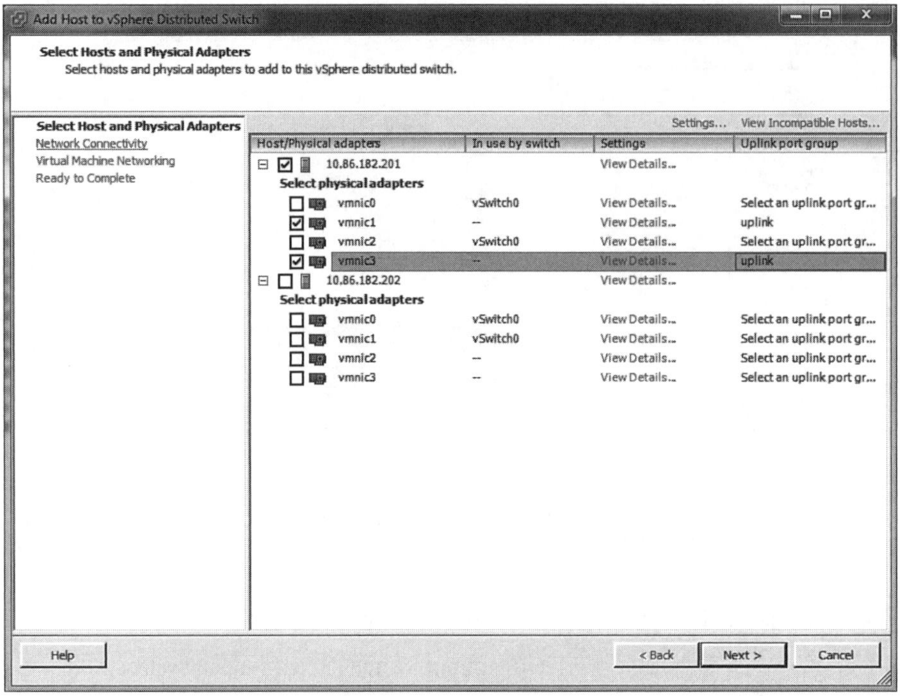

Figure 9-36 *Selecting the ESX Host and the Physical Network Adapters*

a. Migrate Management (vmk) interfaces to port-groups to the Nexus 1000V. vmk0 is not migrated; it will be below for l3control. Click **Next** (see Figure 9-37).

b. Migrate the virtual machines to the Nexus 1000V. Select the correct port-group for each virtual machine, as shown in Figure 9-38.

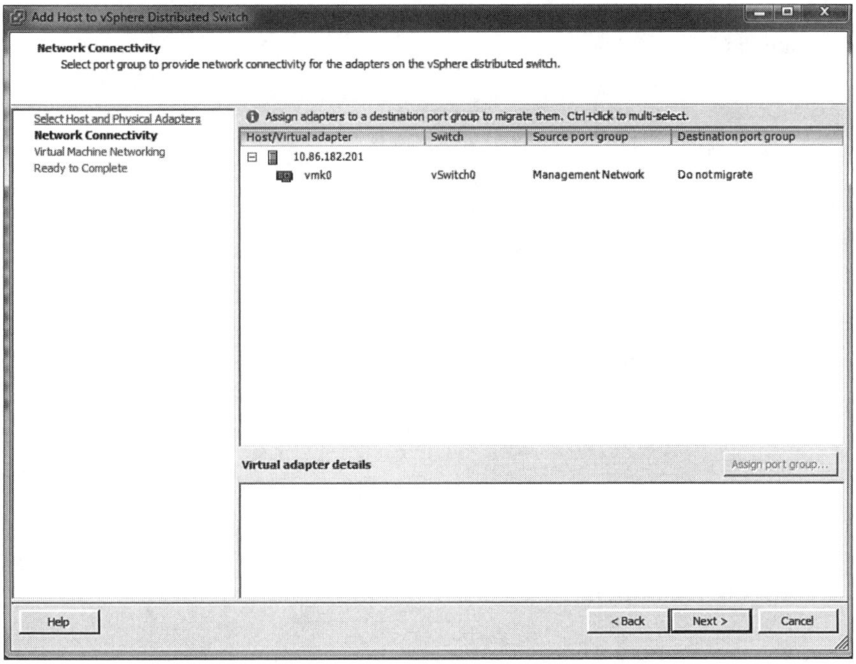

Figure 9-37   *Selecting the ESX Host and the Physical Network Adapters*

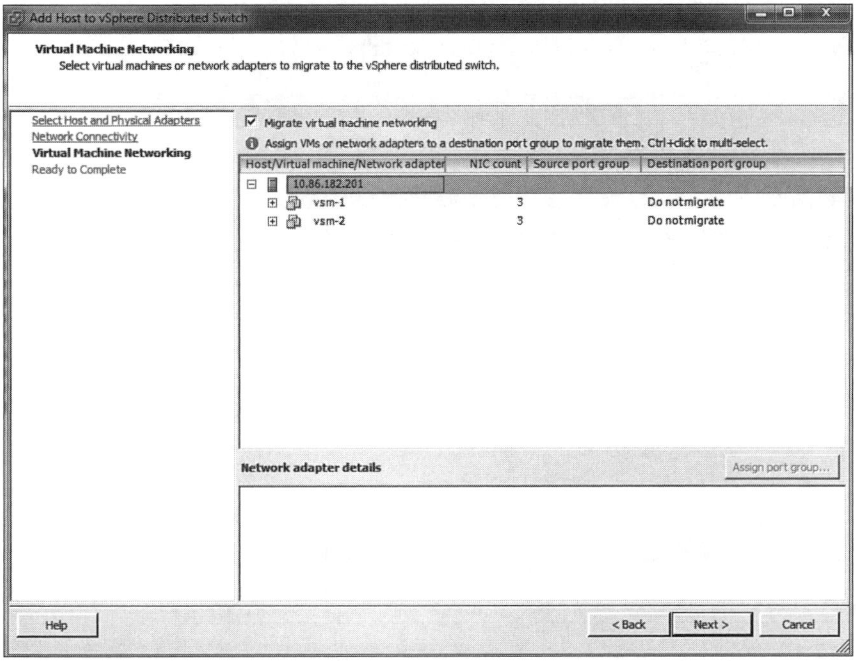

Figure 9-38   *Selecting the VM to Migrate the Nexus 1000v VEM*

3. Verify the settings for the new VEM to be installed, and click the **Finish** button, as demonstrated in Figure 9-39.

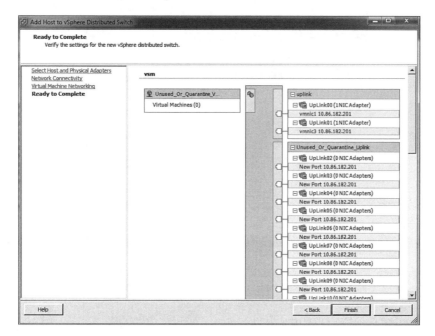

Figure 9-39 *Verifying the Settings for the New VEM to Be Installed*

4. Verify that the ESX host was added to the Hosts tab of vsm, as shown in Figure 9-40.

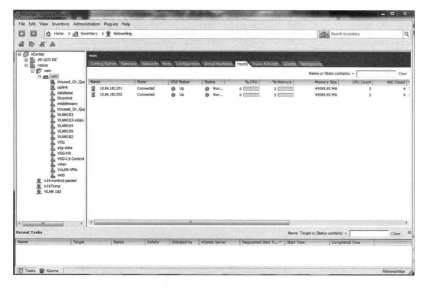

Figure 9-40 *Verifying That the ESX Host Was Added to the "Hosts" Tab of vsm*

5. Verify the VEM was added to the VSM, **vsm.** The following example shows the VEM being powered up on vsm:

```
vsm# 2012 Aug 23 02:05:33 vsm %VEM_MGR-2-VEM_MGR_DETECTED: Host 10.86.182.201
detected as module 3

2012 Aug 23 02:05:33 vsm %VIM-5-IF_ATTACHED: Interface Ethernet3/2 is attached to
vmnic1 on module 3

2012 Aug 23 02:05:33 vsm %VIM-5-IF_ATTACHED: Interface Ethernet3/4 is attached to
vmnic3 on module 3

2012 Aug 23 02:05:33 vsm %VEM_MGR-2-MOD_ONLINE: Module 3 is online

2012 Aug 23 02:05:33 vsm %ETHPORT-5-SPEED: Interface Ethernet3/2, operational speed
changed to 10 Gbps

2012 Aug 23 02:05:33 vsm %ETHPORT-5-IF_DUPLEX: Interface Ethernet3/2, operational
duplex mode changed to Full

2012 Aug 23 02:05:33 vsm %ETHPORT-5-IF_RX_FLOW_CONTROL: Interface Ethernet3/2, oper-
ational Receive Flow Control state changed to on

2012 Aug 23 02:05:33 vsm %ETHPORT-5-IF_TX_FLOW_CONTROL: Interface Ethernet3/2, oper-
ational Transmit Flow Control state changed to on

2012 Aug 23 02:05:33 vsm %ETHPORT-5-SPEED: Interface Ethernet3/4, operational speed
changed to 10 Gbps

2012 Aug 23 02:05:33 vsm %ETHPORT-5-IF_DUPLEX: Interface Ethernet3/4, operational
duplex mode changed to Full

2012 Aug 23 02:05:33 vsm %ETHPORT-5-IF_RX_FLOW_CONTROL: Interface Ethernet3/4, oper-
ational Receive Flow Control state changed to on

2012 Aug 23 02:05:33 vsm %ETHPORT-5-IF_TX_FLOW_CONTROL: Interface Ethernet3/4, oper-
ational Transmit Flow Control state changed to on

2012 Aug 23 02:05:33 vsm %ETHPORT-5-IF_UP: Interface Ethernet3/2 is up in mode trunk

2012 Aug 23 02:05:33 vsm %ETHPORT-5-IF_UP: Interface Ethernet3/4 is up in mode trunk
```

```
vsm# show module
Mod  Ports  Module-Type                      Model             Status
---  -----  -------------------------------  ----------------  -----------
1    0      Virtual Supervisor Module        Nexus1000V        active *
2    0      Virtual Supervisor Module        Nexus1000V        ha-standby
3    248    Virtual Ethernet Module          NA                ok


Mod  Sw                 Hw
---  -----------------  ---------------------------------------------
1    4.2(1)SV1(5.1a)    0.0
2    4.2(1)SV1(5.1a)    0.0
3    4.2(1)SV1(5.1a)    VMware ESXi 5.0.0 Releasebuild-469512 (3.0)


Mod  MAC-Address(es)                        Serial-Num
---  -------------------------------------  ----------
1    00-19-07-6c-5a-a8 to 00-19-07-6c-62-a8  NA
2    00-19-07-6c-5a-a8 to 00-19-07-6c-62-a8  NA
```

```
3     02-00-0c-00-03-00 to 02-00-0c-00-03-80   NA


Mod   Server-IP       Server-UUID                          Server-Name
---   -------------   ------------------------------------ --------------------
1     10.86.182.152   NA                                   NA
2     10.86.182.152   NA                                   NA
3     10.86.182.201   ba5eba11-9999-0001-0000-000000000001 NA


* this terminal session
vsm#


vsm# show module 3
Mod   Ports  Module-Type                       Model              Status
---   -----  --------------------------------  -----------------  -----------
3     248    Virtual Ethernet Module           NA                 ok


Mod  Sw                 Hw
---  -----------------  ---------------------------------------------
3    4.2(1)SV1(5.1a)    VMware ESXi 5.0.0 Releasebuild-469512 (3.0)


Mod  MAC-Address(es)                       Serial-Num
---  ------------------------------------  ----------
3    02-00-0c-00-03-00 to 02-00-0c-00-03-80  NA


Mod   Server-IP       Server-UUID                          Server-Name
---   -------------   ------------------------------------ --------------------
3     10.86.182.201   ba5eba11-9999-0001-0000-000000000001 NA
vsm#
```

Example 9-5 shows how to install the Nexus 1000V license. A Cisco Nexus 1000V license is required for each server CPU in your system.

Example 9-5   *Installing the Nexus 1000V License*

```
vsm# copy tftp://10.1.4.10/N1KVFEAT20091108140613428.lic bootflash:
Enter vrf (If no input, current vrf 'default' is considered): management
Trying to connect to tftp server......
Connection to Server Established.
|
TFTP get operation was successful
vsm# conf t
vsm-VSM(config)# exit
vsm# install license bootflash:N1KVFEAT20091108140613428.lic
Installing license .....done
vsm# show license
```

```
N1KVFEAT20091108140613428.lic:
SERVER this_host ANY
VENDOR cisco
INCREMENT NEXUS1000V_LAN_SERVICES_PKG cisco 1.0 permanent 2 \
        HOSTID=VDH=4459104771250635013 \
        NOTICE="<LicFileID>20091108140613428</LicFileID><LicLineID>1</LicLineID> \
        <PAK>FXPAK2485D0</PAK>" SIGN=BD161668DEB2

vsm# dir bootflash:
       146     Nov 08 20:11:21 2009   .ovfconfigured
       253     Nov 08 22:09:38 2009   N1KVFEAT20091108140613428.lic
     77824     Nov 08 20:10:58 2009   accounting.log
     16384     Aug 18 22:34:51 2009   lost+found/
   1335170     Aug 18 22:35:40 2009   nexus-1000v-dplug-mzg.4.0.4.SV1.2.bin
  21732352     Aug 18 22:35:42 2009   nexus-1000v-kickstart-mzg.4.0.4.SV1.2.bin
  73375005     Aug 18 22:35:53 2009   nexus-1000v-mzg.4.0.4.SV1.2.bin

Usage for bootflash://sup-local
  211210240 bytes used
 1383665664 bytes free
 1594875904 bytes total
vsm#
```

Note There is a 60-day evaluation license part of the OVF VSM installation, which can be verified with the following command:

```
vsm# show mod vem internal license-info
License Sync Initiator     : VEM 3
License Sync Stages        : Complete
Num of Def Licenses in Use : 0
Num of Sync participants   : 2
License Host-ID            : 3730446821259416248
Eval time remaining        : 47 days
Installed lic count        : 0
--------------------VEM License Info ----------------------
Vem    Current License Operation       License Status  License Flags
---    -------------------------       --------------  -------------
 3                     None            licensed  None
 4                     None            licensed  None


----------------VEM Socket License Info ------------------
Vem    Sync   License Usage   Sockets License Version
---    ----   -------------   ------- ---------------
 3     Yes              2          2          1.0
 4     Yes              1          1          1.0
```

Enabling the Telnet Server Process

Example 9-6 shows how to enable the Telnet server, which is disabled by default.

Example 9-6 *Enabling Telnet Server*

```
vsm# conf t
vsm(config)# telnet server enable
vsm(config)# exit
vsm# show telnet server
telnet service enabled
vsm#
```

Changing the VSM Hostname

Example 9-7 shows how to change the Nexus 1000V VSM hostname.

Example 9-7 *Changing the Nexus 1000V VSM Hostname*

```
Change Nexus 1000V Hostname
switch# conf t
switch(config)# hostname vsmvsm
vsmvsm(config)# exit
vsmvsm#
```

Layer 3 Control

The Nexus 1000V software release 4.0(4)SV1(2) adds the capability for Layer 3 Control between the VEMs and VSM; Layer 3 Control no longer requires the Control and Packet VLANs. Layer 3 Control capability offers the following capabilities and requirements:

- The transport mode for the VSM domain can be configured for Layer 3.

- The VEM VM kernel NIC must connect to the Layer 3 control port profile when adding the host to the Cisco Nexus 1000V DVS.

- Only one VM kernel NIC can be assigned to the Layer 3 Control port-profile per host.

- The VLAN assigned to the Layer 3 Control port profile must be a system VLAN.

- The port-profile must be an access port profile; it cannot be a trunk port profile.

- Different hosts can use different VLANs for Layer 3 Control.

Figure 9-41 shows the Cisco Nexus 1000V Series Architecture for L3 Control:

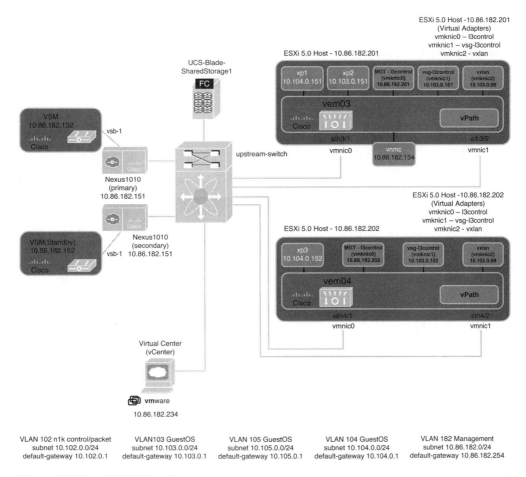

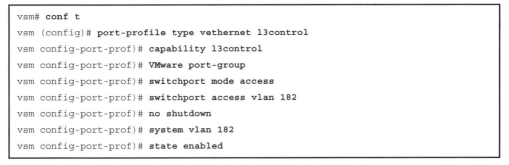

Figure 9-41   *1000V-Topology*

Example 9-8 shows how to create a port-profile for Layer 3 Control mode.

Example 9-8   *Create a Port-Profile for L3 Control Mode*

```
vsm# conf t
vsm (config)# port-profile type vethernet l3control
vsm config-port-prof)# capability l3control
vsm config-port-prof)# VMware port-group
vsm config-port-prof)# switchport mode access
vsm config-port-prof)# switchport access vlan 182
vsm config-port-prof)# no shutdown
vsm config-port-prof)# system vlan 182
vsm config-port-prof)# state enabled
```

Example 9-9 shows how to verify the Layer 3 Control port-profile.

Example 9-9   *Verifying the Layer 3 Control Port-Profile*

```
vsm(config-port-prof)# show port-profile name l3control
port-profile l3control
 type: Vethernet
 description:
 status: enabled
 max-ports: 32
 min-ports: 1
 inherit:
 config attributes:
  switchport mode access
  switchport access vlan 182
  no shutdown
 evaluated config attributes:
  switchport mode access
  switchport access vlan 182
  no shutdown
 assigned interfaces:
 port-group: l3control
 system vlans: 182
 capability l3control: yes
 capability iscsi-multipath: no
 capability vxlan: no
 capability l3-vn-service: no
 port-profile role: none
 port-binding: static
vsm(config-port-prof)#
```

Example 9-10 shows how to enable SVS Layer 3 mode feature level.

Example 9-10   *Enabling SVS L3 Mode Feature Level*

```
vsm(config)# system update vem feature level 1
old feature level: 4.0(4)SV1(1) new feature level: 4.0(4)SV1(2)
vsm(config)#
```

Example 9-11 shows how to nullify the Control and Packet VLANs, which will show both Control and Packet VLANs as 1; this is OK.

Example 9-11   *Nullifying the Control and Packet VLANs*

```
vsm(config-svs-domain)# no packet vlan
vsm(config-svs-domain)# no control vlan
```

Example 9-12 shows how to change SVS mode from Layer 2 to Layer 3 and specify the Layer 3 Management interface of mgmt0. The Control0 interface could be used as well.

Example 9-12   *Changing SVS Mode from Layer 2 to Layer 3 and Specifying the Layer 3 Management Interface of mgmt0*

```
vsm(config-svs-domain)# svs mode l3 interface mgmt0
```

Example 9-13 shows how to change the system VLAN on the uplink profile.

Example 9-13   *Changing the System VLAN on the Uplink Profile*

```
vsm# conf t
vsm(config)# port-profile uplink
vsm(config-port-prof)# system vlan 182
```

Example 9-14 shows how to verify the L3 Control configuration.

Example 9-14   *Verifying the Layer 3 Control Configuration*

```
vsm# show svs domain
SVS domain config:
  Domain id:    989
  Control vlan: 1
  Packet vlan:  1
  L2/L3 Control mode: L3
  L3 control interface: mgmt0
  Status: Config push to VC successful.
```

Figure 9-42 shows how to add a vmkernel interface to vNetwork Distributed Switch. The vmkernel interface (vmk0) will have an IP address on it for the Layer 3 Control.

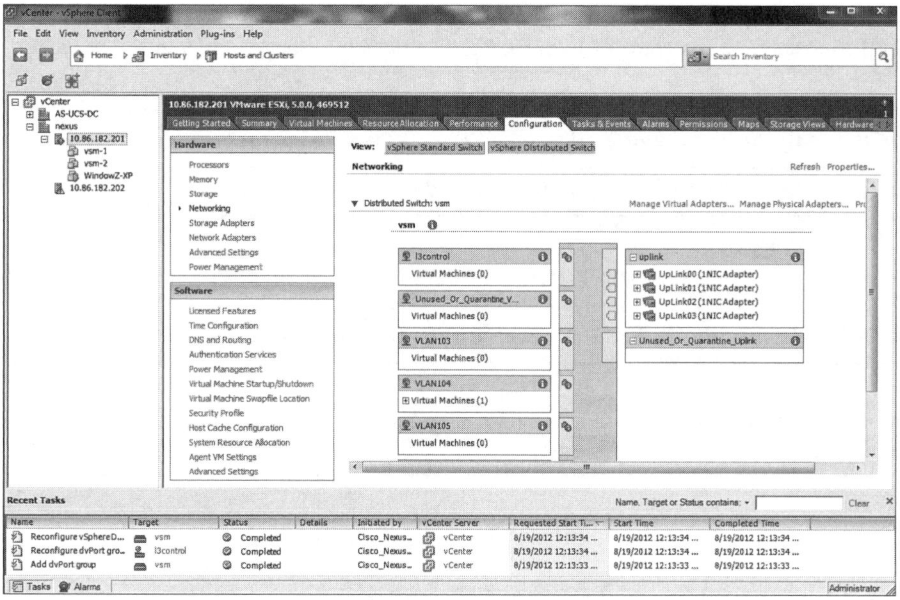

Figure 9-42 *Adding a vmkernel Interface to vNetwork Distributed Switch*

Figure 9-43 shows how to add a vmkernel interface to a vNetwork Distributed Switch. The vmkernel interface (vmk0) will have an IP address on it for the Layer 3 Control.

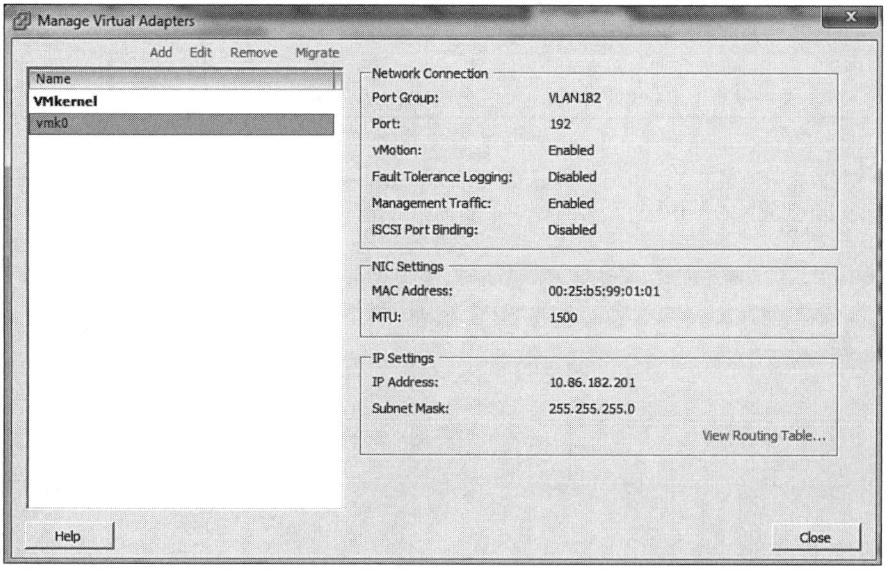

Figure 9-43 *Selecting the vmkernel Interface to Add to the vNetwork Distributed Switch*

Figure 9-44 shows how to select the correct vmware port-group for the vmkernel interface to be migrated to the Cisco vNetwork Distributed Switch VEM.

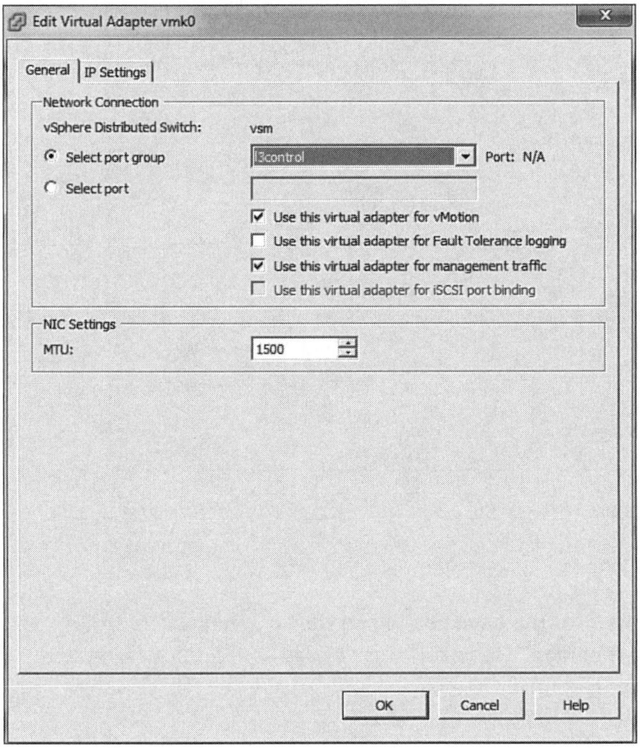

Figure 9-44   *Selecting the Correct vmware port-group for the vmkernel Interface to be Migrated to the Cisco vNetwork Distributed Switch VEM*

Figure 9-45 shows that the vmk0 was added successfully to the vmware port-group l3control.

Example 9-15 shows the VSM output for vmk0 interface attaching for l3control.

Example 9-15   *Running-Configuration for the Layer 3 Control Configuration*

```
vsm(config-port-prof)#

2012 Aug 23 22:29:33 vsm %VIM-5-IF_DETACHED: Interface Vethernet2 is detached

2012 Aug 23 22:29:33 vsm %ETHPORT-5-IF_DOWN_NON_PARTICIPATING: Interface Vethernet2
is down (Non participating)

2012 Aug 23 22:29:33 vsm %VIM-5-IF_CONFIG_PURGE_AUTO: Configuration on interface
Vethernet2 has been auto purged (port-profile changed)

2012 Aug 23 22:29:33 vsm %VIM-5-IF_ATTACHED: Interface Vethernet2 is attached to
vmk0 on port 1 of module 3 with dvport id 224
```

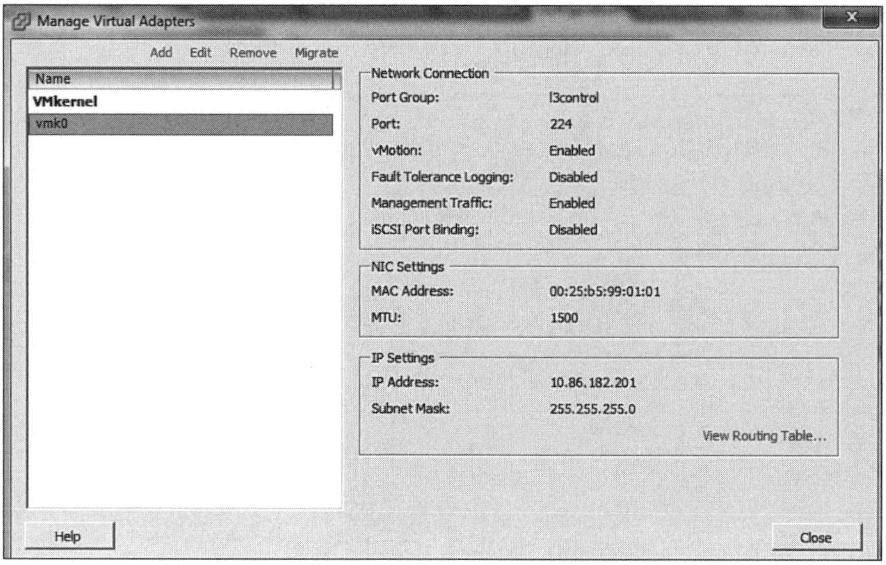

Figure 9-45 *Verifying That the vmk0 Was Successfully Added to the vmware port-group l3control*

The mgmt0 interface will be used for the Layer 3 Control traffic; interface control0 can be used as well. Port-profile named "l3control" was created and defined the system VLAN of 182 and capability of l3control.

1000V Port Profiles

Port profiles are used to configure interfaces on the VEM. A port profile can be assigned to multiple interfaces; this allows for standardized interface configurations across multiple VEMs. When changes are applied to a port profile, the changes can be propagated automatically to the configuration of any interface assigned to it.

In the VMware vCenter Server, a port profile is represented as a port group. The vEthernet or Ethernet interfaces are assigned in vCenter Server to a port profile for

■ Defining port configuration by policy

■ Applying a single policy across a large number of ports

■ Supporting both VEthernet and vEthernet ports

Port profiles that are configured as uplinks can be assigned by the server administrator to physical ports (a vmnic or a physical NIC [PNIC]). Port profiles that are not configured as uplinks can be assigned to a VM virtual port.

Note   Manual interface configuration overrides the port-profile configuration; it is recommended to use this method for temporary changes or configuration changes.

Port profiles have two states, enabled and disabled. When a port-profile state is disabled, the port-profile has the following behavior:

- Its configuration is not applied to assigned ports.

- If exporting policies to a VMware port group, the port group is not created on the vCenter Server.

When a port-profile state is enabled, the port-profile has the following behavior:

- Its configuration is applied to assigned ports.

- If inheriting policies from a VMware port group, the port group is created on the vCenter Server.

Note   The default state of a port-profile is disabled.

A port profile can have the following characteristics defined:

- ACL

- Capability (uplink, l3control)

- Channel-group

- Description

- Inherit

- Default, resets characteristics to default settings

- Interface state (shutdown/no shutdown)

- Name

- Netflow

- Port-security

- Private-VLAN

- QoS policy

- State (enabled/disabled)

- Switchport mode (access port or trunk port)

- System VLAN

- VLAN configuration

- VMware max-ports

- VMware port-group name

Port Profile Inheritance enables one port profile to inherit the policies from another port profile. The characteristics of the parent profile become the default settings for the child. The inheriting port profile ignores any nonapplicable configuration.

Table 9-1 lists the port profile characteristics that can and cannot be inherited.

Table 9-1   *Port Profile Characteristic Inheritance Properties*

Port Profile Characteristics That Can Be Inherited	Port Profile Characteristics That Cannot Be Inherited
ACL	Capability
Channel-group	Description
Default	State
Inherit	System vlan list
Interface state	VMware max-port
Name	VMware port-group name
Netflow	
Port-security	
QoS	
Private vlan	
Switchport mode	
VLAN configuration	

A system port profile is designed to establish vCenter Server connectivity. The system port-profile carries the following VLANs:

- System VLANs or VNICs used when bringing up the ports before communication is established between the VSM and VEM.

- The uplink that carries the control VLAN.

- Management uplink(s) used for VMware vCenter Server connectivity or SSH or Telnet connections. There can be more than one management port or VLAN—for example, one dedicated for vCenter Server connectivity, one for SSH, one for SNMP, a switch interface, and so forth.

■ VMware kernel NIC for accessing VMFS storage over iSCSI or NFS.

The system port-profile system VLANs have the following characteristics:

■ System VLANs cannot be deleted when the profile is in use.

■ Non-system VLANs in a system port profile can be freely added or deleted, even when the profile is in use; that is, one or more DVS ports are carrying that profile.

■ System VLANs can always be added to a system port profile or a non-system port profile, even when the profile is in use.

■ The native VLAN on a system port profile may be a system VLAN or a non-system VLAN.

Example 9-16 shows how to create the port-profile on the VSM.

Example 9-16   *Creating the Port-Profile on the VSM*

```
vsm(config)# port-profile HR-APPS
SVS domain config:
vsm(config-port-prof)# vmware port-group
vsm(config-port-prof)# switchport mode access
vsm(config-port-prof)# switchport access vlan 701
vsm(config-port-prof)# service-policy type qos output qos-stat
vsm(config-port-prof)# no shutdown
vsm(config-port-prof)# system vlan 701
vsm(config-port-prof)# state enabled
vsm(config-port-prof)# exit


vsm(config)# port-profile Web
vsm(config-port-prof)# vmware port-group
vsm(config-port-prof)# switchport mode access
vsm(config-port-prof)# switchport access vlan 78
vsm(config-port-prof)# ip flow monitor IPv4Monitor input
vsm(config-port-prof)# service-policy type qos output qos-stat
vsm(config-port-prof)# no shutdown
vsm(config-port-prof)# state enabled
vsm(config-port-prof)# exit


vsm(config)# port-profile NAS
vsm(config-port-prof)# vmware port-group
vsm(config-port-prof)# switchport mode access
vsm(config-port-prof)# switchport access vlan 702
vsm(config-port-prof)# ip flow monitor IPv4Monitor input
vsm(config-port-prof)# service-policy type qos output mark-control-packet-vlans
vsm(config-port-prof)# no shutdown
vsm(config-port-prof)# system vlan 702
```

```
vsm(config-port-prof)# state enabled
vsm(config-port-prof)# exit
vsm(config)# port-profile ERSPAN
vsm(config-port-prof)# capability l3control
vsm(config-port-prof)# vmware port-group
vsm(config-port-prof)# switchport mode access
vsm(config-port-prof)# switchport access vlan 702
vsm(config-port-prof)# no shutdown
vsm(config-port-prof)# system vlan 702
vsm(config-port-prof)# state enabled
vsm(config-port-prof)# exit
```

Example 9-17 shows how to verify the port-profiles on the VSM.

Example 9-17   *Verifying the Port-Profiles on the VSM*

```
vsm# show port-profile usage


-------------------------------------------------------------
Port Profile            Port        Adapter         Owner
-------------------------------------------------------------
HR-APPS                 Veth3       Net Adapter 1   Demo-Testsrv2
Web                     Veth2       Net Adapter 1   Demo-Testsrv1
l3control               Veth1       vmk2            Module 4
uplink                  Eth4/2      vmnic1          demolab-vm1.csc.dublin.ci
vsm#
vsm# show running-config interface vethernet 3
version 4.0(4)SV1(2)

interface Vethernet3
  inherit port-profile HR-APPS
  description Demo-Testsrv2, Network Adapter 1
  vmware dvport 160

vsm# show running-config interface vethernet 2
version 4.0(4)SV1(2)

interface Vethernet2
  inherit port-profile Web
  description Demo-Testsrv1, Network Adapter 1
  vmware dvport 192

vsm# show running-config interface vethernet 1
version 4.0(4)SV1(2)
```

```
interface Vethernet1
  inherit port-profile l3control
  description VMware VMkernel, vmk2
  vmware dvport 100

vsm# show int vethernet 3
Vethernet3 is up
    Port description is Demo-Testsrv2, Network Adapter 1
    Hardware is Virtual, address is 0050.5686.3f96
    Owner is VM "Demo-Testsrv2", adapter is Network Adapter 1
    Active on module 4
    VMware DVS port 160
    Port-Profile is HR-APPS
    Port mode is access
    5 minute input rate 168 bits/second, 0 packets/second
    5 minute output rate 0 bits/second, 0 packets/second
    Rx
    45 Input Packets 0 Unicast Packets
    3 Multicast Packets 42 Broadcast Packets
    5932 Bytes
    Tx
    1 Output Packets 0 Unicast Packets
    1 Multicast Packets 0 Broadcast Packets 1 Flood Packets
    60 Bytes
    0 Input Packet Drops 0 Output Packet Drops

vsm# show port-profile usage
----------------------------------------------------------------------
Port Profile            Port        Adapter         Owner
----------------------------------------------------------------------
HR-APPS                 Veth3       Net Adapter 1   Demo-Testsrv2
Web                     Veth2       Net Adapter 1   Demo-Testsrv1
l3control               Veth1       vmk2            Module 4
uplink                  Eth4/2      vmnic1          demolab-vm1.csc.dublin.ci
vsm# show port-profile name web
ERROR: port-profile web does not exist
vsm# show port-profile name Web
port-profile Web
  description:
  type: vethernet
  status: enabled
  capability l3control: no
  pinning control-vlan: -
  pinning packet-vlan: -
  system vlans: none
```

```
  port-group: Web
  max ports: 32
  inherit:
  config attributes:
    switchport mode access
    switchport access vlan 78
    ip flow monitor IPv4Monitor input
    service-policy type qos output qos-stat
    no shutdown
  evaluated config attributes:
    switchport mode access
    switchport access vlan 78
    ip flow monitor IPv4Monitor input
    service-policy type qos output qos-stat
    no shutdown
  assigned interfaces:
    Vethernet2
vsm# show int brie


-------------------------------------------------------------------
Port      VRF          Status IP Address              Speed   MTU
-------------------------------------------------------------------
mgmt0      --           up      10.2.9.11               1000    1500


----------------------------------------------------------
Ethernet    VLAN   Type Mode   Status  Reason             Speed    Port
Interface                                                           Ch #
-------------------------------------------------------------------
Eth4/2       1     eth  trunk  up      none                1000(D)  --


-------------------------------------------------------------------
Interface   VLAN   Type Mode   Status  Reason             MTU
-------------------------------------------------------------------
Veth1       702    virt access up      none               1500
Veth2       78     virt access down    inactive           1500
Veth3       701    virt access up      none               1500


-------------------------------------------------------------------
Port      VRF          Status IP Address              Speed   MTU
-------------------------------------------------------------------
ctrl0      --           up      --                      1000    1500
vsm#
```

Figure 9-46 shows the port-profiles that were created on the VSM pushed to Virtual Center port-groups.

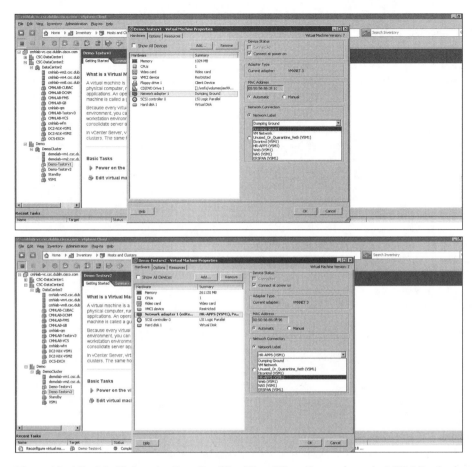

Figure 9-46 *Verifying the Port-Profiles That Were Created on the VSM Pushed to Virtual Center Port-Groups*

Example 9-18 shows port-profile mobility; virtual machine "Demo-Testsrv2" was vMotioned to another ESX host. Interface Vethernet 3 is now installed on another VEM; the interface counters were not changed.

Example 9-18 *Port-Profile Mobility, Virtual Machine "Demo-Testsrv2" Was vMotioned to Another ESX Host*

```
vsm# show int vethernet 3
Vethernet3 is up
    Port description is Demo-Testsrv2, Network Adapter 1
    Hardware is Virtual, address is 0050.5686.3f96
    Owner is VM " Demo-Testsrv2", adapter is Network Adapter 1
    Active on module 5
    VMware DVS port 160
```

```
    Port-Profile is HR-APPS
    Port mode is access
    Rx
    116110 Input Packets 102386 Unicast Packets
    15 Multicast Packets 13709 Broadcast Packets
    21252722 Bytes
    Tx
    1162978 Output Packets 125195 Unicast Packets
    72181 Multicast Packets 965602 Broadcast Packets 0 Flood Packets
    169423238 Bytes
    98 Input Packet Drops 0 Output Packet Drops

vsm# show int vethernet 3
Vethernet3 is up
    Port description is Demo-Testsrv2, Network Adapter 1
    Hardware is Virtual, address is 0050.5686.3f96
    Owner is VM " Demo-Testsrv2", adapter is Network Adapter 1
    Active on module 4
    VMware DVS port 160
    Port-Profile is HR-APPS
    Port mode is access
    Rx
    116113 Input Packets 102386 Unicast Packets
    18 Multicast Packets 13709 Broadcast Packets
    21252902 Bytes
    Tx
    1163004 Output Packets 125196 Unicast Packets
    72185 Multicast Packets 965623 Broadcast Packets 6 Flood Packets
    169425525 Bytes
    100 Input Packet Drops 0 Output Packet Drops
```

Example 9-19 shows a sample QoS policy that was part of the port-profiles configured.

Example 9-19 *Sample QoS Policy That Was Part of the Port-Profiles Configured*

```
Sample QoS Configure for the QoS
ip access-list match-control-vlans
  statistics per-entry
  10 permit ip 10.1.12.0/24 any
  20 permit ip any 10.1.12.0/24
class-map type qos match-any EF
  match dscp 46
class-map type qos match-any CS3
  match dscp 24
class-map type qos match-any cs0
```

```
  match dscp 0
class-map type qos match-any cs1
  match dscp 8
class-map type qos match-any cs2
  match dscp 16
class-map type qos match-any cs3
  match dscp 24
class-map type qos match-any cs4
  match dscp 32
class-map type qos match-any cs5
  match dscp 40
class-map type qos match-any cs6
  match dscp 48
class-map type qos match-any cs7
  match dscp 56
class-map type qos match-any AF31
  match dscp 26
class-map type qos match-any af11
  match dscp 10
class-map type qos match-any af12
  match dscp 12
class-map type qos match-any af13
  match dscp 14
class-map type qos match-any af21
  match dscp 18
class-map type qos match-any af22
  match dscp 20
class-map type qos match-any af23
  match dscp 22
class-map type qos match-any af31
  match dscp 26
class-map type qos match-any af32
  match dscp 28
class-map type qos match-any af33
  match dscp 30
class-map type qos match-any af41
  match dscp 34
class-map type qos match-any af42
  match dscp 36
class-map type qos match-any af43
  match dscp 38
class-map type qos match-any match-control-vlans
  match access-group name match-control-vlans
policy-map type qos qos-stat
  class cs7
```

```
      class cs6
      class cs5
      class cs4
      class cs3
      class cs2
      class cs1
      class af43
      class af42
      class af41
      class af33
      class af32
      class af31
      class af23
      class af22
      class af21
      class af13
      class af12
      class af11
      class EF
      class cs0
  policy-map type qos mark-control-packet-vlans
      class match-control-vlans
        set cos 6
```

As you can see in Example 9-19, port-profiles offer a tremendous amount of flexibility, control, and details on a per–virtual machine basis. Example 9-19 demonstrates a detailed QoS policy that can be customized to meet different requirements and applications.

Virtual Network Management Center

Virtual Network Management Center (VNMC) is a centralized management application that enables the management of virtualized security services. VNMC aligns with current enterprise operational models for security, server, and network operational models. VNMC manages Virtual Security Gateway (VSG) and the virtual Adaptive Security Appliance (vASA) to deploy virtualized services in a secure multitenant data center Private/Public Cloud business model. The operational models can be achieved in the following manner:

■ Security administrators can create, define, monitor, and manage security profiles.

■ Network administrators can create, define, monitor, and manage network profiles that integrate directly into the security policies defined by the security admin organization.

■ Server administrators can associate the security and network policies to the proper virtual machine resources and application in the tool they use; for example, this can be performed in VMware vCenter management application.

Installing Virtual Network Management Center Software from OVA Downloaded from Cisco.com

The list that follows outlines how to install the VNMC security management application suite. VNMC provides centralized multidevice and policy management for Cisco network virtual services. VNMC provides automation of processes, scalability, standardization, consistent security policies, and centralized logging:

1. Log in to Virtual Center, and deploy a New OVF Template from the File menu. Figure 9-47 shows how to create a new OVF Template with Virtual Center.

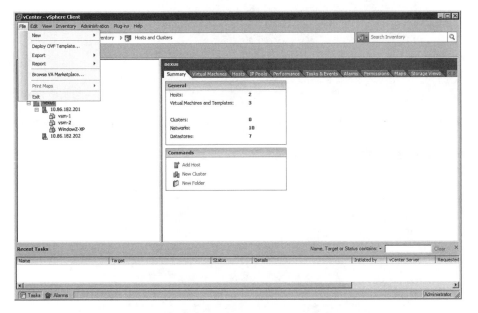

Figure 9-47   *Creating a New OVF Template with Virtual Center*

2. Browse to the VNMC .OVA image that was downloaded from www.cisco.com.

   Figure 9-48 shows how to point to the .OVA file source that was downloaded from www.cisco.com.

3. Verify the OVF details for VNMC, and click **Next**, as shown in Figure 9-49.

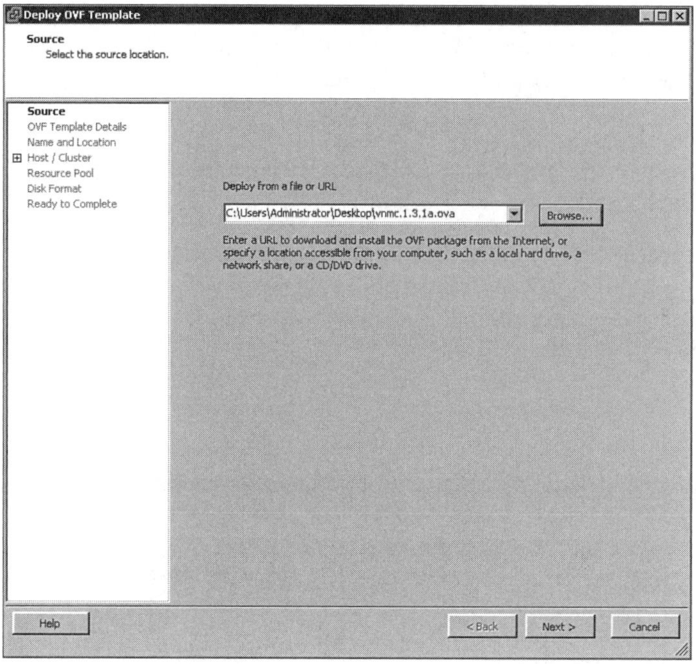

Figure 9-48 *Selecting the .OVA File Source That Was Downloaded from www.cisco.com*

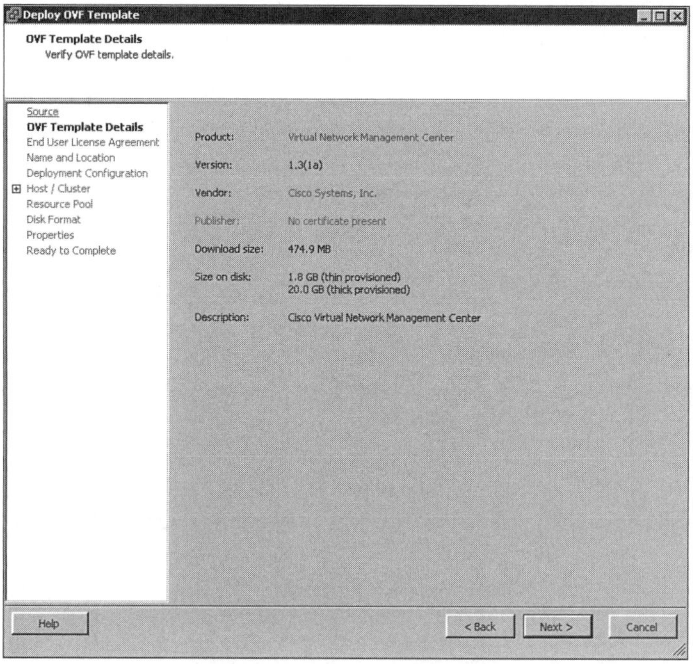

Figure 9-49 *Verifying the OVF Deployment Details*

4. Accepts the License Agreement, as shown in Figure 9-50.

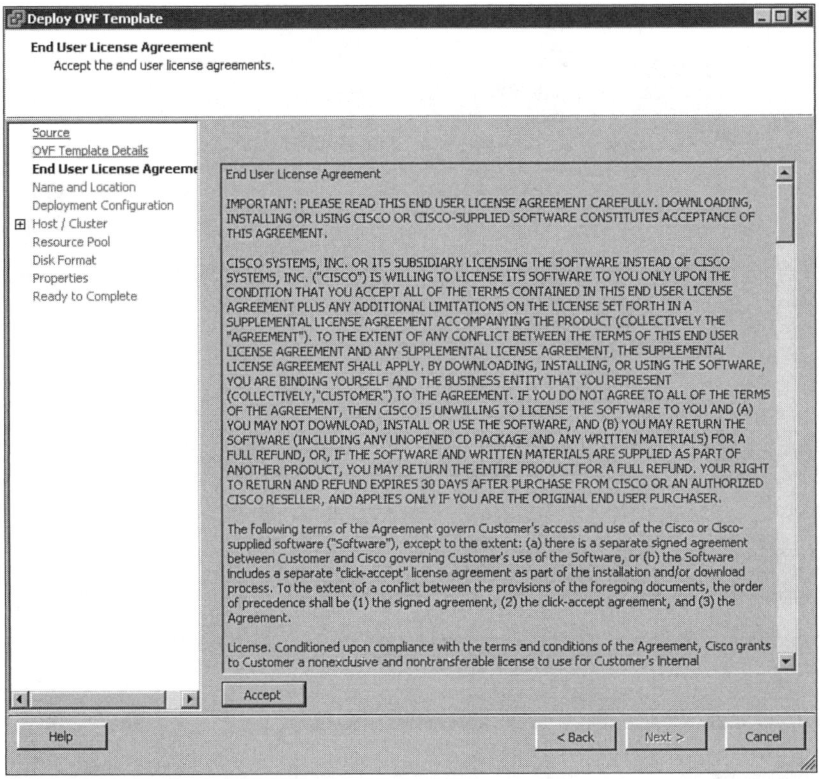

Figure 9-50 *Accepting the License Agreement*

5. Specify the Data Center container location to deploy the OVA template, as shown in Figure 9-51.

6. Specify the VMMC Installer Script Wizard for installation of VMMC, as shown in Figure 9-52.

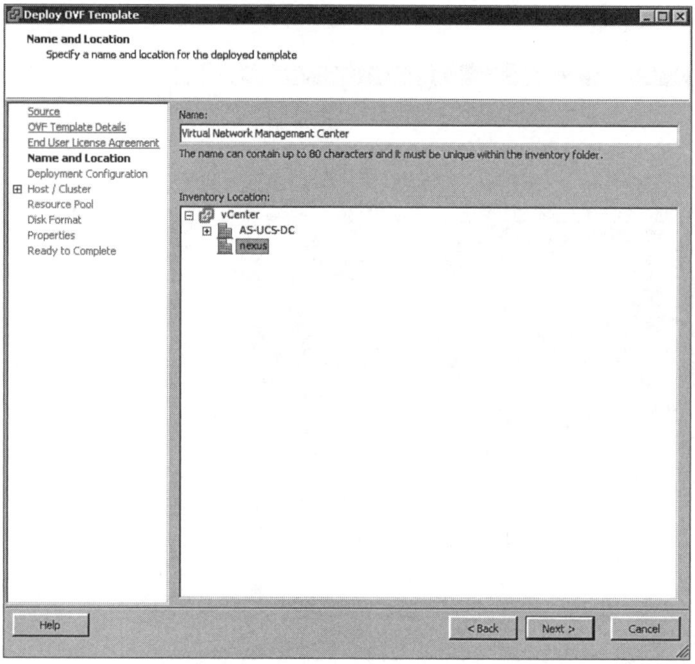

Figure 9-51 *Specifying the Data Center Container Location to Deploy the OVF Template Within Virtual Center*

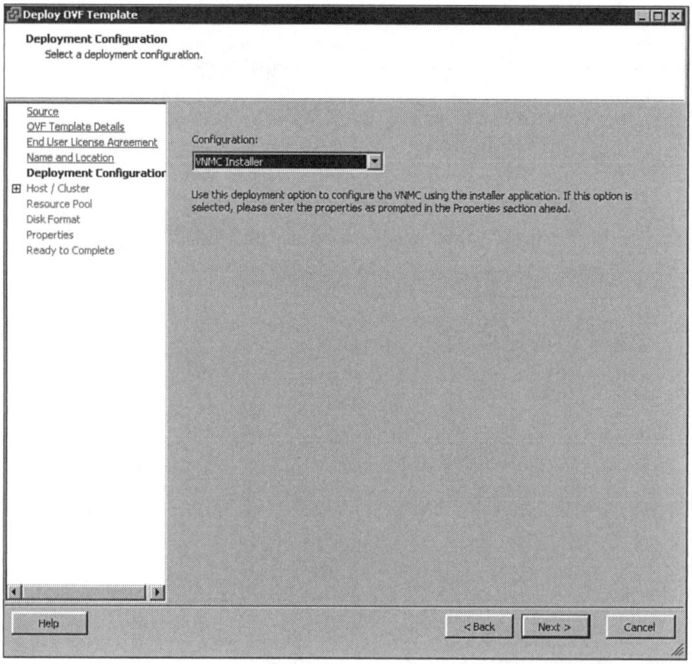

Figure 9-52 *Specifying the VNMC Installation GUI Script*

7. Specify the specific ESX Host or ESX Cluster to install the VNMC Software, as shown in Figure 9-53.

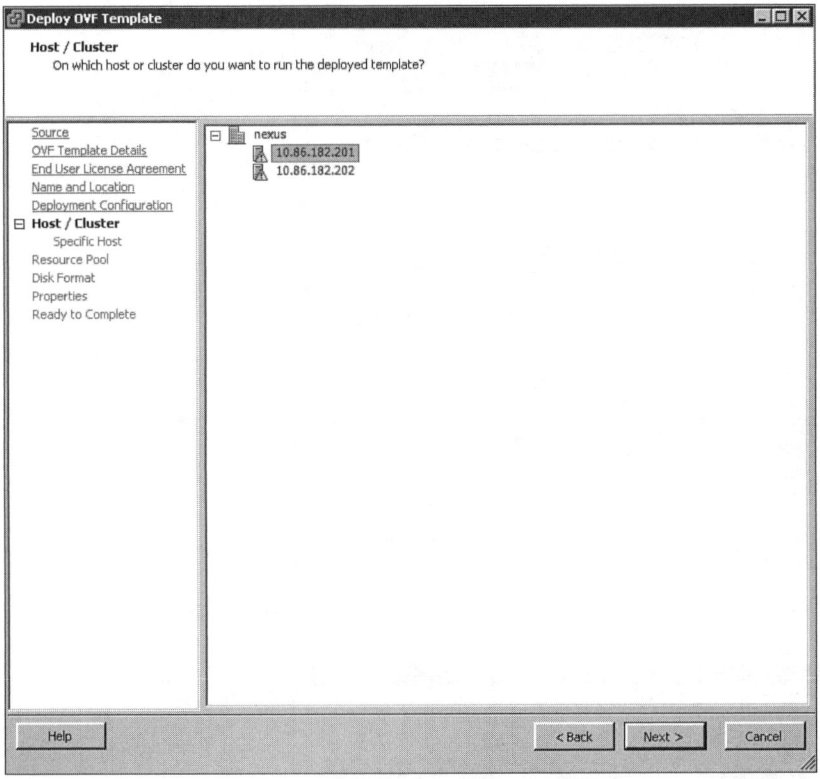

Figure 9-53 *Specifying the Specific ESX Host or ESX Cluster to Install the VNMC Software*

8. Specify the datastore for the virtual machine to be installed, as shown in Figure 9-54.

9. Specify the datastore disk format for the virtual machine, as shown in Figure 9-55.

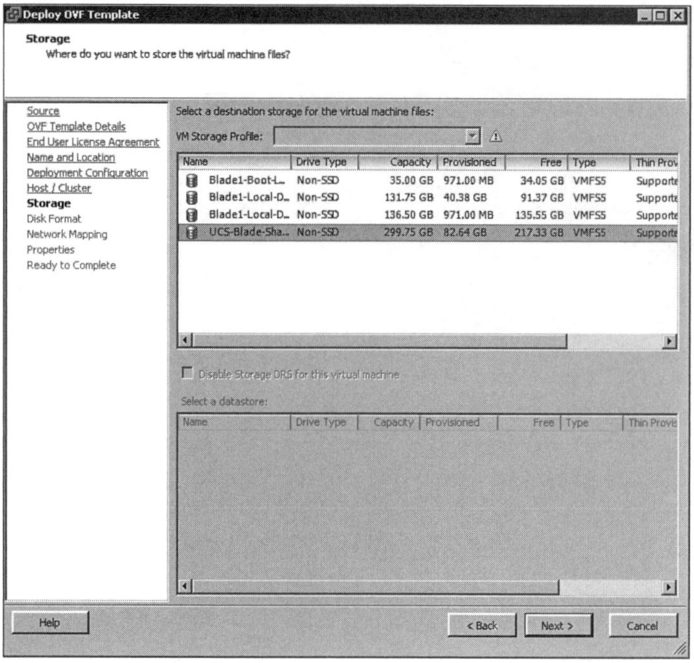

Figure 9-54   *Specifying the Datastore for the Virtual Machine Installation*

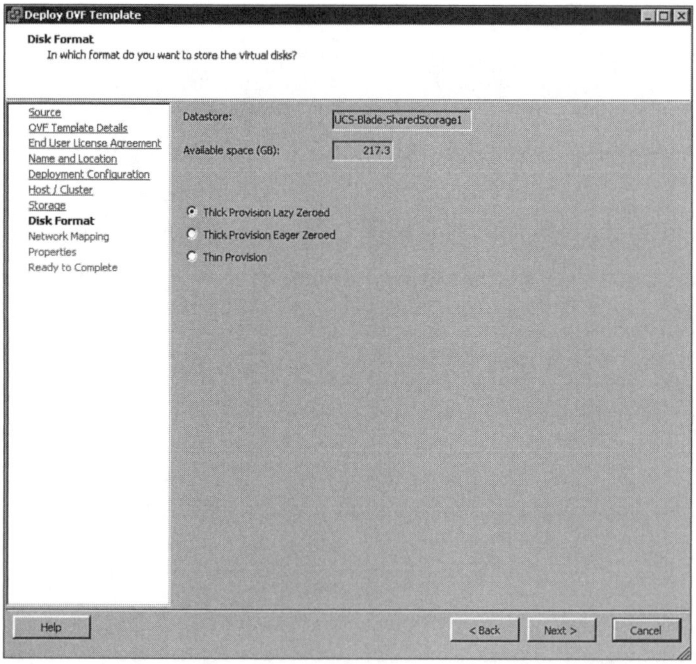

Figure 9-55   *Specifying the Datastore Disk Format for the Virtual Machine*

10. Specify the proper network port-group for the VNMC connectivity, as shown in Figure 9-56.

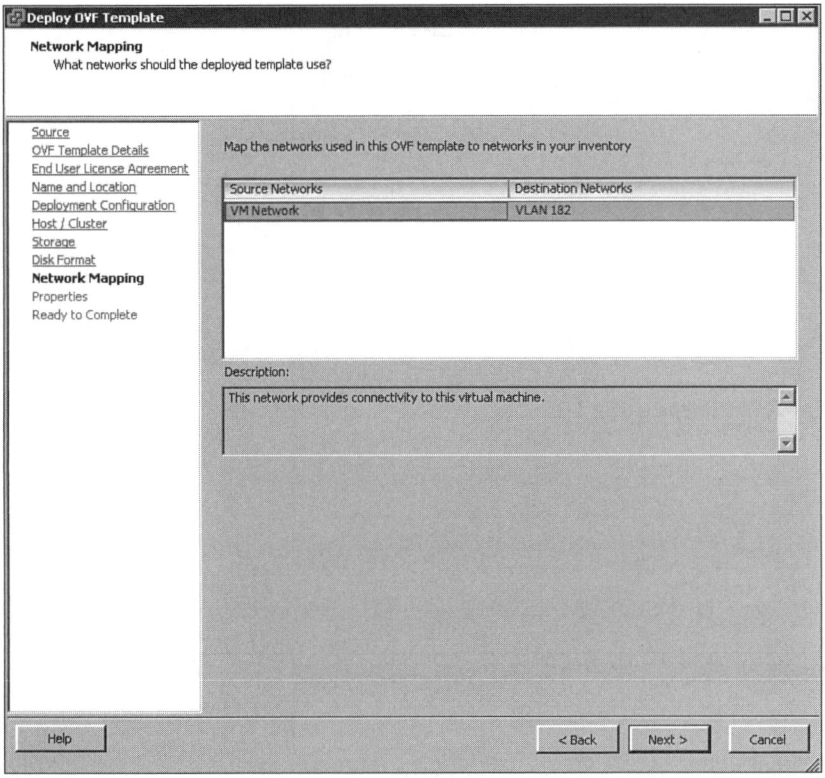

Figure 9-56 *Specifying the Correct Network Port-Group for the VNMC Connectivity.*

11. Specify the proper Network IP Address information for the VNMC management interface:

   a. Specify the IP address information for the VNMC management interface for the network selected in step 10, as shown in Figure 9-57.

   b. Specify the hostname, administrator password, and secret, as shown in Figure 9-58. The secret will be used for the communication to vCenter.

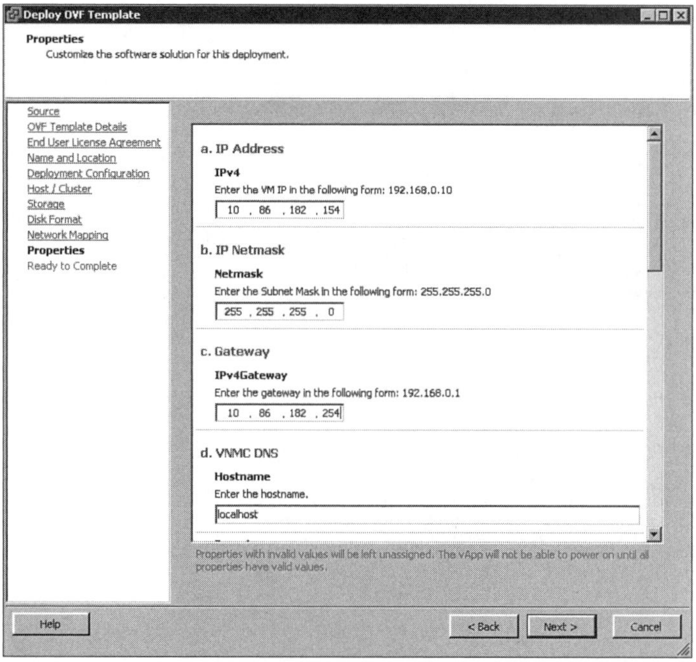

Figure 9-57 *Specifying the IP Address Information for the VNMC Management Interface*

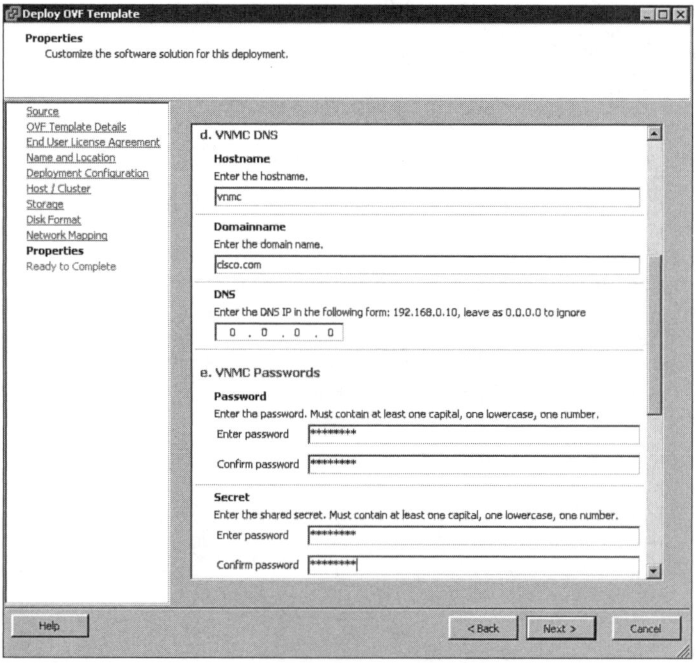

Figure 9-58 *Specifying the Hostname, Administrator Password, and Secret*

12. Verify the information before deployment of the OVF template for VNMC, as shown in Figure 9-59.

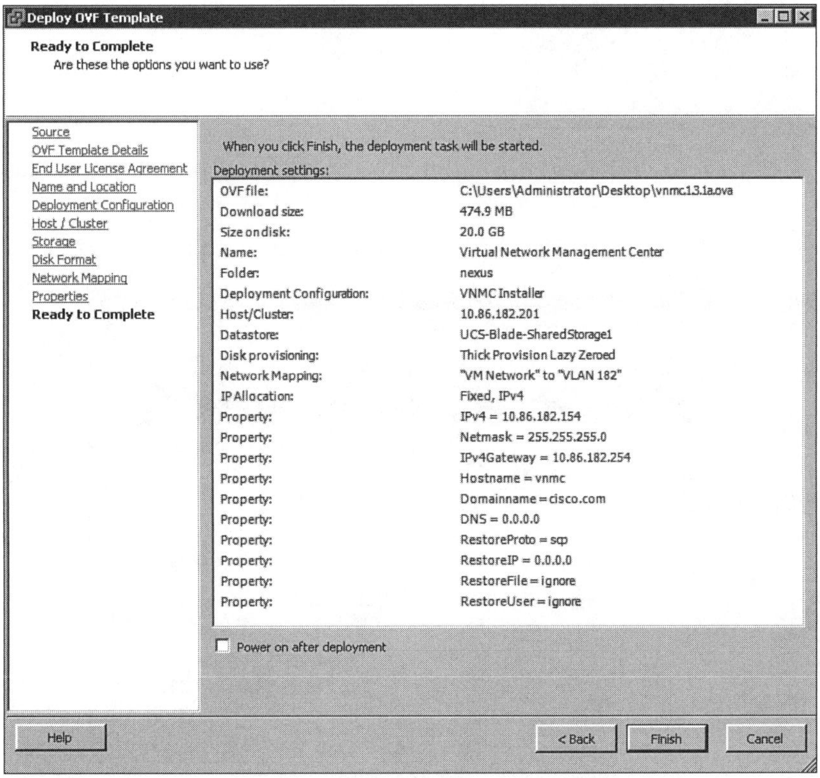

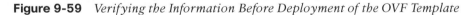

Figure 9-59 *Verifying the Information Before Deployment of the OVF Template*

13. Display the OVF deployment of VNMC.

Figure 9-60 shows the OVF deployment of VNMC to the datastore that was selected.

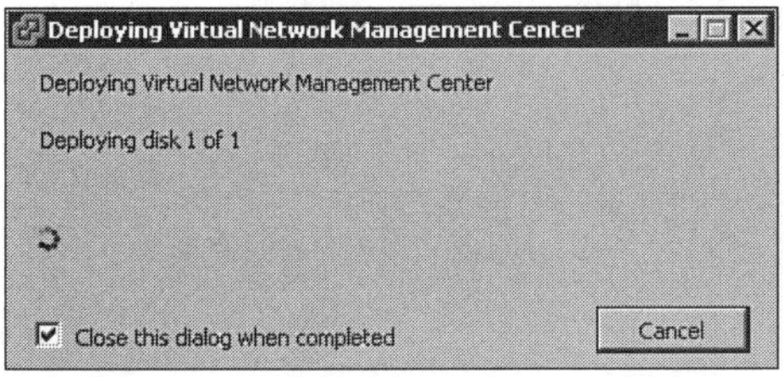

Figure 9-60 *Displaying the OVF Deployment of VNMC to the Datastore That Was Selected*

Figure 9-61 shows the OVF deployment progress of VNMC to the datastore that was selected.

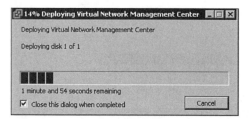

Figure 9-61   *Displaying the OVF Deployment Progress of VNMC to the Datastore That Was Selected*

14. Power on the newly created VNMC Virtual Machine, as shown in Figure 9-62.

Figure 9-62   *Powering On the Newly Created VNMC Virtual Machine*

15. View the VNMC VM booting in the Virtual Machine Console, as shown in Figure 9-63.

16. Verify that the VNMC VM has successfully booted and at the login prompt, as shown in Figure 9-64.

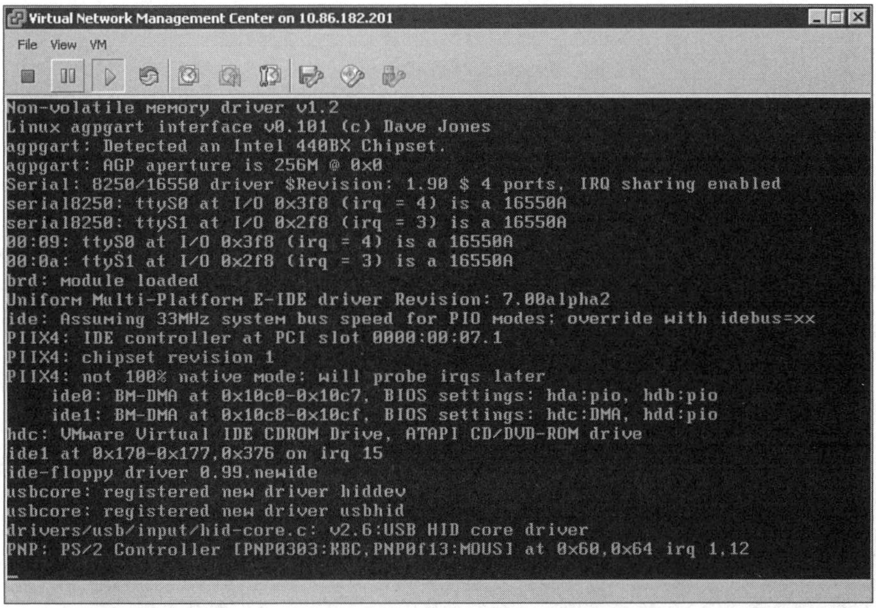

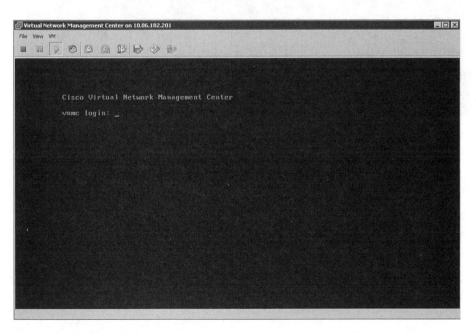

Figure 9-63 *Displaying the VNMC Virtual Machine Booting in the Virtual Machine Console*

Figure 9-64 *Confirming that the VNMC VM Has Successfully Booted and at the Login Prompt*

Adding the VM-Manager for vCenter Connectivity in VNMC Management Application

The VNMC VM-Manager connects to the vCenter. The vCenter extension file is required to establish a connection between the VNMC VM-Manager and vCenter. The extension file is exported from Cisco VNMC and linked on the VM-Managers within VNMC. The plug-in will be installed on all vCenter servers that require these services.

The following steps show how to add vCenter as a VM-Manager for VNMC:

1. Open your web browser, and point the VNMC Management interfaces configured during the OVF installation, as shown in Figure 9-65. In this example VNMC has a IP address of 10.86.182.154; enter **https://10.86.182.154** into your web browser.

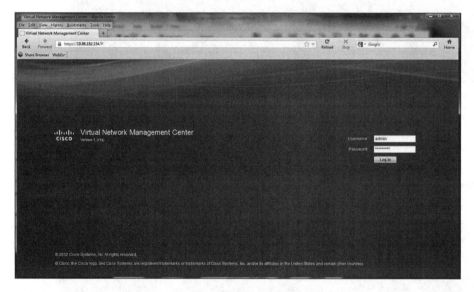

Figure 9-65 *Browse to the VNMC Management Interface and Log In As Admin*

2. Navigate to Administrator and VM Managers within the VNMC Management Application, as shown in Figure 9-66.

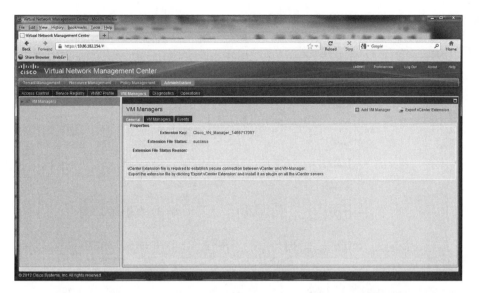

Figure 9-66 *Navigating to Administrator and VM Managers Within the VNMC Management Application*

3. Save the Extension Key in the VNMC Management Application (see Figure 9-67).

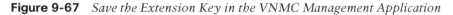

Figure 9-67 *Save the Extension Key in the VNMC Management Application*

4. Navigate to the plug-in and then Manage Plug-ins with vCenter to install the Extension Key downloaded from VNMC (see Figure 9-68).

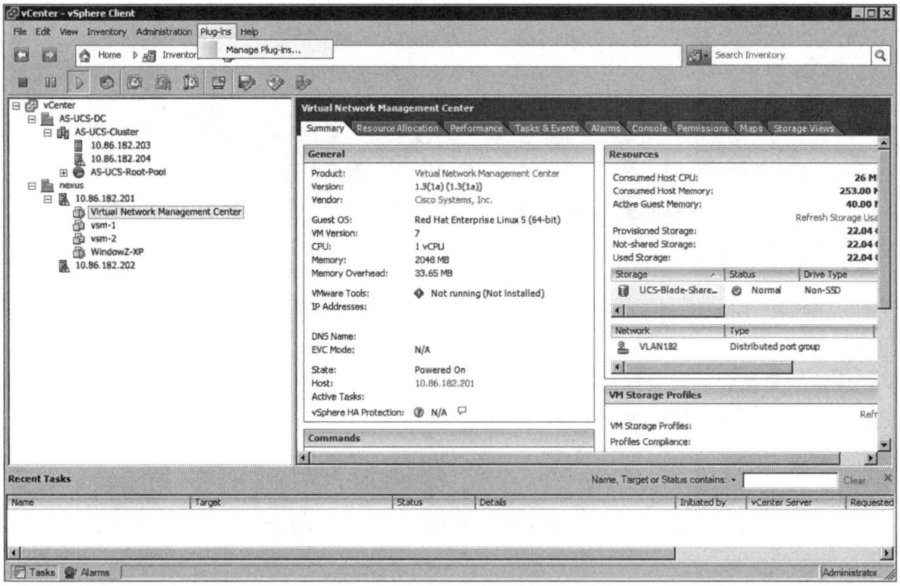

Figure 9-68   *Install the Extension Key Downloaded from VNMC*

5. Select the Extension Key downloaded from VNMC. Right mouse-click in the Manage Plug-In Manager Windows and select new Plug-In (see Figure 9-69).

Figure 9-69   *Select the Extension Key Downloaded from VNMC*

6. Register the Plug-in displayed on the screen (see Figure 9-70).

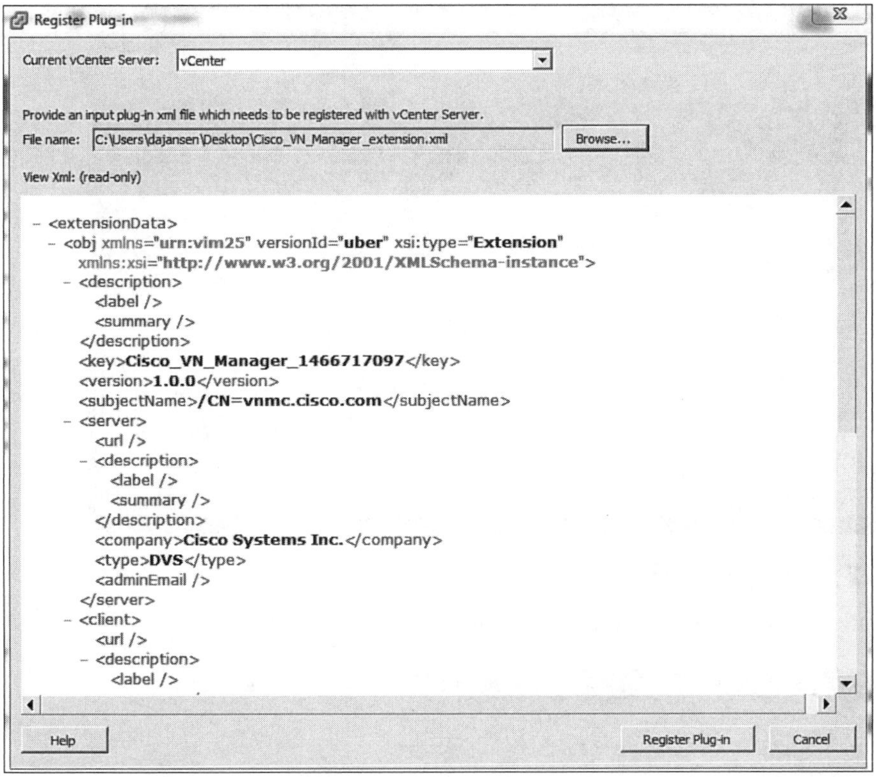

Figure 9-70 *Register the Plug-In*

7. Confirm that the plug-in was successfully registered (see Figure 9-71).

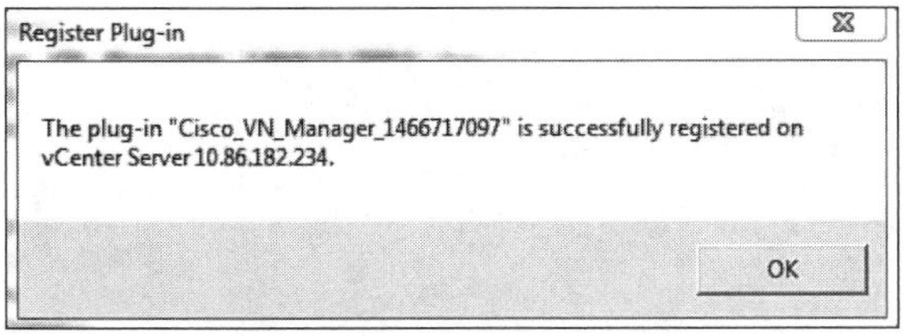

Figure 9-71 *Confirm the Plug-In Was Successfully Registered*

8. Add vCenter VM Manager in VNMC (see Figure 9-72).

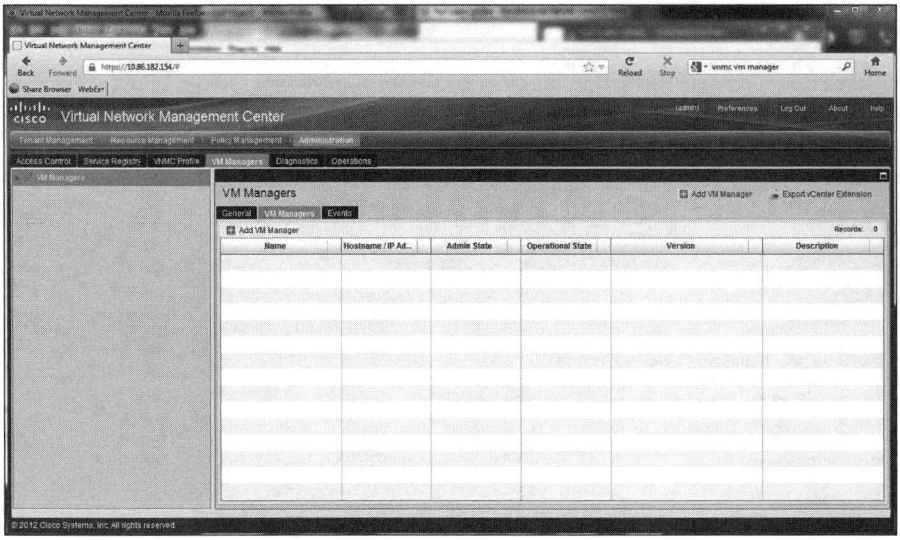

Figure 9-72 *Adding vCenter VM Manager in VNMC*

   9. Enter the Name and IP address of vCenter (see Figure 9-73).

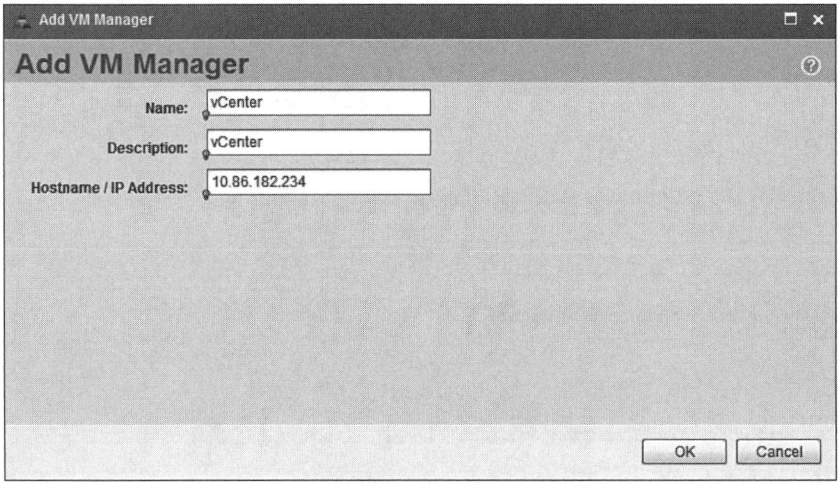

Figure 9-73 *Enter the Name and IP Address of vCenter in the Add VM Manager Dialog Box*

   10. Display the Status of UP for the newly created vCenter VM Manager (see Figure 9-74).

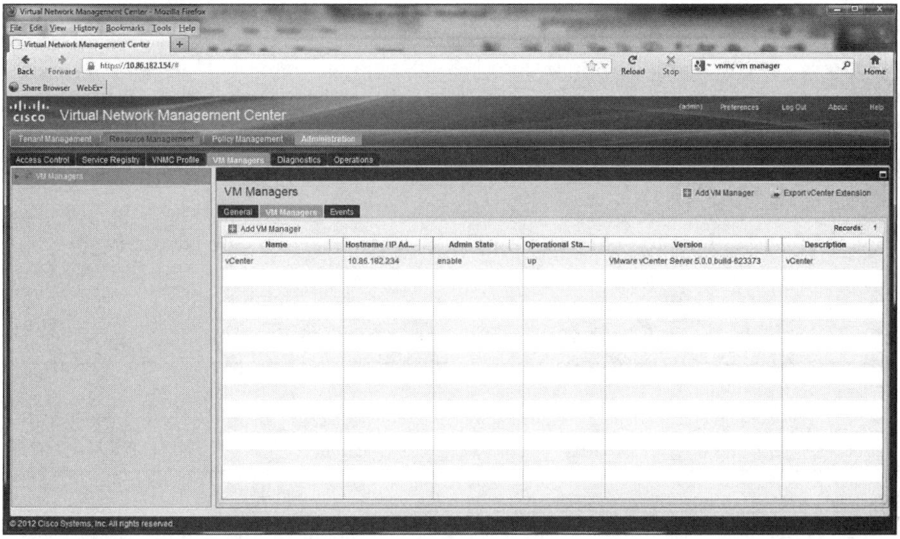

Figure 9-74 *Display the Status of UP for the Newly Created vCenter VM Manager*

> **11.** View the vCenter ESX Hosts in the VNMC Resource Management Resources (see Figure 9-75).

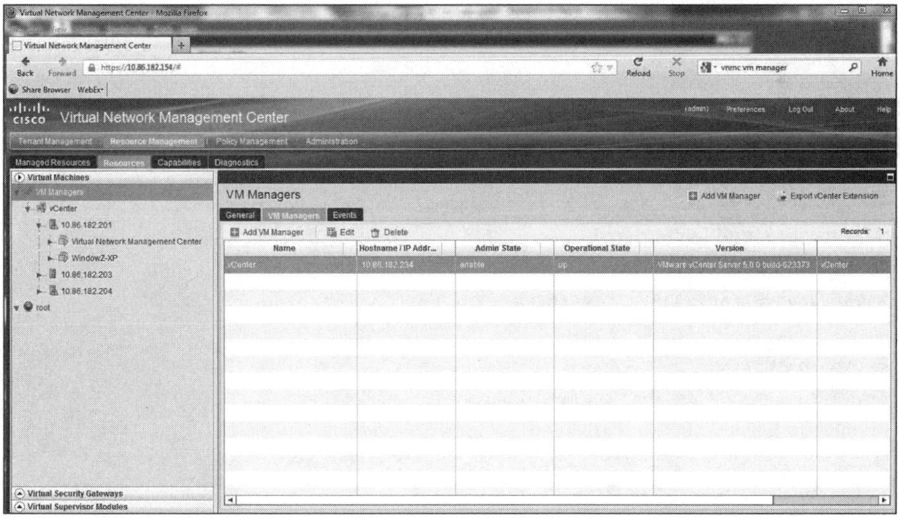

Figure 9-75 *Display vCenter ESX Hosts in the VNMC Resource Management Resources*

Configuring the Cisco VNMC Policy-Agent on the 1000v VSM

The policy-agent (PA) is implemented as an NX-OS plug-in. The policy-agent runs on the VSM to communicate with the VNMC; the PA resides on bootflash: of the VSM. The VSM PA is stateless; it does not need to sync any data to the standby VSM. If VSM HA pair is deployed, the PA needs to be installed on the standby VSM because the PA is stateless.

Example 9-20 shows how to verify that the PA has been copied to the Nexus 1000v VSM.

Example 9-20   *Verify the Policy-Agent Is Copied to the VSM Bootflash*

```
vsm# dir

   17416906     Aug 23 00:39:13 2012  vnmc-vsmpa.1.3.1d.bin
```

Example 9-21 shows the location of the VNMC policy-agent on the Nexus 1000v VSM.

Example 9-21   *Configure the VNMC Policy-Agent on the Nexus 1000v VSM*

```
vsm# show vnm-pa status
VNM Policy-Agent status is - Not Installed

vsm# conf t
Enter configuration commands, one per line.  End with CNTL/Z.
vsm(config)# vnm-policy-agent
vsm(config-vnm-policy-agent)# registration-ip 10.86.182.154
vsm(config-vnm-policy-agent)# shared-secret cisco.123
vsm(config-vnm-policy-agent)# policy-agent-image bootflash:/vnmc-vsmpa.1.3.1d.bin
vsm(config-vnm-policy-agent)# end
vsm# copy running-config startup-config
[#######################################] 100%

vsm# show vnm-pa status
VNM Policy-Agent status is - Installed Successfully. Version 1.3(1d)-vsm

vsm#
```

Example 9-22 shows how to configure the port-profiles on the Nexus 1000v for the VSG Communication.

Example 9-22 *Create the Cisco VSG Port-Profiles on the Nexus 1000v VSM. Port-Profile "VSG" Is the Data VLAN*

```
vsm(config)# port-profile VSG
vsm(config-port-prof)# vmware port-group
vsm(config-port-prof)# switchport mode access
vsm(config-port-prof)# switchport access vlan 102
vsm(config-port-prof)# no shutdown
vsm(config-port-prof)# state enabled
vsm(config-port-prof)#


vsm(config)# port-profile VSG-HA
vsm(config-port-prof)# vmware port-group
vsm(config-port-prof)# switchport mode access
vsm(config-port-prof)# switchport access vlan 102
vsm(config-port-prof)# no shutdown
vsm(config-port-prof)# state enabled
vsm(config-port-prof)# exit
vsm(config)#
```

Example 9-23 shows how to configure the port-profiles on the Nexus 1000v for the VSG Communication.

Example 9-23 *Do No Forget to Add the VSG-Data and HA VLANs to the Ethernet Profile. This Example uses "uplink" port-profile*

```
vsm(config)# port-profile type ethernet uplink
vsm(config-port-prof)# switchport trunk allowed vlan add 100, 200
vsm(config-port-prof)# exit
```

Virtual Security Gateway

Virtual Security Gateway (VSG) is a multitenant security firewall to secure virtualized workloads. Deployment of virtualized workloads enables mobility between rack and rows within a data center and across a data center. The VSG security policy moves with the mobile virtualized workloads. With the VSG, workloads can be monitored and conform to compliance and regulatory regulations with the enterprise/cloud deployment.

VSG secures virtualized environments by decoupling the control-plane and data-plane operations to leverage capabilities built into the VEM deployed in the ESX/ESXi Hypervisor. vPath is embedded in the 1000v VEM distributed virtual switch; VSG leverages vPath to steer the traffic to provide highly available, scalable tenant-aware security architecture.

Because VSG is multitenant-aware, vPath can steer different traffic flows for client-server communication and server-server communication. VSG scales in many ways; for example, only the initial packet is sent to the VSG for policy enforcements. The policy will either permit or deny the traffic. The response to the initial packet, permit or deny, is offloaded directly to vPath on the VEM. In addition, VSG scales to provide security policy across multiple servers within the infrastructure with a centralized instance of VSG. vPath supports both Layer 2 and Layer 3. For Layer 2, the vPath encapsulation is Mac-in-Mac Layer 2 encapsulation. For Layer 3, the vPATH encapsulation is MAC-in-UDP Tunnel.

vPath offers the following benefits:

- Granular enforcement of network, security, and operational policies.

- vPath support for multitennant deployment.

- Offload policy and enables data-plane acceleration for services scale.

- Enables virtual machine mobility to have policy follow the movement of each workload.

- vPath 2.0 enables services chaining.

vPath 2.0 service chaining enables two services to be chained with the first release. vPath 2.0 enables VSG and vASA security services to be chained. The chaining configured enables the sequence mode of operation—for example, which service is first. vASA enables edge firewall services that are not provided by VSG, such as Network Address Translation (NAT) and IP Security (IPsec).

VSG offers flexible deployment options including both Layer 2 and Layer 3 deployment configuration. The Layer 2 or Layer 3 configuration refers to the communication between the VEM and the VSG Firewall.

VSG can be placed on a dedicated appliance (Nexus 1010 or 1010-X) as an OVF or as a virtual machine on a traditional vSphere Guest to meet security requirements. VSG deployed on the Nexus 1010 as a VSB for VSG is covered in this section.

VSG supports a traditional 5-tuple (Source IP address, Source port, Destination IP address, Destination port, and Protocol) security policy. VSG also supports a security model to decouple VLAN and IP address information from the security policy. The security administrator can define policy based upon the following schema attributes from vCenter:

- Name of the virtual machine

- Name of the ESX Host

- Name of the guest operating system

- Name of the associated vAPP

Security policies can be defined in new ways, defining polices that state the operating system type of Windows can have access only to the Active Directory, and operating system type of Linux has access only to LDAP.

Figure 9-76 shows the Virtual Security Gateway system architecture.

VSG System Architecture

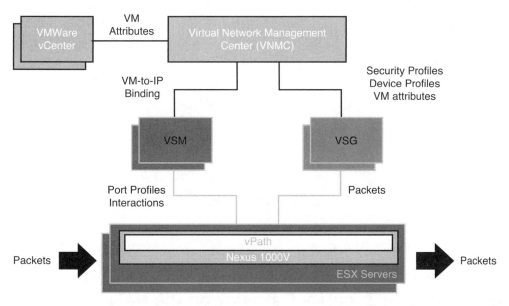

Figure 9-76 *VSG System Architecture*

Figure 9-77 shows the communication between the different components for the entire solution.

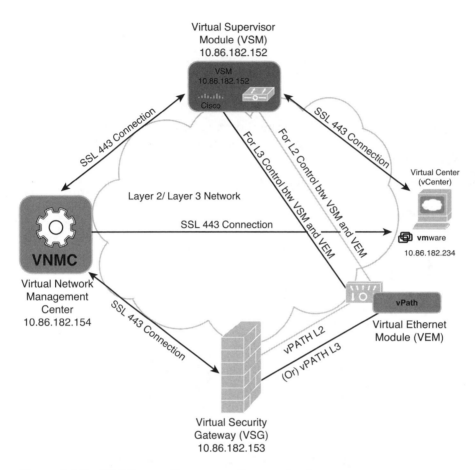

Figure 9-77 *VSG System Component Communication*

Install Virtual Security Gateway on the Nexus 1010

Virtual Security Gateway provides secure virtualized data centers, and public and private clouds, multitennant environments. The following deployment of VSG on the Nexus 1010 is to meet the following requirements of dynamic policy-based operations, mobility-transparent enforcement, and scale-out deployment for multitenancy.

Figure 9-78 shows the VSG topology deployed on Nexus 1010s for the configurations shown in this section.

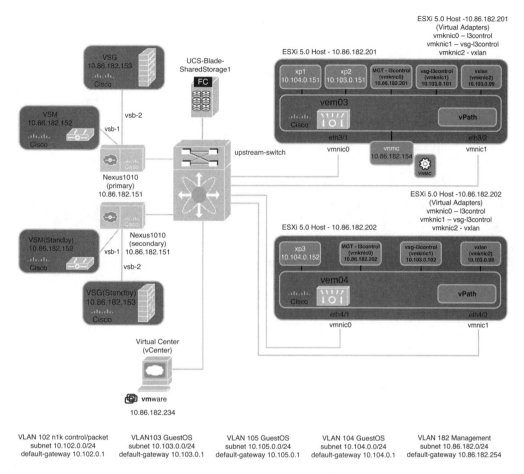

Figure 9-78   *VSG Topology Deployed on Nexus 1010s*

The following steps show how to install the Cisco VSG on the Nexus 1010 appliance.

Example 9-24 shows that the VSG is copied to the "repository" directory on the Nexus 1010 appliance where the Cisco VSG will be installed.

Example 9-24   *Verifying the VSG Nexus1010 .iso Is Copied to the Nexus1010 bootflash:/repository Directory*

```
Nexus1010# dir repository

 107161600     Aug 08 02:33:26 2012   nexus-1000v.VSG1.3.1a.iso
```

Example 9-25 shows how to create a new Virtual Services Blade for the VSG firewall application.

Example 9-25   *Create a New Virtual Services Blade for VSG on the Nexus 1010*

```
Nexus1010(config-vsb-config)# virtual-service-blade-type new nexus-1000v.VSG1.3
.                        1a.iso
Nexus1010(config-vsb-config)# interface data vlan 104



  Nexus1010(config-vsb-config)# interface ha vlan 102
```

Note   When deploying the VSG on the Nexus 1010, the VSG on the Nexus 1010 inherits management VLAN of Nexus 1010 (VLAN182). It is recommended not to change management VLAN on a VSB.

Example 9-26 shows the initial configuration for the VSG VSB installation.

Example 9-26   *Initiate the Configuration Script for the VSG VSB*

```
Nexus1010(config-vsb-config)# enable
Enter vsb image: [nexus-1000v.VSG1.3.1a.iso]
Enter HA id[1-4095]: 989
Management IP version [V4/V6]: [V4] V4
Enter Management IP address: 10.86.182.153
Enter Management subnet mask: 255.255.255.0
IPv4 address of the default gateway: 10.86.182.254
Enter HostName: vsg
Enter the password for 'admin': Cisco123
Note: VSB installation is in progress, please use show virtual-service-blade com-
mands to check the installation status.
Nexus1010(config-vsb-config)#
```

Example 9-27 shows how to verify the VSG VSB installation.

Example 9-27   *Verify the VSG VSB Configuration and Status*

```
Nexus1010# show virtual-service-blade name VSG
virtual-service-blade VSG
  Description:
  Slot id:       2
  Host Name:     VSG
  Management IP: 10.86.182.153
  VSB Type Name : VSG-1.2
  vCPU:          1
  Ramsize:       2048
  Disksize:      3
```

```
Heartbeat:      176756
-----------------------------------------------------------------
     Interface        Type  VLAN       State         Uplink-Interface
                                   Primary  Secondary   Oper  Admin
-----------------------------------------------------------------
VsbEthernet2/1         data   104       up                    Po2   Po2
VsbEthernet2/2   management   182       up                    Po1   Po1
VsbEthernet2/3           ha   102       up                    Po2   Po2
        internal        NA    NA        up
virtual-service-blade:
  HA Status: ACTIVE
  Status:       VSB POWERED ON
  Location:     PRIMARY
  SW version:   4.2(1)VSG1(3.1a)
VSB Info:
  Domain ID : 989

Nexus1010#
```

Configuring the Cisco VNMC Policy-Agent on the VSG

The policy-agent (PA) is implemented as an NX-OS plug-in. The PA runs on the VSG to communicate with the VNMC; the PA resides on bootflash: of the VSG.

The following steps show how to configure the VNMC PA on the VSG.

Example 9-28 shows the VNMC PA is on the Cisco VSG.

Example 9-28   *Verify the Policy-Agent Is Copied to the VSG bootflash:*

```
vsg# dir

  20053444     Aug 22 15:09:06 2012   vnmc-vsgpa.1.3.1d.bin
```

Example 9-29 shows the initial status of the VNMC policy-agent on the VSG.

Example 9-29   *Configure the Policy-Agent on the VSG Pointing to VNMC*

```
vsg# show vnm-pa status
VNM Policy-Agent status is - Not Installed


vsg# conf t
Enter configuration commands, one per line.  End with CNTL/Z.
vsg(config)# vnm-policy-agent
```

```
vsg(config-vnm-policy-agent)# registration-ip 10.86.182.154
vsg(config-vnm-policy-agent)# shared-secret cisco.123
vsg(config-vnm-policy-agent)# policy-agent-image bootflash:vnmc-vsgpa.1.3.1d.bin
vsg(config-vnm-policy-agent)# end

vsg# show vnm-pa status
VNM Policy-Agent status is - Installed Successfully. Version 1.3(1d)-vsg

vsg#
```

Verify That the VSG and VSM Are Registered Clients in VNMC

The following steps show how to verify that the VSM and VSG are registered with the VNMC application.

Verify that both the VSG and the VSM policy-agents are registered with the VNMC application, as illustrated in Figure 9-79.

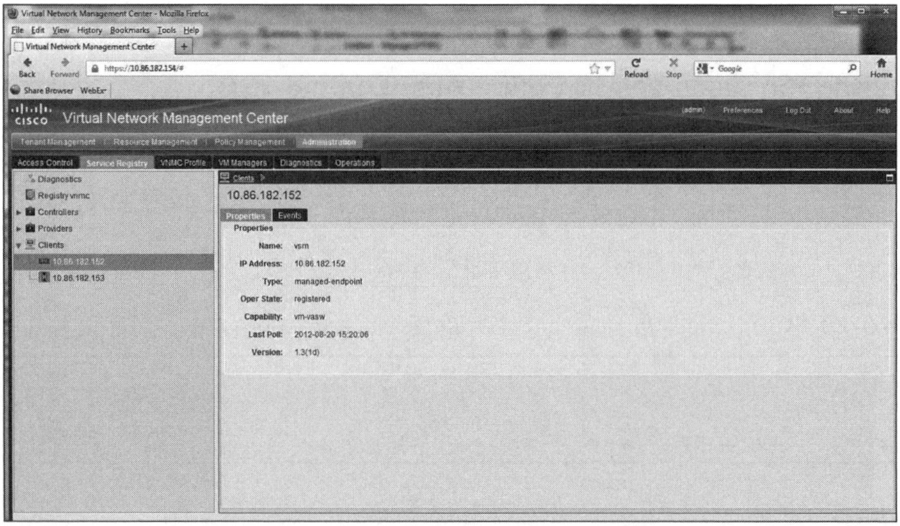

Figure 9-79 *VSM Successfully Registered with VNMC*

Next, ensure that the VSG successfully registered with VNMC, as illustrated in Figure 9-80.

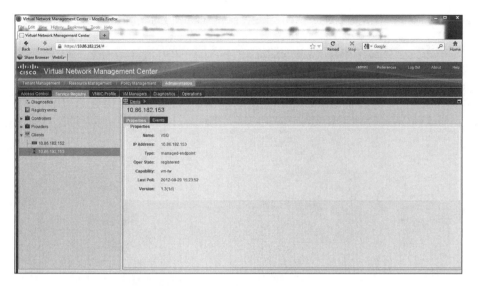

Figure 9-80 *VSG Successfully Registered with VNMC*

Creating a Tenant in VMMC

The following steps show how to create, configure, and deploy security with the VSG Firewall.

Figure 9-81 shows how to create a Tenant for VSG Firewall services through the VNMC management application.

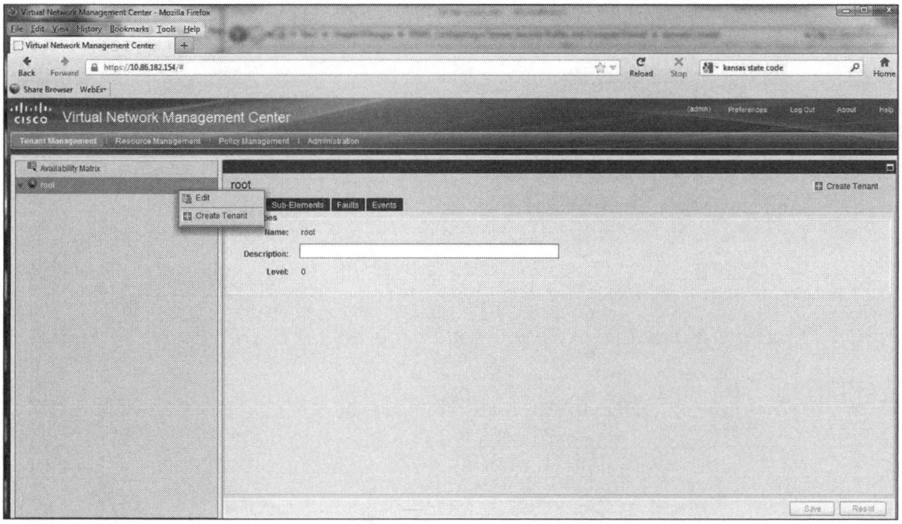

Figure 9-81 *Creating a Tenant in VNMC*

Figure 9-82 shows how to create a Tenant in VNMC named Enterprise.

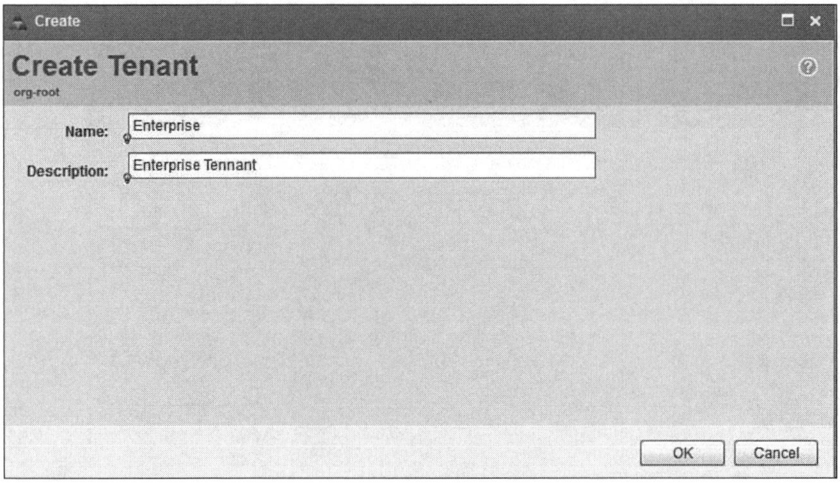

Figure 9-82 *Creating a Tenant in VNMC Named Enterprise*

Figure 9-83 shows how to create a Virtual Data Center in VNMC.

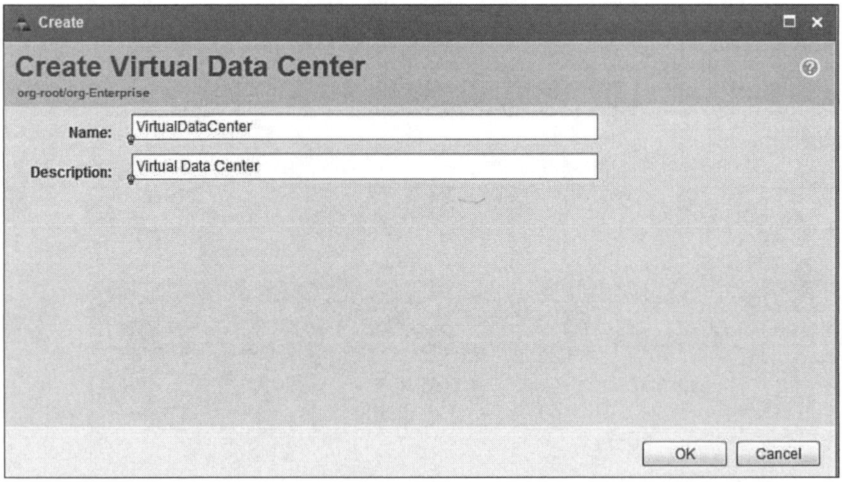

Figure 9-83 *Creating a Virtual Data Center Under the Tenant Hierarchy*

Figure 9-84 shows how to create an Application under the Virtual Data Center in VNMC.

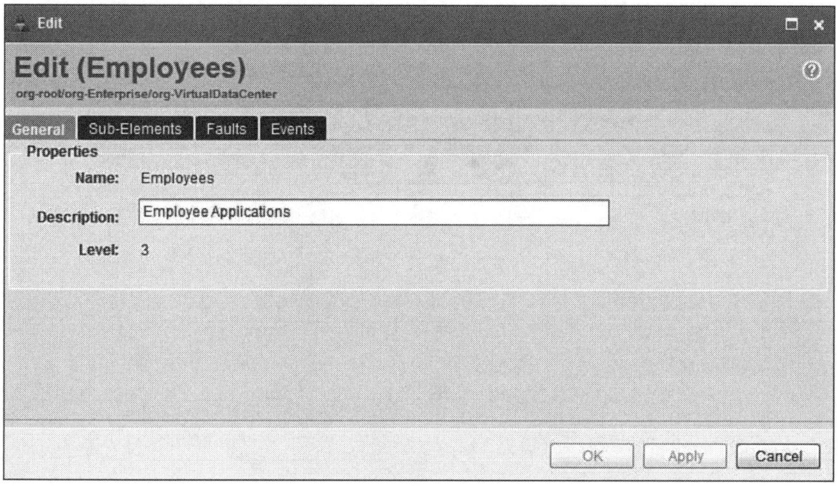

Figure 9-84 *Creating an Application Under the Virtual Data Center in VNMC*

Figure 9-85 shows how to create an Application under the Virtual Data Center in VNMC.

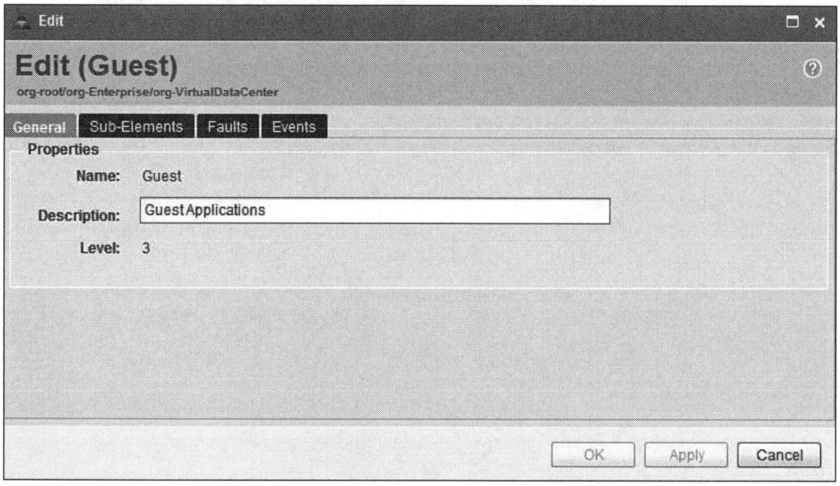

Figure 9-85 *Creating an Application Under the Virtual Data Center in VNMC*

Figure 9-86 and Figure 9-87 show how to create a Security Profile under the Application and Tenant shown previously in Figure 9-85.

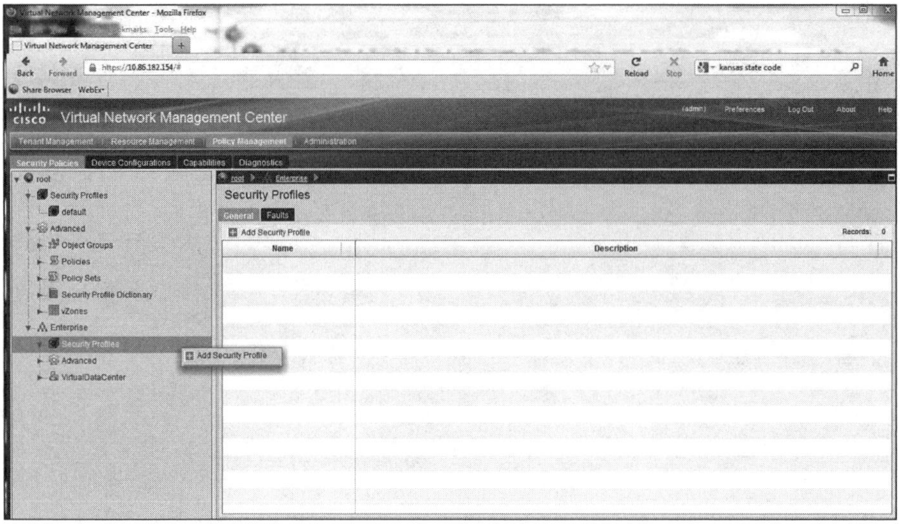

Figure 9-86   *Create a Security Profile Under the Application and Tenant Above*

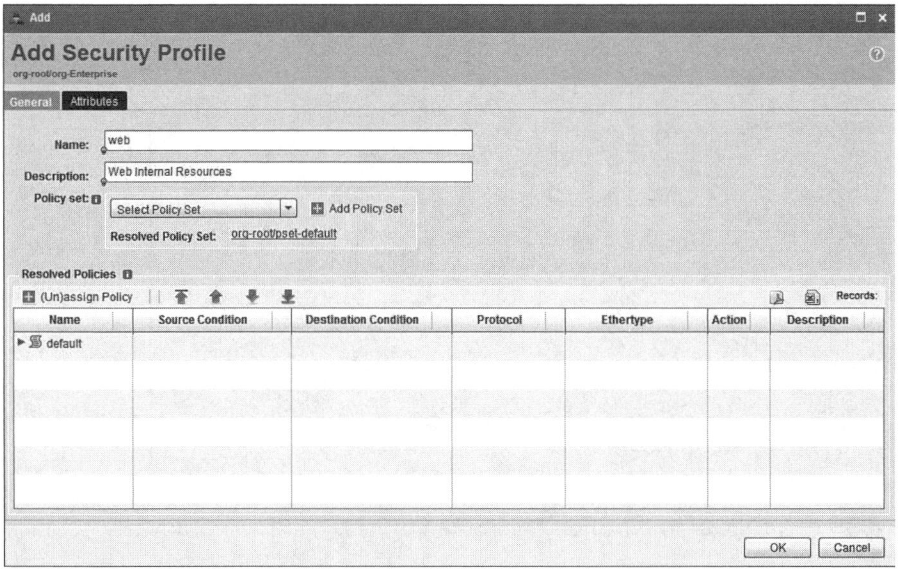

Figure 9-87   *Create a Security Profile Web Under the Preceding Application and Tenant*

Figure 9-88 shows how to create a Security Profile under the Application and preceding Tenant.

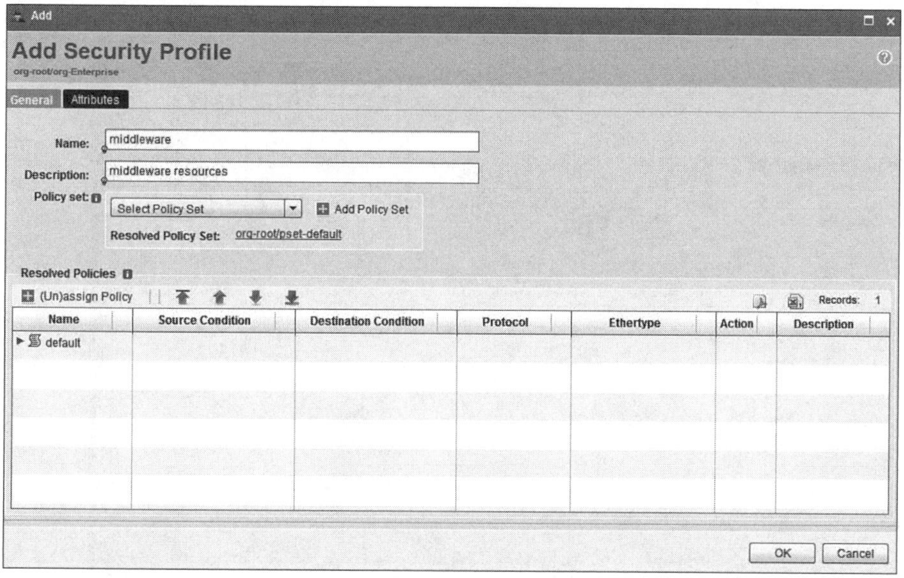

Figure 9-88 *Creating a Security Profile Middleware Under the Application and Preceding Tenant*

Figure 9-89 shows how to create a Security Profile under the Application and preceding Tenant.

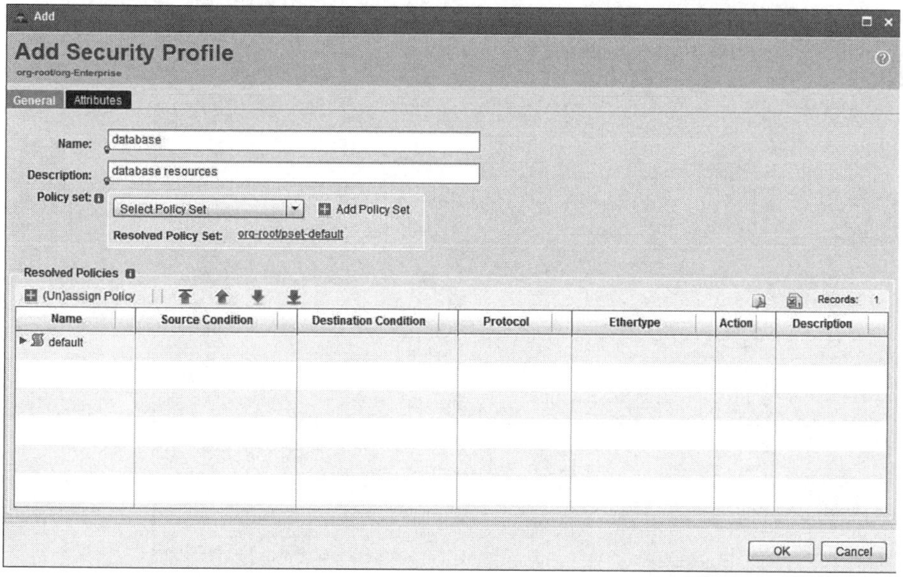

Figure 9-89 *Creating a Security Profile Database Under the Application and Preceding Tenant*

Figure 9-90 shows how to add the Compute Firewall to the Enterprise Tenant.

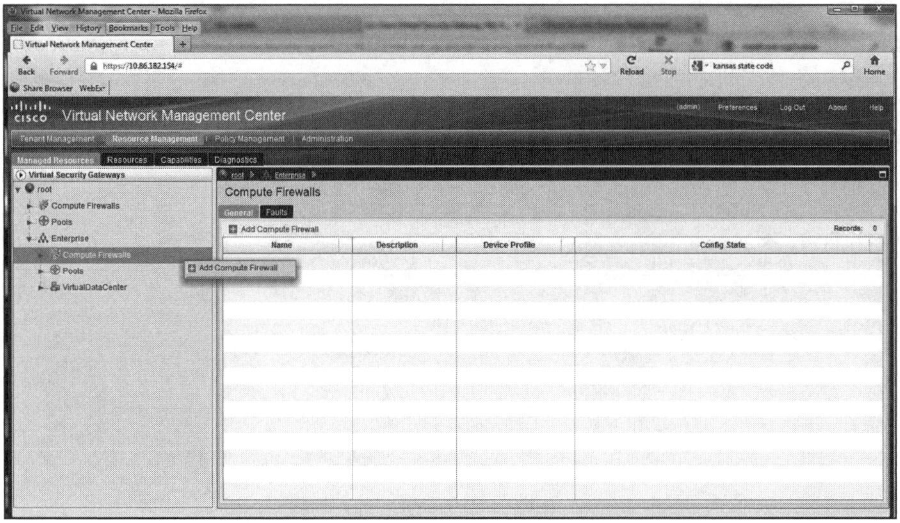

Figure 9-90 *Adding the Compute Firewall to the Enterprise Tenant*

Figure 9-91 shows how to add naming, description, and IP addressing information for the Compute Firewall to the Enterprise Tenant.

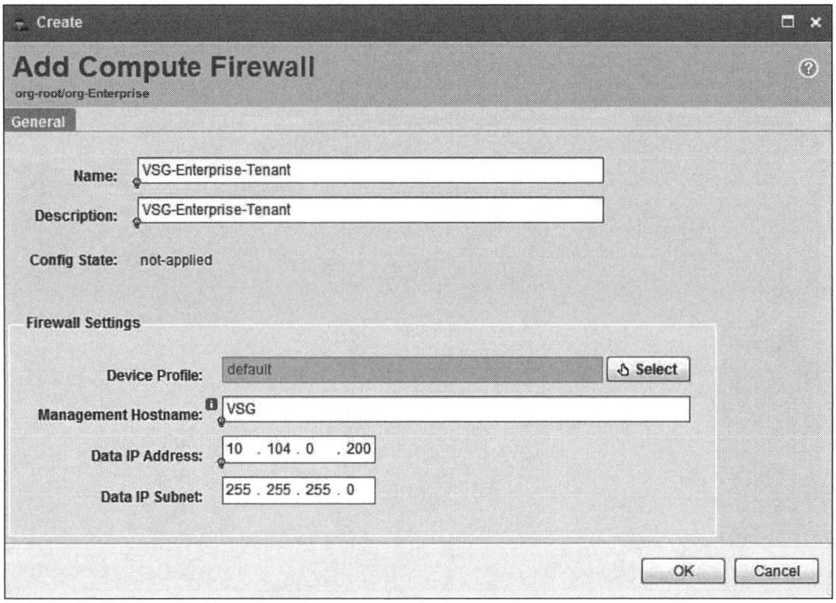

Figure 9-91 *Adding Name, Description, and IP Addressing Information for the Compute Firewall*

Note   When the compute firewall is added, the IP address provided will be deployed and configured on the VSG data0 interface.

```
VSG# show running-config int data 0
!Command: show running-config interface data0
!Time: Thu Aug 30 17:50:50 2012


version 4.2(1)VSG1(3.1a)


interface data0
  ip address 10.104.0.200/24
```

Figure 9-92 shows how to assign the VSG to the Enterprise Tenant.

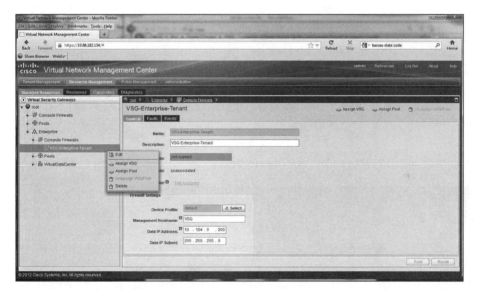

Figure 9-92   *Assigning the VSG to the Enterprise Tenant*

Figure 9-93 shows how to assign the VSG to the Enterprise Tenant.

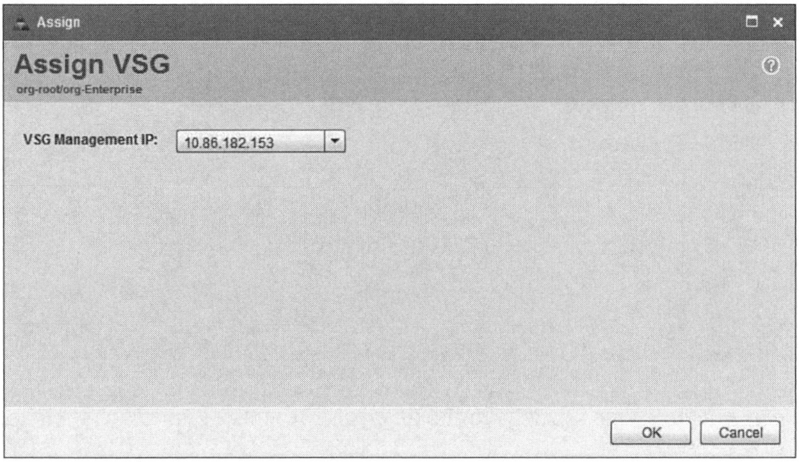

Figure 9-93   *Assigning the VSG to the Enterprise Tenant*

Note   Only one VSG can be assigned to a Tenant. If there are multiple Tenants, additional VSGs will have to deployed and configured with different IP Address. For example, if you have five Tenants, five VSGs will be needed.

Figure 9-94 shows how to add a Policy Set in VNMC for web, middleware, and database.

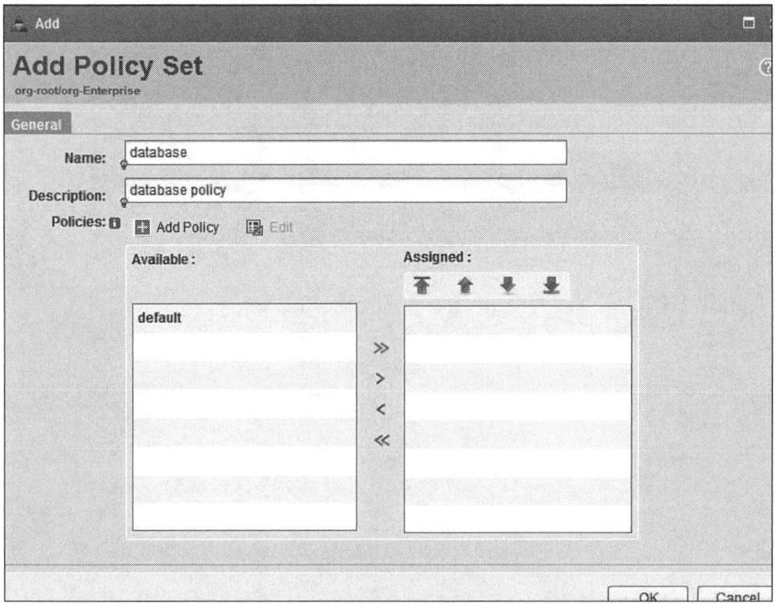

Figure 9-94   *Adding a Policy Set in VNMC for Database*

Figure 9-95 shows how to add a Policy to permit any rule in VNMC for Web, middleware, and database.

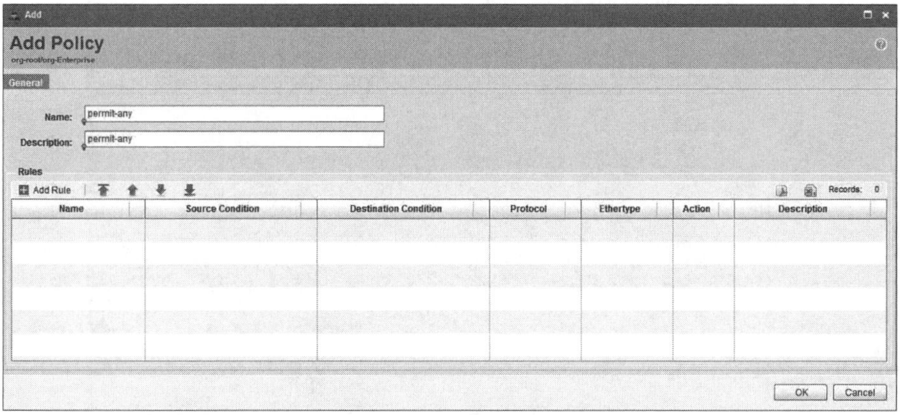

Figure 9-95 *Adding a Policy in VNMC for Web, Middleware, and Database; Permit Any Rule*

Figures 9-96 through 9-98 show how to verify the Policy and Policies within VNMC.

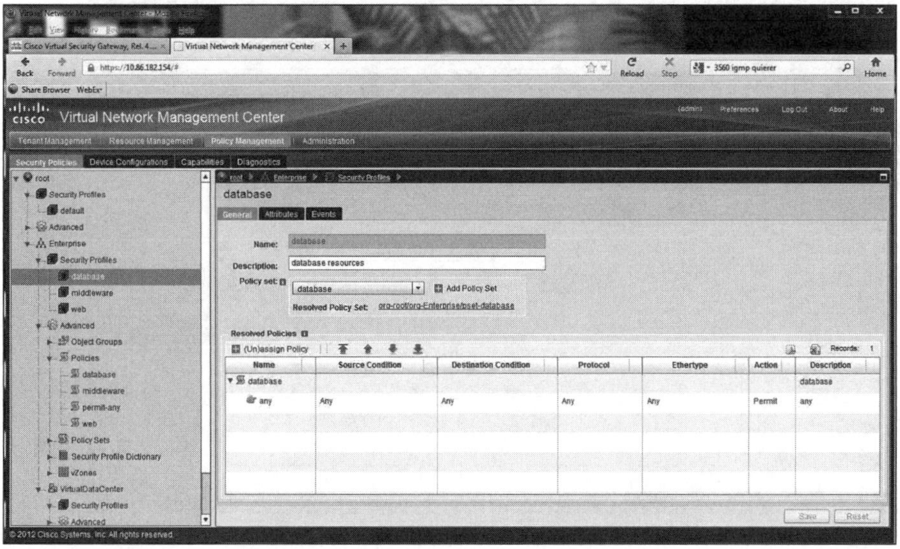

Figure 9-96 *Verifying the Policy and Policies Within VNMC for Database*

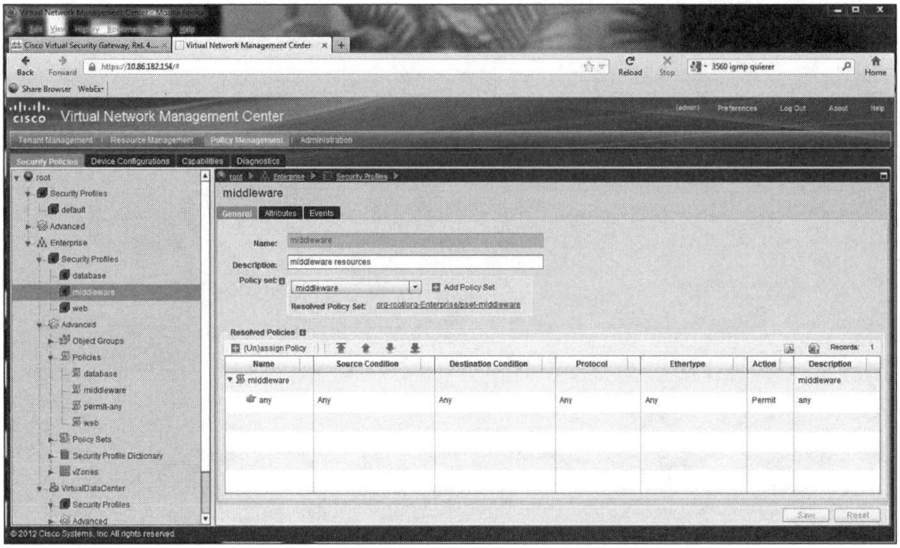

Figure 9-97   *Verifying the Policy and Policies Within VNMC for Middleware*

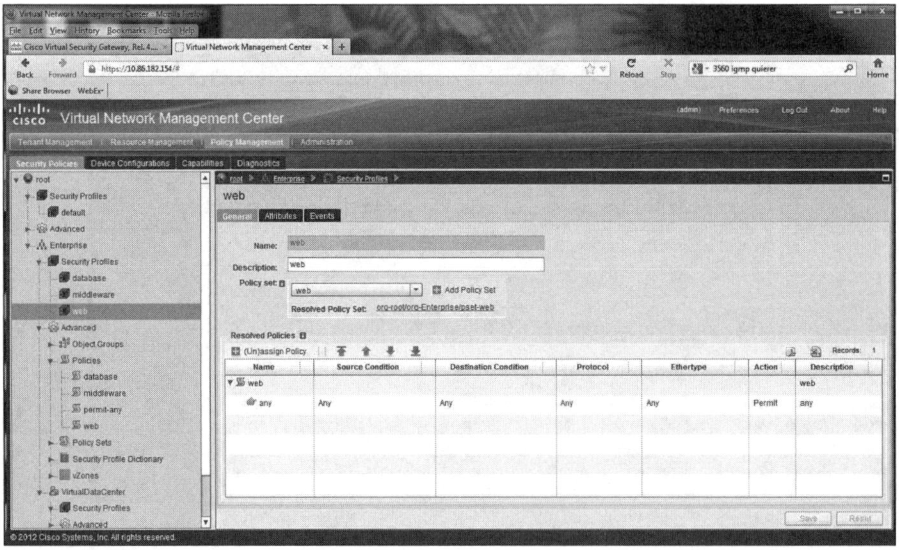

Figure 9-98   *Verifying the Policy and Policies within VNMC for Web*

Verify the Policies created in VNMC on the VSG Firewall running on the Nexus 1010, as demonstrated in Example 9-30.

Example 9-30 *Verifying the Policies Created in VNMC on the VSG Firewall Are Running on the Nexus 1010*

```
VSG# show running-config | begin security
security-profile database@root/Enterprise
  policy database@root/Enterprise
  custom-attribute vnsporg "root/enterprise"

security-profile default@root
  policy default@root
  custom-attribute vnsporg "root"

security-profile middleware@root/Enterprise
  policy middleware@root/Enterprise
  custom-attribute vnsporg "root/enterprise"

security-profile web@root/Enterprise
  policy web@root/Enterprise
  custom-attribute vnsporg "root/enterprise"
rule database/any@root/Enterprise
  action 10 permit
rule default/default-rule@root
  action 10 drop
rule middleware/any@root/Enterprise
  action 10 permit
rule web/any@root/Enterprise
  action 10 permit
policy default@root
  rule default/default-rule@root order 2
policy database@root/Enterprise
  rule database/any@root/Enterprise order 101
policy middleware@root/Enterprise
  rule middleware/any@root/Enterprise order 101
policy web@root/Enterprise
  rule web/any@root/Enterprise order 101
vnm-policy-agent
  registration-ip 10.86.182.154
  shared-secret **********
  policy-agent-image bootflash:/vnmc-vsgpa.1.3.1d.bin
  log-level info
logging logfile messages 2 size 4194303
```

Example 9-31 shows the security policy that was created in VNMC was successfully pushed to the Cisco VSG Firewall running on the Nexus 1010 VSB.

The following steps show how to configure and verify the policy-agent for the Cisco VSG and VSM Communication.

Example 9-31 *Verify the Policy-Agent Is Copied to the VSG bootflash*

```
vsg# dir

   20053444    Aug 22 15:09:06 2012  vnmc-vsgpa.1.3.1d.bin
```

Example 9-32 shows how to create the port-profiles on the Nexus 1000v VSM for the VSG policy enforcement. The port-profile enables the VM Traffic for the Firewall Policy. vPath on the installed VEM performs this functionality. The port-profile will be assigned to the virtual machine.

Example 9-32 *Port-profile Enables the VM Traffic for the Firewall Policy*

```
vsm# conf t
Enter configuration commands, one per line.  End with CNTL/Z.
vsm(config)# port-profile VLAN104
vsm(config-port-prof)# vn-service ip-address 10.104.0.200 vlan 104 security-profile
Employee
vsm(config-port-prof)# org root/Employee
vsm(config-port-prof)# show runn port-profile VLAN104

!Command: show running-config port-profile VLAN104
!Time: Sun Aug 26 20:47:03 2012

version 4.2(1)SV1(5.1a)
port-profile type vethernet VLAN104
  vmware port-group
  switchport mode access
  switchport access vlan 104
  org root/Employees
  no shutdown
  vn-service ip-address 10.104.0.200 vlan 104 security-profile Employee
  state enabled


vsm(config-port-prof)#
```

Example 9-33 shows how to verify the port-profile created VSG services.

Example 9-33 *Verify port-profile VLAN104 Configuration*

```
vsm# show running-config port-profile VLAN104
!Time: Sun Aug 26 20:47:03 2012

version 4.2(1)SV1(5.1a)
port-profile type vethernet VLAN104
  vmware port-group
  switchport mode access
  switchport access vlan 104
  org root/Employees
  no shutdown
  vn-service ip-address 10.104.0.200 vlan 104 security-profile Employee
  state enabled

vsm(config-port-prof)#
```

Example 9-34 shows how to create the port-profiles on the Nexus 1000v VSM for the Cisco VSG data VLAN and the Cisco VSG high-availability port-profiles.

Example 9-34 *Create the VSG Data and HA port-profiles on the VSM*

```
vsm# conf t
Enter configuration commands, one per line.  End with CNTL/Z.
vsm(config)# port-profile type vethernet VSG-HA
vsm(config-port-prof)#  vmware port-group
vsm(config-port-prof)#  switchport mode access
vsm(config-port-prof)#  switchport access vlan 102
vsm(config-port-prof)#  no shutdown
vsm(config-port-prof)#  state enabled


vsm# conf t
Enter configuration commands, one per line.  End with CNTL/Z.
vsm(config)#port-profile type vethernet vsg-data
vsm(config-port-prof)#  vmware port-group
vsm(config-port-prof)#  switchport mode access
vsm(config-port-prof)#  switchport access vlan 104
 vsm(config-port-prof)# no shutdown
vsm(config-port-prof)#  state enabled
```

Add the port-profile VLAN104 to the virtual machine, as shown in Figure 9-99, and verify, as shown in Example 9-35.

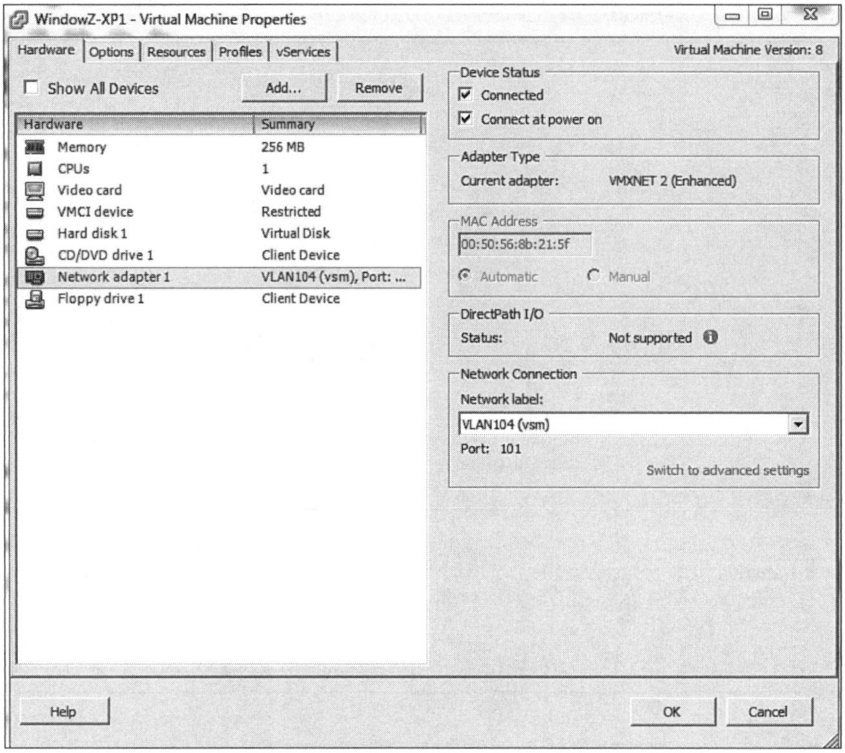

Figure 9-99 *Adding the port-profile VLAN104*

Example 9-35 *Verify the Virtual Services Node on the vsm; Notice the State of Up*

```
vsm# show vsn bri
  VLAN          IP-ADDR          MAC-ADDR    FAIL-MODE  STATE  MODULE
  104       10.104.0.200   00:02:3d:72:2b:06    Close      Up    3


vsm# show vsn port vethernet 4
Veth             : Veth4
VM Name          : windowz-xp1
VM uuid          : 50 0b c9 f8 7a 60 03 97-bd 38 fb 0f 79 48 33 f4
DV Port          : 101
DVS uuid         : ed 5d 0b 50 26 85 42 50-73 78 8e 28 b9 e6 36 dd
Flags            : 0x248
VSN Data IP      : 10.104.0.200
Security Profile : Employess
Org              : root/Employees
VNSP id          : 2
```

```
IP addresses:
    10.104.0.100


vsm#
```

Example 9-35 showed that the port-profile VLAN104 and the VSG data0 interface VLAN104 are L2 adjacent in the same VLAN. If there is a requirement for L3. Example 9-36 shows the configurations to enable L3 mode. VLAN103 will be used for L3 Control for VSG.

Example 9-36 *Configuring the port-profiles for VSG L3-Control. On the Uplink port-profile, VLAN103 Needs to be Added as a System VLAN*

```
vsm# conf t
Enter configuration commands, one per line.  End with CNTL/Z.
vsm(config)# port-profile type ethernet uplink
vsm(config-port-prof)#  vmware port-group
vsm(config-port-prof)#  switchport mode trunk
vsm(config-port-prof)#  switchport trunk vsm(config-port-prof)#  allowed vlan 102-
105,182
 vsm(config-port-prof)#  no shutdown
vsm(config-port-prof)#    system vlan 102, 103
vsm(config-port-prof)#    state enabled


vsm(config-port-prof)#    port-profile type vsm(config-port-prof)#    vethernet VSG-
L3-Control
vsm(config-port-prof)#      vmware port-group
vsm(config-port-prof)#      capability l3-vn-service
vsm(config-port-prof)#      switchport mode access
vsm(config-port-prof)#      switchport access vlan 103
vsm(config-port-prof)#      no shutdown
vsm(config-port-prof)#      state enabled


vsm(config-port-prof)#    port-profile type vethernet VLAN103
vsm(config-port-prof)#      vmware port-group
vsm(config-port-prof)#      switchport mode access
vsm(config-port-prof)#      switchport access vlan 103
vsm(config-port-prof)#      org root/Enterprise
vsm(config-port-prof)#      no shutdown
vsm(config-port-prof)#      vn-service ip-address 10.104.0.200 l3-mode security-pro-
file web
vsm(config-port-prof)#      state enabled
```

Next, create a vmk interface on the ESX host, and assign the vmk interface to port-profile VSG-L3-Control, as shown in Figure 9-100.

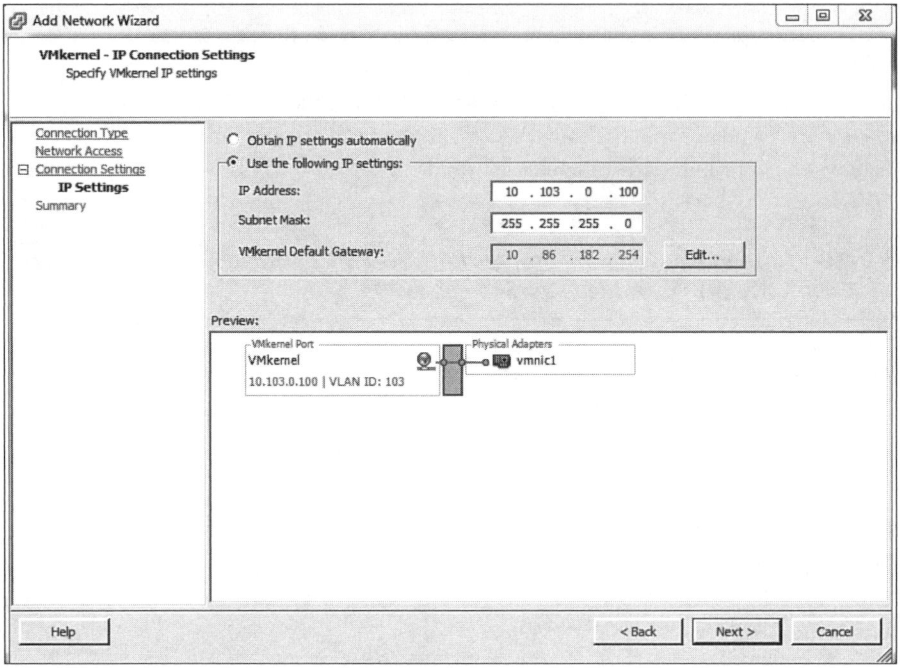

Figure 9-100 *Create a vmk Interface on the ESX Host and Assign the vmk Interface to port-profile VSG-L3-Control*

Because there are multiple vmk interfaces on the ESX host and you can have only one default-gateway, a static route needs to be added on the ESX host to reach 10.104.0.250 VSG from VLAN103, as demonstrated in Example 9-37.

Example 9-37 *A Static Route Needs to be Added on the ESX Host to Reach 10.104.0.250 VSG from VLAN103*

```
~ # esxcfg-route -a 10.104.0.250/32 10.103.0.1
Adding static route 10.104.0.250/32 to VMkernel
```

Assign the virtual machine to VLAN103 port-profile, as shown in Figure 9-101.

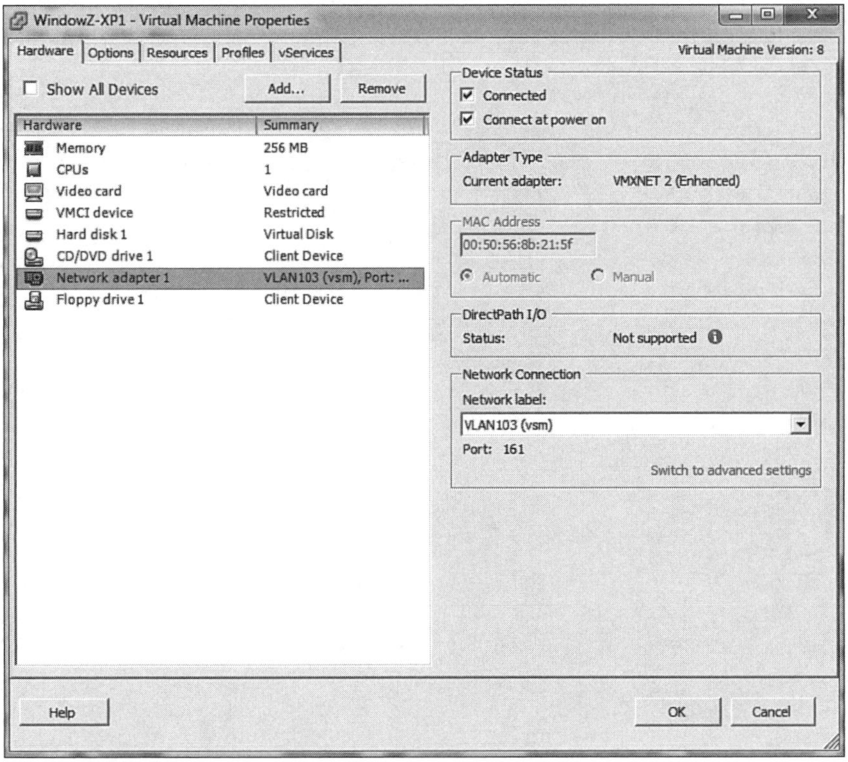

Figure 9-101   *Assigning the Virtual Machine to VLANM103*

Example 9-38 demonstrates l3-control status on the Nexus 1000v VSM has been successfully configured.

Example 9-38   *Verify That the L3 Control Traffic from the Virtual Machine via vPath Is in State Up*

```
vsm# show vsn brief
   VLAN        IP-ADDR        MAC-ADDR  FAIL-MODE  STATE  MODULE
     -       10.104.0.200        -        Close     Up    3
```

Example 9-39 demonstrates the vPath information for each VEM on the Nexus 1000v VSM.

Example 9-39   *Verify the vPath Information on the VSM for Both L2 and L3 Control*

```
vsm# show vsn statistics vpath module 3
#VSN  VLAN: 104, IP-ADDR: 10.104.0.200
  Module: 3
    #VPath Packet Statistics     Ingress         Egress          Total
    Total Seen                     2446            121             2567
    Policy Redirects                426              0              426
    No-Policy Passthru             1812            121             1933
    Policy-Permits Rcvd               0              0                0
    Policy-Denies  Rcvd             426              0              426
    Permit Hits                       0              0                0
    Deny   Hits                     208              0              208
    Decapsulated                    426              0              426
    Fail-Open                         0              0                0
    Badport Err                       0              0                0
    VSN Config Err                    0              0                0
    VSN State Down                    0              0                0
    Encap Err                         0              0                0
    All-Drops                       208              0              208
    Flow Notificns Sent                                              0
    Total Rcvd From VSN                                            426
    Non-Cisco Encap Rcvd                                             0
    VNS-Port Drops                                                 426
    Policy-Action Err                                                0
    Decap Err                                                        0
    L2-Frag Sent                                                     0
    L2-Frag Rcvd                                                     0
    L2-Frag Coalesced                                                0
    Encap exceeded MTU                                               0
    ICMP Too Big Rcvd                                                0

    #VPath Flow Statistics
    Active Flows               0  Active Connections                 0
    Forward Flow Create      405  Forward Flow Destroy             405
    Reverse Flow Create      405  Reverse Flow Destroy             405
    Flow ID Alloc            810  Flow ID Free                     810
    Connection ID Alloc      405  Connection ID Free               405
    L2 Flow Create             0  L2 Flow Destroy                    0
    L3 Flow Create           320  L3 Flow Destroy                  320
    L4 TCP Flow Create         0  L4 TCP Flow Destroy                0
    L4 UDP Flow Create       490  L4 UDP Flow Destroy              490
    L4 Oth Flow Create         0  L4 Oth Flow Destroy                0
    Embryonic Flow Create      0  Embryonic Flow Bloom               0
    L2 Flow Timeout            0  L2 Flow Offload                    0
```

```
    L3 Flow Timeout              331  L3 Flow Offload              160
    L4 TCP Flow Timeout            0  L4 TCP Flow Offload            0
    L4 UDP Flow Timeout          578  L4 UDP Flow Offload          266
    L4 Oth Flow Timeout            0  L4 Oth Flow Offload            0
    Flow Lookup Hit              229  Flow Lookup Miss             810
    Flow Dual Lookup            1039  L4 TCP Tuple-reuse             0
    TCP chkfail InvalACK           0  TCP chkfail SeqPstWnd          0
    TCP chkfail WndVari            0
    Flow Classify Err              0  Flow ID Alloc Err              0
    Conn ID Alloc Err              0  Hash Alloc Err                 0
    Flow Exist                     0  Flow Entry Exhaust             0
    Flow Removal Err               0  Bad Flow ID Receive            0
    Flow Entry Miss                0  Flow Full Match Err            0
    Bad Action Receive             0  Invalid Flow Pair              0
    Invalid Connection             0
    Hash Alloc                     0  Hash Free                      0
    InvalFID Lookup                0  InvalFID Lookup Err            0
    Deferred Delete                0
#VSN  VLAN: 0, IP-ADDR: 10.104.0.200
  Module: 3
    #VPath Packet Statistics    Ingress       Egress       Total
    Total Seen                     82            2           84
    Policy Redirects               23            0           23
    No-Policy Passthru             21            1           22
    Policy-Permits Rcvd             0            0            0
    Policy-Denies  Rcvd            23            0           23
    Permit Hits                     0            0            0
    Deny   Hits                    20            0           20
    Decapsulated                   23            0           23
    Fail-Open                       0            0            0
    Badport Err                     0            0            0
    VSN Config Err                  0            0            0
    VSN State Down                 19            0           19
    Encap Err                       0            0            0
    All-Drops                      38            1           39
    Flow Notificns Sent                                      0
    Total Rcvd From VSN                                     23
    Non-Cisco Encap Rcvd                                     0
    VNS-Port Drops                                         23
    Policy-Action Err                                       0
    Decap Err                                               0
    L2-Frag Sent                                            0
    L2-Frag Rcvd                                            0
    L2-Frag Coalesced                                       0
    Encap exceeded MTU                                      0
```

```
     ICMP Too Big Rcvd                                    0

     #VPath Flow Statistics
     Active Flows                 0  Active Connections         0
     Forward Flow Create         20  Forward Flow Destroy      20
     Reverse Flow Create         20  Reverse Flow Destroy      20
     Flow ID Alloc               40  Flow ID Free              40
     Connection ID Alloc         20  Connection ID Free        20
     L2 Flow Create               0  L2 Flow Destroy            0
     L3 Flow Create               8  L3 Flow Destroy            8
     L4 TCP Flow Create           0  L4 TCP Flow Destroy        0
     L4 UDP Flow Create          32  L4 UDP Flow Destroy       32
     L4 Oth Flow Create           0  L4 Oth Flow Destroy        0
     Embryonic Flow Create        0  Embryonic Flow Bloom       0
     L2 Flow Timeout              0  L2 Flow Offload            0
     L3 Flow Timeout              9  L3 Flow Offload            4
     L4 TCP Flow Timeout          0  L4 TCP Flow Offload        0
     L4 UDP Flow Timeout         43  L4 UDP Flow Offload       19
     L4 Oth Flow Timeout          0  L4 Oth Flow Offload        0
     Flow Lookup Hit             23  Flow Lookup Miss          40
     Flow Dual Lookup            63  L4 TCP Tuple-reuse         0
     TCP chkfail InvalACK         0  TCP chkfail SeqPstWnd      0
     TCP chkfail WndVari          0
     Flow Classify Err            0  Flow ID Alloc Err          0
     Conn ID Alloc Err            0  Hash Alloc Err             0
     Flow Exist                   0  Flow Entry Exhaust         0
     Flow Removal Err             0  Bad Flow ID Receive        0
     Flow Entry Miss              0  Flow Full Match Err        0
     Bad Action Receive           0  Invalid Flow Pair          0
     Invalid Connection           0
     Hash Alloc                   0  Hash Free                  0
     InvalFID Lookup              0  InvalFID Lookup Err        0
     Deferred Delete              0
vsm#


vsm# show vsn statistics vpath
#VSN  VLAN: 104, IP-ADDR: 10.104.0.200
  Module: 3
    #VPath Packet Statistics    Ingress      Egress        Total
    Total Seen                     2448         122         2570
    Policy Redirects                426           0          426
    No-Policy Passthru             1814         122         1936
    Policy-Permits Rcvd               0           0            0
    Policy-Denies  Rcvd             426           0          426
    Permit Hits                       0           0            0
```

```
Deny   Hits                       208               0             208
Decapsulated                      426               0             426
Fail-Open                           0               0               0
Badport Err                         0               0               0
VSN Config Err                      0               0               0
VSN State Down                      0               0               0
Encap Err                           0               0               0
All-Drops                         208               0             208
Flow Notificns Sent                                                 0
Total Rcvd From VSN                                               426
Non-Cisco Encap Rcvd                                                0
VNS-Port Drops                                                    426
Policy-Action Err                                                   0
Decap Err                                                           0
L2-Frag Sent                                                        0
L2-Frag Rcvd                                                        0
L2-Frag Coalesced                                                   0
Encap exceeded MTU                                                  0
ICMP Too Big Rcvd                                                   0


#VPath Flow Statistics
Active Flows                     0    Active Connections              0
Forward Flow Create            405    Forward Flow Destroy          405
Reverse Flow Create            405    Reverse Flow Destroy          405
Flow ID Alloc                  810    Flow ID Free                  810
Connection ID Alloc            405    Connection ID Free            405
L2 Flow Create                   0    L2 Flow Destroy                 0
L3 Flow Create                 320    L3 Flow Destroy               320
L4 TCP Flow Create               0    L4 TCP Flow Destroy             0
L4 UDP Flow Create             490    L4 UDP Flow Destroy           490
L4 Oth Flow Create               0    L4 Oth Flow Destroy             0
Embryonic Flow Create            0    Embryonic Flow Bloom            0
L2 Flow Timeout                  0    L2 Flow Offload                 0
L3 Flow Timeout                331    L3 Flow Offload               160
L4 TCP Flow Timeout              0    L4 TCP Flow Offload             0
L4 UDP Flow Timeout            578    L4 UDP Flow Offload           266
L4 Oth Flow Timeout              0    L4 Oth Flow Offload             0
Flow Lookup Hit                229    Flow Lookup Miss              810
Flow Dual Lookup              1039    L4 TCP Tuple-reuse              0
TCP chkfail InvalACK             0    TCP chkfail SeqPstWnd           0
TCP chkfail WndVari              0
Flow Classify Err                0    Flow ID Alloc Err               0
Conn ID Alloc Err                0    Hash Alloc Err                  0
Flow Exist                       0    Flow Entry Exhaust              0
Flow Removal Err                 0    Bad Flow ID Receive             0
```

Flow Entry Miss	0	Flow Full Match Err		0
Bad Action Receive	0	Invalid Flow Pair		0
Invalid Connection	0			
Hash Alloc	0	Hash Free		0
InvalFID Lookup	0	InvalFID Lookup Err		0
Deferred Delete	0			

#VSN VLAN: 0, IP-ADDR: 10.104.0.200

Module: 3

#VPath Packet Statistics	Ingress	Egress	Total
Total Seen	84	2	86
Policy Redirects	24	0	24
No-Policy Passthru	22	1	23
Policy-Permits Rcvd	0	0	0
Policy-Denies Rcvd	24	0	24
Permit Hits	0	0	0
Deny Hits	20	0	20
Decapsulated	24	0	24
Fail-Open	0	0	0
Badport Err	0	0	0
VSN Config Err	0	0	0
VSN State Down	19	0	19
Encap Err	0	0	0
All-Drops	38	1	39
Flow Notificns Sent			0
Total Rcvd From VSN			24
Non-Cisco Encap Rcvd			0
VNS-Port Drops			24
Policy-Action Err			0
Decap Err			0
L2-Frag Sent			0
L2-Frag Rcvd			0
L2-Frag Coalesced			0
Encap exceeded MTU			0
ICMP Too Big Rcvd			0

#VPath Flow Statistics			
Active Flows	0	Active Connections	0
Forward Flow Create	21	Forward Flow Destroy	21
Reverse Flow Create	21	Reverse Flow Destroy	21
Flow ID Alloc	42	Flow ID Free	42
Connection ID Alloc	21	Connection ID Free	21
L2 Flow Create	0	L2 Flow Destroy	0
L3 Flow Create	8	L3 Flow Destroy	8
L4 TCP Flow Create	0	L4 TCP Flow Destroy	0
L4 UDP Flow Create	34	L4 UDP Flow Destroy	34

L4 Oth Flow Create	0	L4 Oth Flow Destroy	0
Embryonic Flow Create	0	Embryonic Flow Bloom	0
L2 Flow Timeout	0	L2 Flow Offload	0
L3 Flow Timeout	9	L3 Flow Offload	4
L4 TCP Flow Timeout	0	L4 TCP Flow Offload	0
L4 UDP Flow Timeout	45	L4 UDP Flow Offload	20
L4 Oth Flow Timeout	0	L4 Oth Flow Offload	0
Flow Lookup Hit	23	Flow Lookup Miss	42
Flow Dual Lookup	65	L4 TCP Tuple-reuse	0
TCP chkfail InvalACK	0	TCP chkfail SeqPstWnd	0
TCP chkfail WndVari	0		
Flow Classify Err	0	Flow ID Alloc Err	0
Conn ID Alloc Err	0	Hash Alloc Err	0
Flow Exist	0	Flow Entry Exhaust	0
Flow Removal Err	0	Bad Flow ID Receive	0
Flow Entry Miss	0	Flow Full Match Err	0
Bad Action Receive	0	Invalid Flow Pair	0
Invalid Connection	0		
Hash Alloc	0	Hash Free	0
InvalFID Lookup	0	InvalFID Lookup Err	0
Deferred Delete	0		

```
vsm# show vsn port vethernet 4
Veth            : Veth4
VM Name         : windowz-xp1
VM uuid         : 50 0b c9 f8 7a 60 03 97-bd 38 fb 0f 79 48 33 f4
DV Port         : 161
DVS uuid        : ed 5d 0b 50 26 85 42 50-73 78 8e 28 b9 e6 36 dd
Flags           : 0x348
VSN Data IP     : 10.104.0.200
Security Profile : web
Org             : root/Enterprise
VNSP id         : 4
IP addresses:
    10.103.0.151




vsm# show vsn port vm windowz-xp1
Veth            : Veth4
VM Name         : windowz-xp1
VM uuid         : 50 0b c9 f8 7a 60 03 97-bd 38 fb 0f 79 48 33 f4
DV Port         : 161
```

```
DVS uuid          : ed 5d 0b 50 26 85 42 50-73 78 8e 28 b9 e6 36 dd
Flags             : 0x348
VSN Data IP       : 10.104.0.200
Security Profile  : web
Org               : root/Enterprise
VNSP id           : 4
IP addresses:
    10.103.0.151


vsm# show vsn brief
  VLAN         IP-ADDR           MAC-ADDR   FAIL-MODE  STATE  MODULE
  104      10.104.0.200  00:02:3d:72:2b:06    Close     Up    3
    -      10.104.0.200             -         Close     Up    3
```

Virtual Extensible LAN

Virtual Extensible LAN (VXLAN) uses a 24-bit LAN segment identifier that enables additional scale compared to a current 802.1Q VLAN 12-bit identifier that is limited to 4096 VLANs. VXLAN enables the creation of Layer 2 network isolation with the 24-bit segment identifier to scale beyond the 4096 limitations of VLANs. VXLAN creates LAN segments by using an overlay MAC-in-IP encapsulation of 50 bytes. The VEM is responsible for the encapsulation of the original Layer 2 frame from the VM.

Figure 9-102 shows the VXLAN packet format.

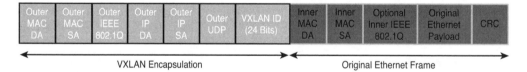

Figure 9-102   *VXLAN Packet Format*

A virtual vmknic network adapter is created on the ESX host and assigned to the VEM. This enables the VEM to encapsulate the original L2 frame with the VXLAN identifier. Today, VXLAN is supported only on the Nexus 1000v; if there is a requirement for external communication of the VXLAN segment the following solutions are available:

■ Deploy a multihomed virtual machine with two interfaces. One interface would reside in the VXLAN network, and the second interface would reside in the VLAN network.

- Deploy a VXLAN gateway; the Virtual ASA (vASA 1000v) or Cloud Services Router (CSR 1000v) can be deployed as a VXLAN gateway.

The following requirements are needed to deploy VXLAN:

- The MTU needs to be increased by 50 bytes to enable the VLAN MAC-in-IP encapsulation.

- Recommend using LACP port-channels for the PNICs.

- The upstream physical switches from the VEMs need to have IGMP querier-enabled.

- Proxy-ARP needs to be enabled on the Layer3 Interfaces (SVI) upstream routers for the port-profiles that are capability vxlan-enabled.

- Multicast routing needs to be enabled on the upstream switches or routers if the VEMs are separated by routers and require VXLAN connectivity.

- Enable 5 Tuple Hashing for optimal load balancing for LACP; the encapsulation will generate a source UDP port based on a hash of inner packet 5-tuples.

The default setting for the VM vNICs (vEthernet) MTU is 1500 bytes. This is also true for the uplink pNICS (Physical Ethernet) uplink interfaces. With the default setting of 1500 byes on the edge MTU, a minimum of 1550 bytes is needed to allow for the VXLAN encapsulation. On the Nexus 1000v, the additional MTU can be enabled on the Ethernet uplink profile assigned to the physical ESX hosts; nothing else needs to be configured on the VM or host side. The physical upstream switches that provide the connections need to have jumbo frames enabled as well. Another option is to set the edge MTU on the VM vNICs to 1450 bytes, which would be 50 bytes less than the default 1500 bytes.

For proxy-arp, it is enabled by default on IOS-based devices. For NX-OS platforms, proxy-arp is disabled by default and needs to be enabled.

For the Multicast, multicast queries need to come into the vmk NIC for the VXLAN transport VLAN. This requires that IGMP snooping querier be configured for the transport VLAN. Without the querier enabled or configured, the multicast will not work and there will not be any remote IP interfaces learned for VXLAN operation.

Figure 9-103 shows the VXLAN topology used throughout this section.

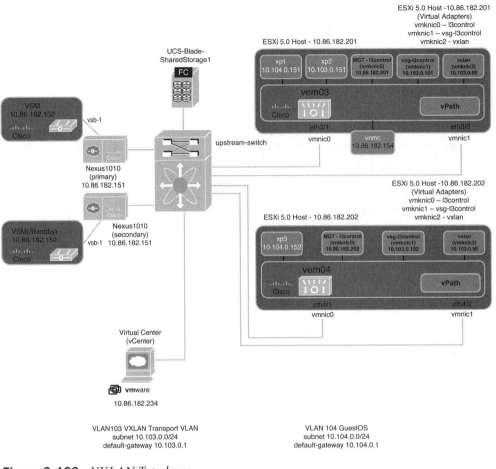

Figure 9-103   *VXLAN Topology*

Note   If there are firewalls in the middle, VXLAN uses a destination UDP port of 8472 for the MAC-in-IP encapsulation. This must be opened allowed for proper operations.

Deploying Virtual Extensible LAN

What follows are the configuration steps to deploy VXLAN on Nexus 1000v:

1. Enable the VXLAN feature on the Nexus 1000v VSM:

```
vsm# conf t
Enter configuration commands, one per line.  End with CNTL/Z.
vsm(config)# feature segmentation
```

```
vsm(config)# 2012 Aug 29 01:05:54 vsm %SEG_BD-2-SEG_BD_ENABLED: Feature
Segmentation enabled
vsm(config)#
```

2. Create a VXLAN, and define the bridge-domain and Multicast group on the Nexus 1000v VSM:

```
vsm# conf t
Enter configuration commands, one per line.  End with CNTL/Z.
vsm(config)# bridge-domain 10
vsm(config-bd)# segment id 60133
vsm(config)# group 239.1.1.1
```

Note The Multicast group is used for broadcasts and flooding; reserved multicast addresses are not allowed.

3. Enable jumbo frames on the Ethernet uplink to PNICs to allow for the additional 50 bytes for VXLAN:

```
vsm# conf t
Enter configuration commands, one per line.  End with CNTL/Z.
vsm(config)# port-profile type ethernet uplink
vsm(config-port-prof)# vmware port-group
vsm(config-port-prof)# switchport mode trunk
vsm(config-port-prof)# switchport trunk allowed vlan 102-105,182
vsm(config-port-prof)# mtu 9000
vsm(config-port-prof)# no shutdown
vsm(config-port-prof)# system vlan 102-103,182
vsm(config-port-prof)# state enabled
```

4. Configure the transport VLAN port-profile for the VXLAN encapsulated traffic:

```
vsm# conf t

Enter configuration commands, one per line.  End with CNTL/Z.
vsm(config)# port-profile type vethernet vxlan
vsm(config-port-prof)# vmware port-group
vsm(config-port-prof)# switchport mode access
vsm(config-port-prof)# switchport access vlan 103
vsm(config-port-prof)# capability vxlan
vsm(config-port-prof)# no shutdown
vsm(config-port-prof)# state enabled
```

5. Create a port-profile to assign each virtual machine for the same VXLAN bridge-domain:

```
vsm# conf t

Enter configuration commands, one per line.  End with CNTL/Z.
vsm(config)#port-profile VxLAN-VMs
vsm(config-port-prof)#vmware port-group
vsm(config-port-prof)# switchport mode access
vsm(config-port-prof)# switchport access bridge-domain 10
vsm(config-port-prof)# no shutdown
vsm(config-port-prof)# state enabled
```

6. Enable Multicast on the upstream switch router:

```
upstream-switch#show run | i igmp
ip igmp snooping querier address 10.103.0.1
ip igmp snooping querier

upstream-switch##show ip igmp snooping group
Vlan    Group               Type      Version    Port List
----------------------------------------------------------------
103     239.1.1.1           igmp                 Te0/1
105     239.255.255.250     igmp                 Te0/1, Te0/2
182     239.255.255.253     igmp                 Gi0/1, Te0/1
183     239.255.255.250     igmp                 Gi0/1
```

7. Enable jumbo frames on the upstream switch router:

```
upstream-switch#conf t

upstream-switch(config)#system jumbomtu 9216
```

8. Create vmknic on the upstream switch or router:

```
upstream-switch#conf t

upstream-switch(config)#system jumbomtu 9216
```

9. Create vmknic on each ESX host 10.86.182.201 for the VXLAN transport VLAN, as shown in Figure 9-104.

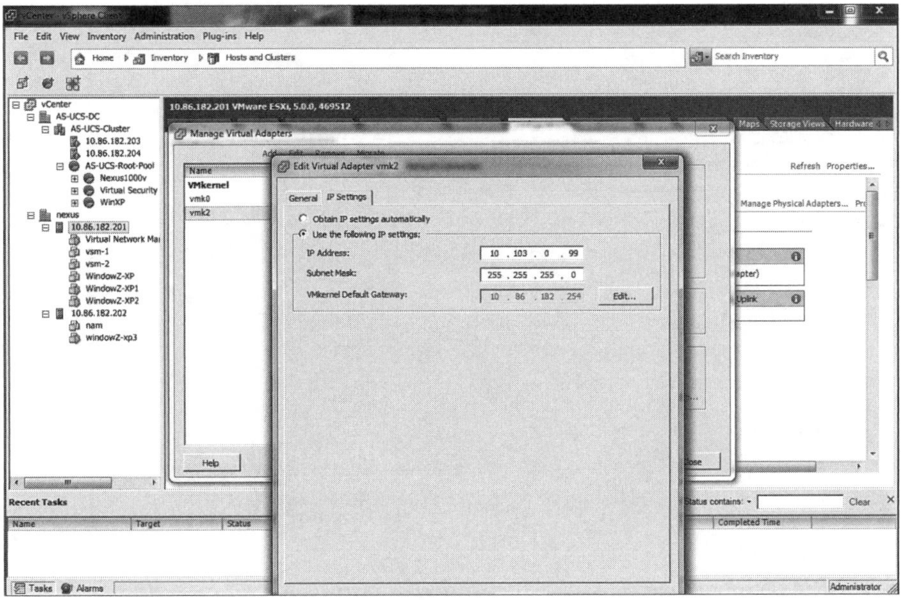

Figure 9-104 *Creating vmknic on Each ESX Host 10.86.182.201 for the VXLAN Transport VLAN*

   10. Assign vmknic 10.103.0.99 to vxlan port-group on ESX host 10.86.182.201, as shown in Figure 9-105.

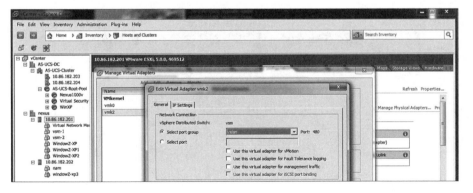

Figure 9-105 *Assigning vmknic 10.103.0.99 to vxlan port-group on ESX Host 10.86.182.201*

   11. Assign vmknic 10.103.0.98 to vxlan port-group on ESX host 10.86.182.202, as shown in Figure 9-106.

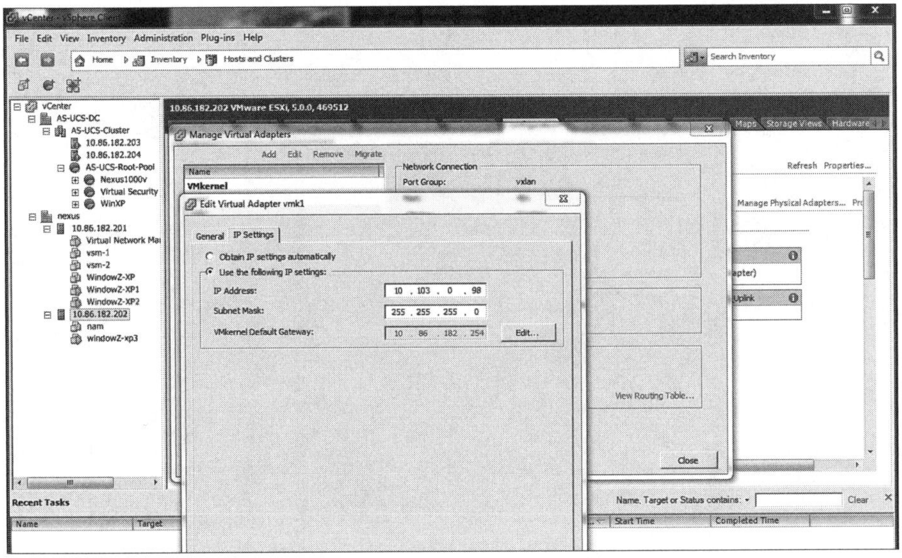

Figure 9-106 *Assigning vmknic 10.103.0.98 to vxlan port-group on ESX Host 10.86.182.202*

12. Create vmknic on each ESX host 10.86.182.202 for the VXLAN transport VLAN, as shown in Figure 9-107.

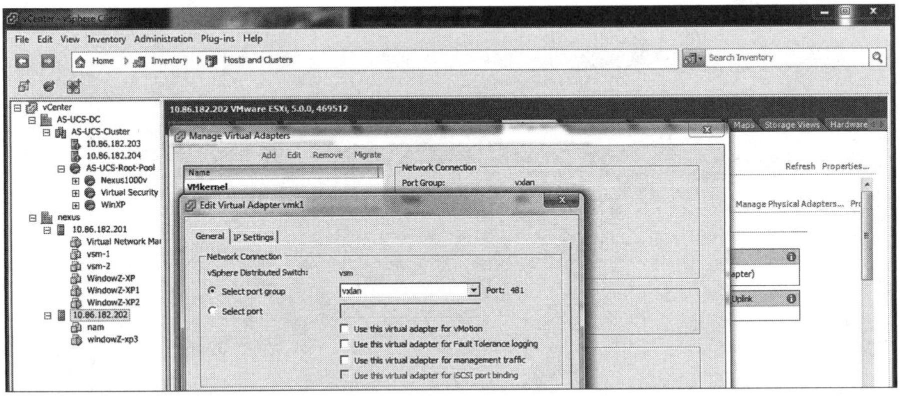

Figure 9-107 *Creating vmknic on each ESX host 10.86.182.202 for the VXLAN Transport VLAN*

13. Assign the VxLAN-VMs port-group to the virtual machine on ESX 10.86.183.201, as shown in Figure 9-108.

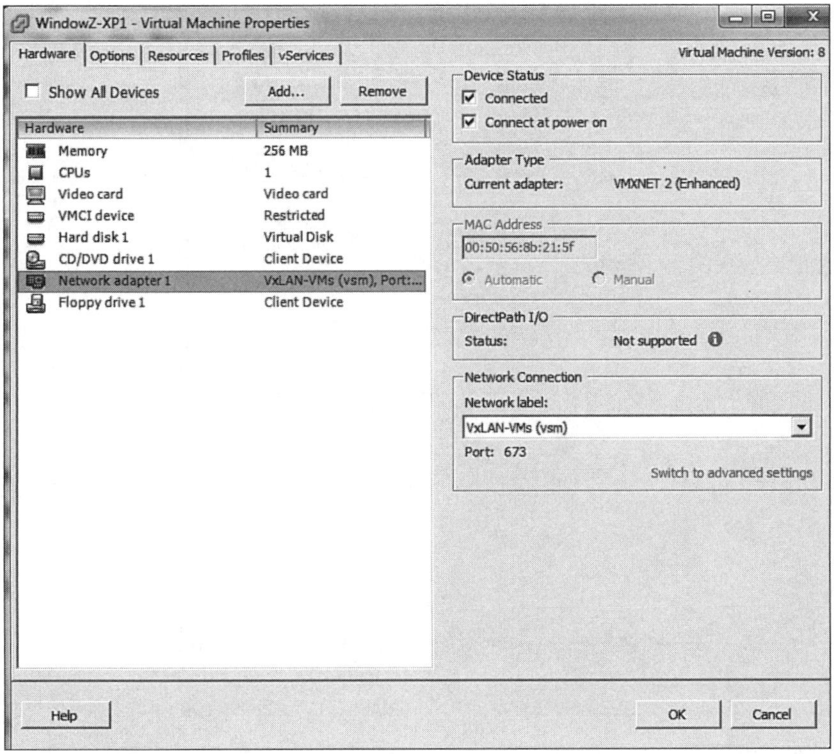

Figure 9-108 *Assigning the VxLAN-VMs port-group to the Virtual Machine on ESX 10.86.183.201*

14. Assign the VxLAN-VMs port-group to the virtual machine on ESX 10.86.183.202, as shown in Figure 9-109.

15. Display the the VMs and ESX host layout, as shown in Figure 9-110.

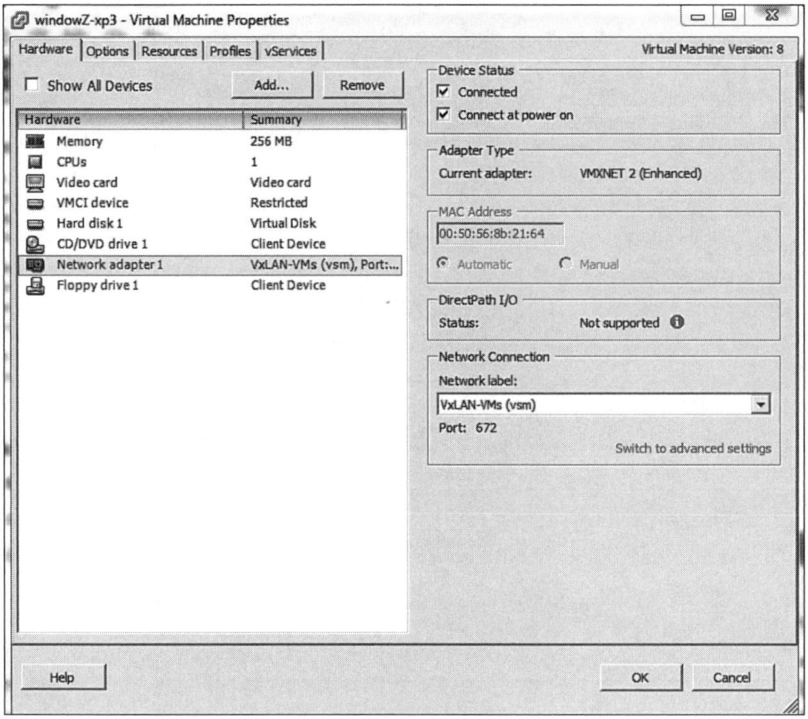

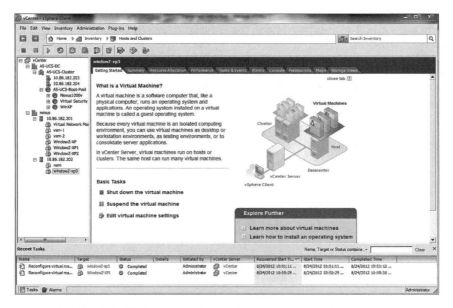

Figure 9-109 *Assigning the VxLAN-VMs port-group to the VM on ESX 10.86.183.202*

Figure 9-110 *The VMs and ESX Host Layout*

16. Verifiy the VM IP address information and the reachability across VXLAN, as shown in Figure 9-111.

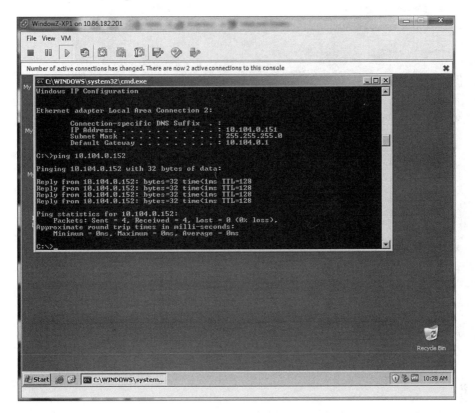

Figure 9-111 *Verifying the VM IP Address Information and the Reachability Across VXLAN*

17. Verify the VM IP address information and the reachability across VXLAN, as shown in Figure 9-112.

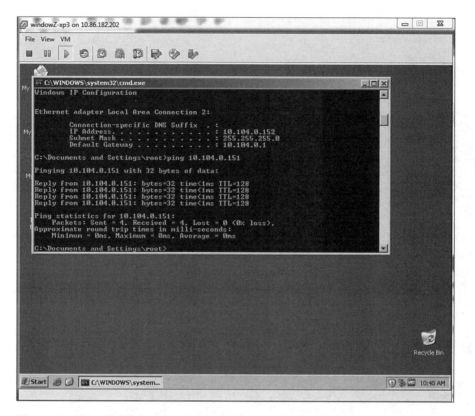

Figure 9-112 *Verifying the VM IP Address Information and the Reachability Across VXLAN*

18. Confirm ESX host 10.86.182.201 VEM VXLAN information, the VM IP address information and the reachability across VXLAN:

```
~ # vemcmd show port
   LTL    VSM Port  Admin Link   State  PC-LTL   SGID  Vem Port    Type
    19     Eth3/3    UP    UP     F/B*      0            vmnic2
    49     Veth2     UP    UP     FWD       0            vmk0
    50     Veth3     UP    UP     FWD       0            Virtual Networ...nt Center.eth0
    51     Veth5    DOWN   UP     BLK       0            WindowZ-XP2.eth0
    52     Veth4     UP    UP     FWD       0            WindowZ-XP1.eth0
    53     Veth6     UP    UP     FWD       0            vmk2   VXLAN

* F/B: Port is BLOCKED on some of the vlans.
 Please run "vemcmd show port vlans" to see the details.


~ # vemcmd show vxlan-stats
   LTL  Ucast   Mcast    Ucast    Mcast     Total
```

```
      Encaps  Encaps  Decaps  Decaps   Drops
  51        0      76       0       0       0
  52    51059     152   51006     242       0
  53    51988     842   51984     477       0
```

```
~ # vemcmd show vxlan interfaces
LTL          IP       Seconds since Last
                      IGMP Query Received
(* Interface on which IGMP Joins are sent)
-----------------------------------------
  53    10.103.0.99         38          *
```

```
~ # vemcmd show vxlan-stats ltl 52
VXLAN Port Stats for LTL 52
Unicast Encapsulations: 51082
Multicast Encapsulations: 152
Unicast Decapsulations: 51029
Multicast Decapsulations: 242
IP Pre-fragmentations: 0
TSO Processed Packets: 0
ICMP Pkt Too Big msgs from upstream: 0
ICMP Pkt Too Big msgs sent to VM: 0

Drop Statistics:
MTU Exceeded: 0
Generic Encap Fail: 0
No VMKNIC for Encap: 0
ARP Miss for Encap IP: 0
VXLAN BD Error: 0
Can't map packet: 0
Generic Decap Fail: 0
Encap source IP is one of ours: 0
Segment BD Error: 0
Dest Mcast IP not Segment Group IP: 0
Mcast Pkt for non-0th VXLAN Interface: 0
Pinning Failed on Decap: 0
Can't get uplink MTU: 0
TSO Processing Failure: 0
PreFrag Processing Failure: 0
~ # vemcmd show vxlan-stats ltl 53
VXLAN Port Stats for LTL 53
Unicast Encapsulations: 52022
```

```
Multicast Encapsulations: 842
Unicast Decapsulations: 52018
Multicast Decapsulations: 477
IP Pre-fragmentations: 0
TSO Processed Packets: 0
ICMP Pkt Too Big msgs from upstream: 0
ICMP Pkt Too Big msgs sent to VM: 0

Drop Statistics:
MTU Exceeded: 0
Generic Encap Fail: 0
No VMKNIC for Encap: 0
ARP Miss for Encap IP: 0
VXLAN BD Error: 0
Can't map packet: 0
Generic Decap Fail: 0
Encap source IP is one of ours: 0
Segment BD Error: 0
Dest Mcast IP not Segment Group IP: 0
Mcast Pkt for non-0th VXLAN Interface: 0
Pinning Failed on Decap: 0
Can't get uplink MTU: 0
TSO Processing Failure: 0
PreFrag Processing Failure: 0
~ #
```

19. Confirm ESX host 10.86.182.202 VEM VXLAN information, the virtual machine IP address information, and the reachability across VXLAN:

```
~ # vemcmd show port
    LTL   VSM Port  Admin Link   State  PC-LTL   SGID  Vem Port   Type
    17    Eth4/1    UP    UP     F/B*     0             vmnic0
    49    Veth7     UP    UP     FWD      0             vmk0
    50    Veth8     UP    UP     FWD      0             vmk1       VXLAN
    51    Veth9     UP    UP     FWD      0             windowZ-xp3.eth0

    * F/B: Port is BLOCKED on some of the vlans.
     Please run "vemcmd show port vlans" to see the details.


    ~ # vemcmd show vxlan-stats
    LTL   Ucast   Mcast   Ucast   Mcast   Total
          Encaps  Encaps  Decaps  Decaps  Drops
    50    52130    486    52134    327     0
    51    51152    265    51205    153     1
```

```
~ # vemcmd show vxlan interfaces
LTL            IP        Seconds since Last
                                 IGMP Query Received
(* Interface on which IGMP Joins are sent)
----------------------------------------
  50    10.103.0.98        57         *


~ # vemcmd show vxlan-stats ltl 50
VXLAN Port Stats for LTL 50
Unicast Encapsulations: 52149
Multicast Encapsulations: 486
Unicast Decapsulations: 52153
Multicast Decapsulations: 327
IP Pre-fragmentations: 0
TSO Processed Packets: 0
ICMP Pkt Too Big msgs from upstream: 0
ICMP Pkt Too Big msgs sent to VM: 0

Drop Statistics:
MTU Exceeded: 0
Generic Encap Fail: 0
No VMKNIC for Encap: 0
ARP Miss for Encap IP: 0
VXLAN BD Error: 0
Can't map packet: 0
Generic Decap Fail: 0
Encap source IP is one of ours: 0
Segment BD Error: 0
Dest Mcast IP not Segment Group IP: 0
Mcast Pkt for non-0th VXLAN Interface: 0
Pinning Failed on Decap: 0
Can't get uplink MTU: 0
TSO Processing Failure: 0
PreFrag Processing Failure: 0
~ # vemcmd show vxlan-stats ltl 51
VXLAN Port Stats for LTL 51
Unicast Encapsulations: 51175
Multicast Encapsulations: 265
Unicast Decapsulations: 51228
Multicast Decapsulations: 153
IP Pre-fragmentations: 0
TSO Processed Packets: 0
```

```
ICMP Pkt Too Big msgs from upstream: 0
ICMP Pkt Too Big msgs sent to VM: 0

Drop Statistics:
MTU Exceeded: 0
Generic Encap Fail: 0
No VMKNIC for Encap: 0
ARP Miss for Encap IP: 1
VXLAN BD Error: 0
Can't map packet: 0
Generic Decap Fail: 0
Encap source IP is one of ours: 0
Segment BD Error: 0
Dest Mcast IP not Segment Group IP: 0
Mcast Pkt for non-0th VXLAN Interface: 0
Pinning Failed on Decap: 0
Can't get uplink MTU: 0
TSO Processing Failure: 0
PreFrag Processing Failure: 0
~ #
```

20. Verify bridge-domain and active vEthernet interfaces:

```
vsm# show bridge-domain

Bridge-domain 10 (2 ports in all)
Segment ID: 60133 (Manual/Active)
Group IP: 239.1.1.1
State: UP              Mac learning: Enabled
Veth4, Veth9
```

21. Verify vEthernet interface information for the bridge-domain 10:

```
vsm# show port-profile name VxLAN-VMs

port-profile VxLAN-VMs
 type: Vethernet
 description:
 status: enabled
 max-ports: 32
 min-ports: 1
 inherit:
 config attributes:
  switchport mode access
  switchport access bridge-domain 10
```

```
 no shutdown
evaluated config attributes:
 switchport mode access
 switchport access bridge-domain 10
 no shutdown
assigned interfaces:
 Vethernet4
 Vethernet9
port-group: VxLAN-VMs
system vlans: none
capability l3control: no
capability iscsi-multipath: no
capability vxlan: no
capability l3-vn-service: no
port-profile role: none
port-binding: static


vsm# show interface vethernet 4
Vethernet4 is up
  Port description is WindowZ-XP1, Network Adapter 1
  Hardware: Virtual, address: 0050.568b.215f (bia 0050.568b.215f)
  Owner is VM "WindowZ-XP1", adapter is Network Adapter 1
  Active on module 3
  VMware DVS port 673
  Port-Profile is VxLAN-VMs
  Port mode is access
  5 minute input rate 600 bits/second, 0 packets/second
  5 minute output rate 600 bits/second, 0 packets/second
  Rx
    52590 Input Packets 186343 Unicast Packets
    75 Multicast Packets 1801 Broadcast Packets
    4118765 Bytes
  Tx
    53176 Output Packets 51944 Unicast Packets
    623 Multicast Packets 13218 Broadcast Packets 1225 Flood Packets
    4162531 Bytes
    0 Input Packet Drops 1 Output Packet Drops


vsm# show interface vethernet 9
Vethernet9 is up
  Port description is windowZ-xp3, Network Adapter 1
  Hardware: Virtual, address: 0050.568b.2164 (bia 0050.568b.2164)
  Owner is VM "windowZ-xp3", adapter is Network Adapter 1
```

```
        Active on module 4
        VMware DVS port 672
        Port-Profile is VxLAN-VMs
        Port mode is access
        5 minute input rate 600 bits/second, 0 packets/second
        5 minute output rate 600 bits/second, 0 packets/second
        Rx
          52254 Input Packets 51749 Unicast Packets
          17 Multicast Packets 488 Broadcast Packets
          4086724 Bytes
        Tx
          52055 Output Packets 51729 Unicast Packets
          0 Multicast Packets 326 Broadcast Packets 326 Flood Packets
          4054975 Bytes
          0 Input Packet Drops 0 Output Packet Drops
```

22. Verify VXLAN transport VLAN and vmknic vEthernet interface information:

```
vsm# show port-profile name vxlan

port-profile vxlan
 type: Vethernet
 description:
 status: enabled
 max-ports: 32
 min-ports: 1
 inherit:
 config attributes:
  switchport mode access
  switchport access vlan 103
  capability vxlan
  no shutdown
 evaluated config attributes:
  switchport mode access
  switchport access vlan 103
  capability vxlan
  no shutdown
 assigned interfaces:
  Vethernet6
  Vethernet8
 port-group: vxlan
 system vlans: none
 capability l3control: no
 capability iscsi-multipath: no
 capability vxlan: yes
```

```
 capability l3-vn-service: no
 port-profile role: none
 port-binding: static


vsm# show interface vethernet 6
Vethernet6 is up
  Port description is VMware VMkernel, vmk2
  Hardware: Virtual, address: 0050.5672.d60a (bia 0050.5672.d60a)
  Owner is VMware VMkernel, adapter is vmk2
  Active on module 3
  VMware DVS port 480
  Port-Profile is vxlan
  Port mode is access
  5 minute input rate 1000 bits/second, 0 packets/second
  5 minute output rate 992 bits/second, 0 packets/second
  Rx
    54190 Input Packets 51826 Unicast Packets
    1453 Multicast Packets 911 Broadcast Packets
    6854180 Bytes
  Tx
    53775 Output Packets 51759 Unicast Packets
    1910 Multicast Packets 106 Broadcast Packets 1522 Flood Packets
    6789587 Bytes
    0 Input Packet Drops 0 Output Packet Drops


vsm# show interface vethernet 8
Vethernet8 is up
  Port description is VMware VMkernel, vmk1
  Hardware: Virtual, address: 0050.5670.2bce (bia 0050.5670.2bce)
  Owner is VMware VMkernel, adapter is vmk1
  Active on module 4
  VMware DVS port 481
  Port-Profile is vxlan
  Port mode is access
  5 minute input rate 992 bits/second, 0 packets/second
  5 minute output rate 1000 bits/second, 0 packets/second
  Rx
    53722 Input Packets 51762 Unicast Packets
    1374 Multicast Packets 586 Broadcast Packets
    6787314 Bytes
  Tx
    53573 Output Packets 51829 Unicast Packets
    1708 Multicast Packets 36 Broadcast Packets 1405 Flood Packets
    6751109 Bytes
    0 Input Packet Drops 0 Output Packet Drops
```

23. Verify MAC address information on the VSM and that the IP address information is being learned via VXLAN:

```
vsm# show mac address-table
VLAN      MAC Address       Type    Age      Port                        Mod
---------+-----------------+-------+--------+---------------------------+---
1         0002.3d13.dd02    static  0        N1KV Internal Port           3
1         0002.3d23.dd00    static  0        N1KV Internal Port           3
1         0002.3d23.dd02    static  0        N1KV Internal Port           3
1         0002.3d33.dd02    static  0        N1KV Internal Port           3
1         0002.3d43.dd02    static  0        N1KV Internal Port           3
1         0002.3d63.dd00    static  0        N1KV Internal Port           3
1         0002.3d83.dd02    static  0        N1KV Internal Port           3
102       0002.3d83.dd02    static  0        N1KV Internal Port           3
102       0002.3d72.2b00    dynamic 0        Eth3/3                       3
102       0002.3d72.2b03    dynamic 0        Eth3/3                       3
102       0002.3d72.2b07    dynamic 0        Eth3/3                       3
102       001d.70d7.1f80    dynamic 1        Eth3/3                       3
103       0050.5672.d60a    static  0        Veth6                        3
103       001d.70d7.1f80    dynamic 2        Eth3/3                       3
103       0050.5670.2bce    dynamic 0        Eth3/3                       3
104       001d.70d7.1f80    dynamic 1        Eth3/3                       3
105       001d.70d7.1f80    dynamic 1        Eth3/3                       3
105       0050.568b.1c32    dynamic 46       Eth3/3                       3
105       0050.568b.1c33    dynamic 56       Eth3/3                       3
105       0050.568b.1c34    dynamic 61       Eth3/3                       3
182       0025.b599.0101    static  0        Veth2                        3
182       0050.568b.1c42    static  0        Veth3                        3
182       0002.3d72.2b01    dynamic 0        Eth3/3                       3
182       0002.3d72.2b02    dynamic 0        Eth3/3                       3
182       0002.3d72.2b05    dynamic 0        Eth3/3                       3
182       0006.285a.2201    dynamic 40       Eth3/3                       3
182       000c.29ce.4d7d    dynamic 109      Eth3/3                       3
182       000e.0c3c.d59b    dynamic 1        Eth3/3                       3
182       0010.8378.ca00    dynamic 67       Eth3/3                       3
182       0011.bbb6.7f00    dynamic 2        Eth3/3                       3
182       0013.21cb.eb94    dynamic 142      Eth3/3                       3
182       0014.4f9b.8d52    dynamic 143      Eth3/3                       3
182       001a.2f8d.15c0    dynamic 3        Eth3/3                       3
182       001a.6d05.6308    dynamic 4        Eth3/3                       3
182       001c.c4fb.d6bc    dynamic 43       Eth3/3                       3
182       0025.b599.0201    dynamic 1        Eth3/3                       3
182       0050.568b.1c39    dynamic 15       Eth3/3                       3
182       0050.568b.1c3b    dynamic 15       Eth3/3                       3
182       0050.569e.0007    dynamic 156      Eth3/3                       3
```

```
182        0050.569e.0026    dynamic 1        Eth3/3                                    3
182        0050.569e.0027    dynamic 18       Eth3/3                                    3
182        0050.569e.0032    dynamic 1        Eth3/3                                    3
182        0050.569e.0033    dynamic 1        Eth3/3                                    3
182        0050.569e.003e    dynamic 1        Eth3/3                                    3
182        0050.569e.004a    dynamic 2        Eth3/3                                    3
182        0050.569f.0723    dynamic 188      Eth3/3                                    3
182        00c0.9f9a.b9a7    dynamic 34       Eth3/3                                    3
182        00d0.c9c3.4a10    dynamic 35       Eth3/3                                    3
182        547f.ee64.3461    dynamic 8        Eth3/3                                    3
182        8843.e17d.d80f    dynamic 9        Eth3/3                                    3
182        f0f7.5544.94ca    dynamic 272      Eth3/3                                    3


Bridge-domain: 10
           MAC Address       Type    Age      Port            IP Address      Mod
-------------------------+-------+---------+---------------+---------------+---
           0050.568b.215f    static  0        Veth4           0.0.0.0         3

           0050.568b.2164    dynamic 1        Eth3/3          10.103.0.98     3


VLAN       MAC Address       Type    Age      Port                            Mod
---------+-----------------+-------+---------+----------------------------+---
1          0002.3d13.dd03    static  0        N1KV Internal Port              4
1          0002.3d23.dd03    static  0        N1KV Internal Port              4
1          0002.3d33.dd03    static  0        N1KV Internal Port              4
1          0002.3d43.dd03    static  0        N1KV Internal Port              4
1          0002.3d63.dd00    static  0        N1KV Internal Port              4
1          0002.3d83.dd03    static  0        N1KV Internal Port              4
102        0002.3d83.dd03    static  0        N1KV Internal Port              4
102        0002.3d72.2b00    dynamic 0        Eth4/1                          4
102        0002.3d72.2b03    dynamic 1        Eth4/1                          4
102        0002.3d72.2b07    dynamic 0        Eth4/1                          4
102        001d.70d7.1f80    dynamic 1        Eth4/1                          4
103        0002.3d83.dd03    static  0        N1KV Internal Port              4
103        0050.5670.2bce    static  0        Veth8                           4
103        001d.70d7.1f80    dynamic 3        Eth4/1                          4
103        0050.5672.d60a    dynamic 1        Eth4/1                          4
104        001d.70d7.1f80    dynamic 1        Eth4/1                          4
105        001d.70d7.1f80    dynamic 2        Eth4/1                          4
105        0050.568b.1c32    dynamic 47       Eth4/1                          4
105        0050.568b.1c33    dynamic 57       Eth4/1                          4
105        0050.568b.1c34    dynamic 61       Eth4/1                          4
182        0002.3d83.dd03    static  0        N1KV Internal Port              4
182        0025.b599.0201    static  0        Veth7                           4
182        0002.3d72.2b01    dynamic 0        Eth4/1                          4
```

```
182       0002.3d72.2b02    dynamic 0        Eth4/1                      4
182       0002.3d72.2b05    dynamic 0        Eth4/1                      4
182       0006.285a.2201    dynamic 40       Eth4/1                      4
182       000c.29ce.4d7d    dynamic 110      Eth4/1                      4
182       000e.0c3c.d59b    dynamic 0        Eth4/1                      4
182       0010.8378.ca00    dynamic 68       Eth4/1                      4
182       0011.bbb6.7f00    dynamic 2        Eth4/1                      4
182       0013.21cb.eb94    dynamic 142      Eth4/1                      4
182       0014.4f9b.8d52    dynamic 142      Eth4/1                      4
182       001a.2f8d.15c0    dynamic 3        Eth4/1                      4
182       001a.6d05.6308    dynamic 3        Eth4/1                      4
182       001c.c4fb.d6bc    dynamic 44       Eth4/1                      4
182       0025.b599.0101    dynamic 1        Eth4/1                      4
182       0050.568b.1c39    dynamic 15       Eth4/1                      4
182       0050.568b.1c3b    dynamic 15       Eth4/1                      4
182       0050.569e.0007    dynamic 156      Eth4/1                      4
182       0050.569e.0026    dynamic 1        Eth4/1                      4
182       0050.569e.0027    dynamic 18       Eth4/1                      4
182       0050.569e.0032    dynamic 1        Eth4/1                      4
182       0050.569e.0033    dynamic 1        Eth4/1                      4
182       0050.569e.003e    dynamic 0        Eth4/1                      4
182       0050.569e.004a    dynamic 1        Eth4/1                      4
182       0050.569f.0723    dynamic 188      Eth4/1                      4
182       00c0.9f9a.b9a7    dynamic 35       Eth4/1                      4
182       00d0.c9c3.4a10    dynamic 36       Eth4/1                      4
182       547f.ee64.3461    dynamic 8        Eth4/1                      4
182       8843.e17d.d80f    dynamic 10       Eth4/1                      4
182       f0f7.5544.94ca    dynamic 273      Eth4/1                      4


Bridge-domain: 10
          MAC Address     Type    Age      Port            IP Address      Mod
-------------------------+-------+---------+---------------+---------------+---
          0050.568b.2164  static  0        Veth9           0.0.0.0          4

          0050.568b.215f  dynamic 1        Eth4/1          10.103.0.99      4

Total MAC Addresses: 106
```

24. View the full running-config of the VSM for VXLAN:

```
vsm# show running-config

!Command: show running-config
!Time: Thu Aug 30 19:31:32 2012
```

```
version 4.2(1)SV1(5.1a)
no feature telnet
feature segmentation

username admin password 5 $1$Sx5LsG2Q$DS.HLmmfy1wUIkK9do2Af/  role network-admin

banner motd #Nexus 1000v Switch#

ssh key rsa 2048
ip domain-lookup
hostname vsm
vem 3
  host vmware id ba5eba11-9999-0001-0000-000000000001
vem 4
  host vmware id ba5eba11-9999-0002-0000-000000000002
bridge-domain 10
  segment id 60133
  group 239.1.1.1
snmp-server user admin network-admin auth md5 0xe90e1fbf4aa6dd0ccde9bb8f2db21c3f
 priv 0xe90e1fbf4aa6dd0ccde9bb8f2db21c3f localizedkey

vrf context management
  ip route 0.0.0.0/0 10.86.182.254
vlan 1,102-105,182
vlan 1
vlan 102
  name control-packet
vlan 103
  name GuestOS
vlan 104
  name DB
vlan 105
  name App
vlan 182
  name mgt-vmk

port-channel load-balance ethernet source-mac
port-profile default max-ports 32
port-profile default port-binding static
port-profile type ethernet Unused_Or_Quarantine_Uplink
  vmware port-group
  shutdown
  description Port-group created for Nexus1000V internal usage. Do not use.
  state enabled
port-profile type vethernet Unused_Or_Quarantine_Veth
```

```
    vmware port-group
    shutdown
    description Port-group created for Nexus1000V internal usage. Do not use.
    state enabled
port-profile type ethernet uplink
    vmware port-group
    switchport mode trunk
    switchport trunk allowed vlan 102-105,182
    mtu 9000
    no shutdown
    system vlan 102-103,182
    state enabled
port-profile type vethernet VLAN103
    vmware port-group
    switchport mode access
    switchport access vlan 103
    org root/Enterprise
    no shutdown
    vn-service ip-address 10.104.0.200 l3-mode security-profile web
    state enabled
port-profile type vethernet VLAN104
    vmware port-group
    switchport mode access
    switchport access vlan 104
    org root/Enterprise
    no shutdown
    vn-service ip-address 10.104.0.200 vlan 104 security-profile database
    state enabled
port-profile type vethernet VLAN105
    vmware port-group
    switchport mode access
    switchport access vlan 105
    no shutdown
    state enabled
port-profile type vethernet VSG-L3-Control
    vmware port-group
    switchport mode access
    switchport access vlan 103
    no shutdown
    capability l3-vn-service
    state enabled
port-profile type vethernet VLAN182
    vmware port-group
    switchport mode access
    switchport access vlan 182
```

```
  no shutdown
  state enabled
port-profile type vethernet l3control
  capability l3control
  vmware port-group
  switchport mode access
  switchport access vlan 182
  no shutdown
  system vlan 182
  state enabled
port-profile type vethernet VSG
  vmware port-group
  switchport mode access
  switchport access vlan 102
  no shutdown
  state enabled
port-profile type vethernet VSG-HA
  vmware port-group
  switchport mode access
  switchport access vlan 102
  no shutdown
  state enabled
port-profile type vethernet vsg-data
  vmware port-group
  switchport mode access
  switchport access vlan 104
  no shutdown
  state enabled
port-profile type vethernet database
  vmware port-group
  switchport mode access
  switchport access vlan 104
  org root/Enterprise
  no shutdown
  vn-service ip-address 10.104.0.200 vlan 104 security-profile database
  state enabled
port-profile type vethernet web
  vmware port-group
  switchport mode access
  switchport access vlan 104
  org root/Enterprise
  no shutdown
  vn-service ip-address 10.104.0.200 vlan 104 security-profile web
  state enabled
port-profile type vethernet middleware
```

```
      vmware port-group
      switchport mode access
      switchport access vlan 104
      org root/Enterprise
      no shutdown
      vn-service ip-address 10.104.0.200 vlan 104 security-profile middleware
      state enabled
port-profile type vethernet vxlan
      vmware port-group
      switchport mode access
      switchport access vlan 103
      capability vxlan
      no shutdown
      state enabled
port-profile type vethernet VLAN103-vxlan
      vmware port-group
      switchport mode access
      switchport access bridge-domain VLAN103
      no shutdown
      state enabled
port-profile type vethernet VxLAN-VMs
      vmware port-group
      switchport mode access
      switchport access bridge-domain 10
      no shutdown
      state enabled

vdc vsm id 1
      limit-resource vlan minimum 16 maximum 2049
      limit-resource monitor-session minimum 0 maximum 2
      limit-resource vrf minimum 16 maximum 8192
      limit-resource port-channel minimum 0 maximum 768
      limit-resource u4route-mem minimum 1 maximum 1
      limit-resource u6route-mem minimum 1 maximum 1
      limit-resource m4route-mem minimum 58 maximum 58
      limit-resource m6route-mem minimum 8 maximum 8

interface mgmt0
      ip address 10.86.182.152/24

interface Vethernet1
      inherit port-profile VLAN103
      description WindowZ-XP, Network Adapter 1
      capability l3-vn-service
      vmware dvport 160 dvswitch uuid "ed 5d 0b 50 26 85 42 50-73 78 8e 28 b9 e6 36
```

```
dd"
  vmware vm mac 0050.568B.1C30


interface Vethernet2
  inherit port-profile l3control
  description VMware VMkernel, vmk0
  vmware dvport 224 dvswitch uuid "ed 5d 0b 50 26 85 42 50-73 78 8e 28 b9 e6 36
dd"
  vmware vm mac 0025.B599.0101


interface Vethernet3
  inherit port-profile VLAN182
  description Virtual Network Management Center, Network Adapter 1
  vmware dvport 192 dvswitch uuid "ed 5d 0b 50 26 85 42 50-73 78 8e 28 b9 e6 36
dd"
  vmware vm mac 0050.568B.1C42


interface Vethernet4
  inherit port-profile VxLAN-VMs
  description WindowZ-XP1, Network Adapter 1
  vmware dvport 673 dvswitch uuid "ed 5d 0b 50 26 85 42 50-73 78 8e 28 b9 e6 36
dd"
  vmware vm mac 0050.568B.215F


interface Vethernet5
  inherit port-profile VLAN103-vxlan
  description WindowZ-XP2, Network Adapter 1
  vmware dvport 513 dvswitch uuid "ed 5d 0b 50 26 85 42 50-73 78 8e 28 b9 e6 36
dd"
  vmware vm mac 0050.568B.215E


interface Vethernet6
  inherit port-profile vxlan
  description VMware VMkernel, vmk2
  vmware dvport 480 dvswitch uuid "ed 5d 0b 50 26 85 42 50-73 78 8e 28 b9 e6 36
dd"
  vmware vm mac 0050.5672.D60A


interface Vethernet7
  inherit port-profile l3control
  description VMware VMkernel, vmk0
  vmware dvport 225 dvswitch uuid "ed 5d 0b 50 26 85 42 50-73 78 8e 28 b9 e6 36
dd"
  vmware vm mac 0025.B599.0201
```

```
interface Vethernet8
  inherit port-profile vxlan
  description VMware VMkernel, vmk1
  vmware dvport 481 dvswitch uuid "ed 5d 0b 50 26 85 42 50-73 78 8e 28 b9 e6 36
dd"
  vmware vm mac 0050.5670.2BCE

interface Vethernet9
  inherit port-profile VxLAN-VMs
  description windowZ-xp3, Network Adapter 1
  vmware dvport 672 dvswitch uuid "ed 5d 0b 50 26 85 42 50-73 78 8e 28 b9 e6 36
dd"
  vmware vm mac 0050.568B.2164

interface Ethernet3/3
  inherit port-profile uplink

interface Ethernet4/1
  inherit port-profile uplink

interface control0
line vty
line console
boot kickstart bootflash:/nexus-1000v-kickstart-mz.4.2.1.SV1.5.1a.bin sup-1
boot system bootflash:/nexus-1000v-mz.4.2.1.SV1.5.1a.bin sup-1
boot kickstart bootflash:/nexus-1000v-kickstart-mz.4.2.1.SV1.5.1a.bin sup-2
boot system bootflash:/nexus-1000v-mz.4.2.1.SV1.5.1a.bin sup-2
monitor session 1 type erspan-source
  source vlan 103-104,182 rx
  destination ip 10.86.182.155
  erspan-id 101
  ip ttl 64
  ip prec 0
  ip dscp 0
  mtu 1500
  header-type 2
  no shut
svs-domain
  domain id 989
  control vlan 1
  packet vlan 1
  svs mode L3 interface mgmt0
svs connection nexus
  protocol vmware-vim
  remote ip address 10.86.182.234 port 80
```

```
  vmware dvs uuid "ed 5d 0b 50 26 85 42 50-73 78 8e 28 b9 e6 36 dd" datacenter-n
ame nexus
  max-ports 8192
  connect
vsn type vsg global
  tcp state-checks
vnm-policy-agent
  registration-ip 10.86.182.154
  shared-secret **********
  policy-agent-image bootflash:/vnmc-vsmpa.1.3.1d.bin
  log-level info
vsm#
```

If services are needed and or required with VXLAN, vPath is VXLAN-aware. Because vPath is VXLAN-aware, Layer2 flow interception and adjacency is supported to inter-cept L2 frames on the VXLAN interface or the VM. The VXLAN tunnel is between the VEMs, and the VMs do not see the VXLAN-id. The actual VXLAN encapsulation and de-encapsulation are performed on the VEM; they use the IP address of the vmk inter-faces associated with the VXLAN and transports VLAN.

Nexus 1000v Network Analysis Module

With more and more workloads moving to virtual servers, visibility into these workloads is critical. With the edge of the network moving into the server, end-to-end service vis-ibility, service levels, features, policy, and control becomes critical. The Network Analysis Module (NAM) enables administrators to effectively manage VM networks with the fol-lowing capabilities:

- Analyze network usage behavior by application.

- Analyze host and VM conversations and performance.

- Visibility for VM-to-VM traffic and virtual interface statistics.

- Support for QoS, Netflow, SPAN, ERSPAN, NDE, RMON, and DSMON.

- Port-profile monitoring.

- Troubleshooting tools and performance issues.

The Nexus 1000v NAM can be deployed on a dedicated appliance (Nexus 1010 or 1010-X) or as an OVF VM.

Figure 9-113 shows the NAM topology used throughout this section.

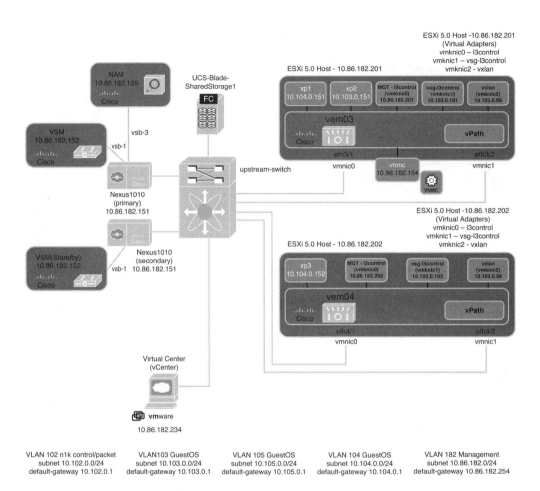

Figure 9-113 *NAM Topology*

Installing Nexus 1000v Network Analysis Module

The following steps are for the deployment and configuration for the NAM to be deployed as an OVF Template VM:

1. Install and deploy the OVF NAM VM.

    a. Create a new VM with the following custom attributes:

        VM version 7.

        VM type Other Linux 64-bit.

        2 vCPUs, 1GB RAM.

        2 NICs (You can configure both in the same VLAN; the first one is the one used for management traffic, and the second interface is for the data port.)

53GB HDD.

Leave the rest default.

b. After VM creation, modify the VM properties to mount the ISO image (nam-app-x86_64.5-1-2.iso") on its CD drive, as shown in Figure 9-114.

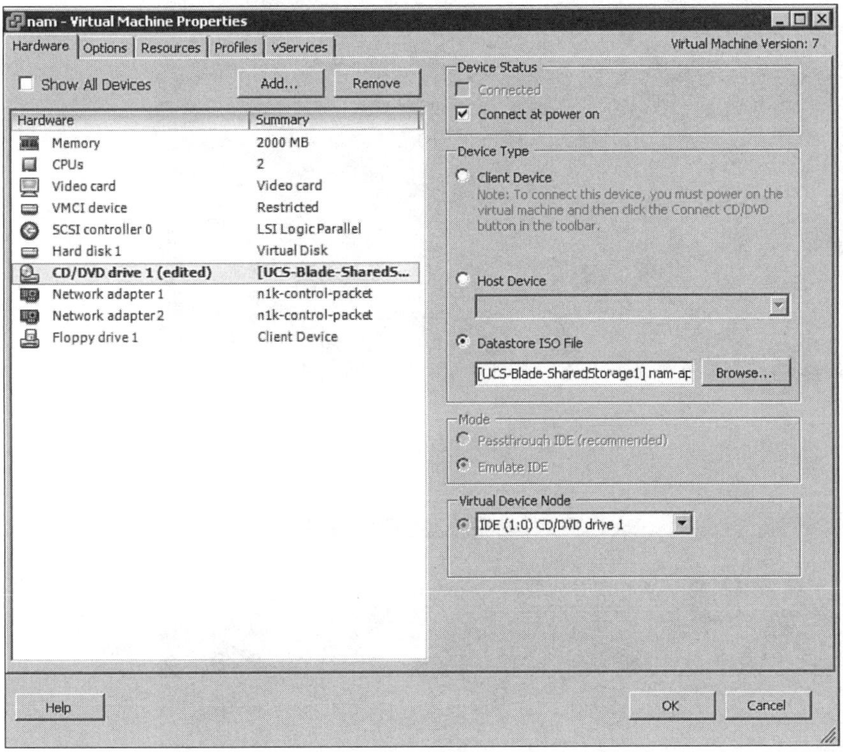

Figure 9-114 *Modifying the VM Properties to Mount the ISO Image on Its CD Drive*

2. Install the NAM software:

a. Boot the VM.

b. If the VM tries to PXE-boot, it means you probably forgot to mount the ISO image properly.

c. What you should actually see is a menu offering different options to install the NAM software, as shown in Figure 9-115.

d. Choose "3" to install the NAM software out of the CD, as shown in Figure 9-116.

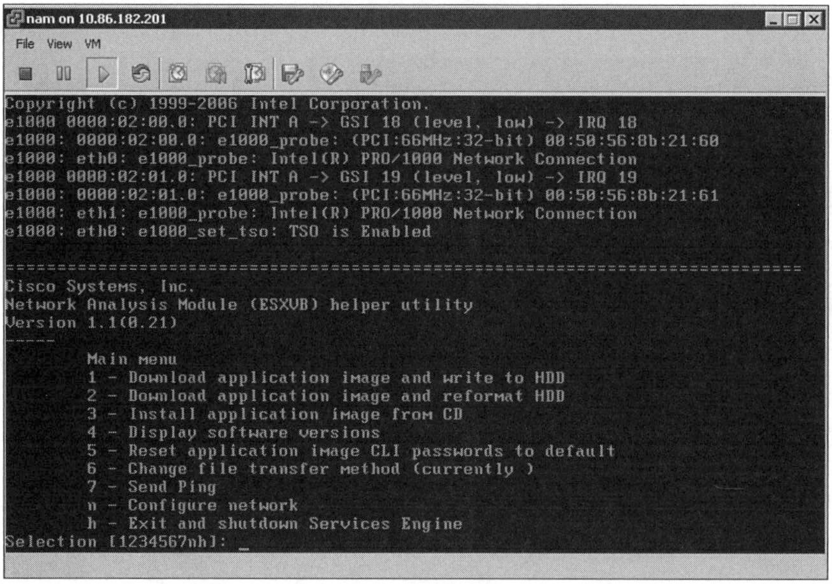

Figure 9-115 *Options for Installing NAM Software*

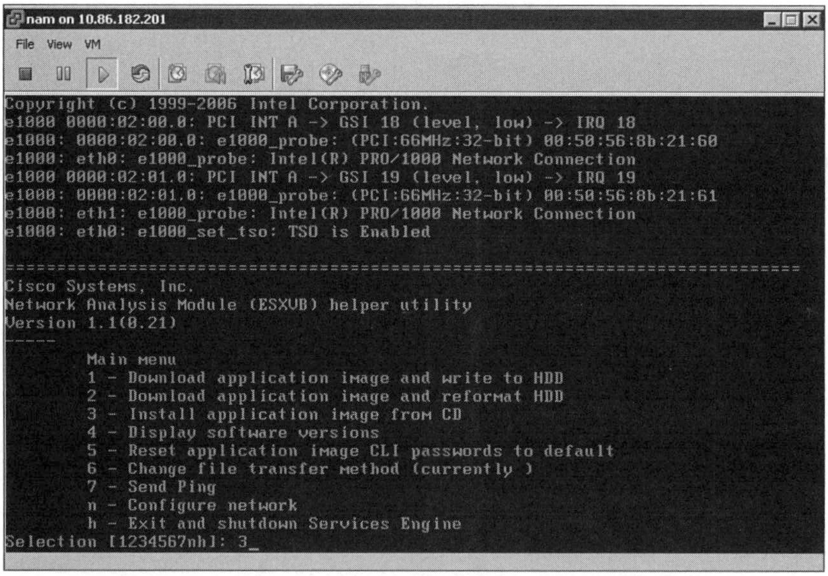

Figure 9-116 *Option to Install the NAM Software Out of the CD*

    e. When the installation is finished, choose the option "h" to shut down the VM, as shown in Figure 9-117.

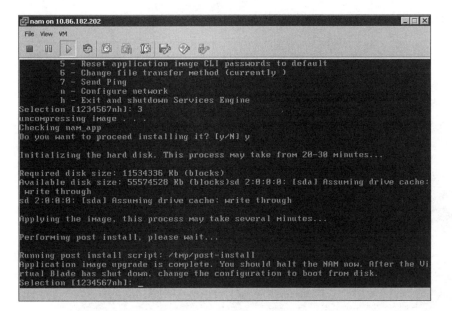

Figure 9-117 *Shutting Down the VM After Installation*

    f. When the VM is powered off, make sure to unmount the CD so that the VM boots from its HDD the next time it is powered on.

  3. Configure the NAM software for the initial configuration:

    a. Boot the NAM VM; you should see a login prompt, as shown in Figure 9-118.

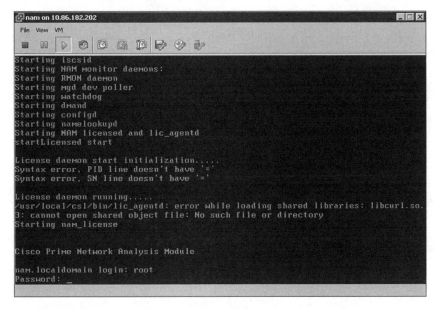

Figure 9-118 *Login Prompt After Booting the VM*

b. User is "root"; password is "root."

c. Use the **ip** commands to set up the name, domain, IP address, default gateway, and DNS server. After this, you should ping your NAM.

d. Use the **ip http server enable** command to activate the HTTP server and define a web user, as shown in Figure 9-119.

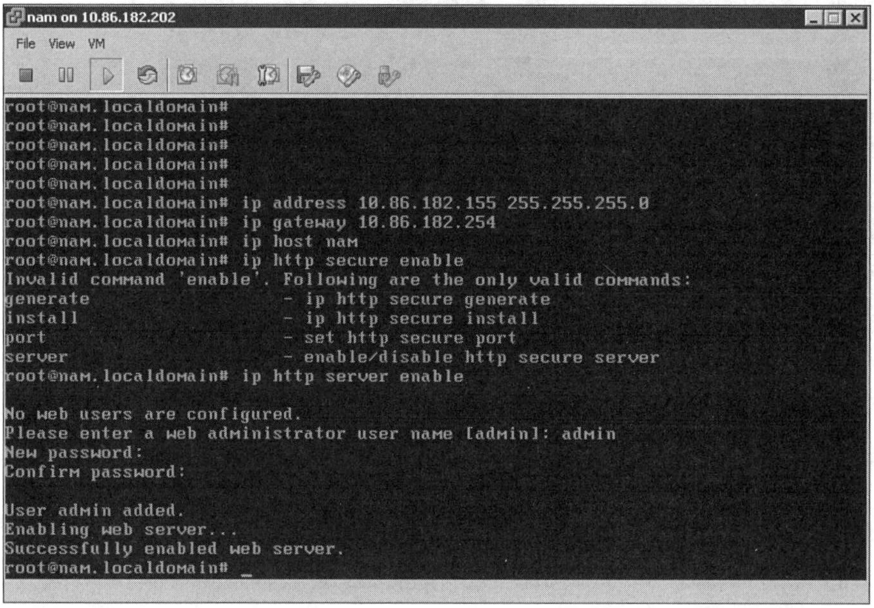

Figure 9-119 *Activate the HTTP Server and Define a Web User*

4. Verify NAM functionality and start with the NAM application configuration:

a. Configure a device to send data to your NAM, for example, a simple ERSPAN session on an N1Kv with a couple of VLANs as the source:

```
vsm(config)# monitor session 1 type erspan-source
vsm(config-erspan-src)# source vlan 103,104,182 rx
vsm(config-erspan-src)# destination ip 10.86.182.155
vsm(config-erspan-src)# erspan-id 101
vsm(config-erspan-src)# ip ttl 64
vsm(config-erspan-src)# ip prec 0
vsm(config-erspan-src)# ip dscp 0
vsm(config-erspan-src)# mtu 1500
vsm(config-erspan-src)# header-type 2
vsm(config-erspan-src)# no shutdown
vsm(config-erspan-src)#
```

```
verify monitor session on the Nexus 1000v vsm:
vsm# show monitor session 1
   session 1
---------------
type              : erspan-source
state             : up
source intf       :
   rx             :
   tx             :
   both           :
source VLANs      :
   rx             : 103-104,182
   tx             :
   both           :
source port-profile :
   rx             :
   tx             :
   both           :
filter VLANs      : filter not specified
destination IP    : 10.86.182.155
ERSPAN ID         : 101
ERSPAN TTL        : 64
ERSPAN IP Prec.   : 0
ERSPAN DSCP       : 0
ERSPAN MTU        : 1500
ERSPAN Header Type: 2


vsm# show monitor session 1 brief
   session 1
---------------
type              : erspan-source
state             : up
source intf       :
source VLANs      :
   rx             : 103-104,182
   tx             :
   both           :
source port-profile :
   rx             :
   tx             :
   both           :
filter VLANs      : filter not specified
destination IP    : 10.86.182.155
ERSPAN ID         : 101
ERSPAN TTL        : 64
```

```
ERSPAN IP Prec.   : 0
ERSPAN DSCP       : 0
ERSPAN MTU        : 1500
ERSPAN Header Type: 2
vsm#


vsm# show monitor
Session  State       Reason                 Description
-------  ----------  ---------------------  --------------------------------
1        up          The session is up
vsm#
```

    b. Browse to the IP address you defined previously: http://10.86.182.155. Log in
        with the web user credentials you defined, as shown in Figure 9-120.

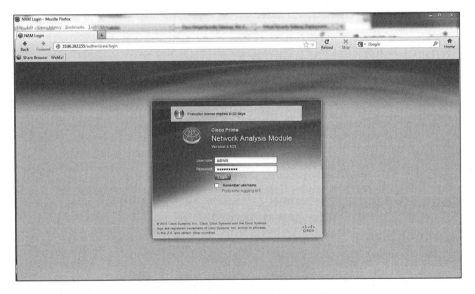

Figure 9-120 *Logging In to the Network Analysis Module*

    c. "Auto-create" should be enabled per default. You should see the IP addresses
        of your ESX hosts (ERSPAN data is sent out of the VEMs, not the VSM) under
        Setup – NAM data sources. With "auto-create" on, NAM will have automatically
        created these sources upon receiving the ERSPAN packets, as shown in
        Figure 9-121 and Figure 9-122.

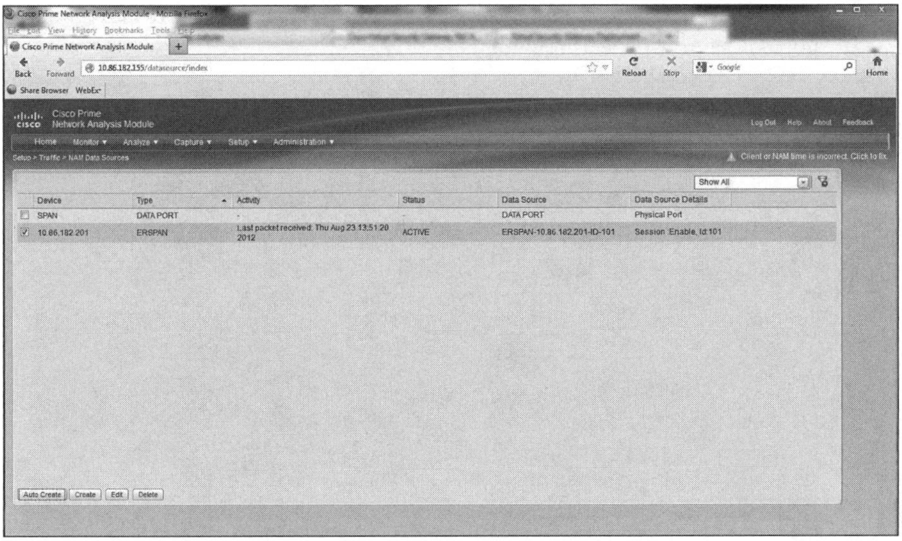

Figure 9-121   *Selecting or Changing Data Sources for the NAM*

Note   "Auto-create" is enabled by default, which enables visibility of the IP addresses of the ESX hosts. ERSPAN data is sent out of the VEMs, not the VSM. The "auto-create" enables the NAM to automatically create these sources upon receiving the ERSPAN packets.

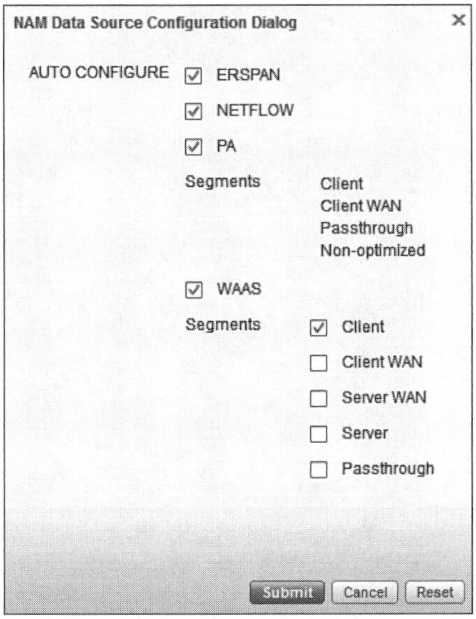

Figure 9-122   *Defining a Site on the NAM*

d. Define a Site (Setup – Sites) for your servers (typically the IP address is enough), as shown in Figure 9-123 through Figure 9-126.

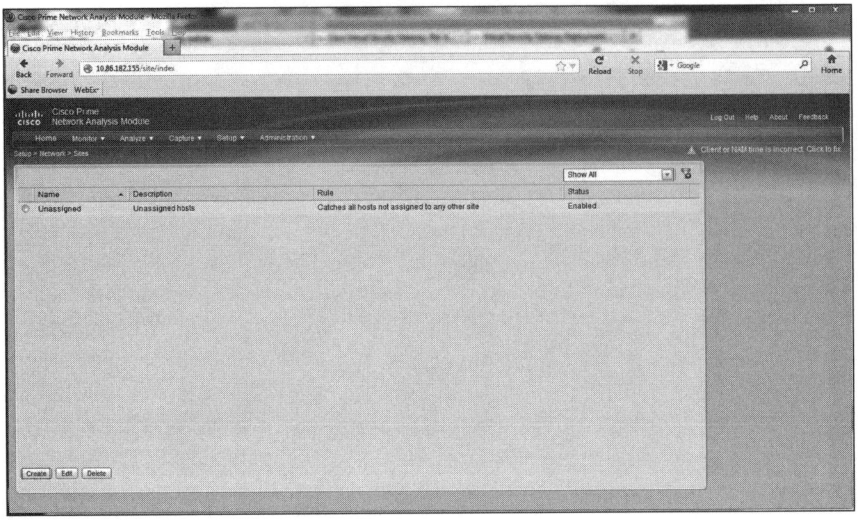

Figure 9-123   *Defining a Site for Servers*

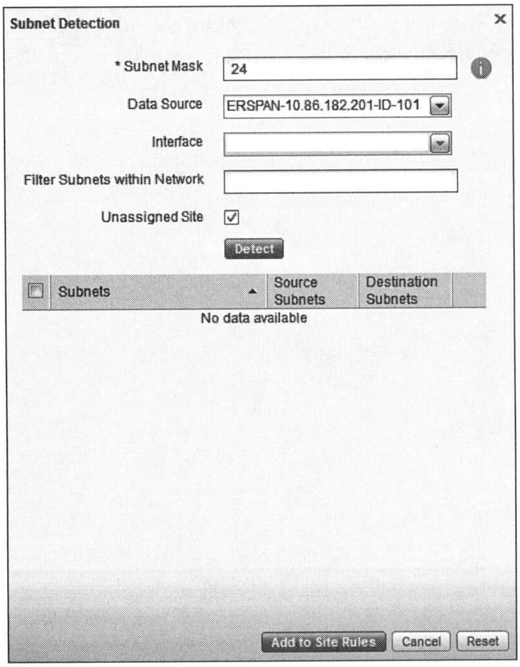

Figure 9-124   *Defining the Subnet Information for the NAM Data Source*

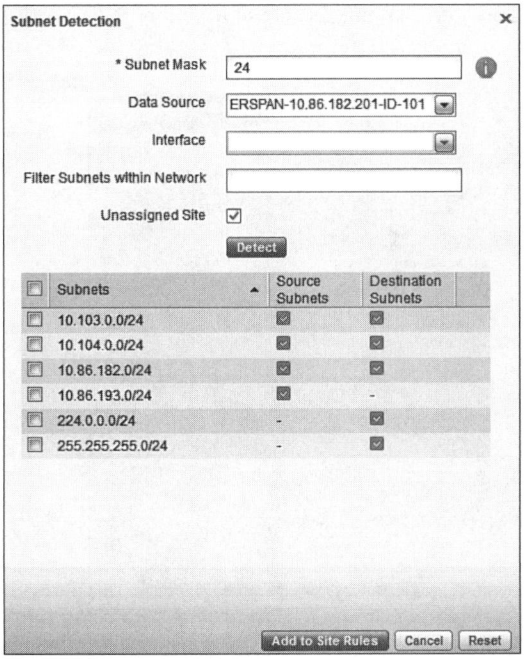

Figure 9-125 *Properly Configured Subnets for Monitoring Within the NAM Application*

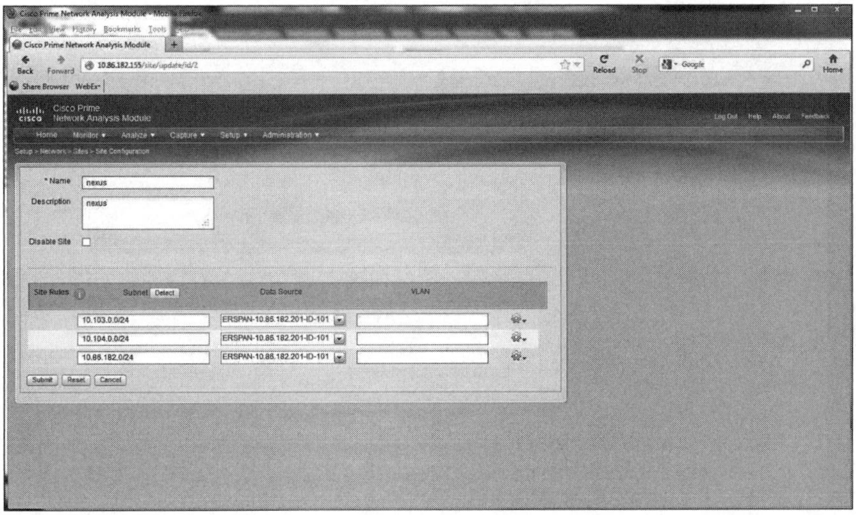

Figure 9-126 *Monitoring and Traffic Statistics Within the NAM Application*

   e. Go to the dashboards (Monitor) and start playing, as shown in Figure 9-127 and Figure 9-128.

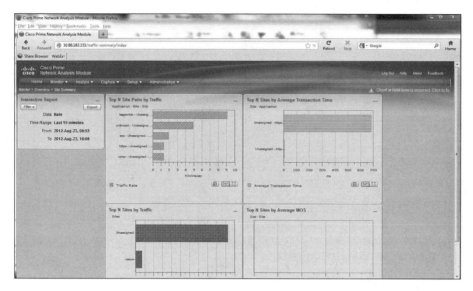

Figure 9-127 *Sample Output from the NAM*

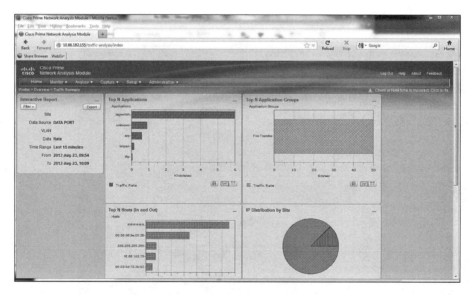

Figure 9-128 *Another Sample View for a Server Monitoring Traffic from the NAM*

Deploying the Nexus 1000v NAM as a Virtual Services Blade on the Nexus 1010

The following steps show how to install the NAM as a virtual appliance on the Nexus 1010.

Example 9-40 shows the configuration for deploying the Nexus 1000v NAM as a Virtual Services Blade on the Nexus 1010.

Example 9-40 *Configuring the Nexus 1000v NAM as a Virtual Services Blade*

```
Nexus1010# dir bootflash:/repository
     16384    Mar 04 09:45:13 2012  lost+found/
  183412736   Mar 04 09:49:10 2012  nam-app-x86_64.5-1-1.iso
  169666560   Mar 04 09:50:30 2012  nexus-1000v.4.2.1.SV1.4a.iso
  119234068   Aug 08 01:57:44 2012  nexus-1000v.4.2.1.SV1.5.1a.1010.ova
  139923456   Aug 22 23:45:31 2012  nexus-1000v.4.2.1.SV1.5.1a.iso
  108810240   Mar 04 09:51:21 2012  nexus-1000v.VSG1.2.iso
  107161600   Aug 08 02:33:26 2012  nexus-1000v.VSG1.3.1a.iso
  246831104   Aug 07 16:45:57 2012  nexus-1010.4.2.1.SP1.4a.iso
      9498    Aug 23 00:36:00 2012  ovf-env-va-1.xml
      9482    Aug 24 19:07:53 2012  ovf-env-va-2.xml
       642    Aug 24 19:07:54 2012  vmpresults.txt


Usage for bootflash://sup-local
  521707520 bytes used
 3469672448 bytes free
 3991379968 bytes total


Nexus1010# conf t

Nexus1010(config)# virtual-service-blade nam
Nexus1010(config-vsb-config)# virtual-service-blade-type new nam-app-x86_64.5-1-1.
iso
Nexus1010(config-vsb-config)# interface data vlan 104
Nexus1010(config-vsb-config)# en
enable    end
Nexus1010(config-vsb-config)# enable
Enter vsb image: [nam-app-x86_64.5-1-1.iso]
Enter Management IPV4 address: 10.86.182.155
Enter Management subnet mask: 255.255.255.0
IPv4 address of the default gateway: 10.86.182.254
Enter HostName: nam
Setting Web user/passwd will enable port 80. Enter[y|n]: [n] y
Web User name: [admin]
Web User password: cisco.123
```

```
Note: VSB installation is in progress, please use show virtual-service-blade com-
mands to check the installation status.
Nexus1010(config-vsb-config)#


nam login root default password is cisco
root with the default password cisco
```

Summary

The Nexus 1000V offers tight integration between server and network environments; this integration helps to ensure consistent, policy-based network capabilities to all servers in your data center. The chapter covered several benefits such as policy-based virtual machine connectivity, mobile VM security, network policy, and operation models. Having real-time coordinated configurations of network and security services enables enterprises to increase the scale of the VM deployments and have the tools to maintain, monitor, and troubleshoot these dynamic environments.

## Chapter 10

Quality of Service (QoS)

This chapter covers the following topics:

- Nexus 7000 quality of service configuration

- Nexus 5000 quality of service configuration

- Nexus 1000V quality of service configuration

In the past, QoS in a data center environment has been frequently overlooked. Data centers were built with large bandwidth links, and most applications were isolated to the data center and centralized. Virtualization is changing all those rules because applications are more mobile within and between data centers. Technology enables applications that may have been distributed in the past to be centralized, and the need to differentiate between applications to meet service-level agreements (SLA) is becoming critical.

The Nexus family of switches provides a rich set of tools to the network administrator to classify, queue, and police traffic in a data center. This chapter describes common QoS mechanisms used and illustrates their configurations. The differences in platform and hardware capabilities are also discussed where relevant.

A solid foundation of QoS terminology and theory is helpful because QoS fundamentals will not be described in this chapter.

As a family of products, the Nexus line shares some common attributes, not the least of which is NX-OS. With NX-OS providing an opportunity to set new defaults, the engineers enabled QoS by default. In addition, Nexus switches "trust" QoS markings by default. These two settings simplify life for network administrators who had to enable QoS and configure trust in the past.

The QoS structure in the Nexus family is based on the Modular QoS CLI (MQC) The MQC is consistent with other Cisco platforms and provides a familiar and consistent interface for configuration of QoS policies. Using the MQC involves a three-step process to first classify traffic using various attributes such as access lists, Class of Service (CoS), or Differentiated Services Code Point (DSCP). After the traffic is classified, a policy map is used to determine what is done with the matched traffic, and finally the policy map is applied to an interface or VLAN to take effect.

Example 10-1 illustrates a simple application of the MQC where the goal is to match Telnet traffic from a specific network and set the CoS to 5.

Example 10-1   *Basic MQC Usage*

```
N7K-2# config
Enter configuration commands, one per line.  End with CNTL/Z.
N7K-2(config)#
N7K-2(config)# ip access-list acl-match-telnet
N7K-2(config-acl)# 10 permit tcp 10.100.1.0/24 eq telnet any
N7K-2(config-acl)# class-map type qos match-all cm-match-telnet
N7K-2(config-cmap-qos)# match access-group name acl-match-telnet
N7K-2(config-cmap-qos)# policy-map type qos pm-match-telnet
N7K-2(config-pmap-qos)# class cm-match-telnet
N7K-2(config-pmap-c-qos)# set cos 5
N7K-2(config-pmap-c-qos)# int e4/1
N7K-2(config-if)# service-policy input pm-match-telnet
N7K-2(config-if)# end
N7K-2# show policy-map interface e4/1 type qos


Global statistics status :    enabled

Ethernet4/1

  Service-policy (qos) input:    pm-match-telnet
    SNMP Policy Index:  285215169

    Class-map (qos):    cm-match-telnet (match-all)
      Match: access-group acl-match-telnet
      set cos 5


N7K-2#
```

The first step creates an access list to define the traffic you want to have the switch take an action against. Then a class map is created that refers to the access list. Next, the policy map is created, which refers to the class map and specifies the action to take. In this example, the goal is to mark the traffic with CoS 5. Finally, the last step applies the policy map to interface E4/1 for inbound traffic. The policy map can be verified by using the **show policy-map** command, as shown in Example 10-1.

> **Note**   It is helpful to prepend MQC entries with their function and give them meaningful names. It helps the network to be "self-documenting" and comes in handy at 3:00 a.m. when reviewing configurations. In Example 10-1, the access control list (ACL) name is **acl-match-telnet**, the class map name is **cm-match-telnet**, and the policy map name is **pm-match-telnet**.

Nexus devices enable class maps to be applied for different applications lending additional flexibility. These types fall into three distinct categories:

- QoS for packet classification

- Network-QoS for systemwide marking and congestion control

- Queuing for scheduling of traffic

The Nexus 7000 also supports an additional type for the control plane. Example 10-2 shows these types.

Example 10-2   *QoS Types*

```
N7K-2# show policy-map type ?
  control-plane  Command is for copp policy
  network-qos    Type network-qos
  qos            Type qos
  queuing        Type queuing

N7K-2#
```

Looking at these types more closely shows that each type has its specific function and role within the switch. The **qos** type is used for classification and marking of traffic. This is usually the first step in defining a QoS policy and allows for granular control of what traffic is classified or marked to a specific value. Referring to Example 10-1, you see the access list was very specific to match traffic from a subnet that was also Telnet traffic. Access lists can be broad or as focused as required.

QoS classes are not restricted to just using ACLs to classify traffic. Additional granularity can be added by matching against cos, dscp, ip rtp ports, precedence, or predefined protocols, as shown in Example 10-3.

Example 10-3   *Classification Matches*

```
N5K-1# config
Enter configuration commands, one per line.   End with CNTL/Z.
N5K-1(config)# class-map cm-match-telnet
N5K-1(config-cmap-qos)# match ?
  access-group  Access group
  cos           IEEE 802.1Q class of service
```

```
   dscp        DSCP in IP(v4) and IPv6 packets

   ip          IP

   precedence  Precedence in IP(v4) and IPv6 packets

   protocol    Protocol


N5K-1(config-cmap-qos)#
```

> **Note**   The Nexus 7000 supports additional classification match options such as MPLS experimental bits and matching on packet length. This is due to different hardware and software capabilities between the platforms.

The network-qos policy is used to define global queuing and scheduling parameters for the entire switch. Configuration parameters such as a no-drop class and default queuing policies are defined in the network-qos policy. The network-qos policy should be consistent across the entire network, especially in cases where no-drop traffic classes are used, such as for Fibre Channel over Ethernet (FCoE). Platform-specific network-qos settings are discussed under each platform.

> **Note**   In Nexus 7000 devices the network-qos policy is defined in the default Virtual Device Context (VDC) or Admin VDC, and the policy applies to all ports in all VDCs.

The queuing policies define platform-specific CoS-to-queue mappings. Platform-specific queuing settings are discussed under each platform.

QoS on Nexus 7000

The Nexus 7000 series of modular switches provide a full set of QoS mechanisms for network administrators to deploy. The QoS implementation follows the MQC described earlier in this chapter. QoS capabilities between Nexus devices can vary based on hardware and software capabilities. This section focuses on Nexus 7000-specific configuration.

Forwarding Architecture

The forwarding architecture of the Nexus 7000 uses the concept of virtual output queues managed by centralized arbitration to forward traffic across the internal components of the switch. The I/O modules installed in a chassis connect into the fabric modules to create a three-stage switching fabric. This architecture enables the switch to manage traffic across the switch in a granular fashion and avoids a situation referred to as head-of-line blocking (HOLB). HOLB can occur in a fabric when congestion on an egress port prevents (blocks) ingress traffic bound for other destinations. One of the goals of the Nexus family of switches was to engineer a platform that would avoid head-of-line blocking. In addition, the ability to have an arbitrated fabric enables guaranteed traffic within the switch. This enables the switch to offer lossless services over Ethernet as the switch can ensure that traffic will not be dropped as it traverses the switch.

To accomplish these goals, the Nexus 7000 uses a centrally arbitrated fabric and a concept of Virtual Output Queues (VOQ). The arbitrator grants permission and tracks capacity across the fabric to the VOQs to ensure reliable delivery. This is accomplished for traffic on ingress to the switch to provide buffering for destinations across the fabric referred to as the Virtual Queuing Index (VQI). The switch dequeues the traffic into the fabric based on the destination VQI and traffic priority. This is an efficient mechanism to grant access to the fabric and prevent HOLB because each VQI can be scheduled independently.

A VQI is a destination on the egress module and is dependent on the model of line card to determine what a VQI is. This means that the definition of a VQI could be different depending on the line card, as described in the following list:

- M1 48 port modules have 12 front-panel ports as a VQI for a total of 4 VQI per module.

- M1 8 port modules have a single front-panel port as a VQI for a total of 8 VQI per module.

- M1 32 port modules use a single front-panel port in dedicated mode as a VQI or group of 4 ports when in shared mode for a total of 8 VQIs per module.

- M2 24 port modules have a VQI per interface for a total of 24 VQI per module.

- M2 6 port modules have a VQI per interface when in 40G mode for a total of 6 VQI per module.

- M2 6 port modules have a VQI per interface when in 10G mode for a total of 24 VQI per module if all 6 ports are in 10G mode.

- M2 2 port modules have a VQI per interface when in 100G mode for a total of 2 VQI per interface.

- M2 2 port modules have a VQI per interface when in 40G mode for a total of 4 VQI per module if both ports are in 40G mode.

- M2 2 port modules have a VQI per interface when in 10G mode for a total of 20 VQI per module if both ports are in 10G mode.

- F1 32 port modules have a VQI per interface for a total of 32 VQI per module.

- F2/F2e 48 port modules have a VQI per interface for a total of 48 VQI per module.

A centralized arbitration mechanism used to provide access to the fabric relies on the supervisor module to track, grant, and deny access to the fabric (VQI) based on traffic. This arbitration is performed on a dedicated arbitration path between the supervisor modules and every I/O module in the chassis and is done on a per-destination, per-priority basis. Unicast traffic is controlled using centralized arbitration, but multidestination traffic such as ingress broadcast, multicast, and unknown unicast are sent unarbitrated. Although this might sounds like it could be problematic, the possibility of HOLB increases if you arbitrate for multidestination traffic because a single congested egress port could impact noncongested ports. The modules in a Nexus 7000 have reserved "shared" VQIs for multidestination traffic to prevent contention issues with unicast traffic delivery.

Network-QoS Policies

The network-qos policy defines queuing and scheduling across the switch. You can select from four policies, as shown in Example 10-4.

Example 10-4   *Nexus 7000 network-qos Policies*

```
N7K-2# config
Enter configuration commands, one per line.  End with CNTL/Z.
N7K-2(config)# system qos
N7K-2(config-sys-qos)# service-policy type network-qos ?
  default-nq-4e-policy  Default 4-ethernet policy (4-drop 4-nodrop CoS)
  default-nq-6e-policy  Default 6-ethernet policy (6-drop 2-nodrop CoS)
  default-nq-7e-policy  Default 7-ethernet policy (7-drop 1-nodrop CoS)
  default-nq-8e-policy  Default 8-ethernet policy (8-drop CoS)
N7K-2(config-sys-qos)#
```

The default network-qos policy is the default-nq-8e-policy, which does not specify a no-drop policy. The other policies enable one, two, or four no-drop policies depending on the network's requirements. This configuration is performed in the default or admin VDC on the Nexus 7000 and is systemwide.

Note   A policy with no-drop capabilities can be configured in a chassis with modules that support no-drop applications. At press time, three modules support the no-drop class. The F1, F2, and F2e modules have hardware support for no-drop classes. All M-series modules do not.

Verification of the system network-qos policy can be performed, as shown in Example 10-5.

Example 10-5   *Verification of Systemwide network-qos policy*

```
N7K-2# show policy-map system type network-qos

 Type network-qos policy-maps
 ==============================
 policy-map type network-qos default-nq-8e-policy
```

```
      class type network-qos c-nq-8e
        match cos 0-7
        congestion-control tail-drop
        mtu 1500
N7K-2#
```

When the default policy is changed to a no-drop policy, notable changes can be observed, as shown in Example 10-6.

Example 10-6   *Configuring a No-Drop Systemwide network-qos Policy*

```
N7K-2# config
Enter configuration commands, one per line.  End with CNTL/Z.
N7K-2(config)# system qos
N7K-2(config-sys-qos)# service-policy type network-qos default-nq-7e-policy
N7K-2(config-sys-qos)# show policy-map system type network-qos


  Type network-qos policy-maps
  ============================
  policy-map type network-qos default-nq-7e-policy
    class type network-qos c-nq-7e-drop
      match cos 0-2,4-7
      congestion-control tail-drop
      mtu 1500
    class type network-qos c-nq-7e-ndrop-fcoe
      match cos 3
      match protocol fcoe
      pause
      mtu 2112



N7K-2(config-sys-qos)#
```

Comparing the two policies, the primary difference is the addition of a no-drop class for FCoE traffic on CoS 3. This is FCoE's default CoS—notice the larger MTU to accommodate the bigger frame sizes. The application of this policy also shows on Ethernet interfaces, as shown in Example 10-7, where Ethernet 3/1 is a F1 module capable of supporting FCoE, and Ethernet 4/1 is an M series module that cannot support FCoE.

Example 10-7   *MTU Differences in a System with No-Drop Class*

```
N7K-2# show int e3/1
Ethernet3/1 is down (Administratively down)
admin state is down, Dedicated Interface
  Hardware: 1000/10000 Ethernet, address: e8b7.48cc.08bc (bia e8b7.48cc.08bc)
```

```
    MTU bytes (CoS values):  MTU  1500(0-2,4-7) bytes  MTU  2112(3) bytes
    BW 10000000 Kbit, DLY 10 usec, reliability 255/255, txload 1/255, rxload 1/255
    Encapsulation ARPA, medium is broadcast

<snip>

N7K-2# show int e4/1
Ethernet4/1 is down (Administratively down)
admin state is down, Dedicated Interface
  Hardware: 10000 Ethernet, address: 0024.98eb.ff41 (bia f866.f2ac.5aa8)
  MTU 1500 bytes, BW 10000000 Kbit, DLY 10 usec
  reliability 255/255, txload 1/255, rxload 1/255
  Encapsulation ARPA, medium is broadcast
N7K-2#
```

Queuing Policies

The Nexus 7000 supports a variety of modules that can be grouped into two families:

- M-Series modules, which have a hybrid ingress and egress buffering model
- F-Series modules, which have a primarily ingress buffering model

These different models impact where traffic is queued in the network, which is apparent in the examples. The queuing capability of different modules within the same family can be different based on the hardware implementation. The queuing capability displays as a string of numbers and letters that can be confusing. A good example is 1P7Q4T. This is shorthand for **One Priority(1P)** queue, **Seven Queues(7Q)** with **Four Thresholds(4T)** per queue. Table 10-1 shows the queuing structure for the available modules in the Nexus 7000.

Table 10-1 *Module Queuing Structures and Sizes*

Module Type	Model No.	Port Queuing Structure (Ingress/ Egress)	Per-Port Buffer Capacity (Ingress/ Egress)	Fabric Queuing Structure	VOQ Buffer Capacity
M1 8-port 10 G	N7K-M108X2-12L	8q2t 1p7q4t	96 MB / 80 MB	1p3q1t	32 MB
M1 32-port 10 G	N7K-M132XP-12	8q2t 1p7q4t	1 MB + 65 MB / 80 MB	1p3q1t	32 MB

Module Type	Model No.	Port Queuing Structure (Ingress/ Egress)	Per-Port Buffer Capacity (Ingress/ Egress)	Fabric Queuing Structure	VOQ Buffer Capacity
M1 48-port 1G	N7K-M148GT-11 N7K-M148GS-11 N7K-M148GS-11L	2q4t / 1p3q4t	7.56 MB / 6.15 MB	1p3q1t	16 MB
F1 32-port 10 G	N7K-F132XP-15	N/A	N/A	2q4t ingress 1p3q1t egress	40 MB
F2/F2e 48-port 10 G	N7K-F248XP-25 N7K-F248XP-25E	N/A	N/A	2q4t ingress 1p3q1t egress	72 MB
M2 24-port 10 G	10 G	8q2t / 1p7q4t	4.5 MB/ 4.5 MB	1p3q1t	64 MB
M2 6-port 40 G	40 G	8q2t / 1p7q4t	18 MB/ 18 MB	1p3q1t	64 MB
	10 G (Break out cable)	8q2t / 1p7q4t	4.5 MB/ 4.5 MB	1p3q1t	64 MB
M2 2-port 100 G	100 G	8q2t / 1p7q4t	54 MB/ 54 MB	1p3q1t	64 MB
	40 G	8q2t / 1p7q4t	18 MB/ 18 MB	1p3q1t	64 MB
	10 G (Break out cable)	8q2t / 1p7q4t	4.5 MB/ 4.5 MB	1p3q1t	64 MB

The queues are hardware components used to segregate and hold traffic mapped into the queue until the scheduler services the queue. The queues can have different behavior depending on the implementation. The thresholds 1P7Q4T signify the number of thresholds per queue for managing congestion using either Weighted Random Early Detection (WRED) or tail drops.

Depending on the module, the Nexus 7000 priority queue (1P) can a strict priority queue. When configured for strict priority queuing, all traffic classified into this queue will be serviced before any other traffic is on the link. This is useful when running a network with requirements for latency-sensitive traffic, such as voice to ensure voice traffic is not delayed in the switch. The primary consideration for using the strict priority queue is to be careful about what traffic is mapped into the priority queue. Inadvertently mapping too much traffic into the priority queue can create a situation called queue starvation. In *queue starvation*, the strict priority queue constantly has traffic in it that needs to be serviced, and the other queues on the interface do not get access to transmit their data and in essence starve.

The M-series modules can support the 1P queue as a strict priority queue when the **priority** command is added to the queue; otherwise, it is a regular queue. This is default behavior as illustrated by the priority level 1 command. Example 10-8 illustrates the use of the **priority** command on the queue.

Example 10-8   *Displaying a Strict priority Queue on an M Series Module*

```
N7K-2# show mod 4 | i Mod
Mod  Ports  Module-Type                    Model            Status
4    8      10 Gbps Ethernet XL Module     N7K-M108X2-12L   ok
N7K-2# show policy-map int e4/2 type queuing


Global statistics status :    enabled


Ethernet4/2

  Service-policy (queuing) input:    default-in-policy
    SNMP Policy Index:  301991185

    Class-map (queuing):    in-q1 (match-any)
      queue-limit percent 50
      bandwidth percent 80
      queue dropped pkts : 0


    Class-map (queuing):    in-q-default (match-any)
      queue-limit percent 50
      bandwidth percent 20
      queue dropped pkts : 0


  Service-policy (queuing) output:    default-out-policy
    SNMP Policy Index:  301991194

    Class-map (queuing):    out-pq1 (match-any)
      priority level 1
      queue-limit percent 16
      queue dropped pkts : 0
```

```
    Class-map (queuing):   out-q2 (match-any)
      queue-limit percent 1
      queue dropped pkts : 0


    Class-map (queuing):   out-q3 (match-any)
      queue-limit percent 1
      queue dropped pkts : 0


   Class-map (queuing):   out-q-default (match-any)
      queue-limit percent 82
      bandwidth remaining percent 25
      queue dropped pkts : 0




 N7K-2#
```

The F-series modules always support a strict priority queue and don't require any configuration change like the M-series modules. One key difference that the F-series modules offer is the capability to shape the traffic in the strict priority queue, which can help avoid the aforementioned queue starvation. Example 10-9 illustrates shaping a strict priority queue on an F-series module.

Example 10-9   *Shaping a Strict Priority Queue on an F-Series Module*

```
N7K-2-F2# qos copy policy-map type queuing default-4q-8e-out-policy suffix -testing
N7K-2-F2# conf t
Enter configuration commands, one per line.  End with CNTL/Z.
N7K-2-F2(config)# policy-map type queuing 4q-8e-out-testing
N7K-2-F2(config-pmap-que)# class type queuing 1p3q1t-8e-out-pq1
N7K-2-F2(config-pmap-c-que)# shape percent 10
N7K-2-F2(config-pmap-c-que)# int e 9/1
N7K-2-F2(config-if)# service-policy type queuing output 4q-8e-out-testing
N7K-2-F2(config-if)#
N7K-2-F2(config-if)# exit
N7K-2-F2(config)# exit
N7K-2-F2# show policy-map int e9/1 type queuing



Global statistics status :   enabled

Ethernet9/1
```

```
    Service-policy (queuing) input:   default-4q-8e-in-policy

      Class-map (queuing):   2q4t-8e-in-q1 (match-any)
        queue-limit percent 10
        bandwidth percent 50
        queue dropped pkts : 0


      Class-map (queuing):   2q4t-8e-in-q-default (match-any)
        queue-limit percent 90
        bandwidth percent 50
        queue dropped pkts : 0

    Service-policy (queuing) output:   4q-8e-out-testing

      Class-map (queuing):   1p3q1t-8e-out-pq1 (match-any)
        priority level 1
        shape average percent 10
        queue dropped pkts : 0


      Class-map (queuing):   1p3q1t-8e-out-q2 (match-any)
        bandwidth remaining percent 33
        queue dropped pkts : 0


      Class-map (queuing):   1p3q1t-8e-out-q3 (match-any)
        bandwidth remaining percent 33
        queue dropped pkts : 0


      Class-map (queuing):   1p3q1t-8e-out-q-default (match-any)
        bandwidth remaining percent 33
        queue dropped pkts : 0

N7K-2-F2#
```

With the priority queues explained, there are still more queues to understand. You can
use the remaining queues to schedule traffic based on COS or DSCP for transmission.
M-series modules differ somewhat from F-series modules for queuing policies. Both
families of modules trust the COS or DSCP marking on traffic. Example 10-10 shows the
default queuing policies for M-series modules, whereas Example 10-11 shows the default
queuing policies for F-series modules.

Example 10-10 *Default M-Series Modules Queuing Policies*

```
N7K-2# show mod 8 | i Mod
Mod   Ports  Module-Type                   Model            Status
8     24     10 Gbps Ethernet Module       N7K-M224XP-23L   ok


N7K-2# show policy-map interface e8/1 type queuing


Global statistics status :    enabled

Ethernet8/1

  Service-policy (queuing) input:   default-in-policy
    SNMP Policy Index:  301991785

    Class-map (queuing):   in-q1 (match-any)
      queue-limit percent 50
      bandwidth percent 80
      queue dropped pkts : 0

    Class-map (queuing):   in-q-default (match-any)
      queue-limit percent 50
      bandwidth percent 20
      queue dropped pkts : 0

  Service-policy (queuing) output:   default-out-policy
    SNMP Policy Index:  301991794

    Class-map (queuing):   out-pq1 (match-any)
      priority level 1
      queue-limit percent 16
      queue dropped pkts : 0

    Class-map (queuing):   out-q2 (match-any)
      queue-limit percent 1
      queue dropped pkts : 0

    Class-map (queuing):   out-q3 (match-any)
      queue-limit percent 1
      queue dropped pkts : 0

    Class-map (queuing):   out-q-default (match-any)
      queue-limit percent 82
      bandwidth remaining percent 25
```

```
             queue dropped pkts : 0


N7K-2#
```

Example 10-11 *Default F-Series Module Queuing Policies*

```
N7K-2# show module 3 | i Mod
Mod  Ports  Module-Type                   Model           Status
3    32     1/10 Gbps Ethernet Module     N7K-F132XP-15   ok
N7K-2# show policy-map int e3/1 type queuing


Global statistics status :   enabled

Ethernet3/1

  Service-policy (queuing) input:   default-4q-8e-in-policy

    Class-map (queuing):   2q4t-8e-in-q1 (match-any)
      queue-limit percent 10
      bandwidth percent 50
      queue dropped pkts : 0


    Class-map (queuing):   2q4t-8e-in-q-default (match-any)
      queue-limit percent 90
      bandwidth percent 50
      queue dropped pkts : 0


  Service-policy (queuing) output:   default-4q-8e-out-policy

    Class-map (queuing):   1p3q1t-8e-out-pq1 (match-any)
      priority level 1
      queue dropped pkts : 0


    Class-map (queuing):   1p3q1t-8e-out-q2 (match-any)
      bandwidth remaining percent 33
      queue dropped pkts : 0


    Class-map (queuing):   1p3q1t-8e-out-q3 (match-any)
      bandwidth remaining percent 33
      queue dropped pkts : 0
```

```
     Class-map (queuing):   1p3q1t-8e-out-q-default (match-any)
       bandwidth remaining percent 33
       queue dropped pkts : 0



N7K-2#
```

Changing the default queuing policy may be preferred and enables flexible application of QoS policies.

Note Changes to the queuing policy are disruptive to traffic transiting the ports being modified.

The default queuing policies cannot be modified directly. There are two options to make changes to the default queuing policies. The first option is to copy the default policy to a new policy and then modify the new policy. This makes it possible to revert back to the defaults in the event the changes made need to be reversed. Example 10-12 describes how to copy a default policy to a new policy for editing.

Example 10-12 *Copying the Default Queuing Policies to a New Policy*

```
N7K-2# qos copy policy-map type queuing default-4q-8e-in-policy suffix -testing
N7K-2# show policy-map type queuing ?
  <CR>
  4q-8e-in-testing           Policy map name (type queuing)
  4q-8e-inchanged            Policy map name (type queuing)
  >                          Redirect it to a file
  >>                         Redirect it to a file in append mode
  default-4q-8e-in-policy    Default 8-ethernet input queuing policy
  default-4q-8e-out-policy   Default 8-ethernet output queuing policy
  default-in-policy          Policy map name (type queuing)
  default-out-policy         Policy map name (type queuing)
  |                          Pipe command output to filter

N7K-2# show policy-map type queuing 4q-8e-in-testing


  Type queuing policy-maps

  ========================


  policy-map type queuing 4q-8e-in-testing
    class type queuing 2q4t-8e-in-q1
      queue-limit percent 10
```

```
      bandwidth percent 50
   class type queuing 2q4t-8e-in-q-default
     queue-limit percent 90
     bandwidth percent 50
N7K-2#
```

The second option would be to define a new policy with a unique name and apply it. There is no functional difference between the two options other than simplified use with the first option and changing an already existing policy. Advanced network administrators may want to use the second option.

Using the first option after the policy has been copied, changes can be made. In Example 10-13, the copy made from the default template is modified to adjust queue depth.

Example 10-13 *Modifying Queue Depth on Copied Policy*

```
N7K-2# show int e3/1
N7K-2# config
Enter configuration commands, one per line.  End with CNTL/Z.

N7K-2(config)# policy-map type queuing 4q-8e-in-testing
N7K-2(config-pmap-que)# class type queuing  2q4t-8e-in-q1
N7K-2(config-pmap-c-que)# queue-limit percent 20
N7K-2(config-pmap-c-que)# show policy-map type queuing 4q-8e-in-testing


  Type queuing policy-maps
  ========================

  policy-map type queuing 4q-8e-in-testing
    class type queuing 2q4t-8e-in-q1
      queue-limit percent 20
      bandwidth percent 10
    class type queuing 2q4t-8e-in-q-default
      queue-limit percent 90
      bandwidth percent 50
N7K-2(config-pmap-c-que)# end
N7K-2#
```

Example 10-14 shows an entirely new queuing policy is created, which specifies different queue depths for various COS.

Example 10-14 *Creating a New Queuing Policy*

```
N7K-2# config
Enter configuration commands, one per line.  End with CNTL/Z.
N7K-2(config)#
N7K-2(config)# policy-map type queuing m2-10g-egress-queuing
N7K-2(config-pmap-que)#
N7K-2(config-pmap-que)# class type queuing 1p7q4t-out-pq1
N7K-2(config-pmap-c-que)#
N7K-2(config-pmap-c-que)# priority
N7K-2(config-pmap-c-que)#
N7K-2(config-pmap-c-que)# queue-limit percent 5
N7K-2(config-pmap-c-que)#
N7K-2(config-pmap-c-que)# class type queuing 1p7q4t-out-q2
N7K-2(config-pmap-c-que)#
N7K-2(config-pmap-c-que)# bandwidth remaining percent 60
N7K-2(config-pmap-c-que)# queue-limit percent 20
N7K-2(config-pmap-c-que)#
N7K-2(config-pmap-c-que)# class type queuing 1p7q4t-out-q3
N7K-2(config-pmap-c-que)# bandwidth remaining percent 25
N7K-2(config-pmap-c-que)# queue-limit percent 25
N7K-2(config-pmap-c-que)#
N7K-2(config-pmap-c-que)# class type queuing 1p7q4t-out-q-default
N7K-2(config-pmap-c-que)# bandwidth remaining percent 15
N7K-2(config-pmap-c-que)# queue-limit percent 50
N7K-2(config-pmap-c-que)#
N7K-2(config-pmap-c-que)# int e8/1
N7K-2(config-if)# service-policy type queuing output m2-10g-egress-queuing
N7K-2(config-if)# end
N7K-2# show policy-map int e8/1


Global statistics status :    enabled


Ethernet8/1

  Service-policy (queuing) input:   default-in-policy
    SNMP Policy Index:  301991785

    Class-map (queuing):   in-q1 (match-any)
      queue-limit percent 50
      bandwidth percent 80
      queue dropped pkts : 0
```

```
         Class-map (queuing):   in-q-default (match-any)
           queue-limit percent 50
           bandwidth percent 20
           queue dropped pkts : 0

      Service-policy (queuing) output:   m2-10g-egress-queuing
        SNMP Policy Index:  301991809

         Class-map (queuing):   1p7q4t-out-pq1 (match-any)
           priority level 1
           queue-limit percent 5
           queue dropped pkts : 0

         Class-map (queuing):   1p7q4t-out-q2 (match-any)
           bandwidth remaining percent 60
           queue-limit percent 20
           queue dropped pkts : 0

         Class-map (queuing):   1p7q4t-out-q3 (match-any)
           bandwidth remaining percent 25
           queue-limit percent 25
           queue dropped pkts : 0

         Class-map (queuing):   1p7q4t-out-q-default (match-any)
           bandwidth remaining percent 15
           queue-limit percent 50
           queue dropped pkts : 0
N7K-2#
```

As mentioned earlier, the Nexus family of switches by default trust the COS and DSCP markings they receive. In some cases it is preferable to re-mark all traffic to zero when it is received. This can prevent unwanted QoS markings from a host or application from interfering with the company's QoS policy. Example 10-15 shows how to set DSCP to 0 for all inbound packets on an access port.

Note   This policy can work on an access port because no COS is received. For a trunk port, the queuing policy would need to be changed to reset the COS.

Example 10-15   *Setting DSCP to 0 for Untrusted Sources*

```
N7K-2# config
Enter configuration commands, one per line.  End with CNTL/Z.
N7K-2(config)# policy-map type qos notrust
```

```
N7K-2(config-pmap-qos)# class class-default
N7K-2(config-pmap-c-qos)# set dscp 0
N7K-2(config-pmap-c-qos)# int e4/3
N7K-2(config-if)# service-policy type qos input notrust
N7K-2(config-if)# end
N7K-2# show policy-map int e4/3 type qos


Global statistics status :    enabled


Ethernet4/3

  Service-policy (qos) input:   notrust
    SNMP Policy Index:  285214610


    Class-map (qos):   class-default (match-any)
      set dscp 0
N7K-2#
```

QoS and Nexus 2000 Fabric Extenders

The Nexus 7000 supports Nexus 2000 series fabric extenders (FEX) to provide additional options for server connectivity and Top of Rack (ToR) cabling architectures. The FEX is considered a remote patch panel because it has no local switching capability, limited buffering, and a minimal control plane. The FEX's intelligence is derived from the upstream or parent switch it is connected to. To provide this connectivity, there are two new types of ports made available to the network administrator:

■ **FEX Host Interface (HIF):** The ports on a FEX where servers and downstream devices connect

■ **FEX Network Interface (NIF):** The ports on a FEX used to connect to the parent switch (uplinks)

From a QoS perspective, there are some restrictions for what types of policies can be applied to a FEX configuration. Starting with the HIF

■ Classification and marking are supported on HIFs through the QOS type policies.

■ Queuing type policies are not supported on FEX HIF.

The NIF interfaces on a FEX have the following considerations:

■ Queuing type policies can be applied in both ingress and egress directions.

■ Queuing on FEX NIFs connected to an F2 module support two queues on ingress and four queues on egress.

- Queuing on FEX NIFs connected to an M1 or M2 series module support eight queues on both ingress and egress.

Example 10-16 illustrates the results of changing the queuing policy on a FEX HIF, whereas Example 10-17 shows the application of a qos type policy to a FEX HIF.

Example 10-16   *Changing the Queuing Policy on a FEX HIF*

```
N7K-1-Agg1# config
Enter configuration commands, one per line.  End with CNTL/Z.
N7K-1-Agg1(config)#
N7K-1-Agg1(config)# int e101/1/1
N7K-1-Agg1(config-if)# service-policy type queuing in default-in-policy
ERROR: Cannot apply queuing policy to
fex port interface: Ethernet101/1/1
N7K-1-Agg1(config-if)# end
N7K-1-Agg1#
```

Example 10-17   *Applying a QoS policy to a FEX HIF*

```
N7K-1-Agg1# config
Enter configuration commands, one per line.  End with CNTL/Z.
N7K-1-Agg1(config)# policy-map type qos notrust
N7K-1-Agg1(config-pmap-qos)# class class-default
N7K-1-Agg1(config-pmap-c-qos)# set dscp 0
N7K-1-Agg1(config-pmap-c-qos)# int e101/1/1
N7K-1-Agg1(config-if)# service-policy type qos input notrust
N7K-1-Agg1(config-if)# end
N7K-1-Agg1# show policy-map int e101/1/1 type qos


Global statistics status :   enabled

Ethernet101/1/1

  Service-policy (qos) input:   notrust

    Class-map (qos):   class-default (match-any)
      set dscp 0
N7K-1-Agg1#
```

QoS and Nexus 7000 Virtual Device Contexts

The Nexus 7000 supports the capability to create multiple Virtual VDC that virtualize the switch and provide a myriad of options for network administrators to take advantage of. The majority of Nexus 7000 features work and operate specifically in the VDC they are configured in; QoS is both VDC-specific and systemwide so it requires some additional consideration. This section explores these considerations to help ensure your QoS implementation is successful.

As mentioned, the majority of QoS parameters are VDC-specific, although some are systemwide. COS-to-queue mapping is systemwide and must be done from the admin VDC or the default VDC. When this change is made, it is applied immediately and across all VDCs. Ensure that if you do change the CoS to queue mapping that you have a queuing policy in all VDCs that defines behavior for all queues with COS values mapped. If not, performance could suffer and packets could be dropped because of inconsistent QoS policies.

The network-qos used to change the systemwide QoS policy is configurable only in the default or admin VDC.

As of the writing of this chapter, you cannot change CoS-to-queue mappings in a device that has a VDC with a mix of M1/M2/F1 modules. This capability changes in future software releases, and it would be best to check the documentation on Cisco.com for release-specific information.

As illustrated, the Nexus 7000 offers a rich set of QoS features for network administrators to take advantage of. Comprehensive queuing, classification, and scheduling are available and depending on the modules used will determine configuration specifics.

QoS on Nexus 5x00

The Nexus 5x00 series of switches provides a full set of QoS mechanisms for network administrators to deploy. The QoS implementation follows the MQC described earlier in this chapter. QoS capabilities between Nexus devices can vary based on hardware and software capabilities. This section focuses on Nexus 5x00-specific configuration.

Forwarding Architecture

The forwarding architecture of the Nexus 5000 uses the concept of *virtual output queues* managed by centralized arbitration to forward traffic across the internal components of the switch. The Nexus 5x000 series switches uses a Unified Port Controller (UPC) to connect into the crossbar fabric to create a three-stage switching fabric. This architecture enables the switch to manage traffic across the switch in a granular fashion and avoids a situation referred to as HOLB. HOLB can occur in a fabric when congestion on an egress port prevents (blocks) ingress traffic bound for other destinations. One of the goals of the Nexus family of switches was to engineer a platform that would avoid HOLB. In addition, the ability to have an arbitrated fabric enables guaranteed traffic within the switch. This enables the switch to offer lossless services over Ethernet because the switch can ensure that traffic will not be dropped as it traverses the switch. The Nexus 5x00 switches uses an ingress buffered architecture, similar to the Nexus 7000 F1 and F2/F2e modules. In an ingress buffered device, traffic is stored in ingress buffers until the egress port has capacity to accept the traffic. The Nexus 5x00 also uses the same VOQ architecture as the Nexus 7000 with centralized arbitration from the Supervisor of the switch. Each front-panel port has eight VOQs for traffic.

The Nexus 5x00 uses the same MQC structure as described earlier in the chapter with network-qos, queuing, and qos policies available for configuration. Nexus 5x00 supports eight CoS, one per CoS, and depending on the model of switch, they can have different default settings.

The Nexus 5010 and 5020 switches have QoS enabled by default, and you cannot turn it off. In addition, four default CoS values are defined. The first two are for CoS 6 and 7 for control traffic, CoS 3 for FCoE, and a default Ethernet class for all other CoS values. Up to four additional system classes can be defined to meet the network's requirements. Because FCoE is defined by default, it is guaranteed 50 percent of all bandwidth. If FCoE is not in use, you might want to change this allocation.

Note   Control traffic in CoS 6 and COS 7 is treated as a strict priority and is serviced ahead of other traffic.

The Nexus 5548 and 5596 series of switches have QoS enabled, and like the 5010 and 5020, it cannot be disabled. Three default CoS values are defined. The first two are for CoS 6 and 7 for control traffic and a default Ethernet class for all other CoS values. Up to five additional system classes can be defined to meet the network's requirements. FCoE queues are not pre-allocated on the 5500 series.

Network-QoS Policies

The network-qos policy defines queuing and scheduling across the switch. By default on the Nexus 5000, FCoE is enabled, as shown in Example 10-18.

Example 10-18   *Nexus 5000 network-qos Policy*

```
5010-1# show policy-map type network-qos


  Type network-qos policy-maps
  ================================

  policy-map type network-qos default-nq-policy
    class type network-qos class-fcoe
```

```
      pause no-drop
      mtu 2158
   class type network-qos class-default

      mtu 1500
5010-1#
```

The default network-qos policy specifies no-drop behavior for class-fcoe, which enables lossless Ethernet and also accommodates a larger MTU for FCoE.

In a Nexus 5500, the default network-qos policy does not configure FCoE. Example 10-19 shows the default network-qos policy on a Nexus 5500.

Example 10-19 *Verification of Systemwide network-qos Policy*

```
cmhlab-dc2-tor2# show policy-map system type network-qos


  Type network-qos policy-maps
  ================================

  policy-map type network-qos default-nq-policy
    class type network-qos class-default
      match qos-group 0

      mtu 1500
      multicast-optimize
cmhlab-dc2-tor2#
```

When the default policy on a Nexus 5000 is used, and the bandwidth is reserved for FCoE, you can see notable changes, as shown in Example 10-20.

Example 10-20 *Configuring a No-Drop Systemwide network-qos Policy*

```
5010-1# show policy-map int e1/1 type queuing

Global statistics status :   disabled

 NOTE: Type qos policy-map configured on VLAN will take precedence
       over system-qos policy-map for traffic on the VLAN



Ethernet1/1

  Service-policy (queuing) input:   default-in-policy
```

```
       policy statistics status:    enabled

   Class-map (queuing):    class-fcoe (match-any)
     Match: qos-group 1
     bandwidth percent 50

   Class-map (queuing):    class-default (match-any)
     Match: qos-group 0
     bandwidth percent 50

 Service-policy (queuing) output:    default-out-policy
   policy statistics status:    enabled

   Class-map (queuing):    class-fcoe (match-any)
     Match: qos-group 1
     bandwidth percent 50

   Class-map (queuing):    class-default (match-any)
     Match: qos-group 0
     bandwidth percent 50



5010-1#
```

Changing the MTU per CoS is possible through the application of a network-qos policy,
which is then applied to the system qos policy. Example 10-21 shows how to set jumbo
frames in the Nexus 5x00 switches.

Example 10-21 *Enabling Jumbo Frames on a Nexus 5x00 Switch*

```
5010-1# config
Enter configuration commands, one per line.  End with CNTL/Z.
5010-1(config)# policy-map type network-qos jumbo
5010-1(config-pmap-nq)# class type network-qos class-default
5010-1(config-pmap-nq-c)# mtu 9216
5010-1(config-pmap-nq-c)# system qos
5010-1(config-sys-qos)# service-policy type network-qos jumbo
5010-1(config-sys-qos)# end
5010-1# show policy-map system type network-qos


  Type network-qos policy-maps
  ================================


  policy-map type network-qos jumbo
```

```
    class type network-qos class-fcoe
      match qos-group 1

      pause no-drop
      mtu 2158
    class type network-qos class-default
      match qos-group 0

      mtu 9216
5010-1#
```

Queuing Policies

The Nexus 5x00 switches support the ability to queue traffic based on classification and support setting a queue to a strict priority and bandwidth sharing. When configured for strict priority queuing, all traffic classified into this queue will be serviced before any other traffic in on the link. The one exception is the default system-defined strict priority queues for CoS 6 and 7, which are serviced before the user-defined strict priority queue. This is useful when running a network with requirements for latency-sensitive traffic such as voice to ensure voice traffic is not delayed in the switch. The primary consideration for using the strict priority queue is to be careful about what traffic is mapped into the priority queue. Inadvertently mapping too much traffic into the priority queue can create a situation called queue starvation. In queue starvation, the strict priority queue constantly has traffic in it that needs to be serviced and the other queues on the interface do not get access to transmit their data and in essence starve.

Example 10-22 shows how to define a strict priority queue for voice traffic.

Example 10-22 *Defining a Strict Priority Queue*

```
5010-1# config
Enter configuration commands, one per line.  End with CNTL/Z.
5010-1(config)# class-map type qos match-all voice
5010-1(config-cmap-qos)# match cos 5
5010-1(config-cmap-qos)# class-map type queuing voice
5010-1(config-cmap-que)# match qos-group 5
5010-1(config-cmap-que)# exit
5010-1(config)# policy-map type queuing voice
5010-1(config-pmap-que)# class type queuing voice
5010-1(config-pmap-c-que)# priority
5010-1(config-pmap-c-que)# system qos
5010-1(config-sys-qos)# service-policy type queuing input voice
5010-1(config-sys-qos)# show policy-map system type queuing
```

```
   Service-policy (queuing) input:    voice
     policy statistics status:    disabled

     Class-map (queuing):    voice (match-any)
       Match: qos-group 5
       priority

     Class-map (queuing):    class-fcoe (match-any)
       Match: qos-group 1
       bandwidth percent 50

     Class-map (queuing):    class-default (match-any)
       Match: qos-group 0
       bandwidth percent 50

   Service-policy (queuing) output:    default-out-policy
     policy statistics status:    enabled

     Class-map (queuing):    class-fcoe (match-any)
       Match: qos-group 1
       bandwidth percent 50

     Class-map (queuing):    class-default (match-any)
       Match: qos-group 0
       bandwidth percent 50
5010-1(config-sys-qos)#
```

QoS and Nexus 2000 Fabric Extenders

The Nexus 5x00 supports Nexus 2000 series FEX to provide additional options for server connectivity and ToR cabling architectures. The FEX is considered a remote patch panel because it has no local switching capability, limited buffering, and a minimal control plane. The FEX's intelligence is derived from the upstream or parent switch to which it is connected. The Nexus 5x00 switches enable the configuration of Nexus 2000 port buffers. This tuning should be done with care because changing the FEX queue limits provide better burst absorption but have a trade-off of less starvation prevention from a congested receiver.

To configure the FEX port buffers, you can specify the number of bytes to use, as shown in Example 10-23.

Example 10-23 *Tuning FEX Buffers*

```
5010-1# config
Enter configuration commands, one per line.  End with CNTL/Z.
5010-1(config)# system qos
5010-1(config-sys-qos)# no fex queue-limit
5010-1(config-sys-qos)# fex 101
5010-1(config-fex)# hardware ?
  N2148T      Fabric Extender 48x1G 4x10G SFP+ Module
  N2224TP     Fabric Extender 24x1G 2x10G SFP+ Module
  N2232P      Fabric Extender 32x10G SFP+ 8x10G SFP+ Module
  N2232TM     Fabric Extender 32x10GBase-T 8x10G SFP+ Module
  N2232TM-E   Fabric Extender 32x10GBase-T 8x10G SFP+ Module
  N2248T      Fabric Extender 48x1G 4x10G SFP+ Module
  N2248TP-E   Fabric Extender 48x1G 4x10G SFP+ Module
  NB22FJ      Fabric Extender 16x10G SFP+ 8x10G SFP+ Module
  NB22HP      Fabric Extender 16x10G SFP+ 8x10G SFP+ Module

5010-1(config-fex)# hardware  N2232P queue-limit 5120
5010-1(config-fex)#end
5010-1#
```

Table 10-2 offers a comparison of the FEX Buffer capabilities.

Table 10-2 *Fabric Extender Buffer Sizes*

Model No.	Interfaces	Per-Port Buffer Capacity (Network-to-Host/ Host-to-Network)
N2K-C2148T-1GE	48 1GE RJ-45	320 KB per four ports
N2K-C2224TP	24 100/1GE RJ-45	640 KB/480 KB per four ports
N2K-C2248TP	48 100/1GE RJ-45	800 KB/480 KB per eight ports
N2K-C2248TP-E	48 100/1GE RJ-45	32 MB Shared across all ports
N2K-C2232PP	32 1G/10G SFP+	1280 KB/1280 KB per eight ports
N2K-C2232TM	32 1G/10G RJ-45	1280 KB/1280 KB per eight ports
N2K-C2232TM-E	32 1G/10G RJ-45	1280 KB/1280 KB per eight ports
N2K-B22HP	16 1G/10G Internal	1280 KB/1280 KB per eight ports

QoS on Nexus 1000V

The Nexus 1000V switch provides a full set of QoS mechanisms for network administrators to deploy. The QoS implementation follows the MQC described earlier in this chapter. QoS capabilities between Nexus devices can vary based on hardware and software capabilities. This section focuses on Nexus 1000V specific configuration.

Forwarding Architecture

The forwarding architecture of the Nexus 1000V is distributed from the Virtual Supervisor Module (VSM) to the Virtual Ethernet Modules (VEMs). The VSM is the control plane for the switch and pushes the QoS configuration to the VEMs for enforcement and application of policy. By default, the Nexus 1000V doesn't have any QoS configuration with the exception of marking traffic used for control between the VSM and VEM with COS 6 because of its critical nature. Because the Nexus 1000V is a software component, it has no hardware queues or controls to manipulate. All classification, queuing, and policy enforcement are done in software on the VEM.

Classification in Nexus 1000V

The Nexus 1000V offers a full set of classification tools for marking traffic in the network. The QoS engine in the Nexus 1000V uses the MQC similar to the other Nexus family of switches and as such uses the class map, policy-map, and service-policy structure to configure QoS. When classifying traffic, the options to determine which traffic receives which marking include CoE, IP Precedence, DSCP, QoS groups, discard classes, ACLs, packet length, IP RTP port ranges, and specific class-maps. Example 10-24 shows the options available in the CLI.

Example 10-24   *Classification Options with Nexus 1000V*

```
demolab-vsm1# config
Enter configuration commands, one per line.  End with CNTL/Z.
demolab-vsm1(config)# class-map type qos match-any cm-marking
demolab-vsm1(config-cmap-qos)# match ?
  access-group    Access group
  class-map       Class map
  cos             IEEE 802.1Q class of service
  discard-class   Discard class
  dscp            DSCP in IP(v4) and IPv6 packets
  ip              IP
  not             Negate this match result
  packet          Packet
  precedence      Precedence in IP(v4) and IPv6 packets
  qos-group       Qos-group
demolab-vsm1(config-cmap-qos)
```

In Example 10-25, the classification policy matches against IP precedence 0, and the counters on the virtual interface increment as matches are made.

Example 10-25 *Classification Using IP Precedence on Nexus 1000V*

```
demolab-vsm1# config
Enter configuration commands, one per line.  End with CNTL/Z.
demolab-vsm1(config)# class-map type qos match-any cm-marking
demolab-vsm1(config-cmap-qos)# match precedence 0
demolab-vsm1(config-cmap-qos)# exit
demolab-vsm1(config)# policy-map type qos pm-marking
demolab-vsm1(config-pmap-qos)# class cm-marking
demolab-vsm1(config-port-prof)# service-policy type qos input pm-marking
demolab-vsm1(config-port-prof)# end
demolab-vsm1# show policy-map int vethernet 2


Global statistics status :   enabled


Vethernet2

  Service-policy (qos) input:    pm-marking
    policy statistics status:    enabled

    Class-map (qos):   cm-marking (match-any)
      142 packets
      Match: precedence 0
        142 packets
demolab-vsm1#
```

In addition, using the MQC marking policies can be made where traffic is matched and then marked with specific values. Marking can be implemented on the following fields: DSCP, IP Precedence, CoS, QoS group, Discard Class, or ingress and egress ports. Example 10-26 builds on the classification policy and marks the IP Precedence 0 traffic to IP Precedence 1.

Example 10-26 *Marking IP Precedence in Nexus 1000V*

```
demolab-vsm1# config
Enter configuration commands, one per line.  End with CNTL/Z.
demolab-vsm1(config)# policy-map type qos pm-mark-ipprecedence
demolab-vsm1(config-pmap-qos)# class cm-marking
demolab-vsm1(config-pmap-c-qos)# set precedence priority
demolab-vsm1(config-pmap-c-qos)# port-profile vlan301
demolab-vsm1(config-port-prof)# service-policy type qos input pm-mark-ipprecedence
```

```
demolab-vsm1(config-port-prof)# end
demolab-vsm1# show policy-map int v2


Global statistics status :   enabled

Vethernet2

  Service-policy (qos) input:   pm-mark-ipprecedence
    policy statistics status:   enabled

    Class-map (qos):   cm-marking (match-any)
      34 packets
      Match: precedence 0
        34 packets
      set prec priority
demolab-vsm1#
```

The Nexus 1000V also supports Class-Based Weighted Fair Queuing (CBWFQ), which enables network administrators to define QoS policies that can avoid queue starvation. In addition, bandwidth guarantees for each traffic class can be configured, and the uplink bandwidth can be used effectively. CBWFQ extends the functionality from Weighted Fair Queuing by enabling user-defined classes. The CBWFQ configuration in the Nexus 1000V uses the MQC that drives the QoS configuration in Nexus switches.

Note   CBWFQ policies can be applied only on an uplink in the egress or outbound direction.

Predefined protocol classes are frequently seen in a VMware network and may be preferable to classify and queue. They are the Nexus 1000V control, management, and packet traffic and various VMware vmkernel traffic. Example 10-27 shows the complete list.

Example 10-27   *Class-Based Weighted Fair Queuing Protocols*

```
demolab-vsm1# config
Enter configuration commands, one per line.  End with CNTL/Z.
demolab-vsm1(config)# class-map type queuing match-any cm-cbwfq ?
  <CR>

demolab-vsm1(config)# class-map type queuing match-any cm-cbwfq
demolab-vsm1(config-cmap-que)# match ?
  cos       IEEE 802.1Q class of service
  protocol  Protocol
```

```
demolab-vsm1(config-cmap-que)# match protocol ?
  n1k_control   N1K control traffic
  n1k_mgmt      N1K management traffic
  n1k_packet    N1K inband traffic
  vmw_ft        VMware fault tolerance traffic
  vmw_iscsi     VMware iSCSI traffic
  vmw_mgmt      VMware management traffic
  vmw_nfs       VMware NFS traffic
  vmw_vmotion   VMware vmotion traffic
```

With the ability to match and queue protocol-specific traffic, the network administrator can start to implement policies that provide more control than generic queuing. In Example 10-28, VMotion traffic will be guaranteed at least 50 percent of the bandwidth on the uplink.

Example 10-28   *Guaranteeing Uplink Bandwidth for VMotion*

```
demolab-vsm1# config
Enter configuration commands, one per line.  End with CNTL/Z.
demolab-vsm1(config)# class-map type queuing match-any cm-vmotion
demolab-vsm1(config-cmap-que)# match protocol vmw_vmotion
demolab-vsm1(config-cmap-que)# exit
demolab-vsm1(config)# policy-map type queuing pm-vmotion
demolab-vsm1(config-pmap-que)# class type queuing cm-vmotion
demolab-vsm1(config-pmap-c-que)# bandwidth percent 50
demolab-vsm1(config-pmap-c-que)# end
demolab-vsm1# show policy-map type queuing pm-vmotion


  Type queuing policy-maps
  ========================


  policy-map type queuing pm-vmotion
    class type queuing cm-vmotion
      bandwidth percent 50
demolab-vsm1#
```

Summary

The Nexus family of switches shares a common infrastructure for implementation of QoS policies through the Modular QoS CLI. The ability to classify, mark, and queue traffic is available across the platforms and provides a rich set of tools for network administrators to configure their QoS policy:

- **Nexus 7000:** Offers a comprehensive suite of capabilities across multiple families of line cards. The three-stage crossbar switching architecture is engineered to avoid head-of-line blocking and facilitates lossless traffic. This provides a solid foundation for Unified Fabric and other application that can leverage lossless topologies.

- **Nexus 5x00:** Uses VOQ and an ingress buffered platform to deliver the foundation for FCoE and Unified Fabric and the ability to avoid head-of-line blocking.

- **Nexus 1000V:** Offers insight, visibility, and control in a virtualized infrastructure. A complete set of classification, marking, and queuing features including Class-Based Weighted Fair Queuing provide the network administration the tools it needs to be successful.

This chapter showed the basic Nexus 7000, Nexus 5x00, and Nexus 1000V configurations to provide a foundation for classification, marking, and queuing in a modern data center. Common deployments were illustrated and detailed examples provided.

## Chapter 11

Overlay Transport Virtualization (OTV)

This chapter covers the following topics:

- Introduction to OTV
- OTV terminology and concepts
- OTV control plane
- OTV data plane
- Multihoming with OTV
- OTV and ARP
- FHRP localization
- Ingress routing optimization

Overlay Transport Virtualization (OTV) is an IP-based innovation to provide a Layer 2 extension between data centers. OTV is transport agnostic, meaning that the transport infrastructure between data centers can be dark fiber, MPLS, IP routed WAN, ATM, Frame Relay, and so on. The only requirement is that the data centers must have IP reachability between them. OTV enables multipoint services for Layer 2 extension and independent Layer 2 domains between data centers, preserving the fault-isolation, resiliency, and load-balancing benefits of an IP-based interconnection.

Unlike traditional Layer 2 extension technologies, OTV introduces the concept of Layer 2 MAC routing. The MAC-routing concept enables a control-plane protocol to advertise the reachability of Layer 2 MAC addresses. The MAC-routing concept has tremendous benefits over traditional Layer 2 extension technologies that traditionally leveraged data plane learning, hence, flooding of Layer 2 traffic across the transport infrastructure.

As customers consolidate data centers, there is still a driving requirement for multipoint support, meaning more than two locations sharing the same Layer 2 information. OTV provides multipoint connectivity and IP multicast capabilities to provide optimal multicast traffic replication to multiple sites. The benefit of multicast replication for multipoint services is the elimination of head-end replication, which provides suboptimal bandwidth utilization.

Multihoming has always been a requirement to provide redundancy within a given data center. Historically, building Layer 2 solutions with multihoming required additional configuration to provide for end-to-end Layer 2 loop prevention. OTV has a built-in loop detection and suppression mechanism that offers transparent multihoming that does not require additional configuration.

In addition, OTV offers failure boundary and site independence preservation. Because OTV uses a control-plane protocol to advertise MAC address reachability, OTV does not rely on traffic flooding to propagate reachability information for MAC addresses. With the control-plane MAC address learning, OTV does not flood unknown unicast traffic, and Address Resolution Protocol (ARP) traffic is forwarded only in a controlled manner. Because OTV does not forward or propagate Spanning Tree Bridge Protocol Data Units (BPDUs) across the overlay; this enables data center simplification and Spanning Tree Root Bridge independence per data center for all virtual local area networks (VLANs) extended across OTV.

Figure 11-1 shows a common deployment and topology deployed in many Enterprise accounts. Having an OTV Virtual Device Context (VDC) is a best practice; this is a mandatory requirement if the VLANs extended via OTV require a Layer 3 Switched Virtual Interface (SVI) to a given VLAN. The topology in Figure 11-1 is explained and referenced throughout the rest of the chapter.

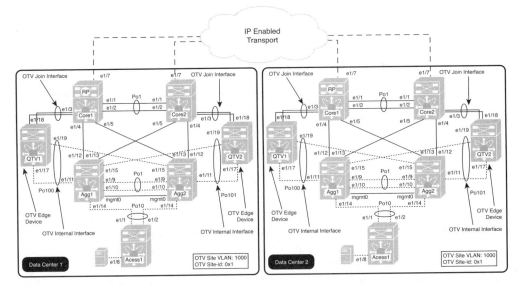

Figure 11-1 *OTV Topology*

OTV Terminology and Concepts

Before understanding and learning the OTV control-plane and data-plane operations, the OTV terminology needs to be defined and understood:

- **OTV Edge Device:** The OTV Edge Device performs the OTV function and operations. The OTV Edge Device receives the Layer 2 Ethernet traffic for all VLANs that need to be extended between OTV peers and dynamically encapsulates the Ethernet frames into IP packets that are then sent across the transport infrastructure. Because the OTV Edge Device needs to see the Layer 2 traffic, it is recommended to place the Edge Device at the Layer 2 or Layer 3 boundary of the data center aggregation layer. However, the OTV Edge Device can be positioned in different places of the data center network and is extremely flexible based on the requirements and data center topology. It is recommended but not required to deploy the OTV Edge Device in pairs for redundancy, load balancing, and resiliency. The OTV edge device is typically carved up into a VDC on each Nexus 7000.

- **OTV internal interfaces:** The internal interfaces are the interfaces of the OTV Edge Devices that face the local site and carry the VLANs extended through OTV. The OTV internal interfaces are typically Layer 2 trunk interfaces carrying multiple VLANs. OTV internal interfaces are regular Layer 2 interfaces; there is not any OTV-specific configuration to the OTV internal interfaces. For example, the OTV internal interfaces perform traditional Layer 2 functions such as local switching, spanning tree operation, data-plane learning, and flooding.

  Example 11-1 shows how to configure the OTV internal interfaces that transport across the OTV. Port-channels are used to leverage vPC running at the data center aggregation layers.

Example 11-1 *Sample Configuration for the OTV Internal Interface*

```
interface port-channel1002
  description L2 to 101 and 102
  switchport
  switchport mode trunk
  switchport trunk native vlan 699
  switchport trunk allowed vlan 10,12,14,18-19,24,34,37,52,56-69,1000
  spanning-tree port type normal
  mac packet-classify

interface Ethernet4/26
  switchport
  switchport mode trunk
  switchport trunk native vlan 699
  switchport trunk allowed vlan 10,12,14,18-19,24,34,37,52,56-69,1000
  spanning-tree port type normal
  channel-group 1002 mode active
```

```
  no shutdown

interface Ethernet7/26
  switchport
  switchport mode trunk
  switchport trunk native vlan 699
  switchport trunk allowed vlan 10,12,14,18-19,24,34,37,52,56-69,1000
  spanning-tree port type normal
  channel-group 1002 mode active
  no shutdown
```

- **OTV join-interface:** The OTV join-interface is the uplink interface of the Edge Device to the Layer 3 core of the network. The OTV join-interface is a Layer 3 point-to-point routed interface, subinterface, or port-channel or a port-channel sub-interface. (Loopback interfaces are not supported today.) The OTV join-interface is used to source the OTV encapsulated traffic and send it to the Layer 3 core of the network of the data center network. The join interface can be associated with a given OTV overlay or associated with multiple overlays. The OTV join interface is configured as an IGMP client that initiates the join to the multicast group configured on the OTV overlay interface; this results in a "join" across the overlay network and discovers the other remote OTV Edge Devices. After the control planes are fully adjacent, this enables the locations to send and receive MAC reachability information and send and receive unicast and multicast traffic.

Example 11-2 demonstrates an OTV join interface configuration. A port-channel is used for high availability.

Example 11-2   *Sample Configuration for the OTV Join Interface*

```
interface port-channel1001
  mtu 1600
  ip address 192.168.205.45/30
  ip ospf network point-to-point
  ip router ospf 1 area 0.0.0.0
  ip igmp version 3

interface Ethernet4/28
  mtu 1600
  channel-group 1001 mode active
  no shutdown

interface Ethernet7/28
  mtu 1600
  channel-group 1001 mode active
  no shutdown
```

■ **OTV overlay interface:** The overlay interface is a logical virtual interface where all
the OTV configuration is placed. The overlay interface encapsulates the site Layer 2
frames in IP unicast or multicast packets that are then sent to the other sites. Every
time the OTV Edge Device receives a Layer 2 frame destined for a remote data
center site, the frame is logically forwarded to the overlay interface. This instructs
the Edge Device to perform the dynamic OTV encapsulation on the Layer 2 packet
and send it to the join interface toward the routed domain. Example 11-3 provides a
sample configuration on how to create the OTV interface in the OTV VDC.

> **Note** The OTV feature is disabled by default. OTV needs to be enabled with the feature
> otv cli.

Example 11-3 *Sample Configuration for the OTV Overlay Interface*

```
feature otv

interface Overlay1
  otv join-interface port-channel1001
  otv control-group 239.1.1.1
  otv data-group 232.0.0.0/24
  otv extend-vlan 10, 12, 14, 18-19, 24, 34, 37, 52, 56-69, 75-79, 86-87, 99, 102-
103, 106, 116, 120, 122
  no shutdown
```

■ **OTV site VLAN:** The OTV site-VLAN is used to discover other Edge Devices in a
multihomed topology. OTV Edge Devices within the same site establish an OTV
adjacency over the site VLAN and elect the Authoritative Edge Device (AED) for
each extended VLAN. The OTV site VLAN needs to be trunked on the OTV internal interfaces of the OTV Edge Device. It is recommended that the OTV site VLAN
is unique per location and does not overlap with any other VLANs in the topology,
meaning the VLAN chosen to be the OTV site VLAN serves only this purpose.
Example 11-4 shows how to configure the OTV site VLAN on the OTV VDC; the
site VLAN needs to be allowed on the OTV internal interfaces as well.

Example 11-4 *Sample Configuration for the OTV Site VLAN*

```
vlan 1000
name otv-site-vlan
otv site-vlan 1000
```

■ **OTV site-id:** With NX-OS release 5.2.1 and later, a second OTV adjacency is maintained, the overlay adjacency. The overlay adjacency is established over the OTV
join-interfaces across the Layer 3 network. Each OTV Edge Device located in the

same site must be configured with the same site-identifier (site-id). The new site-id is advertised in IS-IS hello packets as a part of OTV and is sent over both the overlay and on the OTV site VLAN. The second adjacency protects against when the OTV site VLAN is partitioned between the OTV Edge Devices in the same site. The site-identifier is mandatory to configure on each OTV Edge Device. Example 11-5 shows how to configure the OTV site identifier.

Example 11-5 *Sample Configuration for the OTV Site-Identifier*

```
OTV(config)# otv site-identifier 0x1
```

- **OTV Authoritative Edge Device:** The AED is responsible for the forwarding of Layer 2 traffic including unicast, multicast, and broadcast traffic. The AED is also responsible for the advertisement of mac-address reachability to the remote locations for the VLANs it is active for. The site-vlan is used to discover other Edge Devices in a multihomed site; the discovery elects an ordinal value of either 0 (zero) or 1 (one). This value cannot be manually configured. The AED that has the ordinal value of 0 will be the AED for all the even-numbered VLANs; the AED that has the ordinal value of 1 will be the AED for all the odd-numbered VLANs.

In addition to the OTV site-vlan, with NX-OS release 5.2 (1) and later, each OTV device maintains a second adjacency with other OTV Edge Devices belonging to the same data center. With 5.2.1 and later, there are now two adjacencies established:

- **Site adjacency:** The OTV Edge Devices continue to use the site VLAN for discovering and establishing adjacency with other OTV Edge Devices in the same site.

- **Overlay adjacency:** Established across the OTV join interfaces across the L3 network domain.

The site-id for the overlay adjacency is mandatory when running NX-OS 5.2.1 and later. The site-identifier value can be a value from 0x1 to 0xffffffff (the default is 0x0); the format can be hexadecimal or a MAC address format. If the site-id is not configured, the overlay interface does not come up. All Edge Devices must be configured with the same site-id; the site-id is advertised in IS-IS hello packets sent over both the overlay and on the site VLAN. The combination of the site-id and the IS-IS system-id is used to identify a neighbor Edge Device in the same site.

The dual adjacency provides additional resiliency to avoid a single point of failure of the site VLAN going down or removed to the internal interfaces. The dual adjacency also informs its neighbor about local failures such as the join interfaces going down, the AED is down, initializing, or the internal VLAN is down or removed. As long as the following two conditions are met, the Edge Devices can continue normal operations in a nonfailed environment:

- At least one of the adjacencies needs to be up.

- The Edge Devices are AED-capable.

Because both OTV edge devices are up in data center 1, the VLANs will be divided between them (odd and even); the "*" sign in front of VLANs indicates the AED for each VLAN, as shown in Example 11-6.

Example 11-6   *OTV AED Output*

```
otv-1# show otv site
Site Adjacency Information (Site-VLAN: 1000) (* - this device)
Overlay1 Site-Local Adjacencies (Count: 2)
  Hostname                      System-ID      Up Time   Ordinal
  ------------------------------ -------------- --------- ----------
  otv-2                 f866.f208.c742  1w4d       0
* otv-1                 f866.f209.e243  28w4d      1


otv-1# show otv vlan
OTV Extended VLANs and Edge Device State Information (* - AED)
VLAN   Auth. Edge Device                  Vlan State      Overlay
----   ---------------------------------- ----------      -------
  10   otv-2                              inactive(NonAED)Overlay1
  12   otv-2                              inactive(NonAED)Overlay1
  14   otv-2                              inactive(NonAED)Overlay1
  18   otv-2                              inactive(NonAED)Overlay1
  19*  otv-1                              active          Overlay1
  24   otv-2                              inactive(Non AED)Overlay1
  34   otv-2                              inactive(Non AED)Overlay1
  37*  otv-1                              active          Overlay1
  52   otv-2                              inactive(Non AED)Overlay1
  56   otv-2                              inactive(Non AED)Overlay1
  57*  otv-1                              active          Overlay1
  58   otv-2                              inactive(Non AED)Overlay1
  59*  otv-1                              active          Overlay1
  60   otv-2                              inactive(Non AED)Overlay1
  61*  otv-1                              active          Overlay1
  62   otv-2                              inactive(Non AED)Overlay1
  63*  otv-1                              active          Overlay1
  64   otv-2                              inactive(Non AED)Overlay1
  65*  otv-1                              active          Overlay1
  66   otv-2                              inactive(Non AED)Overlay1
  67*  otv-1                              active          Overlay1
  68   otv-2                              inactive(Non AED)Overlay1
  69*  otv-1                              active          Overlay1
```

OTV Control Plane

The core principles on which OTV operates are the use of a control protocol to advertise MAC address reachability information (instead of using data-plane learning) and packet switching of IP encapsulated Layer 2 traffic (instead of using circuit switching) for data forwarding. These features are a significant departure from the core mechanics of traditional Layer 2 VPNs. In traditional Layer 2 VPNs, a static mesh of circuits is maintained among all devices in the VPN to enable flooding of traffic and source-based learning of MAC addresses. This full mesh of circuits is an unrestricted flood domain on which all traffic is forwarded. Maintaining this full mesh of circuits severely limits the scalability of existing Layer 2 VPN approaches. At the same time, the lack of a control plane limits the extensibility of current Layer 2 VPN solutions to properly address the requirements for extending LANs across data centers.

OTV uses a control protocol to map MAC address destinations to IP next hops that are reachable through the network core. OTV can be thought of as MAC routing in which the destination is a MAC address, the next hop is an IP address, and traffic is encapsulated in IP, so it can simply be carried to its MAC routing next hop over the core IP network. Thus, a flow between source and destination host MAC addresses is translated in the overlay into an IP flow between the source and destination IP addresses of the relevant Edge Devices. This process is called *encapsulation* rather than *tunneling* because the encapsulation is imposed dynamically, and tunnels are not maintained. Because traffic is IP forwarded, OTV is as efficient as the core IP network and can deliver optimal traffic load balancing, multicast traffic replication, and fast failover just like the core would.

The mappings of the MAC address to the IP next hop in the forwarding table are advertised by a control protocol, thus eliminating the need for flooding of unknown unicast traffic across the overlay. The control protocol is extensible and includes useful MAC address-specific information such as VLAN, site ID, and associated IP address (for IP hosts). These requirements are needed to eliminate failure domains and fate-sharing; OTV provides the intelligence to implement multihoming, load-balancing, end-to-end loop-prevention, localize First-Hop Resiliency Protocol (FHRP) capability, and even localize ARP traffic without creating additional operational overhead for each function. Thus, OTV can be used to provide connectivity based on
MAC-address destinations while preserving most of the characteristics of a Layer 3 interconnection.

However, before MAC reachability information can be exchanged, all OTV Edge Devices must become "adjacent" to each other from an OTV perspective. This can be achieved in two ways, depending on the nature of the transport network interconnecting the various sites:

- **Multicast mode:** If the transport is multicast-enabled, a specific multicast group can be configured to exchange the control protocol messages between the OTV Edge Devices.

■ **Unicast mode:** Starting with NX-OS release 5.2(1) and later, the adjacency server was introduced. If the transport is not multicast-enabled, a Nexus 7000 OTV Edge Device can be configured as an adjacency server to which all other Edge Devices register and communicates belonging to a given overlay.

Example 11-7 through Example 11-10 demonstrate the OTV control-plane configuration and verification.

Example 11-7 *Show OTV ISIS Control-Plane Information*

```
show otv isis
ISIS process : default
VPN: Overlay1
  System ID : f866.f209.e243   IS-Type : L1
  SAP : 439   Queue Handle : 11
  Maximum LSP MTU: 1392
  Graceful Restart enabled. State: Inactive
  Last graceful restart status : none
  Metric-style : advertise(wide), accept(narrow, wide)
  Area address(es) :
    00
  Process is up and running
  VPN ID: 171
  Incremental update routes during SPF run
  Stale routes during non-graceful controlled restart
  Interfaces supported by OTV-IS-IS :
    Overlay1
Level 1
Authentication type and keychain haven't been configured
Authentication check is specified
  Address family IPv4 unicast :
    Number of interface : 1
    Adjacency check disabled
    Distance : 115
  Address family IPv6 unicast :
    Number of interface : 1
    Adjacency check disabled
    Distance : 115
  Address family MAC unicast :
    Number of interface : 1
    Adjacency check disabled
    Redistributing :
      all            policy OTV_HSRP_filter
    Distance : 115
  L1 Next SPF: Inactive
```

Example 11-8 *Show OTV Adjacencies*

```
otv-1# show otv adj
Overlay Adjacency database
Overlay-Interface Overlay1  :
Hostname                      System-ID     Dest Addr      Up Time    State
otv-2                    f866.f208.c742 192.168.205.50  28w4d      UP
otv-4                    0026.980d.06c2 192.168.205.53  28w4d      UP
otv-3                    108c.cf1c.f943 192.168.205.58  7w4d       UP
```

Example 11-9 *Show OTV Control-Plane Adjacencies*

```
otv-1# show otv overlay 1
OTV Overlay Information
Overlay interface Overlay1
 VPN name              : Overlay1
 VPN state             : UP
 Extended vlans        : 10 12 14 18-19 24 34 37 52 56-69
 (To
 Control group         : 239.1.1.1
 Data group range(s)  : 232.0.0.0/24
 Join interface(s)     : Po1001 (192.168.205.45)
 Site vlan             : 1000 (up)
```

Example 11-10 *Show All MAC Addresses Learned Locally and the OTV Overlay*

```
otv-1# show otv route
OTV Unicast MAC Routing Table For Overlay1
VLAN MAC-Address     Metric  Uptime    Owner      Next-hop(s)
---- -------------- ------  --------  ---------  -----------
  19 001b.1700.0117  1       00:05:50  site       port-channel1002
  37 0000.0c9f.f005  1       1w4d      site       port-channel1002
  37 0017.a43a.4d3b  42      1w4d      overlay    otv-3
  37 0017.a43b.2025  42      1w4d      overlay    otv-3
  37 0017.a43b.30f3  1       01:40:26  site       port-channel1002
  37 0017.a4a7.8241  42      1w4d      overlay    otv-3
  37 0025.9019.ad8f  42      1w4d      overlay    otv-3
  37 0025.9019.ad9b  42      1w4d      overlay    otv-3
  37 0026.980d.06c3  42      1w4d      overlay    otv-3
  37 108c.cf1c.f942  42      1w4d      overlay    otv-3
  37 f866.f208.c743  1       1w4d      site       port-channel1002
  37 f866.f209.e242  1       1w4d      site       port-channel1002
  57 001b.1700.011d  1       1w4d      site       port-channel1002
  57 0050.5657.a45c  42      1w4d      overlay    otv-3
```

```
57  0050.5657.a45e   42    1w4d       overlay   otv-3
57  0050.5692.0ef9   42    1w4d       overlay   otv-3
57  0050.5692.117b   42    1w4d       overlay   otv-3
57  0050.5692.20e4   42    1w4d       overlay   otv-3
57  0050.5692.2c8b   42    1w4d       overlay   otv-3
57  0050.5692.48d1   42    1w4d       overlay   otv-3
57  0050.5692.5040   42    1w4d       overlay   otv-3
57  0050.5692.5244   42    1w4d       overlay   otv-3
57  0050.5692.5db1   42    1w4d       overlay   otv-3
57  0050.5692.6096   42    1w4d       overlay   otv-3
57  0050.5692.6276   42    1w4d       overlay   otv-3
57  0050.5692.68ae   42    1w4d       overlay   otv-3
57  0050.5692.722d   42    1w4d       overlay   otv-3
57  0050.5692.7c15   42    1w4d       overlay   otv-3
59  0000.5e00.013b   42    1w4d       overlay   otv-3
59  000c.2976.0c7b   1     1w4d       site      port-channel1002
59  000c.298e.b1f6   1     1w4d       site      port-channel1002
59  000c.298f.429c   1     3d05h      site      port-channel1002
59  0017.65ba.2e00   42    1w4d       overlay   otv-3
59  0017.65ba.2e01   42    00:45:23   overlay   otv-3
59  0017.a477.0448   1     1w4d       site      port-channel1002
59  0017.a477.044a   1     1w4d       site      port-channel1002
59  0017.a477.0818   42    1w4d       overlay   otv-3
59  0017.a477.081a   42    1w4d       overlay   otv-3
59  001a.4ba7.e942   1     1w4d       site      port-channel1002
59  0050.5657.042c   1     1w4d       site      port-channel1002
59  0050.5657.042e   1     1w4d       site      port-channel1002
59  0050.5657.0430   1     1w4d       site      port-channel1002
59  0050.5657.0432   1     1w4d       site      port-channel1002
59  0050.5657.0808   42    1d16h      overlay   otv-3
59  0050.5657.080a   42    1d16h      overlay   otv-3
59  0050.5657.080c   42    1w4d       overlay   otv-3
59  0050.5657.080e   42    1w4d       overlay   otv-3
59  0050.5657.0860   42    1w4d       overlay   otv-3
59  0050.5657.0862   42    1w4d       overlay   otv-3
59  0050.5657.0c1c   42    1w2d       overlay   otv-3
59  0050.5657.0c1e   42    1w2d       overlay   otv-3
59  0050.5657.0c28   42    1w4d       overlay   otv-3
59  0050.5657.0c2a   42    1w4d       overlay   otv-3
59  0050.5657.1008   1     1w4d       site      port-channel1002
59  0050.5657.100a   1     1w4d       site      port-channel1002
59  0050.5657.100c   1     1w4d       site      port-channel1002
59  0050.5657.100e   1     1w4d       site      port-channel1002
59  0050.5657.1010   1     1w4d       site      port-channel1002
59  0050.5657.1012   1     1w4d       site      port-channel1002
```

```
59 0050.5657.7428  42    1w4d      overlay   otv-3
59 0050.5657.742a  42    1w4d      overlay   otv-3
59 0050.5657.7440  42    1w4d      overlay   otv-3
59 0050.5657.7442  42    1w4d      overlay   otv-3
59 0050.5657.7450  42    1w4d      overlay   otv-3
59 0050.5657.7452  42    1w4d      overlay   otv-3
59 0050.5657.a470  42    1w4d      overlay   otv-3
59 0050.5657.a472  42    1w4d      overlay   otv-3
59 0050.5657.c44c  1     1w4d      site      port-channel1002
59 0050.5657.c44e  1     1w4d      site      port-channel1002
59 0050.5657.d000  1     1w4d      site      port-channel1002
59 0050.5657.d002  1     1w4d      site      port-channel1002
59 0050.5657.d004  1     1w4d      site      port-channel1002
59 0050.5657.d006  1     1w4d      site      port-channel1002
59 0050.5657.d034  1     1w4d      site      port-channel1002
59 0050.5657.d036  1     1w4d      site      port-channel1002
59 0050.5692.059e  42    1w4d      overlay   otv-3
59 0050.5692.09d0  42    1w4d      overlay   otv-3
59 0050.5692.0ae3  42    1w4d      overlay   otv-3
59 0050.5692.119a  42    1w4d      overlay   otv-3
59 0050.5692.1b04  42    1w4d      overlay   otv-3
59 0050.5692.50d6  42    1w4d      overlay   otv-3
59 0050.5692.5635  42    1w4d      overlay   otv-3
59 0050.5692.5e5b  42    1w4d      overlay   otv-3
59 0050.5692.6995  42    1w4d      overlay   otv-3
59 0050.5692.7680  42    1w4d      overlay   otv-3
59 0050.569c.13a1  1     1w0d      site      port-channel1002
59 0050.569c.2902  1     4d00h     site      port-channel1002
59 0050.569c.31a1  1     1w4d      site      port-channel1002
59 0050.569c.4b6c  1     00:22:39  site      port-channel1002
59 0050.569c.59de  1     1w4d      site      port-channel1002
59 0050.569c.6759  1     1w4d      site      port-channel1002
59 0050.569c.6b37  1     4d00h     site      port-channel1002
59 0050.569c.71ea  1     4d00h     site      port-channel1002
59 0050.569c.76cf  42    13:26:07  overlay   otv-3
59 0050.569c.7796  1     1w4d      site      port-channel1002
59 0050.569c.7c89  1     1w4d      site      port-channel1002
59 0050.56bb.0ce1  1     05:08:32  site      port-channel1002
59 0050.56bb.13e4  1     1w4d      site      port-channel1002
59 0050.56bb.1e1f  1     00:55:49  site      port-channel1002
59 0050.56bb.2c7e  1     01:09:59  site      port-channel1002
59 0050.56bb.3010  1     1w4d      site      port-channel1002
59 0050.56bb.4044  1     1w4d      site      port-channel1002
59 0050.56bb.44b7  1     07:08:21  site      port-channel1002
59 0050.56bb.6c62  1     00:56:54  site      port-channel1002
```

```
59 0050.56bb.760b  1    1w4d       site      port-channel1002
59 0050.56bb.77ae  1    1w4d       site      port-channel1002
59 0050.56bd.0df1  42   1w4d       overlay   otv-3
59 0050.56bd.1df9  42   1w4d       overlay   otv-3
59 0050.56bd.2fc8  1    1w4d       site      port-channel1002
59 0050.56bd.396b  1    11:23:10   site      port-channel1002
59 0050.56bd.3df0  42   1d13h      overlay   otv-3
59 0050.56bd.4bc3  1    1w4d       site      port-channel1002
59 0050.56bd.5696  42   1w4d       overlay   otv-3
59 0050.56bf.4c10  1    1d13h      site      port-channel1002
61 0000.5e00.013d  1    1w4d       site      port-channel1002
61 0014.4f56.99e2  42   1w4d       overlay   otv-3
61 0014.4f56.9a81  42   1w4d       overlay   otv-3
61 0014.4f56.9a83  42   1w4d       overlay   otv-3
61 0014.4f56.9df2  42   1w4d       overlay   otv-3
61 0014.4f5e.988b  1    1w4d       site      port-channel1002
61 0014.4f5e.9b96  1    04:36:56   site      port-channel1002
61 0014.4f5e.9b98  1    01:18:42   site      port-channel1002
61 0014.4f63.c09f  1    1w4d       site      port-channel1002
61 0016.3e25.b2e1  42   1w4d       overlay   otv-3
61 0016.3e40.ae3d  1    1w4d       site      port-channel1002
61 0016.3e54.6fa1  1    1w4d       site      port-channel1002
61 0016.3e70.c9a4  1    1w4d       site      port-channel1002
61 0016.3e7b.a490  42   1w4d       overlay   otv-3
61 0017.65b6.bd00  42   1w4d       overlay   otv-3
61 0017.65bb.5400  1    1w4d       site      port-channel1002
61 0017.65bb.5401  1    18:09:00   site      port-channel1002
61 0017.65bb.541f  1    18:16:24   site      port-channel1002
61 0018.74cf.dc00  1    1w4d       site      port-channel1002
61 0050.5657.0844  42   1w4d       overlay   otv-3
61 0050.5657.0846  42   1w4d       overlay   otv-3
61 0050.5657.1014  1    1w4d       site      port-channel1002
61 0050.5657.1016  1    1w4d       site      port-channel1002
61 0050.5692.7055  42   1w4d       overlay   otv-3
61 0050.56bb.094c  1    1w4d       site      port-channel1002
61 00e0.814d.1b9a  1    1w4d       site      port-channel1002
61 00e0.81c2.4a74  42   1w4d       overlay   otv-3
61 5452.0027.3e71  42   1w4d       overlay   otv-3
```

Multicast-Enabled Transport Infrastructure

With multicast-enabled transport, all OTV Edge Devices will be configured to join a specific Any Source Multicast (ASM) multicast group. With the ASM multicast group, each OTV Edge Device will be a multicast receiver and a multicast source. All interfaces in the path must be configured with PIM sparse-mode (**ip pim sparse-mode**), and each device must specify the SSM group to be used with the command **ip pim ssm** *range*. The sparse-mode and SSM groups should be groups that are currently unused. It is recommended to use a group in the private range 239.0.0.0/8 for the sparse mode group and 232.0.0.0/8 for the SSM group. A Rendezvous Point (RP) must be defined for the sparse mode group, and it is recommended to deploy at least two RPs for redundancy. Redundancy can be accomplished by using Anycast RP, where PIM anycast (**ip pim anycast-rp** *anycast-rp-address anycast-rp-peer-address*) is used to ensure that both RPs are aware of all registered sources. The RP addresses can either be coded statically on each device or can be distributed dynamically using Auto-RP or BSR. The RPs can be placed in a single site in a two-site deployment or can be placed in two separate sites so that a loss of connectivity to one site does not impact other sites.

Because each OTV Edge Device is a multicast source, each OTV Edge Device performs the following steps to become adjacent with the other OTV Edge Devices with multicast transport:

1. Each OTV Edge Device sends an IGMP report to join the specific ASM group used to carry control protocol exchanges. The Edge Devices join the group as hosts, leveraging the join interface. PIM is not enabled on the join interface in the OTV VDC; it is enabled and configured on the upstream Layer 3 interface. The ASM multicast group is specified only in the overlay-interface configuration.

2. The OTV control protocol running generates hello packets that need to be sent to all other OTV Edge Devices; this enables each Edge Device to communicate about its existence to establish a full-mesh of control plane adjacencies per overlay interface.

3. The OTV hello messages are sent across the logical overlay to reach all OTV remote devices; the original frames will be OTV-encapsulated, adding an external IP header (42 bytes). The source IP address of the OTV-encapsulated header is the IP address of the join interface of the Edge Device; the destination is the multicast address of the ASM group dedicated to carry the control protocol. This will result in the multicast frame to be sent to the join interface toward the Layer 3 network core.

4. The multicast frames are carried across the transport and optimally replicated to reach all the OTV Edge Devices that joined that multicast group specified on the overlay interface configuration.

5. The receiving OTV Edge Devices decapsulates the packets.

6. The hellos are passed to the control protocol process.

Note The control-plane routing protocol used to implement the OTV is IS-IS, which has TLV support to carry MAC address information and is a standard-based protocol. The customer or end user does not need to configure any IS-IS information to get OTV to work.

The use of the ASM group to transport the Hello messages enables the Edge Devices to discover each other as if they were deployed on a shared LAN segment.

Although data centers offer forms of physical security access controls and are controlled environments, you can leverage the IS-IS HMAC-MD5 authentication feature to add an HMAC-MD5 digest to each OTV control protocol message. The digest enables authentication at the IS-IS protocol level, which prevents the unauthorized routing message from being injected into the network routing domain. As a result, only authenticated devices will be allowed to successfully exchange OTV control protocol messages between them and become part of the same overlay network. Because the OTV Edge Devices have a full mesh of adjacencies, here is how the MAC address advertisement happens from each OTV Edge Device:

1. The OTV Edge Devices learn new MAC addresses on the internal interface; this is traditional Layer2, switching data-plane learning.

2. An OTV Update message is created containing information for the MAC addresses that were learned in the OTV internal interfaces. The MAC addresses are OTV encapsulated and sent to the Layer 3 core. Again, the IP destination address of the packet in the outer header is the multicast group configured under the OTV overlay interface used for control protocol exchanges.

3. The OTV Update is optimally replicated in the transport and delivered to all remote Edge Devices that decapsulate it and hand it to the OTV control process.

4. The MAC reachability information is populated in the MAC address hardware tables of the OTV Edge Devices. The only difference is that a traditional MAC address is associated with a physical interface; OTV-learned remote MAC addresses have MAC address entries associated to the IP address of the join interface of the originating Edge Device.

Because you advertise reachability of MAC addresses from the control-plane IS-IS protocol, the same logic can be applied for MAC address withdraw and MAC address movements from one data center to another.

Note   The Nexus 7000 has a default Layer 2 MAC address aging time of 1800 seconds (30 minutes) and a default ARP aging timer of 1500 seconds (25 minutes). By setting the default ARP < CAM, timeout results in refreshing the CAM entry before it expires and preventing unicast-flooding in the network.

Example 11-11 shows each OTV edge device as a multicast source to the group configured under the OTV interface.

Example 11-11   *OTV Multicast Mode to Show All the OTV Edge Devices as Sources to the Multicast Group*

```
(*, 239.1.1.1/32), uptime: 1w4d, mrib pim igmp ip
 Incoming interface: loopback200, RPF nbr: 192.168.205.70
 Outgoing interface list: (count: 1)
   port-channel1001, uptime: 1w4d, igmp


(192.168.205.45/32, 239.1.1.1/32), uptime: 1w4d, mrib pim ip
 Incoming interface: port-channel1001, RPF nbr: 192.168.205.45, internal
 Outgoing interface list: (count: 3)
   port-channel1001, uptime: 1w4d, mrib, (RPF)
   Ethernet4/10, uptime: 1w4d, pim
   port-channel1005, uptime: 1w4d, pim


(192.168.205.50/32, 239.1.1.1/32), uptime: 1w4d, mrib pim ip
 Incoming interface: port-channel1005, RPF nbr: 192.168.205.74, internal
 Outgoing interface list: (count: 1)
   port-channel1001, uptime: 1w4d, mrib


(192.168.205.53/32, 239.1.1.1/32), uptime: 1w4d, mrib pim ip
 Incoming interface: Ethernet4/10, RPF nbr: 192.168.205.38, internal
 Outgoing interface list: (count: 2)
   port-channel1001, uptime: 1w4d, mrib
   port-channel1005, uptime: 1w4d, pim


(192.168.205.58/32, 239.1.1.1/32), uptime: 1w4d, mrib pim ip
 Incoming interface: port-channel1005, RPF nbr: 192.168.205.74, internal
 Outgoing interface list: (count: 1)
   port-channel1001, uptime: 1w4d, mrib
```

For the Multicast-enabled transport, a best practice is to leverage AnyCast-RP. With the AnyCast-RP configuration in Example 11-12, you can leverage native PIM between the RPs; this means that there is not any MSDP protocol and MSDP cache; the (S's, G's) are added to the PIM/MRIB tables. You can verify the PIM RP redundancy and display the created state or registrations with the following **show ip pim route** and **show ip mroute** commands.

Example 11-12   *Sample Multicast PIM-SM Configuration Leveraging Native PIM for RP Redundancy*

```
Core-1 #feature pim
feature eigrp
feature bfd
interface loopback0
```

```
   ip address 40.1.1.6/32
   ip router eigrp 10
   ip pim sparse-mode
interface loopback1
   ip address 40.10.10.50/32
   ip router eigrp 10
   ip pim sparse-mode
router eigrp 10
  bfd
ip pim rp-address 40.10.10.50 group-list 224.0.0.0/4
ip pim ssm range 232.0.0.0/8
ip pim bfd
ip pim anycast-rp 40.10.10.50 40.1.1.4
ip pim anycast-rp 40.10.10.50 40.1.1.6
Core-2:
Anycast-RP 2:
feature pim
feature eigrp
feature bfd
interface loopback0
   ip address 40.1.1.4/32
   ip router eigrp 10
   ip pim sparse-mode
interface loopback1
   ip address 40.10.10.50/32
   ip router eigrp 10
   ip pim sparse-mode
router eigrp 10
  bfd
ip pim rp-address 40.10.10.50 group-list 224.0.0.0/4
ip pim ssm range 232.0.0.0/8
ip pim bfd
ip pim anycast-rp 40.10.10.50 40.1.1.4
ip pim anycast-rp 40.10.10.50 40.1.1.6
```

Unicast-Enabled Transport Infrastructure

In situations in which multicast transport services are not available, OTV can be
deployed with unicast-only transport starting with NX-OS 5.2(1) release and greater. The
main difference with unicast-enabled transport is that each OTV device needs to create
multiple copies of each control-plane packet and unicast them to each remote OTV
Edge Device as part of the same logical overlay interface. The unicast updates sent
to each remote Edge Device are referred to as *head-end replication*; by leveraging a

multicast-enabled transport head end, replication is eliminated as the core replicates the updates.

For OTV Edge Devices to communicate with each other, each OTV Edge Device needs to know a list of neighbors to replicate the control packets to. Remember, even in unicast mode (same as multicast) each OTV Edge Device needs to discover each other forming a full-mesh of control-plane adjacencies. For a unicast neighbor definition, the concept and feature of adjacency server is introduced. Adjacency is not an external server or function; it is a function running on the Nexus 7000 OTV VDC. An OTV Edge Device needs to be designated as the OTV adjacency server. Every OTV device wanting to join a specific OTV logical overlay interface needs to first "register" with the adjacency server by sending OTV hello messages. The reception of these hello messages helps the adjacency server to build up the list of all the OTV devices that should be part of the same overlay (named *unicast-replication-list*). This list is periodically sent in unicast fashion to all the listed OTV devices, so that they can dynamically be aware about all the OTV neighbors in the network.

Although high availability and redundancy is always preferred, a pair of adjacency servers can be deployed between two different Nexus 7000 Edge Devices. There is not any state information shared between a pair of OTV adjacency servers; they are completely stateless. Because there is not any state between the OTV adjacency servers, each OTV Edge Device needs to register with both of the OTV adjacency servers. Although an OTV Edge Device (client) can register with multiple adjacency servers, the remote OTV client cannot process an alternative server's replication list until it detects that the primary adjacency server has timed out. The timeout value is 10 minutes; if the primary adjacency server comes back up within 10 minutes, OTV always reverts back to the primary replication list. If an adjacency server is rebooted or misconfigured, the adjacency server has a graceful exit mechanism. By exiting the remote client gracefully, the remote OTV client can start to use the secondary adjacency server and does not need to wait for the 10-minute adjacency timeout. Figure 11-2 shows the topology for an OTV adjacency server.

Example 11-3 show how to configure the primary OTV adjacency server.

Example 11-13 *Sample Configuration for the Primary OTV Adjacency Server*

```
ADJ_Primary# feature otv
otv site-identifier 0x1
otv site-vlan 1000
interface Overlay1
  otv join-interface port-channel1001
  otv adjacency-server unicast-only
  otv extend-vlan 10, 12, 14, 18-19, 24, 34, 37, 52, 56-69, 75-79, 86-87, 99, 102-
103, 106, 116, 120, 122
```

Example 11-14 shows how to configure the secondary OTV adjacency server.

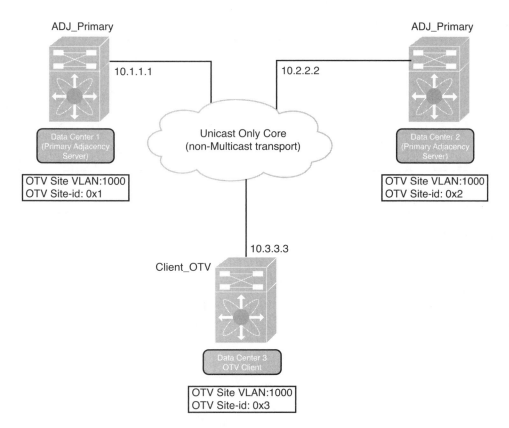

Figure 11-2 *OTV Adjacency Server Topology*

Example 11-14 *Sample Configuration for the Secondary OTV Adjacency Server*

```
ADJ_Secondary# feature otv
otv site-identifier 0x2
otv site-vlan 1000
interface Overlay1
  otv join-interface port-channel1001
  otv adjacency-server unicast-only
  otv use-adjacency-server 10.1.1.1 unicast-only
  otv extend-vlan 10, 12, 14, 18-19, 24, 34, 37, 52, 56-69, 75-79, 86-87, 99, 102-
103, 106, 116, 120, 122
```

Example 11-15 shows the configuration for the OTV client that is not an adjacency server.

Example 11-15   *Sample Configuration for OTV Client Nonadjacency Server*

```
Client_OTV# feature otv
otv site-identifier 0x3
otv site-vlan 1000
interface Overlay1
  otv join-interface port-channel1001
  otv use-adjacency-server 10.1.1.1 10.2.2.2 unicast-only
  otv extend-vlan 10, 12, 14, 18-19, 24, 34, 37, 52, 56-69, 75-79, 86-87, 99, 102-
103, 106, 116, 120, 122
```

Example 11-16 shows how to verify the primary OTV adjacency server.

Example 11-16   *Verify the Primary OTV Adjacency Server*

```
ADJ_Primary# show otv overlay 1
OTV Overlay Information
Site Identifier 0000.0000.0001
Overlay interface Overlay1
 VPN name             : Overlay1
 VPN state            : UP
 Extended vlans       : 10, 12, 14, 18-19, 24, 34, 37, 52, 56-69, 75-79, 86-87, 99,
102-103, 106, 116, 120, 122 (Total:37)
 Join interface(s)    : port-channel1001 (10.1.1.1)
 Site vlan            : 1000 (up)
 AED-Capable          : Yes
 Capability           : Unicast-Only
 Is Adjacency Server  : Yes
 Adjacency Server(s)  : [None] / [None]
```

Example 11-17 shows how to verify the secondary OTV adjacency server.

Example 11-17   *Verify the Secondary OTV Adjacency Server*

```
ADJ_Secondary# show otv overlay 1
OTV Overlay Information
Site Identifier 0000.0000.0002
Overlay interface Overlay1
 VPN name             : Overlay1
 VPN state            : UP
 Extended vlans       : 10, 12, 14, 18-19, 24, 34, 37, 52, 56-69, 75-79, 86-87, 99,
102-103, 106, 116, 120, 122 (Total:37)
 Join interface(s)    : port-channel1001 (10.2.2.2)
 Site vlan            : 1000 (up)
 AED-Capable          : Yes
 Capability           : Unicast-Only
```

```
   Is Adjacency Server : Yes
   Adjacency Server(s) : 10.1.1.1 / [None]
```

Example 11-18 shows how to verify the OTV client.

Example 11-18 *Verify the OTV Client Nonadjacency Server*

```
Client_OTV# show otv overlay 1
OTV Overlay Information
Site Identifier 0000.0000.0003
Overlay interface Overlay1
 VPN name            : Overlay1
 VPN state           : UP
 Extended vlans      : 10, 12, 14, 18-19, 24, 34, 37, 52, 56-69, 75-79, 86-87, 99,
102-103, 106, 116, 120, 122 (Total:37)
 Join interface(s)   : port-channel1001 (10.3.3.3)
 Site vlan           : 1000 (up)
 AED-Capable         : Yes
 Capability          : Unicast-Only
 Is Adjacency Server : No
 Adjacency Server(s) : 10.1.1.1 / 10.2.2.2
```

OTV Data-Plane

All the OTV edge devices need to be fully adjacent with each other. With the adjacencies formed, now the OTV data plane can exchange mac-address reachability information. There are now two different scenarios:

- You still have local Layer 2 switching for devices that want to talk to each other locally within the same VLAN and the same data center: *intrasite -data center.*

- You have remote Layer 2 switching between devices between the data center within the same VLAN: *intersite -data center.*

For an intrasite Data Center Layer 2 communication, the Ethernet frame is received at the aggregation layer device and the standard Layer 2 destination lookup is performed to determine how to reach the local mac-address destination. For intersite Data Center Layer 2 communication, OTV is in between the data center communication paths. A different mechanism is required to establish Layer 2 communication between the data center. The following procedure details that relationship:

1. The Layer 2 frame is received at the OTV edge device. A Layer 2 lookup is performed, but this time the MAC information in the MAC table does not point to a local Ethernet interface but to the IP address of the remote OTV edge device that advertised the MAC reachability information.

2. The OTV edge device encapsulates the original Layer 2 frame: The source IP of the outer header is the IP address of its join interface, whereas the destination IP is the IP address of the join interface of the remote edge device.

3. The OTV encapsulated frame (a regular unicast IP packet) is carried across the transport infrastructure and delivered to the remote OTV edge device.

4. The remote OTV edge device decapsulates the frame exposing the original Layer 2 packet.

5. The edge device performs another Layer 2 lookup on the original Ethernet frame and discovers that it is reachable through a physical interface, which means it is a MAC address local to the site.

6. The frame is delivered to the remote destination.

The Ethernet frames are carried across the IP transport infrastructure because they were encapsulated by the AED. You must understand that the OTV encapsulation adds an additional 42 bytes; it is the OTV data-plane encapsulation performed on the original Ethernet frame, as illustrated in Figure 11-3.

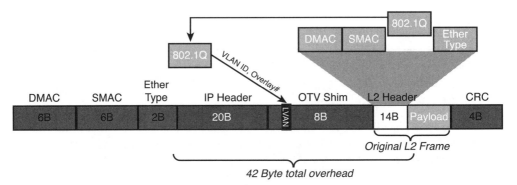

Figure 11-3   *OTV Data Plane Encapsulation*

OTV encapsulation increases the overall MTU size of 42 bytes; as a result, the path from AED to AED must accommodate the additional 42 bytes of MTU end to end. The OTV Edge Device removes the CRC and the 802.1Q fields from the original Layer 2 frame and adds an OTV header. The OTV header contains the VLAN information, overlay ID information, and IP header.

The MTU is important to spend additional time on because the OTV control and data-plane encapsulation originate from an OTV Edge Device and set the Don't Fragment (DF) bit set. Because the DF bit is set, fragmentation and reassembly are not supported on the Nexus 7000 today. Mechanisms such as Path MTU Discovery (PMTUD) are not an option in this case because the MTU must be increased on all the physical interfaces along the path between the source and destination endpoints to account for introducing the extra 42 bytes by OTV.

Consider the following example: If the edge MTU is set to 1500 bytes; the MTU end to end needs to be 1500 bytes + 42 bytes for a total of 1542 bytes minimum MTU. If the transport does not support an MTU greater than 1500 bytes, here are a couple thoughts or recommendations:

■ Set the edge (server) MTU to 1458 bytes; this enables 1458 bytes + 42 bytes for a total of 1500 bytes.

■ Leverage OTV on the ASR1000 because you can support fragmentation and reassembly on the ASR platform. Be aware of potential performance issues and out-of-order packet delivery.

Data-Plane Multicast Traffic

Many applications have a requirement to support Layer 2 multicast communication between data centers that have Layer 2 extended between them. The implementation details depend on whether you have OTV configured for multicast transport or unicast transport.

For Multicast-enabled transport, a multicast source sending traffic to a specific group is deployed in a VLAN in data center 1, and a multicast receiver belonging to the same VLAN is placed in data centers that have a requirement to receive traffic for the same group.

For the Layer 2 multicast communication between senders and receivers between data centers, the Layer 2 multicast traffic must go across the OTV overlay network. Because you have multicast-enabled transports, you do not have suboptimal head-end replication to support Layer 2 multicast communication between multiple data centers for application server requirements. Source Specific Multicast (SSM) is used for the data plane application Layer 2 Multicast requirements. The SSM multicast is different than the ASM Multicast groups for the OTV control-plane adjacencies. For the data-plane requirements with multicast-enabled transport; a multicast source is activated on the data center and starts streaming traffic to the multicast-group (G). The local OTV edge device receives the first multicast frame and creates a mapping between the group Gs and a specific SSM group Gd available in the transport infrastructure; the multicast group from source (Gs) is mapped to SSM data group (Gd). The range of SSM groups to be used to carry Layer 2 multicast data streams are specified during the configuration of the overlay interface.

To configure the range of an SSM data, use the following command under the overlay interface created in the OTV VDC:

```
OTV-VDC-A(config-if)# otv data-group 232.1.1.0/26
```

You need to plan for the amount of data-group multicast and multicast state. For the data grouping, a single data group can be used in the core to carry all the (S,G) site multicast streams; the remote sites would receive all the streams as soon as a receiver joined a specific group. If a dedicated data group were used for each (S,G) site group, each site would receive multicast traffic only for the specific groups joined by local receivers.

For Unicast-enabled transport, multicast capabilities are not enabled in the transport infrastructure. This means that the Layer 2 multicast traffic can be sent across the OTV overlay where the multicast source is located; this results in head-end replication. IGMP Snooping ensures that the Layer 2 multicast packets are sent only to remote data centers where there are active receivers; IGMP Snooping reduces the amount of required head-end replication.

OTV and QoS

To clarify the behavior of OTV from a QoS perspective, you should distinguish between control- and data-plane traffic:

- **Control plane:** The control plane frames are always originated by the OTV Edge Device and statically marked with CoS = 6/DSCP = 48.

- **Data plane:** The assumption is that the Layer 2 frames received by the Edge Device to be encapsulated have already been properly marked (from a CoS and DCSP perspective).

When OTV encapsulates the packet, the QoS marking transfers to the header of the encapsulated packet in the following two ways:

- With 802.1p tagged packets the L2-CoS is copied to the outer DSCP, and the inner DSCP is preserved as is across the overlay.

- With 802.1p untagged packets the outer DSCP is zero (TOS = 0x00) and the inner DSCP is preserved as it is across the tunnel.

Failure Isolation

One of the main requirements of every LAN extension solution is to provide Layer 2 connectivity between remote sites without giving up the advantages of resiliency, stability, scalability, and so on obtained by interconnecting sites through a routed transport infrastructure.

OTV achieves this goal by providing four main functions: Spanning Tree Protocol (STP) isolation, Unknown Unicast traffic suppression, broadcast policy control, and ARP optimization.

STP Isolation

By default, STP Bridge BPDU are not sent across the OTV overlay network. Because you do not need to send BPDUs, this allows each data center to have its own spanning tree root for each VLAN extended between data centers. This also allows each data center to compute its spanning tree locally and independent of the other data centers. In addition to spanning tree control-plane information not being sent across the overlay, the follow traffic is also not sent across the overlay:

- Unknown unicast floods

- CDP

- LACP

- IGMP

- VTP

Unknown Unicast Handling with OTV

OTV uses a control-plane protocol to advertise MAC address reachability information between the OTV edge devices. The MAC address reachability for remote MAC addresses is a mapping of MAC address destinations to IP address next hop that are reachable across the IP network. With the implementation of a control-plane protocol, the OTV Edge Device behaves like a router instead of a Layer 2 bridge, much like how you learn Layer 3 prefixes with routing protocols.

If an OTV Edge Device receives a frame where the destination MAC is an unknown unicast, the Layer 2 traffic is flooded out the OTV internal interfaces only and not the OTV overlay interface. The reason the traffic is flooded out the OTV internal interfaces is that the OTV internal interfaces behave like regular Ethernet interfaces. There is also an assumption that there are not any silent or unidirectional devices attached to the network.

For specific applications that require the flooding of Layer 2 traffic, unknown unicast mode, a workaround is to statically configure the cluster Virtual MAC on the remote data center OTV Edge Device:

```
Site-B-*OTV-ED*(config)# mac address-table static _Cluster MAC_ vlan vlan-name
interface OTV-internal-interface
```

This enables the OTV Edge Device in the remote site to advertise the Cluster MAC to the OTV edge devices in the primary data center, enabling communication. This results in the unknown unicast MAC not being unknown anymore.

Broadcast Traffic Handling with OTV

Layer 2 broadcast traffic is sent across the overlay network. With Multicast-enabled transport, the broadcast frames are sent to all remote OTV Edge Devices to the same ASM multicast group in the transport already configured for the OTV control-plane adjacency.

For unicast-only transport infrastructure deployments, head-end replication performed on the OTV device in the site originating the broadcast would ensure traffic delivery to all the remote OTV Edge Devices part of the unicast-only list.

Multihoming with OTV

Deploying devices in pairs for high availability is always preferred in data center networks. Because you do not send any spanning tree BPDU control-plane information across the OTV overlay network, you must have a method to support multihoming in which there are two (or more) OTV Edge Devices that provide LAN extension services to a given site to prevent an end-to-end data-plane loop.

To support multihoming, an AED is elected on a per-VLAN basis. A site-vlan is created for the AED communication; each AED gets an ordinal value. The ordinal value is either "0" or "1"; the AED that has an ordinal value of "0" is the AED for all the even VLANs extended across OTV, and the AED that has the ordinal value of "1" is the AED for all the off VLANs extended across OTV. The AED is responsible for sending and receiving Unicast, Multicast, and broadcast traffic if an AED that is nonauthoritative for a given VLAN that receives Unicast, Multicast, and broadcast traffic drops the traffic. The OTV Edge Device is the mechanism that enables multihoming and prevents the end-to-end loop between multiple data centers on a per VLAN basis. For the site-vlan, it is recommended to carry the site VLAN on the same interfaces as the extended VLANs; this ensures that if the site-vlan goes down, so will the extended-vlans. Another deployment recommendation is for the site-vlan to use the same VLAN as the site-vlan on all OTV Edge Devices between data centers; remember do not extend the site-vlan across an OTV.

Note   As of today, with the latest NX-OS releases supporting OTV (5.2.5, 6.0.4, and 6.1.1), you cannot change to AED odd-and-even AED load-balancing.

Starting with NX-OS release 5.2.1 and later, a second adjacency is added in addition to the site-vlan adjacency. The second adjacency is the *overlay adjacency*; this adjacency is established over the OTV Layer 3 join interfaces. The overlay adjacency is required to configure and deploy OTV; all OTVE Devices in the same data center must be configured with the same site-id. The site-id configured is advertised in the IS-IS hello packets sent; this advertisement is over both the overlay and on the site VLAN.

Note   If you run the OTV with versions of NX-OS prior to 5.2.1, In-Service Software Upgrade (ISSU) cannot be performed. The OTV Edge Device is forced into a down state until the site-id is configured the same on both AEDs in the same data center.

OTV and ARP

OTV introduces several enhancements to reduce the overall amount of traffic that traverses the inter-DC links. One of these enhancements is ARP optimization. ARP optimization enables each AED to snoop and cache initial ARP replies from hosts located at a remote site. Because the reply information is cached, a local AED can then reply in proxy to ARP requests for remote hosts, thus reducing ARP traffic across the inter-DC links. The caching process functions as follows:

1. A device in Datacenter 2 site sources an ARP request to determine the MAC of the host with address IP A.

2. The ARP request is a Layer 2 broadcast frame and is sent across the OTV overlay to all remote sites, eventually reaching the machine with address IP A in Datacenter 1, which creates an ARP reply message. The ARP reply is sent back to the originating host in the Datacenter 2.

3. The OTV Edge Device in Datacenter 2 snoops the ARP reply and caches the contained mapping information (MAC 1, IP A) in a local data structure named ARP Neighbor-Discovery (ND) Cache.

4. A subsequent ARP request is originated from Datacenter 2 for the same IP A address.

5. The request is not forwarded to the remote sites but is locally answered via proxy by the local OTV Edge Device on behalf of the remote device IP A.

This caching process does, however, introduce some potential caveats. In a situation in which the ARP aging timer is set longer than the CAM aging timer, traffic might be blackholed because of OTV dropping unknown unicast frames. Recommended practice dictates that the ARP aging-timer is set lower than the CAM aging-timer to eliminate this caveat. The default aging timers on the Nexus 7000 follow:

- **OTV ARP aging-timer:** 480 seconds / 8 minutes

- **MAC aging-timer:** 1800 seconds / 30 minutes

These timers differ on other Cisco platforms, such as the Nexus 5000 or an IOS-based device such as a Catalyst 6500. In deployments in which the host's default gateway is placed on a device different than the Nexus 7000, you must set the ARP aging-timer of the device to a value lower than its MAC aging-timer. The OTV ARP caching behavior is enabled by default. It can be disabled via the **otv suppress-arp-nd** command inside of the OTV overlay interface subconfiguration.

Example 11-19 shows the OTV ARP Cache for the OTV Edge Device.

Example 11-19   *Verifying OTV ARP-ND Caching*

```
switch# show otv arp-nd-cache
OTV ARP/ND L3->L2 Address Mapping Cache


Overlay Interface Overlay1
VLAN   MAC Address       Layer-3 Address       Age        Expires In
10     000f.206c.54a6    10.46.12.13           00:14:09   00:02:50
10     000e.7ffd.f82f    10.46.100.11          28w4d      00:07:21
```

10	000f.206b.ada1	10.46.112.225	00:08:39	0.589306
10	000f.206b.ada1	10.46.112.227	12w5d	00:07:40
10	4a3b.3781.b20b	10.46.120.1	20:23:41	00:00:22
10	4a3b.30a4.9f0b	10.46.120.2	05:50:39	00:00:06
10	4a3b.30a4.9f0b	10.46.120.5	1d01h	00:00:21
10	0009.6b1b.6c42	10.46.120.14	1w0d	00:07:55
10	0009.6b1b.6b3e	10.46.120.15	00:02:29	00:05:30

Example 11-20 shows how to disable OTV ARP Cache under the OTV overlay interface.

Example 11-20   *Disabling OTV ARP-ND Caching*

```
interface Overlay1
  otv join-interface port-channel1001
  otv control-group 239.1.1.1
  otv data-group 232.0.0.0/24
  no otv suppress-arp-nd
  otv extend-vlan 10, 12, 14, 18-19, 24, 34, 37, 52, 56-69, 75-79, 86-87, 99, 102-
103, 106, 116, 120, 122
  no shutdown
```

First-Hop Routing Protocol Localization

A second enhancement employed by OTV to reduce the amount of traffic that traverses the inter-DC links is a method to localize the Virtual default-gateway IP address (VIP) of the FHRP. *FHRP* is a general term for a protocol that defines the default gateway IP address. It encompasses any of the well-known protocols such as Hot-Standby Router Protocol (HSRP), Virtual Router Redundancy Protocol (VRRP), and Global Load Balancing Protocol (GLBP). In a spanned Layer 2 environment, it is important to retain the same default-gateway IP and MAC address at each site to allow for seamless live migrations of virtual resources between sites. With HSRP deployed as the FHRP, the vMAC is derived from the HSRP group number. So, if data center 1 has HSRP group number x between the two routers and data center 2 has the same HSRP group number of X, both data center, will have the same vMAC programmed locally. With a server cluster that fails over or when a virtual machine moves from one data center to another (assuming all of the back-end storage is in place for this to happen), the mac-address of its default gateway is cached. There will not be any traffic disruption as the end host will have the same gateway vMAC address.

Note   HSRP and VRRP assign gateway virtual MAC addresses in a deterministic fashion. GLBP, by default, assigns virtual MAC addresses to the various gateways via the active virtual gateway (AVG). Because of this difference in behavior, FHRP localization currently requires that either HSRP or VRRP be deployed.

This functionality causes the OTV AEDs to filter FHRP messages across the overlay network to enable the co-existence of the default gateway VIP at each OTV site. Without filtering enabled, FHRP messages would be sent across the overlay leading to the election of a single active device to serve as the default gateway. This behavior would then force any traffic destined for the default gateway to the site where the Active node was elected—leading to suboptimal traffic flow and also a high amount of data traversing the inter-DC links creating unnecessary use of those links. However, with filtering enabled, FHRP messages are dropped at the AED, and the gateway VIP can be considered active-active at each OTV site—thus eliminating hair-pinning of traffic destined for the default gateway between sites. In addition, with the HSRP filtering only the local routers in each data center will know about each other; the routers in the other data centers do not know anything about the others. This can result in active or active HSRP (with vPC in this sample topology) configuration and cannot have HSRP "listeners" as you filter all the HSRP Multicast hellos.

FHRP filtering functionality should be deployed with an equivalent method to optimize inbound traffic flows to avoid asymmetric traffic behavior. (This would be unwanted especially in deployments leveraging stateful services such as firewalls or load balancers across data centers.) The next section covers several methods for ingress routing optimization.

Example 11-21 shows how to prevent HSRP messages to perform HSRP localization.

Example 11-21   *Define HSRPv1 and HSRPv2 to Block HSRP Hello Messages Between the OTV Edge Devices*

```
ip access-list ALL_IPs
  10 permit ip any any
!
mac access-list ALL_MACs
  10 permit any any
!
ip access-list HSRP_IP
  10 permit udp any 224.0.0.2/32 eq 1985
  20 permit udp any 224.0.0.102/32 eq 1985
vlan access-map HSRP_Local 10
      match ip address HSRP_IP
      action drop
vlan access-map HSRP_Local 20
      match ip address ALL
      action forward
```

Example 11-22 shows how to block HSRP gratuitous ARP for the HSRP virtual IP address.

Example 11-22 *Prevent Duplicate HSRP Gratuitous ARP from HSRP VIP*

```
This is the error message and the following ACL presents this:

Message without: %ARP-3-DUP_VADDR_SRC_IP:  arp [3849]  Source address
of packet received from 0000.0c07.ac1f on Vlan10(port-channel10) is
duplicate of local virtual ip, 192.168.10.1

arp access-list HSRP_VMAC_ARP
  10 deny ip any mac 0000.0c07.ac00 ffff.ffff.ff00
  20 deny ip any mac 0000.0c9f.f000 ffff.ffff.f000
  30 permit ip any mac any
feature dhcp
ip arp inspection filter HSRP_VMAC_ARP 10,11,600, 601, 700, 701
```

Example 11-23 shows how to block the HSRP vMAC from being advertised to other routers.

Example 11-23 *Filter Learning HSRP Virtual MAC Address Across OTV*

```
mac access-list HSRP_VMAC
  10 permit 0000.0c07.ac00 0000.0000.00ff any
  20 permit 0000.0c9f.f000 0000.0000.0fff any
!
vlan access-map HSRP_Localization 10
        match mac address HSRP_VMAC
        match ip address HSRP_IP
        action drop
!
vlan access-map HSRP_Localization 20
        match mac address ALL_MACs
        match ip address ALL_IPs
        action forward
!
vlan filter HSRP_Local vlan-list 10,11,600, 601, 700, 701

mac-list HSRP_VMAC_Deny seq 5 deny 0000.0c07.ac00 ffff.ffff.ff00
mac-list HSRP_VMAC_Deny seq 10 deny 0000.0c9f.f000 0000.0000.0fff
mac-list HSRP_VMAC_Deny seq 15 permit 0000.0000.0000 0000.0000.0000
!
route-map stop-HSRP permit 10
match mac-list HSRP_VMAC_Deny
!
otv-isis default
vpn Overlay0
redistribute filter route-map stop-HSRP
```

Inbound Path Optimization

Inbound path optimization is equally important to optimizing outbound routing in an OTV environment to provide proper flow symmetry. An additional level of intelligence is required to provide information on which specific location an IP address is available and avoid a suboptimal traffic path across the L2 connection established between OTV sites.

Server virtualization and high availability across geographically dispersed data centers are common in data center deployments today. Workload virtualization requires location independence for server resources and requires the flexibility to move these server resources from one data center to another to meet increasing workloads and to support disaster recovery. This brings the challenge of route optimization when the virtual servers move to route traffic to its current location. It also keeps the server's identity (IP address) the same across moves, so the clients can continue to send traffic regardless of the server's current location.

Several methods exist to control and manage inbound routing, including Route Health Injection (RHI), Null Aggregation, and Locator Identity Separation Protocol (LISP). These methods are discussed from a high-level standpoint; additional details for RHI and Null Aggregation are outside the scope of this book. LISP is covered in detail in Chapter 13, "LISP."

One simple way to redirect traffic to a specific IP address in an OTV extended VLAN environment is to dynamically inject a host route for the individual endpoint IP address into the routing protocol. Load balancers with the RHI function implemented on them can provide an automated mechanism for detecting real-server reachability, dynamically reacting to moves (VM-Mobility) and injecting the necessary host routes as applicable. In an OTV environment, this allows remote hosts and routers to use this routing-specific information to take the most optimal path to a specific IP address that is part of an extended VLAN. When combined with FHRP isolation, this enables complete end-to-end routing symmetry.

Note   This approach, although simple, pollutes the routing tables considerably and causes a large amount of churn in the routing protocol. Forcing churning of the routing protocol is a risky proposition because it can lead to instabilities and overall loss of connectivity, together with adding delays to roaming handoffs.

Null Aggregation provides another extremely simple mechanism for providing optimal inbound path selection. In a Null Aggregation deployment for a typical dual-DC deployment leveraging OTV, a VLAN's Layer 3 subnet is logically split into two more specific subnets along a logical boundary—creating two logical ranges of IP addresses—one range to be used per site. Hosts at each site are addressed inside of that site's specific range but retain the larger subnet mask and the same default gateway. The split range boundary is statically defined in the routing table pointing to Null0, creating a more-specific inbound path for a particular subnet—thus drawing the traffic into a particular site in an OTV extended VLAN environment. This method is similar to the RHI approach previously described but without any sort of dynamic behavior. It is also bound at the subnet level and not to an individual host level. As this method is static in nature, strict administrative oversight is required to ensure hosts are addressed into the correct IP range to maintain symmetry.

Due to this, the Null Aggregation approach works well in OTV deployments leveraging geographically dispersed clusters because IP addresses would stay "stuck" to a particular site. This method quickly breaks in VM-Mobility environments as individual IP addresses float dynamically between sites.

Example 11-24 shows the Null route information for Datacenter 1.

Example 11-24   *Null Aggregation Datacenter 1 Configuration Example Leveraging the Subnet 10.1.64.0/24 and EIGRP for Redistribution*

```
interface Vlan64
  no shutdown
  description ERP-PROD
  no ip redirects
  ip address 10.1.64.2/24
  ip router eigrp 1
  ip passive-interface eigrp 1
  hsrp version 2
  hsrp 600
    preempt
    priority 105
    ip 10.1.64.1

ip prefix-list otv-local-prefix seq 10 permit 10.1.64.0/25
route-map redist-otv-subnets permit 10
  match ip address prefix-list otv-local-prefixes

ip route 10.1.64.0/25 Null0 250

router eigrp 1
  router-id 10.0.0.250
  redistribute static route-map redist-otv-subnets
```

Example 11-25 shows the Null route information for Datacenter 2.

Example 11-25   *Null Aggregation Datacenter 2 Configuration Example Leveraging the Subnet 10.1.64.0/24 and EIGRP for Redistribution*

```
interface Vlan64
  no shutdown
  description ERP-PROD
  no ip redirects
  ip address 10.1.64.3/24
  ip router eigrp 1
  ip passive-interface eigrp 1
  hsrp version 2
  hsrp 600
    ip 10.1.64.1

ip prefix-list otv-local-prefix seq 10 permit 10.1.64.128/25
route-map redist-otv-subnets permit 10
  match ip address prefix-list otv-local-prefixes

ip route 10.1.64.128/25 Null0 250

router eigrp 1
  router-id 10.0.0.251
  redistribute static route-map redist-otv-subnets
```

Finally, LISP is a new routing architecture that creates a new paradigm by splitting the device identity, known as an Endpoint Identifier (EID), and its location, known as its Routing Locator (RLOC), into two different numbering spaces. This capability brings renewed scale and flexibility to the network in a single protocol, enabling the areas of mobility, scalability, and security. It provides end-to-end path optimization in an OTV environment, without any of the sacrifices of RHI or Null Aggregation.

Specifically for enterprises leveraging OTV, LISP provides several key benefits, including simplified Layer 2 extension with ingress Traffic Engineering (TE) capabilities and IP Mobility for geographically disperses data centers and Disaster Recovery (DR). LISP is covered in great detail in Chapter 13.

Summary

This chapter discussed how you can deploy OTV to provide multipoint Layer 2 LAN extension between data centers. It also discussed the deployment options and recommended topologies.

OTV can extend Layer 2 networks over any IP-enabled network and provide ease of configuration and deployment, multihoming, optimal multicast replication, and HSRP localization. OTV also can preserve Layer 3 boundaries and site scale.

## Chapter 12

Layer 3 Virtualization and Multiprotocol Label Switching (MPLS)

This chapter covers the following topics:

- Virtual Routing and Forwarding (VRF):

    - VRF, VRF-Lite, VRF Import-Export

    - Configuration examples

- Multiprotocol Label Switching (MPLS):

    - Introduction

    - Terminology

    - Layer 3 virtual private networks (VPNs), Traffic Engineering, 6PE and 6VPE, high-availability

    - Management and Troubleshooting: LSP Ping/Trace and TE Tunnel Ping/Trace

    - Configuration examples

- Nexus hardware requirements and NX-OS licensing for MPLS and VRF

Virtual Routing and Forwarding

Virtual Routing and Forwarding provides logical network segmentation by virtualizing both the routing control plane and data plane functions into autonomous instances. Routing protocols and interfaces, both physical and logical, become members of a specific VRF instance via configuration. For each VRF, IPv4 and IPv6 tables are created automatically and independent routing and forwarding decisions are made. NX-OS supports up to 1000 unique VRF instances, whether defined in a single Virtual Device Context (VDC) or spread across multiple VDCs.

In NX-OS, all components were designed from the ground up to be VRF-capable. This includes management services, network services, routing protocols, and uniform configuration and operational parameters, such as the following:

- VRF-Specific Static ARP
- VRF-Aware Ping
- PBR-set VRF
- VRF-Aware SCP
- VRF-Aware AAA (RADIUS)
- VRF-Aware SNMP Agent
- VRF-Aware AAA (TACACS+)
- VRF-Aware SSH
- VRF-Aware BGP
- VRF-Aware Syslog
- VRF-Aware DHCP
- VRF-Aware Telnet
- VRF-Aware DNS
- VRF-Aware Traceroute
- VRF-Aware FTP / TFTP
- -VRF-Aware uRPF
- VRF-Aware NTP
- VRF-Aware FHRP protocols
- VRF-Aware OSPF
- VRF-Aware WCCP

Predefined VRFs

NX-OS has two predefined VRFs, as shown in Example 12-1. Unlike IOS, which has a global routing table, NX-OS has a VRF named *default* that encompasses all the predefined aspects of the systems. Unless another VRF is specified or configured, all Layer 3 interfaces, routing protocols, routing context, and **show** commands run in the default VRF. Also, any new interfaces added to the system over time as the result of installing additional linecard modules automatically become members of the default VRF. Example 12-2 outlines the interface-to-VRF bindings.

Note   When an interface is configured to become a member of a different VRF, any existing Layer 3 configuration is lost.

Example 12-1   *Viewing NX-OS Predefined VRFs*

```
N7k-1# show vrf
VRF-Name                        VRF-ID State    Reason
default                              1 Up       --
management                           2 Up       --
```

Example 12-2   *Leveraging the show vrf interface Command to View Interface to VRF Mappings*

```
N7k-1# show vrf interface
Interface        VRF-Name                 VRF-ID  Site-of-Origin
Vlan1            default                       1  --
Vlan50           default                       1  --
Vlan60           default                       1  --
Vlan70           default                       1  --
Ethernet10/1     default                       1  --
Ethernet10/2     default                       1  --
Ethernet10/3     default                       1  --
Ethernet10/4     default                       1  --
Ethernet10/5     default                       1  --
Ethernet10/6     default                       1  --
Ethernet10/7     default                       1  --
Ethernet10/8     default                       1  --
Ethernet10/9     default                       1  --
Ethernet10/11    default                       1  --
Ethernet10/12    default                       1  --
Ethernet10/13    default                       1  --
Ethernet10/14    default                       1  --
Ethernet10/15    default                       1  --
Ethernet10/16    default                       1  --
Ethernet10/17    default                       1  --
Ethernet10/19    default                       1  --
Ethernet10/20    default                       1  --
Ethernet10/21    default                       1  --
Ethernet10/22    default                       1  --
Ethernet10/23    default                       1  --
Ethernet10/24    default                       1  --
Ethernet10/25    default                       1  --
Ethernet10/26    default                       1  --
Ethernet10/27    default                       1  --
Ethernet10/28    default                       1  --
Ethernet10/29    default                       1  --
Ethernet10/30    default                       1  --
Ethernet10/31    default                       1  --
```

```
Ethernet10/32    default                              1   --
mgmt0            management                           2   --
loopback100      vrf-customer1                        6   --
loopback200      vrf-customer2                        7   --
```

A second predefined VRF exists in NX-OS, named *management*. As the name implies, this VRF is used only for out-of-band system management purposes. Transient traffic, or traffic not destined to the switch, is not permitted in the management VRF. Only the interface *mgmt0*, which is found on the Nexus 7000 Supervisor Module, the Nexus 5000, and Nexus 3000, is permitted as a member interface to the management VRF. Other interfaces, such as an Ethernet interface or Switched Virtual Interface (SVI) cannot be configured as a member of the predefined management VRF. Furthermore, only static routing is permitted inside of the management VRF; no additional routing protocols are supported and no route import/export (leak) functionality is supported. Example 12-3 illustrates the configuration of the mgmt0 interface with static routing inside of the management VRF. As you can see in Example 12-4, the management VRF is completely isolated from the default VRF from a Layer 3 perspective.

Example 12-3 *NX-OS mgmt0/Interface and VRF Configuration*

```
N7k-1(config)# int mgmt0
N7k-1(config-if)# ip address 10.91.86.180/25
N7k-1(config-if)# vrf context management
N7k-1(config-vrf)# ip route 0.0.0.0/0 10.91.86.129
N7k-1(config)# end
```

Example 12-4 *NX-OS Default and Management VRF Routing Table Isolation*

```
N7k-1# show ip route
IP Route Table for VRF "default"
'*' denotes best ucast next-hop
'**' denotes best mcast next-hop
'[x/y]' denotes [preference/metric]

172.17.22.0/24, ubest/mbest: 1/0, attached
    *via 172.17.22.2, Vlan50, [0/0], 12w4d, direct
172.17.22.1/32, ubest/mbest: 1/0
    *via 172.17.22.1, Vlan50, [0/0], 5w0d, hsrp
172.17.22.2/32, ubest/mbest: 1/0, attached
    *via 172.17.22.2, Vlan50, [0/0], 12w4d, local
172.17.23.0/24, ubest/mbest: 1/0, attached

N7k-1# show ip route vrf management
IP Route Table for VRF "management"
```

```
'*' denotes best ucast next-hop
'**' denotes best mcast next-hop
'[x/y]' denotes [preference/metric]


0.0.0.0/0, ubest/mbest: 1/0
    *via 10.91.86.129, [1/0], 12w4d, static
10.91.86.128/25, ubest/mbest: 1/0, attached
    *via 10.91.86.180, mgmt0, [0/0], 12w4d, direct
10.91.86.180/32, ubest/mbest: 1/0, attached
    *via 10.91.86.180, mgmt0, [0/0], 12w4d, local
```

VRF Operational Commands

Because NX-OS was built from the ground up with VRF support in mind, operational commands have a specific, consistent placement of a keyword at the end of a command to specify a VRF. As mentioned earlier, the *default* VRF is used when no VRF is specified in a particular command. To continue to provide the network engineer with a more streamlined configuration approach, NX-OS also supports a routing-context mode, which sets the scope for any subsequent **show** or EXEC commands. Example 12-5 shows how to leverage the **routing-context** command to simplify operations.

Example 12-5   *Using the vrf Keyword and Routing-Context Scope for EXEC and show Commands*

```
N7k-1# ping 10.100.5.20 vrf management
N7k-1# show ip arp 10.100.5.20 vrf management
N7k-1# show routing vrf management


N7k-1# routing-context vrf management
N7k-1%management# ping 10.100.5.20
N7k-1%management# sh ip arp 10.100.5.20
N7k-1%management# show routing
```

VRF-Lite

VRF-Lite provides a simple and scalable method for virtualizing routing in many environments. However, VRF-Lite does not require MPLS. VRF-Lite is one of the most common deployments of VRF technology in most enterprise networks today. VRF-Lite is typically found on MPLS CE routers, in environments in which multitenancy and routing isolation are required, or in environments requiring support for overlapping IP ranges.

Following is a listing of steps to configure basic elements of VRF-Lite:

1. Create a new VRF context.

2. [Optional] Configure Route Targets for Import/Export Functionality.

3. Configure any necessary static routing inside of the VRF context as part of the appropriate address-family.

4. Assign interfaces to the newly created VRF.

5. Configure Interior Gateway Protocol (IGP) for the newly created VRF.

6. [Optional] If configuring Route Import/Export, configure MP-BGP.

To configure Multi-VRF, create a VRF table and then specify the Layer 3 interface associated with that VRF. You can also optionally configure any static routing associated to the VRF. Example 12-6 describes these key configuration elements. Remember to assign the VRF first before any IP addresses to the interface. Next, you enable the newly created VRF inside of a routing protocol, as shown in Example 12-7 for OSPF, Example 12-8 for EIGRP, and Example 12-9 for IS-IS.

Example 12-6 *Basic VRF-Lite Configuration Example Using Two VRFs, vrf-customer1 and vrf-customer2*

```
N7k-1(config)# vrf context vrf-customer1
N7k-1(config-vrf)# ip route 192.168.0.0/16 172.16.21.254


N7k-1(config)# vrf context vrf-customer2
N7k-1(config-vrf)# ip route 10.100.0.0/16 172.16.10.254


N7k-1(config)# interface Ethernet18/48
N7k-1(config-if)# vrf member vrf-customer1


N7k-1(config)# interface Ethernet18/1
N7k-1(config-if)# vrf member vrf-customer2
```

Example 12-7 *Basic OSPF VRF Configuration*

```
N7k-1(config)# feature ospf


N7k-1(config)# router ospf 20
N7k-1(config-router)# router-id 192.168.100.254
N7k-1(config-router)# vrf vrf-customer1
N7k-1(config-router-vrf)# router-id 192.168.200.254
```

Example 12-8 *Basic EIGRP VRF Configuration*

```
N7k-1(config)# feature eigrp


N7k-1(config)# router eigrp 1
```

```
N7k-1(config-router)# router-id 192.168.100.1
N7k-1(config-router)# vrf vrf-customer2
N7k-1(config-router-vrf)# router-id 192.168.200.1
N7k-1(config-router-vrf)# autonomous-system 200
```

Example 12-9 *Basic IS-IS VRF Configuration*

```
N7k-1(config)# feature isis

N7k-1(config)# router isis 1
N7k-1(config-router)# net <net name 1>
N7k-1(config-router)# vrf vrf-customer3
N7k-1(config-router-vrf)# net <net name 2>
```

Beginning in NX-OS 5.2(1), support was added for the ability to import and export (or *leak*) routes between different VRFs. Route import/export functionality does not require any additional licensing. However, Route import/export functionality does require that MP-BGP is running and that prefixes are either directly installed or redistributed into BGP. A configuration example is provided in the following text.

Note   When configuring VRF-Lite, the RD is tied to the MPLS license in NX-OS and is not required for VRF-Lite and local Route Import/Export functionality.

Figure 12-1 outlines a typical topology where routes are both imported and exported between two VRFs: vrf-customer1 and vrf-customer2. Example 12-10 covers the configuration aspects of this topology. The **route-target** command uses an extended community format. The **route-target import** command specifies routing information *from* a target extended community, whereas the **route-target export** command specifies routing information *to* a target extended community.

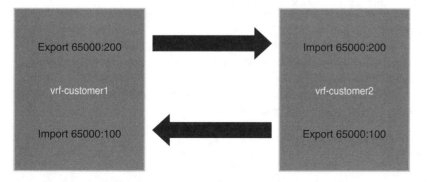

Figure 12-1 *Sample VRF-Lite Route Import/Export Topology*

Example 12-10   *Basic VRF-Lite Route Import/Export Functionality*

```
N7k-1(config)# feature bgp

N7k-1(config)# vrf context vrf-customer1
N7k-1(config-vrf)#address-family ipv4 unicast
N7k-1(config-vrf-af-ipv4)# route-target import 65000:200
N7k-1(config-vrf-af-ipv4)# route-target export 65000:100

N7k-1(config)# vrf context vrf-customer2
N7k-1(config-vrf)# address-family ipv4 unicast
N7k-1(config-vrf-af-ipv4)# route-target import 65000:100
N7k-1(config-vrf-af-ipv4)# route-target export 65000:200

N7k-1(config)# interface Loopback100
N7k-1(config-if)# vrf member vrf-customer1
% Deleted all L3 config on interface loopback100
N7k-1(config-if)# ip address 192.168.100.1/32

N7k-1(config)# interface Loopback200
N7k-1(config-if)# vrf member vrf-customer2
% Deleted all L3 config on interface loopback200
N7k-1(config-if)# ip address 192.168.200.1/32

N7k-1(config-if)# router bgp 65000
N7k-1(config-router)# vrf vrf-customer1
N7k-1(config-router-vrf)# router-id 192.168.100.1
N7k-1(config-router-vrf)# address-family ipv4 unicast
N7k-1(config-router-vrf-af)# network 192.168.100.1/32
N7k-1(config-router-vrf-af)# vrf vrf-customer2
N7k-1(config-router-vrf)# router-id 192.168.200.1
N7k-1(config-router-vrf)# address-family ipv4 unicast
N7k-1(config-router-vrf-af)# network 192.168.200.1/32
```

Example 12-11 shows the verification of the configuration. Route 192.168.100.1 was exported using 65000:100 from VRF vrf-customer1. VRF vrf-customer2 imported this route using the 65000:100 extended community. Conversely, route 192.168.200.1 was exported using the 65000:200 extended community from VRF vrf-customer2. VRF vrf-customer1 imported this route using 65000:200.

Example 12-11   *VRF-Lite Route Import/Export Verification*

```
N7k-1# show ip bgp vrf vrf-customer1 192.168.200.1
BGP routing table information for VRF vrf-customer1, address family IPv4 Unicast
BGP routing table entry for 192.168.200.1/32, version 5
```

```
Paths: (1 available, best #1)
Flags: (0x00001a) on xmit-list, is in urib, is best urib route

  Path type: local, path is valid, is best path
            Imported from 192.168.200.1/32 (VRF vrf-customer2)
  AS-Path: NONE, path locally originated
    0.0.0.0 (metric 0) from 0.0.0.0 (0.0.0.0)
      Origin IGP, MED not set, localpref 100, weight 32768
      Extcommunity:
          RT:65000:200

  Not advertised to any peer


N7k-1# show ip bgp vrf vrf-customer2 192.168.100.1
BGP routing table information for VRF vrf-customer2, address family IPv4 Unicast
BGP routing table entry for 192.168.100.1/32, version 4
Paths: (1 available, best #1)
Flags: (0x00001a) on xmit-list, is in urib, is best urib route

  Path type: local, path is valid, is best path
            Imported from 192.168.100.1/32 (VRF vrf-customer1)
  AS-Path: NONE, path locally originated
    0.0.0.0 (metric 0) from 0.0.0.0 (0.0.0.0)
      Origin IGP, MED not set, localpref 100, weight 32768
      Extcommunity:
          RT:65000:100

  Not advertised to any peer
```

MPLS Introduction

Multiprotocol Label Switching is a widely adopted high-performance, scalable transport mechanism that enables inherit virtualization by enabling a host of advanced features across a single infrastructure. MPLS was designed as a transport-agnostic solution with the capability to integrate with existing physical transport mediums, including ATM, Frame Relay, and Ethernet. Furthermore, MPLS was aimed to be highly efficient across these varying transport mediums—specifically by eliminating costly processor cycles associated with examining Layer 2 or Layer 3 headers. Instead, MPLS makes forwarding decisions based on a new label placed on the packet. When subsequent devices within the MPLS network receive these labeled packets, they can make a forwarding decision based only on the label of the packet without regard to source, destination, or type of traffic contained within the packet.

The core of MPLS is decoupled and consists of two primary areas:

■ **Control plane:** Leverages protocols to construct the Forwarding Table, whereas the forwarding plane forwards packets to the appropriate destination.

■ **Forwarding table:** Lists label values, which are each associated with determining the outgoing interface for every network prefix. Cisco NX-OS Software supports two signaling mechanisms to distribute labels: Label Distribution Protocol (LDP) and Resource Reservation Protocol/Traffic Engineering (RSVP / TE).

MPLS is composed of the following major components:

■ **MPLS Virtual Private Networks (Layer 3 VPN):** Provides secure segmentation of different traffic types and classes, shared services, and route import/export between VPNs

■ **MPLS Traffic Engineering (TE):** Enables on-demand bandwidth for applications, optimized link sharing and protection, fast convergence, and capacity planning

■ **MPLS quality of service (QoS):** Supports classification and prioritization of traffic flows, ability to preserve or remark traffic flows, and ability to police and to conform to service-level agreements (SLAs)

Integration of MPLS application components, including Layer 3 VPNs, Traffic Engineering, QoS, and mVPN, enables the development of highly efficient, scalable, and secure networks that guarantee SLAs.

MPLS Terminology

Before understanding and learning MPLS configurations and operations, the MPLS terminology needs to be defined and understood:

■ **Label:** An MPLS label is a 4-byte header placed on a data packet, which contains basic information about how to forward the packet. The label contains a value, which identifies the packet, traffic class for QoS purposes, and Time-To-Live (TTL). A packet can be marked with multiple labels, for example, an outer label, which contains forwarding information about the packet, and an inner label, which identifies a specific customer VPN that the packet is destined for. The label also contains a bit, which signifies whether it is the last or if subsequent labels are contained within the packet. Labels can also be aggregated so that many different packets may be assigned the same label; for example, packets going to the same destination network or belonging to the same VPN. These packets are part of the same forwarding equivalency class (FEC) and are treated the same throughout the MPLS network.

- **Label Distribution Protocol (LDP):** Each device determines the unique label that it uses for a particular FEC. For end-to-end label switching to occur, the Label Switching Router (LSR) must disseminate its local label bindings to adjacent devices. LDP is the standard protocol used to propagate this information.

- **Label Switching Router (LSR):** An LSR is a device that uses labels to determine the forwarding path a particular packet should take. LSRs can be either provider (P) or provider edge (PE).

- **Label Switched Path (LSP):** A set of hops within an MPLS network for a particular FEC. Labels may be added (pushed), removed (popped), or swapped throughout the LSP.

- **Provider router (P):** A provider router or P device is a device that relies solely on label information to make forwarding decisions. Its routing table is limited to a small amount of routes, which provide path information for other P or PE devices. P routers usually contain a little amount of routing state associated with end host networks.

- **Provider Edge (PE) routers:** These devices represent the demarcation point between the MPLS network and the traditional networks for which they are transporting traffic. These devices perform the initial encapsulation or push the first MPLS labels onto the packet. They form routing adjacencies with devices on traditional networks and prepare the traffic to be transmitted across the MPLS network.

- **Resource Reservation Protocol (RSVP):** RSVP, which operates at each LSP hop, is used to signal and maintain LSPs based on the calculated path.

- **Customer Edge (CE) routers:** CE devices are traditional L2 or L3 devices, which form adjacencies with PE devices to interconnect transparently with other CE devices.

- **Route Distinguisher (RD):** An RD is a single, unique identifier prepended to MPLS VPN routes and is defined inside of a VRF. The RD can be either an AS number and an arbitrary number (xxxxx:y) or an IP address and arbitrary number (A.B.C.D:y).

- **Route Target (RT):** A RT looks similar to an RD and is configured in the same format but has a completely different purpose. One or many RTs can be configured to reference specific policies to support Importing and Exporting route prefixes between VRFs.

Figure 12-2 shows a typical MPLS deployment and illustrates the relationship between devices.

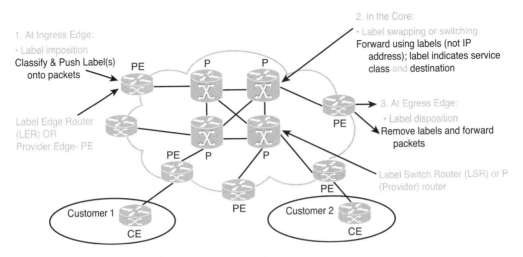

Figure 12-2   *MPLS Deployment: Device Relationships*

LDP and Layer 3 VPNs

Probably the most widely deployed application of MPLS is the capability to share a common network infrastructure across multiple customers by defining VPNs for customer resources. RFC 4364 defines the use of MPLS and BGP to achieve such functionality. MPLS VPNs are widely deployed by service provider networks and offered as an alternative to traditional wide area network (WAN) interconnect technologies such as Frame Relay or ATM. Enterprise adoption of MPLS VPNs has also been on the rise in recent years as a result of organizations grappling with the scale, security, and emergence of shared services data centers where lines of business IT operations need to be consolidated while still maintaining existing levels of separation.

The following is a listing of steps to configure basic elements of MPLS on a Nexus 7000, with examples of each step in Example 12-12:

1. Install the MPLS Feature set in the default Virtual Device Context (VDC).

2. [Optional] After the Feature set is installed, limit MPLS to specific target VDCs via per-VDC configuration. This is accomplished via the **no-allow feature-set** command under the VDC configuration, which restricts the feature set from being enabled inside of the VDC.

3. Enable the MPLS feature set inside of the target VDC.

4. Enable the MPLS feature inside of the target VDC. Make sure to enable the LDP, L3VPN, and TE features during this step as well.

Example 12-12 *Enabling the MPLS Feature in NX-OS*

```
N7k-1(config)# install feature-set mpls


N7k-1(config)# vdc Lab
N7k-1(config-vdc)# no allow feature-set mpls


N7k-1(config)# feature-set mpls


N7k-1(config)# feature mpls ?
  l3vpn                Enable/Disable Layer 3 Virtual
                       Private Networks
  ldp                  Enable/Disable Label Distribution
                       Protocol
  traffic-engineering  Enable/Disable MPLS Traffic
                       Engineering


N7k-1(config)# feature mpls <ldp | l3vpn | te>
```

Many of the features introduced in NX-OS 5.2(1) for the Nexus 7000 revolved around adding support for MPLS Layer 3 VPNs including basic MPLS label switching functionality (LSR) and the LDP (Label Distribution Protocol). LDP is used to exchange label bindings between adjacent nodes, sets up LSPs to carry VPN traffic from PE to PE, and interfaces with other NX-OS system components to program labels for forwarding. Additional support includes advanced features such as IGP synchronization, session protection, label filtering, static label binding, and MD5 authentication.

The following is a listing of steps to configure LDP on a Nexus 7000, with examples of each step in Example 12-13:

1. Ensure the LDP service was enabled while configuring the MPLS feature.

2. Enable LDP on an interface.

3. Enable LDP synchronization for the IGP, which ensures that LDP is fully established before the IGP routing path is used. This helps to minimize MPLS packet loss.

Example 12-13 *Configuring LDP with OSPF as an IGP*

```
N7k-1(config)# feature mpls ldp


N7k-1(config)# interface Ethernet10/18
N7k-1(config-if)# mpls ip
N7k-1(config-if)# ip address 192.168.0.1/30
N7k-1(config-if)# ip router ospf 1 area 0.0.0.0
N7k-1(config-if)# no shutdown
```

```
N7k-1(config)# router ospf 1
N7k-1(config-router)# mpls ldp sync
```

Example 12-14 shows several useful LDP operational commands. The first command, **show mpls ldp bindings**, shows the IP prefixes with their corresponding MPLS labels, which is called the Label Information Base (LIB). The local binding shows the label assigned by the router, which is, in turn, advertised to neighbors. The remote binding refers to a label-prefix learned via LDP from a neighbor. The command **show mpls ldp discovery** enables the network administrator to easily verify if LDP is running correctly. This command lists the interfaces in which LDP is running and also verifies that the interfaces are transmitting and receiving LDP Hello packets. Lastly, the command **show mpls ldp neighbor** displays useful information about the status of LDP peers, including the neighborship state and operation LDP discovery sources.

Example 12-14   *Important LDP Operational Commands*

```
N7k-1# sh mpls ldp bindings

  lib entry: 1.1.1.1/32, rev 2
        local binding:  label: imp-null
        remote binding: lsr: 2.2.2.2:0, label: 16
  lib entry: 2.2.2.2/32, rev 6
        local binding:  label: 16
        remote binding: lsr: 2.2.2.2:0, label: imp-null


N7k-1# sh mpls ldp discovery
 Local LDP Identifier:
    1.1.1.1:0
    Discovery Sources:
    Interfaces:
        Ethernet10/18 (ldp): xmit/recv
            LDP Id: 2.2.2.2:0

N7k-1# sh mpls ldp neighbor
    Peer LDP Ident: 2.2.2.2:0; Local LDP Ident 1.1.1.1:0
        TCP connection: 2.2.2.2.56735 - 1.1.1.1.646
        State: Oper; Msgs sent/rcvd: 8/10; Downstream
        Up time: 00:02:50
        LDP discovery sources:
          Ethernet10/18, Src IP addr: 192.168.0.2
        Addresses bound to peer LDP Ident:
          192.168.0.2     2.2.2.2
```

From a CE to PE IPv4 routing protocol support perspective, the Nexus 7000 supports all well-known IGP protocols for IPv4 deployments including OSPF, EIGRP, and ISIS. In addition, static routing and BGP are also both supported for IPv4 and IPv6 6PE and 6VPE deployments. Example 12-15 outlines a typical CE-to-PE design leveraging BGP. You see the command **address-family ipv4 unicast** listed twice in the output. The first instance activates the IPv4 unicast address family for the VRF. The neighbor statements are not nested under this and also must be activated for the IPv4 unicast address family, which is configured under the neighbor statement.

Example 12-15 *Sample VRF-Based CE-PE BGP Configuration*

```
router bgp 65505
  log-neighbor-changes
  vrf i-vrf
    router-id 1.1.1.1
    address-family ipv4 unicast
    neighbor 192.168.1.9 remote-as 36067
      address-family ipv4 unicast
    neighbor 192.168.1.17 remote-as 36067
      address-family ipv4 unicast
```

Quality of Service

MPLS for the Nexus 7000 also brings overall alignment from a Quality of Service (QoS) perspective. From a classification, marking, and policing perspective, MPLS is fully supported based on MPLS EXP bits (in addition to CoS, IP Precedence, IP DSCP, and IP ACL where applicable). Because the Nexus 7000 is a hardware-based forwarding platform, certain feature sets apply to the type and generation of the linecards installed in the system.

Note Current Nexus 7000 hardware does not support QoS-based traffic shaping that is traditionally configured on Service Provider edge routers. Only policing is supported.

Traffic Engineering

In addition to the performance of MPLS, one of the bigger advantages of MPLS over traditional routing protocols is the flexibility that it gives administrators in controlling how traffic flows through the network. Rather than simply computing a loop free path, and following the shortest path to a particular destination, MPLS gives administrators the option of placing constraints on a particular path for the amount of bandwidth available, the latency of a path, or specifying an explicit primary and backup path for traffic of a particular class. This flexibility gives administrators the ability to ensure strict SLA across different customers and traffic characteristics.

MPLS Traffic Engineering (TE) functions by learning the topology and resources available in a network and then mapping traffic flows to a particular path, called a label switched path (LSP). The LSP is a unidirectional tunnel from a source MPLS node (head-end) to a destination MPLS node (tailend). The tunnel calculation uses a link-state database that contains flooded topology, and resource information operates at the LSP head-end node. This mapping can be based on resource requirements and network resources, such as bandwidth.

One of the other concepts of MPLS TE is the capability to protect a link, a node, and even to protect a complete end-to-end path via TE. MPLS TE uses extensions to either IS-IS or OSPF. If configured, OSPF or IS-IS can automatically route the traffic onto the LSPs. RSVP can be leveraged as part of MPLE TE to automatically establish and maintain the LSPs.

Finally, one interesting feature supported with NX-OS and MPLS TE is AutoBandwidth. The AutoBandwidth feature enables traffic to be mapped to a specific LSP based on the QoS class and policy set configured on the system. This functionality enables complete class-based tunnel selection.

MPLS TE requires one of the IGP features (OSPF or ISIS) to be enabled. Enabling **feature mpls traffic-engineering** can automatically enable other required NX-OS components (RSVP, OAM, MPLS MGR, and ULIB).

The following is a listing of steps to configure LDP on a Nexus 7000, with examples of each step:

1. Enable the TE feature (see Example 12-16).

2. Disable/Enable MPLS TE globally (enabled by default) (refer to Example 12-16).

3. Configure TE for the IGP (IS-IS or OSPF), as shown in Example 12-17 and Example 12-18.

Example 12-16   *Enabling MPLS TE*

```
N7k-1(config)# feature mpls traffic-engineering

N7k-1(config)# mpls traffic-eng configuration
N7k-1(config-te)# [no] shutdown

N7k-1(config)# interface loopback0
N7k-1(config-if)# ip address 1.1.1.1/32
```

Example 12-17   *Configuring MPLS TE for IS-IS*

```
N7k-1(config)# router isis p1
N7k-1(config-router)# mpls traffic-eng level-2
N7k-1(config-router)# mpls traffic-eng router-id loopback0
```

Example 12-18 *Configuring MPLS TE for OSPF*

```
N7k-1(config)# router ospf p1
N7k-1(config-router)# mpls traffic-eng area 0
N7k-1(config-router)# mpls traffic-eng router-id loopback0
```

MPLS and IPv6: 6PE and 6VPE

Over the next few years, a transition to IPv6 is imminent because IPv4 address space is nearing exhaustion. One of the key features introduced with MPLS Layer 3 VPN and TE support in NX-OS 5.2(1) for the Nexus 7000 is the capability to implement IPv6 on routers across a IPv4 transport, which is known as 6PE, and native IPv6 VPNs over MPLS, which is known as 6VPE. Leveraging 6PE enables the capability to aid in migration to IPv6 by supporting IPv6 transport across both data center and in the campus networks on top of an existing IPv4 infrastructure. This is possible with minimal operational overhead whether a dual stack or a tunnel-based IPv4 to IPv6 transition mechanism is in place. 6PE also has the capability to further traffic separation between IPv4 and IPv6. 6PE and 6VPE are two completely different features, although each has similar acronyms. While 6PE is leveraged in environments with existing IPv4 MPLS configurations, if native IPv6 VPNs are deployed, 6VPE can be leveraged.

> **Note** At press time, static routes and BGPv6 are supported as a CE-PE routing protocol for 6PE and 6VPE.

Management and Troubleshooting

NX-OS and the Nexus 7000 support a number of tools to help enable support, management, and troubleshooting of the platform. One feature included in NX-OS is Ethanalyser, which is a built-in protocol analyser that can be leveraged to capture inbound control plane packets for troubleshooting and debugging.

NX-OS includes OAM services along with tools such as LSP ping and LSP traceroute for a label-switched path and traffic engineering tunnel troubleshooting. NX-OS also supports a number of SNMP MIBs based on both RFCs and certain IETF. These include LSR MIB, LDP MIB, Traffic Engineering MIB, and FRR MIB (IETF draft).

High Availability

NX-OS brings support for many unparalleled high-availability features, including In-Service Software Upgrades (ISSU) and Non-Stop Forwarding (NSF). ISSU provides the ability to perform software upgrades with zero packet loss and no service disruptions. These high-availability functions are carried into various MPLS components. MPLS

Layer 3 VPNs, TE, and 6PE/6VPE are all stateful system services operating in NX-OS; in addition, these services are fully compatible with ISSU and NSF.

Nexus Hardware Requirements and NX-OS Licensing for MPLS and VRF

The Nexus platforms support different hardware and software features based on their intended position within the Cisco overall data center portfolio. Now focus on MPLS and VRF-Lite functionality across the Nexus 7000, 5500, and 3000 series platforms.

On the Nexus 7000, the M-series linecards support rich Layer 2 and Layer 3 feature sets. MPLS is supported in hardware on any of the M1- or M2-series linecards offered on the platform. The F1-, F2-, and F2e-series linecards do not natively support MPLS because they are instead aimed at high-performance, unified fabric deployments. The F1 linecard, being Layer 2 natively, would however support MPLS when operating in proxy Layer 3 mode by taking advantage of routing resources with an M1- or M2-series linecard for MPLS forwarding. MPLS was introduced as a feature in NX-OS 5.2(1) for the Nexus 7000. MPLS does require a specific MPLS license, along with the Layer 3 Enterprise license.

On the Nexus 7000, VRF and VRF-Lite have both been supported since NX-OS version 4.0(1) and are supported on any M1 or M2 modules, along with the F2 and F2e. As new features have been introduced to the Nexus 7000 platform over time, VRF support has also expanded to support them. VRF-Lite Route Import/Export functionality, as discussed earlier, was introduced along with MPLS in NX-OS 5.2(1).

Note   The predefined "default" and "management" VRFs are always enabled on the Nexus 7000, regardless of linecard options or licensing levels.

With the appropriate hardware and licensing configuration, both the Nexus 5500 and the Nexus 3000 can support VRF-Lite. The Nexus 5548P, 5548UP, and 5596UP support an optional Layer 3 daughtercard that provides Layer 3 support for the systems. With this daughtercard installed, the Advanced Layer 3 license installed and NX-OS Software running version NX-OS 5.0(3) N1(1) or later, it is possible to leverage VRF-Lite. However, as mentioned earlier specific to the Nexus 7000, predefined VRFs, *default* and *management*, are enabled on the Nexus 5500 and Nexus 3000 platforms, regardless of hardware options or licensing levels.

Note   The Advanced Layer 3 license for the Nexus 5500 requires that the Base Layer 3 license be installed first.

The Nexus 3016, 3048, and 3064 also can support VRF-Lite starting in software version 5.0(3)U1(1). The Nexus 5500 and 3000 both do not currently support MPLS, and VRF-Lite Route Import/Export functionality is also not currently supported at the time of this writing.

Note   At press time, the Nexus 3000 platforms do not support VRF-Lite with EIGRP.

Summary

MPLS is a proven, standards-based technology that when deployed in data center environments can provide efficient network virtualization, consolidation, and segmentation. MPLS support in NX-OS combines the past strengths of MPLS in other Cisco platforms along with the inherit virtualization, high-density, manageability, and high-availability found in the Nexus 7000. Furthermore, built-in VRF features from the ground up provide the feature sets necessary to enable network engineers to build next-generation network infrastructures.

## Chapter 13

LISP

This chapter covers the following topics:

- LISP overview
- LISP terminology
- LISP prerequisites
- LISP control plane
- Communicating between LISP and non-LISP sites
- LISP Host Mobility with an Extended Subnet
- Deployment of best practices

LISP Overview

Locator/ID Separation Protocol (LISP) is a new routing architecture and paradigm shift that decouples the server identity and the server location. This decoupling enables mobility, scalability, and security. As endpoints become detached from the physical infrastructure and are mobile, the LISP routing architecture enables IP addresses to move freely and efficiently across the infrastructure. Although more server virtualization is deployed within the Enterprise and the service providers, the movement of the virtualized workloads to meet high availability and disaster recovery is significantly increasing. LISP decouples the server identity and the server location into two different address spaces: The Endpoint Identifier (EID) is the server identity and the server location is the Routing Locator (RLOC).

Although LISP has many use cases in addition to workload mobility, the focus of this chapter is only for server mobility and how to influence the ingress routing to these mobile resources.

This chapter assumes that you have Layer 2 extended between a data center location via Overlay Transport Virtualization (OTV) or another L2 extension technology. The challenge that arises when Layer 2 virtual local area networks (VLANs) are extended between data centers is that the upper routers to do not know that the subnets and VLANs are shared; hence, this results in nonoptimal and asymmetric traffic flows. The consequences of nonoptimal, asymmetrical traffic flows follow:

■ Utilization of expensive interconnect transport.

■ State devices see only half connections and drop the connections.

With LISP Host Mobility, the network can detect movement and provide optimal routing between clients and the IP end point that moved, regardless of its location.

LISP Terminology

LISP is an overlay routing protocol that encapsulates the original packet and adds an additional 36 bytes for IPv4 and 56 bytes for IPv6. The LISP encapsulation is dynamic and does not require static tunnels to be predefined, which enables LISP to be scalable. A LISP-enabled network includes the following components:

■ **EID addresses:** The IP addresses and prefixes that identifying the hosts; this is part of the LISP name space.

■ **RLOC addresses:** The IP addresses and prefixes identifying the different routers in the IP network; this is part of the LISP name space as well.

■ **Ingress Tunnel Router (ITR):** A LISP speaking site edge device that receives packets from site-facing interfaces (internal hosts) and encapsulates them to remote LISP sites, or natively forwards them to non-LISP sites.

■ **Egress Tunnel Router (ETR):** A LISP speaking site edge device that receives packets from core-facing interfaces (the transport infrastructure), decapsulates LISP packets, and delivers them to local EIDs at the site.

■ **xTR (ITR and ETR):** A LISP device that implements ITR and ETR functionality on the same device to enable the establishment of bidirectional communication.

■ **Map-Server (MS):** The LISP ETRs register their EID prefixes. The EID prefixes are stored and registered in the mapping-server (MS) database and associated to the proper RLOCs; all LISP sites use the LISP mapping system to resolve EID-to-RLOC mappings.

■ **Map-Resolver (MR):** The LISP ITRs send LISP Map-Request queries when resolving EID-to-RLOC mappings.

■ **Proxy ITR (PITR):** A LISP device that provides connectivity between non-LISP sites and LISP sites by attracting non-LISP traffic destined to LISP sites encapsulating this traffic to ETRs devices deployed at LISP sites.

■ **Proxy ETR (PETR):** A LISP Infrastructure device that enables EIDs at LISP sites to successfully communicate with devices located at non-LISP sites.

An analogy for the LISP mapping services is equivalent to how DNS services are provided and function today.

Figure 13-1 shows the LISP components used throughout this chapter.

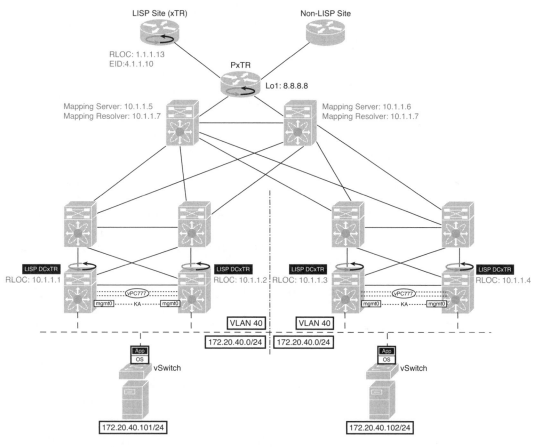

Figure 13-1 *LISP Components*

LISP Prerequisites

The following hardware and software requirements need to be fully understood before deploying LISP on the Nexus 7000 for host mobility:

■ LISP was first introduced on the Nexus 7000 with NX-OS software release 5.2.1; it is recommended to start with a minimum of NX-OS 5.2.7.

- From a Nexus point of view, LISP is supported only on the N7K-M132XP-12 and in N7K-M132XP-12L modules. It is the M1-32 module that can perform the LISP encapsulation/decapsulation in hardware.

Note   The Nexus 3000, Nexus 5000, and Nexus 5500 do not support LISP.

- It is highly recommended to run the latest electronic programmable logic device (EPLD) images on the M1-32 modules to support LISP.

Note   Consult the following link to the NX-OS EPLD release notes:
http://www.cisco.com/en/US/docs/switches/datacenter/sw/5_x/epld/epld_rn_5.2.html.

- If F1 modules are installed as the same VDC as M1-32 modules, L3 Proxy is supported for LISP.
- With L3 proxy-mode for LISP, it is recommended to not have any other M1 modules installed in the Virtual Device Context (VDC). If there are modules other than M1-32s doing L3-Proxy, it is critical to disable the L3 proxy functionality for the non-M1-32 modules. For example, if module 18 is an N7K-M148GT-11L (non-M132) and LISP is a requirement, you need to exclude the L3 proxy routing with the following NX-OS command in that VDC:

hardware proxy layer-3 forwarding exclude module 18

LISP Control Plane

Figure 13-2 shows the LISP control plane sequence of events as defined in the list that follows:

1. (Map-Register) The LISP ETR in the data center send a Map-Register message to the LISP Mapping-Server (MS) for the dynamic-eid space defined, 172.20.40.0 /24.

2. (Map-Request) The client wants to send the packet to the 172.20.40.0 /24 EID space that the ETR registered to the MS. The ITR LISP router sends a Map-Request to the Map-Resolver (MR); the MR then forwards the Map-Request to the MS.

3. (Map-Request) The LISP Mapping-Server (MS) forwards the original Map-Request to the ETR (10.1.1.1) in the data center that sent the last registration message of the EID 172.20.40.0 /24.

4. (Map-Reply) The LISP ETR sends the ITR the Map-Reply mapping information.

5. (Map-Cache Entry) The LISP ITR installs the mapping information in its local map-cache; this starts the LISP encapsulation of traffic toward the data center EID destination of 172.20.40.0 /24.

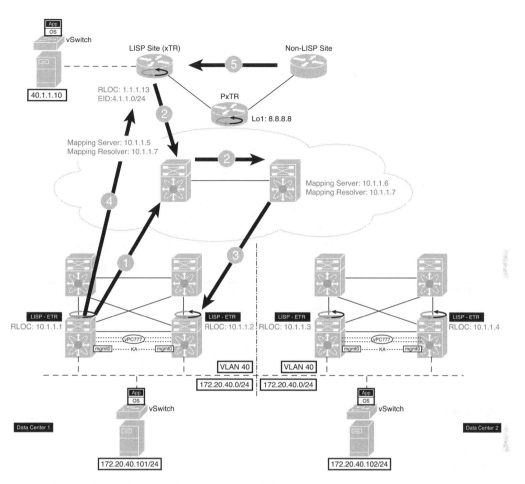

Figure 13-2 *LISP Control Plane Sequence of Events*

LISP Data Plane

LISP leverages a UDP encapsulation where the src port value is dynamically created and associated to each original flow to ensure better load-balancing of traffic across the transport infrastructure.

Figure 13-3 shows the LISP communication sequence of events as described in the list that follows.

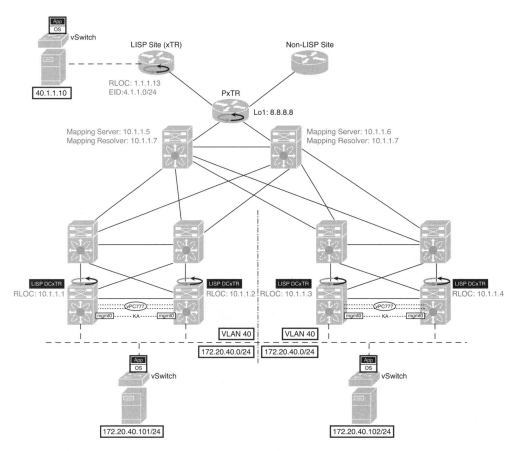

Figure 13-3   *LISP Communication Sequence of Events*

1. The client in the LISP site requests services from a server; the server IP address is 172.20.40.101. The client can use the IP address of the server or enter the DNS address for the server to return the IP address.

2. The client sends the packet to the router with the source IP address 40.1.1.10 and destination IP address 172.20.40.101.

3. The LISP device performs a lookup for the destination (172.20.40.101) in the routing table. The destination is a LISP EID subnet; it is not injected in the RLOC space, so the lookup does not return any match, triggering the LISP control plane. The ITR receives mapping information from the Mapping database (MS) and populates the local map-cache. The destination EID subnet (10.17.1.0/24) is associated with the ROLCs. The ITR LISP router has a mapping entry of the following:

```
EID-prefix: 172.20.40.0/24
Locator-set:
10.1.1.1, priority: 1, weight: 50
10.1.1.2, priority: 1, weight: 50
```

4. The ITR LISP router encapsulating into LISP has a mapping entry of the following:

```
1.1.1.13 -> 10.1.1.1 (LISP)

40.1.1.10 -> 172.20.40.101 (Inside LISP Packet)
```

5. The ETR LISP router in the Data Center de-encapsulates the LISP packet and sees the following:

```
40.1.1.10 -> 172.20.40.101
```

Figure 13-4 shows the format of the UDP LISP encapsulated packet.

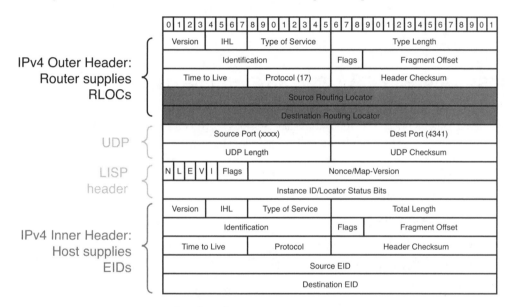

Figure 13-4 *LISP Encapsulated Packet Format*

The ITR performs LISP encapsulation of the original IP traffic and sends it into the transport infrastructure, destined to one of the RLOCs of the data center ETRs. The ETR receives the packet, decapsulates it, and sends it into the site toward the destination EID.

Communicating Between LISP and non-LISP Sites

Because LISP introduces an encapsulation, there needs to be a way to have LISP-enabled sites to communicate with non-LISP enabled site, and resources. Because LISP deployments happen in phases in the Enterprise space, not all the devices will be configured at once; there will be a period of time when some devices and resources are LISP-enabled and others are not. For LISP and non-LISP sites and resources to communicate with each other, the LISP role of the Proxy Tunnel routers is placed within the IP network. Similar to the xTR example, there is a PxTR: PITR, as well as Proxy Egress Tunnel Router (PETR) devices.

The traffic needs to reach the PITR device; this traffic follows the current IGP/BGP routing domain. When the traffic reaches the PITR, the process of getting traffic to the EID address space in the data center is the same. It is vital that all the traffic originated from the non-LISP sites be directed toward the PITR LISP device. Having the traffic directed toward the PITR LISP devices, the PITR can advertise the proper routing information for the data center EID address space for the non-LISP sites.

Note   For a complete deployment guide for PxTR services, refer to the following link: http://www.cisco.com/en/US/docs/solutions/Enterprise/Data_Center/DCI/whitepaper/ PxTR_Redundancy/PxTR-Redundancy.pdf.

LISP Host Mobility with an Extended Subnet Mode

Before all the details are defined for host mobility, the business drivers and use cases need to be defined. The applications and business drivers for the Extended Subnets between data centers follow (not all-inclusive):

- Extending operating system/file system clusters

- Extending database clusters

- Virtual machine mobility

- Physical machine mobility

- Physical to Virtual (PtoV) migrations

- Legacy devices/apps with embedded IP addressing

- Time to deployment and operational reasons

- Extend DC to solve power/heat/space limitations

- Data center colocation

Because LISP decouples host identity and the location, this LISP defines a new routing architecture. Historically, the identity of the server (IP address) was associated with a given location, which made it difficult to control and influence the inbound routing decisions at scale. The decoupling of the server IP address identity, EIDs, location, and RLOC enable a dynamic mapping mechanism between these two address families providing mobility. EIDs can change locations dynamically and are reachable via different RLOCs. The LISP RLOC is part of and reachable via the traditional IP routing topology; when a host moves between locations (RLOC), it is only the mapping to the host (EID) and RLOC that are updated dynamically. The ability to dynamically have the network detect movement allows traffic to be sent to the new location without any impact to the underlying routing infrastructure. The EID-to-RLOC mapping is performed by the LISP MS.

The following configuration assumes that the Nexus 7000 runs LISP; here are the configuration details and steps for the LISP configuration on the Nexus 7000:

Because NX-OS is a modular operating system, the LISP service needs to be enabled.

1. Enable the LISP feature on the Nexus 7000, as shown in Example 13-1.

Example 13-1 *Enabling LISP Feature/Process*

```
xTR#
xTR# conf t
Enter configuration commands, one per line. End with CNTL/Z.
xTR(config)# feature lisp
xTR(config)# show feature | i lisp
lisp               1          enabled
xTR(config)# exit
xTR# copy running-configuration startup-configuration
```

2. Configure the ITR and ETR functionality on the Nexus 7000, as shown in Example 13-2.

Example 13-2 *Configure ITR and ETR Functionality*

```
xTR#
xTR# conf t
Enter configuration commands, one per line. End with CNTL/Z.
xTR(config)# ip lisp itr-etr
xTR(config)# exit
xTR# copy running-configuration startup-configuration
```

3. Define the global mappings for the servers IP Address space, as shown in Example 13-3.

Example 13-3 *Define the Global Mapping That Identifies the IP Subnets in the Data Center Assigned to the Servers*

```
xTR#
xTR# conf t
Enter configuration commands, one per line. End with CNTL/Z.
xTR(config)# ip lisp database-mapping 172.20.0.0/16 10.1.1.1 priority 1 weight 50
xTR(config)# ip lisp database-mapping 172.20.0.0/16 10.1.1.2 priority 1 weight 50
xTR(config)# exit
xTR# copy running-configuration startup-configuration
```

The mapping configuration enables the aggregate prefix 172.20.0.0/16 to the two RLOC IP addresses; the RLOC IP addresses identifies the data center xTR LISP devices. The priority and weight are centrally configured and managed; this allows the administrator to influence the inbound traffic to a specific xTR. Example 13-3 has the priority and weights the same for both xTRs that enable load-balancing across both the data center xTRs.

4. Define the map-server (MS) and map-resolvers (MR) on the Nexus 7000, as shown in Example 13-4.

Example 13-4   *Define the Map-Servers and Map-Resolvers*

```
xTR#
xTR# conf t
Enter configuration commands, one per line. End with CNTL/Z.
xTR(config)# ip lisp itr map-resolver 10.1.1.7
xTR(config)# ip lisp etr map-server 10.1.1.5 key cisco
xTR(config)# ip lisp etr map-server 10.1.1.6 key cisco
xTR(config)# exit
xTR# copy running-configuration startup-configuration
```

The map-servers are deployed in a redundant fashion; map-servers do not share state information. Because the map-servers are stateless, the two entries are needed to define both map-servers in the Layer 3 infrastructure to have each xTR register the EID prefixes with both map-servers. The map-resolvers are configured with the Anycast IP address; the MR requests will be serviced by the closest MR defined by the Layer 3 routing domain.

5. Configure Proxy-ETR, as shown in Example 13-5.

Example 13-5   *Configure the LISP Proxy ETR Functionality*

```
xTR#
xTR# conf t
Enter configuration commands, one per line. End with CNTL/Z.
xTR(config)# ip lisp use-petr 8.8.8.8
xTR(config)# exit
xTR# copy running-configuration startup-configuration
```

6. Define the dynamic mapping for the servers' mobile subnets, as shown in Example 13-6.

Example 13-6 *Define the Dynamic Mapping for the Server Subnets That Move Between the Layer 2 Extended Between the Data Centers*

```
xTR#
xTR# conf t
Enter configuration commands, one per line. End with CNTL/Z.
xTR(config)# lisp dynamic-eid EXTVLAN40
xTR(config-lisp)# database-mapping 172.20.40.0/24 10.1.1.1 priority 1 weight 50
xTR(config-lisp)# database-mapping 172.20.40.0/24 10.1.1.2 priority 1 weight 50
xTR(config-lisp)# map-notify-group 239.192.1.1
xTR(config)# exit
xTR# copy running-configuration startup-configuration
```

The map-notify-group multicast address must be defined and associated to the dynamic-eid mapping; the map-notify-group has to be the same across all the xTRs. The map-notify-group is used for the LISP control plane communication between all the xTRs for the "EXTVLAN40" Extended Subnet. Because the Nexus 7000 is deployed at the Layer 2/Layer 3 boundary, the configuration will be applied to the Layer 3 SVI interface.

Note The multicast frames need to traverse the Layer 2 network between data centers; this is a mandatory requirement for Layer 2 extension technology deployed.

7. Configure the Layer 3 interfaces for the servers' default gateway, as shown in Example 13-7.

Example 13-7 *Define the Layer 3 LISP Information for the Mobile Subnet Configuration*

```
xTR#
xTR# conf t
Enter configuration commands, one per line. End with CNTL/Z.
xTR(config)# lisp dynamic-eid EXTVLAN40
xTR(config)# interface Vlan40
xTR(config-if)#      no shutdown
xTR(config-if)#      description Server Farm VLAN 40
xTR(config-if)#      ip address 172.20.40.2/24
xTR(config-if)#      lisp mobility EXTVLAN40
xTR(config-if)#      lisp extended-subnet-mode
xTR(config-if)#   hsrp 40
xTR(config-if-hsrp)#   priority 120
xTR(config-if-hsrp)#   ip 172.20.40.1
xTR(config-if)# exit
xTR# copy running-configuration startup-configuration
```

The **lisp mobility** command is used to attach the dynamic-eid construct to this interface, whereas **lisp extended-subnet-mode** is used to specify that the mobile subnet is extended across data center sites.

> **Note**   There are not any requirements to enable PIM for the map-notify-group; **lisp mobility** allows for the multicast frames.

Example 13-8 shows the full running LISP configuration inclusive of all the preceding steps.

Example 13-8   *The Full Running Configuration for the Nexus 7000*

```
feature lisp
ip lisp itr-etr
ip lisp use-petr 8.8.8.8
ip lisp database-mapping 172.20.0.0/16 10.1.1.1 priority 1 weight 50
ip lisp database-mapping 172.20.0.0/16 10.1.1.2 priority 1 weight 50
ip lisp itr map-resolver 10.1.1.7
ip lisp etr map-server 10.1.1.5 key 3 9125d59c18a9b015
ip lisp etr map-server 10.1.1.6 key 3 9125d59c18a9b015
ip lisp map-request-source 10.1.1.1
lisp dynamic-eid EXTVLAN40
  database-mapping 172.20.40.0/24 10.1.1.1 priority 1 weight 50
  database-mapping 172.20.40.0/24 10.1.1.2 priority 1 weight 50
  map-notify-group 239.192.1.1

interface Vlan40
  no shutdown
  description Server Farm VLAN 40
  ip address 172.20.40.2/24
  lisp mobility EXTVLAN40
  lisp extended-subnet-mode
 hsrp 40
    priority 120
    ip 172.20.40.1
```

Example 13-9 and Example 13-10 show the map-server and map-resolver configuration on Nexus 7000-1 and Nexus 7000-2.

Example 13-9   *The Map-Server and Map-Resolver Configuration on Nexus 7000-1*

```
feature lisp
ip lisp map-resolver
ip lisp map-server
```

```
lisp site Branch
  eid-prefix 4.1.1.0/24
  authentication-key 3 9125d59c18a9b015
lisp site Datacenter
  eid-prefix 172.20.0.0/16 accept-more-specifics
  authentication-key 3 9125d59c18a9b015
```

Example 13-10   *The Map-Server and Map-Resolver Configuration on Nexus 7000-2*

```
feature lisp

ip lisp map-resolver
ip lisp map-server
lisp site Branch
  eid-prefix 4.1.1.0/24
  authentication-key 3 9125d59c18a9b015
lisp site Datacenter
  eid-prefix 172.20.0.0/16 accept-more-specifics
  authentication-key 3 9125d59c18a9b015
```

Example 13-11 shows the proxy configuration on the Nexus 7000 pointing to the LISP proxy router.

Example 13-11   *The PxTR Configuration*

```
router lisp
 eid-table default instance-id 0
  map-cache 4.1.1.0/24 map-request
  map-cache 172.20.0.0/16 map-request
  exit
 ipv4 map-request-source 8.8.8.8
 ipv4 proxy-etr
 ipv4 proxy-itr 8.8.8.8
 ipv4 itr map-resolver 10.1.1.7
 exit
```

Example 13-12 shows the LISP-enabled branch configuration.

Example 13-12   *LISP Branch Configuration*

```
router lisp
 database-mapping 4.1.1.0/24 1.1.1.13 priority 1 weight 100
 ipv4 itr map-resolver 10.1.1.7
 ipv4 itr
```

```
ipv4 etr map-server 10.1.1.5 key cisco
ipv4 etr
```

Examples 13-13 through 13-18 show the LISP output to verify that LISP works properly.

Example 13-13 *Verifying That the xTRs Successfully Registered Their EID Subnets with the Mapping Server*

```
MS# sh lisp site
LISP Site Registration Information for VRF "default"
* = truncated IPv6 address, -x = more-specifics count


Site Name      Last       Actively   Who last     EID-prefix
               Registered Registered Registered
Branch         00:00:19   yes        1.1.1.13     4.1.1.0/24
Datacenter     00:00:09   yes        10.1.1.2     172.20.0.0/16
```

The host sends out an IP packet that is intercepted by one of the xTRs and punted to the CPU, triggering a data plane–driven EID discovery event. The host IP traffic is the source IP address of the EID space defined for LISP. This EID is discovered and is added to the dynamic-eid table of the discovering xTR, as shown in Example 13-14.

Example 13-14 *Dynamic-eid Discovered as the VM Moves Between Locations*

```
N7K1# show lisp dyn summ
LISP Dynamic EID Summary for VRF "default"
* = Dyn-EID learned by site-based Map-Notify
Dyn-EID Name   Dynamic-EID    Interface   Uptime     Last      Pending
                                                     Packet    Ping Count
EXTVLAN40      172.20.40.101  Vlan40      00:19:28   00:02:58  0
EXTVLAN40      172.20.40.102  Vlan40      00:09:40   00:09:39  0
```

Example 13-15 *LISP Installs in the Routing Table of the Discovering xTR a Local /32 Route Associated to the EID*

```
N7K1# show ip route 172.20.40.101
IP Route Table for VRF "default"
'*' denotes best ucast next-hop
'**' denotes best mcast next-hop
'[x/y]' denotes [preference/metric]


172.20.40.101/32, ubest/mbest: 1/0, attached
    *via 172.20.40.101, Vlan40, [250/0], 01:16:31, am
     via 172.20.40.101, Vlan40, [251/0], 00:19:11, lisp, dyn-eid
```

```
N7K1# show ip route 172.20.40.102
IP Route Table for VRF "default"
'*' denotes best ucast next-hop
'**' denotes best mcast next-hop
'[x/y]' denotes [preference/metric]


172.20.40.102/32, ubest/mbest: 1/0, attached
    *via 172.20.40.102, Vlan40, [250/0], 00:09:14, am
     via 172.20.40.102, Vlan40, [251/0], 00:09:25, lisp, dyn-eid
```

Example 13-16 *The xTR That Discovered the EID Sends a Map-Notify-Group*
Multicast Message to 239.192.1.1

```
N7K2# show lisp dyn summ
LISP Dynamic EID Summary for VRF "default"
* = Dyn-EID learned by site-based Map-Notify
Dyn-EID Name    Dynamic-EID      Interface      Uptime     Last      Pending
                                                           Packet    Ping Count

EXTVLAN40       *172.20.40.101   Vlan40         00:04:33   00:00:36  0

N7K2# show ip route 172.20.40.101
IP Route Table for VRF "default"
'*' denotes best ucast next-hop
'**' denotes best mcast next-hop
'[x/y]' denotes [preference/metric]


172.20.40.101/32, ubest/mbest: 1/0, attached
    *172.20.40.101, Vlan40, [251/0], 00:09:14, lisp, dyn-eid
```

Note   Dynamic-eid entries have an * on the HSRP standby router. The HSRP active does not have an * for the dynamic-eid entry.

Example 13-17   *The xTRs in the Other Data Center Have a /32 Null0 Route Installed for the EID Because the Workload Has Been Discovered in the Other Data Center*

```
N7K2A# show ip route lisp
IP Route Table for VRF "default"
'*' denotes best ucast next-hop
'**' denotes best mcast next-hop
'[x/y]' denotes [preference/metric]
```

```
172.20.40.101/32, ubest/mbest: 1/0, attached
    *via Null0, [252/0], 00:00:07, lisp, dyn-eid
172.20.40.102/32, ubest/mbest: 1/0, attached
    *via Null0, [252/0], 00:00:07, lisp, dyn-eid
172.20.40.128/25, ubest/mbest: 1/0
    *via Null0, [251/0], 00:17:53, lisp, dyn-eid
```

Example 13-18   *The Map-Server Adds the Specific EID Information to the Database*

```
andrey-ad-l2span02-lisp# show lisp site detail
LISP Site Registration Information for VRF "default"
* = truncated IPv6 address, -x = more-specifics count


Site name:   "Branch"
Description: none configured
Allowed configured locators: any
  Configured EID-prefix: 4.1.1.0/24, instance-id: 0
    Currently registered:     yes
    First registered:         17:54:37
    Last registered:          00:00:19
    Who last registered:      1.1.1.13
    Routing table tag:        0x00000000
    Proxy Replying:           no
    Wants Map-Notifications:  no
    Registered TTL:           1440 minutes
    Registered locators:
      1.1.1.13 (up), priority: 1, weight: 100
    Registration errors:
      Authentication failures: 0
      Allowed locators mismatch: 0

Site name:   "Datacenter"
Description: none configured
Allowed configured locators: any
  Configured EID-prefix: 172.20.0.0/16, instance-id: 0
    More-specifics registered: 2
    Currently registered:     yes
    First registered:         17:55:26
    Last registered:          00:00:09
    Who last registered:      10.1.1.2
    Routing table tag:        0x00000000
```

```
    Proxy Replying:             no
    Wants Map-Notifications:    yes
    Registered TTL:             1440 minutes
    Registered locators:
        10.1.1.1 (up), priority: 1, weight: 50
        10.1.1.2 (up), priority: 1, weight: 50
    Registration errors:
        Authentication failures: 0
        Allowed locators mismatch: 0
More-specific EID-prefix: 172.20.40.101/32, instance-id: 0
    Currently registered:       yes
    First registered:           14:52:05
    Last registered:            00:00:25
    Who last registered:        10.2.2.2
    Routing table tag:          0x00000000
    Proxy Replying:             no
    Wants Map-Notifications:    yes
    Registered TTL:             1440 minutes
    Registered locators:
        10.1.1.1 (up), priority: 1, weight: 50
        10.1.1.2 (up), priority: 1, weight: 50
    Registration errors:
        Authentication failures: 0
        Allowed locators mismatch: 0
More-specific EID-prefix: 172.20.40.102/32, instance-id: 0
    Currently registered:       yes
    First registered:           14:49:08
    Last registered:            00:00:25
    Who last registered:        10.2.2.2
    Routing table tag:          0x00000000
    Proxy Replying:             no
    Wants Map-Notifications:    yes
    Registered TTL:             1440 minutes
    Registered locators:
        10.1.1.1 (up), priority: 1, weight: 50
        10.1.1.2 (up), priority: 1, weight: 50
    Registration errors:
        Authentication failures: 0
        Allowed locators mismatch: 0
```

LISP Deployment Best Practices

LISP Host Mobility with Extended Subnet is deployed at the L2/L3 boundary at the data center aggregation layer on the Nexus 7000. The data center aggregation layer enables the LISP xTR functionality to be deployed at the first Layer 3 gateway for the LISP Mobility Extended Subnet. Some of the best practices for deploying LISP follows:

- Deploy the MS with redundancy, each having its own IP address.

- Deploy the MR with redundancy leveraging Anycast IP; this would provide for redundancy and allow each ITR to reach the closest MR via the L3 IGP/BGP routing domain.

- Deploy the MS/MR functions colocated on the same device; this allows each xTR to register with both Map-Servers' LISP EID namespace.

- OTV must run in a separate VDC to support SVIs for IP routing on extended VLANs.

- Enable LISP in the Aggregation VDC, separate from OTV, just like any other IP routing service.

- The prefix length of the dynamic-eid mappings must always be larger (more specific) than the prefix length of the global mappings defined on a given xTR.

- Only add to the mobility configuration those prefixes that require mobility.

- For LISP MR, use Anycast, iTRs Anycast Map Request.

- All services such as FWs, LBs, and DPI should be deployed south of the LISP xTRs; services must receive nonencapsulated traffic.

- Design the core with symmetric ECMPs that allow fast failover convergence of the RLOC space.

- The recommendation is to define a loopback interface on each device as the RLOC so that communication to that IP address remains successful as long as a valid L3 path connects the xTR to the L3 domain of the network.

Summary

This chapter focused on a specific use case and demonstrated how to leverage LISP to have the network detect movement within the fabric and influence the inbound routing decision when Layer 2 networks are extended. LISP has many other real-world use cases, including aiding in Enterprise IPv6 migrations and enabling Virtual Machine Mobility (VM-Mobility). Using the same LISP attributes as Extended Subnet mode, VM-Mobility enables a virtual machine to freely move between data centers and even different organizations, regardless of its IP address and subnet, without the need for traditional Layer 2 extension using LISP VM-Mobility across the Subnet feature. Although the focus of this chapter and the book is on data center and NX-OS, EID space was defined as the server address space. LISP VM-Mobility is another incremental solution that allows VM-Mobility across subnets (ASM) without the need or requirement for L2 extension between the data centers. LISP ASM is currently used to address cold migration scenarios to support disaster recovery and workload mobility based on demand. From a LISP architectural point of view, the EID space can be any EID, which define "who" the device is that can solve any mobility use case from Enterprise WAN, the Internet, IPv6 and IPv4 connectivity, mobile devices application deployment, and tracking.

You can find additional LISP use cases, including VM-Mobility, at:

http://lisp.cisco.com/
http://lisp.cisco.com/lisp_over.html

Chapter 14

Nexus Migration Case Study

The case study in this chapter demonstrates a migration from a traditional Catalyst-based data center infrastructure to a next-generation Nexus-based data center. This case study brings together a great deal of the topics discussed individually throughout this book and combines them with work performed by the authors in Cisco engineering labs and multiple real-world customer scenarios, including their requirements, designs, and deployments. This case study can provide a foundation for organizations looking to make a similar migration.

Existing Environment

Acme, Inc., is a large global enterprise with many diverse lines of business. Its information technology group is a centralized group that provides technology services to all lines of business. Acme, Inc., has been a long-time Cisco customer with a great track record of success with the Catalyst 6500 switching family. Acme, Inc., has chosen to use the industry-leading practice of a three-tier design.

The server access is spread between six pairs of Catalyst 6509 switches. Each pair of 6509s serves a specific area (region) of the data center and is distributed throughout the data center accordingly. Each region of the data center contains a defined set of approximately four to five virtual local area networks (VLANs) dedicated to specific server types and functions, that is, a VLAN for UNIX, a VLAN for Windows, and so on. Each pair of 6509s provides redundancy for the servers' default gateway by using Hot-Standby Router Protocol (HSRP).

To optimize traffic flows for server-to-server communication within the data center, an L3 server distribution layer has been introduced. The primary role of this layer is to interconnect each of the six access pairs and provide network connectivity to the core layer. All connectivity to this layer is achieved using routed point-to-point links.

The core layer provides connectivity to the campus network and connects to various WAN routers for remote office connectivity. This layer is completely Layer 3 routed using

EIGRP as the IGP. All connectivity into this layer is done with routed point-to-point links. Figure 14-1 shows the existing environment.

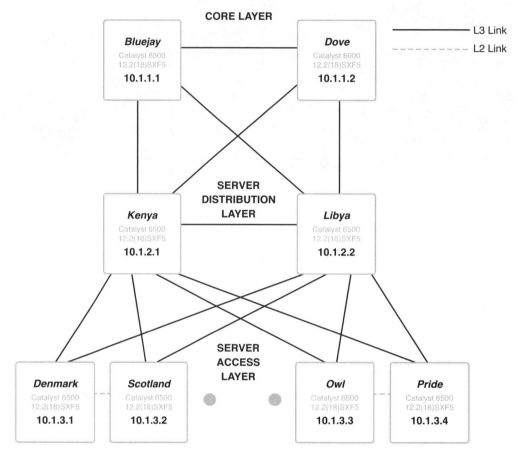

Figure 14-1 *Existing Data Center Environment for Acme, Inc.*

Design Goals

Acme, Inc., wants to modernize its data center and has the following goals that must be met as part of the next-generation data center design:

- **Scalability:** Recent acquisitions combined with organic growth have increased demand on the existing network. Acme, Inc., would like to right size its infrastructure for today's demands and account for future growth.

- **Performance:** The refresh of network appliances and server assets have created a requirement for more 10 Gbps connectivity. Acme, Inc., also would like to future-proof its environment for 40 and 100 Gbps deployments in the future. This requires that Acme, Inc., re-evaluate its server access layer offering and make appropriate upgrades to the core infrastructure to accommodate this level of throughput.

■ **Availability:** Acme, Inc., can no longer schedule routine maintenance windows on a regular monthly basis as it could in years past. Downtime windows are becoming shorter and further between. The next-generation infrastructure must provide high availability through network design and product selection. The next-generation design must also be incrementally deployable so that long maintenance windows are not required to migrate services to the new design.

■ **Flexibility:** Currently, Acme, Inc., has faced several challenges related to the capacity of its data center; many of the regions are at full capacity with space and power consumption at nearing 100 percent. Clustering applications require L2 adjacencies that cannot be accomplished unless the servers physically reside in the same region of the data center. In addition, recent efforts to optimize data center operations and lower costs have resulted in large-scale server virtualization efforts. These virtualization efforts have led to challenges associated with the L2 adjacency requirements of its virtualization solution. Acme, Inc., would like the future design to provide the ability to extend VLANs between regions of the data center and provide future abilities of extending VLANs to its disaster recovery data center. Fibre Channel over Ethernet (FCoE) is also something that Acme will be evaluating over the next several months, and it would like the new solution to provide this functionality.

The Design

To accomplish the design goals, Acme, Inc., has chosen the Cisco Nexus lines of switches because of the alignment that exists between Acme's design goals and the Nexus product family.

The existing Core Layer will remain intact because it currently meets all the Campus connectivity requirements. New linecards will be installed to connect to the aggregation switches at 10 Gbps.

The aggregation layer will receive the most dramatic change; the Catalyst 6500s will be replaced with Nexus 7010 switches based on the current and future capacity demands of Acme, Inc. vPC technology will be leveraged to enable an active/active topology and eliminate any Spanning Tree Protocol (STP) blocked links.

The existing access switches will stay in place until they are fully depreciated and all of the hosts have been migrated off of them. New access layer 5596UPs have been chosen to provide next-generation server connectivity. Each region switch pair within the data center will be replaced with a pair of Nexus 5596UPs and will aggregate Nexus 2248 and 2232 Fabric Extenders that are placed strategically in the top of various racks within the data center.

Migration Plan

Acme's business is such that it cannot afford extended outage windows for the migration to occur and therefore has approved several smaller outage windows of approximately 1 hour each. The IT management team would like to see the actual impact of the changes to be made to be considerably less than 1 hour but are preparing for worst-case scenarios. There also must be an easy back-out strategy with each change made to the environment to eliminate as much risk as possible. This project has high visibility within the entire organization and must go smoothly. With this in mind the network team has provided the following high-level plan for migration.

Prior to the first maintenance window, the new Nexus 7000 aggregation switches and 5596 access switches will be configured in the lab and allowed to burn in for several weeks.

The first maintenance window will be used to move the Nexus 7000s and 5596s from the lab to the data center, powering them on; cabling them to new linecards, which will be installed in the existing 6500 core switches; and establishing Layer 3 connectivity to the existing environment.

The second maintenance window will be used to establish L2 connectivity between one of the region 6500 pairs and the new Nexus aggregation layer. Routing for the region VLANs will be migrated to the Nexus 7000. New links will be turned up from the existing access switches to the Nexus 7000 switch.

The last step will be to bring the first pair of Nexus 5596s and Nexus 2000s online.

Based on the results of these maintenance windows, plans will be made to accelerate the migration of the remaining access pairs. Acme, Inc., will make a decision to migrate the remaining access switches in one slightly longer maintenance window or will continue migrating one pair per maintenance window.

After the access switches have been converted to L2 and migrated to the Nexus aggregation environment, hosts can be migrated on a one-by-one basis to the Nexus 5000/2000 devices, which can then host any of the data center VLANs. Acme has chosen to do this because some hosts will require 10G upgrades sooner than others and this will allow Acme to fully depreciate its 6500 assets where they are still meeting host connectivity requirements.

For the purposes of this case study, this chapter takes you through the first two maintenance windows, demonstrating procedures to accomplish the migration and discussing design considerations that were taken into account during the planning stages.

Premigration Steps

During lab testing basic configurations were placed on the Nexus 7000 and Nexus 5000 devices. These are the basic Layer 2 and virtual port-channel configuration, which will be used in production.

Example 14-1 shows the base configuration for Egypt.

Example 14-1 *Egypt Base Configuration*

```
egypt# show running-config

!Command: show running-config
!Time: Sun Dec  2 19:00:01 2012


feature lacp
feature pim
feature vpc
vrf context VPCKA
vpc domain 1
  role priority 4096
  peer-keepalive destination 10.255.255.2 source 10.255.255.1 vrf VPCKA
  peer-gateway
interface port-channel1
  switchport
  switchport mode trunk
  vpc peer-link
  spanning-tree port type network
interface port-channel5
  vrf member VPCKA
  ip address 10.255.255.1/30
interface Ethernet1/1,Ethernet10/1
  switchport
  switchport mode trunk
  channel-group 1 mode active
  no shutdown
interface Ethernet4/12,Ethernet7/12
  channel-group 5 mode active
  no shutdown

ip pim rp-address 10.131.243.117 group-list 224.0.0.0/4
```

Example 14-2 shows the base configuration for Italy.

Example 14-2 *Italy Base Configuration*

```
italy# show running-config

!Command: show running-config
!Time: Sun Dec  2 19:00:01 2012

```

```
feature lacp
feature pim
feature vpc
vrf context VPCKA
vpc domain 1
  role priority 8192
  peer-keepalive destination 10.255.255.1 source 10.255.255.2 vrf VPCKA
  peer-gateway
interface port-channel1
  switchport
  switchport mode trunk
  vpc peer-link
  spanning-tree port type network
interface port-channel5
  vrf member VPCKA
  ip address 10.255.255.1/30
interface Ethernet1/1,Ethernet10/1
  switchport
  switchport mode trunk
  channel-group 1 mode active
  no shutdown
interface Ethernet4/12,Ethernet7/12
  channel-group 5 mode active
  no shutdown

ip pim rp-address 10.131.243.117 group-list 224.0.0.0/4
```

Maintenance Window #1

During the first maintenance window, the Nexus 7000s and 5500s are physically moved into the data center, racked, and powered on. New linecards are installed in the existing 6500 to provide 10G connectivity to the new environment. The following steps will be performed.

In Example 14-3, the physical interfaces between Bluejay and the Nexus 7000 aggregation devices (Egypt and Italy) are placed into port-channels, which have point-to-point routed subnets configured, and are placed in an administratively down state.

Example 14-3 *Build Port-Channels on Bluejay*

```
bluejay# conf t
bluejay(config)# interface TenGigabitEthernet3/2
bluejay(config-if)# descr to AG1 (Egypt)
bluejay(config-if)# no ip address
bluejay(config-if)# channel-group 3 mode on
```

```
bluejay(config-if)#
bluejay(config-if)# interface TenGigabitEthernet3/3
bluejay(config-if)#  descr to AG2 (Italy)
bluejay(config-if)#  no ip address
bluejay(config-if)#  channel-group 4 mode on
bluejay(config-if)#
bluejay(config-if)# interface Port-channel3
bluejay(config-if)#  shutdown
bluejay(config-if)#  ip pim sparse-mode
bluejay(config-if)#  description to AGG1 (Egypt)
bluejay(config-if)#  ip address 10.198.2.1 255.255.255.252
bluejay(config-if)#
bluejay(config-if)# interface Port-channel4
bluejay(config-if)#  shutdown
bluejay(config-if)#  ip pim sparse-mode
bluejay(config-if)#  description to AGG2 (Italy)
bluejay(config-if)#  ip address 10.198.2.5 255.255.255.252
bluejay(config-if)#  end
bluejay#
```

Design Note   Acme, Inc., has elected to use port-channels between these devices, even though initially it will use only a single 10 G member in each port-channel. This gives them flexibility to incrementally add bandwidth in the future by simply adding additional members. To decrease the impact of a single module failure, the aggregation links to the core are placed on different linecards. On the core side of these links, diversity is achieved by redundant chassis, each with a single linecard. Cost was a major driver for this decision, but by making these links port-channels, in the future, Acme may purchase additional modules, at which time additional links from the new modules can be added to the port-channels and increase the redundancy.

Example 14-4 performs the same task on Dove.

Example 14-4   *Build Port-Channels on Dove*

```
dove# conf t
dove(config)# interface TenGigabitEthernet3/2
dove(config-if)# descr to AG1 (Egypt)
dove(config-if)#  no ip address
dove(config-if)#   channel-group 3 mode on
dove(config-if)#
dove(config-if)# interface TenGigabitEthernet3/3
dove(config-if)#  descr to AG2 (Italy)
dove(config-if)#  no ip address
```

```
dove(config-if)#  channel-group 4 mode on
dove(config-if)#
dove(config-if)# interface Port-channel3
dove(config-if)#  shutdown
dove(config-if)#  ip pim sparse-mode
dove(config-if)#  descr to AG1 (Egypt)
dove(config-if)#  ip address 10.198.2.9 255.255.255.252
dove(config-if)#
dove(config-if)# interface Port-channel4
dove(config-if)#  shutdown
dove(config-if)#  ip pim sparse-mode
dove(config-if)#  descr to AG2 (Italy)
dove(config-if)#  ip address 10.198.2.13 255.255.255.252
dove(config-if)#  end
dove#
```

Note No additional configuration for Enhanced Interior Gateway Routing Protocol (EIGRP) is necessary here because Acme already has network statements that cover the new routed links present in its EIGRP configuration.

Examples 14-5 and 14-6 show the configuration for the routed (Layer 3) interfaces.

Example 14-5 *Build L3 Port-Channels on AGI (Egypt)*

```
egypt# conf t
Enter configuration commands, one per line.  End with CNTL/Z.
egypt(config)# interface ethernet1/2
egypt(config-if)# desc to CS1 (BLUEJAY)
egypt(config-if)# channel-group 2 mode on
egypt(config-if)# no shutdown
egypt(config-if)#
egypt(config-if)# interface port-channel2
egypt(config-if)#   descr to CS1 (BLUEJAY)
egypt(config-if)#   no shutdown
egypt(config-if)#   ip address 10.198.2.2/30
egypt(config-if)#   ip router eigrp 1341
egypt(config-if)#
egypt(config-if)# interface e10/2
egypt(config-if)#   desc to CS2 (DOVE)
egypt(config-if)#   channel-group 3 mode on
egypt(config-if)#   no shutdown
egypt(config-if)#
egypt(config-if)# interface port-channel3
```

```
egypt(config-if)#   description to CS2 (DOVE)
egypt(config-if)#   no shutdown
egypt(config-if)#   ip address 10.198.2.10/30
egypt(config-if)#   ip router eigrp 1341
egypt(config-if)# end
egypt#
```

Example 14-6 *Build L3 Port-Channels on AG2 (Italy)*

```
italy# conf t
Enter configuration commands, one per line.  End with CNTL/Z.
italy(config)# interface ethernet1/2
italy(config-if)# desc to CS1 (BLUEJAY)
italy(config-if)# channel-group 2 mode on
italy(config-if)# no shutdown
italy(config-if)#
italy(config-if)# interface port-channel2
italy(config-if)#   descr to CS1 (BLUEJAY)
italy(config-if)#   no shutdown
italy(config-if)#   ip address 10.198.2.6/30
italy(config-if)#   ip router eigrp 1341
italy(config-if)#
italy(config-if)# interface e10/2
italy(config-if)#   desc to CS2 (DOVE)
italy(config-if)#   no shutdown
italy(config-if)#   channel-group 3 mode on
italy(config-if)#
italy(config-if)# interface port-channel3
italy(config-if)#   description to CS2 (DOVE)
italy(config-if)#   no shutdown
italy(config-if)#   ip address 10.198.2.14/30
italy(config-if)#   ip router eigrp 1341
italy(config-if)# end
italy#
```

Examples 14-7 and 14-8 can enable the port channel interfaces.

Example 14-7 *Configure Port-Channels on CS1 (Bluejay)*

```
bluejay# conf t
bluejay(config)# interface range port 3-4
bluejay(config-if-range)# no shutdown
bluejay(config-if-range)# end
bluejay#
```

Example 14-8   *Configure Port-Channels on CS2 (Dove)*

```
dove# conf t
dove(config)# interface range port 3-4
dove(config-if-range)# no shutdown
dove(config-if-range)# end
dove#
```

Additional verification in the way of **show** commands is also performed, as shown in Examples 14-9 and 14-10.

Example 14-9   *Verification Performed on Egypt*

```
egypt# show interface status | inc CS
Eth1/2        to CS1 (BLUEJAY)    connected routed    full   10G    10g
Eth10/2       to CS2 (DOVE)       connected routed    full   10G    10g
Po2           to CS1 (BLUEJAY)    connected routed    full   10G    --
Po3           to CS2 (DOVE)       connected routed    full   10G    --
egypt# show cdp neigh

Capability Codes: R - Router, T - Trans-Bridge, B - Source-Route-Bridge
                  S - Switch, H - Host, I - IGMP, r - Repeater,
                  V - VoIP-Phone, D - Remotely-Managed-Device,
                  s - Supports-STP-Dispute

Device-ID             Local Intrfce Hldtme Capability  Platform     Port ID
italy(TBM12162116)    Eth1/1         121    R S I s     N7K-C7010    Eth1/1
bluejay               Eth1/2         171    R S I       WS-C6506     Ten3/2
ghana(FLC12200419)    Eth1/4         176    S I s       N5K-C5020P-BF Eth1/1
italy(TBM12162116)    Eth1/9         121    R S I s     N7K-C7010    Eth1/9
italy(TBM12162116)    Eth4/12        122    R S I s     N7K-C7010    Eth4/12
italy(TBM12162116)    Eth7/12        122    R S I s     N7K-C7010    Eth7/12
italy(TBM12162116)    Eth10/1        122    R S I s     N7K-C7010    Eth10/1
dove                  Eth10/2        174    R S I       WS-C6506     Ten3/2
italy(TBM12162116)    Eth10/9        123    R S I s     N7K-C7010    Eth10/9

egypt#
egypt# show ip eigrp neighbor

IP-EIGRP neighbors for process 1341 VRF default
H   Address              Interface     Hold  Uptime    SRTT  RTO  Q    Seq
                                       (sec)           (ms)       Cnt  Num
2   10.198.2.9           Po3           14    00:00:33  106   636  0    9356
0   10.198.2.1           Po2           12    00:00:39  1     200  0    9194
1   10.198.2.18          Po4           13    02:14:04  4     200  0    446
```

```
egypt#
```

Example 14-10 *Verification Performed on Italy*

```
italy# show interface status | inc CS

Eth1/2       to CS1 (BLUEJAY)   connected routed    full    10G    10g
Eth10/2      to CS2 (DOVE)      connected routed    full    10G    10g
Po2          to CS1 (BLUEJAY)   connected routed    full    10G    --
Po3          to CS2 (DOVE)      connected routed    full    10G    --

italy# show cdp neigh

Capability Codes: R - Router, T - Trans-Bridge, B - Source-Route-Bridge
                  S - Switch, H - Host, I - IGMP, r - Repeater,
                  V - VoIP-Phone, D - Remotely-Managed-Device,
                  s - Supports-STP-Dispute


Device-ID            Local Intrfce Hldtme Capability  Platform      Port ID
egypt(TBM12162118)   Eth1/1        141    R S I s     N7K-C7010     Eth1/1
bluejay              Eth1/2        171    R S I       WS-C6506      Ten3/3
ghana(FLC12200419)   Eth1/4        176    S I s       N5K-C5020P-BF Eth1/2
egypt(TBM12162118)   Eth1/9        141    R S I s     N7K-C7010     Eth1/9
egypt(TBM12162118)   Eth4/12       142    R S I s     N7K-C7010     Eth4/12
egypt(TBM12162118)   Eth7/12       142    R S I s     N7K-C7010     Eth7/12
egypt(TBM12162118)   Eth10/1       142    R S I s     N7K-C7010     Eth10/1
dove                 Eth10/2       174    R S I       WS-C6506      Ten3/3
egypt(TBM12162118)   Eth10/9       142    R S I s     N7K-C7010     Eth10/9


italy# show ip eigrp neigh

IP-EIGRP neighbors for process 1341 VRF default
H   Address              Interface       Hold  Uptime    SRTT  RTO  Q   Seq
                                         (sec)           (ms)       Cnt Num
1   10.198.2.13          Po3             14    00:00:33  74    444  0   9357
0   10.198.2.5           Po2             12    00:00:39  1     200  0   9189
2   10.198.2.17          Po4             11    02:14:04  8     200  0   398
```

Maintenance Window #1 Summary

During this maintenance window, Acme, Inc., engineers successfully integrated the Nexus 7000 switches into the existing data center without issue. Physical links were brought up, and EIGRP was configured and verified such that full communication exists at Layer 3 between the new environment and the old. Establishing this connectivity allows Acme to migrate routing for a single VLAN at a time and ensures that dependencies between VLANs that have been migrated can still communicate with those that have not.

Figure 14-2 shows the current topology after this maintenance window.

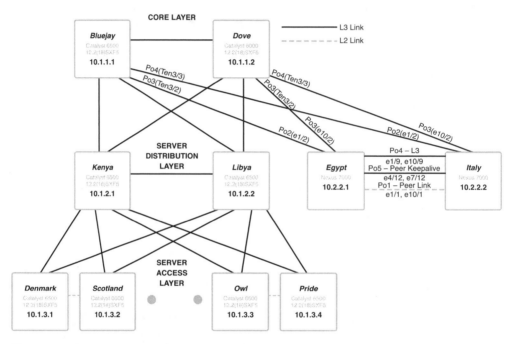

Figure 14-2 *Current Topology*

Maintenance Window #2

During the second maintenance window, the first access pair (Denmark and Scotland) will be physically connected to the new aggregation 7000s at Layer 2. The Layer 2 topology will be modified so that the Nexus 7000s will be the root bridge for all VLANs that live on Denmark and Scotland. Acme, Inc., has chosen to connect the Catalyst 6500s to the Nexus 7000s using the Virtual Port-Channel (vPC) feature that was discussed in Chapter 2, "Layer 2 Support and Configurations." Additional links have been pre-cabled between the aggregation and access devices so that the cutover can occur as seamlessly as possible and ensuring that to back these changes out, these links can simply be shut down if necessary. As with previous steps, these port-channels will be configured on both sides and set to administratively disabled on the 6500 side of the link initially, and then enabled in a controlled fashion.

Design Note   Care has been given to distribute port-channel members across multiple linecards. This ensures that no single module failure results in a major L2 topology change.

One additional concern of Acme, Inc., is that its existing devices have been left with per-VLAN spanning-tree (PVST). As discussed in Chapter 2, the Nexus switches support only Rapid-PVST+ and MST. Although Rapid-PVST+ is backward compatible with PVST, Acme views relying on this backward compatibility as unwanted. Because of the increased reliance on Layer 2 in the new design, the existing devices will be converted to Rapid-PVST+. This will ensure the fastest possible reconvergence should the Layer 2 topology change.

Examples 14-11 and 14-12 illustrate the interface configuration elements of Denmark and Scotland for their migration to the Nexus switches.

Example 14-11   *Port-Channel Configuration on SSA (Denmark)*

```
denmark# conf t
denmark(config)# interface GigabitEthernet1/3
denmark(config-if)#  description VPC member
denmark(config-if)#  switchport
denmark(config-if)#  switchport trunk encapsulation dot1q
denmark(config-if)#  switchport trunk allowed vlan 26,57,208,209
denmark(config-if)#  switchport mode trunk
denmark(config-if)#  channel-group 100 mode passive
denmark(config-if)#
denmark(config-if)#  interface GigabitEthernet1/4
denmark(config-if)#  description VPC member
denmark(config-if)#  switchport
denmark(config-if)#  switchport trunk encapsulation dot1q
denmark(config-if)#  switchport trunk allowed vlan 26,57,208,209
denmark(config-if)#  switchport mode trunk
denmark(config-if)#  channel-group 100 mode passive
denmark(config-if)#
denmark(config-if)#  interface GigabitEthernet2/3
denmark(config-if)#  description VPC member
denmark(config-if)#  switchport
denmark(config-if)#  switchport trunk encapsulation dot1q
denmark(config-if)#  switchport trunk allowed vlan 26,57,208,209
denmark(config-if)#  switchport mode trunk
denmark(config-if)#  channel-group 100 mode passive
denmark(config-if)#
```

```
denmark(config-if)#  interface GigabitEthernet2/4
denmark(config-if)#   description VPC member
denmark(config-if)#   switchport
denmark(config-if)#   switchport trunk encapsulation dot1q
denmark(config-if)#   switchport trunk allowed vlan 26,57,208,209
denmark(config-if)#   switchport mode trunk
denmark(config-if)#   channel-group 100 mode passive
denmark(config-if)#
denmark(config-if)#  interface Port-channel100
denmark(config-if)#   shutdown
denmark(config-if)#   switchport
denmark(config-if)#   switchport trunk encapsulation dot1q
denmark(config-if)#   switchport trunk allowed vlan 26,57,208,209
denmark(config-if)#   switchport mode trunk
denmark(config-if)#   end
denmark#
```

Example 14-12 *Port-Channel Configuration on SSB (Scotland)*

```
scotland# conf t
scotland(config)# interface GigabitEthernet1/3
scotland(config-if)#  description VPC member
scotland(config-if)#   switchport
scotland(config-if)#   switchport trunk encapsulation dot1q
scotland(config-if)#   switchport trunk allowed vlan 26,57,208,209
scotland(config-if)#   switchport mode trunk
scotland(config-if)#   channel-group 100 mode passive
scotland(config-if)#
scotland(config-if)#   interface GigabitEthernet1/4
scotland(config-if)#   description VPC member
scotland(config-if)#   switchport
scotland(config-if)#   switchport trunk encapsulation dot1q
scotland(config-if)#   switchport trunk allowed vlan 26,57,208,209
scotland(config-if)#   switchport mode trunk
scotland(config-if)#   channel-group 100 mode passive
scotland(config-if)#
scotland(config-if)#   interface GigabitEthernet2/3
scotland(config-if)#   description VPC member
scotland(config-if)#   switchport
scotland(config-if)#   switchport trunk encapsulation dot1q
scotland(config-if)#   switchport trunk allowed vlan 26,57,208,209
scotland(config-if)#   switchport mode trunk
scotland(config-if)#   channel-group 100 mode passive
scotland(config-if)#
```

```
scotland(config-if)#  interface GigabitEthernet2/4
scotland(config-if)#   description VPC member
scotland(config-if)#   switchport
scotland(config-if)#   switchport trunk encapsulation dot1q
scotland(config-if)#   switchport trunk allowed vlan 26,57,208,209
scotland(config-if)#   switchport mode trunk
scotland(config-if)#   channel-group 100 mode passive
scotland(config-if)#
scotland(config-if)#  interface Port-channel100
scotland(config-if)#   shutdown
scotland(config-if)#   switchport
scotland(config-if)#   switchport trunk encapsulation dot1q
scotland(config-if)#   switchport trunk allowed vlan 26,57,208,209
scotland(config-if)#   switchport mode trunk
scotland(config-if)#   end
scotland#
```

With the physical links in place and ready to be enabled, the focus now shifts to the VLANs that are present on Denmark and Scotland. By examining the configuration, you can see that the following VLANs are present and routed by Denmark and Scotland. Example 14-13 and Example 14-14 show the Layer 2 VLAN configuration for Denmark and Scotland, respectively.

Example 14-13 *VLAN Spanning Tree Configuration on Denmark*

```
denmark# show run

<snip>
vlan 26,57,208-209

<snip>
spanning-tree mode pvst
spanning-tree vlan 26,57,208-209,300-301 priority 8192
```

Example 14-14 *VLAN/Spanning Tree Configuration on Scotland*

```
scotland# show run

<snip>
vlan 26,57,208-209

<snip>
spanning-tree mode pvst
spanning-tree vlan 26,57,208-209,300-301 priority 16384
```

These VLANs must be configured on the Nexus aggregation devices with priorities that will not initially cause an STP root change. Acme has chosen to use 61440 as the initial value. This value has been determined to be higher than all configured devices and the default value of 32768 for most switches. Example 14-15 demonstrates the configuration that will be placed on Egypt and Italy.

Example 14-15   *VLAN/Spanning Tree Configuration on Egypt and Italy*

```
egypt# sh run

!Command: show running-config
!Time: Sun Dec  2 19:32:57 2012

<snip>
vlan 26,57,208-209
spanning-tree vlan 26,57,208-209 priority 61440
```

Design Note   Care has been given to port-channel numbers, physical interface placement, and so on so that the configuration between the Nexus devices can be almost exactly the same. The only differences between AG1 and AG2 will be unique identifiers such as loopbacks and physical interface addresses.

The next step involves building the corresponding vPC configuration for the port-channels that were created on Denmark and Scotland. Example 14-16 demonstrates the configuration. This side of the port-channel will remain administratively enabled so that the turnup/turndown of these links can be controlled from a smaller number of boxes (Denmark and Scotland).

Example 14-16   *vPC Configuration on Egypt and Italy*

```
egypt# conf t
Enter configuration commands, one per line.  End with CNTL/Z.
egypt(config)# interface Ethernet4/1,E7/1
egypt(config-if)#    switchport
egypt(config-if)#    switchport mode trunk
egypt(config-if)#    switchport trunk allowed vlan 26,57,208-209
egypt(config-if)#    channel-group 101 mode active
egypt(config-if)#    no shutdown
egypt(config-if)#
egypt(config-if)# interface port-channel101
egypt(config-if)#    switchport
egypt(config-if)#    switchport mode trunk
egypt(config-if)#    vpc 101
```

```
egypt(config-if)#    switchport trunk allowed vlan 26,57,208-209
egypt(config-if)#
egypt(config-if)# interface Ethernet4/2,E7/2
egypt(config-if)#    switchport
egypt(config-if)#    switchport mode trunk
egypt(config-if)#    switchport trunk allowed vlan 26,57,208-209
egypt(config-if)#    channel-group 102 mode active
egypt(config-if)#    no shutdown
egypt(config-if)#
egypt(config-if)# interface port-channel102
egypt(config-if)#    switchport
egypt(config-if)#    switchport mode trunk
egypt(config-if)#    vpc 102
egypt(config-if)#    switchport trunk allowed vlan 26,57,208-209
egypt(config-if)# end
egypt#
```

With this configuration in place, the port-channel between Denmark and the Nexus vPC domain will be enabled, as shown in Example 14-17. No impact is expected during this step.

Example 14-17 *Enable the vPC Port-Channel on SSA (Denmark)*

```
denmark# conf t
denmark (config)# interface port-channel 100
denmark (config-if)# no shut
denmark (config)# end
denmark #
```

With this link enabled, verification can be performed to ensure that the port-channel comes online, as shown in Example 14-18.

Example 14-18 *Verification*

```
denmark# show etherchannel summary
Flags:  D - down        P - bundled in port-channel
        I - stand-alone s - suspended
        H - Hot-standby (LACP only)
        R - Layer3       S - Layer2
        U - in use       N - not in use, no aggregation
        f - failed to allocate aggregator

        M - not in use, no aggregation due to minimum links not met
        m - not in use, port not aggregated due to minimum links not met
        u - unsuitable for bundling
```

```
        d - default port

        w - waiting to be aggregated
Number of channel-groups in use: 4
Number of aggregators:           4


Group  Port-channel  Protocol    Ports
------+-------------+-----------+------------------------------------------------
1      Po1(SU)          -         Gi1/24(P)     Gi2/24(P)
2      Po2(RU)          -         Gi1/1(P)      Gi2/1(P)
3      Po3(RU)          -         Gi1/2(P)      Gi2/2(P)
100    Po100(SU)      LACP        Gi1/3(P)      Gi1/4(P)        Gi2/3(P)
Gi2/4(P)
```

To decrease the impact of the spanning-tree root change, enable Rapid-PVST+ on the access switches. Example 14-19 demonstrates the configuration required to accomplish this.

Example 14-19   *Enable Rapid-PVST+ on Denmark and Scotland*

```
denmark# conf t
denmark (config)# spanning-tree mode rapid-pvst
denmark (config)# end
denmark #
```

The next step is to move the spanning-tree root for the VLANs you are working with to the Nexus 7000 aggregation switches. Example 14-20 shows this configuration.

Example 14-20   *Configure Egypt and Italy with a Lower Root Priority*

```
egypt# conf t
Enter configuration commands, one per line.  End with CNTL/Z.
egypt(config)# vpc domain 1
egypt(config-vpc-domain)# peer-switch
egypt(config-vpc-domain)# !
egypt(config-vpc-domain)# spanning-tree vlan 26,57,208-209 priority 4096
egypt(config)# end
egypt#
```

Verification will be performed on Egypt, Italy, and Denmark, as shown in Examples 14-21 through 14-23.

Example 14-21 *Spanning-Tree Root Verification on Egypt*

```
egypt# show spanning-tree root


                                 Root  Hello Max Fwd
Vlan                  Root ID    Cost  Time  Age Dly  Root Port
---------------- -------------------- ------- ----- --- ---  ----------------
VLAN0001         32769 0023.04ee.be01    0     2    20  15   This bridge is root
VLAN0026          4122 0023.04ee.be01    0     2    20  15   This bridge is root
VLAN0057          4153 0023.04ee.be01    0     2    20  15   This bridge is root
VLAN0208          4304 0023.04ee.be01    0     2    20  15   This bridge is root
VLAN0209          4305 0023.04ee.be01    0     2    20  15   This bridge is root


egypt#
```

Example 14-22 *Spanning-Tree Root Verification on Italy*

```
italy# show spanning-tree root


                                 Root  Hello Max Fwd
Vlan                  Root ID    Cost  Time  Age Dly  Root Port
---------------- -------------------- ------- ----- --- ---  ----------------
VLAN0001         32769 0023.04ee.be01    0     2    20  15   This bridge is root
VLAN0026          4122 0023.04ee.be01    0     2    20  15   This bridge is root
VLAN0057          4153 0023.04ee.be01    0     2    20  15   This bridge is root
VLAN0208          4304 0023.04ee.be01    0     2    20  15   This bridge is root
VLAN0209          4305 0023.04ee.be01    0     2    20  15   This bridge is root


italy#
```

Example 14-23 *Spanning-Tree Root Verification on Denmark*

```
denmark# show spanning-tree root


                                 Root Hello Max Fwd
Vlan                  Root ID    Cost Time Age Dly  Root Port
---------------- -------------------- ------ ----- --- ---  ----------------
VLAN0001         49152 0003.a0ed.5401    0    2    20  15
VLAN0026          4122 0023.04ee.be01    3    2    20  15   Po100
VLAN0057          4153 0023.04ee.be01    3    2    20  15   Po100
```

```
VLAN0208          4304 0023.04ee.be01        3    2    20   15   Po100
VLAN0209          4305 0023.04ee.be01        3    2    20   15   Po100
denmark#
```

Acme, Inc., now has L2 configured between the first access pair and the Nexus aggregation switches, as shown in Figure 14-3.

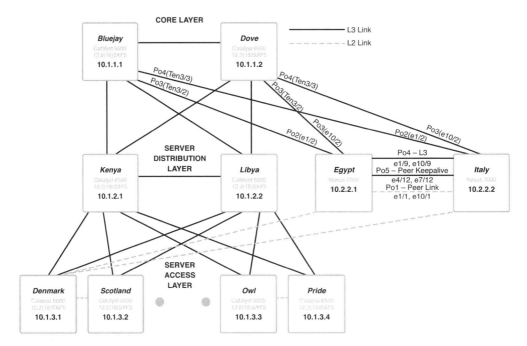

Figure 14-3 *Updated Topology Configuration*

Design Note   L3 routing will be migrated prior to turning up the vPC from Scotland to the Nexus aggregation devices. The reasoning behind this decision is that you want to keep the traffic pattern the same for as long as you can to minimize disruptions to the existing flows. Assuming that Denmark is the active HSRP router, the hosts connected to Scotland have a L2 path of Scotland to Denmark to get to their default gateway. If the vPC is turned up between Scotland and Egypt/Italy, the link between Denmark and Scotland would become blocked by STP, and the L2 path for hosts connected to Scotland would be Scotland to Egypt/Italy to Denmark to get to their default gateway. Doing it this way ensures that servers must take only the extra hop to aggregation after their default gateway resides there.

The next step in the process is to convert the Switched Virtual Interface (SVI) interfaces from the 6500 access switches to the Nexus 7000 aggregation devices. Start by examining the existing 6500 configuration and making the necessary changes to move these interfaces to the Nexus 7000. Example 14-24 shows the current SVI configuration from Denmark.

Example 14-24 *SVI Configuration on Denmark*

```
denmark# show run

<snip>

interface Vlan26
 ip address 10.198.26.254 255.255.255.0
 ip pim sparse-dense-mode
 ip cgmp
 standby 26 ip 10.198.26.1
 standby 26 priority 110
 standby 26 preempt
 arp timeout 240
!
interface Vlan57
 ip address 10.198.57.248 255.255.255.0
 ip helper-address 10.198.67.50
 ip helper-address 10.198.64.98
 ip pim sparse-dense-mode
 ip cgmp
 standby 57 ip 10.198.57.1
 standby 57 priority 110
 standby 57 preempt
 arp timeout 240
!
interface Vlan208
 ip address 10.198.208.2 255.255.255.0
 ip helper-address 10.198.67.167
 ip helper-address 10.198.64.73
 standby 208 ip 10.198.208.1
 standby 208 priority 110
 standby 208 preempt
 standby 209 priority 110
 arp timeout 240
!
interface Vlan209
 ip address 10.198.209.2 255.255.255.0
 ip helper-address 10.198.67.167
```

```
ip helper-address 10.198.64.73
standby 209 ip 10.198.209.1
standby 209 priority 110
standby 209 preempt
arp timeout 240
```

The configuration calls for four distinct features to be enabled on the Nexus 7000 because of the modular nature of NX-OS: interface-vlan, PIM, HSRP, and DHCP. These features are enabled using the configuration shown in Example 14-25.

Example 14-25   *Enable the Interface-VLAN, PIM, HSRP, and DHCP Features on Egypt and Italy*

```
egypt# conf t
Enter configuration commands, one per line.  End with CNTL/Z.
egypt(config)# feature pim
egypt(config)# feature dhcp
egypt(config)# feature hsrp
egypt(config)# feature interface-vlan
egypt(config)# end
egypt#
```

Example 14-26 highlights the migrated SVI configuration with commented explanations.

Example 14-26   *SVI Configuration on Egypt and Italy*

```
egypt# conf t
Enter configuration commands, one per line.  End with CNTL/Z.
egypt(config)#interface Vlan26
! We want ensure that the SVI is shutdown
egypt(config-if)#shutdown
! NX-OS supports slash notation for IP addresses
egypt(config-if)#ip address 10.198.26.251/24
egypt(config-if)#ip pim sparse-mode
! IOS defaults to having proxy-arp enabled by default,
whereas, NX-OS ! disables this feature by default - we
want to ensure a smooth !migration for hosts which may
have an incorrect default gateway !configuration
egypt(config-if)#ip proxy-arp
egypt(config-if)#no ip redirects
! In lieu of "router eigrp" mode configuration we use interface
! commands to specify how this interface will participate in EIGRP
egypt(config-if)#ip router eigrp 1341
egypt(config-if)#ip passive-interface eigrp 1341
! We want this to be an undesirable path initially
```

```
egypt(config-if)#ip delay eigrp 1341 2000
! The "standby" branch of commands is replaced with an HSRP
! configuration sub mode
egypt(config-if)#hsrp 26
egypt(config-if-hsrp)#   ip 10.198.26.1
! Configure initially with a low priority so that we can gracefully
! move routing over through preemption later
egypt(config-if-hsrp)#   priority 1
egypt(config-if-hsrp)#   end
egypt#
```

Design Note   Available IP addresses for each VLAN have been reserved for the SVIs that are being configured on the Nexus 7000s. This enables you to have both the access and aggregation SVIs up for a period of time without introducing any duplicate IP addresses. After the access SVIs have been decommissioned, the IP addresses of the Nexus 7000s will be changed to those previously configured in the access layer. This allows Acme, Inc., to reclaim the temporary IP addresses and accounts for any hosts that may be pointing to a physical IP address as opposed to the HSRP VIP.

With these considerations in place, the full configurations for Egypt and Italy are shown in Examples 14-27 and 14-28.

Example 14-27   *SVI 26 Configuration Followed by Configuration of Remaining SVI Interfaces*

```
egypt# sh run int vlan26

!Command: show running-config interface Vlan26
!Time: Sun Dec  2 19:45:57 2012

version 5.2(3a)

interface Vlan26
 shutdown
 ip address 10.198.26.251 255.255.255.0
 ip pim sparse-mode
 ip proxy-arp
 no ip redirects
 ip router eigrp 1341
 ip passive-interface eigrp 1341
 ip delay eigrp 1341 2000
 hsrp 26
    priority 1
```

```
      ip 10.198.26.1

egypt# conf t
Enter configuration commands, one per line.  End with CNTL/Z.
egypt(config)# interface Vlan57
egypt(config-if)#  shutdown
egypt(config-if)#  ip address 10.198.57.239 255.255.255.0
egypt(config-if)#  ip dhcp relay address 10.198.67.50
egypt(config-if)#  ip dhcp relay address 10.198.64.98
egypt(config-if)#  ip pim sparse-mode
egypt(config-if)#  ip proxy-arp
egypt(config-if)#  no ip redirects
egypt(config-if)# ip router eigrp 1341
egypt(config-if)# ip passive-interface eigrp 1341
egypt(config-if)# ip delay eigrp 1341 2000
egypt(config-if)#  hsrp 57
egypt(config-if-hsrp)#    priority 1
egypt(config-if-hsrp)#    ip 10.198.57.1
egypt(config-if-hsrp)#
egypt(config-if-hsrp)#
egypt(config-if-hsrp)# interface Vlan208
egypt(config-if)#  shutdown
egypt(config-if)#  ip address 10.198.208.4 255.255.255.0
egypt(config-if)#  ip dhcp relay address 10.198.67.167
egypt(config-if)#  ip dhcp relay address 10.198.64.73
egypt(config-if)#  ip pim sparse-mode
egypt(config-if)#  ip proxy-arp
egypt(config-if)#  no ip redirects
egypt(config-if)#  ip router eigrp 1341
egypt(config-if)#  ip passive-interface eigrp 1341
egypt(config-if)#  ip delay eigrp 1341 2000
egypt(config-if)#   hsrp 208
egypt(config-if-hsrp)#    priority 1
egypt(config-if-hsrp)#    ip 10.198.208.1
egypt(config-if-hsrp)#
egypt(config-if-hsrp)#
egypt(config-if-hsrp)# interface Vlan209
egypt(config-if)#  shutdown
egypt(config-if)#  ip address 10.198.209.4 255.255.255.0
egypt(config-if)#  ip dhcp relay address 10.198.67.167
egypt(config-if)#  ip dhcp relay address 10.198.64.73
egypt(config-if)#  ip pim sparse-mode
egypt(config-if)#  ip proxy-arp
egypt(config-if)#  no ip redirects
egypt(config-if)#  ip router eigrp 1341
```

```
egypt(config-if)#  ip passive-interface eigrp 1341
egypt(config-if)#  ip delay eigrp 1341 2000
egypt(config-if)#  hsrp 209
egypt(config-if-hsrp)#      priority 1
egypt(config-if-hsrp)#      ip 10.198.209.1
egypt(config-if-hsrp)# end
egypt#
```

Example 14-28 *Configure the Initial SVI Configuration on AG2 (Italy)*

```
italy# conf t
Enter configuration commands, one per line.  End with CNTL/Z.
italy(config)# interface Vlan26
italy(config-if)#  shutdown
italy(config-if)#  ip address 10.198.26.252 255.255.255.0
italy(config-if)#  ip pim sparse-mode
italy(config-if)#  ip proxy-arp
italy(config-if)#  no ip redirects
italy(config-if)#  ip router eigrp 1341
italy(config-if)#  ip passive-interface eigrp 1341
italy(config-if)#  ip delay eigrp 1341 2000
italy(config-if)#  hsrp 26
italy(config-if-hsrp)#      priority 1
italy(config-if-hsrp)#      ip 10.198.26.1
italy(config-if-hsrp)#
italy(config-if-hsrp)# interface Vlan57
italy(config-if)#  shutdown
italy(config-if)#  ip address 10.198.57.240 255.255.255.0
italy(config-if)#  ip dhcp relay address 10.198.67.50
italy(config-if)#  ip dhcp relay address 10.198.64.98
italy(config-if)#  ip pim sparse-mode
italy(config-if)#  ip proxy-arp
italy(config-if)#  no ip redirects
italy(config-if)#  ip router eigrp 1341
italy(config-if)#  ip passive-interface eigrp 1341
italy(config-if)#  ip delay eigrp 1341 2000
italy(config-if)#  hsrp 57
italy(config-if-hsrp)#      priority 1
italy(config-if-hsrp)#      ip 10.198.57.1
italy(config-if-hsrp)#
italy(config-if-hsrp)# interface Vlan208
italy(config-if)#  shutdown
italy(config-if)#  ip address 10.198.208.5 255.255.255.0
italy(config-if)#  ip dhcp relay address 10.198.67.167
```

```
italy(config-if)#  ip dhcp relay address 10.198.64.73
italy(config-if)#  ip pim sparse-mode
italy(config-if)#  ip proxy-arp
italy(config-if)#  no ip redirects
italy(config-if)#  ip router eigrp 1341
italy(config-if)#  ip passive-interface eigrp 1341
italy(config-if)#  ip delay eigrp 1341 2000
italy(config-if)#
italy(config-if)# interface Vlan209
italy(config-if)#  shutdown
italy(config-if)#  ip address 10.198.209.5 255.255.255.0
italy(config-if)#  ip dhcp relay address 10.198.67.167
italy(config-if)#  ip dhcp relay address 10.198.64.73
italy(config-if)#  ip pim sparse-mode
italy(config-if)#  ip proxy-arp
italy(config-if)#  no ip redirects
italy(config-if)#  ip router eigrp 1341
italy(config-if)#  ip passive-interface eigrp 1341
italy(config-if)#  ip delay eigrp 1341 2000
italy(config-if)#  hsrp 209
italy(config-if-hsrp)#     priority 1
italy(config-if-hsrp)#     ip 10.198.209.1
italy(config-if-hsrp)# end
italy#
```

After the SVIs are configured on both Nexus 7000 devices, they can be enabled and verified as operational, as shown in Example 14-29 through 14-32.

Example 14-29 *Enable SVIs on Egypt*

```
egypt# conf t
Enter configuration commands, one per line.  End with CNTL/Z.
egypt(config)# interface Vlan26,Vlan57,Vlan208,Vlan209
egypt(config-if-range)#     no shutdown
egypt(config-if-range)# end
egypt#
```

Example 14-30 *Enable SVIs on Italy*

```
italy# conf t
Enter configuration commands, one per line.  End with CNTL/Z.
italy(config)# interface Vlan26,Vlan57,Vlan208,Vlan209
italy(config-if-range)#     no  shutdown
italy(config-if-range)# end
italy#
```

Example 14-31 *Verify That SVIs Are Operational on Egypt*

```
egypt# show ip int brief | exc un

IP Interface Status for VRF "default"(1)
Interface           IP Address      Interface Status
Vlan26              10.198.26.251   protocol-up/link-up/admin-up
Vlan57              10.198.57.239   protocol-up/link-up/admin-up
Vlan208             10.198.208.4    protocol-up/link-up/admin-up
Vlan209             10.198.209.4    protocol-up/link-up/admin-up
loopback0           10.2.2.1        protocol-up/link-up/admin-up
port-channel2       10.198.2.2      protocol-up/link-up/admin-up
port-channel3       10.198.2.10     protocol-up/link-up/admin-up
port-channel4       10.198.2.17     protocol-up/link-up/admin-up
```

Example 14-32 *Verify That SVIs Are Operational on Italy*

```
italy# show ip int brief | exc un

IP Interface Status for VRF "default"(1)
Interface           IP Address      Interface Status
Vlan26              10.198.26.252   protocol-up/link-up/admin-up
Vlan57              10.198.57.240   protocol-up/link-up/admin-up
Vlan208             10.198.208.5    protocol-up/link-up/admin-up
Vlan209             10.198.209.5    protocol-up/link-up/admin-up
loopback0           10.2.2.2        protocol-up/link-up/admin-up
port-channel2       10.198.2.6      protocol-up/link-up/admin-up
port-channel3       10.198.2.14     protocol-up/link-up/admin-up
port-channel4       10.198.2.18     protocol-up/link-up/admin-up


italy#
```

Although the SVIs on Egypt and Italy are operational now, because of the high delay configured for these networks, the core still prefers the path through the access switches, which is verified on Bluejay in Example 14-33.

Example 14-33 *Verify Routing Table on Bluejay*

```
bluejay# show ip route
<snip>
D       10.198.26.0/24
            [90/3328] via 10.198.0.2, 00:03:47, TenGigabitEthernet4/2
            [90/3328] via 10.198.0.10, 00:03:47, TenGigabitEthernet4/3
```

```
D       10.198.57.0/24
              [90/3328] via 10.198.0.2, 00:03:47, TenGigabitEthernet4/2
              [90/3328] via 10.198.0.10, 00:03:47, TenGigabitEthernet4/3
<output truncated>
bluejay#
```

With the SVIs operational, and EIGRP adjacencies formed, Acme can now adjust the delay used for the EIGRP calculation so that the paths through both the access switches and Nexus aggregation are equal, as shown in Example 14-34. The result of this change will be equal cost multipathing (ECMP).

Example 14-34 *Modify EIGRP Delay on Egypt/Italy*

```
egypt# conf t
Enter configuration commands, one per line.  End with CNTL/Z.
egypt(config)# interface Vlan26,Vlan57,Vlan208,Vlan209
ip delay eigrp 1341 2
egypt(config-if-range)# ip delay eigrp 1341 2
egypt(config-if-range)# end
egypt#
```

Design Note The goal here is to make the EIGRP metrics equal. In this example a delay of 2 accomplishes this because the bandwidths are equal. Depending on the topology, additional manipulation by way of bandwidth may be necessary to influence route selection.

Now that the EIGRP metrics have been manipulated, the core devices can see four paths to the networks being migrated: two via the existing access switches and two via the new Nexus Aggregation switches, as shown in Example 14-35.

Example 14-35 *Verify ECMP on Bluejay*

```
bluejay# show ip route

<snip>

D       10.198.26.0/24
              [90/3328] via 10.198.0.2, 00:00:08, TenGigabitEthernet4/2
              [90/3328] via 10.198.0.10, 00:00:08, TenGigabitEthernet4/3
              [90/3328] via 10.198.2.2, 00:00:08, Port-channel3
              [90/3328] via 10.198.2.6, 00:00:08, Port-channel4
D       10.198.57.0/24
              [90/3328] via 10.198.0.2, 00:00:08, TenGigabitEthernet4/2
```

```
        [90/3328] via 10.198.0.10, 00:00:08, TenGigabitEthernet4/3
        [90/3328] via 10.198.2.2, 00:00:08, Port-channel3
        [90/3328] via 10.198.2.6, 00:00:08, Port-channel4
```

While inbound traffic is being distributed between the Nexus and 6500 devices, all traffic leaving the VLANs is still being routed by the 6500 because it is the active HSRP
device. By adjusting the HSRP priority, Acme can force HSRP to become active on the
Nexus aggregation switches. To accomplish this, Acme must configure the HSRP priority,
which is higher than any of the other HSRP routers, and enable preemption, as shown in
Example 14-36 and verified in Example 14-37.

Example 14-36   *Configure AG1 (Egypt) as the Active HSRP Router*

```
egypt# conf t
Enter configuration commands, one per line.  End with CNTL/Z.
egypt(config)# interface Vlan26
egypt(config-if)#   hsrp 26
egypt(config-if-hsrp)#     priority 200
egypt(config-if-hsrp)#     preempt
egypt(config-if-hsrp)#
egypt(config-if-hsrp)# interface Vlan57
egypt(config-if)#   hsrp 57
egypt(config-if-hsrp)#     priority 200
egypt(config-if-hsrp)#     preempt
egypt(config-if-hsrp)#
egypt(config-if-hsrp)# interface vlan208
egypt(config-if)#   hsrp 208
egypt(config-if-hsrp)#     priority 200
egypt(config-if-hsrp)#     preempt
egypt(config-if-hsrp)#
egypt(config-if-hsrp)# interface vlan209
egypt(config-if)#   hsrp 209
egypt(config-if-hsrp)#     priority 200
egypt(config-if-hsrp)#     preempt
egypt(config-if-hsrp)# end
egypt#
```

Example 14-37   *Verify That HSRP Is Active on Egypt*

```
egypt# show hsrp brief
                     P indicates configured to preempt.
                     |
Interface   Grp Prio P State    Active addr     Standby addr    Group addr
```

```
Vlan26       26  200  P Active   local              10.198.26.252   10.198.26.1
(conf)
Vlan57       57  200  P Active   local              10.198.57.240   10.198.57.1
(conf)
Vlan208     208  200  P Active   local              10.198.208.5    10.198.208.1
(conf)
Vlan209     209  200  P Active   local              10.198.209.2    10.198.209.1
(conf)


egypt#
```

To complete the default gateway migration, Acme will also make sure that Italy is configured with the second highest priority and becomes the standby router, as shown in Example 14-38 and verified in Example 14-39.

Example 14-38 *Configure Italy as the Standby HSRP Router*

```
italy# conf t
Enter configuration commands, one per line.  End with CNTL/Z.
italy(config)# interface Vlan26
italy(config-if)#   hsrp 26
italy(config-if-hsrp)#      priority 190
italy(config-if-hsrp)#      preempt
italy(config-if-hsrp)#
italy(config-if-hsrp)# interface Vlan57
italy(config-if)#   hsrp 57
italy(config-if-hsrp)#      priority 190
italy(config-if-hsrp)#      preempt
italy(config-if-hsrp)#
italy(config-if-hsrp)# interface vlan208
italy(config-if)#   hsrp 208
italy(config-if-hsrp)#   priority 190
italy(config-if-hsrp)#   preempt
italy(config-if-hsrp)#
italy(config-if-hsrp)# interface vlan209
italy(config-if)#   hsrp 209
italy(config-if-hsrp)#   priority 190
italy(config-if-hsrp)#   preempt
italy(config-if-hsrp)# end
italy#
```

Example 14-39   *Verify That HSRP Is Standby on Italy*

```
italy# show hsrp brief

                      P indicates configured to preempt.
                      |
Interface    Grp Prio P State    Active addr     Standby addr   Group addr
Vlan26       26  190  P Standby  10.198.26.251   local          10.198.26.1
(conf)
Vlan57       57  190  P Standby  10.198.57.239   local          10.198.57.1
(conf)
Vlan208      208 190  P Standby  10.198.208.4    local          10.198.208.1
(conf)
Vlan209      209 190  P Standby  10.198.209.4    local          10.198.209.1
(conf)


italy#
```

With the default gateway migration complete, Acme can now remove the paths to the migrated networks through the access switches by adjusting the EIGRP metric again. This time the goal in metric manipulation is to make these paths unwanted. This time, the bandwidth will be manipulated to "poison" these paths, as shown in Example 14-40.

Example 14-40   *Configure the Bandwidth on Denmark and Scotland*

```
denmark# conf t
denmark(config)# interface vlan26
denmark(config-if)# bandwidth 5
denmark(config-if)# interface vlan57
denmark(config-if)# bandwidth 5
denmark(config-if)# interface vlan208
denmark(config-if)# bandwidth 5
denmark(config-if)# interface vlan209
denmark(config-if)# bandwidth 5
denmark(config-if)# end
denmark#
```

From the core switches, Acme verifies that there are now two paths via the Nexus aggregation switches to reach the migrated networks, as shown in Example 14-41.

Example 14-41 *Verify Routing on Bluejay*

```
bluejay# show ip route

<snip>

D       10.198.26.0/24 [90/3328] via 10.198.2.2, 00:00:10, Port-channel3
                       [90/3328] via 10.198.2.6, 00:00:10, Port-channel4
D       10.198.57.0/24 [90/3328] via 10.198.2.2, 00:00:10, Port-channel3
                       [90/3328] via 10.198.2.6, 00:00:10, Port-channel4

<output truncated>
bluejay#
```

With the routing migration complete, Acme returns its focus to the L2 topology. Recall in previous steps that the vPC between Scotland and the Nexus aggregation was deferred while routing was being migrated. In the next phase of the migration, Acme enables the vPC between Scotland and the vPC domain. This results in Scotland seeing a better path to the root bridge via the vPC and moves its port-channel to Denmark into a blocking state. While it remained down, the configuration for this was staged on both Nexus switches and Scotland in previous steps. Enabling the port-channel is the only step remaining, as shown in Example 14-42.

Example 14-42 *Enabling the Port-Channel to the vPC Domain on Scotland*

```
denmark# conf t
denmark(config)# interface Port-Channel 100
denmark(config-if)# no shutdown
denmark(config-if)# end
denmark#
```

With this port-channel enabled, Scotland sees a superior root path via the new port-channel, as shown in Example 14-43.

Example 14-43 *Verify Spanning-Tree Topology on Scotland*

```
scotland# show spanning-tree root

                             Root Hello Max Fwd
Vlan                Root ID  Cost  Time Age Dly  Root Port
---------------- -------------------- ------ ----- --- ---  ----------------
VLAN0001        49152 0003.a0ed.5401   3003    2   20  15  Po1
VLAN0026         4122 0023.04ee.be01      3    2   20  15  Po100
VLAN0057         4153 0023.04ee.be01      3    2   20  15  Po100
VLAN0208         4304 0023.04ee.be01      3    2   20  15  Po100
VLAN0209         4305 0023.04ee.be01      3    2   20  15  Po100
scotland#
```

In addition, Acme verifies that the topology is loop-free and that the path to Denmark is put into a blocking state, as shown in Example 14-44.

Example 14-44   *Verify Spanning-Tree Topology on Scotland*

```
scotland# show spanning-tree blocked


Name                     Blocked Interfaces List
-------------------- -----------------------------------
VLAN0026                 Po1
VLAN0057                 Po1
VLAN0208                 Po1
VLAN0209                 Po1


Number of blocked ports (segments) in the system : 4


scotland#
```

Acme feels that in vPC a resilient topology exists and therefore sees no need to keep the link between the two access switches in place. After verifying that the link is blocking, it is also administratively shut down, as shown in Example 14-45.

Example 14-45   *Shut Down port-channel Between Denmark and Scotland*

```
denmark# conf t
denmark(config)# interface Port-channel1
denmark(config-if)# shutdown
denmark(config-if)# end
denmark#
```

Acme now allows a period of time in which it monitors the input and output rates on the SVIs. Because all traffic has been migrated, these rates should be low after this is confirmed. The SVIs on Denmark and Scotland can be shut down, as shown in Example 14-46.

Example 14-46   *Shut Down Migrated SVIs on Denmark and Scotland*

```
denmark# conf t
denmark(config)# interface vlan26
denmark(config-if)# shutdown
denmark(config-if)# interface vlan57
denmark(config-if)# shutdown
denmark(config-if)# interface vlan208
denmark(config-if)# shutdown
denmark(config-if)# interface vlan209
```

```
denmark(config-if)# shutdown
denmark(config-if)# end
denmark#
```

A similar process is done with the uplinks on Denmark and Scotland. Routing proto-col hellos should be the only traffic on these links and can be shut down, as shown in Example 14-47.

Example 14-47   *Routed Uplinks Are Shut Down on Denmark and Scotland*

```
denmark# conf t
denmark(config)#interface range port-channel2-3
denmark(config-if)# shutdown
denmark(config-if)# end
denmark#
```

Design Note   When the routed uplinks are down, the 6500 loopback addresses that were previously used to manage the devices are unreachable. A single SVI in one of the existing (or a new) VLANs is created and used to manage the devices moving forward.

The migration of Denmark and Scotland is now complete, as shown in Figure 14-4.

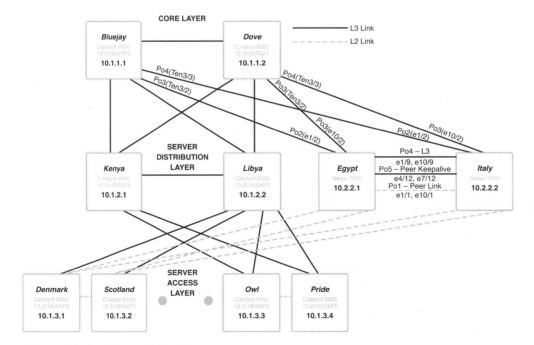

Figure 14-4   *Migrated Topology*

One final cleanup task remains, which is to reconfigure the physical IP addresses of the Nexus to match what was previously configured on the 6500 switches, as shown in Example 14-48 and Example 14-49. This ensures that hosts that do not use the HSRP address as their default gateway can continue to work and also allows Acme to reclaim the temporary addresses assigned to the Nexus switches.

Example 14-48   *Configure Egypt with Denmark's SVI Addresses*

```
egypt# conf t
Enter configuration commands, one per line.  End with CNTL/Z.
egypt(config)# interface Vlan26
egypt(config-if)# ip address 10.198.26.254 255.255.255.0
egypt(config-if)#
egypt(config-if)# interface Vlan57
egypt(config-if)#   ip address 10.198.57.241 255.255.255.0
egypt(config-if)#
egypt(config-if)# interface Vlan208
egypt(config-if)# ip address 10.198.208.2 255.255.255.0
egypt(config-if)#
egypt(config-if)# interface Vlan209
egypt(config-if)# ip address 10.198.209.2 255.255.255.0
egypt(config-if)# end
egypt#
```

Example 14-49   *Configure Italy with Scotland's SVI Addresses*

```
italy# conf t
Enter configuration commands, one per line.  End with CNTL/Z.
italy(config)#  interface Vlan26
italy(config-if)# ip address 10.198.26.253 255.255.255.0
italy(config-if)#
italy(config-if)# interface Vlan57
italy(config-if)#   ip address 10.198.57.242 255.255.255.0
italy(config-if)#
italy(config-if)# interface Vlan208
italy(config-if)# ip address 10.198.208.3 255.255.255.0
italy(config-if)#
italy(config-if)# interface Vlan209
italy(config-if)# ip address 10.198.209.3 255.255.255.0
italy(config-if)# end
italy#
```

The next step of the migration will be to bring the first set of Nexus 5596 switches online and the Nexus 2000 for connectivity to the migrated VLANs. The topology diagram in Figure 14-5 shows the physical connectivity that will be configured to accomplish this.

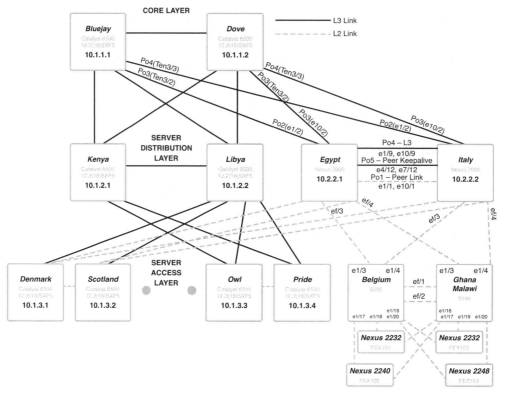

Figure 14-5   *Topology with 5K/2K Devices in Place*

First, vPCs will be created on the Nexus 7000 aggregation switches (Egypt and Italy), as shown in Example 14-50.

Example 14-50   *vPC Configuration on Egypt and Italy*

```
egypt# conf t
Enter configuration commands, one per line.  End with CNTL/Z.
egypt(config)# interface port-channel150
egypt(config-if)#    switchport
egypt(config-if)#    switchport mode trunk
egypt(config-if)#    vpc 50
egypt(config-if)# interface Ethernet1/3 - 4
egypt(config-if-range)#    switchport
egypt(config-if-range)#    switchport mode trunk
egypt(config-if-range)#    channel-group 50 mode active
egypt(config-if-range)#    no shutdown
```

```
egypt(config-if-range)# end
egypt#
```

The corresponding vPC configuration will be placed on Belgium and Ghana, as shown in
Example 14-51 and Example 14-52.

Example 14-51   *vPC Configuration on Belgium*

```
belgium# conf t
Enter configuration commands, one per line.  End with CNTL/Z.
belgium(config)# feature lacp
belgium(config)# feature vpc
belgium(config)# vpc domain 2
belgium(config-vpc-domain)#   peer-keepalive destination 30.1.130.106 source
30.1.131.105
belgium(config-vpc-domain)# interface port-channel1
belgium(config-if)#   switchport mode trunk
belgium(config-if)#   vpc peer-link
belgium(config-if)#   spanning-tree port type network
belgium(config-if)#
belgium(config-if)# interface port-channel50
belgium(config-if)#   switchport mode trunk
belgium(config-if)#   vpc 50
belgium(config-if)#   speed 10000
belgium(config-if)#
belgium(config-if)# interface Ethernet1/1 - 2
belgium(config-if-range)#   switchport mode trunk
belgium(config-if-range)#   channel-group 1 mode active
belgium(config-if-range)#
belgium(config-if-range)# interface Ethernet1/3 - 4
belgium(config-if-range)#   switchport mode trunk
belgium(config-if-range)#   channel-group 50 mode active
belgium(config-if-range)#
belgium(config-if-range)# interface mgmt0
belgium(config-if)# ip address 30.1.131.105/16
belgium(config-if)#end
belgium#
```

Example 14-52   *vPC Configuration on Ghana*

```
ghana# conf t
Enter configuration commands, one per line.  End with CNTL/Z.
ghana(config)# feature lacp
ghana(config)# feature vpc
```

```
ghana(config)# vpc domain 2
ghana(config-vpc-domain)#   peer-keepalive destination 30.1.130.105 source
30.1.131.106
ghana(config-vpc-domain)# interface port-channel1
ghana(config-if)#   switchport mode trunk
ghana(config-if)#   vpc peer-link
ghana(config-if)#   spanning-tree port type network
ghana(config-if)#
ghana(config-if)# interface port-channel50
ghana(config-if)#   switchport mode trunk
ghana(config-if)#   vpc 50
ghana(config-if)#   speed 10000
ghana(config-if)#
ghana(config-if)# interface Ethernet1/1 - 2
ghana(config-if-range)#   switchport mode trunk
ghana(config-if-range)#   channel-group 1 mode active
ghana(config-if-range)#
ghana(config-if-range)# interface Ethernet1/3 - 4
ghana(config-if-range)#   switchport mode trunk
ghana(config-if-range)#   channel-group 50 mode active
ghana(config-if-range)#
ghana(config-if-range)# interface mgmt0
ghana(config-if)# ip address 30.1.131.106/16
ghana(config-if)#end
ghana#
```

After the vPC peer link and uplinks into the Nexus 7000 aggregation are in place, the
fabric extension (FEX) configuration will be placed on both Nexus 5596s to host physical server connections. Example 14-53 shows the configuration to be placed on both
Belgium and Ghana.

Example 14-53   *FEX Configuration on Belgium and Ghana*

```
belgium# show running-config fex

!Command: show running-config fex
!Time: Sun Dec  2 19:00:01 2012


feature fex
fex 100
  pinning max-links 1
  description "FEX0100"
fex 101
  pinning max-links 1
  description "FEX0101"
```

```
fex 102
  pinning max-links 1
  description "FEX0102"
fex 103
  pinning max-links 1
  description "FEX0103"
interface port-channel100
  switchport mode fex-fabric
  vpc 100
  fex associate 100

interface port-channel101
  switchport mode fex-fabric
  vpc 101
  fex associate 101

interface port-channel102
  switchport mode fex-fabric
  vpc 102
  fex associate 102

interface port-channel103
  switchport mode fex-fabric
  vpc 103
  fex associate 103
interface Ethernet1/17
  switchport mode fex-fabric
  fex associate 100
  channel-group 100

interface Ethernet1/18
  switchport mode fex-fabric
  fex associate 101
  channel-group 101

interface Ethernet1/19
  switchport mode fex-fabric
  fex associate 102
  channel-group 102

interface Ethernet1/20
  switchport mode fex-fabric
  fex associate 103
  channel-group 103
```

Ongoing Maintenance Windows

Future maintenance windows will follow the exact same procedures to migrate additional access pairs or VLANs. With the VLANs migrated to the Nexus environment, hosts attached to legacy 6500 devices can be physically rehomed to 5K/2K devices, without requiring an IP address change. This allows Acme to re-home hosts on an as-needed basis over time. The additional maintenance windows will not be covered in the case study but will consist of configuring port-level characteristics covered throughout this book.

Summary

Acme has created a migration plan in which a pair of L3 access switches can be connected to the new Nexus environment in a controlled fashion with minimal outages. A similar procedure will be followed for the remaining switch pairs, IP addresses, and VLAN numbers; interface names will change, but the methodology will remain identical. The remaining migrations will be omitted from this case study. However, this case study demonstrates that the topics discussed throughout this book can be tied together in a way that enables Acme and other organizations to migrate to next data center networks and take advantage of the features of the Nexus family of switches.

Index

NUMBERS

A

B

E

M

ciscopress.com: Your Cisco Certification and Networking Learning Resource

Subscribe to the monthly Cisco Press newsletter to be the first to learn about new releases and special promotions.

Visit **ciscopress.com/newsletters.**

While you are visiting, check out the offerings available at your finger tips.

—Free Podcasts from experts:
  - OnNetworking
  - OnCertification
  - OnSecurity

View them at **ciscopress.com/podcasts.**

—Read the latest author **articles** and **sample chapters** at ciscopress.com/articles.

—Bookmark the Certification Reference Guide available through our partner site at **informit.com/certguide.**

Connect with Cisco Press authors and editors via Facebook and Twitter, visit informit.com/socialconnect.

cisco.

NX-OS and Cisco Nexus Switching

Next-Generation Data Center Architectures

Second Edition

Ron Fuller, CCIE® No. 5851
David Jansen, CCIE® No. 5952
Matthew McPherson

ciscopress.com

Safari
Books Online

FREE
Online Edition

Your purchase of **NX-OS and Cisco Nexus Switching: Next-Generation Data Center Architectures** includes access to a free online edition for 45 days through the **Safari Books Online** subscription service. Nearly every Cisco Press book is available online through **Safari Books Online**, along with thousands of books and videos from publishers such as Addison-Wesley Professional, Exam Cram, IBM Press, O'Reilly Media, Prentice Hall, Que, Sams, and VMware Press.

Safari Books Online is a digital library providing searchable, on-demand access to thousands of technology, digital media, and professional development books and videos from leading publishers. With one monthly or yearly subscription price, you get unlimited access to learning tools and information on topics including mobile app and software development, tips and tricks on using your favorite gadgets, networking, project management, graphic design, and much more.

Activate your FREE Online Edition at informit.com/safarifree

STEP 1: Enter the coupon code: RGAJGWH

STEP 2: New Safari users, complete the brief registration form.
Safari subscribers, just log in.

If you have difficulty registering on Safari or accessing the online edition,
please e-mail customer-service@safaribooksonline.com